QUINTILIAN

BOOK I

M. FABII QUINTILIANI
INSTITUTIONIS ORATORIAE
LIBER I

EDITED WITH INTRODUCTION AND COMMENTARY

BY

F. H. COLSON, M.A.,

FORMERLY FELLOW OF ST JOHN'S COLLEGE, CAMBRIDGE

CAMBRIDGE
AT THE UNIVERSITY PRESS
1924

CAMBRIDGE
UNIVERSITY PRESS

University Printing House, Cambridge CB2 8BS, United Kingdom

Published in the United States of America by Cambridge University Press, New York

Cambridge University Press is part of the University of Cambridge.

It furthers the University's mission by disseminating knowledge in the pursuit of education, learning and research at the highest international levels of excellence.

www.cambridge.org
Information on this title: www.cambridge.org/9781107689060

© Cambridge University Press 1924

First published 1924
First paperback edition 2014

A catalogue record for this publication is available from the British Library

ISBN 978-1-107-68906-0 Paperback

CARISSIMAE

"If the nineteenth century has said anything on this subject as well worth hearing, as wise, as humane, as full of sympathy and judgement as these reflections and animadversions of a scholar of the first half or quarter of the seventeenth, I have not chanced to meet it."

SWINBURNE, *on the sections in Ben Jonson's* Discoveries *on education, translated or sometimes paraphrased from Quintilian, the source of which Swinburne did not recognise, and believed them to be the thoughts of Jonson himself.*

"Quintilian...is little read and seldom sufficiently appreciated. His book is a kind of encyclopaedia of the thoughts of the ancients on the whole field of education and culture: and I have retained through life many valuable ideas, which I can distinctly trace to my reading of him even at that early age."—MILL'S *Autobiography.*

PREFACE

THIS edition of the First Book of Quintilian has been prepared under the conviction that seldom have sixty pages of equal importance and interest lain so long neglected. The great educational principles of the Prooemium and first three chapters—principles which at various times and particularly at the Renaissance have had enormous influence—the remarkable philological disquisition of the next four chapters, which with all its imperfections gives us an admirable bird's-eye view of the language-science of the Ancients—the literary criticism and thoughts on the teaching of literature in the eighth—the school practice in the ninth—the discussion of music and mathematics in the tenth—carry the reader into most of the chief branches of ancient culture, while the two remaining chapters have many points of educational interest. Further they abound, especially chapters 4–10, in difficult problems, which require for their elucidation more illustration from parallel and mostly obscure sources, than I believe they have ever yet received. There are other parts of Quintilian of great interest, notably the first chapter of the tenth book, the only part, I believe, with which the ordinary scholar is familiar. Next come the second and twelfth books, but they must, I think, yield the palm to the first.

The commentary is mainly exegetical. The scholar who attempts the exegesis of any but the tenth book has practically only Spalding to work upon. Spalding absorbed all that was valuable in the earlier commentaries, and his edition, at any rate that part of it which he lived to complete himself, will remain a standard work. But he left a vast number of doubtful points untouched, and there are many sources of illustration which he either did not know or did not use. Moreover he lacked two things which the present editor enjoys. One is the invaluable *Lexicon Quintilianeum* which Bonnell added to Spalding's edition: the other is the indexes to Keil's *Grammatici Latini*, which immensely facilitate any comparative study of the grammatical chapters. But from commentaries proper I have gained little apart from Spalding. Fierville's edition—the only one of the first book separately which has preceded this—has two excellent features. The account of the MSS. is admirably complete, and the sketch of the "Fortleben" of Quintilian has been of great service to me in making my own, as, apart from the actual information given, it has often put me on the right track. But the notes themselves are weak, while, to take the other two commentaries which have appeared since Spalding's, the exegesis of Meyer is meagre and that of Gernhard negligible.

In textual matters the case is very different. The three editions of Halm, Meister and Radermacher have set the text on a firm foundation. As I have tried to shew in the last chapter of the Introduction, there is a general and, I believe, a just agreement, that the sources of the external evidence for most of this book may be limited to two, and the work of the commentator on the textual side is mainly concerned with the internal evidence. There are plenty of textual notes in this commentary, but they are of the kind which is akin to exegesis— based on the consideration of what the sense of the passage or its parallels demands. The work of the above-mentioned editors absolves me, I hope, from the duty of recording the many variants which were current in the old editions before the days of Halm and of collating hitherto unexplored MSS., a work for which I am very ill suited. I have made indeed one small and one larger exception to this last. I have collated the Harleianus 2664, first brought into notice by Peterson, for the small portion in which it is perhaps one of our two primary authorities. And as it happens that the one MS. easily accessible to me, the Joannensis in my own college library, has through a chapter of accidents been less known to editors than any ancient codex of its type, I have collated it throughout the book. But neither of these collations, the objects of which are fully explained on p. xcvii. of the Introduction and p. 184 of the Appendix, has really added anything of importance to my knowledge of the text, and if my work on this side has any value at all, it lies in the discussion of the internal evidence.

During many years of reading round the subject I have accumulated a considerable body of illustrative matter and a good part of this has been embodied in the introduction and notes. I trust that this neither is nor will be set down as due to vanity. The primary use of illustration is no doubt to prove or elucidate a point, and I hope that a considerable part of the quotations and references given serve this purpose. But apart from the fact that a scholar can rarely resist the attraction of an apt parallel, I believe that there is a special reason for making the citation of parallels a leading feature in a commentary on this book. I am convinced that any independent student of the methods and principles of education in the imperial period should take Quintilian as his primary authority, and I hope that such a student will be glad of some guidance to the many secondary sources. Much the same may be said of the grammatical chapters. These, as I have said, do not shew Quintilian at his best. He is moving, sometimes rather confusedly, in a region where his knowledge is more wide than profound. Still his compressed sketch is the best starting-point for anyone who wishes to understand—not indeed what the Latin language is—but what the Latins themselves thought about their language and language in general; and I think that to such a person a good deal of reference to Varro and the later Latin grammarians, as well as to the parallel Greek authorities, may be of service.

I do not feel so sure about the appropriateness of one part of my book, which is elaborated on a scale unusual in editions of the classics. I mean that part of the Introduction which deals with the " Fortleben "—I repeat the word because I do not know of any real English equivalent—of Quintilian. It will not be much apology to say that this has given me more pleasure than any other side of what has been throughout an enjoyable task, but I do hope that the vicissitudes,—unparalleled, I think, in the case of any classical writer—through which the reputation of Quintilian has passed may be sufficient justification. I should add that I am quite aware that its scope is somewhat ambitious; and though I have taken great pains to ensure accuracy, I hold it to be almost certain that there are actual mistakes, still more certain that some things are set in their wrong perspective, most certain of all that there are gaps as serious as blunders. May readers and reviewers, who are specialists in one or other of the periods traversed, have mercy!

There are certain omissions, or what may be thought to be omissions, which should be noted.

1. I had intended to add a translation, and indeed much of it had been completed. But the publication of a translation by Prof. H. E. Butler in the Loeb series led me to change my plans. The Loeb version presents Quintilian to the English reader in an easy and pleasant form, and in this respect I could not hope to better it. I have therefore contented myself with giving my own views on the places in which I question its accuracy or adequacy, and in these cases I have usually, but not always, set the Loeb version side by side with mine. Where there is no note of this kind my readers may take it that I acquiesce.

2. I have not given any formal critical apparatus, and have confined myself to stating in the notes the main manuscript evidence on important or doubtful points. I have hesitated much on this matter, and probably many will think that my decision is wrong. The textual student who has access to Halm and Fierville will be able to repair the omission, and also I think that he will find the conspectus of various readings in recent editions on pp. 180–183 of use. I may also be blamed for not separating my critical from my exegetical notes. On this matter I feel more confidence in my judgment. To me at any rate it seems difficult to make any logical distinction between the two.

3. The information as to MSS. is meagre in comparison with that supplied by Peterson and Fierville. On this point I may refer to what is said on p. xci. of the Introduction.

4. I have not added any general account of Quintilian's linguistic usages or peculiarities, but have confined myself to commenting on such as actually occur. There are two excellent dissertations of this kind already in existence; one in the opening pages of Bonnell's *Lexicon*, the other in Peterson's Introduction to his edition of the tenth book.

5. It is possible that some of the subject-matter of Book I. may be so unfamiliar even to good scholars, that I shall seem to have left unexplained what requires explanation. I can

only hope this is not so. Those who find the connexion of the thought difficult will, I think, get assistance from the analysis which follows the commentary.

I have to give my best thanks to the well-known scholar, Mr J. D. Duff, Fellow of Trinity College, for valuable help. He has read the proofs with great care, and made many substantial suggestions, besides correcting numerous minor inaccuracies. Also I have to thank Mr Previté-Orton, Librarian and late Fellow of St John's College. His help was indispensable to me in my study of the Johnian manuscript, and this I have acknowledged in the proper place, but his services have not been limited to this. Finally, there is the Reader of the Pitt Press, whose knowledge and insight, extending to points far beyond those on which one expects a reader's help, have impressed me as much as I know them to have impressed others.

F. H. C.

CAMBRIDGE,
February, 1924.

[*Abbreviations.* A few of the most important of these are explained on p. xcviii. Abbreviations of the names of authors and books will be understood by reference to Indexes I–III.]

CONTENTS

INTRODUCTION

CHAPTER I

BIOGRAPHICAL[1]

§ 1. QUINTILIAN'S EARLY LIFE

THE only data of any value for this are (*a*) the two following passages from the Hieronymian Chronicle:

> (*a*) Against the year 68 'M. Fabius Quintilianus Romam a Galba perducitur.'
>
> (*β*) Against the year 88 'Quintilianus ex Hispania Cala-gurritanus primus Romae publicam scholam et sala-rium e fisco accepit et claruit';

and the following from the *Institutio* itself:

> (*b*) 'egregieque nobis adulescentibus dixisse accusator Cos-sutiani Capitonis videbatur,' VI. I, 14.
>
> (*c*) (*a*) 'Domitio Afro...quem adulescentulus senem colui,' V. 7, 7.
>
> (*β*) 'Vidi...Domitium Afrum valde senem cotidie aliquid ex ea, quam meruerat, auctoritate perdentem,' XII. 11, 3.

From the first two it would appear that Quintilian, before he settled at Rome, belonged to Calagurris in Spain, a view which is supported by a line of Ausonius:

> Adserat usque licet Fabium Calagurris alumnum[2].

As to (*b*) we may accept the statement of Tacitus *Ann.* XIII. 33 that the trial mentioned took place in 57 A.D. But as 'adu-lescens' is an extremely elastic term, these words hardly enable us to fix the limits of Quintilian's birth more closely than somewhere between 30 and 40 A.D. This conclusion is more or less confirmed by (*c*). For Domitius Afer is stated by Jerome to have died in 58, and the two passages here quoted

---

[1] The remarks that follow are not intended to give a continuous life of Quintilian, which may be found in any biographical dictionary, so much as to distinguish between certainties and uncertainties. It seems to me that an extraordinary number of doubt-ful or even unsupported statements have been made by various writers on the subject.

[2] *Prof. Burd.* I. 7.

evidently imply that Quintilian joined Domitius some considerable time before his death. We certainly cannot on the evidence of these place the birth later than 40. The commonly accepted date of *c.* 35 is perhaps good enough for a central point, but 'circum' must be interpreted elastically.

From (*c*) we also learn that Quintilian spent some part of his early life at Rome, and it has been generally assumed that the whole of his boyhood and education is to be placed there. While there is little or no evidence against this, there is, in my opinion, as little in favour of it. Two positive facts are indeed sometimes alleged on this side. The first is that in M. Seneca's *Controversiae* a *rhetor* Quintilianus is mentioned[1]. It is assumed that this person is our Quintilian's father, and a theory has been constructed that after practising at Calagurris he removed to Rome while his son was an infant. Now it is a fair though not certain presumption from the witticism of his recorded in *Inst.* IX. 3, 73 that Quintilian's father was a 'rhetor,' but his identity with the Quintilianus of Seneca, or at any rate the theory just mentioned, is really very improbable. Seneca's death lies between 39 and 43. His reminiscences belong to his better years and concern persons whom the sons for whom he writes have never known. Even if we admit exceptions to this, we have obviously but a short time for the rhetor of Calagurris, transplanted to Rome, to find his way into Seneca's gallery[2]. The second point is a statement by the scholiast on Juv. VI. 452 *Palaemonis artem*, to the effect that Quintilian was the pupil of Palaemon. While not denying the possibility of its truth, I look upon the unsupported statement of a late and unknown writer with great suspicion, which is increased by observing that this scholiast found Palaemon and Quintilian given in his author as typical examples of the two kinds of schoolmasters and that it was natural enough to imagine that the later teacher was a pupil of the earlier[3]. Is it supported by

---

[1] *Contr.* X. Pr. 2, ib. 33, 19.

[2] I do not know that we can rule out the possibility that S. heard Quintilian senior declaim in Spain, like Gavius Silo (*Contr.* X. Pr. 14), but the result for my present argument would be the same.

[3] The tendency to assign distinguished men to some distinguished teacher without real evidence is not confined to scholiasts, as the imaginations about the relations of Juvenal and Tacitus to Quintilian (mentioned below) shew.

Quintilian himself? Quite the contrary. In I. 4, 20 he quotes the authority of Palaemon on one point of grammar. In I. 7, 26 he notes the usage of 'nostri praeceptores' on another, without a word to suggest that the two are identical. Considering the pride he shews in his later connexion with Domitius, I find it difficult to believe that he would thus treat an earlier connexion with the greatest grammarian of his time.

It is possible that this view as to Quintilian's early youth and education (a view which, I am bound to say, has been accepted so universally that I dissent with considerable diffidence) is really based on two unspoken assumptions. It may be thought, firstly, that it is unlikely that a person of his educational attainments was brought up in a distant province, and, secondly, that his connexion with Domitius in early manhood suggests a Roman education throughout. Neither of these assumptions, if they really are made, appears to me to have any solid weight. We do not indeed know much about details of education in Spain at this time[1], but we do know that as Mommsen says[2], Roman civilisation gained ground in Spain earlier and more powerfully than in any other province, especially in regard to literature. We do know that an extraordinary number of literary men were Spanish by origin, and this in itself goes some way to show that a society existed, which would naturally produce schools of learning. Long before the time that Quintilian would be attending a 'schola grammatica,' Horace seems to recognise the existence of such schools in Spain[3]. Some thirty or forty years later Tacitus makes one of his interlocutors remark how rapidly oratorical *sententiae* and *loci* circulate through the provinces[4], a statement which creates a presumption at any rate that 'scholae rhetoricae' were to be found there. Of his 'schola grammatica' Quintilian tells us nothing except that two particular forms of spelling

---

[1] Bouchier *Spain under the Roman Empire* p. 155 gives several instances of inscriptions recording the names of 'grammatici' and 'rhetores' in various towns. But I can see no evidence of date for these.

[2] *Provinces under Roman Empire* I. p. 75.

[3] I think this is the natural meaning of *Odes* II. 20, 19
 'me peritus
 Discet Iber Rhodanique potor'
as opposed to the *noscent* applied to the uneducated nations.

[4] *Dial.* 20.

were in use there¹. Of his 'schola rhetorica' he tells us a little
more. He notes with approval the method of taking places in
class and also a certain form of 'progymnasma².' I know of
no reason why these should not be in vogue in a provincial
school³.

As to the second point, what Quintilian means by the phrase
'colui Domitium' is shewn by the advice given X. 5, 19 to his
readers 'quare iuvenis qui rationem inveniendi eloquendique
a praeceptoribus diligenter acceperit,...exercitationem quoque
modicam fuerit consecutus, oratorem sibi aliquem, quod apud
maiores fieri solebat, deligat, quem sequatur, quem imitetur.'
But can we infer anything from this as to the earlier stages?
This last stage corresponds roughly to the life of the medical
student at the hospital or the articled clerk. When we are
told that a young man has gone to London for any of
these purposes, we do not infer that he was a schoolboy there.
I know of no reason for thinking that this common-sense
principle does not apply to ancient as much as to modern
life.

At the same time I must not be understood to be maintaining
positively that Quintilian's early life and education belong to
Spain. I regard the question as absolutely uncertain. One
fact only seems to me to point positively in that direction.
It is certainly one of the best authenticated facts in the life of
Quintilian that he went back to Spain and lived there for some
time before finally settling in Rome⁴. Why did he go back to
Spain? Many possibilities may be imagined, but the one which
will occur to everyone first is that he went to carry on his profession as a 'rhetor,' and if so it is perhaps more probable that
his family had maintained throughout its connexion with the

---

¹ I. 7, 26, 27.   ² I. 2, 23; II. 4, 26.

³ The old idea that I. 5, 57 ' "gurdos," quos pro stolidis accipit vulgus, ex Hispania
duxisse originem audivi' tended to disprove his Spanish birth is now, I think,
abandoned. Possibly it may be thought that a boyhood spent in Spain would give
it some force. I do not see that a lifetime spent there would enable him to testify
to the *original* source of a word current in vulgar Latin. Also he may well mean
" Some say it is Spanish in origin. I have no personal evidence for it."

⁴ 'Romam a Galba perducitur' can hardly mean, as some have supposed, that he
went in Galba's suite and returned with him, and the second entry in the Chronicle
confirms the natural inference from the first, viz. that he was domiciled in Spain
before his return with Galba.

place. I think this constitutes a slight presumption—I should not say more—in favour of his Spanish education[1].

§ 2. QUINTILIAN AT ROME

As we have seen, the Hieronymian Chronicle gives against the year 88 the entry 'Quintilianus ex Hispania Calagurritanus primus Romae publicam scholam et salarium e fisco accepit et claruit.' While the date of this entry must be wrong[2], if we accept Suetonius' statement (*Vesp.* 18) that it was Vespasian who 'primus e fisco Latinis Graecisque rhetoribus annua centena constituit,' the entry may be otherwise accurate. But to speak of Quintilian as the first to hold the professorship of rhetoric at Rome is a little misleading. The grant seems to have been rather of the nature of a subsidy to the worthier members of an existing profession than the endowment of a professor's chair. And while Quintilian may have been actually the first to receive the allowance, the plural 'rhetoribus,' as well as what we know of subsequent practice, implies that it was soon after given to others[3]. At the same time we cannot doubt that he held in general estimation the premier place amongst the *rhetores* of Rome. This is indeed definitely stated by Martial in an epigram, which is usually dated about 84 A.D.:

> Quintiliane, vagae moderator summe iuventae,
> Gloria Romanae, Quintiliane, togae[4].

But it is also implied by the way in which Juvenal uses his name, by the honours bestowed on him[5], and perhaps also by

---

[1] Perhaps I should mention VI. 3, 57 'nobis pueris Iunius Bassus, homo in primis dicax, "asinus albus" vocabatur.' There may be a slight presumption that if Quintilian really means that he heard this in his boyhood and not that he knew that the date of the witticism was in his boyhood, he is more likely to have heard it at Rome. But it is very slight evidence. Still less is that of the speeches which, X. 1, 24, 'nobis pueris insignes ferebantur.' All this means is 'in my early student days these speeches were highly thought of.'

[2] It has been emended by the insertion of 'qui' before 'primus' and the omission of 'et' before 'claruit.' This is no doubt possible. Pauly-Wissowa and Teuffel hold that the text is right and that Jerome has confused the retirement with the grant of salary. Perhaps the simplest supposition is that Jerome has here as elsewhere assigned a wrong date to an otherwise correctly stated fact.

[3] v. Julius Capitolinus, *Anton. Pius*, 11.   [4] II. 90.

[5] 'Quintilianus consularia per Clementem ornamenta sortitus honestamenta nominis potius videtur quam insignia potestatis habuisse,' Ausonius, *Gratiarum Actio* 7. Whether there is an allusion to this in Juv. 7, 197 seems to me doubtful.

the wealth which on Juvenal's testimony[1] we may believe him to have possessed, though we have to remember that some of this may have been acquired by his practice as an advocate.

But however successful it may have been it is well to remember that Quintilian's school in the proper sense of the word can hardly have been what we should call a large one, according to the evidence of Book II. 1–10. The younger pupils wrote 'progymnasmata' of various types. These were looked over individually and corrected, and Quintilian gives us some account of the comments he used to make[2]. There were the reading-lessons in the historians and orators. The close detailed interpretation of these he found was uncongenial and he employed it only occasionally[3], but when the pupils had read the speech or portion aloud, there were comments from the rhetorical point of view interspersed with questions to avoid 'securitas[4].' Passages were learnt by heart and presumably heard[5]. There were also lectures on the theory of rhetoric, no doubt after the manner of the *Institutio* itself[6]. Last of all came the declamations. Here the skeleton (partitio) dictated by the teacher, and the model at a later point delivered by him, did not, as he himself remarks, necessitate any limitation of the audience[7]. But the individual declamations of the pupils must have taken up a great deal of time for hearing and comment. Did he employ assistants? Though he notes that Greek rhetoricians used such 'adiutores' his language gives us no reason to suppose that he did so himself[8]. When we remember

---

[1] Juv. 7, 188 ff. This is evidently true, as the fact cuts clean against Juvenal's argument of the poverty of the *rhetores*, and can only be mentioned because it was too well known to be ignored. It is noteworthy that Juvenal shews no knowledge of the state subsidy to Quintilian or other *rhetores*.

[2] II. 4, 13–14.   [3] II. 5, 1.

[4] II. 5, 5–13. It is possible however that he means to include this in the counsels of perfection, which he found he could only carry out in exceptional cases.

[5] II. 7.   [6] Prooem. 7.   [7] I. 2, 13; cf. II. 6, 1.

[8] II. 5, 3. The assistant-master (hypodidascalus, subdoctor, proscholus) was no doubt to be found in Roman schools; v. evidence collected in Grasberger *Erziehung* II. 145 ff. Most of the examples there quoted probably apply to the grammatical schools, though possibly Quintilian's account of his own experiences in I. 1, 23–25, may imply a rhetorical school with a staff of more than one. It seems to me that it would be quite in accordance with Quintilian's principles, that he would not think of delegating the real teaching work to persons of inferior attainments. I can well imagine however that he would employ 'preparation masters' ('studiorum exactores,' I. 3, 14).

his work as an advocate[1] and apparently also as a public declaimer[2], his industry, even on the supposition that his school was small and select, is astonishing.

The 'studiosi iuvenes,' who went through a course such as that described above, were Quintilian's pupils in the fuller sense. But there seems also to have been a looser relation, that of 'auditores' who sat under him when he declaimed or perhaps lectured to a larger public. In one of the two places in which Pliny speaks of his relations with Quintilian, he tells how a certain Naso, who was evidently a grown man at the time, used to be pointed out to himself 'vixdum adulescentulo' in the lecture-rooms of Quintilian and Nicetes Sacerdos which they both frequented[3]. This can hardly refer to the regular classes of the rhetoric school. It may refer to public lectures on rhetoric, but the association with Nicetes, a travelling sophist from Asia, and rather a tub-thumper at that (ὑπόβακχος καὶ διθυραμβώδης Philostratus calls him)[4], points rather to declamations. In this looser sense half Rome may have heard him, but in the closer sense we cannot assign to him any single person as pupil except possibly Pliny, who speaks of him elsewhere as 'praeceptor meus' and records one of his reminiscences[5]. The suggestions frequently made and occasionally treated as certainties, that Tacitus and Juvenal[6] were his pupils, have no foundation of any kind that I have been able to discover.

[1] I have not dwelt on this side of Quintilian's work. The reader will find it dealt with adequately in Peterson, Intr. pp. vi., vii. The references given to the *I. O.* are IV. 2, 86; VII. 2, 24; IX. 2, 74.

[2] XI. 2, 39.   [3] *Ep.* 6, 6.

[4] *Vit. Soph.* I, 19; v. also Tac. *Dial.* 15. Peterson and others can hardly be right in identifying him with the Nicetes of Sen. *Suas.* III. 6 who is too early in date. Mommsen in his index to Pliny distinguishes the two.

[5] *Ep.* 2, 14.

[6] Pliny's correspondence gives no such suggestion. In 7, 20 he writes to Tacitus saying how greatly in early youth he had admired his distinguished senior, but gives no hint that they had the tie of the same instruction. In 6, 9 it appears that Tacitus favoured the same Naso's candidature, but no allusion is made to the lecture-room of Quintilian, as was made in 6, 6. I expect the idea arises from the supposed similarity of ideas in the *Dialogue* and *Institutio*. What this amounts to is discussed on pp. xli. xlii.

As to Juvenal, I think it is possible that *Sat.* 14, 32 ff. may contain a reminiscence of *Inst.* I. 2, 4 ff., but to have read the first two chapters of the book does not imply study in Quintilian's school. The blessing on 'qui praeceptorem sancti voluere parentis | esse loco' is sometimes compared with *Inst.* II. 2, 4. But the sentiment is a commonplace in antiquity. Probably every schoolboy wrote a 'chria' on the

§3. Retirement and Composition of the *Institutio*

From Quintilian himself we have the following facts : (1) he retired after 20 years' labour expended *iuvenibus erudiendis*[1], (2) for a long time he refused to yield to the invitation to compose his treatise[1], (3) he spent more than two years on its composition[2], (4) he then kept it by his side for some time before publishing it[2]. As the items 2–4 can hardly cover less than three years and may cover a good deal more, as 20 years from his return to Rome will bring us to 88, and as the book was presumably published before Domitian's death in 96, it would seem at first sight that we are shut up within the limits of 91 or 92 and 95 or 96 for the publication. This has been the general conclusion and it is probable enough. My reason for doubting its absolute validity is that on the hypothesis that he practised as a rhetor in Spain, I cannot feel sure that the 20 years do not include some unknown period there[3]. If I am right in thinking that this datum is not so conclusive as is usually supposed[4], what other data have we? One as we have said is that the book was certainly composed and almost certainly published[5] before Domitian's death. The others are that it was after his assumption of the title of Germanicus in 84[6], and after the institution of the 'quinquennale certamen Capitolino Iovi' mentioned by Suetonius (*Dom.* 4) and dated by Censorinus in 86[7]. It is then between these limits of 86 and 95, that I should

words of Aristotle that teachers were more to be honoured than parents, Τοὺς μὲν γὰρ τὸ ζῆν, τοὺς δὲ τὸ καλῶς ζῆν παρασχέσθαι. Juvenal's allusions to Quintilian in 6. 75; 6. 280 and 7. 186 ff. amount to statements (1) that Quintilian was the last person a fast woman would make love to, (2) that he was a well-known advocate, (3) that he was unusually rich for a 'rhetor,' but owed it to his luck. Observe that Juvenal was flogged, or says he was, by his 'rhetor.' Contrast with 1. 3, 13.

[1] Prooem. 1.   [2] Ep. to Trypho 1, but v. note there.

[3] In 11. 12, 12 to the words 'quando et praecipiendi munus iam pridem deprecati sumus' he adds 'et in foro quoque dicendi,' which can only refer to Rome. If they were found in Prooem. 1, we could have no doubt to what the 20 years referred.

[4] The doubt may seem perverse; yet I cannot help feeling that a Canadian scholar, who had studied at Cambridge, then held an appointment in Canada and was finally called to a chair in Cambridge, would, if he then wrote a treatise on his subject and stated that he had taught it for so many years, include in that number his Canadian as well as his English years.

[5] At least it seems unlikely that if the murder had taken place before publication the complimentary passages would have been allowed to remain.

[6] X. 1, 91.

[7] III. 7, 4 'an laudes Capitolini Iovis, perpetua sacri certaminis materia, vel dubiae

fix as a matter of certainty the publication of the book. If the ordinary interpretation of the 'viginti annos' is right we can of course be more definite[1,2].

The retirement and the composition of the book are closely connected with some other events in his life. His young wife and the younger of his two sons (only 5 years old) died much about the time that he retired. The elder boy followed them not more than four years later, and the father's lament for him appears in a well-known passage in the beginning of Book VI. Again a little time before this last event, he had been entrusted by the emperor with the care of his grand-nephews and heirs, the sons of Flavius Clemens[3], and it is probable enough that we should associate with this another honour, that of his receiving the Consular insignia, which, as noted above, according to Ausonius he owed to Clemens[3].

sunt vel non oratorio genere tractantur?' compared with Suet. *Dom.* 4 'certabant enim et prosa oratione Graece Latineque.' Dodwell inferred from 'perpetua' that the contest must have been held twice when Quintilian's words were written, thus bringing their date up to 91. I think however that 'perpetua' *need* not be more than a complimentary addition designed to shew that Domitian's institution would last for ever.

[1] It will be observed that *if* the text of the Hieronymian Chronicle is emended by the insertion of 'qui' and omission of 'et,' and *if* we identify 'claruit' with Quintilian's retirement, we get the accepted year of the retirement. But both these are too doubtful to add to the argument.

Another datum is the fact that Vibius Crispus is spoken of as lately dead in X. 1, 119, while he certainly lived well into Domitian's reign (Juv. 4). Teuffel gives the date of his death as *c.* 90, but I know no evidence for this and suspect that Teuffel is merely working backwards from the accepted date of the *Inst.*

[2] No inference as to the date of the book can be drawn I think from the expulsion of the philosophers, though many have thought so, v. note on p. xxv.

[3] This has no bearing, as has sometimes been thought, on the date of the book. Clemens fell from favour and was put to death at the end of Domitian's reign, but there is no evidence as to the age of his sons at the time, or at what point in the reign their selection as heirs took place.

As Peterson's edition is generally accepted as an authority, it is perhaps only right that I should notice the extraordinary theory which, following the French editor Hild, he puts forward on this point. It is briefly this. In the prooem. to Book I. Quintilian tells Marcellus that one purpose of the work is to help in the education of Marcellus' son Geta. In the prooem. to Book IV. he tells him that he has now the additional stimulus of the education of the two princes. In the prooem. to Book VI. he laments the loss of his one remaining son. Now, say Hild and Peterson, when he wrote this last prooem., if the young princes had still been with him, he would have been sure to mention them, and therefore during the interval the fall of Clemens and his family had taken place. Surely the natural conclusion is very different. If the two boys entrusted to him with *éclat* had been removed to disgrace and probably death within a few months, a veil would have been drawn

Of his subsequent life we know nothing. It is very unlikely that the Quintilianus of Pliny 6, 32 is our author. On the other hand the idea of Peterson and others that he must have been dead when Pliny wrote 2, 14 and 6, 6 (v. above p. xv) seems to me quite baseless. Surely one may write to a friend and recall some word or action of a former master or tutor, or the fact that some third person used to be in the same class, without implying that the said master or tutor is dead.

As to Quintilian's other writings, apart from an early published *actio* (VII. 2, 24) and piratical circulations of his lectures and other speeches (Pr. 7, III. 6, 68, VII. 2, 24), we have five allusions in the *Institutio* to *alius liber* on rhetorical or educational matters. In two of these (VI. Pr. 3 and VIII. 6, 76) the title of the book is definitely given as *De Causis corruptae Eloquentiae*. In two others, though the title is not stated, the topics which are noticed as having been discussed leave no doubt that the same book is referred to[1]. The fifth passage is not quite so clear. Speaking of declamations (II. 4, 42) Quintilian observes that while this sort of exercise undoubtedly arose in Greece in the time of Demetrius Phalereus, he does not know whether it was actually invented by him, 'ut alio quoque libro sum confessus.' This would have no direct connexion with the subject of the *De Causis*, but as V. 12, 23 shews that this treatise did discuss declamations as they then were, a historical note of this sort would not have been out of place.

over such a painful incident and the prooem. to Book IV. cancelled. But as a matter of fact the princes are obviously alluded to in the prooem. of VI. Quintilian, recapitulating what he has said in the other two introductions, remarks that he had begun the work at the request of Marcellus and also with the hope of aiding 'boni iuvenes,' and 'novissime paene etiam necessitate quadam officii delegati mihi.' He then adds that behind all these he had thoughts of the use it might have in a more distant future to his own boy. This hope has now gone. Thus he can no longer find personal value in the book, and 'haec cura alienas necessitates spectat.'

The oddest part of this odd theory is that Geta too, not being definitely mentioned in the prooem. of VI., is supposed to have died in the interval between the writing of Books IV. and VI. 'Dans la préface du VIᵉ livre ceux-ci (i.e. the princes) et Géta ont également disparu' (Hild). 'The opening words of the sixth book shew that they are all gone' (Peterson). That is to say, Quintilian and his friend have both lost their sons at the same time. Yet Quintilian can write to Marcellus and dwell as he does on the sorrow of his own bereavement without a word for the bereavement of his friend. Surely this would be inexcusable egoism. Happily Mommsen seems to have found Geta alive as a *Frater Arvalis* in 118.

[1] V. 12, 23 the frequent unreality of declamations; VIII. 3, 58 κακόζηλον.

I see no reason therefore to postulate (as Peterson seems half inclined to do) more than one other rhetorical work of Quintilian's in addition to the *Institutio*[1].

Editors and biographers have generally either condemned or apologised for Quintilian's flattery of Domitian. It is a point on which every reader can form his own judgment, without any assistance from me. The passages concerned are III. 7, 9, IV. Pr. 3, X. 1, 91[2].

[1] The *De Causis* must have been written either shortly before or shortly after the retirement. Some, e.g. Dodwell and Peterson, have positively affirmed that the latter is the case. This is going too far. The data are as follows: (1) He began the book at the time when he lost his younger son (VI. Pr. 3); (2) This boy was then 'quintum *egressus* annum.' In connexion with the elder boy's death we are told that, in comparison with the promise (flosculi) of the younger, 'iam decimum aetatis ingressus annum certos ac deformatos fructus ostenderat.' It is not quite clear whether this is meant to be the date of the boy's death, or the beginning of his eight months' illness. Supposing that it is the latter and that the elder was about a year older than the other, we should get something from three to four years between the two deaths; (3) The death of the elder is worked into the structure of the *Institutio* at the beginning of the sixth book. I do not indeed think that we should take this too literally. I do not conceive of Quintilian as steadily working through the *Institutio* as we have it and as having exactly reached the end of the third and fifth books, when the events occurred which occasion these *prooemia*. Rather the *prooemia* are literary embellishments, very probably added when the work was otherwise finished. But we may, I think, suppose that the setting roughly corresponds with the facts and conclude (1) that his appointment to teach the princes and the loss of the elder boy occurred comparatively early in the period at which he was at work on the *Institutio*, (2) that the first of these two events preceded the second. If so it is quite possible that the death of the younger boy and the composition of the *De Causis* are to be dated two or even three years before he began the *Institutio*, and whether this will bring us to a time before the retirement depends on the length of time implied by 'diu sum reluctatus' (Pr. 1).

Dodwell was sure that Quintilian could not have found time to write it before the retirement, and what I have said above on Quintilian's industry tends to support this. Still a modern professor would hardly endorse this argument. Observe that in Pr. 1, Quintilian does not say that he had for his refusal to undertake the *Institutio* the excellent reason that he was engaged on another book.

[2] I ought not perhaps to conclude this chapter without mentioning the extant declamations. But they do not really concern the first book, and I have not studied them in a way that would enable me to speak with conviction on the internal evidence. The main points are as follows. The belief that these or other declamations were the genuine work of Quintilian is as early as the beginning of the fourth century, and three at least of the quotations or allusions given are to declamations which appear in the extant collection of the Decl. Majores, 19 in number (Ritter *Die Quint. Decl.* p. 209 f.). On the other hand the internal evidence is generally supposed to be against their authenticity, though Ritter makes exceptions. For the Decl. Min. originally numbering 388, of which 145 survive, the external evidence is nil. There are no clear quotations from those which we possess. As to internal testimony, Ritter has put together a body of evidence, which certainly seems to shew that they

are from the hand of one who had made a very close study of Quintilian, if not from Quintilian himself. The only point on which I would speak positively is that I do not think Ritter can be right (p. 217) in identifying this collection with the second of the 'libri artis rhetoricae' mentioned in Prooem. 7, and again in III. 6, 68. The book in question consisted of notes of Quintilian's lectures taken down imperfectly in shorthand by his pupils and then published. Ritter produces some evidence that an 'ars' or τέχνη might include examples and possibly even some complete specimens of declamations, but the context makes it clear that the book thus published was of the same scope and character as the rhetorical part of the *Institutio,* which differs totally in these respects from the Decl. Min.

If either collection or both are genuine, the silence of Quintilian on the subject, while he speaks freely of other publications, makes it very improbable that he had published them when he wrote the *Institutio.* But there is nothing to forbid the supposition that he collected and edited them after the publication of his great work.

CHAPTER II

THE *INSTITUTIO ORATORIA*

§ 1. THE EDUCATIONAL SYSTEM OF QUINTILIAN'S TIME AND HIS RELATIONS TO IT

THE *Institutio Oratoria* seems to me one of the most remarkable and interesting products of Roman common sense. This is a judgment which I think would hardly have been disputed till perhaps the last century or so, when the book fell into comparative neglect. Its interest is twofold, as a treatise firstly on education, secondly on rhetoric. It is the first aspect with which this edition is mainly concerned, though something must also be said with regard to the second.

In estimating Quintilian's relation to the educational ideas of the time, the great basic fact is the existence of the ἐγκύκλιος παιδεία, the curriculum which included (1) 'grammatice,' originally the literary and critical study of the poets, historians and orators, but tending more and more to include scientific grammar in our sense of the word; (2) rhetoric, including the theory and carefully graduated exercises culminating in the declamation; (3) geometry, which included arithmetic and a certain amount of astronomy; (4) dialectic of a sort; (5) music, to which adhered something of, but by no means all, the virtue which Plato and Aristotle ascribed to it, while drawing, on which the latter laid considerable stress, had dropped out of the curriculum. The Encyclopaedia, if I may be allowed to use this barbarism, cannot be said to embody any theory of education. It is simply the sum total of the branches of knowledge which had reached such a degree of reputation, that the ordinary parent wished his children to know them. In this respect it probably resembled most systems of popular education. But we do find two real theories of education which, accepting the Encyclia in practice, endeavour to justify the acceptance on general principles. The first of these is the rhetorical or sophistical theory, which we find in Quintilian. It holds that 'eloquentia' or a mastery of language is the chief

factor of success in life and that to give this is the main object
of education. Now the idea of 'eloquentia' always carried with
it wealth of thought as well as wealth of words, and the rhetorical
ideal is not so narrow as we are wont to think. But to square
it with the facts of life Quintilian and Cicero had to carry the
theory a step further. They could not ignore the popularity
of the Encyclia: probably indeed they were too much attached
to them to wish to do so. Accordingly Quintilian agrees that
as there is no subject on which the orator may not have to
speak, literature, history, grammar, geometry, music and astronomy are all necessary parts of his education.

In opposition to this we have the philosophical view, which
holds that right conduct is the one thing needful and philosophy
the one true study for mankind. But this theory too had to
face the facts of life. Philosophy in Quintilian's time as a whole
could not afford, whatever the Epicureans and earlier Stoics
may have done, to throw the Encyclia overboard. So we get
the theory that the Encyclia are προπαιδεύματα, the handmaids
of philosophy. We find this theory in the treatise περὶ ἀγωγῆς
παίδων, generally bound up with the *Moralia* of Plutarch.
This treatise has many resemblances to the early chapters of
Quintilian, so much so that it has been thought that they drew
from the same source. But the general outlook of the two is
widely different[1]. In ps.-Plutarch the whole of the 'Encyclopaedia' has to be taken, but only ἐκ παραδρομῆς ὡσπερεὶ
γεύματος ἕνεκεν. He quotes with approval the saying of Bion
that those who spend their time on προπαιδεύματα are like
the suitors of Penelope, who when they were unable to win the
mistress contented themselves with the maids.

The philosophical view is perhaps presented most effectively
in Philo, particularly in the treatise *De Congressu*. Here
Philo, adapting the allegory of Bion, took Abraham for the
Human Soul and Sarah for Philosophy. At first Abraham
finds Sarah barren and accordingly mates with Hagar who
represents the Encyclia. The union is fruitful, for the soul
which in its earliest years cannot grasp philosophy may be
prepared by the ordinary subjects of education. But there
comes a time when Sarah can bear Abraham a son, and then

---

[1] v. § 5 below.

the bondmaid and her son must be cast out. In the same treatise Philo explains what Ishmael is, or in other words what the Encyclia can do for the soul. 'Grammatice,' dealing with poets and prose-writers, produces intelligence and wide knowledge (πολυμαθία), and teaches us through the heroic examples of literature to despise misfortunes. Music brings the soul to harmony. Geometry creates a love for Justice. Rhetoric trains and welds thought to expression, and thus makes the man truly λογικός. Dialectic, the twin of rhetoric, shews us how to distinguish truth from falsehood[1].

Quintilian would have quarrelled with none of these estimates, though he would have laid more stress on some other aspects. Thus the attitude assumed by the two schools of thought to the ordinary curriculum was practically the same in spite of the difference of general outlook. And a further approximation was caused by the doctrine on which Quintilian lays such stress, that moral goodness was inseparably bound up with eloquence. Not only ought the orator to be 'bonus' (for otherwise he will be a very dangerous person) but he will actually be so, if he is to attain real success[2]. For a bad life is incompatible with the 'prudentia' which is demanded of the orator and the 'diligentia' required for intellectual study, and furthermore no one can speak persuasively, except where he feels.

This attack upon the enemy's citadel is carried two points further. Firstly Quintilian agrees with the philosophers that virtue cannot be fully acquired without a study of ethics. As the rhetoricians in the past have unfortunately left this to the philosophers, this knowledge can only be acquired from the philosophers of the past; but it does not follow that education should be in the hands of the philosophers of the present[3]. The true teacher of oratory is now ready to take up his responsibilities. Secondly he urges that the 'virtus' which the boy will acquire under the rhetorician is really of a higher kind. The philosophers have always shewn a tendency to separate themselves from public and civil life. His school will

---

[1] I have treated the thoughts of Philo on this subject more fully in an article on 'Philo on Education,' in the *Journal of Theological Studies*, January 1917.

[2] v. particularly XII. I.   [3] I. Pr. 17.

produce the 'Romanus sapiens qui non secretis disputationibus sed rerum experimentis atque operibus vere civilem virum exhibeat[1].'

The normal practice was that, if a course of philosophy was taken at all, it was after the student had passed successively through the schools of the 'grammaticus' and the 'rhetor.' Whether the philosopher encroached on the two earlier forms of training is not, I think, clear. It is *prima facie* probable that if Chrysippus held that nurses ought to be professed philosophers[2], many parents may have felt that *a fortiori* pedagogues and teachers ought to be of the same kind, and that thus scholastic ability may have been sacrificed to philosophical seriousness, real or supposed. And I find it difficult to account for Quintilian's strong feeling on the subject, without postulating some practical opposition of this kind. But I know of no evidence to this effect in the first century. We hear of the philosopher as director, but not as schoolmaster[3]. On the other hand Quintilian apparently would eliminate the formal philosophical course altogether and send the boy straight from the 'rhetor' into practical life. But he does not make it clear how the future orator is to get philosophy without the help of the living philosopher. The regular course of philosophical reading recommended in XII. 2 seems to be outside the rhetorical school. In X. 1 indeed philosophical books are to be read, apparently in private, during the rhetorical course, but this is for the purpose of cultivating style. It is not suggested that formal philosophy should be taught by the 'rhetor[4].' As I take it, the meaning is that rhetoric in the wider sense is so saturated by philosophical ideas that the true orator cannot fail to make it his own, and the true 'rhetor' cannot fail to teach it.

Quintilian's view of the superiority of the 'rhetor' to the philosopher is clearly reflected in two events of the time. The first of these is the endowment of rhetoric by Vespasian[5]. The

---

[1] XII. 2, 7.   [2] I. 1, 4.

[3] At a later period we have perhaps a hint of this in Luc. *De merc. cond.* 19; cf. Alciphron 3, 64.

[4] The only suggestion of the sort that I know is in Augustine *Conf.* III. 7 'usitato iam discendi ordine perveneram in librum cuiusdam Ciceronis,' i.e. the *Hortensius.*

[5] Suet. *Vesp.* 18, v. p. xiii.

other is the expulsion of the philosophers from Rome about A.D. 94[1]. The latter, whatever its other causes may have been, was certainly from one point of view a triumph for Quintilian's educational views.

Quintilian's views on this subject are no doubt largely based on Cicero's. But it would be as wrong to call them Ciceronian as to call them original. He voices the age-long antithesis between rhetoric and philosophy. Necessarily opponents, it was inevitable in an educational age that they should struggle 'for the soul of the child.' The conflict indeed bears a close analogy to the modern controversy between the partisans of religious or clerical, and those of secular or anti-clerical education.

§ 2. QUINTILIAN'S EDUCATIONAL PRINCIPLES

While Quintilian's book is the great representative of the rhetorical school of educational thought and indeed of ancient pedagogy in general, it must be remembered that it is not as a whole a treatise on education, not even indeed a treatise on how to *teach* rhetoric. The greater part of it, Book II. 14–XI., is a treatise *on* rhetoric. This section of the work has indeed very great interest and very marked features of its own and of these I shall speak presently, but its scope is quite different from that of the rest. Further in Quintilian's own view the strictly educational part is subordinate. He frequently tells us that his book as a whole is for 'iuvenes studiosi,' not for the 'rhetor,' still less for the 'grammaticus' or the 'grammatistes.'

---

[1] But the frequent attempts to draw inferences as to the date of the book from the date of the expulsion seem to me as misconceived as they are contradictory. The publication, says Dodwell, must have preceded the expulsion: otherwise he would not have spoken so favourably of a body under imperial displeasure. It must have been subsequent, say Hild and Peterson, otherwise he would not have spoken of them so harshly, though they add that the milder references I. 4, 5; X. 1, 35 and 123 were probably written before the event. There is no doubt that there is a relation between Domitian's action and Quintilian's views, but it is not one that can be stated in terms of a few months or years. One important point which appears is that Domitian's action was not mere wanton tyranny, but did have a certain support from an important body of opinion. The combination of praise for the early, with condemnation of the later, philosophers seems to have strangely puzzled many writers on Quintilian. I take it that his attitude is much the same as that of a sound Protestant to the Christian fathers, or at any rate to such men as Boniface, Bede and Bernard.

In fact this, its most valuable part, seems to have slipt from him almost involuntarily. It is as if the writer of a treatise on chemistry should preface his work by a chapter on how to teach chemistry and another on his conception of the best early training for the future chemist from the cradle upwards.

Again, the educational part of the work may be grouped under two heads: (*a*) general principles, (*b*) remarks on the method of teaching 'eloquentia' or a mastery of language, through three stages, the elementary or 'grammatistice,' the middle or 'grammatice,' and the higher or 'rhetorice.' It is his treatment of the first of these two heads which has given Quintilian his place among educational thinkers. This part of the book abounds in admirable and sensible ideas. These ideas are not perhaps original. Quintilian makes indeed little claim to originality, nor is he to any large extent a reformer. The teacher of to-day, as he reads each sentence, may if he will dismiss it with the thought 'this is merely what I have always said and believed.' And yet the sum total of wise thoughts incisively put is so great, that I venture to think that no teacher can fail to gain by reading them.

Amongst the educational principles of Quintilian, I should select the following as the most noteworthy:

The great object of education is to create or foster mental activity in the student (implied *passim*, e.g. in the phrase 'acuere ingenia').

Teaching must be accommodated to the power of the student. Further his individual characteristics must be considered and the methods and forms of study shaped accordingly. (I. 2, 27 ff., I. 3.)

Knowledge can only be acquired step by step, dropped in, not poured in. (I. 2, 28.)

At the same time it must be remembered that one function of education is to correct the weak points of nature. (II. 8.)

Relaxation and amusement are necessary. Games are a valuable indication of character. (I. 3. 8 ff.)

A good foundation is necessary in the earliest stages. (I. Pr. 4.)

In the earliest or infant stage all mental work should take the form of amusement. (I. 1, 20.)

In the middle or 'grammatical' stage, the curriculum should

be varied and different subjects taught concurrently. Change of study promotes activity, and the capacity of the young for congenial work is very large. (I. 12¹.)

Corporal punishment should be avoided. The true motives are (1) Competition, (2) Commendation, (3) Affection for the teacher, (4) Interest aroused by the subject. (I. 3, II. 9.)

The average child is intelligent and eager for knowledge. It is the fault of his training if he ceases to be so. (I. I, I ff.)

Class is better than private or individual teaching. Boys learn from each other and large classes stimulate the teacher. (I. 2.)

Don't over-teach, or intervene needlessly between the student and his studies. (I. 2, 11 and elsewhere.)

The attainment is always lower than the ideal aimed at, and therefore the ideal must be pitched high. (I. Pr. 20.)

Richness, fluency, *élan* etc. in a pupil, even if accompanied by crudity and bad taste, are better than aridity. (II. 4.)

Good education is desirable in those who are brought into contact with the child in earlier years. (I. I, 4 ff.)

Ability and learning are desirable in the teacher, not merely at the higher but also at the lower stages. (II. 3.)

In the teacher we also require (*a*) strict morality, (*b*) friendliness combined with the maintenance of proper respect, (*c*) clearness, (*d*) patience, (*e*) quiet insistence without violent pressure, (*f*) generosity without extravagance in bestowing praise. (II. 2.)

Whilst few will differ widely from Swinburne in his judgment of these 'reflections and animadversions²,' it is probable that many will fail to appreciate Quintilian's ideal of education. 'All this,' it may be asked, 'to produce an orator?'

¹ It is interesting to note that Quintilian limits this principle to the middle stage, or at least considers that it is most easily carried out there. In I. 12, 12 he points out that the pupil's work at that time is mainly of a receptive kind: 'His aetatibus omnis in audiendo profectus est' (though to judge from the exercises prescribed in I. 9, the 'omnis' is a little too absolute). When the time for original thought and creation arrives in the rhetorical school ('Cum generabit ipse aliquid et componet') this distraction of studies is far less possible or congenial. His view in fact corresponds very closely with the instinct which has led the Board of Education to prescribe generalization (School Certificate) up to the age of about 16, specialization (Higher Certificate) after that age. I do not however remember that the Board has ever assigned this reason for the difference of treatment of the two stages, though it is quite applicable to modern conditions.

² v. quotation from Swinburne on the back of the title-page.

To those who look upon ancient rhetoric as essentially in-
sincere, the *Institutio* may seem, as one critic has phrased it,
a treatise on 'Lying as a Fine Art for those fully conscious of
their own rectitude.' But even those who have a better appreciation of Quintilian's conception of 'eloquentia' may still
feel his aim to be inadequate. On the other hand, to the
scientific student of rhetoric, the idealization of the subject may
seem mere loose thinking. Whately in his *Rhetoric*, whilst
admitting Quintilian to be a 'judicious writer,' and 'no mean
proficient in the conduct of education,' was evidently repelled
by this looseness. The conception that the orator must be a
good man is a 'fantastic' idea. As for the view that the knowledge of what has to be said is part of the art of rhetoric, you
might as well say that the possession of building materials is
part of the art of architecture. All this glorification of the art
was in Whately's opinion ἀλαζονεία or pedantry. While I
can quite understand this point of view, I still think that this
so-called 'pedantry' is one of Quintilian's chief claims to our
respect. The belief that 'eloquentia' was the most splendid
of human gifts was deeply rooted in the Roman mind and was
hardly if at all shaken by the fact that political oratory had
ceased to have much practical value—any more than the belief
of Western Europe in the Classics was for centuries shaken
by the fact that the Classics had ceased to be to us, what they
had been to the men of the Renaissance, the repository of
scientific knowledge and the only great literature. To harmonise this belief with the Encyclopaedic doctrine of general
culture—to save rhetoric from its natural tendency to degenerate into a study of ingenious and elegant phrasing, or a rigid
system of rules—to represent 'eloquentia' as something even
greater and broader than

> 'Cet grand art des Romains, cette auguste science
> D'embellir la raison, de forcer les esprits[1],'

is the main aim of this most practical of educationists.

---

[1] Voltaire in a letter to Frederick the Great. Quoted by Ernesti s.v. *eloquentia*.

§ 3. SCHEME OF TEACHING THE MOTHER TONGUE LAID DOWN IN THE *INSTITUTIO*

Besides these general principles we have, in the first two books, as remarked above, a complete scheme of teaching the mother tongue through the three stages of *grammatistice, grammatice* and *rhetorice.* The first of these requires little discussion. We may notice that Quintilian, who never mentions the name of the 'grammatistes' or 'literator,' evidently takes it for granted that in his *clientèle* this stage will be undertaken by the "pedagogue" or at any rate by some private teacher. In his remarks on first lessons in reading and writing he notes that the shapes of the letters should be taught concurrently with the names, and that writing should be practised first on grooved tablets. He also recommends that these early lessons should be utilized for acquiring a wider vocabulary and some knowledge of easy poetry and valuable maxims[1]. The next two stages involve more complicated questions.

I have said above that the 'Encyclopaedia' as a whole was not an educational system, but merely the sum of the things which an educated man was expected to know. And now it may be added that the two most important branches, 'grammatice' and 'rhetoric,' did not originally stand to each other in the relation which we find in Quintilian's time. 'Grammatice' was originally a study of literature, and its aim was to preserve the knowledge and understanding of the classical Greek writers; rhetoric was the art of using language effectively. But it was felt from early times that a certain amount of knowledge of the nature of the words which make up a book was necessary for the understanding of the book. Further, as the Greek language decayed or seemed to decay from the standard of the Classics, the idea gained ground that

---

[1] Quintilian says nothing of the elementary training in numeration, which is usually supposed to have been part of 'grammatistice.' The evidence for this for Roman schools is meagre. The most relevant passage is Aug. *Conf.* 1. 13 'illas primas (sc. litteras) ubi legere et scribere et numerare discitur...iam vero unum et unum duo, duo et duo quattuor odiosa cantio erat.' Jul. Cap. *Pertinax* 1. sometimes adduced is hardly relevant, nor is the well-known arithmetical lesson in Hor. *A. P.* 325, which may easily belong to a later stage. Still it is intrinsically probable that this was the case, and Quintilian's silence may perhaps be due merely to the fact that he had no valuable ideas on the subject.

one of the functions of 'grammatice' was to preserve the laws of correct speech. The combination of these two ideas slowly transformed the old view of 'grammatice,' till ultimately what we call 'grammar' swamped literature. While originally grammar had been merely an aid in understanding the books, ultimately the books became little more than the quarry to which the grammarian went for his facts. In Quintilian's time we find this process in mid-way: 'grammatice' is divided into 'recte loquendi scientia' and 'enarratio poetarum.' These two are kept very distinct, and the balance maintained evenly enough. But the fact that the 'ars recte loquendi' had risen to be a half of the whole subject had already had some momentous consequences. It changed the relations of 'grammatice' and rhetoric. While originally the two would naturally be studied concurrently, the view that the former gave the 'ars recte loquendi,' the latter the 'ars bene dicendi,' made the first a primary, the other a secondary study. Boys were sent to the 'grammaticus' first and to the 'rhetor' later, and by Quintilian's time, if not before, the 'grammaticus' is an inferior profession, worse paid and of lower social status. And to this subordination of 'grammatice' to rhetoric we may perhaps trace one of the most important facts in Roman education. 'Grammatice' had originally included prose as well as verse. It had been the study of ποιηταὶ καὶ συγγραφεῖς. But if the grammatical school was but the preliminary to the rhetorical, where necessarily prose was mainly studied, it followed that the 'grammaticus' would do well to restrict himself to the poets. At any rate this seems to have been the general if not universal practice in the Roman schools[1].

A further complication was introduced into the Western schools by the existence of Greek *grammatici* and *rhetores*

---

[1] The substance of this paragraph will be found more fully treated in my article on 'The Grammatical Chapters in Quintilian' in *Classical Quarterly*, January 1914.

I should note however two possible exceptions to the rule that prose was excluded (mentioned by Hulsebos *De Educatione* etc., p. 92). One is Cic. *ad Q. F.* III. 1, 11, where Cicero says of one of his speeches 'praesertim cum...meam (sc. orationem, apparently the *in Pisonem*) in illum pueri omnes tanquam dictata perdiscant.' Perhaps we need not take this very seriously, or if we do 'pueri' were not excluded from rhetorical schools. The other is Ausonius *Id.* 4 (' Lib. protrepticus') 60–65, where Sallust follows the list of poets which his grandson is to read, apparently in school, though whether the last item is to be taken 'apud grammaticum' is not perfectly clear.

beside the Roman[1]. Indeed, if the struggle between philosophical and rhetorical education has some resemblance to the
struggle between religious and secular education in our own
times, there is a still closer analogy between the opposition of
Greek to Latin studies then and that of classical to modern
now. 'Grammatice,' indeed, at Rome was originally entirely
Greek, and even when the idea that their native language and
literature was worth the same elaborate study as Greek dawned
upon the Romans, they continued to apply the same principles
of instruction. For instance, as Greek education had always
begun with Homer, the Latin grammarians continued to employ Livius Andronicus' translation of the *Odyssey* as a text-
book down to the days of Horace. Probably it was largely
the fact that the *Aeneid* supplied them with a worthy counter-
part for educational purposes that gave it its instantaneous
popularity, and such opposition as was made to it may well
have come, if not from the Greek 'grammatici' themselves,
from those amongst the Roman public who did not wish to see
Homer superseded by a modern poem.

The study of Greek 'grammatice' was begun earlier[2] than
the Latin. Otherwise, as I have said, we know of no difference of method[3]. On the other hand, between the Greek and
Latin ' rhetors,' there were in Quintilian's time distinct differences of practice, which may perhaps have originated at a
much earlier date. School rhetoric of any kind seems to have
won its way into Roman education with difficulty. In 162 B.C.
we find rhetoricians classed with philosophers and like them
under sentence of expulsion. Seventy years later we have the
well-known edict of Crassus against the newly-risen Latin
'rhetors' with the implication that Greek 'rhetors' were quite an
ancestral institution. The motives for this preference for Greek

[1] For the position held by Greek in education at Rome v. examples collected
by Mayor on Juv. 15, 110, though most of these imply rather than mention directly
actual instruction in school. To these add Livy 9, 36 'habeo auctores vulgo tum
Romanos pueros, sicut nunc Graecis, ita Etruscis literis erudiri solitos'; also the
frequent mention of Greek *rhetores* and *grammatici* in Suetonius and elsewhere.
The fact that Greek studies of a sort continued to be forced on boys in the West
in the fourth century, in spite of obvious reluctance, as shewn by Augustine and
Ausonius, shews how deeply the system was rooted.

[2] I. 1, 13 and 4, 1 ; v. also Petronius *Sat.* 5, though possibly this refers mainly
to Naples.

[3] Except the tendency amongst the Latins to encroach on rhetoric mentioned below.

are twice stated by Cicero. In *De Or.* 3, 94 he puts into the mouth of Crassus a statement to the effect that, though the Greek 'rhetors' were without that general knowledge of life which he held to be essential to true oratory, they had a certain 'doctrina et humanitate digna scientia,' while the Latins taught nothing but impudence. Elsewhere (*Ep. ad Titinnium*, Suet. *De Rhet.* 2) he says that as a boy he had wished to hear Plotius Gallus, the earliest of these rhetors, 'continebar autem doctissimorum hominum auctoritate, qui existimabant Graecis exercitationibus ali melius ingenia posse[1].' This is rather vague. It may be that the declamation system from the first took a hold on the Latin schools, which the more conservative thought pernicious. But perhaps we can find an adequate explanation in the tradition that Greek culture was the only possible culture, with the probable consequence that the earliest Latin teachers were a different type of men from their established Greek rivals. Apart from these passages I know of nothing to shew any difference between the two schools till we come to Quintilian's time. He notes two important differences of practice between the two. The first concerns the progymnasmata or graded preliminary exercises in composition described in I. 9 and II. 4. According to the original conception of the two arts, these belonged entirely to rhetoric, and so they are treated by the Greek progymnasmatists Theon and Hermogenes. When 'grammatice' became on one side the 'ars recte loquendi' it was only natural that some elementary exercises in composition should be associated with it. But the Latin *grammatici* appropriated *all* these exercises with the utmost goodwill on the part of the Latin 'rhetors,' who wished to concentrate all their efforts on the full-dress declamation. 'The Greek "rhetors" understood better the limits and requirements of their profession[2].'

The other difference was that the Greek 'rhetors' did attempt to give some careful lectures on prose writers. As we have seen the practice had grown up of restricting 'grammatice' on its literary side to poetry. But the Latin 'rhetors' apparently

---

[1] Apparently Cicero in after years still taught his son rhetoric in Greek in preference to Latin, v. opening of *De Part. Or.*
[2] I. 9, 6; cf. II. 1, 1-3.

did not accept the corollary that they should expound the orators and historians, as the 'grammatici' expounded the poets, though we may suppose that they required that their pupils should read them. Quintilian himself, who felt that this was a serious defect, found himself unable, in view of the feelings of parents and pupils, to do much to remedy it[1].

All this points to a marked contrast between the two systems. Though the upper classes at Rome may have known Greek a good deal better than ours know French, the Greek and Latin 'rhetors' served different purposes. The declamation system with all its show and advertisement dominated the Latin schools. However much men like Quintilian might protest, parents and pupils tended to express Latin education in terms of declamation[2]. It was not likely to be so with Greek, and though probably declamation in Greek was common enough, it had not the same absorbing interest. Thus Greek rhetoric worked in a more educational atmosphere than Latin and was less likely to be influenced by superficial considerations.

The educational position then in Quintilian's time is that 'grammatice' in its wider sense has come to be regarded as preliminary to 'rhetorice' and that Latin studies in both are on a par with Greek, with the probable corollary that the former are more popular and less austere than the latter. As to the method of teaching we may note the following points.

A. *Grammatice.*

The two departments, the 'scientia recte loquendi' and the 'enarratio poetarum,' could not of course be kept entirely distinct. Quintilian's scheme of teaching literature includes parsing and some other points which belong rather to 'grammar' than to 'literature,' as also does the earlier scheme of Dionysius Thrax. But there were also presumably formal lessons in 'grammar.'

Quintilian's account notes, among the subjects discussed, the lore of the parts of speech, interchanges of vowels and consonants, the value of analogy as a guide in language,

---

[1] II. 5, 1 ff.

[2] v. my article on 'Declamare—*κατηχεῖν*,' *Classical Review*, August 1922. The suggestion there made that 'declamatio' originally meant the rhetorical instruction as a whole is admittedly a conjecture, but the general facts are, I think, as there stated.

curiosities in etymology, various points in spelling and other things far too numerous to be given in detail here[1]. All these points were no doubt treated at any rate by the better type of 'grammaticus.' But Quintilian's sketch of the 'ars recte loquendi,' interesting as it is, cannot be taken to shew the way in which it actually was taught or even the way in which he thought it should be taught. He is chiefly exercised in shewing that it is a subject full of interest. And indeed the main point to remember is that grammar was then a living study. The process—surely one of the very greatest achievements of Graeco-Roman culture—by which the laws of what we call grammar were laid down for the two languages, and to some extent for all languages, was not yet complete. The study of language apart from literature was still vitalised by controversy, such as that between the Analogists and Anomalists. It held in fact in the mental outlook of the student of the time much the same position as Science does to-day.

Turning to the literary side we find Quintilian's scheme in such close agreement with the course laid down by Dionysius Thrax a century-and-a-half earlier, that we can have little doubt that it represents general practice. It includes expressive, well-toned and well-punctuated reading, parsing, scansion, the study of figures and tropes, the explanation of difficult words (glosses) and allusions (historiae) which occur in the reading; and finally literary criticism, including the discussion of the structure, incidents, vocabulary, characterization and style of the poem[2]. Further lessons in reading and reciting might be given by a specialist[3].

I have already spoken of the 'progymnasmata' or graduated exercises in composition, which in the Roman schools at any rate were taken at this stage. As I said above, all these exercises are in their nature rhetorical, but even in the Greek schools practical exigencies must have brought such an elementary exercise as the 'Aesop's fable' described by Theon and Hermogenes within the sphere of the 'grammaticus.' Perhaps we may surmise that their practice was what Quintilian himself advocates, viz. that besides the 'fable,' the 'chria,' etc., i.e. the development of some philosophical text, should be

---

[1] v. ch. 4–7.   [2] Ch. 8.   [3] Ch. 11.

correlated with the poets read in the grammatical school, and regarded as belonging to it.

B. *Rhetoric.*

The course adopted by Quintilian consists of:

(*a*) A further graduated course of exercises in composition culminating in the declamation.

(*β*) Reading of prose authors corresponding to the reading of the poets in the grammatical school, but not including attention to literary or grammatical points. Quintilian, however, recommends on his own authority a similar treatment so far as criticism is concerned.

(*γ*) The theory of rhetoric (under the five heads of 'inventio,' 'dispositio,' 'elocutio,' 'memoria' and 'pronuntiatio') to be imparted by means of lectures.

To these are appended various suggestions as to the practical work by which the student will convert this theoretical knowledge into a ἕξις, i.e. the mastery which habit gives. This is particularised as (1) general reading to be distinguished from that earlier reading under the professor mentioned in (*β*), (2) judicious imitation of what he reads, (3) careful composition, written not dictated, (4) revision, (5) judicious choice of the forms of composition, translation from the Greek and paraphrasing of Latin authors being specially mentioned, (6) meditation, (7) improvisation. These methods are given primarily as suitable to the rhetorical school, though they may be carried on to the stage when the student has entered practical life[1].

[1] These suggestions, which occupy Book X., are given as an appendix to 'elocutio' and are followed by the discussion of 'memoria' and 'pronuntiatio.' They are perhaps mainly concerned with 'elocutio,' but not exclusively so, and a better place for them would have been either in Book II. or after Book XI.

I take the opportunity of saying that it is to be regretted that Book X. should have been so frequently selected for editing and reading. Chapter I indeed with its famous literary conspectus may be quite properly taken out of its surroundings, but the rest of the book cannot be fully appreciated without a knowledge of Books I. and II.

At this point it is well to take some note of Book XII., a book in many ways as interesting as any of its predecessors, though it does not either contain what we ordinarily call 'educational principles' or make part of the scheme for teaching 'eloquentia.' Having traced the orator's course from the cradle to the time when he enters public life, Quintilian now wishes to follow him to the grave. He speaks of the necessity that he should be a 'vir bonus'—of the value of formal philosophical study for this purpose—of other studies to be pursued after school years, such as

While the general principles of Quintilian have on the whole received ample attention from educational writers, I do not think the same can be said of the scheme of language-teaching just described, which, though not his alone, is best seen in his book. And therefore, without attempting to give any complete estimate of its value, I will indicate some of the main characteristics as they appear to me.

In the first place the system is constructed with extraordinary care and minuteness from beginning to end. I do not say that this elaboration is necessarily a virtue. I point it out as a fact for the student of educational method. The nicety with which the 'progymnasmata' are graded deserves study if not imitation by modern teachers of English. I should be inclined to say rather more of the directions as to the teaching of literature (note especially the analysis of literary criticism in I. 8, 17). The adjustment of oral and written composition in the earlier stages is an excellent feature, and while we should all admit that oral eloquence was given too much weight in the later stages, is it not true that we have swung too much to the other side, and that the debating society cannot take the place of the class-room in teaching young people to speak?

But the main feature of the ancient system is the distinction between the 'ars recte loquendi' and the 'ars bene dicendi.' In other words it assumes that the art of effective speech, which it distinguishes from the art of merely coherent speech, is the main object of education, and that this aim cannot be attained without a careful study and application of the principles and methods which have constituted effectiveness in the writings and speeches of the past. Unhappily this art of 'rhetoric,' as they called it, has in England, at any rate of late years, been almost universally confused with the modern meaning of rhetoric as

law and history—of the other qualities which he requires, when he begins public speaking—how he should deal with his case—when he should retire—and how he should spend his leisure. After this we have a semi-final chapter (10) on the 'genus dicendi,' or the characteristics of the different styles, Attic and Asian, 'tenue,' 'medium,' and 'grande.' In introducing this Quintilian refers to the classification by which in II. 15 he divided rhetoric into 'ars,' 'artifex' and 'opus.' The 'ars' has been treated in Books III.–XI., the 'artifex' in XII. 1–9, and the 'opus' in this XII. 10. But this classification is not satisfactory. The three cannot really be separated, and the matter of XII. 10 belongs to 'elocutio,' and should have been dealt with in that part of the work.

unreal and exaggerated oratory, and its scientific character has been constantly ignored. Moreover the trivial character of the declamations preserved to us (though the triviality is, I think, often exaggerated) has gendered the idea that nothing else but clever turns of expression was or could be learnt in the rhetorical schools. That many or most of the schools may have at times shewn this weakness is probable enough. We have already seen that the declamation system tended to gain undue prominence in the Latin schools, and certainly most of the contemporary criticism, Petronius, Tacitus, Persius, Juvenal, goes on the assumption that the pupils of the 'rhetor never did anything but produce or listen to such declamations. But this weakness is not inherent in the system. For above all the modern reader should remember that rhetoric dealt with 'inventio' and 'dispositio' quite as much as with 'elocutio' and that its golden rule was 'rem tene, verba sequentur.' Even now it is, I think, true, that many useful lessons can be learnt from the theory of rhetoric, as Quintilian and his contemporaries understood it. It is perhaps only during the last 150 years or so that it has fallen into neglect, and it is quite possible that in the future it will recover something of its old reputation.

Besides the above-mentioned causes of the depreciation of the ancient schools, I mean the evil associations of the word 'rhetoric' and the weaknesses of the declamation literature, there is another which should be mentioned. It is frequently thought, I imagine, that these schools led merely to decadence in poetry and fustian in oratory and finally landed their students in the night of barbarism. This seems to me wide of the mark. In the earlier centuries the schools took a large part in moulding the great Augustan school of literature. In the later centuries, so far as the schools were bound up with decaying paganism they decayed, but in their vigorous stepchild Christianity they gained new life. The system which produced Origen, Jerome, Augustine and the Cappadocian fathers cannot be dismissed on the ground of the feebleness of its children, even by those to whom those children seem unlovely. How much Christian Biblical exegesis owes to the grammatical schools and Christian preaching to the rhetorical will not easily be calculated, and it was, partly at least, the strength that she drew from the

d 2

schools which armed the Church, when 'capta ferum victorem cepit.'

§ 4. The *INSTITUTIO* REGARDED AS A TREATISE ON RHETORIC

I said above that the main part of the *Institutio Oratoria* is not in the proper sense of the word an educational work, but a treatise on rhetoric. In this part of the work, i.e. Book III.–XI., Quintilian ceases in the main to address the teacher and turns to the student. Moreover, like most writers on the subject, he allows himself to be too much occupied with forensic rhetoric to the exclusion of other forms. The present volume is not properly speaking concerned with that side of Quintilian's work. Still the position the *Institutio* occupies amongst rhetorical treatises is unique and deserves a few words.

The book may be said to stand midway between the *De Oratore* on the one hand and the ordinary 'artes' on the other. Of these last Cicero's *De Inventione* may be taken as a satisfactory example, though indeed it is less dry than most. The *De Oratore* with its dramatic form and its framework of distinguished men of the past may be fairly said, in Mommsen's words, to have solved the problem of combining didactic instruction with amusement. From its richness and brightness Quintilian evidently learnt much, though wisely enough he did not attempt to imitate its form.

Quintilian very truly describes the main characteristic of his own book, when he writes of his method (I. Prooem. 23) as a 'docendi ratio, quae non eorum modo scientia...studiosos instruat, et...ius ipsum rhetorices interpretetur, sed alere facundiam, vires augere eloquentiae possit.' He goes on to contrast it with the 'nudae artes,' which 'omnem sucum ingenii bibunt, et ossa detegunt, quae ut esse et adstringi nervis suis debent, sic corpore operienda sunt.'

The sap and body will be easily realised by the reader who takes any one section of Quintilian's text-book and compares it with the treatment of the same point in the *De Inventione* or the other 'artes.' I might suggest as one instance out of many possible, the treatment of the qualities of 'narratio' in IV. 2, 31–65 compared with *De Inventione* I. 27–30. Quintilian gives us a discussion rather than a lecture. The result is a length three or four times that of the other, but at the same time far more personal and human.

Another quality of the text-book may be noticed here. Quintilian does not regard the rules he lays down as absolute. They are not καθολικά, i.e. universally and absolutely true, but merely general rules which have perpetually to be modified by private judgment. This doctrine affects not only the scientific character of his treatment of rhetoric, but also its literary expression. The absence of dogmatism strengthens the appeal of the book to the general reader. At the same time it is probably true that the very virtues of the treatise have detracted from its value for school use. So far as I can judge, throughout the centuries during which rhetoric was really studied, it was certainly not always, perhaps not even generally, the favourite text-book. Both teachers and students probably preferred their rules in a cut-and-dried form, rather than in Quintilian's human, personal and (in spite of the many incisive, forcible and aphoristic remarks which lighten it) sometimes garrulous style.

A third characteristic is the amount of purely literary criticism, not merely in the chapters (I. 8, II. 5 and X. I) which definitely treat of the value of various writers, but throughout most of the books, particularly VIII. to X. All writers on rhetoric are necessarily to some extent literary critics, but none, I think, not even Cicero, to the extent of Quintilian[1]. To this aspect of his work I shall have to return in a later part of this introduction. Meanwhile I cannot, I think, describe it better than by quoting the words of the Historian of Criticism.

' It would be possible by a process of mere " lifting out," with hardly any important garbling of phrase, to extract from the *Institutions* a " Treatise on Composition and Critical Reading," which would be of no mean bulk, of no narrow range, and would contain a very large proportion of strictly relevant and valuable detail. And this treatise would be illuminated—for practically the only time, in the range of ancient literature on the subject, to any considerable extent—by that searchlight

---

[1] Treatises like the *De Compositione* of Dion. Hal. or the *De Sublimitate* can hardly be reckoned amongst writings on formal rhetoric.

of criticism, the comparative method ; while it would also display, throughout, the other illuminative powers of wide reading, sound judgment, and an excellent and by no means merely pedestrian common-sense[1].'

§ 5. Comparison with Plutarch's *De Liberorum Educatione* and Tacitus' *Dialogus de Oratoribus*

There are two more or less contemporary works which challenge comparison with the educational side of Quintilian. One is the *De Liberorum Educatione* bound up with the *Moralia* of Plutarch. The other is the *Dialogus de Oratoribus* of Tacitus.

As to the first, which we may for convenience call ' Plutarch,' I have already pointed out that it differs fundamentally from Quintilian in that it represents the philosophical as opposed to the rhetorical ideal. It also differs in that it is mainly or wholly addressed to the parent rather than the teacher, and thus deals with many questions with which Quintilian is not concerned. At the same time the two agree on several points of detail. Plutarch like Quintilian (1) dilates on the necessity for care in choosing nurses, 'paedagogi,' and the 'vernae' with whom the child associates (Ch. 5–7), (2) objects to flogging (Ch. 12), (3) shews the need of relaxation (Ch. 13), (4) the importance of cultivating the memory (ib.). In (1) (2) and (4) there are some fairly close resemblances of detail. For while Plutarch lays more stress on character in the attendant servants than does Quintilian, his solicitude about the correctness of speech in the 'vernae' (περίτρανα λαλεῖν) is very like Quintilian. Both writers base their objection to flogging on its servile nature, and the phrase ' thesaurus eloquentiae,' quoted by Quintilian (XI. 2, 1) as a proverbial description of memory, is perhaps the equivalent of the παιδείας ταμιεῖον of Plutarch. On the other hand there are many important differences of opinion. Plutarch's attitude to bodily exercise is widely different from that of the other, and the non-committal line which he adopts on παιδεραστία is one with which we cannot imagine that Quintilian would agree. He evidently objects altogether to

[1] Saintsbury *History of Criticism* Vol. I. p. 319.

the declamations which he calls πανηγυρικοὶ λῆροι and in particular to improvisation (αὐτοσχέδιος λόγος). As I noted above
his philosophical bias led him to the view that all the ἐγκύκλια
should be treated ἐκ παραδρομῆς ὡσπερεὶ γεύματος ἕνεκεν, and
while Quintilian might have accepted this in regard to music
and mathematics, he would have rejected it strenuously in
regard to 'grammatice' as well as rhetoric. Further Quintilian
would by no means approve of the attitude which Plutarch
assumes to the teachers, though he would of course have agreed
that they should be chosen with care. The Plutarchian parent
does not trust the teacher. 'Every few days' he will test how
the pupils are getting on, knowing well the truth of the proverb
that 'nothing keeps the horse in such good condition as the
master's eye' (Ch. 13). There is not much chance under such
a *régime* for cultivating those relations of love and respect
which Quintilian describes in II. 2.

Altogether the two treatises are the work of writers who
have fundamentally little in common. It will be of course quite
compatible with this that in the points where they agree, one
is reminiscent of the other or both of some common source.
But I do not myself think that the agreements above noted
are sufficiently strong, either as to thought or language, to
warrant any definite conclusion on the point.

The *Dialogue* of Tacitus, or rather the speech of Messalla
in the *Dialogue*, has also several points of contact with the
Institutio, but again there is little real agreement. The book
touches a different side of Quintilian's educational work from
that touched by Plutarch. It is not concerned with ethical
questions, but with the education of the orator. Tacitus fully
agrees with Cicero and Quintilian that wide knowledge, in
which philosophy is an important element, is the true foundation
of oratory. But the methods of acquiring this wide knowledge
which he proposes are very different. Messalla sketches (28)
the old *régime* under which the parent superintended the boy's
education himself, and the boy thus trained was sent to his ap-
prenticeship in the Forum under some distinguished orator (34).
Now the early education is entrusted to worthless slaves (29),
the stages of 'grammatistice 'and 'grammatice' are passed per-
functorily (30), and the boy is sent to the rhetor's school with

its atmosphere of complacency and mutual admiration and its absurd declamations (35). Thus on what we know from Quintilian himself to have been two leading practical questions, viz. home teaching *v.* school teaching, and the value of declamations, Messalla gives his views, and if I mistake not they are the very opposite of Quintilian's. It is true that the *Dialogue* does not suggest in so many words that 'grammatice' should be learnt at home. But the ideal youth of the past came to the Forum 'imbutus domestica disciplina,' and the objection to the rhetorical school that 'in condiscipulis nihil profectus' applies almost as well to the grammatical and is the very opposite of Quintilian's view that boys learn from each other. On the declamation question it is only a superficial examination that will find real agreement. It is true that both take much the same view of the abuses of the system. But with Quintilian they are only abuses neither universal nor necessary. With Messalla they *are* the system, and the point he works up to is that the *rhetores*, including presumably Quintilian himself, should be eliminated. It would be fanciful to suppose that the book was written in definite hostility to Quintilian, but such a theory would be much less preposterous than the idea frequently put forward that the resemblances between the *Dialogue* and the *Institutio* suggest that the writer of the former was a pupil of the writer of the latter[1].

----

[1] Nowadays it is hardly necessary to notice the old theory that the *Dialogue* is the lost *De Causis* of Quintilian.

CHAPTER III

KNOWLEDGE AND USE OF QUINTILIAN UP TO THE
DISCOVERY BY POGGIO OF THE COMPLETE TEXT IN
1416

§ 1. Use by Authors till the End of the Thirteenth Century

IT is a remarkable fact that we can find no clear allusion to
or sign of knowledge of the *Institutio* for something like 300
years. The contemporary allusions to the man Quintilian tell
us nothing of his writings, nor is there any certain sign of his
influence. As I have already said Juvenal 14, 32–58 is sufficiently akin to *I. O.* I. 2, 4–8 to suggest a certain probability
that Juvenal had read that chapter of the *Institutio*. In the
next two centuries we hear nothing of him[1]. When we come
to the fourth century we find Lactantius, Trebellius Pollio,
Sidonius, Ausonius[2] and Jerome alluding to him as a writer,
but except in the case of the last it is either the Declamations
that are mentioned, or else the reference is uncertain. I am
inclined to think however that Lactantius knew the *Institutio*[3].
In his *Div. Inst.* V. 9 he speaks of Seneca as 'morum vitiorum-
que publicorum et descriptor verissimus et accusator acerrimus.'
Compare this with *I. O.* X. 1, 129 on Seneca 'egregius tamen
vitiorum insectator fuit.' Again we have of Cyprian (*D. I.* V. 1)
'ingenio facili copioso suavi, et quae sermonis maxima est
virtus, aperto.' Compare this with *I. O.* X. 1, 128 (of Seneca)
'ingenium facile et copiosum' and II. 3, 8 'prima est eloquentiae virtus perspicuitas.' Again while Quintilian says of Cicero
(X. 1, 123) 'Platonis aemulus exstitit,' Lactantius says (ib. I.
15) 'M. Tullius solus exstitit Platonis imitator.' Lactantius

---

[1] It may perhaps be said that the fact that a mass of declamations usually held
to be largely if not entirely spurious were tacked on to the name of the author of
the *Institutio* is in itself a sign of the great reputation of the book.

[2] These will be found in the *Testimonia et Elogia* at the beginning of the editions
of Capperonnier and Burman.

[3] It is never safe to quote a story as evidence that the narrator has found it in
any particular book. Still it may be noted that the story of Carneades' double
oration at Rome for justice and injustice, which appears in *D. I.* 5, 15, does not
seem to come in any earlier authority except *I. O.* XII. 1, 35.

(ib. II. 13) couples Empedocles in Greek with Lucretius and Varro in Latin as writers on natural science, exactly as Quintilian does in I. 4, 4. Finally both quote (*D. I.* III. 17 ; *I. O.* VIII. 5, 5) the otherwise unknown line :

'Mors misera non est; aditus ad mortem est miser.

None of these points is at all conclusive in itself, but cumulatively they do, I think, suggest that Lactantius knew and used the *I. O.*

M. Fierville remarks that we have to come to St Hilary of Poitiers (died 368) and St Jerome (died 420) to find any express mention of the *I. O.* I am afraid part of this statement is too strong, for the only connexion of Hilary with Quintilian seems to lie in the words of Jerome (*Ep.* 70 Migne) ' Hilarius meorum confessor temporum et episcopus duodecim Quintiliani libros et stylo imitatus est et numero.' Jerome is here enumerating the chief ecclesiastical writers both Greek and Latin and commending their secular learning, but I cannot help feeling that this remark about Hilary is mere fancy. The treatise *De Trinitate* has indeed 12 books, but after reading a considerable part of it, I can find no more connexion in style than in subject[1]. Elsewhere indeed (*Ep.* 58) he refers to Hilary by no means so favourably, and I suspect that the comparison with Quintilian is but a chance suggestion to balance the Ciceronian character just before ascribed to Lactantius. For, as we shall see presently, amongst prose-writers on serious and semi-philosophical subjects Quintilian stands very high in Jerome's estimation[2], and the compliment to Hilary may merely mean that he deals with his subject as ably as does Quintilian with his.

Jerome has some general allusions to Quintilian, two of which became apparently stereotyped in the Middle Ages. One of these is the 'acumina Quintiliani' of *Ep.* 125, the

---

[1] It is just possible that the way in which Hilary at the end of his first book summarises the contents of the remaining eleven may have seemed to Jerome to resemble Quintilian's announcement in Prooem. 21–22.

[2] To judge from the quotations collected by Lübeck *Hieronymus quos noverit scriptores et ex quibus hauserit*, a collection by no means complete, Quintilian stands second and Sallust third among prose-writers, Cicero of course being first. In *Ep.* 125 Jerome notes as favourite writers 'Quintiliani acumina, Ciceronisque fluvios, gravitatemque Frontonis et lenitatem Plinii.' As a matter of fact however he does not seem to quote Fronto at all, nor either Pliny extensively.

other is a passage in *Ep.* 36, 14 where the 'flosculi Quintiliani' are coupled with the 'argumenta Aristotelis' and the 'flumen Tullianum eloquentiae.' No doubt in the former he refers primarily to the *Institutio,* and in the latter to the *Declamations.* But besides such allusions and also direct quotations from the *Declamations,* there are others from the *Institutio* adapted to different contexts in a way that shews that he was thoroughly familiar with his author. Thus 'velut laeto gramine sata strangulant' in *Inst.* VIII. Prooem. 23 is quoted without acknowledgment in *Ep.* 57, 6. So too ib. 31 'iacere sensus in oratione, in qua verba laudantur' appears slightly altered in *Ep.* 58, 8 and with the addition 'ut quidam ait.' In *Ep.* 53, 1 the phrase 'T. Livium lacteo eloquentiae fonte manantem' is an adaptation of *Inst.* X. 1, 32[1], while in *Ep.* 66, 9 the words 'felices, inquit Fabius, essent artes, si de illis soli artifices iudicarent[2]' seem to be a free version of XII. 10, 50. Elsewhere (Pref. to Comm. on Obadiah) he couples the *Inst.* with Origen on the Cantica and Tertullian *Contra Marcionem* as instances of maturer works which superseded earlier attempts (evidently alluding to Prooem. 7). But by far the most important use of Quintilian by Jerome is to be found in the letter to Laeta (107)[3]. Here Jerome, wishing to make suggestions for the training of a Christian girl, pays Quintilian the high compliment of not so much quoting as adapting his educational views. The importance of first associations, with the same Horatian illustrations, the injunctions as to the careful selection of companions, the use of letters of ivory as playthings, the need to use love of praise and ambition as a stimulus, the danger of creating dislike for study are all modelled on Quintilian both in thought and language. In other cases he gives Quintilian's advice a different turn. As with his predecessor the nouns used in the first writing lessons should be such as are worth learning; but while with Quintilian these are the 'lingua secretior,' with Jerome they are the genealogies in the 1st and 3rd gospels.

---

[1] This is often quoted in later times, and as the words in Quintilian referred to lay in the great lacunas its origin remained unsuspected.

[2] The same phrase ascribed to 'disertissimus rhetor' opens the preface to Book XVI. of the Commentary on Isaiah. Ritter would trace it to a lost declamation.

[3] In another educational letter to Gaudentius (128) the influence of Quintilian is fairly obvious in the first section at least.

Like Quintilian's boy this girl is to begin with Greek, to be followed shortly by Latin, but the Greek is to be the Greek scriptures. In some cases he has either mistaken his authority or deliberately differed from him. Thus methods of teaching the letters and writing which Quintilian thinks wrong or unnecessary are recommended, though in obviously borrowed language. The whole letter, in spite of much that seems to us monkish, has a great deal of human charm and beauty and must have exercised considerable influence on Christian education. That it should recognise Quintilian as its model, even though *mutatis mutandis*, is perhaps the highest tribute paid to him till the Renaissance, or at any rate till the days of John of Salisbury[1].

Did Jerome's great contemporary know Quintilian? I have never seen any definite quotation produced from Augustine, though I have suggested myself on I. 8, 5 that we may find a reminiscence of it in *De Civ.* 1, 3. In the *De Ordine* to some extent, and still more in the *De Doct. Christ.*, there is a good deal which may be closely illustrated from Quintilian, but it is matter more or less common to rhetoricians. The most likely allusion that I have noticed lies in *De Doct. Christ.* 4, 7, 21 where the doctrine that rhetoric merely observes phenomena and does not create them is mentioned. This appears in Cic. *De Or.* 1, 146, but as it is more prominent in Quintilian (*v.* note on I. 6, 16) and Aug. attributes it to 'quidam disertissimi et acutissimi viri,' there is some reason for supposing that he has Quintilian in his mind[2].

I now turn to the use of Quintilian by the grammarians and rhetoricians. As to the former, Quintilian was not a grammarian by profession and it is not remarkable that his sketch in

---

[1] The adducing in *Ep.* 69, 8 of the definition of the orator as the 'Vir bonus dicendi peritus' is given by Lübeck as from Quintilian XII. 1, 1. But it must be remembered that Jerome was acquainted with the elder Seneca, who also gives it as Cato's. I should suspect however that the addition 'ut rhetores quidam definiunt' implies that he knew it from both. When this definition is found in the Middle Ages it may be derived from Jerome, or quite as probably from Cassiodorus or Isidore.

[2] *Conf.* III. 17 'peccata proficientium, quae bene iudicantibus et vituperantur ex regula perfectionis et laudantur spe frugis sicut herba segetis' may have been inspired by *I. O.* II. 4, 13–14. But the thought is so natural (something like it had been said by Cicero), that we cannot lay stress on it.

I. 4–8 did not attract particular notice. On the contrary it is rather to be wondered at, that we actually find Priscian quoting it once[1]. The other quotations[2] are all concerned either with figures and tropes or metrical points and are drawn from Books VIII. and IX.

As to the rhetoricians, it may safely be assumed that they all had read and knew Quintilian, but the extent to which they used and reproduced him may be fairly[3] gauged by the list of quotations in the index to Halm's *Latini Rhetores minores*. Of the 135 references there Fortunatianus has one[4], three belong to Rufinus on metres, three to Isidore, about thirty are merely 'flosculi' from Quintilian inserted in MSS. of Cassiodorus, and all the rest belong to Julius Victor, who alone among the rhetoricians quotes copiously and indeed transcribes whole passages from Quintilian.

Turning to the well-known names of the next few centuries after Jerome, we find no sign in Martianus Capella, nor yet in Boethius, of Quintilian's influence. Cassiodorus on the other hand knew and used him to a considerable extent. His eulogy on him in his *De Artibus ac Disciplinis liberalium Litterarum* (v. Halm op. cit. p. 498) has often been quoted. After noting the *De Inventione*, with the commentary of Victorinus as his primary authority, he goes on: 'Quintilianus tamen doctor egregius, qui post fluvios Tullianos singulariter valuit implere quae docuit, virum bonum dicendi peritum a prima aetate suscipiens per cunctas artes ac disciplinas nobilium litterarum erudiendum esse monstravit, quem merito ad defendendum totius civitatis vota requirerent.' The continuation is still more important : ' Libros autem duo Ciceronis de arte rhetorica et Quintiliani duodecim institutionum iudicavimus esse iungendos, ut nec codicis excresceret magnitudo, et utrique dum

---

[1] Prisc. K. II. 18, where *Inst.* I. 4, 15 is quoted; v. note thereon.

[2] v. Index Auctorum, Keil.

[3] I say 'fairly,' for this index is not perfect. In Clodius *De Statibus* (p. 590) there is a reference, unnoticed in the index, to *Inst.* III. 6, 68, in Grillus (p. 598) to Prooem. 13, in Julius Severianus (p. 355) to Prooem. 27 (v. note). The account of 'exercitatio' in Fortunatianus (p. 122) seems to be a summary of the scheme of Book X. Note too that of the anonymous *Schemata dianoeas*, pp. 71–77, about a quarter are taken verbatim from Quintilian and are not transcribed by Halm.

[4] Halm, p. 122 'Vir perfectissimus dixit "verbis utendum est ut nummis publica moneta signatis,"' a loose version of I. 6, 3.

necessarii fuerint, parati semper occurrant.' This is for the library of his monastery of Viviers. For those who want their rhetoric in a more condensed form he has Fortunatianus bound in a single volume. Cassiodorus also wrote a short treatise on orthography, in which he notes the chapter of Quintilian (I. 7) as an accepted authority, though he does not make any extracts from it.

Next comes Isidore, whose *Origines* or *Etymologies* was the chief encyclopaedia of the Middle Ages. After defining rhetoric (Migne 82, 124, Halm op. cit. p. 507) he goes on 'Haec autem disciplina a Graecis inventa est, et translata in Latinum a Tullio videlicet et Quintiliano[1], sed ita copiose, ita varie, ut eam lectori admirari in promptu sit, comprehendere impossibile.' In the short sketch that follows there is a little but only a little which can be traced to Quintilian exclusively[2], but his influence is clearer in other parts of the *Etymologies*. This is particularly the case with the chapter on Analogy (I. 28, Migne, p. 104) and that on 'quid possit musica' (III. 17, Migne, p. 164) where the adaptations from *I. O.* I. 6 and I. 10 respectively are patent.

The authority of Cassiodorus and Isidore could not fail to establish Quintilian's position at any rate as a rhetorician. Yet we have to wait more than two centuries before we hear of him again. Aldhelm gives no evidence of having read him in any way, and though his quotations from Latin prose-writers are far less numerous than those from the poets, they are numerous enough to make the absence significant. Bede does not seem to use him. When we come to Alcuin, it is to be observed that Quintilian's name does not occur in the famous hexametric catalogue of the Library at York (Migne 101,843-4), and though there are 'perplures alii' omitted, including Isidore himself, when we remember how easily the alternative names Fabius and Quintilianus fit into verse, the omission is noteworthy. The treatise of Alcuin on rhetoric at first sight seems to reproduce Quintilian, notably the remark 'licet ipsa vitium

---

[1] Some MSS. and Edd. insert 'et Titiano,' an early corruption, which was read by Conrad von Hirschau (12th century), v. page lv. The addition was possibly a deduction from the juxtaposition of Quintilian and Titianus by Ausonius in the passage of the *Grat. Act.*, part of which was quoted above, p. xiii.

[2] v. Halm *Lat. Rhet.* p. 518.

sit ambitio, frequenter tamen causa virtutum est[1]' (I. 2, 22), but inspection will shew that this and other passages are transcribed from Julius Victor and not from Quintilian direct. Nor can I find anything in Rabanus Maurus. His remarks on rhetoric are really transcripts of Augustine *De Doct. Christ.* His definition of 'grammatica,' often noted as shewing an appreciation of the literary side better than that of Alcuin, might seem tó reproduce Quintilian. But it is really nothing but the traditional definition given by Marius Victorinus and Sergius, itself a translation of Dionysius Thrax. It is only when we come to that interesting seeker after learning, Servatus Lupus of Ferrières (d. about 860), that we find authentic traces of Quintilian[2]. In his letters he twice[3] mentions the *Institutio.* In the first case he writes to the Abbot of York, asking for a copy of the 12 books. In the second he writes to the Pope and asks for a complete copy of this and the *De Oratore*, adding that he already possessed both works in an incomplete form[4].

Then again there is a great gap. Neither in the tenth nor in the eleventh centuries can I find any clear indication of a knowledge of Quintilian. At the end of the tenth Gerbert quotes a large number of writers, but Quintilian is not among them, and when he wishes for a rhetorical treatise, it is that of Victorinus. One may however perhaps conjecture, that when his biographer, Richer, writes of him 'cum ad rhetoricam suos provehere vellet, id sibi suspectum erat quod sine locutionum modis, qui in poetis discendi sunt, ad oratoriam artem perveniri non queat,' he means that Gerbert followed in training his pupils the principles of Quintilian as to the relations of 'grammatice' and rhetoric (Migne 138, p. 103). For in no other writer, so far as I know, would he find this principle so clearly emphasized. We may perhaps go further and

---

[1] Both this and the allusion in Hincmar (v. *infra*) had been remarked by Spalding, who failed however to notice the sources from which Alcuin and Hincmar drew their knowledge.

[2] Lupus' contemporary Hincmar of Rheims has been credited by his editor in Migne (125, p. 993) with a quotation from *I. O.* I. 1, 9 (the story of Alexander and Leonides), but evidently his statement is a rather rash interpretation of Jerome, v. note on that passage.

[3] Migne 119, pp. 526 and 579.   [4] v. *inf.* p. lxiii.

suggest that Gerbert's pupil Fulbert[1], who founded the school of Chartres, carried there his master's conception of the value of literature and created the tradition which his later successors in the school certainly followed.

It was in 1119 that Bernard of Chartres succeeded to the headship of that school. Of his methods and those of his successors, William of Conches and Richard l'Évêque, we have a well-known description in the *Metalogicus* of John of Salisbury (I. 24). In the first part of this chapter John gives a description of what a 'praelectio' should be—a description which largely repeats *Inst.* I. 8, 13 ff., with some reminiscence of I. 4, 4–5, and shews that the student of every 'discipline' will find the essence of what he seeks in literature, and conversely that a knowledge of these disciplines will enable him to bring out more clearly the true significance of literature. He then describes how Bernard followed this method, always however considering (as in *Inst.* II. 8) the capacities of his hearers. He would mark carefully the distinction between 'propria' and 'translata' (*Inst.* I. 5,7). He would demand each day from every pupil some points of yesterday's lesson (cf. perhaps *Inst.* II. 2, 8). Above all he would dwell on the literary value of the authors read, and here John repeats almost word for word the admirable classification of the subjects of literary judgment which we have in *Inst.* I. 8, 17. He then takes Quintilian's remarks in the same chapter about the need of discrimination in dealing with 'histories,' but (doubtless through mistaking the meaning of the word) applies these remarks to the choice of authors in general: finally the book is concluded by a lengthy quotation of the 'laus grammaticae' from *Inst.* I. 4, 5–6[2].

Whether the exercises, mentioned in addition to the 'praelectio,' are also reminiscent of Quintilian is more doubtful. The 'vespertinum exercitium' or 'declinatio' presumably consisted of rigid grammatical catechizing on some given material,

---

[1] Clerval (*Écoles de Chartres*, p. 115) says that Fulbert apparently did not know Quintilian. I know of no definite evidence one way or the other.

[2] The fact that John knew Quintilian has been noticed by Fierville and others, but the close dependence of Bernard's scheme on him seems to have been frequently or generally ignored. Neither Clerval (*Écoles de Chartres*) nor Norden (*Kunstprosa*) nor Poole (*Illustrations of History of Mediaeval Thought and Learning*), though they quote or comment on the scheme, seem to recognise the connexion with Quintilian. But v. Sandys *Hist. Class. Schol.* I. 539.

and may have been founded on the 'nomina declinare et verba inprimis pueri sciant' of I. 4, 22 and the 'declinatio' of the 'chriae' in I. 9, 5. The material is to be of an edifying character (again from the 'chriae'?). There is more definite ground for supposing that the 'exercitium' or original composition in prose and verse is based on Quintilian's principles as explained in I. 8, II. 4, and II. 10; and the eulogy of the competitive element in these, as well as the description of Bernard's encouraging method of correction, seem to me suggestive of I. 2, 21 and II. 4, 10 respectively[1].

The evidence of Chartres does not stand alone in this century. The fact that a monk of Bec, Stephen of Rouen, reduced the mutilated version, which alone was at his disposal, to an abstract of about one-third, shews that at Bec the educational value of the work was understood. Stephen, it may be observed, was not a mere rhetorician. He was also a poet of some reputation. His introduction[2] is of considerable interest and defends the undertaking by pointing out the attention given to pagan writers by Augustine, Ambrose, Origen, Alcuin and Charles the Great. With Stephen's work perhaps we may group an early collection of 'flores,' largely from the first two books, of an educational character, of which four copies survive (v. Fierville, p. xxxi.).

Another[3] valuable tribute during the same century comes from Wibald, abbot of Stavelot and Corvey (d. 1158), an undoubted lover of learning. His letter (Migne 189, ep. 147) 'ad Mangoldum scholae magistrum' brings out the educational use of the book. It is no small matter, he says, to know

[1] We have another witness to the school of Chartres in the *Eptateuchon* of Bernard's brother and (though not immediate) successor Theodoric. The *Eptateuchon* is preserved in MS. at Chartres. According to Clerval's account of this work, which is an encyclopaedic description of the Seven Arts, though Quintilian is cited in the rhetorical portion, he is not one of the text-books which form its basis. The whole treatment as described by Clerval seems narrower and drier than Bernard's.

[2] Partly in verse and partly in prose. Some of the former is quoted by Fierville, p. xxviii. and some of the latter by Comparetti, *Virgil in the Middle Ages*, Eng. Trans., pp. 84, 85.

[3] 'Peter of Blois,' mentioned by Fierville, p. xvi., as having known Quintilian, must be eliminated. Allusions indeed appear in nos. 101 and 150 of these letters (the genuineness of which seems to be more than doubtful), but comparison with the *Metalogicus* of John of Salisbury will shew that they, as apparently most of 'Peter's' literary embellishments, are borrowed from John.

the power and character of different pupils, to stimulate the indolent, to hold back the impetuous, and to guide them with a strong rein. Then he goes on 'Lege Quintilianum de institutione oratoria, qui ab utero matris susceptum infantem limare incipit et formare in substantiam oratoris perfecti.' The same letter contains a clear though unacknowledged adaptation from X. 5, 19 'si gloria dicendi tangeris, elige quem sequaris.'

Giraldus Cambrensis, who may be said to belong to the end of this century, quotes Quintilian twice and both times from Book X. (91 and 114). But he quotes so many other authors and so much more copiously, that this can hardly be reckoned amongst the tributes paid to Quintilian[1].

In the thirteenth century[2] the encyclopaedist Vincent of Beauvais shews a very full knowledge of Quintilian. In the *Speculum Historiale*, one of the four divisions of his great work, there are collected (Book IX. 121) some sixty flosculi from him. They are rather of a moral or philosophical character, than rhetorical. In another division, the *Speculum Doctrinale*, many of these recur in various connexions. And it is noteworthy that in the chapters of this *Speculum Doctrinale* which deal with the *Instructio* and *Eruditio Puerorum* he is equally prominent. Still more is this the case in a *Tractatus de Educatione Filiorum regalium*, which forms part of his *Opuscula*[2, 3].

Before closing this section I may note, though I do not know whether its date can be fixed with certainty, another striking use of Quintilian, which stands in a sense by itself. This is the pseudo-Boethian *Liber de Geometria* appended to the two books on geometry ascribed to Boethius. While the authenticity of these last is a matter of dispute among experts, there seems to be no doubt at all as to the spuriousness of

---

[1] v. below, p. lxii.

[2] v. Bassi *Giornale Storico* vol. XXIII., p. 186, where the references to the *Speculum Doctrinale* are given in full. I have verified them, but regret that I have been unable to do the same with the statement about the *Opuscula*. According to Bassi Quintilian is constantly and almost exclusively quoted in a large part of this tractate.

[3] One great writer of the thirteenth century may be mentioned as probably not knowing Quintilian, viz. Roger Bacon. He has such an excellent opportunity of using him, when he deals with the training of the young (*Op. Maj.* VII. 3, 3), and to a less extent when discussing the need of relaxation, that I hardly think he can have read him.

this *Liber de Geometria*. Still the fact remains that in this addition of the thirteenth (?) century to Boethian literature, the writer introduces a large portion of the remarks of Quintilian in I. 10 on the uses of geometry[1]. Perhaps too we may find the use of Quintilian in another pseudo-Boethian work, the *De Scholarium Disciplinis*[2]. This work is certainly earlier than Roger Bacon, who twice quotes it as genuine[3]. It contains at least one remark, which I decidedly suspect to be borrowed from Quintilian[4]. And finally we have to note that this spurious work is itself the subject of an elaborate commentary ascribed to Aquinas himself and reckoned among his 'dubia' by recent editors. This commentary makes unmistakable use of Quintilian.

§ 2. OTHER FORMS OF NOTICE DURING THE SAME PERIOD

Dante, I think, gives no sign of any knowledge of Quintilian, and our next name will be Petrarch; but as that brings us to the period of the Revival, it will be well to go back for a little. Hitherto I have dealt with various writers with a view to ascertaining whether they really knew or used Quintilian, but besides testimonies of this kind, there are other forms of evidence, which can tell us something about the extent to which his name and the general character of his work were known in the centuries which I have been traversing[5]. These are (*a*) passing allusions in literary works or letters, which shew that he was regarded as a great name in rhetoric; (*b*) lists of authors recommended to students; (*c*) library catalogues.

[1] Migne 63, p. 1353.   [2] Migne 64, pp. 1223–1238.
[3] It has been supposed that the true author is 'Thomas Cantimpretensis,' but on what grounds I do not know.
[4] Chap. I., Migne p. 1226 'scientia sine usu prodest parum, usus autem sine scientia prodest multum'; cf. *Inst.* XII. 6, 4 'plusque, si separes, usus sine doctrina quam citra usum doctrina valet.' This passage would be found in the mutilated copies.
[5] I may here take the opportunity of modifying a rather too sweeping statement which I made in *Classical Review*, November 1921, p. 153, as to the wide educational influence of Quintilian during these centuries. I was then too much impressed by the cases of Chartres and Bec and had not realised that elsewhere this influence was not so apparent.

(*a*) In the first of these three classes I have noted a few examples which a wider reading would probably supplement. Several of them appear in complimentary passages. The writer expresses his high opinion of somebody else's powers, by saying that various ancient celebrities could not challenge him. Thus a certain Alvarus in the ninth century writing to Eulogius on his *Memoriale Sanctorum* says 'tibi dulcis cedet illa saecularis lingua Catonis, fervens quoque Demosthenis ingenium et dives Ciceronis olim eloquium floridusque Quintilianus' (Migne 115, p. 735). Again, in the eleventh century, we have Benzo, Bishop of Alba, addressing the Emperor Henry IV. in a panegyrical poem[1], in which he extols his powers, literary and otherwise. In this, after Tully and Donatus, various writers are mentioned who would not have dared to compete with the Emperor. In this list Quintilian appears: so do Virgil, Lucan and Statius; but, as it also includes the Latin *Iliad*[2] and Grillus the commentator on the *De Inventione*, the compliment is not a very high one. Again, in the twelfth century, 'Nigellus Wirecker,' writing on the virtues of Becket, says:

> Tardus ad hunc sanius[3] si certet acumine mentis
> Indoctusque Plato Varroque stultus erit.
> Curio si certet verbis vincetur ab ipso,
> Victus si certet Quintilianus erit.

About the same time Alain-de-Lille in his *Anti-claudianus* puts him in the forefront of rhetoricians (III. 3), while in II. 6, in a general list of accomplished persons, we have 'ut Fabius loquitur, ut Tullius ipse perorat.' Alexander Neckham (died 1217), in his *De Laudibus Divinae Sapientiae*, after noting the powers of rhetoric, goes on, X. 95:

> Pectus Aristotelis miror, linguam Ciceronis,
> Et flores laudo, Quintiliane, tuos...
> ....
> In coniecturis, Quintiliane, vales,
> Nunc confutando nunc confirmando perorans
> Se causa gaudet obtinuisse sua.

---

[1] Given in Pertz *Mon. Germ. Hist.* XI. (XIII.), p. 599.

[2] 'Pindarus seu Homerus.' The Latin version of the *Iliad* was ascribed to 'Pindarus Thebanus.' There is no suggestion, as some have thought, of Greek authors.

[3] *sic* in text. ? Samius = Pythagoras.

These vague generalities do not perhaps amount to very much. In the first place some of them apply mainly or entirely to the Declamations, and secondly one may ask, are we really sure that these people knew anything more about Quintilian than that he was praised by the writer whom they really did know—Jerome? This suspicion is confirmed by the fact that one of the couplets quoted from Neckham is obviously a paraphrase of Jerome, *Ep.* 36 (mentioned on p. xlv.) 'argumenta Aristotelis—flumen Tullianum eloquentiae—flosculi Quintiliani,' and that the 'floridus Quintilianus' of Alvarus comes almost as certainly from the same source[1]. Still, whatever the source of their views of Quintilian, it does remain the fact, I think, that he takes in the eyes of the ordinary student of those ages, a higher place among the classics than he does now. And this conclusion is supported by our second heading.

(*b*) Documents giving lists or descriptions of authors recommended to students. Of these I have seen four, viz. (1) the 'Dialogus super auctores' of Conrad of Hirschau (c. 1100); (2) the so-called 'Sacerdos ad altare' bound up with the works of Johannes de Garlandia, but possibly the work of Alexander Neckham; (3) the 'Biblionomia' of Richard de Fournival (both of these about the end of the twelfth century), and (4) the 'Registrum multorum auctorum' of Hugo of Trimburg (towards the end of the thirteenth). Of these Conrad's dialogue gives a list of twenty-one authors, each of whom is described with some fullness. Quintilian is not amongst these, but neither is any prose writer except Cicero and Sallust. His name appears at the end of the treatise as one of the founders of Latin rhetoric, but the whole passage is merely transcribed from Isidore and couples with the names of Cicero and Quintilian that of the nebulous Titinius.

The 'Sacerdos ad altare' is to be found in a MS. in Caius

---

[1] It is amusing to note with what misleading persistence this phrase of Jerome turns up. Messer (*Quintilian als Didaktiker*) argues that Quintilian must have again become known in Germany (was he ever unknown?) because of an allusion to him in a letter of Gregor Heimburg, for which Messer refers to Voigt II. 288. But on turning to Voigt we find that Heimburg wrote that 'Die göttliche Dinge bedürfen nicht der Bewässerung durch die Fluthen der tullianischen Eloquenz, nicht der Redeblümchen Quintilians.' The letter is unpublished and the original Latin not given, but its source seems obvious.

College Library[1]. Whether its authorship is to be ascribed to Johannes de Garlandia or Alexander Neckham, or someone unknown, hardly matters for our purpose. It belongs at any rate to the end of the thirteenth or the beginning of the fourteenth century, and gives a very full and interesting list of recommended books. The rhetorical section runs: 'In rethorica educandus legat primum Tullii rethoricam et librum ad Herennium et Tullium de oratore et causas Quintiliani et Quintilianum de oratoris institucione.'

The 'Biblionomia,' which may be assumed to represent the author's ideal of a library rather than anything actually existent, has a section corresponding to each of the seven arts. The rhetorical section is headed by Quintilian, followed by a large number of Cicero's works (including his declamations!), Victorinus, Grillus and Sallust's 'Invectives against Catiline[2].'

The 'Registrum' of Hugo includes no prose writers except Cicero, Sallust and Seneca.

(c) The results obtained under (a) and (b) are quite confirmed by the evidence of the Catalogues of Libraries. In about 130 collected by G. Becker (Cat. Bibl. Ant.) ranging from the eighth to the twelfth century Quintilian appears five times (Bec, Michelsburg, Durham, Salzburg, and one of uncertain origin). Judged thus in popularity he comes far behind, not only the chief poets, but also Cicero, Seneca and Sallust, but he is found oftener than Caesar or Livy, or even Aulus Gellius. Nor does he appear to be superseded as a rhetorical handbook by any of the Rhetores Minores except Victorinus on the De Inventione. Fortunatianus occurs only three or four times, and Julius Victor never.

§ 3. USE BY AUTHORS FROM 1300 TO 1416

The fourteenth century, with which we may for convenience range the first quarter of the fifteenth, stands by itself in the history of Quintilian's fortunes. On the one hand the Revival of Latin study, chiefly in Italy, shews us the interest in and appreciation of the book as on a totally different level from that reached in the earlier centuries. On the other hand it is still

---

[1] The document is transcribed by C. H. Haskins (*Harvard Studies in Class. Philol.* 1909, p. 90 ff.).   [2] v. Delisle *Cat. des MSS.* ii. 518.

only the mutilated text that is in the possession of scholars, and we find nothing approaching the enthusiasm, to some extent perhaps artificial, which followed Poggio's discovery at St Gall.

Petrarch heads the list, not only in virtue of his own import- ance, but also of his knowledge of Quintilian. Fierville has called attention to the 'Orkus-Brief' addressed by him to Quintilian, an honour which the latter shares with Cicero, Livy, Horace, Seneca, Virgil and Homer. Petrarch had often heard, he tells us, of Quintilian and he had also read the De- clamations to some extent and wondered at his reputation for 'acumen' (a reminiscence of Jerome). Now an MS. of the *Institutio* 'discerptus et lacer' has come into his hands and he no longer wonders. Comparing the book with the Declama- tions he feels that Quintilian ' melius cotis officio functum esse quam gladii, et oratorem formare potentius quam praestare[1].' Still more interesting, and only known in recent years, is the fact that this 'liber discerptus et lacer' still survives as Parisinus No. 7720[2], and contains Petrarch's often pungent anno- tations. Many of these are quoted by Nolhac and are of some personal interest, as when he uses I. 1, 8 'falsam sibi scientiae persuasionem induerunt' as a text for his dislike of scholastic philosophy 'notate hoc, scholastici de nihilo tumentes.'

Petrarch's letter quoted above implies that it was not always easy to obtain even the mutilated copies of Quintilian, and he again says much the same in the *De Vit. Sol.* I. 4, 3. Here, after quoting *Inst.* X. 3, 28, he adds 'haec Quintilianus, quae libentius inserui, quia secretior locus erat, nam Senecae de hoc ipso vulgatior epistola est.' Salutati seems to have found the same difficulty[3].

The reality of Boccaccio's knowledge of Quintilian has been disputed by Nolhac[4], whose disbelief has been echoed

---

[1] *Ep. Fam.* XXIV. 7, part quoted by Nolhac *Pétrarque et l'humanisme* II. 84.

[2] I state this on the authority of Nolhac, *op. cit.*, who seems to feel no doubt about it. I should have liked the evidence, which I presume is partly handwriting, more definitely stated. But the notes quoted certainly seem to bear out his view.

[3] v. Novati *Epist. di Salutati* I. p. 262 'postquam de Quintiliani spe decidi,' unless indeed this refers to some earlier hope than that noted on p. lxii, of getting a complete copy. [4] op. cit., II. 83.

by other writers. It is admitted that Boccaccio twice claims to be quoting Quintilian in his *De Genealogia Deorum*[1], but Nolhac declared that one of these quotations was borrowed from Petrarch, and that the other could not be found in Quintilian. I feel little doubt that this is an error and that Boccaccio shews a distinct, though I would not say an intimate, knowledge of Quintilian[2].

Besides these two famous names, a few others may be cited as belonging wholly or mainly to this period. Salutati, chancellor of Florence (died 1406), shews a fairly considerable knowledge of Quintilian. He quotes the first and tenth books several times, once at considerable length[3]. His name naturally leads us to two contemporary French humanists. One of them, Jean de Montreuil, was a correspondent and admirer of Salutati. The other, Nicholas de Clemanges, was a close friend of Jean. This last certainly quotes Quintilian once[4]. Nicholas' quotations are more copious, but confined to the twelfth and tenth books. He calls Quintilian (*Ep.* 5) 'alterum artis oratoriae post Ciceronem decus.' But some of his remarks (*Ep.* 4) shew that while he had studied both Cicero and Quintilian

---

[1] It may also be noted that Quintilian's name appears in the *Decameron*, sixth day, 10, where Cipolla, the eloquent friar, might have been called 'Tullio medesimo o forse Quintiliano.' Here I suppose B. had the *Decl.* mainly in view.

[2] The first of these passages is *De Gen. De.* XI. 2, which has to be compared with *Inst.* X. 3, 23–28, and Petr. *De Vit. Sol.* I. 5, 1. B. has garbled his quotation badly, but on the supposition that the quotation was borrowed from P. the garbling would be worse. Quintilian says that woods, etc., though affected by poets, are really distracting to the student and recommends rather 'silentium noctis.' B. states this as though 'silentium noctis' was regarded by Quintilian as equivalent to lonely woodland scenes. But the form in which P. puts the sense does not appear to differ from Quintilian in any way that would account for the mistake. The other passage is *De Gen.* XIV. 10. The fools say that the poets insert fables to shew their eloquence 'quia circa vera vis eloquentiae non potest ostendi. Male profecto noverunt Quintiliani sententiam, cuius maximi oratoris opinio est, circa falsa nullum eloquentiae nervum posse consistere.' I see no difficulty in referring this to v. 12, 17 (a passage contained in the mutilated text) 'declamationes...ab illa vera imagine orandi recesserunt atque ad solam compositae voluptatem nervis carent,' with also some thought of § 20 just below.

[3] v. index to Novati, *Epist. di Sal.* Note that he too uses the familiar Hieronymian expression 'Ciceronis fluvios, Quintiliani acumina.'

[4] *Inst.* X. 3, 10 'cito scribendo non fit ut bene scribatur' is quoted in a letter first published by A. Thomas (Joh. de Monsteriolo). The editor subjoins 'adde multa alia' (sc. de Quintiliano) but I have not been able to find them. Presumably they are to be found in the still unpublished letters.

he did not regard the formal study of rhetoric as so useful as the study of actual oratory, and it is therefore not surprising that the bulk of his quotations come from the literary criticism of X. 1 [1, 2].

To return to Italy, the famous humanist Gasparino da Barzizza who died in 1431 is said on good authority to have put such store on Quintilian that he attempted to supply the sense in the missing parts [3]. Doubtless he dealt with them in the same way as we know him to have dealt with the lacunas in the *De Oratore* and *Orator* [4].

The last name is that of Vergerio, who died in 1428 (?) but wrote not later than 1404 the work which made his name famous, viz. the treatise *De ingenuis Moribus*. Whether this owes much or anything to Quintilian has been much disputed. That there should be some resemblances of thought is inevitable from the nature of the book. The most definite example is the stress laid on the necessity for providing the best teaching at the earliest stage, supported as in Quintilian by the example of Aristotle and Alexander. We have also the story of Timotheus and his practice of charging double fees to those who had been taught by others. And though he might have got this from other sources, such as John of Salisbury who tells it twice, the cumulative evidence makes me think that it is a definite reminiscence of Quintilian. But the general scope and spirit of the book, which strongly advocates military training,

---

[1] v. Sabbadini *Stor. e Crit.* p. 382.

[2] Another Frenchman, Gerson (probably best known to most people because he has sometimes been put forward as the author of the *Imitatio*), is a voluminous writer, who frequently quotes classical writers. Quintilian however is not amongst the writers whom Voigt (*Humanismus*, II. 343) names him as using. While I cannot definitely state a negative, the treatise *De Parvulis trahendis ad Christum* does not suggest that he had Quintilian much in mind. Otherwise the passages on the force of early training or the bad example of parents, garnished as they are by quotations from Virg. and Cic., could hardly have failed to bring out something from him. He quotes the story of Alexander and Leonides, and (*De Puer. Inst.*) assigns the definition of the Orator as 'vir bonus dicendi peritus' to Cic. For both, I suspect, he is dependent on Jerome or intermediate writers.

[3] On the discovery of the full *De Or.* and *Or.* 'liberatus est Gasparinus ingenti quem adsumpserat labore suppeditandi quod poterat librorum de Oratore defectus, sicut diu ante in Quintiliani Institutionibus multo labore suppleverat.' Flavio Biondo *Ital. Ill.* p. 346.

[4] These supplements which are partly marginal and partly at the end still survive. Sabbadini *Stor. e Crit.* p. 110.

is very different from that of the *Institutio Oratoria*. It should be added that the statement that Vergerio made a 'compendium' of Quintilian is almost certainly a mistake[1].

§4. THE MUTILATED TEXT AND THE FORM IN WHICH IT IS USED

I have regarded the discovery of the complete copy of the *Institutio* by Poggio at St Gall in 1416 as the central point in the history of Quintilian, mainly because it roused the enthusiasm of scholars at a critical moment in the history of education and enthroned Quintilian for a time at least as the leading authority on the subject. With this I propose to deal in the next chapter. But there is another reason also. That the mutilated text, which had held the predominance for some centuries, had not that sole possession of the field which is often credited to it, will appear in the sequel. That the mutilation was not so fatal to the use of the book as is sometimes believed, the foregoing pages will have sufficiently shewn. There was no reason indeed why it should be so. The educational part had suffered little and the main losses were those of the sixth and seventh books, the latter of which is perhaps the least interesting part of the work. Still the mutilation and its results form the most important events in the history of the text of the *Institutio*, and as the currency of the mutilated text was brought to a sudden end[2] by Poggio's find, it will be well to take the subject at this point.

Though the classifications of the MSS. given by Halm, Fierville and Peterson may be for the purpose of determining the true text much superior, for our present purpose it may be

---

[1] It seems to have arisen from an erroneous description of the abridgement made by Patrizi in the latter half of the fifteenth century. An edition of this published by Jean du Tillet, Bishop of S. Brieuc, about 1550 was attributed by him to Vergerio. The full discussion of the matter by Bassi (*Riv. di fil.* XXII.) leaves little doubt on the authorship. The compendium is of the complete text, and therefore even if made by Vergerio could have had no influence on his earlier work.

[2] If we accept Fierville's account of the MSS. only one surviving MS. of the mutilated type is posterior to 1416. This is Par. 7721, executed by Jean Poulain in 1465, but very possibly with the intention of filling up the lacunas, v. Fierv. p. lxxiv.

well to adopt another classification of the MSS. written before 1416. A, those which contain the 'great lacunas,' i.e.

1. Prooem. 1 to a point not earlier than I. 1, 6.
2. V. 14, 12–VIII. 3, 64.
3. VIII. 6, 17–VIII. 6, 67.
4. IX. 3, 2–X. 1, 107.
5. XI. 1, 71–XI. 2, 33.
6. XII. 10, 43 (some earlier), to the end.

Fierville enumerates nine or ten MSS. of this type. The chief of these are the Bernensis, Bambergensis Bg and Nostradamensis, all of the tenth or eleventh century.

B, those which contain the same lacunas with the exception of the portion X. 1, 46–107, which is written at the end of the MS. Of this type there are four surviving, viz. Pratensis, (Stephen of Rouen's abridgement, twelfth century), Puteanus (thirteenth), Vossianus I. (thirteenth), Vossianus III.[1] (fourteenth). This fragment X. 1, 46–107 coupled with the immediate sequel, ib. 107 to the end of the chapter, also appears by itself in two MSS. of the twelfth century bound up with other rhetorical matter. These two are given by Fierville as Par. 7231 and 7696.

C, MSS. with the text complete, or originally complete. Of these there are five or six; Ambrosianus I. (tenth century), Bambergensis (Bg and G combined. The lacunas in Bg were filled up from some complete MS. in the eleventh century; these supplements are known as G), Harleianus, Turicensis and Florentinus (also all of the eleventh), Almeloveenianus (?).

The remarkable fact we have now to note is that while the surviving MSS. shew the A type to be predominant, the quotations in authors point rather to the predominance of the B type. In the first place we must remember that the Pratensis is not an ordinary copy, but an abridgement specially made for educational purposes, and this, as we have seen, is of the B kind. Besides this the 'flores' mentioned on p. li. were evidently drawn from an MS. of this kind, for they are all taken from the parts contained in the 'A' MSS. *except the last*, which

[1] The reader should observe that A and B in this section do not, as in the commentary, denote particular MSS. It should also be noted that Prat. and Put., whose main text comes to an end at X. 3, 32, insert at the end another fragment XII. 10, 10–15. But this fragment does not affect our present argument.

belongs to X. 1, 58. So too with Vincent de Beauvais. His 'flosculi' are also drawn from the incomplete text, but conclude with the same X. 1, 58[1]. John of Salisbury quotes X. 1, 90, and this is the only exception to the rule that he does not quote from the lacunas. Giraldus Cambrensis quotes X. 1, 91[2], and Nicholas de Clemanges several passages in these sections. In fact[3] the only author of whom we can say with certainty that he did not have a B text is Petrarch and we are only certain of this because we possess his MS.

It may however be asked, are we so certain that some of these writers did not possess a C text? It is certainly true that this text was not so completely lost to view as has sometimes been supposed. When we consider how the Bambergensis G was grafted on to the Bambergensis Bg in the eleventh century, how the Harleianus was transcribed from the re-united whole, how again the Florentinus and Turicensis were copied from the Harleianus and the former presented by the Bishop of Strasburg to his Cathedral library[4], we certainly find more activity in the preservation of the complete book than we should have supposed from Poggio's account of what he found at St Gall. And there were other copies in existence. Another was found by Poggio soon after his famous discovery[5]. Bartolommeo da Capra apparently found another in 1423[6]. In 1396 Salutati had heard a report that a complete copy had been

---

[1] This may rouse a suspicion that Vincent's collection is merely an anthology from this other anthology, and without further knowledge of the 'flores' it is impossible to be sure. But such little information as M. Fierville gives does not point that way.

[2] According to the index in the Rolls Series, Giraldus' only other quotation is from X. 1, 114. This does not fall within the fragment, but as noted above the MSS. Par. 7231 and 7696 have X. 1, 47—end (131) bound together. It is possible therefore that Gir. had only access to the fragment with this addition, and not even to an ordinary B text.

[3] I do not feel at all certain of Guarino da Verona in his earlier life. It is a curious fact that, though he was the first to hear and take advantage of Poggio's discovery and lived 34 years afterwards, the quotations from Quintilian in his letters are confined to the 'A' parts, except three from X. 1, 80–94. I imagine that he had soaked himself in the Quintilian accessible to him in earlier years and did not add to his stock with ease, v. Index to Sabbadini's *Epistolario di Guar.*

[4] v. Peterson, Intr. to Book X., p. lxiv. ff. In a later *addendum*, however, he suggests Cologne.

[5] 'Sentio te aliud Quintiliani exemplar nactum esse quod apud te est,' Guarino (to Poggio) 1417, Sabbadini *Epist. di Guar.* 1. 158.

[6] v. Sabbadini *Scoperte dei Codici* 1. pp. 101, 104.

brought into Italy[1]. And though this can hardly have been the case[2], the report points to a belief that such copies were in existence. Still this at least is certain that the scholars of the fourteenth century were so keenly alive to their loss that we may be sure a complete copy did not fall into any learned hands. For the earlier period we cannot say anything more than that, while we find definite evidence of the use of a non-C text by Vincent de Beauvais, John of Salisbury, the 'Flores' and Stephen of Rouen, we have nothing positive to the contrary[3]. For a period earlier still it is difficult to resist the belief that the incomplete *Institutio*, which Lupus possessed and which he hoped to supersede by a complete copy, was a non-C text, especially as he couples it with the *De Oratore*, the text of which has had a closely parallel history[4]. This carries the mutilation far back into the ninth century, a result quite in accordance with the evidence of the MSS. But it does not of course tell us how far the mutilated had superseded the complete text. Earlier than this century there is no evidence, I believe, for the mutilation. Our next earliest witnesses, Isidore and the flosculi incorporated with the MSS. of Cassiodorus, shew a C text[5].

[1] Novati *Ep. di Sal.* III. p. 146 'nescio tamen si verum est quod Andreuolus de Arisiis...qui moram in Gallia continuam trahit, repperit totum Quintilianum de Institutione Oratoria, quem habemus admodum deminutum. Quamobrem te exoratum velim quatenus hoc scisciteris, sique reperieris verum esse, fac ut idem Bonaccursus ita copiam habeat, quod cum diligentia faciat exemplar.'

[2] Sabbadini *Stor. e Crit.* p. 381 assumes that this report was true. It seems to me far more probable that it proved delusive. Salutati and his friends would have moved heaven and earth to get transcripts.

[3] Possibly we may find an exception to this in Wibald of Corvey, v. p. li. His 'ab utero matris susceptum infantem limare incipit et formare' comes more naturally from one whose copy included Prooem. 5 'nec aliter quam si studia eius formare ab infantia incipiam' and I. 1, 1–3, than from a possessor of a mutilated text beginning at I. 1, 6. Moreover he is more connected than the other writers mentioned with the district where we know the complete text to have been preserved. Still this is far from being a certainty.

[4] *Ep.* 103 'Petimus etiam Tullium de Oratore et duodecim libros institutionum oratoriarum Quintiliani, qui uno nec ingenti volumine continentur; quorum utriusque auctorum partes habemus, verum plenitudinem per vos desideramus obtinere.'
The words have been taken to mean that Lupus had seen a complete copy at Rome. This seems to me unwarranted, though of course possible. The point of the words seems to be nothing more than that the size of the parcel would not cause difficulty, cf. *Ep.* 76.

[5] v. Halm *Lat. Rhet.* pp. 503, 504, 518. References there given to Books VI., VII., and IX. 3 fall inside the lacunas.

CHAPTER IV

KNOWLEDGE AND USE OF QUINTILIAN AFTER 1416

§ 1. ON THE CONTINENT

THE story of Poggio's discovery has been so fully and frequently told, that I will not dwell upon it. It is enough to say that he visited the monastery of St Gall in 1416 during the Council of Constance and there found the complete Quintilian 'plenum situ et pulvere squalentem...in teterrimo quodam et obscuro carcere.' He made a transcript of it which he sent to Bruni[1]. As mentioned on p. lxii another complete copy fell into his hands soon afterwards, and certainly one more and possibly others were discovered during the next few years.

It is easy to see why 1416 was an epoch in the fortunes of Quintilian. A complete book is naturally more attractive than one which has something, no one knows how much, missing at each end, to say nothing of the gaps in the middle[2]. The interest aroused in the learned world was immense. Of this the most remarkable example during the next half century or so is L. Valla (1407–1457). He tells us that he knew Quintilian almost by heart[3]. In support of his views on philosophers, though he has as witnesses 'locupletissimos auctores,' he puts forward Quintilian 'non tanquam testem sed tanquam terrestre oraculum[4].' A very

---

[1] According to Sabbadini *Scoperte* II., p. 248, the MS. which Poggio discovered is the Turicensis (now at Zurich) which remained at St Gall till the eighteenth century. If so, Poggio did not bring his find to Italy, as has been often supposed. His transcript is lost, but several copies of the transcript survive. The second MS. which he discovered he did bring to Italy. This is lost, but copies remain.

[2] Poggio and his friends were naturally inclined to exaggerate the defects of the mutilated text. He himself compares it in his letter to Guarino to Deiphobus in *Aen.* 6, 495:

                lacerum crudeliter ora,
    Ora, manusque ambas, populataque tempora raptis
    Auribus et truncas inhonesto vulnere nares.

Bruni writing to Poggio goes further and speaks of the old copies as 'cum vix nobis media pars et ea lacera superesset.'

[3] 'Quintilianum quem prope ad verbum teneo,' Ed. 1543, p. 477.

[4] Ib., p. 958. Fierville, Intr. p. xxi., also quotes 'Marcus Fabius quem omnibus, sine controversia, ingeniis antepono,' as from Elegant. I. 19, but the reference is not right, and I have not traced it elsewhere.

early work of his was a comparison between Cicero and Quintilian, which certainly offended Ciceronian orthodoxy[1]. He treats him as a high authority in his 'Elegantiae,' and he tells us himself that his reason for opening a school of eloquence at Rome was to give honour to Quintilian, who, he considered, was unduly depreciated by George of Trebizond, the Papal Secretary[2,3]. Another noticeable case is that of Politian somewhat later in the century. His oration on Quintilian begins (perhaps with reference to Valla) 'Quintilianum vero non nos quidem Ciceroni praetulimus: sed has certe eius institutiones oratorias rhetoricis Ciceronis libris pleniores uberioresque aestimamus[4].'

But it is on the educational side that the discovery produced its greatest effects[5]. It happened indeed at a lucky moment. The Plutarchian treatise on education had been translated into Latin five years before by Guarino, and the two fitted happily together. Above all, humanism entering on a great and new heritage of knowledge was ripe for a new, or what seemed a new, philosophy of education. The result is seen from the first. Vittorino da Feltre, who left no writings to speak of, but became the traditional ideal of the humanist teacher, was at any rate interpreted by his pupils and successors in terms of Quintilian. The short sketch of his life by Platina[6], who succeeded to the headship of Vittorino's school after Ognibene, is saturated in Quintilian. This is particularly the case with the judgments on classical authors ascribed to Vittorino, many of which follow Quintilian almost slavishly[7]. There may be

---

[1] The book is lost. Some interesting remarks on it by Panormita are quoted by Mancini to whom I owe in the first instance the above references (*Vita di Lorenzo Valla* p. 18). I have not at present seen any clear evidence that the book definitely set Quintilian above Cicero, as sometimes stated.   [2] Ib., p. 348.

[3] For Valla's MS. (Par. 7723) and his notes and corrections v. *infra*, p. xcii, and Fierville, Intr. p. cxviii.

[4] Given in the preface to Capperonnier and Burman's editions.

[5] In the next few pages I owe much to some very valuable papers by Messer on 'Quintilian als Didaktiker' in *Neue Jahr. Phil.* 1897, also to Woodward's *Vittorino da Feltre, Erasmus*, and *Studies in Education during the Age of the Renaissance*. But I have, except where otherwise indicated, verified their statements from my own reading and in many cases added to and sometimes corrected them.

[6] 'Commentariolus Platinae de vita Vict. Felt.' (printed in Vairani's *Cremonensium Monumenta Romae exstantia*). Vict. was born in 1378, but his great work at Mantua began in 1423.

[7] It seems to me rather suspicious to find Platina saying 'legebat etiam tragoedos

some imagination in this, but the general accuracy is confirmed by Ambrogio Traversario, Vittorino's friend, who tells us how at his first meeting they discussed Quintilian at great length. It is still more confirmed by the curious poem of his pupil Corraro, which apparently belongs to 1430 and consists of some 300 hexameters. It is entitled 'Quomodo debeant educari pueri' and opens thus:

> haec tibi de libris veterum, germane, relegi,
> quaeque super pueris docuit pater optimus olim
> Victorinus.

A considerable part of the poem is merely versified Quintilian, for instance of I. 1, 15 on the proper age for beginning study:

> nonnullis visum est maiorum infantibus esse
> parcendum, donec iam septima terminet aetas.
> nos aliter ; neque poeniteat, doctissime rhetor
> Quintiliane, tui. tu rite haec, qui sua quaeque
> infanti studia, et nullum qui duxeris esse
> desidiae tempus. cur quae iam moribus aetas
> congruit, haec eadem studii praecepta refutet?
> quare hoc exiguum lucri fastidis, amice?

Or the following combination of II. 2, 4 and I. 2, 5:

> praecipue sumat curamque animumque parentis
> erga discipulos et per compendia ducat.
> praeterea studio vigilanti vir bonus adsit
> adsidue circa mores.

Or of I. 3, 6:

> quippe etiam multi demissi, ni vehementer
> insistas ; quidam imperio indignantur, at illos
> debilitat timor.

I quote this obscure poem not only to shew how Vittorino seemed to his contemporaries to be Quintilian *redivivus*, but also because the fact that a scholar was impelled to versify an eminently prosaic author seems to me to shew better than all

tum Graecos, *tum Latinos*, ob gravitatem sententiarum, verborum pondus ac personarum auctoritatem,' when we remember *Inst.* X. 1, 97 'Tragoediae scriptores veterum Attius atque Pacuvius clarissimi gravitate sententiarum, verborum pondere, auctoritate personarum.' If Platina means anything by 'Latinos,' it must be that Vittorino admired Seneca's tragedies. But I suspect that he did not realise that Attius and Pacuvius were only known by fragments, if known at all at that time.

the many quotations and adaptations in prose treatises the enthusiasm which Quintilian aroused in this generation[1].

Of these prose treatises four may be specially mentioned which appeared in the half-century which followed 1416.

The letter of Aeneas Sylvius Piccolomini (Pope Pius II) to Ladislas, King of Bohemia (1450), *De Liberorum Educatione,* is full of Quintilian[2]. In the first part of the treatise the remarks on the natural capacity of boys, on the importance of early training, on the age for beginning study, on deportment, on memory are all drawn from this source. The letter then proceeds to deal with the Seven Arts. This part begins with a long disquisition on grammar, of which by far the greater part is Quintilian pure and simple, not very judiciously selected. The remarks on rhetoric and dialectic are more independent, but those on music, geometry, arithmetic and astronomy are again mainly from Quintilian. The borrowings are all or nearly all from the first book.

The treatise of the younger Guarino (about 1458)[3], *De Ordine Docendi et Studendi*[4], has the special value that it reports the methods of his more distinguished father's school. It is concerned mainly with the instructional side, and the analogies to Quintilian belong largely though not exclusively to the part of the work which deals with this and especially to the treatment of 'grammatice.' Thus he adopts Quintilian's division of the subject into 'methodice' and 'historice,' a noticeable fact, as the latter term had no support in Priscian or Donatus or the traditional grammar of the Middle Ages. He repeats almost verbatim Quintilian's 'nomina declinare et verba in-

---

[1] Corraro's verses will be found in the appendix to Krampe's *Die italienischen Humanisten* (Breslau, 1895). For Vittorino himself and his bibliography v. Woodward's *Vittorino da Feltre* (Pitt Press).

[2] To realise this the reader must consult the original (Aen. Sylv. *Op.* (1571), pp. 965 ff.). The version given in Woodward's *Vittorino da Feltre* is not a translation, but rather a loose paraphrase, or sometimes a précis. This is indicated, but perhaps somewhat inadequately, by Woodward, p. 180.

[3] I regret that I have been unable to see a copy of this treatise. My knowledge of it is confined to what may be learnt from the remarks of Messer on it (illustrated by a few quotations from the Latin), and the version (apparently a paraphrase rather than translation) in Woodward's *Vittorino da Feltre* p. 161 ff. The editions Hain 8128, 8129 and 8131 are referred to by Messer and Woodward, but they do not appear to be in the British Museum Library.

[4] Messer gives the title as ' de modo et ordine docendi ac dicendi' (*sic*: ?'discendi').

primis pueri sciant, neque enim aliter pervenire ad intellectum sequentium possunt' I. 4, 22. His remarks on teaching Greek take Quintilian as their starting-point, but he observes that the relations of Greek and Latin were very different in Quintilian's time and in his own, and he differs from him as to the advisability of beginning with Homer[1]. Perhaps the most noticeable point is the remark 'ut ait Quintilianus optimum proficiendi genus esse docere quae didiceris.' Of course the words do not come from Quintilian at all. Guarino had read them in Vergerio. But the mistake shews how growing was the belief that any piece of educational wisdom might be expected to come from Quintilian.

Maffeo Vegio's *De Educatione Liberorum et eorum claris moribus* (about 1460) is a book which it is a little difficult to locate with reference to Quintilian[2]. He quotes him definitely on absurdities in etymology and speaks of him as 'ut in omnibus, ita in hoc praesertim gravissimum atque rectissimum,' and there are many other passages where he unquestionably has him in mind. Such are the postponement of comedy (Fol. 31), the value of change (53), the general testimony to the value of music (37). Thus again when he discusses the question of flogging, he does not name Quintilian, but with the Biblical authorities on the side of the rod names also Chrysippus, obviously referring to I. 3, 14. But on the whole he seems to me to be fairly independent of Quintilian and to keep his own point of view. That he takes Monica's training of Augustine as his model is enough to start him on a different path.

The fourth treatise, which is dated somewhat earlier (1435–1440), belongs to a rather different category. This is the *Vita Civile* of Matteo Palmieri. It is not a purely educational treatise like the others, but perhaps it shews the influence of Quintilian in a still stronger light. For Palmieri sets out to describe the ideal citizen, who does not differ widely from Quintilian's orator, and exactly in Quintilian's manner he proceeds to rear him from the cradle. In fact one can hardly doubt that he has modelled the scope of the book as a whole on the *Institutio*, just as he certainly derives most of the educational part from the

---

[1] So Messer. The reader hardly gets this impression from Woodward's version.
[2] v. Messer, pp. 324 ff. His view on the whole agrees with mine.

educational books of Quintilian. How close is the agreement between the first book of the *Vita Civile* and the first two books of the *Institutio* has been shewn in detail by Bassi (*Giorn. Stor. della Litt. Ital.* XXIII. pp. 182–207[1]). Sometimes whole passages are lifted. Others are adapted. The borrowings (which Bassi estimates as constituting half the first book) are perhaps as numerous as those of Aeneas Sylvius, but more judiciously chosen.

No one can read Aeneas Sylvius or Palmieri without asking himself whether these borrowings are to be regarded as plagiarisms. I think Woodward's answer to this question (p. 73) is undoubtedly right. " Where there was no pretence there was no plagiarism. It was not necessary to mention Quintilian ; he was to every humanist a free quarry, and every scholar recognised the rock from which each new building was hewn."

I know of no other Italian work of the fifteenth century which can be said to be inspired by Quintilian: but before passing on I should notice the abridgement made by Patrizi, which has already been mentioned in connexion with Vergerio, to whom it has been sometimes ascribed. Patrizi, who was for the last part of his life bishop of Gaeta, died in 1494. The letter in which he dedicates the epitome to his friend and pupil Francesco Tranchedini explains that he has done so with hesitation, only because Tranchedini had begged for such a help, as the complete Quintilian was too prolix and the text too incorrect. He continues ' sed unum abs te poscere audeo ut commentarios hosce tecum lectites et integros Quintiliani libros neutiquam negligas.' An analysis of the epitome is given by Bassi, and apparently it may be roughly estimated as being a quarter of the whole. In our book every chapter is represented except the prooemium (v. *Riv. di fil.* XXII. p. 438).

To turn to the German humanists, the greatest name is that of Rudolph Agricola, 1444–1485, of whom his biographer Johann von Plenningen says that ' Quintiliani lectioni praecipue, quem quidem dictione sua fere effingit atque exprimit, animum applicuit,' and there is a further statement, the authority of

---

[1] As Bassi shews, Palmieri used a complete text (which indeed was to be expected), for he quotes both from the introductory epistle to Trypho and from I. 1, 1–2, which were not in the mutilated texts. Woodward (*Renaissance*, p. 69) is wrong in saying that he possessed only an ' incomplete Quintilian.'

which I cannot verify, that during his stay at Ferrara he copied out the whole of the *Institutio*. His little treatise *De formando Studio*[1] has some clear quotations from Quintilian and some unacknowledged reminiscences, but I should agree with Messer (p. 363) that these are rarer than one would expect from the devotion to Quintilian attributed to him.

With Agricola we may join two whom I only know through Messer[2], Bebel (1472–1518) and Murmellius of much the same date. Bebel seems in his three treatises *Modus conficiendarum Epistolarum*, *Ars Versificandi* and *De Institutione Puerorum*, to use Quintilian very considerably. In the last mentioned, after reproducing Quintilian's remarks (I. 1, 8) about getting if possible learned teachers, but if not at least those who know their ignorance, he adds 'hoc te non ego, sed optimus iuventutis doctor, Fabius, primo institutionum docet bracteato propheticoque oraculo.' Murmellius in his *Encheiridion Scholasticorum* has many similar borrowings and elsewhere follows Corraro in turning Quintilian into verse. Messer quotes this version of I. 2, 28:

'ars est tradere liberalis artem
angusto memor ore vasculorum,
quae complentur aqua influente sensim ;
quantum discipuli rudes, videto,
doctrinae excipere et tenere possint.'

Hence we may pass to the far greater name of Erasmus (1466–1536).

It is in Erasmus perhaps that we find the influence of Quintilian at its height. That he is known from end to end, that he lies behind Erasmus' thoughts on early training, curriculum, methods of teaching and rhetoric, will be obvious to every reader. Yet perhaps we may say that he does not so much use him, as build upon him, and he is not afraid to differ from him upon occasion[3]. Thus, to take the chief treatises

---

[1] The treatise seems rather to be a working out of the idea of philosophy as divided into ἠθική, φυσική, and λογική. It is discussed by Woodward, pp. 99–103.

[2] Pp. 367–372.

[3] A strong instance is quoted by Messer from *De recta latini graecique Sermonis Pronunciatione* (a treatise by the way full of Quintilian, particularly the grammatical chapters) where Quintilian's statement as to the inferiority of Latin in 'suavitas' is called 'ridiculum,' Er. *Op.* (Leyden 1703 in 10 vols.), Vol. I., p. 954. All subsequent references are to the same volume.

where we should look for this influence—in the *Ciceronianus*
there is clear proof that his doctrine of the conditions of imitation spring from the chapter on the subject in *Inst.* X. 2¹, but
that somewhat meagre discussion is immensely enriched. In
the *De duplici Copia Verborum et Rerum* Quintilian as a rhetorician is much used, but with an enlargement, for which he
apologises on the ground that if Fabius had been minded to
give his precepts fully, the work would have been unnecessary².
It may be noted that while this distribution between 'res' and
'verba,' on which the work is founded, is definitely traced by
him to Quintilian³, he has really given a new meaning to the
words. Much that appears under 'res' in Erasmus is treated
by Quintilian as 'elocutio' or 'verba.' In *De conscribendis
Epistolis*⁴ we again have Quintilian, but with the necessary
adaptation to a form of study for which Quintilian did not
provide. Then we have the *De Ratione Studii*. Here comes the
remark 'video Fabium hisce de rebus diligentissime praecepisse
adeo ut post hunc de iisdem scribere impudentissimum esse
videatur⁵.' As a matter of fact the treatise keeps fairly clear
of Quintilian and perhaps owes more to the 'progymnasmata'
of Aphthonius or Hermogenes⁶, or perhaps we should rather
say that it embodies the methods which the humanists had
adapted from both sources to their special needs. One important lesson Erasmus seems to me to have drawn from
Quintilian. He has understood *Inst.* I. 4, 2–5 better than some
modern readers and learnt that the master must read far more
widely and have a richness of knowledge far beyond the scope
of what he actually has to teach⁷. On the other hand he definitely departs from Quintilian in his choice of authors for first
reading, which has little real relation to I. 8 or even to X. 1⁸.

It is in the *De Pueris statim ac liberaliter instituendis* that

---

¹ Pp. 985 ff.   ² P. 3.   ³ P. 5.   ⁴ Pp. 345 ff.   ⁵ P. 522.
⁶ Aphthonius is given as an authority, p. 525. Er. would also know Hermogenes
from Priscian's version.
⁷ P. 523.
⁸ P. 521; Woodward *Erasmus* p. 111 says 'in the main he reproduces Quintilian's choice of writers, X. 1.' This is only true in the sense that most of the
authors of his choice naturally occur in the full list of X. 1. Lucian, Erasmus' first
choice in Greek, obviously could not occur in a work written many years before L.'s
birth, though Woodward says later 'Quintilian gives less prominence to Lucian and
Sallust than does Erasmus.'

Erasmus seems to me to cling most closely to Quintilian. In two or three passages he borrows from him on as wholesale a scale as his predecessors, and while there is some admixture of Plutarch, there are few sections in which the thoughts do not agree with Quintilian. The main difference lies in their attitude towards schools. Erasmus can apparently find nothing satisfactory in the schools of his time and will not go further with Quintilian than 'oportet scholam aut esse nullam aut publicam[1].' On the other hand no one can read the treatise without feeling how strongly the advice of Quintilian on corporal punishment, which was a stumbling-block to so many, had taken hold of the mind of Erasmus[2].

The name of Juan Luis Vives (d. 1540), who though a Spaniard lived mostly in the north, is in many ways not one which can rank with Erasmus, but his *De tradendis Disciplinis* is perhaps the greatest educational work of the sixteenth century. Its broad and noble ideas of the function of education and the value of encyclopaedic knowledge make it a book which leaves Quintilian in many ways far behind, and yet it is perhaps the greatest tribute to his influence. The quotations are frequent and almost always made with approval, and the reader will feel in most of the sections, especially where he treats of schools and teachers or language, that he has Quintilian at the back of his mind. But of him it may be said with even more truth than of Erasmus that he builds upon him rather than uses him. Quintilian is to him a starting-point, from which he rises into regions where the Roman could never have followed him[3].

Luther's opinion of Quintilian is expressed, so far as I know, only once, but it is an expression of remarkable force. Writing to George Spalatin, who appears to have put to him the rather odd question, whether his pupils' course of reading would suffer

---

[1] pp. 503 ff.

[2] This very inadequate sketch owes much to Messer, op. cit., pp. 372–387. The two last-named treatises are given in an English dress by Woodward (*Erasmus*), but the reader should again be warned that they are not translations, but loose paraphrases.

[3] It has been observed that Vives like Guarino noted, what so many of the humanists failed to note, that when Quintilian prescribed rules for learning Latin, he was dealing with the vernacular. But like nearly all modern critics who have made this observation, he failed to notice that Quintilian accepts the same rules for learning Greek.

more by the omission of Aristotle *De Animalibus* or the omission of Quintilian, he strongly recommends that if one must be abandoned it should be the former, partly because Pliny will supply the loss, partly because 'Quintilianus unus sit, qui optimos reddit adolescentes, imo viros. Hunc unum rogo ante omnia ne derelinquas, sive Phachus, sive Hessus profiteatur, modo sit inter professiones una. Ego prorsus Quintilianum fere omnibus auctoribus praefero, qui simul et instituit, simul quoque eloquentiam monstrat, id est verbo et re docet quam felicissime[1].'

My knowledge of the debt of Melanchthon (1497–1560) to Quintilian is confined to what is said by Woodward, Messer (pp. 409 ff.) and Hartfelder's 'Melanchthon praeceptor Germaniae' (*Mon. Germ. Paed.* Vol. VII.). His doctrine of 'eloquentia' as involving the contents of what is said as well as language, and therefore in practice covering the widest knowledge, is no doubt mainly due to Quintilian. I may quote Hartfelder's words, which will apply in varying degrees to most of the later humanists, when the first tendency to indiscriminate admiration was over. 'Melanchthon ist Quintilian's Schüler, wie ein tüchtiger Mann der Schüler des andern ist. Frei von dem eiteln Streben auf Kosten des Gegenstandes originell sein zu wollen, entleiht er die massgebenden Gedanken, ohne seine Quelle zu verschweigen, aber auch ohne kritiklose Hingabe, die in falsch verstandener Pietät auf eigenes Urteil verzichtet[2].'

It will be clear from all this that the influence of Quintilian, especially with writers and thinkers on education, was throughout this period immense. One is sometimes tempted to think that the place held by Quintilian in the eyes of the scholars of the century is second or third among Latin writers. This might prove to be an exaggeration, but at least it is safe to say that in the case of no classical writer does there exist so great a difference between his reputation in the fifteenth and sixteenth centuries and his reputation in the nineteenth and twentieth.

At the same time it is just as well to note cases where Quintilian's authority is ignored, or where at least traces of his influence are unexpectedly absent. Amongst the Italian

---

[1] De Wette *Briefe von Luther* Vol. I., p. 385.   [2] p. 348.

treatises of the fifteenth and sixteenth centuries, which deal to some extent with education, two of the best known are the *Cura della Famiglia* of Alberti (d. 1472) and the *Il Cortegiano* of Castiglione (1516). In neither of these can I see any clear signs of Quintilian's influence, though in Alberti's first book at least there are plenty of opportunities. Sadoleto's *De Liberis recte instituendis* (1530) is an important treatise, but here again the expected is absent. The first part on general training has little or no affinity. In the latter part, on literary instruction, there are a good many points which remind one of Quintilian, but no really clear dependence. The literary opinions on the whole bear little resemblance.

I should be inclined to class with those just mentioned two names which in general literature stand out above any of those which I have hitherto dealt with in this chapter, Rabelais and Montaigne. Both write incidentally on education, but they do not take Quintilian as the leading authority. In Rabelais we have two well-known passages on the subject, the reformed education of Gargantua in Book I., and the letter of Gargantua to Pantagruel in Book II. Each contains an allusion to Quintilian, but in the first case it is merely the story of Timotheus (II. 3, 3) and in the second an allusion to his view that Greek should be begun before Latin. Both of these were of course matters of common knowledge. Elsewhere I have not noticed that he mentions or quotes him at all.

Montaigne knew Quintilian well in a sense. He quotes from him at least eight times[1], and some of the quotations are both unhackneyed and apt[2]. But considering the great range of quotations from classical writers in Montaigne, he cannot be regarded as one of the essayist's favourites. In I. 25, the principal place in which he deals with education, he appeals to him as an authority against severe punishment, but on the whole the essay is conceived in a very different spirit. Montaigne may perhaps be regarded as belonging to the age on which we now enter, when the influence of Quintilian began to decline[3].

[1] v. Index to Strowski's ed. Miss Norton *Studies in Montaigne* recognises sixteen, but gives no references. Apparently all but one are confined to the 1595 edition, i.e. belong to M.'s latest essays. [2] v. note on 12, 11.
[3] Possibly it may be thought that definite signs of this decline appear somewhat

There is a notable passage in one of the writings of Muretus[1], who died in 1585, in which he contrasts the attention paid to Quintilian in his boyhood with the present usage. In the old days no one was held a good teacher of eloquence, who did not give the first place to Quintilian in exercising his pupils[2]. Now the young have 'insulsi libelli' and 'dispendiosa compendia.' No doubt this refers rather to Quintilian as a rhetorician than as an educationist. But so far as one can judge there is the same decline in his educational position. And probably the prime factor in this is the schools of the Jesuits. In the *ratio studiorum* there are occasional points in the directions as to teaching grammar and rhetoric which remind one of Quintilian, and we may perhaps connect with his teaching the great stress which the Jesuits laid on competition. But the only definite allusion which I have noticed is in the section (Pachtler, Vol. II. p. 162) recommending that Greek should be begun at the same time as Latin, with the reason that 'pueri varietate detinentur auctore Quintiliano.' This is in the earliest form of the *ratio*

earlier. The long feud (Petromachia) between Peter Ramus and Peter Galland, which Rabelais speaks of in the 'New Preface' to the fourth book of *Pantagruel* (1543?) ('Ce Ramus et ce Galland qui brouillent toute cette Académie de Paris'), turned to some extent at any rate in its later stages on the depreciatory attitude adopted by Ramus to Quintilian in his *Distinctiones in Quintilianum* (1550) and elsewhere (v. Waddington *Vita P. R.* p. 51). Ramus is no doubt a name of great importance in the educational literature of the century, but his attacks were equally or more directed against Aristotle and Cicero, v. e.g. Galland's preface to *Oratio contra Novam Academiam P. R.*, 'cum...veterum scriptorum nemini, non Aristoteli, non Quintiliano, non Ciceroni parcat'; and in default of further knowledge I should hold that the fact of Ramus tilting against these three popular idols rather proves the ascendancy of Quintilian than the reverse, and confirms the words of Galland in the preface to his own edition of the *Institutio* (1538) 'a doctissimis in hac civitate praeceptoribus iuventuti proponitur, inculcatur, et nutricum more veluti cibus praemansus in os inseritur.' It is true that Galland (ib. later) adds 'quo magis Ciceronis quibusdam simiis nihil eius praeter larvam et umbram habentibus infensus sum, qui Quintilianum prolixum et nullo certo docentem ordine clamitantes, de manibus studiosorum excutere meditantur.' But this can hardly refer to the followers of Ramus, who was certainly not 'Ciceronis simia,' but to the view which must always have been current to some extent, that the *rhetorica* of Cicero were more suitable for school purposes than the *I. O.*

[1] Lib. xviii. Var. lect. 20. Quoted by Burman and Capperonnier amongst the 'elogia.'

[2] Cp. a statement apparently made by Fabricius (Fierv., Intr. p. xxiv., but I cannot trace his reference) that the 'professor eloquentiae' at Leipzig was called 'professor Quintiliani.' In view of Muretus' words this is likely enough, v. also the remarks on 'professio Quintiliani' in the quotation from Luther above.

(1586). The numerous schemes of authors to be read given by Pachtler shew little use of him as a book for study, and one of the alterations introduced in 1832 to amend the *ratio* of 1599 is to the effect that Quintilian may be studied as well as Cicero and Aristotle as a rhetorical handbook. Sacchini, whose *Pro-trepticon ad Magistros Scholarum inferiorum* (1625) perhaps gives the inwardness of the Jesuit schools better than the codified *ratio*, quotes Quintilian occasionally as he does other writers, but not in a way that suggests any vital dependence[1].

On the other hand there were some educational forces at work in France, outside the Jesuits, which did something to re-dress the balance. The Oratorian schools used Quintilian as a textbook with the *De Oratore* and *Orator* in the highest or 'rhetoric' class[2]. And Bossuet's well-known letter to Inno-cent XI on the methods he employed in the education of the Dauphin states that in adjusting rhetoric to logic 'selecta Aristotelis, Ciceronis, Quintiliani aliorumque praecepta contuli-mus[3].' More important than either of these is the case of the schools of Port Royal. They too restored him to his position

---

[1] The Jesuits appear to have preferred the use of text-books of their own, notably that of Suarès, for instruction in rhetoric, a view which after all is quite intelligible, if rhetoric is regarded as a science, and neglect of Quintilian as a rhetorician may easily have led to neglect of him as an educationist. Some remarks in Burman's preface (1720) are interesting in this connexion. After mentioning as praiseworthy the object of Rollin's abridgment to restore the use of Quintilian in schools he goes on 'sed ut id Galliae aliisque regionibus, ubi pontificis Romani eiusque satellitum auctoritas praevalet, contingat, prius id Jesuitarum ordini, penes quem fere arbitrium et regnum scholarum et institutionis iuvenilis est, persuadeat Rollinus, necessarium credo.' Their habit of substituting text-books of their own for the great masters, he continues, is the main reason for the loss of sound erudition in Catholic countries; v. also Fierville, Intr., p. xxvi.

We need not however infer that there were not plenty of individual Jesuits who gave full value to Quintilian. One instance at least I can give of a well-known Jesuit who quotes him constantly. This is René Rapin (1621–1687) whose *Réflexions sur l'Éloquence* are full of him. Even his chapter on the eloquence of the pulpit fre-quently draws from this source. Thus the necessity of appealing to the terrors of hell (Edition 1693, Vol. II., p. 74) is supported by *Inst.* III. 8, 40 'nescio an etiam naturaliter apud plurimos plus valeat malorum timor quam spes bonorum.'

[2] Barnard *French Tradition in Education* p. 161.

[3] Bossuet *Oeuvres* (1818), Vol. 34, p. 33. The letter as a whole on its secular side would have pleased Quintilian well, and there are, I think, several reminiscences of his language, e.g. 'vestigiis insistere,' 'ossa et nervos' (contrasted with 'caro') of language, 'optimis imbuere,' 'sensim instillare.'

in the rhetorical school[1]. It may be true that two of their tenets—that emulation as a motive should be discouraged[2], and that small schools are to be preferred to large—are hardly in accordance with his views. But one at least of the leading authorities of Port Royal, Coustel's *Règles de l'Éducation des Enfans*, sets much store on him and quotes him frequently[3]. Their most distinguished pupil Racine made a collection of the 'Quintiliani sententiae illustriores' in the year 1656 when he was 17 years old. This collection survives in MS. and M. Fierville has printed that part which comes from the first book. This in itself may amount to some 3000 words. Racine seems to have been a rebel against Port Royal, even as a boy, on the subject of theatres and romances, but this collection, with a similar collection from Tacitus, is described by his son, as 'extraits des auteurs Latins qu'il lisait à Port-Royal[4].' Again Port Royal seems to have done much to inspire Rollin, and Rollin perhaps stands out preeminent in the eighteenth century as an admirer of Quintilian. He also made an abridgment of the 12 books, but his chief tribute may be found in his *Traité des Études*, otherwise called *De la manière d'enseigner et d'étudier les belles-lettres par rapport à l'esprit et au cœur*, a treatise which in its time had considerable celebrity (c. 1726). The last part of this, dealing with the 'interior government of schools and colleges,' treats of the duties of parents, teachers and pupils, and without displaying any great originality has plenty of good sense to which Quintilian has contributed much. He is frequently quoted and still more often silently adapted. Two other names of first-rate importance in the history of education should be mentioned here, the first a name which takes us back

---

[1] Arnauld (ed. 1780), Vol. 41, p. 96 'Rhétorique, Suarès et alternativement la Rhétorique d'Aristote puis de Quintilien'; ib., p. 90 'Aristote, Quintilien, Hermogenes.'

[2] Barnard, however, *Little Schools of Port Royal*, pp. 103 ff., gives evidence to shew that emulation within limits was encouraged.

[3] Coustel's book does not seem to be obtainable in England and I only know it from the extracts translated in H. C. Barnard's *Port Royalists on Education*. In these Quintilian is clearly quoted from or adapted at least fifteen times and in most cases very aptly. There seems however to be some serious confusion either in the original or the translation on pp. 100-102.

[4] Perhaps made as part of the school curriculum, v. Barnard *Little Schools* pp. 138 ff.

to a date about contemporaneous with the foundation of the Port Royal schools—that of John Amos Comenius. Whether in the great mass[1] of his other work the influence of Quintilian may be traced, I do not know, but his *Didactic* (about 1630) certainly gives evidence of it. There are some definite quotations or acknowledged reminiscences, but more significant are his silent adoption in ch. 17, 6, 34 of the parable of the narrow-necked vessel of *Inst.* I. 2, 28 in language clearly borrowed from Quintilian[2], and the twice or thrice repeated application of the analogy of the sun 'qui universis idem lucis calorisque largitur' (I. 2, 14), to class-teaching. Yet if Comenius shews that Quintilian in the seventeenth century was still read and appreciated as a great educationist, he also goes to shew that he no longer holds the position which he held with Erasmus and Vives.

The other name is of course Rousseau, and here I would speak with all caution. Once only, I think in *Émile* (Book II.), does Rousseau quote Quintilian 'id in primis cavere oportebit, ne studia, qui amare nondum potest, oderit' (I. I, 20)—a quotation so well known that he may easily have got it from some intermediate source, though as a matter of fact he would not have found it in Montaigne. In the Essay on the Origin of Language, ch. 12, when speaking of the ancient connexion of music and grammar, he evidently alludes to I. 10, 17[3]. But his classical quotations from many quarters are very numerous, and I see no certain evidence that he had deliberately weighed Quintilian's views on education. Still, while it is obvious that no two schemes of education could possibly differ more than those of Rousseau and Quintilian, there are points in the former, which every now and then remind one of the latter, and I have a tentative belief that Rousseau had not only read but appreciated some chapters[4].

[1] The list given by Keatinge has 127 items.
[2] 'Cum tamen qui oris angusti vasculo, qualibus ingenia puerorum comparantur, vi infundere quam guttatim instillare malit, quid proficiet?'
[3] 'Étoit-il étonnant que les premiers grammairiens soumissent leur art à la musique et fussent à la fois professeurs de l'un et de l'autre?' The word 'soumissent' for 'subiectam' shews that this was drawn from the original and not from Gédoyn's translation. Gédoyn has 'compris dans la musique.'
[4] E.g., the discussion on the treatment of natural differences and idiosyncrasies in *Nouvelle Héloïse* v. 3 may very possibly have Quintilian in the background.

I have dealt in the foregoing pages with the influence of Quintilian in two aspects. The first and main one is Quintilian as an educationist, the second is Quintilian as a writer on rhetoric, and while rhetoric was an acknowledged part of the school curriculum the two were hardly separable. But there is a third method of treatment which we find occasionally, one indeed which, in days when the word rhetoric had not acquired those unfavourable associations which have now gathered round it, was perfectly natural. The principles of rhetoric, as laid down by Quintilian, may easily be regarded as extending beyond the sphere of oratory to the whole of literature and particularly to poetry, and not only the first chapter of the tenth book, which deals definitely with poets, but a large part of the *Institutio*, may be treated as a sort of *Ars Poetica*[1]. We shall find this view fully expressed in Pope, but there are continental writers in the seventeenth and eighteenth centuries who shew clearly enough that Quintilian was widely honoured as a master in criticism. I give three eminent examples of this. A wider reading than mine would probably make large additions to the list.

The first of these is La Fontaine. In the preface to the Fables[2] he defends his principle of brightening (égayer) the fables by the authority of Quintilian who has said 'on ne sauroit trop égayer les narrations.' He is apparently alluding to IV. 2, 116, 'narrationem, ut si ullam partem orationis, omni qua potest gratia et venere exornandam puto.' He goes on 'il ne s'agit pas ici d'en apporter la raison : c'est assez que Quintilien l'ait dit[3].' So in the preface to the second part of

---

In *Émile* II. there is some resemblance to the remarks on spoilt children in *Inst.* I. 2, 6–8, while in the words 'sacrifiez dans le premier âge un temps que vous regagnerez avec usure dans un âge plus avancé,' he may be deliberately *denying* I. 1, 19. If so, it would be like the example of the two dogs in *N. H.* v. 3, which, though of the same litter, shewed totally different characteristics *because their natures differed*. Here, if we remember Rousseau's love for Plutarch (and he was not likely to question the genuineness of the treatise *De Liberis educandis*), we can hardly doubt that he puts into Wolmar's mouth a deliberate reversal of the story in that treatise, where the two dogs differ *because they have been trained differently*.

[1] v. p. xxxix.
[2] Regnier's edition, Vol. I., 14.
[3] I leave it to those who know more of La Fontaine's inwardness than I do, to say whether there is some irony in this or not.

the *Contes*[1] we are told that too much care 'contrevient aux
préceptes de Quintilien,' alluding presumably to XI. 1, 93 and
other remarks on simplicity. Once more there is a letter of
La Fontaine[2] to the famous scholar Daniel Huet, which
should be noticed. Huet had wished to see an Italian translation of the *Institutio* made in the previous century by
Toscanella. La Fontaine sends him a copy with a letter
which begins:

> Je vous fais un présent capable de me nuire.
> Chez vous Quintilien s'en va tous nous détruire.
> Car enfin qui le suit? qui de nous aujourd'hui
> S'égale aux anciens tant estimés chez lui?

The letter goes on to discuss the true value and right use of
the ancients in general, but though this is La Fontaine's main
purpose, rather than Quintilian in particular, still it remains
the fact that Quintilian appears in the rôle of the great *critic*
of antiquity.

The second name, that of Du Bos, is far less familiar. But
his *Réflexions critiques sur la poësie et la peinture* is a book not
only interesting in itself, but of considerable importance in the
history of criticism. Du Bos is saturated in Quintilian, 'qui ne
laisse rien (in the eighth and ninth books) à faire que d'admirer
sa pénétration et son grand sens' (I. ch. 33)—'l'ouvrage que
nous avons cité tant de fois, quoique nous ne l'ayons pas cité
encore aussi souvent qu'il mérite de l'être' (II. ch. 22). Again
Quintilian, he remarks, does not discuss in detail the faults
real or supposed of the writers whom he judges. 'C'est par
l'impression qu'ils font sur le lecteur que ce grand homme les
définit, et le public qui en a toujours jugé par la même voie, a
toujours été de son avis' (II. ch. 34). Du Bos' quotations are extremely apt, and a 'florilegium' of them would give a reader who
does not know Quintilian otherwise a very fair notion of his incisiveness and good sense. The quotations come from nearly all
the books, though particularly from the sixth, ninth and eleventh.
They touch all manner of subjects, but it may perhaps be said
that it is Quintilian's revolt against fixed rules and exaltation
of free judgment in individual cases, which particularly endears

---

[1] Vol. IV., p. 146.   [2] IX. 201.

him to Du Bos[1]. Even when Quintilian is not mentioned we may often suspect his influence[2].

Quintilian was also a high authority with the German critics[3] of the Illumination and my third name is that of Lessing[4]. His critical works contain proofs of actual detailed study and also a good deal which, in view of such knowledge, we may reasonably conjecture to be founded on Quintilian. The most important example of the former kind is his criticism in his *Fabeln* (ch. IV. Von dem Vortrage der Fabeln) of La Fontaine's remarks quoted above. He points out justly enough that the passage in *Inst.* IV. 2 does not apply to the treatment of fables but to the technical 'narratio' in the course of a forensic speech, and that as a matter of fact ancient taste demanded an especially simple style in the treatment of the fable. He goes on to question the correctness of *égayer* as a rendering of 'gratia et venere exornare,' and takes the occasion to note the superficiality with which French scholars read their classics. But perhaps the most significant instance of Lessing's estimate of Quintilian is the fact that in the preface to what is to most of us his best known work, the *Laocoon*, he is ranked with Aristotle, Cicero and Horace as an authority on the relations of painting to eloquence and poetry[5].

[1] E.g. 'varia hominum iudicia in eo, quod non ratione aliqua sed motu animi quodam nescio an inenarrabili iudicatur' (VI. 3, 6); 'nec magis arte traditur iudicium quam gustus aut odor' (VI. 5, 1); 'propter quae mihi semper moris fuit, quam minime alligare me ad praecepta quae καθολικά vocitant' (II. 13, 14).

[2] E.g. Du Bos' limitation of the 'Public' who are the supreme judge to those 'qui ont acquis des lumieres' (II. ch. 22) is probably founded on Quintilian's adoption of 'consensus eruditorum' as the true standard of 'consuetudo' (I. 6, 45).

[3] Perhaps partly or largely owing to the influence of Du Bos. Lombard in his *Du Bos* (p. 191) says 'Les disciples allemands de Du Bos se reconnaîtront à la fréquence des emprunts, qu'ils feront comme lui à l'I. O.'

[4] I owe the references to Lessing to a careful little book lately published by Dr M. Wychgram, *Quintilian in der Deutschen und Französischen Literatur des Barocks und der Aufklärung*. Other German critics of some importance who appear to have made great use of Quintilian are Breitinger and Gottsched. One conclusion drawn by the writer is that in the first third of the eighteenth century Quintilian had something of the same importance for 'Geistesleben,' as in the Renaissance.

[5] Here I may add a quotation from Jules Janin (given by Fierville, p. cxxxii.). He speaks of the *I.O.* as 'ce chef-d'œuvre, l'admiration de Corneille et de Pascal, de Racine et de Despréaux, de Molière et de Fénelon.' I do not know what grounds there are for speaking thus of Corneille, Pascal and Molière. With Racine I have dealt. As for the other two names, Boileau does not as a matter of fact,

I must conclude this section with two explanatory remarks. The first is that I have made no mention here of scholars, editors, or translators. As my object has been to form some idea of the influence of Quintilian on general thought, I have relegated these others to the Bibliography. The second is a more serious matter. I feel that it is almost ridiculous that I should end a survey of this sort at more than a century and a half from our own time. I doubt indeed whether there is *much* to add. M. Fierville, writing in 1890, says (p. cxxxi.) 'aujourd'hui, malgré les éditions savantes qui ont été faites dans ces dernières années, on ne lit guère Quintilien en entier. Tout au plus le dixième livre est-il encore un peu en faveur.' How the matter stands in Germany I am unable to say, but he quotes Enderlein writing in 1865 to the same effect. It is highly probable that in both countries, as in England, this indifference set in much earlier than the date at which these two writers notice it. Still the influence of Quintilian is sufficiently strong at the point at which I have left it, to justify the belief that considerable traces of it lingered in subsequent literature and thought. In the main I can plead nothing better than ignorance of the period, and can only hope that this great *lacuna* will not render valueless what I have been able to say as to earlier times.

I think, quote him extensively, and such quotations as I have seen do not argue a close acquaintance. In the *Dissertation sur Joconde* the well-known remark on Demosthenes (vi. 3, 2) 'non displicuisse illi iocos sed non contigisse' is quoted, and in an attack on Perrault in the *Conclusion des Réflexions critiques*, the equally well-known (x. 1, 26) 'ne damnent quae non intellegunt,' and it is significant that Boileau introduces this with the remark that it is quoted by Racine.

Something more may be said of Fénelon. In his *Dialogues sur l'Éloquence* and in the *Lettre sur les occupations de l'Académie* the general spirit is quite in accordance with Quintilian. He mentions him as an authority, and the one definite allusion (in the section of the latter on poetry), 'J'irois même d'ordinaire avec Quintilien jusqu'à éviter toute phrase que le lecteur entend, mais qu'il pourroit ne pas entendre, s'il ne suppléoit pas ce qui y manque' (based presumably on viii. 2, 19 'at ego vitiosum sermonem dixerim, quem auditor suo ingenio intellegit'), is not of the type which had passed into common knowledge. And as he had evidently read Quintilian, one may conjecture that in some of the thoughts in the treatise *De l'Éducation des Filles*, e.g. the warning against the spirit of mockery, he had Quintilian in his mind. But Fénelon's range of knowledge and quotation is so wide that Quintilian cannot be said to loom so large in him as in many of the other writers with whom I have dealt.

§ 2. In England

Now to turn to England. The earliest educational work I am acquainted with is Elyot's *Governour* 1531. His first book frequently shews the influence of Quintilian. The importance of the surroundings of little children (I. 4), the value of training before the age of seven (5), the need of correct speech in nurses (ib.), the need for the orator of an acquaintance with the 'encyclopaedia' or 'circle of doctrine,' and many other points, are clearly inspired by Quintilian, who indeed is frequently quoted to enforce his views. In I. 11 Quintilian in Latin and Hermogenes in Greek are recommended as the books in which boys over 14 should study rhetoric.

A more celebrated book, Ascham's *Schoolmaster*, seems to me to have much less dependence. In his views on discipline in general, on the value of rhetoric as a stimulus, on precocity, on the encouragement given by parents to depravity in their children, he may have had Quintilian in view, but there is no very close resemblance. He quotes or mentions him several times, but not with much enthusiasm, and on one point, the use of paraphrase, he is strongly opposed. Indeed he very unjustly accuses Quintilian of having 'spitefully' and 'of an envious mind' set his opinion against Cicero's.

Richard Mulcaster, sometimes called the father of English pedagogy, who died in 1611, had no doubt read Quintilian. There are evident reminiscences in the 'positions,' and I imagine that the allegorical treatment of orthography as depending on sound, reason, and custom is partly drawn from him. But the closest connexion I have observed is in the discussion of public and private education[1]. Here the debt is considerable, but on the whole Mulcaster was not the sort of man to follow any authority closely, and he describes his method truly enough, when he says: 'In this kind of argument, wherein I deal, it is no proof that because Plato praiseth it, because Aristotle alloweth it, because Cicero commendeth it, because Quintilian is acquainted with it...that therefore it is for us to use[2].'

To pass on to writers not strictly educational, Bacon knows

[1] Quick's edition, pp. 183–192.   [2] Ib., p. 11.

g

but little of Quintilian, so far as I can judge. In the whole of the *Essays* and *Advancement of Learning* I have only noted two quotations. One of these is the well-known remark on Seneca in *Inst.* X. 1, 130, 'si rerum pondera minutissimis sententiis non fregisset'; it is to be noted that this (which appears in both works, *Essay* 26, *Adv.* I. 4, 6) is quoted very loosely and ascribed in the former to Aulus Gellius.

On the other hand Ben Jonson's knowledge of Quintilian is both considerable and interesting. That curious work, the *Discoveries*, the true nature of which seems so long to have escaped notice, is now known to consist for much the greater part, if not entirely, of thoughts adapted or transcribed from earlier writers. Some of these are of comparatively recent date, as Heinsius, Lipsius and Vives. Others are ancient and amongst these Quintilian is distinctly the favourite, the two Senecas coming next. The most important adaptation of Quintilian[1] comes in the sections 114–118 beginning : 'It pleased your Lordship of late to ask my opinion touching the education of your sons.' How closely this little tractate on education agrees with Quintilian will be fairly obvious to anyone who studies the quotations subjoined in Castelain's edition, though these are by no means complete[2]. But the strangest thing is that, while the thoughts and to a great extent the language are Quintilian unadulterated, the arrangement is very different. Jonson seems to have been so soaked in Quintilian that he could with ease recast and refit the thoughts into the scheme in which the subject presented itself to him.

One of the oddities connected with the *Discoveries* is that, as earlier critics had not seen that the collection was mainly unoriginal, we have their views upon the thoughts written under the impression that they were really products of Jonson's mind. The judgment of Swinburne, which I regard as the finest compliment ever paid to Quintilian, will be found on

---

[1] Other adaptations or transcriptions will be found in §§ 62, 63, 65, 110, 112, 126.

[2] If we exclude the purely prefatory matter, I think it is true to say that in this disquisition of some two thousand words, with their close-packed sense, there is only one statement or thought which does not come from Quintilian. This is the remark in 116 'Spencer, in affecting the ancients, writ no language; yet I would have him read for his matter; but as Virgil read Ennius,' and even this may have some distant reminiscence of I. 8, 8; II. 5, 21, and X. 1, 87, 88.

the title-page of this volume. But he does not stand alone. Sir Adolphus Ward also expresses his appreciation of §§ 114–118 by saying 'that they are very English in spirit[1].' Further, part of § 63, taken from *Inst.* II. 12, is reproduced in the 'address to the reader' prefacing the *Alchemist,* on which Gifford, who did not recognise the source, remarks that 'it is a very spirited production and well worthy of the author[2,3].'

Milton's Sonnet, in which he says that Scotch names like ' Colkitto or Macdonnel or Galasp would have made Quintilian stare and gasp,' has probably served to make his name familiar to readers who would not otherwise have heard of him. But the passage does not indicate any close acquaintance. Euphony is of course dealt with by Quintilian, but is not a leading idea. Milton's short *Tractate on Education* does not contain, so far as I can see, a single idea which can be traced to him. No doubt he is included among the 'old renowned writers' of whom Milton says, 'I will spare to tell you what I have benefited among them,' and we find the following passage: 'And withal to season them and win them early to the love of virtue and true labour...some easy and delightful book of education would be read to them, whereof the Greeks have store, as Cebes, Plutarch and other Socratic discourses. But in Latin we have none of Classic authority, except the two or three first books of Quintilian and some select pieces elsewhere.' But this reference is curiously vague. The third book would have answered but poorly the purpose Milton has in view. Altogether I cannot credit him with any real affection for Quintilian.

Milton's younger contemporary Locke is the author of a book, which is often regarded as the greatest English work on

---

[1] *Eng. Dram. Lit.* I. p. 542 (new ed., II. 33).

[2] Jonson's adaptation of parts of I. 2, 6–8 on the depravity of home surroundings in *Every Man in his Humour* II. 5 is quoted in the note on that passage.

[3] Two other less known educational books of this century may be mentioned. Peacham's *Compleat Gentleman* (1622) takes some notice of Quintilian, and indeed lays stress on his advocacy of gentleness and consideration. But Peacham is a person of wide reading, or at least of wide range of quotation, and the matter from Quintilian is not very prominent. Of the three direct quotations which I have noted, one (a judgment on Horace) is apocryphal. A similar book, Cleland's *Institution of a Young Nobleman,* 1607, uses Quintilian perhaps a little more, but not in a way that shews special consideration.

education. But I do not think that the *Thoughts* shew any
knowledge of Quintilian. There are points no doubt on which
they agree, e.g. flogging, or making early instruction a play,
or play as a revelation of character[1], but the agreement is
not very close and the points are fairly obvious. The only
note appended to the treatise[2] is on 'how much the Romans
thought the education of their children a business that belongs
to the parents themselves,' and this is illustrated by references
to Suetonius, Plutarch and Diodorus but not to Quintilian.
His editor seems to think that the only educational writer he
followed was Montaigne[3].

One great English writer remains, who seems to have really
known and appreciated Quintilian—Pope. The lines in the
Essay on Criticism (669–674) are well known:

> 'In grave Quintilian's copious works we find
> The justest rules and clearest methods join'd:
> Thus useful arms in magazines we place,
> All rang'd in order and dispos'd with grace,
> But less to please the eye, than arm the hand,
> Still fit for use, and ready at command.'

But better evidence is to be found in Pope's own notes on the
essay, which include several quotations from the *Institutio*,
the point of which, though not always obvious, is sufficiently
apt. Thus to take one instance from our own book, line 324 etc.

'Some by old words to fame have made pretence,' etc.

is illustrated by I. 6, 20 'abolita atque abrogata retinere insolentiae cuiusdam est et frivolae in parvis iactantiae.' The
other quotations are taken from the later books, all from the
fifth to the tenth being represented. And with these proofs of
Pope's reading, I think the metaphor of the 'arms in magazines'
may fairly be regarded as a reminiscence of V. 7, 8 'ea res...
veluti tela ad manum subministrabit,' and a similar passage
in XII. 3, 4.

After Pope, with the exception of the tribute from Mill which
I have set at the beginning of this volume, I have little of

---

[1] Compayré *History of Pedagogy*, in his remarks on Quintilian, notes that
his method of teaching to write is practically the same as Locke's.
[2] Quick's edition, p. 45.   [3] Quick, p. xlix.

importance to add[1]. The main exception of any value known to me is the three modern treatises on rhetoric, viz. those of Blair, G. Campbell, and Whately[2], and it is so inevitable that formal treatises on rhetoric should contain references to Quintilian, that in themselves these are hardly worth mentioning here. Still rather more than this may be said of Blair. His lectures which, if not very profound, seem to me to have qualities which easily account for their popularity, are full of Quintilian, who of 'all the ancient writers on the subject of oratory is the most instructive and most useful.' 'I know few books,' he adds, 'which abound more with good sense and discover a greater degree of just and accurate good taste. Almost all the principles of good criticism are to be found there.' The lectures throughout shew the sincerity of this appreciation[3], and though Blair's intellectual gifts may not be such as to make his estimate important, yet it has to be remembered that the great vogue which his writings seem to have had for many years must have served to keep some knowledge of Quintilian alive amongst the English reading public[4]. But apart from this, so far as I can judge, Quintilian must have begun from the middle of the eighteenth century to sink into the obscurity in which he still remains. One great cause for this was the growing indifference to formal rhetoric[5], which Blair perhaps

---

[1] Johnson of course knew Quintilian. Probably he was one of those writers, 'all literature, Sir, all ancient, all manly,' whom he read before he went to Oxford. I have noticed several signs of knowledge both in the *Lives* and in the *Rambler*. The most marked perhaps is the quotation from this 'illustrious precedent,' in the *Rambler*, no. 88. His educational ideas (v. references given s.v. 'Education' in Birkbeck Hill's index to Boswell) have points where he may have Quintilian in mind, whether to agree or disagree. Still there are not the signs of really high appreciation. Boswell on his own account quotes Quintilian once, very superficially, from the opening sections. Is this perhaps a sign that some knowledge of Quintilian was part of the equipment of a scholarly man?

[2] Campbell uses Quintilian much less than Blair, but much more than Whately, who was evidently repelled by Quintilian's conception of rhetoric (v. p. xxviii.).

[3] I might say of Blair, as of Dubos (p. lxxx.), that his quotations would make a very respectable 'florilegium' to illustrate Quintilian's sense and incisiveness. These are much more numerous than the references given in the index to the edition of 1845 would lead one to suppose.

[4] Peterson notes, Intr. p. xix., that Pitt attended a course of lectures on Quintilian at Cambridge in 1773.

[5] Whately observes that, with regard to the two questions raised as to the utility of rhetoric, (1) whether eloquence is on the whole beneficial, (2) whether it can be

managed to surmount by a judicious mixture of topics of a more general interest. And further, I imagine that the other main aspect of the *Institutio* was not very attractive to a generation, perhaps I should rather say, many generations, which seem to have taken little interest in educational theory. While it is true that I had equally little to record of the use of Quintilian in France during the last century and a half, the meagreness of this whole section as compared with what I have written of French use during earlier centuries suggests either that I have been unfortunate in my reading, or that Quintilian was for a prolonged period better known and appreciated in France than in England. I am inclined to think that this last is the truth, and this makes me suspect that while the blankness of my record at the end of the last section was to some extent due to my ignorance, in this section it represents the truth. Further, I believe this is only what we might expect. While the scholarly study of the Classics may have prospered here more than in France, I imagine that we fall behind in various branches which would naturally foster the study of Quintilian. I doubt whether either educational theory or literary criticism has been so active and sustained here as there. The French too, I think, have never had that revolt against rhetoric as an art which has been so marked with us. And possibly we may add that if the French are our inferiors in scientific scholarship, they have a greater genius for extracting from the Classics what is valuable for modern use[1].

learned by systematic study, doubt as to the first was more felt by the ancients, as to the second by the moderns.

[1] With regard to the nineteenth century, Peterson (Intr. p. xix.) gives two instances of recognition of Quintilian. The first of these, 'Macaulay read him in India, along with the rest of classical literature,' seems at first sight not worth mentioning. But the context 'I am busy with Quintilian and Lucan, both excellent writers,' gives it more body, for Macaulay's criticisms on the many books he read then are by no means always complimentary. More significant is the case of Disraeli 'who was very fond of Quintilian, and said it was strange that in the decadence of Roman literature, as it was called, we had three such authors as Tacitus, Juvenal and Quintilian.'

Of my own older contemporaries, I would mention two, both of them Professors of Edinburgh University. The first of these, Simon Laurie, I am glad to name, because it was on a visit to him, nearly 40 years ago, that I was first led to recognise the importance of a writer, of whom, in spite of, I think, an unusually wide reading for the Classical Tripos, I cannot remember having read a line. Laurie's chapter on Quintilian in his *Pre-christian Education* is the best account I know of Quintilian's

Taking Western Europe as a whole, if this survey, which I cannot suppose to be complete, is in any way representative of the facts, one point will emerge. As I have suggested already, there is probably no classical author in whose case we find so wide a difference between his present and his past reputation. If for some hundreds of years after Jerome the signs of the study of Quintilian are fitful and scanty, he rises into considerable prominence in the twelfth and fourteenth centuries in spite of the unhappy mutilation of the text. After the discovery of Poggio, his influence for perhaps the next hundred and fifty years is enormous and even through the next two centuries very considerable. If the foregoing pages and the commentary which follows do ever so little to make him more intelligible and attractive to those who are interested in the matters treated in this book, whether it be the byways of classical culture, or the educational ideas and practices of the past, it will be ample repayment for what, small as the result may seem, has been the work of many years.

educational system. The other is Professor Saintsbury. His chapter on Quintilian as a critic in the first volume of his *History of Criticism* seems to me one of the best and most sympathetic chapters in a book of amazing scope and learning. Of his estimate I have already given a sample (p. xxxix.).

Here I will take the opportunity of expressing my regret that Dr Rutherford, to whose *Chapter in the History of Annotation* I owe much in part of my commentary, should have so little understood, as it seems to me, the value of Quintilian when he writes (p. 5) as follows: 'Wider reading (i.e. than Cicero's) and a considerable knowledge of Greek seem only to have confused the more a mind naturally vague and perplexed and timorous. He cannot think clearly and has read more than he can carry.' I agree that there are times when Quintilian writes, and perhaps thinks, confusedly. But this is quite compatible with the possession of that more than saving common sense, which illuminates the whole book.

Unfortunately Dr Rutherford's off-hand rejection of Quintilian has received a wider circulation than the learned seclusion of the *Chapter* could have given it. His colleague, the late Mr J. Sargeaunt, edited Pope's *Essay on Criticism* for schools. And in this edition the English schoolboy, who there comes across the name of Quintilian, probably for the first and very possibly for the last time, finds the following: 'Marcus Fabius Quintilianus, a critic of the time of Domitian and Trajan, whose chief work was an elaborate treatise on rhetoric, which for long had a much greater reputation than it deserved. The late Dr Rutherford, comparing him with Cicero, wrote, "Wider reading, etc."'

CHAPTER V

In Ch. III, § 4, I spoke of the earlier MSS. with a view to ascertaining what form of text, mutilated, less mutilated, or complete, was in the hands of pre-Poggian users of the *Institutio*. In this chapter I shall discuss what MSS. have been relied on by recent editors to form the text and how far they appear to be justified. I do not propose to give any elaborate account of the various codices. This has been done by Fierville in his introduction for the continental MSS., of which he enumerates over sixty. Peterson in his introduction reproduces with some additions much of what Fierville says, and besides gives a fairly full account of the English MSS. amounting to twelve. Putting these two together, we have a description from which the reader will be able to gather almost everything that is known about the date, provenance and other external characteristics of these codices[1]. As however in the other section I necessarily confined myself to those written before Poggio's discovery, it must be said here that there is a large number of fifteenth century MSS. written presumably after 1416 and generally supposed to derive ultimately from Bamb. (Bg and G), which was itself the ancestor of Poggio's MS. These fifteenth century codices were largely used by earlier editors. Thus Gesner relied largely on the Gothanus (Goth.), Obrecht on the Argentoratensis (S), and Spalding for the first book on the Guelferbytanus (Guelf.). And though Zumpt and Bonnell shewed much more appreciation of the earlier MSS., the era of modern textual criticism of the *Institutio* may be said to begin with Halm's edition published in 1868.

Halm based his text mainly on (1) the Ambrosianus (A), (2) the Bernensis (Bn) with the Bambergensis (Bg), where these are available; elsewhere on A and the later supplement

---

[1] An exception to this, however, is the relation of the earliest part of the Bambergensis to the rest. To get any clear idea of this, it is necessary to refer to Halm *Sitzungsberichte der königl. bayer. Akademie der Wiss. zu München*, 1866, I. pp. 495 ff.

to Bg (G)[1]. But this last does not affect the first book which for critical purposes we may divide into three parts, (1) the very earliest part, where of these we have only A, (2) the next part, where we have A and Bg, (3) the rest of the book, where we have both A and Bn with Bg. As the last of these is by far the largest, I will take it first.

The consensus of Bn and Bg is called by Halm B, and with A forms, as I have said, his main authority. But he also used a few other MSS., notably the fifteenth century S mentioned above, and the Monacensis (M) also of that century. He states, however, that these gave him little beyond a knowledge as to the origin of the emendations which found their way into the printed editions. He also declares that he cites them only where B fails, i.e. in the lacunas; but this is afterwards corrected by the statement that he uses them also in the first book, where B is mostly available. Indeed he cites them very frequently there, especially M. But it is probable that they did not really influence his choice of readings.

B, as I have said, stands for the consensus of Bn and Bg. But in our book, at any rate, it may perhaps be said that the second of these two elements could be discarded with little loss. There are indeed a considerable number of places where the two differ slightly, but they are for the most part either obvious slips made by Bg in his transcript, or obvious corrections of Bn made by him. I know of few, if any, places where Halm's text would have been different had he rested on A and Bn only.

On the other hand A and B differ considerably and the main work of the textual critic is to decide between the two. Various opinions have been expressed as to their relative value. In our own book it may perhaps be said that *prima facie* A stands higher, though only to the extent of overruling B where the internal evidence is balanced. On a rough calculation I should say that in this book Halm adopts the readings of A against those of B in the proportion of 3 to 2[2], and though his successors have reversed his decision in many individual cases, they leave this proportion undisturbed.

---

[1] For this and a few further particulars on these MSS. v. above, p. lxi.

[2] We should hardly expect this from his estimate of the two given in the *Sitzungsberichte*, but the proportion may be different in the later books.

Halm also attached considerable importance to the evidence given by the quotations made from Quintilian by the rhetorician, Julius Victor[1]. Julius Victor is only known to us by a single MS. of the twelfth century. He lived, however, much earlier, perhaps as early as the fourth century, and since it is most unlikely that the scribe should have been influenced by the text of Quintilian current in his own day, the passages transcribed, making due allowance for the fact that he may have often, and certainly has sometimes, quoted loosely, may be taken to give us a primitive text. This however has little bearing on the first book[2].

Meister, who published his edition in 1887, put much the same reliance as Halm on A and B. Indeed he remarks in his preface that in a large part of the work (including that part of the first book with which we are dealing) any other MSS. are almost superfluous. He had before him however some others, notably the collation made by Chatelain and

---

[1] He also paid regard to the 'excerpta rhetorica' of an unknown writer, to which reference is given in his *Rhet. Lat. Min.*, p. 77, and to those found in Cassiodorus. These however do not concern the first book at all.

It may be well to note here that, though of course the much later date makes the question raised a different one, the quotations in John of Salisbury have some textual interest; Halm himself notes that John in *Metalogicus* I. 25 quotes I. 4, 6 without the absurd 'de litteris,' which most of the older MSS. shew after 'elementa,' thus ranging himself with Prat., Put. and Joann. (v. below, p. xcvi.). Also that in quoting I. 3, 4 he has (*Met.* 2, 8) 'haec firmat' not 'ac firmat.' Halm might also have added that John has in the same place 'praecoquum' for 'praecox,' again with Prat. and Joann. But there is one case of more importance, which no one, so far as I know, has observed. In *Policraticus* 763 D (Webb II. p. 320), in the course of a full quotation of *Inst.* X. 1, 125-131 on Seneca, John evidently read 'si *nil aequalium* contempsisset' (§ 130). This variant in a much discussed passage for 'si aliqua contempsisset' (al. 'si obliqua cont.,' Bn 'simile quam cont.') has been rejected, on the ground that it is found only in fifteenth century codd. (v. Peterson). Yet here we apparently find it in several twelfth or thirteenth century codd. (v. Webb's introduction to *Pol.*). Of less interest is § 83 of the same chapter, where 'eloquendi *usus* (or *usu*) suavitate' emended to 'an el. suav.' (Halm, 'el. *vi ac* suav.') appears in John (*Met.* 2, 2) as 'an eloquendi usu, an suavitate eloquii.'

[2] The borrowings in J. V. from this book are (1) the words (2, 22) 'licet ipsa vitium sit ambitio, frequenter tamen causa virtutum est' (Halm *Rhet. Lat. Min.* p. 445); (2) ib. 18, 19 quoted with variations, which cannot represent the original text (Halm, ib.); (3) 11, 3 of which the same may be said (Halm, p. 441); (4) 11, 4 'emendanda sunt' for 'emendet' (Halm, ib.); (5) 11, 8 where the MS. of J. V. has (*a*) 'simpliciter' for Quintilian's 'simplicem,' (*b*) 'inanitatem' which Halm has corrected to Quintilian's 'inanitate,' and 'circumliniri' to which he has corrected Quintilian's 'circumlinire' (Halm, ib.); (6) 11, 10 where J. V. has 'detorqueantur' and 'distendat' with B against the 'dist.' and 'discindat' of A (Halm, 442). Editors have adopted 'distendat' but differ as to 'detorqueantur.'

Lecoultre[1] of the tenth century Nostradamensis (N), which, though mutilated like B, seems to be of a somewhat different family. Of the later MSS. he speaks with something like contempt. He has about eighty different readings in this book from Halm. Many of them are emendations by himself and others (hardly any of which I find myself able to accept) or rejections of Halm's emendations. Others are preferences for the readings of A or B, as the case may be. There are some places in his very meagre apparatus where he cites other MSS. for the reading he adopts, but they are generally of such a kind that one may suspect that exegetical considerations have weighed more with him. Even N seems to have had hardly any influence on his text. In the two cases where he proposes to follow it against A, B, one is 'exeunt' for 'eunt' in 6, 15, a change which other editors and fifteenth century scribes, led by the 'exeant' two lines above, had already made. The other is 'accepimus' for 'accipimus' in 10, 32, a correction which had already been accepted by Halm[2]. In only one case, I think, can he really be said to make a serious correction on MSS. authority outside A, B, and even this is but a return to the text of Spalding and other editors. This is the insertion of 'laesae' in 2, 4, for which he cites the Lassbergensis, though indeed he might have found better authority[3].

Fierville's edition of the first book followed close on Meister's. It is notable not only for the invaluable account of the codices mentioned above, but also for an apparatus criticus far fuller than that of Halm and for bringing into notice the readings not only of N, but of the Pratensis and Puteanus[4] (called by him P). Fierville however in constituting his text does not seem to me to work on any clear principle, and though there are a few cases in which I believe he is right against the other editors discussed in this chapter, I have no great confidence on the whole in his judgment. I pass on to the latest edition, that of Radermacher.

---

[1] Fierville also made a collation of N, which I have not been able to see. His citations of it however in his app. crit. give or ought to give the main results. But I note several cases where his allegations of variances between B and N are not borne out by Chat. and Lec., e.g. 'at' for 'aut' 4, 7 : 'iudicum' for 'iud.' 10, 25.

[2] He fails to notice that N is against the reading he adopts (I think wrongly) in 6, 14 ('non' for 'nomina').

[3] v. below, p. xcvi.   [4] v. ib.

Radermacher's edition of the first six books was published in 1907 and is intended to supersede the old Teubner edition by Bonnell. He gives the primacy to A and B, but includes N in B, and the fact that his apparatus, which though fuller than Meister's is still exceedingly meagre[1], includes very few variances between N and the other two factors of B, confirms the belief, implied by Meister and supported by my own examination, that the important differences are not many[2]. But the most noteworthy characteristic of Radermacher's edition, at first sight at any rate, is his employment of the fifteenth century codex Parisinus 7723 (once the property of L. Valla) which he calls P[3]. Becher had laid down some years before[4] that this codex, in the tenth book at least, exhibited the true text in an unusually large number of cases, and the question arose whether these readings were due to fifteenth century scholarship, or are derived from some other source independent of the tradition of B. Radermacher tells us in the preface that he originally took the former view, but afterwards came to the conclusion that the latter was partially true, through observing how often P agreed with Julius Victor.

That variations in fifteenth century codices may sometimes or often be due to some older and purer tradition is a view which I have not the knowledge or the wish to reject, more especially as I have perhaps in one case acted on it. I refer to the vexed passage 4, 10, where I have a strong conviction that the insertion 'quod nequit' or 'quod nequit fieri' turns incoherence into a coherent argument, an argument, moreover, which is exactly in accordance with the grammatical doctrine of Quintilian's time. Whether this insertion, if right, is likely to have been a scholar's emendation is a question which I discuss elsewhere[5]. But if it is not, we are, I suppose, shut up within the alternatives of either discarding my view of the

---

[1] This want in the edition, which I find very trying, was perhaps not due to the editor. He says 'adnotationem meam brevem atque concisam esse voluit is qui exemplaria excudenda curavit.'

[2] I have however noted one or two cases where N, according to Fierville, differs from Bern. and Bamb., though Rad. has given B without qualification as authority for the reading.

[3] A rather unfortunate name, as Fierville uses P for the Puteanus.

[4] In *Programm des königlichen Gymnasiums zu Aurich* (1891). I have not been able to see this.

[5] v. Additional Note, p. 172.

passage, or postulating the possibility of some purer tradition in the later MSS.

However this may be, it cannot be said that Radermacher's use of P when closely examined throws much doubt on the sufficiency of A and B for determining the text of the first book. He cites P about 170 or 180 times, but it is more often to support B, or sometimes A. Amongst the sixty or so cases in which P is cited by itself or with other later MSS., there are, I think, only six where he adopts the readings cited, and all these are readings which earlier editors have adopted or favourably considered on other grounds[1]. Indeed, if P were to be judged by the first book, I think little doubt would be felt that its variations, where they are not mere errors, were deliberate emendations.

On the whole I doubt whether Radermacher can be said to have made an improvement on his predecessors. There are 70 places in which he differs from both of them[2]. I follow him in about one-third of them, but only in 8 or so with any strong conviction: while on the other hand there are many places in which I believe he goes obviously wrong.

Before passing on I should take some account of the Pratensis (twelfth) and the Puteanus (thirteenth century) which, though ignored by the German editors, are regarded as of great importance by Fierville and Peterson. Their history is of considerable interest. Since (1) Prat. is older than Put., (2) the latter is (apart from the lacunas) a complete codex, while Prat., which consists of extracts, cannot have been copied from it, (3) their resemblance in the common parts shews that they have the same original, (4) Prat. is known to have been the work of a monk of Bec, (5) Bec is known to have possessed at the time an MS. of the *Institutio* brought from Rome[3], we have more information about the provenance of the two than of most of the MSS. They have some striking points. They omit 'de litteris' in 4, 6 and have 'laesae' in 2, 4 and thus lend Meister's reading better authority than he himself claims. In 4, 27 they have 'tenentur,' the least unsatisfactory substitute

---

[1] One of these is 'dividendi' for 'videndi' in 10, 49.

[2] Meister has supplied a list of his variations from Halm, in which I note two omissions: 4, 28 H. et quaedam, M. quaedam; 10, 39 H. geometrica, M. geometria. I have made the list for Radermacher myself.

v. Fierville, p. lxxvii. I have verified his reference to *Gallia Christiana*.

for the 'teruntur' of A, B, N. In a few other passages they are the earliest codices to exhibit what is obviously the correct reading, but I doubt whether there is a single case, except perhaps the 'laesae' and 'tenentur' just mentioned, where his knowledge or ignorance of these MSS. would make any serious difference to an editor in his constitution of the text. I reckon that of the variants ascribed to them by Fierville something like two-thirds are obvious errors.

So with the Joannensis (p. 184 ff.), of which I have made a collation for the first time, I believe, so far as this first book is concerned. That too has the 'laesae' and omits the foolish 'de litteris.' It also comes nearest in 4, 13 with its 'lases et as fuerunt' to the 'lases et asa fuerunt' which I believe to be right. With N it has 'his Syllae' in 7, 19 for the usual 'hi Syllae,' again, I think, rightly. But here its usefulness for my purpose ceases. On the whole we may say of this, as of Prat., Put. and N, that a study of them does not seriously shake the general principle that a judicious choice between A and B, coupled of course with reasonable conjecture, is the basis on which recent editors have formed, and future editors will probably form, their text.

I now turn to the earlier part or parts, where the full evidence of B is not available. Bn begins in its present state with the words 'licet et nihilominus' (2, 5), but according to Halm originally began at an earlier point. 'Perierunt in eo duo priores chartae primi quaternionis.' This point he fixes at 1, 6 'de patribus loquor,' and it is here also that the hand of Bamber-gensis Bg, who transcribes Bn throughout, begins. As this transcript, where we can compare the original, appears to be a faithful one, the loss presumably is not great and we have but to substitute the symbol Bg for B.

In the earliest part up to 1, 6, the Bambergensis is written, according to Halm, in a hand later, not only than Bamb. Bg, but than Bamb. G[1], who filled up the later lacunas. Moreover it is lost altogether up to 'occupaverunt' (Pr. 17), and after this is illegible except for words here and there till, according to Halm, Pr. 27, according to Peterson, throughout. For this part, where Bg is either missing or mainly illegible, the natural

---

[1] Halm however thought it probable that this earliest lacuna had been originally supplied by the scribe of G, but destroyed and afterwards replaced by the work we now have. I follow Halm in citing it as Bg.

substitutes, when Halm wrote, were the Florentinus (F) and the Turicensis (T) (both eleventh century), which he declared to be derived (though not directly), from the complete Bamb., though as a matter of fact he cites the former but little and the latter hardly as much as M and S.

The situation however is somewhat altered since Halm and even since Meister and Fierville published their editions. In 1891 Peterson, in the introduction to his edition of the tenth book, described the Harleianus 2664 (H), now in the British Museum, a complete eleventh century MS. of the *Institutio*, and gave reasons for thinking that it was the link already postulated by Halm between Bg and F, T. If this is so, A[1] and H become our primary authorities for this earliest portion. I have therefore collated H myself for this part and cite its readings where necessary as far as 1, 6[2].

As I stated in the preface this edition is mainly exegetical. I am indeed fully conscious that, before we attempt to explain an author, we must ascertain, as far as possible, what he actually wrote. But though it would be rash to say that this has been completely done, I do think that, except in certain isolated cases, we know the possible alternatives open to our choice. This chapter has been mainly directed to shewing that one of the greatest critical scholars of the last century based his text almost entirely on the authorities we have called A and B, where these were available, and that the careful editors who followed him have, not only in theory but in practice, endorsed his principles, so far at any rate as the first book is concerned. And I may add that my own judgment, whatever it may be

---

[1] A runs from the beginning, but has lost a piece extending from the middle of the *Ep. ad Tryph.* to Pr. 5.

[2] In doing this, I have followed what seemed the best authority in a matter in which I am no expert. I have never seen Peterson's view impugned, though I note that Radermacher, while praising the ' Petersoni egregios labores,' makes no use or at least no mention of H. But his apparatus in this part is reduced to a vanishing point, and contains the serious mistake that Bg begins at Pr. 7 instead of 17. As to Peterson's argument (based on the textual phenomena of IX. 2, 52) to shew that H was the link between Bg and F, T (p. lxvii.), I cannot help feeling great doubts. I observe too that Chatelain *Paléographie des Classiques Latins*, who gives facsimiles of H, F and T, dates F in a century earlier than H. However, if Peterson is wrong, I do not think that the substitution of H for F, T as our second best authority will have affected the text. Though H has certainly more correct readings in a few places, a list of which (I think complete) is given by Peterson, they only serve to confirm either A or the obvious.

worth, does, after a careful study of the apparatus critici of Halm and Fierville, as well as of the Joannensis, approve these principles. It is possible no doubt that some future critical edition may take a different line and assign more value to the variations of the later MSS. But it is a remote possibility for which the long overdue exegesis of Quintilian cannot afford to wait. I feel fairly confident that the conspectus given later[1] of the variations in the recent editions will supply the reader with as certain a knowledge as is possible to-day of the limits within which the true text of the First Book of the *Institutio* is to be found.

It remains to say a few words as to the scope of my own critical work. I have obviously had to choose between the various readings of the three editors. It will be seen that in about 30 cases I have disagreed with all three[2]. In most of these I have been able to support my choice both by MS. authority and the opinion of earlier editors. Of the remaining five, two (9, 3 and 10, 49) show a return to the MS. readings which have been rejected for centuries. In these cases I have given my reasons at, I fear, a wearisome length. The other three, 4, 11, 4, 28 and 8, 6, are emendations of my own, which I have ventured to print, only because their 'transcriptional possibility' is so obvious that considerations of meaning become paramount. As to the other conjectures, suggested in the notes but not embodied in the text, I can only hope that they will not be judged too harshly.

ABBREVIATIONS REGULARLY USED IN THE COMMENTARY

A = Ambrosianus I.	N = Nostradamensis.
B = Consensus of Bn and Bg.	Prat. = Pratensis.
Bg = Bambergensis.	Put. = Puteanus.
Bn = Bernensis.	
H = Harleianus (2664), (not cited after Ch. I. § 6).	L. = Loeb translation (Prof. H. E. Butler).
Joann. or Jo. } = Joannensis.	Rad. = Radermacher.
	Sp. = Spalding.

[1] v. p. 180 ff.

[2] Some of these are cases in which the three editors have expressed doubts and can hardly be called disagreements.

EPISTULA AD TRYPHONEM

M. Fabius Quintilianus Tryphoni suo salutem. Efflagitasti **1** cotidiano convicio, ut libros, quos ad Marcellum meum de institutione oratoria scripseram, iam emittere inciperem. nam ipse eos nondum opinabar satis maturuisse, quibus componendis, ut scis, paulo plus quam biennium tot alioqui negotiis districtus impendi: quod tempus non tam stilo quam inquisitioni instituti operis prope infiniti et legendis auctoribus, qui sunt innumerabiles, datum est. usus deinde Horati consilio, **2** qui in arte poetica suadet, ne praecipitetur editio *nonumque prematur in annum*, dabam iis otium, ut refrigerato inventionis amore diligentius repetitos tamquam lector perpenderem. sed **3** si tanto opere efflagitantur quam tu adfirmas, permittamus vela ventis et oram solventibus bene precemur. multum autem in tua quoque fide ac diligentia positum est, ut in manus hominum quam emendatissimi veniant.

Tryphoni suo. Cf. 'bibliopola Trypho,' Mart. 4, 72.

1. convicio. Cf. IV. 5, 10 'cum convicio efflagitat' of the impatient 'iudex' who calls upon the advocate to come to the main point. There however the word retains its natural sense of angry expostulation, which at first sight appears to be absent here. Sp. quotes (amongst other less relevant passages) Cic. *ad Qu. Frat.* 2, 11 'epistulam hanc convicio efflagitarunt codicilli tui.' Both there and here, I think, a word connoting discourtesy and anger has been deliberately used, but humorously, 'Every day you abuse me roundly for not publishing etc.' Humour is not a quality for which Q. is distinguished, but he may naturally have affected it in a letter of this sort. Apart from these two passages I find no authority for the friendly or neutral sense, which Sp. supposes it to have here.

alioqui, here = 'praeterea' (as often in Q.) rather than 'otherwise,' as Hand *Turs.* I. 237 appears to take it. For other uses of the word in Q. v. Pet. Intr. p. li.

auctoribus. I agree with Nettleship (*Lat. Lex.* s.v.) and Sp. on II. 15, 36, that the word in Q. never quite = 'scrip-tor' but retains some sense of 'authority,' even when no epithet such as 'clarus' is appended, cf. e.g. 2, 12 'tot auctorum notitia.'

2. nonum...annum, *A. P.* 388.

dabam iis otium. Not, I think, as L. 'I proposed to give them time' but 'I *was* giving them a rest.' Q. does not wish to imply that he immediately or even rapidly yields to Trypho's solicitations, any more than to those mentioned in Prooem. 1.

refrigerato...amore. Cf. X. 4, 2 (advice to the advanced student) 'Nec dubium est optimum esse emendandi genus, si scripta in aliquod tempus reponantur, ut ad ea post intervallum velut nova atque aliena redeamus, ne nobis scripta nostra tamquam recentes fetus blandiantur.' 'Inventio' clearly cannot be used in the ordinary technical sense (as e.g. Prooem. 22) of the provision of matter, as opposed to 'elocutio' 'style,' 'expression,' but in the wider sense of 'creation,' 'authorship.' I have not found a similar use of the noun in Q. but such a use of the verb is not uncommon.

3. oram solventibus. So again IV. 2, 41. For this use of 'ora' v. Forc. H. and indeed all MSS. 'auram.'

INSTITUTIONIS ORATORIAE

LIBER PRIMUS

PROOEMIUM

Post inpetratam studiis meis quietem, quae per viginti annos 1
erudiendis iuvenibus inpenderam, cum a me quidam familiariter
postularent, ut aliquid de ratione dicendi componerem, diu
sum equidem reluctatus, quod auctores utriusque linguae
clarissimos non ignorabam multa quae ad hoc opus pertinerent
diligentissime scripta posteris reliquisse. sed qua ego ex causa 2
faciliorem mihi veniam meae deprecationis arbitrabar fore, hac
accendebantur illi magis, quod inter diversas opiniones priorum
et quasdam etiam inter se contrarias difficilis esset electio, ut
mihi si non inveniendi nova, at certe iudicandi de veteribus
iniungere laborem non iniuste viderentur. quamvis autem non 3
tam me vinceret praestandi quod exigebatur fiducia quam
negandi verecundia, latius se tamen aperiente materia plus
quam inponebatur oneris sponte suscepi, simul ut pleniore
obsequio demererer amantissimos mei, simul ne vulgarem viam
ingressus alienis demum vestigiis insisterem. nam ceteri fere, 4

1. post...quietem. L. translates
'Having at length after twenty years
devoted to the training of the young
obtained *leisure for study*.' This suggests, perhaps unintentionally, that the
last three words = 'studiis meis quietem.'
But as the relative 'quae' shews, the
meaning is 'when I was allowed to rest
from my professional activities.' At any
rate the addition 'for study' is unwarranted. Q. does not wish to suggest
that he had any such motive for retirement and may be supposed to imply
what he actually says in II. 12, 12, that his
reason was 'quia honestissimum finem
putabamus desinere, dum desiderare-
mur.' Cf. also XII. 11, 1–4, though it is
true that in both these passages it is
suggested incidentally that the 'emeri-
tus' will find consolation in study or
helping the next generation.
per viginti annos. For the chrono-
logical inference to be drawn from this
v. Intr. p. xvi.
2. ut...viderentur. For this modest
judgment cf. III. 1, 22 where, after enumerating the great writers in rhetoric,

Q. adds 'Non tamen post tot ac tantos
auctores pigebit meam quibusdam locis
posuisse sententiam; neque enim me
cuiusquam sectae velut quadam super-
stitione imbutus addixi, et electuris quae
volent facienda copia fuit, sicut ipse
plurium in unum confero inventa, ubi-
cumque ingenio non erit locus, curae
testimonium meruisse contentus.'
3. alienis...insisterem. Cf. Hor. *Ep.*
I, 19, 21
'Libera per vacuum posui vestigia
princeps,
non aliena meo pressi pede.'
This use of 'demum' for 'only' is frequent in Q. Other instances (apart from
its use with pronouns) are 4, 29; II. 15, 1
'nomen hoc bonis demum tribui volunt.'
According to Hand and others this is a
silver usage, but the addition of 'demum'
to pronouns, for emphasis and without
thought of time, which is common in
earlier writers, is closely akin. Cic.
however distinguishes it from 'solum'
(*ad Att.* 8, 8 'sic enim sentio id demum,
aut potius id solum esse miserum, quod
turpe sit'). When Q. couples it with

qui artem orandi litteris tradiderunt, ita sunt exorsi, quasi
perfectis omni alio genere doctrinae summam [in] eloquentia
manum inponerent, sive contemnentes tamquam parva quae
prius discimus studia, sive non ad suum pertinere officium
opinati, quando divisae professionum vices essent, seu, quod
proximum vero, nullam ingenii sperantes gratiam circa res
etiamsi necessarias, procul tamen ab ostentatione positas, ut
operum fastigia spectantur, latent fundamenta. ego cum
existimem nihil arti oratoriae alienum sine quo fieri non posse
oratorem fatendum est, nec ad ullius rei summam nisi praece-
dentibus initiis pervenire, ad minora illa, sed quae si neglegas,
non sit maioribus locus, demittere me non recusabo nec aliter
quam si mihi tradatur educandus orator, studia eius formare
6 ab infantia incipiam. quod opus, Marcelle Vitori, tibi dicamus,
quem cum amicissimum nobis tum eximio litterarum amore
flagrantem non propter haec modo, quamquam sunt magna,
dignissimum hoc mutuae inter nos caritatis pignore iudica-
bamus, sed quod erudiendo Getae tuo, cuius prima aetas

pronouns, as in 3, 4, there is no need,
I think, to regard it, as Hand does, as
merely emphatic and not exclusive.

4. eloquentia. I have followed Halm
and Meister's text, but without much
conviction. The sense required seems to
me best met by Fierville's 'eloquentiae'
(gen.). H probably (there is a rent here),
and its descendants F, T certainly, have
'in eloquentiae' (A here fails us, v. p.
xcvii n.), and the others vary between
'eloquentiae' and 'in eloquentia.' The
latter is retained by Rad., who seems
to think that it is defended by X. 1, 97
'summa in excolendis operibus manus.'
But the meaning of 'in' as the sphere
in which the 'summa manus' is exhibited
is unsuitable here. Burman suggested
'eloquentia imponeret,' Regius followed
by Sp. 'inde (out of in̄) eloquentiae,'
Kiderlin 'in[stitutione] eloquentiae,'
Andresen 'iam eloquentiae.'

summam...manum. Cf. X. 1, 97 (just
quoted). Cic. *Brut.* § 126 'manus ex-
trema non accessit operibus eius,' and
other exx. in Dict. For this use of 'sum-
mus' = 'extremus' which seems to be
mainly confined to poetry cf. X. 1, 21
'eaque in prima parte actionis dicit,
quae sunt in summa profutura' (where
v. Peterson), VI. 4, 22.

5. nec...locus. The converse of this
truth is given in X. 1, 4 'sed ut perveniri

ad summa nisi ex principiis non potest,
ita procedente opere iam minima incipi-
unt esse quae prima sunt.'

6. Vitori. MSS. and older edd. Victori. Mommsen (*Hermes* XIII. p. 428)
shews from the Acta Arvalium (v. below)
118–120 A.D. that Vit. is the proper
form of the name. 'Victorius' acc. to
M. is a name current in a later period.
Marcellus as appears from Stat. *Silv.* 4,
4, 49 was at one time praetor and afterwards was given the superintendence of
the Via Latina; v. Vollmer.

quamquam sunt. I follow Halm and
Meister against Fierville and Radermacher in reading 'sunt' not 'sint'
though the evidence seems to me closely
balanced. H 'sunt,' also A, but the 'n' is
written by a second hand over an erasure.
'Quamquam' with subj. is fairly common
in Q. e.g. II. 17, 12 (v. Bonnell). The
same doubt arises Pr. 18, though there
the evidence for the ind. is stronger.

Getae. Halm reads 'Getae,' but adds
'Getae A; "nato" rell. libri fere omnes:
cum in Statii Silvis (4, 4, 20) Victorii
filius "Gallus" nominetur, Burman et
Spalding "Gallo" scribendum censue-
runt; nec tamen probari potest eum
unicum Victorii filium fuisse.'

The reading of A is now put beyond
all doubt by the fact that 'Geta' is
actually mentioned as a son of Vitorius.

manifestum iam ingenii lumen ostendit, non inutiles fore libri
videbantur, quos ab ipsis dicendi velut incunabulis per omnis
quae modo aliquid oratori futuro conferant artis ad summam
eius operis perducere destinabamus, atque eo magis, quod duo **7**
iam sub nomine meo libri ferebantur artis rhetoricae neque
editi a me neque in hoc comparati. namque alterum sermonem
per biduum habitum pueri, quibus id praestabatur, exceperant,
alterum pluribus sane diebus, quantum notando consequi

in *Silv.* 4, 4, 72 'parvoque exempla
parabis | magna Getae.' This is the
reading both of the Matritensis and Politian's notes on the now lost Vetus Poggii.
Earlier edd. of Q. (even including Halm)
seem to have been misled by the common
text of Statius, which exhibits 'patriae
...pater' (conjecturally substituted for
the corruption 'gerens'). In the face of
this it is unnecessary to discuss whether
'nato' is admissible in prose. Gallus,
as Mommsen says, is probably a friend
not a son.
  Geta is no doubt rightly identified
by Mommsen (op. cit.) with C. Vitorius
Hosidius Geta whose name appears in
the Acta Arvalium 118-120 A.D.
  manifestum iam ingenii lumen.
Spalding and earlier edd. read 'iter ad'
for 'iam,' explaining 'ingenii lumen' as
= 'eloquentia,' referring to Cic. *Brut.* 59
'ut enim hominis decus ingenium, sic
ingenii ipsius est lumen eloquentia.'
Halm has been followed by later edd.
in adopting the more intelligible reading
of A; v. Add. Note.
  dicendi...incunabulis. This phrase is
probably a reminiscence of Cic. *De Or.*
1, 23 'repetamque non ab incunabulis
nostrae veteris puerilisque doctrinae
quemdam ordinem praeceptorum' and
Or. 42 'non alienum fuit de oratoris
quasi incunabulis dicere.' But Q. gives
the phrase a different turn. In the *De
Or.* the 'incunabula' are the formal rules
of theoretical rhetoric, in the *Or.* oratory
of the epideictic type, unpractical in
itself, but useful as a training for the
forum. Here we have it extended, in
accordance with Q.'s principles, to elementary education.
  dicendi. Gesner and Bonnell 'discendi.' Whilst the authority of MSS.
is for 'dicendi' it is true as Sp. says that
in these words 'quarum frequentissima
confusio non magna est Codd. auctoritas.'
But 'incunabula discendi' seems to me
a strange expression. The gen. after
'incunabula' is naturally either one of

definition as in *De Or.*, or expresses the
goal to which it leads as in *Or.* and, I
think, here; 'inc. disc.' would be neither.
  destinabamus. A 'festinabimus'
which Fierville adopted. Kiderlin rightly remarks that it does not so well agree
with the imperfect 'ferebantur.'
  7. ferebantur. Cf. VII. 2, 24 'nam
ceterae (actiones), quae sub nomine meo
feruntur, negligentia excipientium in
quaestum notariorum corruptae mini-
mam partem mei habent.' The piratical
editions of the 'actiones' there referred
to are of course quite distinct from those
of the rhetorical treatises mentioned
here. These last are alluded to in III. 6,
68 'in ipsis illis sermonibus me nolente
vulgatis.'
  sermonem...habitum. So A, H followed by Halm and later edd. Earlier
edd. including Sp. and Burman, who
objected to the cacophony of the m's,
read 'sermone...habito.' The acc. is
supported by III. 6, 68 just quoted.
  pueri. Clearly slaves, professional
'notarii' as in VII. 2, 24 just quoted.
There is a contrast between the complete
versions made by the 'pueri' ('exceperant') and the incomplete versions
made by the 'iuvenes' ('interceptum').
That the former should, as is usually
understood, be younger pupils seems to
me impossible. Q. would not address
lectures of this type to younger pupils
exclusively nor would they have managed shorthand better than their seniors.
Moreover on this supposition, what is
'id'? I understand it as = 'excipere.'
Presumably Q. wishing to oblige some
friends opened his lectures to the 'notarii' sent by them and the copy thus
obtained was piratically published.
  notando. For the verb in the sense
of writing shorthand cf. Suet. *Aug.* 64
'nepotes et litteras et notare, aliaque
rudimenta per se plerumque docuit, ac
nihil aeque elaboravit, quam ut imita-
rentur chirographum suum.' For the
ancient shorthand v. esp. *Dict. Ant.* on

potuerant, interceptum boni iuvenes, sed nimium amantes mei
8 temerario editionis honore vulgaverant. quare in his quoque
libris erunt eadem aliqua, multa mutata, plurima adiecta, omnia
vero compositiora et quantum nos poterimus elaborata.

9 Oratorem autem instituimus illum perfectum, qui esse nisi
vir bonus non potest, ideoque non dicendi modo eximiam in
10 eo facultatem, sed omnis animi virtutes exigimus. neque enim
hoc concesserim, rationem rectae honestaeque vitae, ut quidam
putaverunt, ad philosophos relegandam, cum vir ille vere civilis
et publicarum privatarumque rerum administrationi accom-
modatus, qui regere consiliis urbes, fundare legibus, emendare
11 iudiciis possit, non alius sit profecto quam orator. quare,
tametsi me fateor usurum quibusdam quae philosophorum
libris continentur, tamen ea iure vereque contenderim esse
12 operis nostri proprieque ad artem oratoriam pertinere. an, si
frequentissime de iustitia, fortitudine, temperantia ceterisque
similibus disserendum est, adeo ut vix ulla possit causa repe-
riri, in quam non aliqua ex his incidat quaestio, eaque omnia
inventione atque elocutione sunt explicanda, dubitabitur, ubi-
cumque vis ingenii et copia dicendi postulatur, ibi partes

'notae.' Cf. Sen. *Ep.* 90, 25 'Quid
verborum notas, quibus quamvis citata
excipitur oratio et celeritatem linguae
manus sequitur? vilissimorum manci-
piorum ista commenta sunt.'
   boni. A and H have 'bini' which
Fierville actually adopts. It seems to
me to be prohibited by the 'sed,' and
would Q. or indeed any prose writer use
'bini' as simply = 'duo'?
   9. vir bonus. Cf. XII. 1, 1 'sit ergo
nobis orator, quem constituimus, is qui
a M. Catone finitur vir bonus dicendi
peritus.' So too in Sen. *Contr.* 1. pr. 9.
Cf. also *De Or.* 2, 85, Jerome *Ep.* 69, 8,
Fronto (Naber p. 121), Fortunatianus
(Halm *Rhet. Lat.* p. 81). This definition is said by Striller (*De Stoic. stud.
rhet.* p. 8) to be Stoic, and no doubt is
quite in accordance with their definitions
of rhetoric as 'scientia bene (or recte)
dicendi.' I think however it is a mistake
to limit its origin thus. The passages
from the *Gorgias* quoted in II. 15, though
in themselves ironical, would naturally
suggest the doctrine. It is in fact latent
in Ar.'s ἦθος τοῦ λέγοντος, though in
Rhet. 1, 2, 4 he holds that ἦθος to be a
genuine part of rhetoric must be ex-

hibited in the speech itself. It appears
more definitely though in rather an
absurd way in *Rhet. ad Alex.* ch. 38, and
much better in Isoc. περὶ ἀντ. 270 etc.
At any rate after Cato's pronouncement
it becomes something more than a Stoic
dogma and exhibits the view which the
rhetoricians in their conflict with the
philosophers eagerly seized on, that
character is an essential element in the
art of ruling and persuading men. It
finds its noblest expression as Q. (XII.
1, 27) and others have pointed out in
the famous simile of *Aen.* 1, 151.
   ideoque. This phrase used 'in transitu' almost = 'itaque' is an idiom particularly characteristic of Q. (v. Hand
Turs. III. p. 181). Bonnell gives between 20 and 30 exx.
   12. an...disserendum est. L. wrongly
translates 'I shall frequently be com-
pelled to speak of such virtues etc.'
The point is rather that all speakers
have to deal with such questions, a point
further developed in XII. 2, 15-20.
   inventione atque elocutione. The
two fundamental parts of eloquence
corresponding to 'res' and 'verba' respectively, here identified with 'vis

oratoris esse praecipuas? fueruntque haec, ut Cicero apertissime 13
colligit, quemadmodum iuncta natura, sic officio quoque copu-
lata, ut idem sapientes atque eloquentes haberentur. scidit
deinde se studium, atque inertia factum est ut artes esse plures
viderentur. nam ut primum lingua esse coepit in quaestu
institutumque eloquentiae bonis male uti, curam morum qui
diserti habebantur reliquerunt : ea vero destituta infirmioribus 14
ingeniis velut praedae fuit. inde quidam contempto bene
dicendi labore ad formandos animos statuendasque vitae leges
regressi partem quidem potiorem, si dividi posset, retinuerunt,
nomen tamen sibi insolentissimum adrogaverunt, ut soli
studiosi sapientiae vocarentur. quod neque summi impera-
tores neque in consiliis rerum maximarum ac totius adminis-
tratione rei publicae clarissime versati sibi umquam vindicare
sunt ausi : facere enim optima quam promittere maluerunt.
ac veterum quidem sapientiae professorum multos et honesta 15

ingenii' and 'copia dicendi' respectively.

13. haec. This does not refer to the
pair just mentioned, but to 'ratio rectae
vitae' i.e. 'sapientia,' on the one hand,
and 'partes oratoris,' i.e. 'eloquentia'
on the other. The latter includes both
'inventio' and 'elocutio.'

ut Cicero apertissime colligit; i.e.
De Or. 3, 50–61, a passage not altogether clear and perhaps an imperfect
adaptation from some Greek source
(v. Arnim *Dio von Prusa* p. 98 ff.,
who suggests Philo the Academician).
But Q. does not follow this passage exclusively. In Cicero the 'discidium' is
attributed to the dislike which the unpractical philosophers notably Socrates
felt for rhetoric because it was associated
with practical life. In Q. the 'discidium'
is primarily attributed to rhetoric, which
corrupted by Mammon forgets ethics.
Ethics in its turn is taken up by weaker
minds, which conceive a contempt for
eloquence. The fact is, I believe, that
he is following not only *De Or.* 3, but
De Inv. 1, 3, 4, where the 'discidium'
is attributed to 'commoditas quaedam
prava virtutis imitatrix.' When this
'sine ratione officii, dicendi copiam con-
secuta est, tum ingenio freta malitia
pervertere urbes et vitas hominum labe-
factare adsuevit.' That Q. in our
passage is rendering 'commoditas' by
'in quaestu' was suggested by the rhetor Grillus in his commentary on he

De Inv. (a well-known book in the
Middle Ages); v. Halm *Rhet. Lat.*
p. 598.

Another point to be noticed is that
Q. does not follow the *De Or.* in classing Socrates among the non-rhetorical
philosophers. As is shewn in II. 15, 24 ff,
he had convinced himself that the Pla-
tonic Socrates in the *Gorgias* supported
rhetoric. I take the 'inferiora ingenia'
to be the whole body of philosophers,
who, though not without their merits, are
on the whole inferior to the 'sapientes'
of former times, while 'quidam' refers
to the post-Platonic schools.

officio. L. 'practice' which perhaps
must serve. But the word does not, I
think, lose its moral sense. In the
standard of practical duties demanded
by men, a man could not be 'sapiens'
unless he was 'eloquens' and vice versa.
scidit. Cf. 'discidium linguae atque
cordis' *De Or.* 3, 61.

inertia...viderentur, 'neglect of
science led to the multiplication of
sciences.' But no translation can be
adequate. The difficulty lies of course
in the fact that the moral sense inherent
in 'ars' (but not in art) makes it easy
to contrast the former with 'iners' and
'inertia,' a contrast which appears also
in Cic. *De Fin.* 2, 115, *De Part.* 10,
35 (both quoted in L. and S.). The
'inertia' is on the part of both rhetors
and philosophers who did not live up to
their 'ars.'

praecepisse et, ut praeceperint, etiam vixisse facile concesserim:
nostris vero temporibus sub hoc nomine maxima in plerisque
vitia latuerunt. non enim virtute ac studiis ut haberentur
philosophi laborabant, sed vultum et tristitiam et dissentientem
16 a ceteris habitum pessimis moribus praetendebant. haec autem
quae velut propria philosophiae adseruntur, passim tractamus
omnes. quis enim non de iusto, aequo ac bono, modo non et
vir pessimus, loquitur? quis non etiam rusticorum aliqua de
causis naturalibus quaerit? nam verborum proprietas ac differentia omnibus, qui sermonem curae habent, debet esse
17 communis. sed ea et sciet optime et eloquetur orator : qui si
fuisset aliquando perfectus, non a philosophorum scholis virtutis praecepta peterentur. nunc necesse est ad eos aliquando
auctores recurrere, qui desertam, ut dixi, partem oratoriae
artis, meliorem praesertim, occupaverunt, et velut nostrum
reposcere, non ut nos illorum utamur inventis, sed ut illos

15. praeceperint. All recent edd.
have adopted this reading of A, but
there is no serious objection to the older
and commoner reading 'praeceperunt';
v. Roby 1777.

sed vultum et tristitiam etc. Cf.
XI. I, 34 of the forms of oratory which
'non conveniant barbae illi atque tris-
titiae.' Gk. σκυθρωπός, σκυθρωπάζω, cf.
Luc. *Pisc.* 37 ᾗ διότι πώγωνας ἔχουσι καὶ
φιλοσοφεῖν φάσκουσι καὶ σκυθρωποί εἰσι,
διὰ τοῦτο χρὴ ὑμῖν εἰκάζειν αὐτούς; The
whole of this dialogue illustrates well
the sense of this section of Q.

16. The argument of this section is
developed more fully in XII. 2, 10–25.
Here however the main point is that the
subject-matter of philosophy is necessary
to the ordinary man. There as in 12
above the orator himself is in view.
Consequently here only the most elementary parts of the three accepted divisions (ἠθική, φυσική and λογική) are
mentioned. There φυσική is extended
to theology.

modo non et vir pessimus, 'unless
he is an utter villain.' This sense is
supported by III. 11, 24 'neque est fere
quisquam, modo non stultus ... quin
sciat,' but 'et' here seems otiose. We
might perhaps as Halm tentatively
suggests amend to 'sit.' Even so there
is in force in Sp.'s remark that Q. was
well aware that the most depraved may
and do discourse on morality. The
translation 'almost even the most depraved' makes excellent sense, if we can

believe that Q. would use 'modo non'
thus. It seems to me doubtful. Sp.'s
suggestion that it = 'utinam non' seems
still more unlikely. The passage is discussed in Hand *Turs.* III. p. 637.

nam. This use of 'nam' to introduce
something which is too obvious to need
argument or goes beyond what has been
mentioned is common in Q. Cf. 5, 67;
11, 9.

proprietas. The 'proprietas' of a
word consists in its being 'cuiusque rei
proprium,' i.e. it exactly expresses the
thing to which it is applied and nothing
else. The varieties of 'proprietas' are
discussed in VIII. 2. This 'proprietas'
has a rhetorical value when the word is
one 'quo nihil inveniri potest significantius.' From this use 'proprietas' comes
to be regarded as a quality of a language
or a particular writer's style. Thus XII.
10, 36 Greek is said to have 'certior
proprietas' than Latin. Servius on *Aen.*
I, 410, after pointing out that 'incuso'
rather than 'accuso' is the right word
for an inferior remonstrating with a
superior, and quoting a similar use from
Terence, goes on to say that Terence
excels the other comedians in 'proprietas.'

17. meliorem praesertim. L. ignores
'praesertim.' Watson 'preeminently.'
I do not think this gives the meaning of
the word, which as usual introduces a
special reason for the action. 'They appropriated it the more willingly because
it was the better part.'

alienis usos esse doceamus. sit igitur orator vir talis, qualis **18** vere sapiens appellari possit, nec moribus modo perfectus (nam id mea quidem opinione, quamquam sunt qui dissentiant, satis non est), sed etiam scientia et omni facultate dicendi. qualis fortasse nemo adhuc fuerit, sed non ideo minus nobis **19** ad summa tendendum est: quod fecerunt plerique veterum, qui etsi nondum quemquam sapientem repertum putabant, praecepta tamen sapientiae tradiderunt. nam est certe aliquid **20** consummata eloquentia neque ad eam pervenire natura humani ingenii prohibet. quod si non contingat, altius tamen ibunt, qui ad summa nitentur, quam qui praesumpta desperatione quo velint evadendi protinus circa ima substiterint.

Quo magis impetranda erit venia, si ne minora quidem illa, **21** verum operi quod instituimus necessaria praeteribo. nam liber primus ea, quae sunt ante officium rhetoris, continebit. secundo prima apud rhetorem elementa et quae de ipsa rhetorices substantia quaeruntur tractabimus. quinque deinceps inventioni **22** (nam huic et dispositio subiungitur), quattuor elocutioni, in cuius partem memoria ac pronuntiatio veniunt, dabuntur. unus accedet, in quo nobis orator ipse informandus est: ubi, qui mores eius, quae in suscipiendis, discendis, agendis causis ratio, quod eloquentiae genus, quis agendi debeat esse finis, quae post finem studia, quantum nostra valebit infirmitas, disseremus. his omnibus admiscebitur, ut quisque locus postulabit, **23** docendi ratio, quae non eorum modo scientia, quibus solis quidam nomen artis dederunt, studiosos instruat et, ut sic

---

18. quamquam sunt. Sp. and Fierville 'sint'; v. on § 6.
scientia et omni facultate dicendi. L. translates 'the science and the art of speaking' and this might be supported by II. 1, 2 'scientiam declamandi ac facultatem' (where L. gives 'theory and practice'). Or perhaps, 'in knowledge and every form of readiness in speech,' the stress being on the need of possession by the orator of that wide extent of knowledge which will enable him always to speak with ease, so far as grasp of his subject is concerned.
20. altius tamen ibunt. For the thought cf. I. 10, 8 and George Herbert's
  'who aimeth at the sky
Shoots higher far than he who means
  a tree.'

22. ubi. MSS. 'ut,' which necessitated the corr. of 'disseremus' to 'disseramus' in older edd. Halm from A (u in ras.) restored 'ubi.' Meister following Meyer 'et.'
23. his...ratio. L.'s translation 'In the course of these discussions, I shall deal in the proper place with the method of teaching by which students will acquire etc.' misses the sense. Rather 'Through all these subjects, according to their respective requirements, I shall employ a method of treatment, which etc.' Cf. III. 1, 3 'in ceteris enim admiscere temptavimus aliquid nitoris,' where he goes on to apply the lines of Lucr. 1, 936–938, v. Intr. p. xxxviii.
docendi. Regius 'dicendi,' which though preferred by Sp. has rightly been rejected by succeeding edd.

dixerim, ius ipsum rhetorices interpretetur, sed alere facundiam,
24 vires augere eloquentiae possit. nam plerumque nudae illae
artes nimiae subtilitatis adfectatione frangunt atque concidunt
quidquid est in oratione generosius, et omnem sucum ingenii
bibunt et ossa detegunt, quae ut esse et adstringi nervis suis
25 debent, sic corpore operienda sunt. ideoque nos non particulam
illam, sicuti plerique, sed quidquid utile ad instituendum
oratorem putabamus, in hos duodecim libros contulimus,
breviter omnia demonstraturi: nam si quantum de quaque re
26 dici potest persequamur, finis operis non reperietur. illud
tamen in primis testandum est, nihil praecepta atque artes
valere nisi adiuvante natura. quapropter ei, cui deerit ingenium, non magis haec scripta sint, quam de agrorum cultu
27 sterilibus terris. sunt et alia ingenita cuique adiumenta, vox,
latus patiens laboris, valetudo, constantia, decor. quae si
modica obtigerunt, possunt ratione ampliari, sed nonnumquam
ita desunt, ut bona etiam ingenii studiique corrumpant: sicut
et haec ipsa sine doctore perito, studio pertinaci, scribendi

ius ipsum. For this conception of technical rhetoric as a code cf. II. 13, 15 'velut decretis technicorum' and VIII. Prooem. 2 'ad certa quasdam dicendi leges adligati.'

24. artes, here 'text-books,' 'manuals' as in II. 13, 1 and 'artem scindes Theodori,' Juv. 7, 177. Below, 26, 'rules' or 'collections of rules' as in II. 5, 14. Bonnell's lexicon does not sufficiently distinguish between these two meanings. **subtilitatis adfectatione.** Cf. III. 11, 21 'haec adfectata subtilitas circa nomina rerum ambitiose laborat.'

ossa...nervis...corpore. If the difference between 'ossa' and 'nervi' is to be pressed, the former are bald isolated rules, the latter reasoning and logical connexion, while 'corpus' in any case represents fullness and richness in style and treatment. In VIII. Prooem. 18 'res' (the material) as opposed to the 'elocutio' are the 'nervi in causis.' The same contrast of 'nervi' or 'artus' with 'corpus' or 'caro' is used in v. 8, 2 and v. 12, 6 in recommending lively treatment of argumentation.

26. nihil...natura. Q.'s views on this point are given more fully in II. 19.

27. ingenita...adiumenta. These are dealt with again in XII. 5 where they are spoken of as 'instrumenta oratoris'; cf. Julius Severianus (Halm

Rhet. Lat. p. 355) where after natural powers of learning we have 'vox, latus, decor, valetudo, frugalitas, laboris patientia.' Did he read 'patientia' here? **cuique.** So A, H. The older edd. have 'quaedam.' The objection that 'non cuique haec adsunt' mistakes the meaning of 'quisque' here. It expresses the fact that these are essentially individual characteristics not found always or all together. **constantia.** Sp. had some doubt as to the genuineness of this word, appearing as it does amongst physical qualities. But it reappears in the same connection XII. 5, 2 as part of (or perhaps identical with) the 'praestantia animi,' which stands first amongst the 'instrumenta oratoris.' Its place on the list is perhaps strange, but 'decor' is also with Q. a gift of the highest importance. **haec.** It is better to refer this to 'vox latus' etc., rather than to the 'bona ingenii studiique.' In the latter case we should have the absurd statement that 'bona studii' are useless 'sine studio.' 'ipsa'=by themselves alone. Observe that we have here the trinity of 'natura' (or 'ingenium'), 'doctrina,' 'studium' (or 'exercitatio') which is one of the commonest of Greek educational ideas. Cf. VII. 10, 14 'sed haec in oratione praestabit, cui omnia adfuerint, natura, doctrina, studium,' III. 5, 1

legendi dicendi multa et continua exercitatione per se nihil prosunt.

I

[QUEMADMODUM PRIMA ELEMENTA TRADENDA SUNT]

Igitur nato filio pater spem de illo primum quam optimam **1** capiat: ita diligentior a principiis fiet. falsa enim est querella, paucissimis hominibus vim percipiendi quae tradantur esse concessam, plerosque vero laborem ac tempora tarditate ingenii perdere. nam contra plures reperias et faciles in excogitando et ad discendum promptos. quippe id est homini naturale, ac sicut aves ad volatum, equi ad cursum, ad saevitiam ferae gignuntur, ita nobis propria est mentis agitatio atque sollertia, unde origo animi caelestis creditur. hebetes vero et indociles **2** non magis secundum naturam hominis eduntur quam prodigiosa corpora et monstris insignia, sed hi pauci admodum. fuerit argumentum, quod in pueris elucet spes plurimorum:

'natura, arte, exercitatione,' XII. 1, 10 'ingenio, studio, doctrina.' So too *De Or.* 3, 77 'ingenio, doctrina, usu.' In Greek we may note ps.-Plut. *De Ed. Lib.* 4 εἰς τὴν παντελῆ δικαιοπραγίαν τρία δεῖ συνδραμεῖν φύσιν καὶ λόγον καὶ ἔθος, καλῶ δὲ λόγον μὲν τὴν μάθησιν, ἔθος δὲ τὴν ἄσκησιν. Aristotle acc. to Diog. Laert. v. 18 τριῶν ἔφη δεῖν παιδείᾳ, φύσεως, μαθήσεως, ἀσκήσεως. The earliest instance seems to be Plat. *Phaedr.* 269 D and it is expanded at some length in Isoc. *Antid.* 187 (200). The doctrine is really best seen in Philo, where it is several times worked out with Isaac, Abraham and Jacob standing respectively for nat., doct., stud. (v. my article 'Philo on Education,'*Journal of Theological Studies,* Jan. 1917). The simpler dyad of 'natura' and 'doctrina' familiar to us from Hor. *Odes* 4, 4 (cf. Pindar *Olymp.* 9, 100) is adopted in Q. XII. 2, 1, where apparently 'studium' and 'disciplina' are subdivisions of 'doctrina.'
I 1. [quemadmodum...sunt.] For these headings (and the brackets) v. Add. Note.
plerosque; here and in 22 = 'most'; elsewhere frequently no more than 'many'; v. exx. in Pet. Intr. p. xlvi.

quippe...creditur. Cf. XII. 11, 12 (speaking of the study of ethics) 'natura enim nos ad mentem optimam genuit, adeoque discere meliora volentibus promptum est, ut vere intuenti mirum sit illud magis, malos esse tam multos. Nam ut aqua piscibus, ut sicca terrenis, circumfusus nobis spiritus volucribus convenit, ita certe facilius esse oportebat, secundum naturam quam contra eam vivere.'
2. hominis. So A (also H and Bg?) which Halm and later edd. have followed. Sp. and others 'homines,' of which Sp. says 'concinnitas videtur poscere ut *prodigiosa corpora* habeant sibi oppositos non *hebetes* sed *hebetes homines.*' But 'hi' shews that the 'prod. corp.' are human.
monstris insignia, an odd use of 'monstrum' for a 'monstrous peculiarity,' at which some edd. have boggled.
fuerit argumentum. This reading suggested as an emendation by Regius is confirmed by Bg, H. Notwithstanding Halm adopted the reading of most MSS. including A 'fuerunt' and Meister and Rad. have followed him. Meister in *Philologus* 1876 was of a different opinion and held, as I should, that the present rather than the past is needed

quae cum emoritur aetate, manifestum est non naturam defe-
3 cisse, sed curam. 'praestat tamen ingenio alius alium.' concedo,
sed plus efficiet aut minus: nemo reperitur, qui sit studio nihil
consecutus. hoc qui perviderit, protinus ut erit parens factus,
acrem quam maxime curam spei futuri oratoris impendat.
4 Ante omnia ne sit vitiosus sermo nutricibus: quas, si fieri
posset, sapientes Chrysippus optavit; certe quantum res pate-
retur, optimas eligi voluit. et morum quidem in his haud dubie
5 prior ratio est, recte tamen etiam loquantur. has primum audiet
puer, harum verba effingere imitando conabitur. et natura
tenacissimi sumus eorum, quae rudibus animis percepimus:
ut sapor quo nova imbuas <vasa> durat, nec lanarum colores,
quibus simplex ille candor mutatus est, elui possunt. et haec
ipsa magis pertinaciter haerent quo deteriora sunt. nam bona

after 'hi pauci admodum.' The considerations however are very closely
balanced.

fuerit...curam. A valuable proof that
the fall off in desire to learn, which is
so often deplored in the modern, was
also observed in the ancient boy, and
then too was set down to schoolmasters
or systems. If Q. had been a 'grammaticus' himself, he might have taken a
different view.

3. sed plus efficiet. Sp. and other
edd. have 'sed ut plus efficiat,' but
while there is some authority for the
subj. it is not clear that there is any
for the 'ut.' Our reading is that of A,
Bg, H.

quam maxime curam. Both A and
Bg have 'quam maxime datur curam,'
though in Bg 'datur' is expunged. H
omits. Rad. retains 'datur' but it is difficult to give it a satisfactory meaning.

4. nutricibus. The nurse in Q. takes
a more prominent place than in ps.-
Plut. (5) who insists strongly on the
mother suckling her child. If however
a nurse is necessary, she must be σπουδαῖος and τοῖς ἤθεσιν Ἑλληνίς. Pl. says
nothing however about correct speech
though he does in the case of the ' vernae '; v. note on § 7.

sapientes, 'professing philosophers'
in the full Stoic sense. Cf. Lactantius
D. I. III. 25 'Stoici, qui et servis et
mulieribus philosophandum esse dixerunt.'

Chrysippus. Q. refers again to this
treatise, inf. 16. 3, 13. 11, 17. From
the last of these it appears that its title

was περὶ παίδων ἀγωγῆς. He may also
be alluding to it in 10, 32. The book
does not appear in Diog. Laert.'s imperfect list of Chr.'s works and is not otherwise known. The only other educational
statement attributed to him is that the
ἐγκύκλια were εὔχρηστα, D. L. vii. 129.
A treatise of Cleanthes περὶ ἀγωγῆς and
one of Zeno περὶ Ἑλληνικῆς παιδείας are
mentioned by D. L.
  The view is sometimes put forward
that the educational part of the *Inst. Or.*
is largely taken from Chr. None of these
five allusions suggest this, and indeed
in two out of the five Q. is at pains
to shew that his point of view is not
the same.

5. primum. A very clear indication
of the extent to which Q. regards the
mother's duties as delegated. For the
use of the adverb v. note on § 15.

animis—'annis' Sp. and earlier edd.,
and, acc. to Halm, MSS. 'deteriores
pauci.'

vasa. I have adopted with Rad. the
excellent emendation of Becher (Meyer?)
by which 'vasa' is inserted after 'imbuas.' The same antithesis of 'animus'
and 'vas' in I. 2, 28.
  Q. is evidently thinking in the first
part of this passage of Hor. *Ep.* 1, 2, 69
and in the 'lanarum colores' of *Odes* 3,
5, 27. Besides the imitation in Jerome
(v. Intr. p. xlv), there is a close parallel
in Philo *quod omnis probus liber sit* § 2
ὥσπερ γάρ φασι τὰ καινὰ τῶν ἀγγείων
ἀναφέρειν τὰς τῶν πρώτων εἰς αὐτὰ ἐγχυ-
θέντων ὀσμάς, οὕτω καὶ αἱ νέων ψυχαί.

quo deteriora sunt. I have followed

facile mutantur in peius: quando in bonum verteris vitia? non
adsuescat ergo, ne dum infans quidem est, sermoni qui dedi-
scendus sit.

In parentibus vero quam plurimum esse eruditionis opta- 6
verim. nec de patribus tantum loquor: nam Gracchorum
eloquentiae multum contulisse accepimus Corneliam matrem,
cuius doctissimus sermo in posteros quoque est epistulis
traditus. et Laelia C. filia reddidisse in loquendo paternam
elegantiam dicitur, et Hortensiae Q. filiae oratio apud trium-
viros habita legitur non tantum in sexus honorem. nec tamen 7
ii, quibus discere ipsis non contigit, minorem curam docendi
liberos habeant, sed sint propter hoc ipsum ad cetera magis
diligentes.

De pueris, inter quos educabitur ille huic spei destinatus,

Halm though doubtfully in accepting
the general MS. reading. The older
editions had 'quae' to which Meister
and Rad. have returned, and which certainly fits in more obviously with the
next sentence. Still the logic of the two
sentences as they stand in the MSS. can
be justified, though it is not so obvious.
    quando. I have followed Meist., Rad.
and Kid. in this reading which is that of
A against Halm, who adopted 'num
quando' on the authority of late MSS.
Bg, H have 'nam quando.' As Kid.
says, this may have been an intrusion
from the 'nam' of the previous clause,
and the suggestion of 'num quando'
that this conversion *never* happens is too
strong for Q.
    6. nec de patribus. Earlier edd. and
MSS. except A, 'verum nec.' The 'verum' has I think been rightly rejected
by Halm and later edd. as a dittography
of 'verim.'
    Gracchorum eloquentiae etc. Q.
evidently refers to Cic. *Brut.* 210, 211:
'Sed magni interest, quos quisque audiat
cotidie domi, quibuscum loquatur in
puero, quemadmodum patres, paedagogi, matres etiam loquantur. Legimus
epistolas Corneliae matris Gracchorum:
apparet filios non tam in gremio educa-
tos quam in sermone matris. Auditus
est nobis Laeliae C. F. saepe sermo.
Ergo illam patris elegantia tinctam vi-
dimus.' Fragments of Cornelia's letters,
if genuine, are preserved by Cornelius
Nepos. A somewhat similar reference is
made to Laelia *De Or.* 3, 45.
    Compare the story in ps.-Plut. (14) of

Eurydice ἥτις Ἰλλυρὶς οὖσα καὶ τριβάρ-
βαρος ὅμως ἐπὶ τῇ μαθήσει τῶν τέκνων ὀψὲ
τῆς ἡλικίας ἥψατο παιδείας.
    Hortensiae Q. filiae. Halm and later
edd. from the 'Hort. que. fil.' of A
and Bg, for the 'Quinti Hortensii filiae'
of Sp. and earlier edd.
    Hortensiae. A version of this speech
delivered against a special tax imposed
on the matrons by the second Trium-
virate is given in Appian *Bell. Civ.*
4, 32.
    in sexus honorem. Sp. appositely
quotes Sen. Rhet. (*Cont.* III. Pr. 8)
'Orationes Sallusti in honorem historiarum leguntur,' i.e. only in consideration
of the merits of the histories.
    7. docendi liberos. 'About the teach-
ing of their sons.' This has been regarded
as a middle gerund, and Cic. *De Or.*
2, 341 'Graeci...legendi...causa scripti-
taverunt,' Tac. *Germ.* 44 'Unus imperitat
non precario iure parendi' have been
compared. Cf. 'fugiendo' I. 2, 2.
Possibly however the peculiar usage
lies rather in the verb than the gerund,
and 'doceo' = διδάσκομαι as perhaps in
Cic. *Tusc.* 5, 58 (Dionysius) 'tondere
filias suas docuit.'
    pueris, i.e. the young 'vernae' whose
natural association with the 'liberi'
was doubtless as important a consideration as in the days of *Uncle Tom's
Cabin.* Cf. Jer. *Ep.* 14, 3 (Migne) 'illi
cum quibus adolevisti, vernaculi.' Ps.-
Plut. *De Lib. Ed.* 6 οὐ τοίνυν οὐδὲ τοῦτο
παραλιπεῖν ἄξιόν ἐστιν, ὅτι καὶ τὰ παιδία
τὰ μέλλοντα τοῖς τροφίμοις (i.e. the young
masters) ὑπηρετεῖν καὶ τούτοις σύντροφα

8 idem quod de nutricibus dictum sit. de paedagogis hoc amplius, ut aut sint eruditî plane, quam primam esse curam velim, aut se non esse eruditos sciant. nihil est peius iis, qui paulum aliquid ultra primas litteras progressi falsam sibi scientiae persuasionem induerunt. nam et cedere praecipiendi partibus indignantur et velut iure quodam potestatis, quo fere hoc hominum genus intumescit, imperiosi atque interim 9 saevientes stultitiam suam perdocent. nec minus error eorum nocet moribus, si quidem Leonides Alexandri paedagogus, ut a Babylonio Diogene traditur, quibusdam eum vitiis imbuit,

γίνεσθαι ζητητέον πρώτιστα μὲν σπουδαῖα τοὺς τρόπους, ἔτι μέντοι 'Ελληνικὰ καὶ περίτρανα λαλεῖν, ἵνα μὴ συναναχρωνύμενοι βαρβάροις καὶ τὸ ἦθος μοχθηροῖς ἐποφέρωνταί τι τῆς ἐκείνων φαυλότητος.

8. paedagogis. For the ordinary duties ol the 'paedagogus' v. *Dict. Ant.* Some useful reff. to Philostratus and Libanius are given in Walden's *Universities of Ancient Greece*, p. 327. Messer ('*Q. als Didaktiker*,' *Neue Jahr. Phil.* 1897, p. 197) infers from this passage and the absence of any mention of the 'grammatistes' that Q. expects reading and writing to be taught by the 'paedagogus.' Q. certainly assumes that, in his clientèle, such teaching is done at home; for the discussion of the advantages of school and school methods only comes under consideration in connection with the next stage, and if the 'paedagogus' is 'plane eruditus' no doubt he would wish him to be employed as teacher of the elements. Whether he would wish the same in the case of the 'paulum aliquid ultra primas litteras progressi,' seems to me very doubtful, considering the views he expresses in 11. 3 on the advantages of a highly educated teacher in the earlier stages. It is possible no doubt to understand 'cedere praecipiendi partibus' as meaning that these pseudo-erudites, having been as a matter of course employed in the first stage, want to undertake the second, but I prefer to understand it that they use their position as 'exactores studiorum' (v. on 3, 15) to interfere in the teaching.

plane. So Bg and most edd. Halm with A 'plene.' But the fact that Q. does not elsewhere use 'plene,' though he does use 'plenius' and 'plenissime,' turns the scale slightly in favour of 'plane.'

cedere praecipiendi partibus, 'to surrender the office of teacher'; cf. II. 1, 5 'rhetorice...opere cedit,' XI. 1, 12 'patria cedere.' I should have thought it unnecessary to note this, but that L. translates 'they disdain to stoop to the drudgery of teaching.' Even if the Latin can mean this, it is clear that Q. would not wish such persons to teach.

partibus. So A, Bg. Sp. and earlier edd. 'peritis.'

velut...quodam. So frequently, v. Bonnell's lexicon. Cic. generally uses 'quasi' or 'tamquam' with 'quidam.' Q. seems to have a general preference for 'velut' as against these two in comparisons.

quo. Sp. 'qua' and so Bg. Halm and later edd. have followed A.

9. Leonides ... persecuta. Jer. *Ep.* 107 in his adaptation of this passage (v. Intr. p. xlv) has 'Graeca narrat historia Alexandrum potentissimum regem orbisque domitorem et in moribus et in *incessu* Leonidis paedagogi sui non potuisse carere vitiis, quibus adhuc parvulus fuerat infectus.' This 'incessu,' from whatever source Jerome drew it, no doubt gave rise to Hincmar's (v. Intr. p. xlix n.) 'Leoniden citatis (? fierce) moribus et incomposito incessu notabilem, quae puer quasi lac adulterinum sugens ab eo sumpsit,' which in its turn was incorporated in the supplement of Freinsheim printed in the older editions of Q. Curtius.

Babylonio Diogene; v. Pauly-Wissowa. I should conjecture that Q. takes this from Diog.'s treatise περὶ εὐγενείας quoted by Athenaeus IV. 168 E. The story given there of the degeneracy of Phocion's son may very well have accompanied this of the effects of bad environment on Al.

quae robustum quoque et iam maximum regem ab illa institutione puerili sunt persecuta.

Si cui multa videor exigere, cogitet oratorem institui, rem 10 arduam etiam cum ei formando nihil defuerit, praeterea plura ac difficiliora superesse: nam et studio perpetuo et praestantissimis praeceptoribus et plurimis disciplinis opus est. qua- 11 propter praecipienda sunt optima, quae si quis gravabitur, non rationi defuerint, sed homini. si tamen non continget quales maxime velim nutrices, pueros, paedagogos habere, at unus certe sit adsiduus loquendi non inperitus, qui, si qua erunt ab his praesente alumno dicta vitiose, corrigat protinus nec insidere illi sinat, dum tamen intellegatur id, quod prius dixi, bonum esse, hoc remedium.

A sermone Graeco puerum incipere malo, quia Latinum, 12 qui pluribus in usu est, vel nobis nolentibus perbibet, simul quia disciplinis quoque Graecis prius instituendus est, unde et nostrae fluxerunt. non tamen hoc adeo superstitiose fieri velim, 13

robustum. This use of the word in antithesis to 'puer,' and without any definite reference to bodily strength appears again in 8, 12 and 12, 9 and elsewhere in Q. Also in Tac. *Dial.* 35. It is not noticed in the Dict.

iam maximum regem. 'Iam' = 'etiam.' So 8, 16 'iam maiore cura discat.' Other exx. in Bonnell.

10. disciplinis; v. note on 2, 5.

11. defuerint. I have followed Halm and A (also Rad.), though Meister has returned to the older reading 'defuerit' with Bg. I do not think that Sp.'s supposition of 'aliquid' understood is satisfactory. The sense, as I take it, is that if the 'praecepta' are dispensed with in practice, they are none the less inherent in the system. For the antithesis with 'homo' cf. II. 17, 40 'non artis sed hominis,' XI. I, 11 'non fuit hoc utile absolutioni, sed, quod est maius, homini.'

nutrices...unus. So A and recent edd. Bg has 'nutrices pueros habere paedagogus at unus' (and so Regius and Sp. originally). But (1) the position of 'at' is hardly tolerable; (2) the same may be said of the asyndeton 'nutrices, pueros'; (3) the sense is not satisfactory when taken with the last section. In the text adopted Q.'s suggestion is somewhat vague, but apparently he postulates some 'amicus' or 'libertus,' as above 2, 5, who will under-

take a general supervision. Cf. also I. 11, 14.

loquendi. Appropriately used rather than 'dicendi'; v. Intr. p. xxxvi.

12. a sermone Graeco, i.e. *at the earliest stage* the boy's lessons (perhaps also his conversation at table and elsewhere) should be conducted in Greek. The second reason given for this is that when he comes to study 'grammatice,' Greek will necessarily take precedence of Latin and therefore he should be familiar with Greek from the first. That this is the meaning, rather than as L. translates 'the fact that Latin learning is derived from Greek is a further reason for his being first instructed in the latter,' seems to me to be shewn by 'quoque,' which in L.'s rendering becomes pointless. In the next section 'loquatur' refers to this earliest stage, 'discat' to the stage of 'grammatice.' For the priority of Greek v. Intr. p. xxxi.

Latinum...perbibet. The reading of some other edd. 'Latinus...se perbibet' does not seem to have good MS. authority and is extremely weak in sense.

13. superstitiose. Q. uses this and 'superstitio' in this general sense several times; v. Bonnell. Forc. does not quote exx. from other authors. The use of 'religio' in I. 6, 1 is not unlike. Both perhaps throw some light on Q.'s men-

ut diu tantum Graece loquatur aut discat, sicut plerisque moris
est. hoc enim accidunt et oris plurima vitia in peregrinum
sonum corrupti, et sermonis, cui cum Graecae figurae adsidua
consuetudine haeserunt, in diversa quoque loquendi ratione
14 pertinacissime durant. non longe itaque Latina subsequi debent
et cito pariter ire. ita fiet ut, cum aequali cura linguam utram-
que tueri coeperimus, neutra alteri officiat.
15   Quidam litteris instituendos, qui minores septem annis essent,
non putaverunt, quod illa primum aetas et intellectum disciplinarum capere et laborem pati posset. in qua sententia
Hesiodum esse plurimi tradunt, qui ante grammaticum

tality. He perceives that the same human
instincts, which create religious ideas
both good and bad, work also in other
spheres.
    hoc. Regius suspected this and read
'hinc' which Meister has adopted. The
phrase 'hinc accidit' occurs II. 1, 3 and
elsewhere as also 'unde accidit.' I think
the MS. reading may be sufficiently
justified as an ablative of efficient cause
(Roby 1228).
    oris...vitia...et sermonis. 'Os' here
signifies 'utterance' 'pronunciation,' in
particular of words and syllables. So
'vitia oris et linguae' I. 5, 32. Contrast
the description of Q.'s own lost son
VI Prooem. 11 'oris suavitas et in utraque
lingua...expressa proprietas omnium
litterarum.' Cf. XI. 3, 30 'os facile,
explanatum, iucundum, urbanum, id est
in quo nulla neque rusticitas neque
peregrinitas resonet.' On the other hand
'sermo' (language) as used by Q. contemplates words as forming an intelligible
whole. The same combination in § 37,
where see note.
    Graecae figurae. Ernesti *Lex. Rhet.*
s.v. 'figura' takes this phrase to mean
'modi conformandi oris' and = 'proprii
et inenarrabiles soni quibus nonnun-
quam nationes deprehendimus' I. 5, 33.
The objection to this is that the clause
'cui...durant' is clearly adjectival to
'sermonis' and not to 'oris.' I think
it is better to explain the term in its
ordinary sense of 'a form of speech departing from the usual and obvious'
(IX. 1, 4), as in X. 5, 3, where, speaking
of the value of translation from Greek,
he remarks 'figuras vero quibus maxime ornatur oratio, multas ac varias
excogitandi etiam necessitas quaedam
est, quia plerumque a graecis romana
dissentiunt.' There however as the pupil

is at a higher stage, 'rhetorical figures'
are mainly thought of: here the 'grammatical figures' described in IX. 3, 1 ff.
Such a case would arise, if a boy through
the influence of Greek used Latin prepositions with a genitive. It is true
indeed that strictly speaking such a
mistake would not be a 'figura' in either
language. In Greek it would be the
'communis conformatio orationis,' in
Latin a 'vitium,' for every figure would be
a 'vitium' 'si non peteretur sed accideret.'
If this is a serious objection, which I do
not think, we may take 'figurae' as = inflexions; cf. I. 5, 64 'graeca figura.'
This I imagine is the view of Sp. whose
explanation is 'structurae verborum ad
Graecum morem factae.'
    15. septem annis; v. Juv. 14, 11
'cum septimus annus | transierit puerum,
nondum omni dente renato,' where v.
Mayor's note, giving quotations as to
the age when boys were sent to school.
To the 20 or more exx. given, I would
add Soranus, *Art. Obs.* 92 πρὸ δὲ τῶν ἐξ
καὶ ἑπτὰ ἐτῶν τούς τε παῖδας καὶ τὰς κόρας
γραμματισταῖς παραδοῦναι πράεσι καὶ
φιλανθρώποις, Chrysostom *De Mut.
Nom.* 2, 1 (Migne, vol. III. p. 125) οὐδὲ
πέντε ἐτῶν ἡλικίαν ἄγοντα...πρὸς μεσημ-
βρίαν μέσην διακαρτερεῖ καὶ ταλαιπω-
ρεῖται ἐν τῷ διδασκαλείῳ καθήμενα.
    illa primum aetas. Here as in § 5
and in VIII. 3, 35 'idem putat a Terentio
primum dictum esse obsequium' Q. uses
the adverb, where normal use, I think,
calls for the adjective. Below, for 'is
primus negavit' A has 'primum,' which
Rad. has adopted. Halm's note 'Obrecht "prima"' is misleading, for what
Obrecht read was 'illa prima aetas...
non posset.' Compare Prooem. 6 'cuius
prima aetas.' This is a plausible but
unnecessary correction.

Aristophanen fuerunt. nam is primus ὑποθήκας, in quo libro
scriptum hoc invenitur, negavit esse huius poetae. sed alii quo- **16**
que auctores, inter quos Eratosthenes, idem praeceperunt. melius
autem, qui nullum tempus vacare cura volunt, ut Chrysippus.
nam is, quamvis nutricibus triennium dederit, tamen ab illis
quoque iam formandam quam optimis institutis mentem infantium iudicat. cur autem non pertineat ad litteras aetas, **17**
quae ad mores iam pertinet? neque ignoro toto illo, de quo
loquor, tempore vix tantum effici, quantum conferre unus
postea possit annus, sed tamen mihi, qui id senserunt, videntur
non tam discentibus in hac parte quam docentibus pepercisse.
quid melius alioqui facient, ex quo loqui poterunt (faciant **18**
enim aliquid necesse est)? aut cur hoc quantulumcumque est
usque ad septem annos lucrum fastidiamus? nam certe quamlibet parvum sit, quod contulerit aetas prior, maiora tamen
aliqua discet puer ipso illo anno, quo minora didicisset. hoc **19**
per singulos prorogatum in summam proficit, et, quantum in
infantia praesumptum est temporis, adulescentiae adquiritur.
idem etiam de sequentibus annis praeceptum sit, ne, quod
cuique discendum est, sero discere incipiat. non ergo perdamus
primum statim tempus, atque eo minus, quod initia litterarum

Aristophanen. For Ar.'s work in
criticism on Hesiod etc. v. Nauck *Ar.
Byz. Frag.* p. 247.

ὑποθήκας. For all that is known of
this Hesiodic poem Χείρωνος ὑποθῆκαι,
called by Pausanias 9, 31 Παραινέσεις
Χείρωνος ἐπὶ διδασκαλίᾳ Ἀχιλλέως, v.
Pauly-Wissowa *Hesiod* p. 1222. The
statement of Sp., repeated by Watson
and others, that 'some of the ancients
attributed the authorship to Chiron' is
an insult to ancient criticism and, so far
as I can see, quite unfounded.

16. Eratosthenes. For this versatile
Alexandrine again see Pauly-Wissowa.
Where and how this opinion was introduced into a writing of his, we have no
certain knowledge. He may have written
on education separately. It does not fit
very well with the known titles of his
philosophical works. Quite possibly
however it may have appeared in prefatory matter to his γραμματικά, which
is mentioned by Clem. Alex. *Strom.* I.
ch. 16.

17. id senserunt. All recent edd.
except Fierville have adopted the un-

supported reading of A, 'dissenserunt.'
To my mind 'dissentio' is not a natural
word here. The persons spoken of are
the orthodox majority, from which Q.
himself is a somewhat isolated dis-
senter. Even Chrysippus does not apparently hold the same opinion as Q.,
who merely argues that Chrys. makes a
concession, which justifies him in the
further demands which he makes of infancy.

19. prorogatum in summam proficit.
The metaphors appear to be from account keeping. 'Prorogare' is to carry
from one account to another. x. 7, 10
'quantumque dicendo consumitur, tantum ex ultimo prorogetur' (is drawn
from the reserve) gives the converse to
this. As to 'in summam proficere' we
have apparently the same use in xi. 2, 41
of the accumulations of memory 'si coeperimus...cotidie adicere singulos versus,
quorum accessio...in summam ad infinitum usque perveniat.' So too in § 23
of this chapter 'pertinere ad summam.'
Still closer is Livy 3, 61 'parvaque certa-
mina in summam totius profecerant spei.'

sola memoria constant, quae non modo iam est in parvis, sed
tum etiam tenacissima est.

20   Nec sum adeo aetatium inprudens, ut instandum protinus
teneris acerbe putem exigendamque plane operam. nam id in
primis cavere oportebit, ne studia qui amare nondum potest
oderit et amaritudinem semel perceptam etiam ultra rudes
annos reformidet. lusus hic sit, et rogetur et laudetur et numquam non fecisse se gaudeat, aliquando ipso nolente doceatur
alius, cui invideat, contendat interim et saepius vincere se
putet: praemiis etiam, quae capit illa aetas, evocetur.

21   Parva docemus oratorem instituendum professi, sed est sua
etiam studiis infantia, et ut corporum mox fortissimorum
educatio a lacte cunisque initium ducit, ita futurus eloquentis-
simus edidit aliquando vagitum et loqui primum incerta voce
temptavit et haesit circa formas litterarum. nec si quid discere

22 satis non est, ideo nec necesse est. quodsi nemo reprehendit
patrem, qui haec non neglegenda in suo filio putet, cur inpro-
betur, si quis ea, quae domi suae recte faceret, in publicum
promit? atque eo magis, quod minora etiam facilius minores
percipiunt, et ut corpora ad quosdam membrorum flexus
formari nisi tenera non possunt, sic animos quoque ad pleraque

23 duriores robur ipsum facit. an Philippus Macedonum rex

20. plane. Sp. and earlier edd.
'plenam,' but with little or no MS.
authority and inferior sense.

fecisse. This, the reading of A, Bg,
was substituted by Halm for the older
edd. 'scisse,' which appears to have
little MS. authority. Meister has followed Halm, but Rad. has returned to
'scisse.' For 'fecisse' Halm appeals to
'qui parva facile faciunt' 3, 4; for
'scisse' others to *De Fin.* 5, 48
'videmusne ut pueri...aliquid scire se
gaudeant?' It would be a better defence
of 'fecisse' that it takes up the 'faciant
aliquid necesse est' of § 18. Children
must be doing and we must see to it that
this doing not only brings but leaves a
sense of joy. With 'scisse,' I can neither
understand the tense nor the omission of
the object. L.'s 'rejoice when he has
done well' impoverishes the sense.

praemiis. Q. does not suggest actual
prizes except at this early stage, nor were
they common to judge from the fact that
Suetonius specially records the use of
them by Verrius Flaccus (*De Gram.* 17).

21. nec si quid...necesse est. L. translates 'Nor does the fact that the capacity
for learning is inadequate prove that it
is not necessary to learn anything,' apparently taking 'satis' with 'discere.'
Even if Q. can use 'est' thus absolutely,
for which I know no authority, it does
not suit the context. Rather 'The in-
adequacy of any form of learning does
not prove that it can be dispensed with.'
These 'parva' carry us but a little way
to the 'orator,' but they are none the
less necessary.

ideo nec. For this use of 'nec' rather
than the less emphatic 'non' following
on a conjunction and calling attention
to a preceding negative, cf. 11. 13, 7
'non negabo autem sic utile esse plerumque, alioqui nec scriberem,' 11. 17,
35 'ita nec'; v. Hand *Turs.* IV. p.
109.

22. faceret. Sp.'s objection to the
imp. subj. and suggestion of 'fecerit'
seem quite needless. Cf. Peterson on X.
1, 111 and 2, 25, and Hor. *Odes* 1, 2, 22
'quo graves Persae melius perirent.'

Alexandro filio suo prima litterarum elementa tradi ab Aristo-tele summo eius aetatis philosopho voluisset, aut ille suscepisset hoc officium, si non studiorum initia et a perfectissimo quoque optime tractari et pertinere ad summam credidisset? fingamus 24 igitur Alexandrum dari nobis, inpositum gremio, dignum tanta cura infantem (quamquam suus cuique dignus est): pudeatne me in ipsis statim elementis etiam brevia docendi monstrare compendia? neque enim mihi illud saltem placet, quod fieri in plurimis video, ut litterarum nomina et contextum prius quam formas parvuli discant. obstat hoc agnitioni earum, non 25 intendentibus mox animum ad ipsos ductus, dum antecedentem memoriam secuntur. quae causa est praecipientibus, ut etiam, cum satis adfixisse eas pueris recto illo, quo primum scribi solent, contextu videntur, retro agant rursus et varia permuta-tione turbent, donec litteras qui instituuntur facie norint, non ordine. quapropter optime sicut hominum pariter et habitus

---

23. quoque. A has 'horum' (or 'orum'). The suggestion that this stands for 'phorum'='philosophorum' is plausible. Rad. suggests however that it is due to 'studiorum' above.
credidisset. Sp. was inclined to read 'credidissent' and Hand *Turs.* I. p. 539 quotes his words with approval. I think later edd. have rightly judged that there is no sufficient reason for the change, slight as it is: but to retain the singular implies treating 'aut ille... officium' as a parenthesis.
24. Alexandrum...inpositum gremio. Q. adopts the form of the story implied by the supposed letter of Philip to Ar. quoted in Aul. Gell. 9, 3, according to which Alexander is entrusted to Ar. from his birth.
brevia docendi monstrare compen-dia. Either 'to point out short and compendious methods of teaching' or 'to give some short rules about teaching.' In the first case the compendiousness belongs to the methods suggested: in the second to Q.'s exposition of them. 'Monstrare' is in favour of the former, but there is nothing particularly com-pendious about the methods: indeed in one of the three points, we are told that no 'compendium' is possible. On the other hand the use of 'compendium' for a 'general precept' is not to be paral-leled in Q., nor as far as I can see else-where, except in Victorinus and the later

rhetoricians (v. Halm's index). I am inclined to think that the true reading is 'brevi viam docendi monstrare com-pendio.' The stages of the corruption are easy and obvious: (1) breviam... compendio, (2) brevia...compendio, (3) brevia...compendia. It should be noted however that the original reading of A is ei * inioreuia, which may point as Havet (quoted by Fierville) suggests to something like 'meliore via.' But Havet does not suggest any satisfactory sense for the whole.
neque...saltem. This phrase is stated by Sp. and others to = 'not even,' and this sense certainly fits most of the passages in Q. Cf. 'sine ulla cogitandi saltem mora' § 31 (several exx. in Sp.'s note in this passage). If that is the sense here we must understand 'in spite of its general acceptance.' But this seems a little forced, and perhaps the addition of 'saltem' merely emphasises the negative. Q. wishes to call special attention to the ne cessity of employing improved methods at the very start. In fact the sense of 'not even,' where it appears, may lie more in the context than the words, as indeed is the case with 'ne...quidem,' v. Hand IV. p. 60.
25. intendentibus...secuntur. In much the same way, at a very different stage, Q. says (X. 7, 10) of the tendency of the unprepared speaker to be thinking during each sentence of what he has got

26 et nomina edocebuntur. sed quod in litteris obest, in syllabis
non nocebit. non excludo autem, id quod est notum, irritandae
ad discendum infantiae gratia, eburneas etiam litterarum formas
in lusum offerre, vel si quid aliud, quo magis illa aetas gaudeat,
inveniri potest, quod tractare, intueri, nominare iucundum sit.
27 Cum vero iam ductus sequi coeperit, non inutile erit eas
tabellae quam optime insculpi, ut per illos velut sulcos ducatur
stilus. nam neque errabit, quemadmodum in ceris (continebitur
enim utrimque marginibus neque extra praescriptum egredi
poterit), et celerius ac saepius sequendo certa vestigia firmabit
articulos neque egebit adiutorio manum suam manu super
28 inposita regentis. non est aliena res, quae fere ab honestis
neglegi solet, cura bene ac velociter scribendi. nam cum sit in
studiis praecipuum, quoque solo verus ille profectus et altis
radicibus nixus paretur, scribere ipsum, tardior stilus cogita-

to say next 'longe enim praecedat oportet
intentio ac prae se res agat.' Cf. also
§ 34 below.
  26. sed...nocebit. The natural meaning of this would be that the practice
of making children learn the letters by
heart and in a fixed order may safely be
applied to the syllables. I imagine that
this would be totally impossible. I take
the meaning to be that Q. sanctions
learning syllables without having the
forms before the eye. When the child
has learnt to associate the names a, b,
c, d with the symbols, there is no harm
in making him repeat b, a, d, bad, c, a,
d, cad, without having the syllables before his eyes.
  notum. Halm has shewn unusual
rashness in printing here 'inventum,'
the conjecture of Heindorf in *De Nat.
De.* 2, 28, 70. Heindorf gave no reason
for his dislike of 'notus' in either
passage, and subsequent edd. of *D. N. D.*
have not followed him there. Radermacher's 'motum' is worse and the
passages he alleges, III. 1, 8, IV. 1, 29,
VII. 4, 37, are not really similar. Schoell's
'novatum' is better but, beyond the fact
that the sentence runs more smoothly
without the comma before 'irritandae,'
I see no reason to object to 'notum,'
which Meister has retained.
  vel si. So Halm with Bg. Meist.
and Rad. 'et si' with A.
  27. ductus sequi. Cf. X. 2, 2 'sic
litterarum ductus, ut scribendi fiat usus,
pueri sequuntur.'

firmabit. So A, adopted by Halm
and later edd. in place of 'formabit.'
  For the whole of this section cf. X. 2, 2
just quoted and V. 14, 31 where stereotyped rules are compared to 'infantes per-
sequentes praeformatas litteras.' Other
illustrations are given by Grasberger
(*Erziehung und Unterricht*, vol. II.
p. 300), e.g. Plat. *Prot.* p. 326 D
ὥσπερ οἱ γραμματισταὶ τοῖς μήπω δεινοῖς
γράφειν τῶν παίδων, ὑπογράψαντες γραμ-
μὰς τῇ γραφίδι, οὕτω τὸ γραμματεῖον δι-
δόασι, καὶ ἀναγκάζουσι γράφειν κατὰ τὴν
ὑφήγησιν τῶν γραμμῶν; and of the other
practice Sen. *Ep.* 94, 51 'pueri ad praescriptum discunt: digiti illorum tenentur,
et aliena manu per litterarum simulacra
ducuntur.'
  28. honestis. Of social position,
elsewhere contrasted with 'humiles,'
IV. 1, 16, XI. 1, 42.
  scribere ipsum. 'Writing one's self.'
A has 'ipsam' which Bonnell adopted
(after a colon), but later edd. have kept
'ipsum' rightly. The meaning of the
words is brought out in Book X. ch. 3,
where the importance of writing out declamations etc. is emphasised. The ease
with which servile labour could be utilised
naturally led not merely to poor handwriting in the upper classes, but to a
distaste for using it. In the 19th section
of that chapter Q. tells us what he
thought 'de illis dictandi deliciis' and
how it interferes with true progress.
'Ipsum' then is evidently masc., though
Meyer is wrong in saying 'sc. puerum.'

tionem moratur, rudis et confusus intellectu caret: unde
sequitur alter dictandi quae transferenda sunt labor. quare 29
cum semper et ubique, tum praecipue in epistulis secretis
et familiaribus delectabit ne hoc quidem neglectum reliquisse.

Syllabis nullum compendium est: perdiscendae omnes nec, 30
ut fit plerumque, difficillima quaeque earum differenda, ut in
nominibus scribendis deprehendantur. quin immo ne primae 31
quidem memoriae temere credendum: repetere et diu inculcare
fuerit utilius et in lectione quoque non properare ad con-
tinuandam eam vel adcelerandam, nisi cum inoffensa atque
indubitata litterarum inter se coniunctio suppeditare sine ulla
cogitandi saltem mora poterit. tunc ipsis syllabis verba conplecti et his sermonem conectere incipiat: incredibile est, 32
quantum morae lectioni festinatione adiciatur. hinc enim
accidit dubitatio, intermissio, repetitio plus quam possunt
audentibus, deinde cum errarunt, etiam iis quae iam sciunt
diffidentibus. certa sit ergo in primis lectio, deinde coniuncta, 33
et diu lentior, donec exercitatione contingat emendata velocitas.
nam prospicere in dextrum, quod omnes praecipiunt, et pro- 34
videre non rationis modo, sed usus quoque est, quoniam
sequentia intuenti priora dicenda sunt, et, quod difficillimum
est, dividenda intentio animi, ut aliud voce, aliud oculis agatur.

Q. means that as personal writing is so
necessary for the advanced student, the
foundations must be laid in boyhood.
L.'s translation ignores the word.
29. ne hoc quidem. Probably
'neither' as constantly in Q., e.g. § 31
below, though here it may have its
commoner sense, implying that handwriting may seem a very small matter.
30. ut...deprehendantur. Sp. takes
this as = 'ut haereant' and quotes XII.
8, 6 'deinde deprehenduntur et causam
...ex adversariis discunt.' But the meaning may possibly be 'that the difficult
syllables are left till they occur
(deprehendo = offendo) in writing out
the nouns' (or 'deprehendere' may = to
grasp).
nominibus. So in § 34. I doubt
whether Q. ever uses 'nomina' = words,
and in both cases I should translate it
'nouns.' Probably the writing lesson
was used for 'declinatio,' and in this
nouns would come first.

31. nisi cum. Watson and Baur
translate 'until,' but this would pre-
maturely anticipate § 33. I know no
evidence of easy reading books, and
probably a beginning was made with
standard works in which a series of
'inoffensae coniunctiones' would be
only occasional.
verba conplecti, an odd expression
for which I cannot find an exact parallel.
I presume the idea is that the whole is
embraced in its parts. Havet (quoted
by Fierville) thought quite needlessly
that the participle of an abl. abs. had
fallen out after 'syllabis.' His idea that
by 'conplecti' is meant 'embrasser le
sens d'un mot' is clearly quite wrong.
34. providere. The suggestion of
Kid. that 'proxima' has fallen out before
'providere' is not impossible, but it may
be argued in defence of the text that
'prospicere' indicates the mechanical and
'providere' the mental action.
dividenda...agatur; v. on § 25.

illud non paenitebit curasse, cum scribere nomina puer, quemadmodum moris est, coeperit, ne hanc operam in vocabulis
35 vulgaribus et forte occurrentibus perdat. protinus enim potest
interpretationem linguae secretioris, quas Graeci γλώσσας
vocant, dum aliud agitur, ediscere et inter prima elementa
consequi rem postea proprium tempus desideraturam. et
quoniam circa res adhuc tenues moramur, ii quoque versus,
qui ad imitationem scribendi proponentur, non otiosas velim
36 sententias habeant, sed honestum aliquid monentis. prose-
quitur haec memoria in senectutem et inpressa animo rudi
usque ad mores proficiet. etiam dicta clarorum virorum et
electos ex poetis maxime (namque eorum cognitio parvis
gratior est) locos ediscere inter lusum licet. nam et maxime
necessaria est oratori, sicut suo loco dicam, memoria, et ea
praecipue firmatur atque alitur exercitatione et in his, de
quibus nunc loquimur, aetatibus, quae nihildum ipsae generare

vocabulis, here perhaps in its technical sense (cf. I. 4, 20) = προσηγορία,
i.e. common as opposed to proper nouns.
The latter would naturally be avoided
in this exercise.
35. linguae...vocant; v. Rutherford
Chapter in the History of Annotation
pp. 356, 357, where he shews how
γλῶττα, originally meaning 'a dialect
word,' came to be applied to 'obsolete,
obsolescent, unfamiliar words.' He
quotes amongst other exx. Galen (Kühn)
19, 66 ἡ γλῶττα παλαιόν ἐστιν ὄνομα τῆς
συνηθείας ἐκπεπτωκός.
versus. If I am right about 'nomina'
above, this must be an exercise taken at
a somewhat higher stage.
otiosas, for 'pointless,' 'profitless,' is
rather a favourite usage with Q. Cf.
12, 18; v. Peterson on X. 1, 76.
36. usque ad mores proficiet. The
phrase is certainly difficult, and Sp.'s
explanation of 'proficiet' = 'penetrabit'
'reaches the character' is not satisfactory. Kid. proposed and Meister has
adopted 'usque ad mortem in mores,'
an adaptation of the old correction of
Alm. 'usque ad mortem' simply. Kid.
for 'in' quoted 'in summam proficit,'
§ 19. But the phrases are not analogous,
and a further improvement might be
'usque ad mortem ad mores.' In this
case 'proficere ad mores' would mean
'useful for character,' like the 'proficit
ad strumam' quoted by Forc. from Pliny.
But any emendation on these lines seems

to me open to the objection that such a
use of the almost duplicates 'senectus'
and 'mors' is hardly in Q.'s manner and
I have preferred with Rad. to retain the
vulgate; which I take to mean that the
impression produced by these maxims
continues to grow till it reaches the status
of fixed laws of conduct. The use of
'mores' in this case is much the same as
'frequens imitatio transit in mores,' 11, 2,
or Ovid's 'abeunt studia in mores.'
inter lusum. I can hardly bring myself to think that Q. is so inhuman as
to regard this exercise as suitable to the
regular playtime, though in 3, 11 he
shews that he has an eye on the intellectual possibilities of children's games.
I should rather think he means, as in
'lusus hic sit' (20 above), that the exercise may be made congenial by treating
it as a game.
suo loco, i.e. XI. 2.
firmatur...exercitatione, v. §§ 40, 41
of that chapter 'si quis tamen unam
maximamque a me artem memoriae
quaerat, exercitatio est et labor: multa
ediscere, multa cogitare, et si fieri potest
cotidie, potentissimum est; nihil aeque
vel augetur cura vel neglegentia intercidit. Quare et pueri statim, ut praecepi,
quam plurima ediscant....' The importance of exercising the memory is
dwelt on by ps.-Plut. *De Ed. Lib.* 13 πάντων δὲ μάλιστα τὴν μνήμην τῶν παίδων
ἀσκεῖν καὶ συνεθίζειν. αὕτη γὰρ ὥσπερ τῆς
παιδείας ἐστὶ ταμεῖον: v. Intr. p. xl.

ex se queunt, prope sola est, quae iuvari cura docentium possit.
non alienum fuerit exigere ab his aetatibus, quo sit absolutius **37**
os et expressior sermo, ut nomina quaedam versusque adfec-
tatae difficultatis ex pluribus et asperrime coeuntibus inter se
syllabis catenatos et veluti confragosos quam citatissime vol-
vant: χαλινοί Graece vocantur. res modica dictu, qua tamen
omissa multa linguae vitia, nisi primis eximuntur annis, in-
emendabili in posterum pravitate durantur.

II

[UTILIUS DOMI AN IN SCHOLIS ERUDIANTUR]

Sed nobis iam paulatim adcrescere puer et exire de gremio **1**
et discere serio incipiat. hoc igitur potissimum loco tractanda
quaestio est, utiliusne sit domi atque intra privatos parietes
studentem continere, an frequentiae scholarum et velut publicis
praeceptoribus tradere. quod quidem cum iis, a quibus claris- **2**
simarum civitatium mores sunt instituti, tum eminentissimis
auctoribus video placuisse. non est tamen dissimulandum, esse

iuvari cura. The reading 'iuvare curam,' 'to sólace the efforts,' which has little MS. authority, though there is some for 'iuvare' itself, would be hardly worth considering, but that Sp. shewed some inclination for it. The collocation 'iuvare memoriam' occurs in XI. 2, 41.

37. absolutius os et expressior sermo; v. on § 13. The χαλινοί serve both to perfect the pronunciation of particular sounds and as a consequence to enable the child to enunciate a whole sentence or passage distinctly, cf. 11, 4.

χαλινοί. The correctness of this reading of A (Bg χααεινοι), which had been corrupted in later MSS. and edd. to χαλεποί, is proved by the occurrence of 'freni' in two passages in Martianus Capella (Halm, pp. 474, 475) 'vitandi etiam freni qui fiunt ex asperrimis litteris in unum concurrentibus.'

II. 1. nobis. For this ethic dative in Q. cf. 'mihi' 11, 14. Bonnell also quotes II. 4, 9 and XII. 2, 31.

velut publicis. Several MSS., including Bg, 'publicatis,' which has no intelligible meaning, as far as I can see. Sp. very properly asks what is the point of 'velut.' He suggests that it may refer to the fact that Q.'s 'salarium' was paid out of the imperial 'fiscus' and

not out of the treasury. But Q. is not speaking of himself in particular, but of the profession generally, especially the 'grammatici.' If he refers to the source of payment at all, he may mean that the profession was working its way to being a branch of the civil service; some of them at any rate being 'publice conducti' (v. Plin. *Ep.* 4, 13) and others provided (as Pl. suggests for Comum) by subscription. But it seems to me more likely that he has no such thought and merely feels that 'publicus praeceptor' is not quite a satisfactory term to express what he means, though he has not a better at his command. He does not seem to use 'publicus' far from its original sense of 'belonging to the whole people.' When he uses it more loosely for 'general' he adds an apologetic adverb as below 'prope publico more,' VIII. 4, 29 'desiderio prope publico.' In this case the word has the additional unsuitability that it does not suggest what was the main differentia of these schoolmasters, viz. that they taught a number of children in special premises, instead of individuals in a private house. Our own use of 'public' and 'private' in relation to education has similar ambiguities.

2. quod...placuisse. As Turnebus

nonnullos, qui ab hoc prope publico more privata quadam per-
suasione dissentiant. hi duas praecipue rationes sequi videntur;
unam, quod moribus magis consulant fugiendo turbam hominum eius aetatis, quae sit ad vitia maxime prona, unde causas
turpium factorum saepe extitisse utinam falso iactaretur:
alteram, quod, quisquis futurus est ille praeceptor, liberalius
tempora sua inpensurus uni videtur quam si eadem in pluris
3 partiatur. prior causa prorsus gravis: nam si studiis quidem
scholas prodesse, moribus autem nocere constaret, potior mihi
ratio vivendi honeste quam vel optime dicendi videretur. sed
mea quidem sententia iuncta ista atque indiscreta sunt: neque
enim esse oratorem nisi bonum virum iudico et fieri, etiam si
potest, nolo. de hac re igitur prius.

4   Corrumpi mores in scholis putant: nam et corrumpuntur
interim, sed domi quoque, et sunt multa eius rei exempla, tam
hercule, quam conservatae sanctissime utrobique opinionis.
natura cuiusque totum curaque distat. da mentem ad peiora
facilem, da neglegentiam formandi custodiendique in aetate

says, Lycurgus and Plato are examples
of the two classes named.

prope...quadam. The apology implied in these words is, I take it, partly
for the loose use of 'publicus,' and
partly arises from a feeling that the
antithesis is artificial. The words are
suggested by the point under controversy, but have little to do with it. That
the advocacy of 'private' education
should be 'private,' i.e. made by isolated
individuals, and that of 'public' made
by the general mass of people, may be
true at any given moment, but is not
necessarily the case. The reverse is in
itself just as likely. I do not think that
the words 'priv. pers.' can possibly
mean (as L.) 'prejudice in favour of
private education.'

fugiendo. The subject of the verb, if
it could be expressed, is presumably 'the
boys'; v. on 'docendi' 1, 7.

hominum. No one has objected to
this, but it seems to me strange. Possibly 'comitum.'

inpensurus videtur. Peterson on x.
1, 46 notes several examples of this use
of 'videri' with the fut. part. instead of
the inf.

3. **iuncta atque indiscreta,** so 'co-
nexa et indiscreta' X. 1, 2.

si potest. The correction 'posset,'
which some edd. including Meister have
adopted, seems to me unnecessary. There
is nothing unnatural in Q. condescend-
ing to the adversary for a moment by
granting the possibility.

4. eius rei, i.e. 'morum in scholis
corruptorum'—Halm. Rather 'morum
utrobique corruptorum.'

tam hercule. So Halm and Rad. following both A and Bg. Some good MSS.
(v. Intr. pp. xciii, xcvi) have 'tam laesae
hercle' and Meister has adopted 'tam hercule laesae,' on the ground that 'laesae'
spelt 'lese' would easily fall out after
'hercule.' The argument would be more
plausible if any MS. read the words in
this order. The objection to 'tam hercule quam,' that the thing compared is
required between 'tam' and 'quam,' is
sufficiently answered by Tac. *Dial.* 8
'imagines ac tituli et statuae, quae neque ipsa tamen negleguntur, tam hercule
quam divitiae et opes,' and so also ib.
21.

opinionis. This passive use of the
word appears again in II. 12, 5 'affert
et ista res opinionem'; v. Peterson on
X. 5, 18.

distat, impersonal or quasi-impersonal
('natura' and 'cura' are abl.). So 'personis modo distat' VI. 4, 21; v. Bonnell's *Lex.* s.v.

prima pudoris, non minorem flagitiis occasionem secreta prae-
buerint. nam et potest turpis esse domesticus praeceptor, nec
tutior inter servos malos quam ingenuos parum modestos conversatio est. at si bona ipsius indoles, si non caeca ac sopita 5
parentium socordia est, et praeceptorem eligere sanctissimum
quemque, cuius rei praecipua prudentibus cura est, et disciplinam, quae maxime severa fuerit, licet, et nihilo minus
amicum gravem virum aut fidelem libertum lateri filii sui
adiungere, cuius adsiduus comitatus etiam illos meliores faciat,
qui timebantur.

Facile erat huius metus remedium. utinam liberorum nos- 6
trorum mores non ipsi perderemus! infantiam statim deliciis
solvimus. mollis illa educatio, quam indulgentiam vocamus,
nervos omnes mentis et corporis frangit. quid non adultus
concupiscet, qui in purpuris repit? nondum prima verba
exprimit, iam coccum intellegit, iam conchylium poscit. ante 7

conversatio. ' Intercourse,' so ' conversatio doctorum ' VI. 3, 17. This use
of the word is found in Tac. e.g. *Dial.*
9, and frequently in Seneca.
5. praeceptorem...sanctissimum; v.
the full discussion of this in II. 2,
1–8.
disciplinam. The word seems here to
approximate more closely than usual to
our ' discipline.' Still perhaps here too
it has reference if not to what is actually
learnt, to the conditions under which it
is learnt. I should therefore translate it
' methods of study.'
amicum...libertum. That Q. can expect to procure the services of such a
person shews that he is thinking of
wealthy magnates as parents. I cannot
find any record of such a person being
employed elsewhere. Grasberger, vol.
II. p. 174, gives several exx. of the higher type of pedagogue, but there is no
evidence that they were ever free men
or even freedmen.
timebantur, so A, followed by Halm
and Rad. Bg ' timebuntur,' which
Meister adopts. I think Kid. rightly
argues for the imp., when he says ' the
constant accompanying will render the
fear a thing of the past.'
6–8. There is a general resemblance
between these sections and Juv. 14,
1–83, where the main point of both is
expressed in ll. 31, 32 ' velocius et citius
nos | corrumpunt vitiorum exempla do-
mestica.' The resemblance was observed

by Ben Jonson who, in *Every man in his
humour*, Act II. Sc. 5, makes a sort of
paraphrase of the two passages combined;
v. esp. for this passage the lines:
' Nay, would ourselves were not the first,
    even parents,
That did destroy the hopes in our own
    children.
....
Ere all their teeth be born, or they can
    speak,
We make their palates cunning; the
    first words
We form their tongues with, are licen-
tious jests.
Can it call whore? cry bastard? O then
    kiss it !
A witty child ! can 't swear? the father's
    darling,
Give it two plums.'
Cf. also Tac. *Dial.* 29 ' nec quisquam
in tota domo pensi habet quid coram
infante domino dicat aut faciat ; quin
etiam ipsi parentes nec probitati neque
modestiae parvulos adsuefaciunt, sed
lasciviae et dicacitati.'
6. coccum, conchylium. Halm explains ' puer cum iam intelligit quid sit
coccus, quaeque vera purpura, spreta
deteriore purpura, vestem conchyliatam
poscit.' To this view, which assumes a
marked superiority in the ' conchyliata,'
for which clearer evidence would be desirable, the alternative is to read ' coquum '
(cocum) and to regard ' conchylium ' as
a dainty, as in Hor. *Epode* 2, 49, *Sat.*

palatum eorum quam os instituimus. in lecticis crescunt: si
terram attigerunt, e manibus utrimque sustinentium pendent.
gaudemus, si quid licentius dixerint: verba ne Alexandrinis
8 quidem permittenda deliciis risu et osculo excipimus. nec
mirum: nos docuimus, ex nobis audiunt, nostras amicas,
nostros concubinos vident, omne convivium obscenis canticis
strepit, pudenda dictu spectantur. fit ex his consuetudo, inde
natura. discunt haec miseri, antequam sciant vitia esse: inde
soluti ac fluentes non accipiunt ex scholis mala ista, sed in
scholas adferunt.

9   'Verum in studiis magis vacabit unus uni.' ante omnia nihil
prohibet esse illum nescio quem unum etiam cum eo, qui in
scholis eruditur. sed etiamsi iungi utrumque non posset, lumen
tamen illud conventus honestissimi tenebris ac solitudini prae-
tulissem: nam optimus quisque praeceptor frequentia gaudet

2, 4, 30 and Plin. *N. H.* 8, 57 'leges
censoriae...cenis ademerant...conchylia'
(one may perhaps add 'a dainty peculi-
arly unwholesome for a child of two!').
So Sp. The context indeed leaves it
doubtful, whether the words develop
the clause before, or lead up to that
which follows. But on the whole the
balance seems decidedly in favour of
the first view. The phrase 'intellegere
coquum' for 'understand the importance
of the cook' seems almost impossible,
and 'musicos intellegunt' I. 10, 4, 'Socrates ab hominibus sui temporis parum
intellegebatur' XI. 1, 10, are very poor
parallels. And though to ascribe extravagance in dress to an infant is a greater
exaggeration than to ascribe gluttony,
the truth is, I think, that Q. has let
himself go in these sections and reproduced a 'locus communis' from a declamation. Cf. Sen. *Contr.* 2, 7 of the
extravagance of the alleged adulteress
'ex omni rupe conchylium contrahitur,
quo vestis cruentetur.'

7. os instituimus. The other reading
'mores' is a not unnatural corruption
(cf. the 'quamores' of A), and is far
less vigorous.

attigerunt. Older edd. 'attigerint'
with less MS. authority.

Alexandrinis deliciis. That pet-slaves
are meant appears clearly from the
passages quoted by Sp. and others,
viz. Petr. 31 and 68, and still more
Stat. *Silv.* 5, 5, 66 where, speaking
of the beloved slaves he had lost, he
says:

'Non ego mercatus Pharia de puppe
    loquaces
delicias, doctumque sui convicia Nili
infantem, lingua nimium salibusque pro-
    tervum
dilexi.'

8. audiunt. So A, which Halm follows, but there is little to choose between
it and the 'audierunt' of other MSS.

fit...natura. So II. 4, 17 'in hoc
consuescat, huius rei sibi naturam faciat';
cf. Sall. *Jug.* 85 'mihi...bene facere iam
ex consuetudine in naturam vertit'; Sen.
De Prov. 4, 15 'nihil miserum est, quod
in naturam consuetudo perduxit'; Stob.
Ecl. II. 220 μελέτη χρονισθεῖσ' εἰς φύσιν
καθίσταται. The earliest form of the
adage seems to be from Evenus quoted
by Ar. *Nic. Eth.* VII. 11
φημὶ πολυχρόνιον μελέτην ἔμεναι, φίλε,
    καὶ δὴ
ταύτην ἀνθρώποισι τελευτῶσαν φύσιν εἶναι.
So id. *Rhet.* I. 11, 3 τὸ εἰθισμένον ὥσπερ πεφυκὸς ἤδη γίγνεται. Here the
looseness of the use of 'nature' is corrected and still more so in the form in
which Cic. has made the adage familiar
to us; v. *De Fin.* 5, 74 'consuetudine
quasi alteram quandam naturam effici'
(cf. *De Inv.* 1, 3).

fluentes. Not used by Q. elsewhere in
this sense; cf. 'delicatis et luxu fluentibus' Sen. *Ep.* 78, 25. So too Liv. 7,
29, 5. Somewhat similar is Sen. *De
Tran.* 17 'incessu ipso ultra morem
muliebrem fluentibus.'

9. nescio quem. Sp. suggests that this
is said in 'ironical admiration.' It seems

ac maiore se theatro dignum putat. at fere minores ex con- 10
scientia suae infirmitatis haerere singulis et officio fungi quodam
modo paedagogorum non indignantur. sed praestet alicui vel 11
gratia vel pecunia vel amicitia, ut doctissimum atque incom-
parabilem magistrum domi habeat, num tamen ille totum in
uno diem consumpturus est? aut potest esse ulla tam perpetua
discentis intentio, quae non ut visus oculorum obtutu continuo
fatigetur, cum praesertim multo plus secreti temporis studia
desiderent? neque enim scribenti, ediscenti, cogitanti prae- 12
ceptor adsistit: quorum aliquid agentibus cuiuscumque inter-
ventus inpedimento est. lectio quoque non omnis nec semper
praeeunte vel interpretante eget: quando enim tot auctorum
notitia contingeret? modicum ergo tempus est, quo in totum 13
diem velut opus ordinetur, ideoque per plures ire possunt etiam
quae singulis tradenda sunt. pleraque vero hanc condicionem
habent, ut eadem voce ad omnis simul perferantur. taceo de
partitionibus et declamationibus rhetorum, quibus certe quan-
tuscumque adhibeatur numerus, tamen unusquisque totum
feret. non enim vox illa praeceptoris ut cena minus pluribus 14

to me to look forward rather to the next two sentences and suggest that the 'unus' is not likely to be of any great value. The sentence, which Watson completely misunderstands, merely means that a private tutor may take the boy out of school hours.

honestissimi, probably the same sense as in 1, 28.

frequentia. Cf. the 'classis numerosa' of Juv. 7, 151.

11. num tamen. So Halm and Meister with A. Rad. 'non' with B.

12. lectio...contingeret. A valuable remark, shewing how important a part was taken by private reading in grammatical and rhetorical education, v. 11. 5, and x. 1.

praeeunte, the first reading over by the teacher, with the necessary minimum of comment (v. note on 8, 2)—'interpretante'—the detailed comment and questioning that followed the pupil's reading. The two together make up the 'praelectio.'

13. ideoque...tradenda sunt. I think the commentators and translators have failed to understand this. I take the meaning to be that the individual pupils are set to different tasks (scribere, ediscere etc.). This will involve a few minutes to each, but so few that a large

number can be dealt with in a short time. Sp. and others wrongly put a colon after 'tradenda sunt.' With 'pleraque' we enter on a new subject, that part of the work, which consists of lectures addressed to the whole class.

partitionibus. Sp. in his preface (correcting the note on the text) takes the view of Ernesti (s.v. partitio) that the word here signifies the lore connected with the classification of 'status,' and other rhetorical distinctions. This is no doubt the sense that the word bears in Cic.'s treatise *De Partitione Oratoria*. But in view of its connection with declamations it seems to me much more probable that his earlier view was nearer the mark. I think the word refers to the scheme or syllabus suggested by the rhetor to the student as a basis for the declamation. This in mere outline would usually be called 'divisio,' but in 11. 6, 1 Q. notes that some not content with this worked it out more fully. As acc. to vII. 1, 1 the difference between 'divisio' and 'partitio' is that the former is 'rerum plurium in singulas discretio,' the latter 'singularum rerum in partes discretio,' 'partitio' is a natural term for an elaborate form of 'divisio.'

14. cena minus pluribus sufficit.

sufficit, sed ut sol universis idem lucis calorisque largitur. grammaticus quoque si de loquendi ratione disserat, si quaestiones explicet, historias exponat, poemata enarret, tot illa 15 discent, quot audient. 'at enim emendationi praelectionique numerus obstat.' sit incommodum (nam quid fere undique placet?): mox illud comparabimus commodis. Nec ego tamen eo mitti puerum volo, ubi neglegatur. sed neque praeceptor bonus maiore se turba, quam ut sustinere eam possit, oneraverit, et in primis ea habenda cura est, ut is omni modo fiat nobis familiariter amicus nec officium in docendo 16 spectet, sed adfectum. ita numquam erimus in turba. nec sane quisquam litteris saltem leviter imbutus eum, in quo studium ingeniumque perspexerit, non in suam quoque gloriam peculiariter fovebit. sed ut fugiendae sint magnae scholae

L.'s 'a dinner which will only suffice for a limited number' seems to me to miss the full force of the words: rather 'the share of each varies inversely with the number that partake.'

quaestiones. I.e. the ζητήματα or προβλήματα, the difficult and disputed points the discussion and solution of which was one of the highest functions of γραμματική. These were often, perhaps usually, on the literary side, but might also be on the grammatical side of the subject ('loquendi ratio'). As Q. deals with some of these last in ch. 4, he is perhaps primarily thinking of them. A very full account of the 'questions' will be found in Lehrs' *Aristarchus* pp. 212–220.

historias. This important term, signifying points which arise for explanation in the subject-matter of a book, or allusions contained in it, will be further elucidated on 8, 18.

poemata enarret. In its wider sense the 'enarratio poetarum' signifies the literary side of γραμματική, as opposed to what we call grammar. So 'enarratio auctorum,' 9, 1. In this sense it would include 'historiae.' Here however it excludes it and we appear to have the same classification of the grammarian's province as in Sext. Emp. *adv. Gram.* 236 into τεχνικόν, ἱστορικόν, and ἰδιαίτερον. The last-named is defined as the art of explaining difficulties in the meaning, sifting the genuine from the spurious, and appreciating the value of the poems read. So Sen. *Ep.* 88, 3 'grammaticus circa curam sermonis ver-

satur, et si latius evagari vult, circa historias, iam ut longissime fines proferat suos, circa carmina,' where Summers is wrong, I think, in restricting 'carmina' to 'laws of verse.'

15. praelectioni. Why should numbers be an obstacle in this? Sp.'s answer is 'intelligitur talis praelectio, qua singulis pueris, quae ipsi sunt pronunciaturi, diligenter praeeunt magistri.' A better answer, I think, is that in the 'praelectio,' the boys were required to scan, parse, and answer other questions (8, 13 etc.). No doubt the term is used rather loosely, as the 'praelectio' clearly included the 'historiarum expositio' and 'enarratio poetarum' in which he has just said that numbers are no obstacle. In fact the 'praelectio' was partly a lecture and partly a class lesson. It would have been clearer to us, if he had said that numbers were an obstacle in parts of the 'praelectio,' but his readers would probably have no doubt about his meaning.

sed neque...oneraverit. The statement is repeated with further explanation X. 5, 22.

nobis familiariter amicus. Unless Q. is suddenly identifying himself with his pupils, he here lays down the important doctrine that personal friendship between teacher and parent is essential to success in education.

16. nec...saltem; v. on 1, 24.

leviter imbutus. Q. evidently contemplates the possibility of a low standard in the 'grammaticus.' So 4, 23; 5, 7.

(cui ne ipsi quidem rei adsentior, si ad aliquem merito con-
curritur), non tamen hoc eo valet, ut fugiendae sint omnino
scholae. aliud est enim vitare eas, aliud eligere.

Et si refutavimus, quae contra dicuntur, iam explicemus **17**
quid ipsi sequamur. ante omnia futurus orator, cui in maxima **18**
celebritate et in media rei publicae luce vivendum est, adsuescat
iam a tenero non reformidare homines neque illa solitaria et
velut umbratica vita pallescere. excitanda mens et attollenda
semper est, quae in eius modi secretis aut languescit et quendam
velut in opaco situm ducit, aut contra tumescit inani persua-
sione: necesse est enim nimium tribuat sibi, qui se nemini
conparat. deinde cum proferenda sunt studia, caligat in sole **19**
et omnia nova offendit, ut qui solus didicerit quod inter multos
faciendum est. mitto amicitias, quae ad senectutem usque **20**
firmissime durant religiosa quadam necessitudine imbutae:
neque enim est sanctius sacris isdem quam studiis initiari.
sensum ipsum, qui communis dicitur, ubi discet, cum se a congressu, qui non hominibus solum, sed mutis quoque animalibus
naturalis est, segregarit? adde quod domi ea sola discere **21**
potest, quae ipsi praecipientur, in schola etiam quae aliis.
audiet multa cotidie probari, multa corrigi, proderit alicuius
obiurgata desidia, proderit laudata industria, excitabitur laude **22**
aemulatio, turpe ducet cedere pari, pulchrum superasse maiores.
accendunt omnia haec animos, et licet ipsa vitium sit ambitio,

non...eo valet. Bonnell wrongly gives
this as an instance of 'eo' = 'propterea,'
a common use in Q. Rather it is as Cic.
De Nat. De. 3, 5 'quod eo, credo, vale-
bat, ut opinionibus, quas a maioribus acce-
peram, defenderem.' 'This pointed to the
conclusion that,' etc.; v. Mayor's note
there.

18. umbratica. So Halm and recent
edd. with A; B and others 'umbratili'
as in Cic. *De Or.* 1, 157. I follow
the former without much conviction.
The common metaphor of sun and shade
is here applied to the contrast between
'public' and 'private' school. Elsewhere very commonly to that between
school and the forum or public life, e.g.
x. 5, 17 (where v. Peterson), and Cic. l.c.
where v. Wilkins.

19. nova offendit. L. translates 'finds
everything new,' but surely 'stumbles
over everything new.'

20. imbutae. As usual with the
thought of 'from the first.'

sensum...communis. The phrase is,
I think, untranslatable. 'Feeling for
others,' 'common human sympathy,'
and the like fail to express the 'tact' or
'savoir vivre' which is implicit in this
popular ('qui dicitur') use of the phrase.
On the other hand the last two terms
fail to express the idea 'homo sum, nihil
humani alienum a me puto' which is at
the bottom of 'communis sensus.' The
nearest passage to this, perhaps, is
Sen. *Ep.* 5, 4 'hoc primum philosophia
promittit, sensum communem, humani-
tatem, congregationem.' Summers' statement that it there represents 'the
opposite of eccentricity' seems to me
inadequate. Duff and Mayor on Juv.
8, 73, Bentley on Hor. *Sat.* 1, 3, 66 are
worth consulting. The disquisition in
Hamilton's edition of Reid, p. 758 etc.,
often referred to, does not seem to me to
help to elucidate this side of the meaning.

22. licet...ambitio. Cf. Sall. *Cat.* 11
'sed primo magis ambitio quam avaritia

23 frequenter tamen causa virtutum est. non inutilem scio servatum esse a praeceptoribus meis morem, qui cum pueros in classis distribuerant, ordinem dicendi secundum vires ingenii dabant, et ita superiore loco quisque declamabat, ut praecedere 24 profectu videbatur. huius rei iudicia praebebantur : ea nobis ingens palma, ducere vero classem multo pulcherrimum. nec de hoc semel decretum erat: tricensimus dies reddebat victo certaminis potestatem. ita nec superior successu curam remittebat, et dolor victum ad depellendam ignominiam concitabat. 25 id nobis acriores ad studia dicendi faces subdidisse quam

animos hominum exercebat ; quod tamen vitium propius virtutem erat': a remark which is amplified in the succeeding words and may possibly have been in Q.'s mind. Q.'s thought does not appear to have been frequently reproduced. The nearest parallel I know of is Young's ' ambition potent source of good and ill.' Tacitus' 'sapientibus cupido gloriae novissima exuitur,' and its Miltonic equivalent have a certain affinity. On Alcuin's use of the words v. Intr. p. xlix.

23. cum...distribuerant. Cf. x. 5, 21 ' consuetudo classium certis diebus audiendarum,' a passage which shews that it is not the division into classes for the purpose of the full-dress declamation which is here regarded as noteworthy, but making the ' ordo dicendi' depend on merit.

classis. Peterson on x. 5, 21 remarks that the word is not used in this sense before the silver age. In fact no instances even then are quoted except from Q. and Juv. 7, 151. But as we have few or no allusions to the minutiae of school practice earlier, the term may well have been current before. For the general use of ' classis' (apart from the Comitia) v. Reid on Acad. ii. 73.

distribuerant. So most edd. with B, except Bonnell who reads 'distribuerent' with A. The ind. may be justified from vii. 1, 4 ' cum haec collocaveram quodam modo in conspectu, non minus pro adversa parte quam pro mea cogitabam.' The plup. is certainly more suitable to the view I have taken of the whole passage, which regards the arrangement within the class, as subsequent to the arrangement into classes.

24. huius...palma. L. translates 'the performances on these occasions were criticised. To win commendation was a tremendous honour,' and so practically

Watson. I do not think this makes good sense. The whole declamation system everywhere rested on criticism and commendation and there would be nothing specially noteworthy. I think the meaning is as follows. The practice of forming classes, no doubt roughly on merit, and making them declaim on fixed days was general. The special point is that in this case the order of declaiming was determined by a previous trial. The most promising boys were allowed to compete for the headship of the class, and to be on this 'select list' is the ' ingens palma.' On the result of this competition, in which possibly the boys as well as the master had a voice, the ' ordo dicendi' on the show day was determined. The words 'huius...praebebantur' mean then ' opportunities for deciding this were provided.' A variant on this would be to take ' palma' as meaning not so much ' prize' as ' competition.' The only difference in this case would be that the whole class competed, not merely a select few. But I doubt whether ' palma' could bear this meaning. It would be given more easily by the ' palmae contentio' read by old edd. and some MSS.

ducere classem. The term ' dux,' which is well known in Scotland and was perhaps in England (it appears in Miss Yonge's *Daisy Chain*), may no doubt have originated independently, but may also quite possibly be directly derived from this passage. Sp. quotes Sen. *Cont.* 1, 1 Prooem. (at the end) ' Latronem meum declamasse memini admodum iuvenem in Marulli schola, cum iam coepisset diem ducere,' where if 'diem' is genuine (MSS. 'ordinem') the reference is presumably to the ' certi dies' of x. 5, 21. Augustine, *Conf.* iii. 6, uses ' maior in schola' for head of, or high up in, the school.

exhortationem docentium, paedagogorum custodiam, vota
parentium, quantum animi mei coniectura colligere possum,
contenderim. sed sicut firmiores in litteris profectus alit aemu- 26
latio, ita incipientibus atque adhuc teneris condiscipulorum
quam praeceptoris iucundior hoc ipso, quod facilior imitatio
est. vix enim se prima elementa ad spem tollere effingendae,
quam summam putant, eloquentiae audebunt: proxima am-
plectentur magis, ut vites arboribus adplicitae inferiores prius
adprendendo ramos in cacumina evadunt. quod adeo verum 27
est, ut ipsius etiam magistri, si tamen ambitiosis utilia prae-
feret, hoc opus sit, cum adhuc rudia tractabit ingenia, non
statim onerare infirmitatem discentium, sed temperare vires
suas et ad intellectum audientis descendere. nam ut vascula 28
oris angusti superfusam umoris copiam respuunt, sensim autem
influentibus vel etiam instillatis conplentur, sic animi puerorum
quantum excipere possint videndum est: nam maiora intellectu
velut parum apertos ad percipiendum animos non subibunt.
utile igitur habere, quos imitari primum, mox vincere velit: 29
ita paulatim et superiorum spes erit. his adicio praeceptores
ipsos non idem mentis ac spiritus in dicendo posse concipere
singulis tantum praesentibus, quod illa celebritate audientium
instinctos: maxima enim pars eloquentiae constat animo. 30
hunc adfici, hunc concipere imagines rerum et transformari

26. sed sicut...imitatio est. The
'ratio comparandi' as Sp. says is not obvious. He puts a comma after 'facilior'
and explains it as an antithesis of
'aemulatio' amongst the older pupils and
'imitatio' amongst the younger and compares it to 'quos imitari primum, mox
vincere velit' of 29. But what is the
point of 'quam praeceptoris'? With my
(Halm's) punctuation, which makes
'aemulatio' common to both members,
it is rather a contrast between following
in the steps of the teacher, and copying
those who are on one's own level. Cf. II.
9, 2 'esse similes concupiscent.' But the
sentence will become much clearer if,
as I am much inclined to suggest, 'pro-
fessoris' has fallen out after 'profectus.'
'Professor' is the natural word for the
higher rhetorical teacher postulated. For
the use of 'profectus' cf. II. 3, 10.
prima elementa. For the metonymy
Sp. quotes 'prima studia' II. 3, 10, a
passage in which Q. repeats and explains
further the substance of this section. ·

27. si tamen. 'If at any rate,' cf. 8, 6.
Other exx. in Bonnell s.v. 'si.'
29. velit. So Meist. and Rad. with A
in ras. Halm 'velis' with B etc. The
balance of sense is slightly for 'velit.'
instinctos. As an example of this
use Dräger, Vol. II. p. 435, quotes Cic.
Tusc. I, 17 'Platonem ferunt...sensisse
idem, quod Pythagoram.' I. 10, 34
quoted by Meyer 'prodesse eam non ut
ceteras artes' is hardly the same.
30. imagines. This word, indeed the
whole section, is well illustrated by VI.
2, 29 'quomodo fiet, ut afficiamur?...
quas φαντασίας Graeci vocant,... per
quas imagines rerum absentium ita
repraesentantur animo, ut eas cernere
oculis ac praesentes habere videamur.
has quisquis bene conceperit, is erit in
adfectibus potentissimus.' Φαντασίαι are
a leading idea of the treatise *De Sublimitate*, v. particularly § 15, where they are
defined ὅταν ἃ λέγεις ὑπ' ἐνθουσιασμοῦ
καὶ πάθους βλέπειν δοκῇς καὶ ὑπ' ὄψιν
τιθῇς τοῖς ἀκούουσιν.

quodam modo ad naturam eorum, de quibus loquitur, necesse
est. is porro quo generosior celsiorque est, hoc maioribus velut
organis commovetur, ideoque et laude crescit et impetu augetur
31 et aliquid magnum agere gaudet. est quaedam tacita dedig-
natio, vim dicendi tantis comparatam laboribus ad unum
auditorem demittere: pudet supra modum sermonis attolli.
et sane concipiat quis mente vel declamantis habitum vel
orantis vocem incessum pronuntiationem, illum denique animi
et corporis motum, sudorem, ut alia praeteream, et fatigationem
audiente uno: nonne quiddam pati furori simile videatur? non
esset in rebus humanis eloquentia, si tantum cum singulis
loqueremur.

III

[QUA RATIONE IN PARVIS INGENIA DINOSCANTUR ET QUAE TRACTANDA SINT]

1   Tradito sibi puero docendi peritus ingenium eius in primis
naturamque perspiciet. ingenii signum in parvis praecipuum
memoria est: eius duplex virtus, facile percipere et fideliter
continere. proximum imitatio: nam id quoque est docilis

loquitur. Meister, 'loquimur,' somewhat needlessly with inferior MS.
authority.

organis. Here as elsewhere in Q.
of musical wind instruments. The soul,
or rather soul in general, is conceived
of as a melody evoked by pipes or stops.

31. sermonis. 'Sermo' here seems
to be used of 'ordinary conversation' as
in IX. 4, 19 where a distinction is drawn
between 'oratio vincta atque contexta,'
and the 'soluta,' which is found usually
'in sermone et epistulis.' But the
analogy of 9, 2 'sermone...nihil se supra
modum extollente' and II. 4, 9 'qui
nihil supra cotidianum sermonem attollere audeant' (where also 'nihil' probably
is adv.) creates a suspicion that Regius
may have been on the right tack in
suggesting 'sermones' (better 'sermonem').

simile videatur. Sp. conjectured
'simile ille,' not improbably.

pati. Used like πάσχειν. Sp. who
notes this quotes 4, 29. It is also found VI.
2, 27 'similes eorum, qui vere patiuntur,
affectibus' and 'irascetur, si nihil ipse,

qui in iram concitat, ei quod exigit,
simile patietur?' The use is not noted
in Forc., and I have not found it in
Cicero.

Vives' remark on the views expressed
in §§ 29–31 may be worth quoting 'non
nego quin ad dicendum frequentia ex-
citetur animus, sed aliud est dicere
quam docere.'

III. 1. tradito...perspiciet. The subject is further developed in II. 8.

perspiciet. The reading of Sp. and
older edd. 'perspiciat' seems to have no
good MS. authority, though there is
much for 'prospiciet.'

facile...continere. The inclusion of
'facile percipere' as a function of memory
may at first sight cause surprise, and
Turnebus noted that Q. includes 'ingenii
acumen' in memory. But this is too
wide. Q. seems to mean the faculty
which can grasp and hold for the time
being a number of facts, and this he
rightly distinguishes from the retentive
memory. A 'whist memory' is a good
example of the first. In the chapter on
memory XI. 2, 1–2 he shews his meaning

naturae, sic tamen, ut ea, quae discit, effingat, non habitum forte et ingressum et si quid in peius notabile est. non dabit 2 mihi spem bonae indolis, qui hoc imitandi studio petet, ut rideatur. nam probus quoque in primis erit ille vere ingeniosus, alioqui non peius duxerim tardi esse ingenii quam mali. probus autem ab illo segni et iacente plurimum aberit. hic 3 meus quae tradentur non difficulter accipiet, quaedam etiam interrogabit: sequetur tamen magis quam praecurret. illud ingeniorum velut praecox genus non temere umquam pervenit ad frugem. hi sunt qui parva facile faciunt et audacia provecti 4 quidquid illud possunt statim ostendunt, possunt autem id demum, quod in proximo est: verba continuant, haec vultu interrito, nulla tardati verecundia proferunt: non multum praestant, sed cito; non subest vera vis nec penitus inmissis 5 radicibus nititur, ut quae summo solo sparsa sunt semina

clearly: 'neque immerito thesaurus hic eloquentiae dicitur, sed non firme tantum continere verum etiam cito percipere multa acturos oportet, nec quae scripseris modo iterata lectione complecti, sed in cogitatis quoque rerum ac verborum contextum sequi, et quae sint ab adversa parte dicta meminisse...extemporalis oratio non alio mihi videtur mentis vigore constare.' Cp. Sen. *Contr.* I, Pro. 3 'nec ad complectenda tantum quae vellem velox mihi erat memoria, sed etiam ad continenda quae acceperat solebat bonae fidei esse.'

2. non...rideatur. Cf. VI. 3, 35 'ea quae dicet vir bonus omnia salva dignitate ac verecundia dicet. Nimium enim risus pretium est, si probitatis impendio constat.'

alioqui...mali. The words have never been questioned, but they seem to me to be rather pointless. Q. hardly needs to tell us that he thinks badness is as bad as stupidity, and the meaning given to 'alioqui' is singularly little. It is true that there are places in Q., where it = 'praeterea,' v. *Ep. ad Tryph.* 1, but there is always some little antithesis, 'to turn to the other side of things.' If it is not too bold, I would suggest 'cati' for 'mali.' This will give an excellent sense. 'If it were not so, I would as soon a boy were stupid as clever.' Cf. Cic. *Ac.* II. 97 'vide quam sit catus is, quem isti tardum putant.'

iacente. For this sense which is, I think, a little different from any given in Forc. cf. § 10 below and VI. 4, 11

'non est res animi iacentis et mollis supra modum frontis.'

3. hic meus. Andresen may perhaps be right in thinking that the stop should be removed after 'aberit' and placed after 'meus.'

4. quidquid illud possunt. Sp. and other edd. 'illic' with very little authority. The 'illud' adds a depreciatory force; so VI. pr. 3 'quidquid hoc est in me infelicium litterarum,' XII. 6, 2 'quidquid est illud adhuc acerbum proferatur' (where the thought is very similar to this). So too Virg. *Aen.* 1, 78 'quodcumque hoc regni,' and (slightly different) Liv. 9, 3, 13 'quidquid istuc praesens necessitas inusserit.'

5. nec subest vera vis. Sp. quotes *Georg.* 2, 49 'quippe solo natura subest,' and points out that Q. reproduces this more closely X. 2, 11 'subest natura et vera vis.' That Q. has some thought of Virg. in his mind is rendered more likely by the resemblance in this section to line 253 'nec se praevalidam primis ostendat aristis,' and the definite quotation of 272 in § 13.

summo. So X. 3, 2 'profectus non a summo petitus studiorum fructus effundit uberius et fidelius continet.'

4–5. Ben Jonson's paraphrase of this passage is as follows: *Disc.* 65. 2 'There be some that are forward and bold; and these will doe every little thing easily; I mean that is hard by and next them; which they will utter unretarded without any shamefastnesse. These never performe much, but quickly. They

celerius se effundunt et imitatae spicas herbulae inanibus
aristis ante messem flavescunt. placent haec annis comparata;
deinde stat profectus, admiratio decrescit.

6   Haec cum animadverterit, perspiciat deinceps, quonam modo
tractandus sit discentis animus. sunt quidam, nisi institeris,
remissi, quidam imperia indignantur, quosdam continet metus,
quosdam debilitat, alios continuatio extundit, in aliis plus
7 impetus facit. mihi ille detur puer, quem laus excitet, quem
gloria iuvet, qui victus fleat. hic erit alendus ambitu, hunc
mordebit obiurgatio, hunc honor excitabit, in hoc desidiam
numquam verebor.

8   Danda est tamen omnibus aliqua remissio, non solum, quia
nulla res est, quae perferre possit continuum laborem, atque
ea quoque, quae sensu et anima carent, ut servare vim suam
possint, velut quiete alterna retenduntur, sed quod studium
9 discendi voluntate, quae cogi non potest, constat. itaque et
virium plus adferunt ad discendum renovati ac recentes et
10 acriorem animum, qui fere necessitatibus repugnat. nec me
offenderit lusus in pueris (est et hoc signum alacritatis), neque
illum tristem semperque demissum sperare possim erectae
circa studia mentis fore, cum in hoc quoque maxime naturali
11 aetatibus illis impetu iaceat. modus tamen sit remissionibus

are what they are on the sudden: they
shew presently like graine, that scatter-
ed on the top of the ground shoots up,
but takes no root; has a yellow blade,
but the eare empty. They are wits of
good promise at first, but there is an
ingenistitium: they stand still at six-
teene, they get no higher.'
6. continuatio. For this absolute use
of the word cf. Plin. *Ep.* 4, 9, 11
'dicentis color et audientis intentio
continuatione servatur.'
7. For the thought cf. Cic. *De Fin.*
5, 61 'indicant pueri, in quibus ut in
speculis natura cernitur. Quanta studia
decertantium sunt! quanta ipsa certa-
mina! ut illi efferuntur laetitia, cum
vicerunt! ut pudet victos! ut se accusari
nolunt! quam cupiunt laudari! quos illi
labores perferunt ut aequalium principes
sint.' *Pro Cael.* 76 'de impetu animi
loquor, de cupiditate vincendi, de ardore
mentis ad gloriam : quae studia in his iam
aetatibus nostris contractiora esse debent,
in adulescentia vero tamquam in herbis
significant, quae virtutis maturitas, et
quantae fruges industriae sint futurae.'

8. For the doctrine of the need of
relaxation. as applied to children cf.
ps.-Plut. 13 δοτέον οὖν τοῖς παισὶν
ἀναπνοὴν τῶν συνεχῶν πόνων, ἐνθυμου-
μένους ὅτι πᾶς ὁ βίος ἡμῶν εἰς ἄνεσιν καὶ
σπουδὴν διῄρηται...καὶ οὐκ ἐπὶ τῶν ζῴων
μόνων τοῦτ᾽ ἄν ἴδοι τις γιγνόμενον, ἀλλὰ
καὶ ἐπὶ τῶν ἀψύχων, καὶ γὰρ τὰ τόξα καὶ τὰς
λύρας ἀνίεμεν, ἵνα ἐπιτεῖναι δυνηθῶμεν.
Aus. *Id.* 4, 4 'sed requie studiique vices
rata tempora servant' (and next 5 lines).
Similar remarks about relaxation in
general in Sen. *De Tranq.* 17; cp. ib. 3
sub fine.
9. acriorem...repugnat. L. translates
'they approach their work with greater
spirit of a kind that will not submit to
be driven.' Rather 'The mind, which
is apt to rebel against compulsion, comes
to its work with keener zest.'
10. nec me offenderit lusus. Cf. Sen.
De Ira 2, 20 'lusus quoque proderunt,
modica enim voluptas laxat animos.'
Phaedr. 3, 14, 12 'sic ludus animo debet
aliquando dari, | ad cogitandum melior
ut redeat tibi.'
11. It is to be noted that the only

ne aut odium studiorum faciant negatae aut otii consuetudinem
nimiae. sunt etiam nonnulli acuendis puerorum ingeniis non
inutiles lusus, cum positis invicem cuiusque generis quaestiun-
culis aemulantur. mores quoque se inter ludendum simplicius 12
detegunt, modo nulla videatur aetas tam infirma, quae non
protinus quid rectum pravumque sit discat, tum vel maxime
formanda, cum simulandi nescia est et praecipientibus facillime
cedit: frangas enim citius quam corrigas quae in pravum
induruerunt. protinus ergo, ne quid cupide, ne quid inprobe, 13
ne quid inpotenter faciat, monendus est puer, habendumque
in animo semper illud Vergilianum:

adeo in teneris consuescere multum est.

game expressly mentioned is a mental
one. The idea of physical development
as an object in itself does not, I think,
appear in Q. So in 11, 16 the palaestra
is only recommended for the end of
oratorical grace; v. the note there.

cuiusque. Bonnell and some other
edd. read 'cuiuscumque,' the use of
which for 'any whatsoever' is well established in Q. It has little MS. authority
here and recent edd. including Sp. retain 'cuiusque.' I do not however find
any close parallel to it. Dräger, vol. 1.
p. 102, who quotes this passage, couples
it with 1. 2, 4 which seems to me different.

12. mores...detegunt. Cf. Locke *Some
Thoughts concerning Education* § 102:
'Begin therefore betimes nicely to observe your son's temper; and that, when
he is least under restraint in his play,
and as he thinks out of your sight.' ib.
§ 123 'you must watch him at play, when
he is out of his place and time of study,
following his own inclinations and see
whether he be stirring and active...or
whether he lazily and listlessly dreams
away his time'; v. Intr. p. lxxxvi.

modo etc. The connexion of
thought is not quite clear. Acc. to Sp.
'this revelation is only useful, if the
master improves the occasion.' Perhaps
rather 'our sympathy with this natural
simplicity must not lead us into dispens-
ing with moral guidance and correction
of childish faults.'

formanda. The suggestion of Kid.
(adopted by Meister in his text) that
'mens est' has dropped out after 'maxime,' would certainly improve the sentence. But the looseness of language
involved in making 'aetas' the subject
is not very great.

frangas...induruerunt. Ben Jonson
Disc. 7 'Natures that are hardned to
evill you shall sooner breake, then make
straight: they are like poles that are
crooked, and dry: there is no attempting
them.'

13. in teneris. The statement of For-
biger on *Georg.* 2, 272 that Q. quotes the
words in the form 'a teneris' has been
repeated in the various issues of Con-
ington's Virgil, and by Papillon. This
is apparently a pure error. Burmann
indeed notes that he found 'a teneris'
in the edition of Locatellius (which I
have not seen), but all the MSS. and
all the editions accessible to me have
'in.'

14–17. caedi vero. Cf. ps.-Plut. 12
κἀκεῖνό φημι δεῖν τοὺς παῖδας ἐπὶ τὰ
καλὰ τῶν ἐπιτηδευμάτων ἄγειν παραινέ-
σεσι καὶ λόγοις, μὴ μὰ Δία πληγαῖς μηδ'
αἰκισμοῖς. δοκεῖ γάρ που τοῖς δούλοις ταῦτα
μᾶλλον ἢ τοῖς ἐλευθέροις πρέπειν. Seneca
De Clem. 1, 16 'uter autem praeceptor
liberalibus studiis dignior qui excarni-
ficabit discipulos, si memoria illis non
constiterit, aut si parum agilis in le-
gendo oculus haeserit; an qui monitioni-
bus et verecundia emendare ac docere
malit?'

The references to corporal punishment, especially in schools, are innumer-
able. Many of them will be found in
Grasberger, vol. II. pp. 92 etc., Mayor
on Juv. 1, 15, Cresollius *Theat. Rhet.*
v. 6, 7.

But apart from these three passages,
though general expressions in approval
of mildness and persuasion as superior
to force are very common, I have not
come across any condemnation of the
practice. Indeed it should be noticed

14   Caedi vero discentis, quamlibet et receptum sit et Chrysippus
non inprobet, minime velim, primum quia deforme atque
servile est et certe (quod convenit, si aetatem mutes) iniuria :
deinde quod, si cui tam est mens inliberalis, ut obiurgatione
non corrigatur, is etiam ad plagas ut pessima quaeque mancipia
durabitur: postremo quod ne opus erit quidem hac castigatione,
15 si adsiduus studiorum exactor adstiterit. nunc fere neglegentia
paedagogorum sic emendari videtur, ut pueri non facere quae
recta sunt cogantur, sed cur non fecerint puniantur. denique
cum parvulum verberibus coegeris, quid iuveni facias, cui nec
16 adhiberi potest hic metus et maiora discenda sunt? adde quod
multa vapulantibus dictu deformia et mox verecundiae futura
saepe dolore vel metu acciderunt, qui pudor frangit animum
17 et abicit atque ipsius lucis fugam et taedium dictat. iam si
minor in eligendis custodum et praeceptorum moribus fuit
cura, pudet dicere, in quae probra nefandi homines isto caedendi
iure abutantur, quam det aliis quoque nonnumquam occasionem
hic miserorum metus. non morabor in parte hac: nimium est
quod intellegitur. quare hoc dixisse satis est: in aetatem

that Q. and Sen. are speaking of its
employment in cases of idleness or stupidity, though Plut. seems to speak
more generally. Nor does Sen. absolutely condemn it. His words are such
as nearly all schoolmasters would endorse, even though they held to flogging
as a last resort.

On the other hand I know of very little
definite approval. It is recommended
by Arist. *Pol.* 4, 15 for disobedience,
and Ausonius *Id.* 4 seems to regard it
at least with equanimity.

14. discentis. A (and so Halm and
later edd.), 'discipulos' B. 'Discentes'
brings out better what I take to be Q.'s
meaning, that he is only speaking of the
use of the rod in the schoolroom.

quamlibet et. MSS. vary between
this, 'quamlibet id' and 'quamquam
illud.' Halm 'quamlibet rec.'

iniuria. So Meister and Rad. A, B
'iniuriae,' which Halm taking as 'iniuria ē' prints as 'iniuria est,' but the
repetition of 'est' seems to me awkward.

adsiduus ... adstiterit. L. 'if the
master is a thorough disciplinarian.'
But what then is the point of the next
sentence? I understand Q. to expect
that the 'paedagogus' should act as a

superintendent of the boy's industry at
home and possibly in the schoolroom,
when the pupil is set to private study,
like a 'preparation' master in a modern
school. As the 'paedagogus' certainly
often accompanied his charge to school
and waited for him, it would be natural
to utilise him in this way. I do not
however know of any other evidence of
such a practice. v. Intr. p. xiv n.

15. cur non fecerint. So apparently
all MSS. Sp. and others 'cum,' but
Halm and his successors have returned
to the MS. reading. I feel some doubt.
Horace's 'irascar...cur...properent' (*Ep.*
I, 8, 9), Pliny's 'repeto me correptum
cur ambularem' (*Ep.* 3, 5, 16), and
Cic.'s use of 'cur' after 'accuso' are
not quite the same. In all these cases
the idea of interrogation may be latent.
'Damnari cur' (Spartian *Sev.* 14) is a
further extension, but does not go to
the length of 'puniantur cur' (v. Hand
Turs. II. p. 177, Dräger II. p. 481).

16. frangit. So A. Sp. 'refringit,'
a correction for 'refrangit' of most
MSS.

lucis fugam. Cf. 'lucifugus'=unsoci-
able, Cic. *De Fin.* I, 61. So *Pro Sull.*
74 'pudore hominum aspectum lucem-
que vitare.'

infirmam et iniuriae obnoxiam nemini debet nimium licere. nunc quibus instituendus sit artibus qui sic formabitur, ut fieri 18 possit orator, et quae in quaque aetate incohanda, dicere ingrediar.

IV

[DE GRAMMATICE]

Primus in eo, qui scribendi legendique adeptus erit facul- 1 tatem, grammatici est locus. nec refert de Graeco an de Latino loquar, quamquam Graecum esse priorem placet: utrique eadem via est. haec igitur professio, cum brevissime in duas partis 2 dividatur, recte loquendi scientiam et poetarum enarrationem, plus habet in recessu quam fronte promittit. nam et scribendi 3 ratio coniuncta cum loquendi est, et enarrationem praecedit emendata lectio, et mixtum his omnibus iudicium est: quo

---

17. nemini debet licere. 'Debere' adopted by Sp. seems unnecessary. For the use of the personal 'debet' with the impers. 'licere' to form a single impersonal expression I have not found any exact parallels, but it is analogous to 'poterat persuaderi alicui' and the like.

IV. The grammatical chapters 4–8 teem with difficulties both as to their general structure and still more as to points of detail. I have dealt with some of them in two articles in the *Classical Quarterly* Jan. 1914 and Jan. 1916. I refer to these when required as Art. 1914 and Art. 1916 respectively.

1. grammatici. So Halm and Meister with A. Rad. with B 'grammaticis.'

de Graeco an de Latino. The edict of Gratian, Mommsen Cod. Theod. 13, 3, 11, shews that in the fourth century the two sets of teachers maintained a general equality. Their pay is fixed at the same rate, except at Trèves, where it is suggested that a capable Greek grammarian is hardly obtainable.

priorem; v. on 1, 12 and Intr. p. xxxi.

2. duas partis. Called in 9, 1 respectively 'methodice' and 'historice.' For this all-important distinction v. Art. 1914. Here it is enough to say that in earlier times, as late as Cicero and after him Philo, the literary side of 'grammatice,' here put second, was predominant. See also notes on 9, 1.

poetarum enarrationem. Greek

ἐξήγησις, so 'enarratio syllabarum,' Sen. *Ep.* 88, 3. Augustine's commentary on the Psalms is called 'Enarrationes in psalmos'; cf. 2, 14.

3. loquendi. This is Madvig's correction for 'loquendo' (adopted by Meister, but not by Rad.). No parallel to 'cum' with the gerund seems to be known, nor does it here make good sense.

enarrationem. B and most other MSS. 'narrationem.' Halm does not say what A has. Rad. who says that A has 'enarrationem,' incomprehensibly reads 'narrationem.' But the correction to en- is necessary, even if there is no MS. authority. 'Narratio'=διήγησις, and is impossible here.

emendata lectio. A consideration of ch. 8, where the order of studies is explained in detail, makes it perfectly clear that this phrase means 'good and correct reading' and has no reference, as some have thought, to textual emendation. It is true that 'emendatio' in this sense (διόρθωσις) was a regular function of the 'grammatici' as scholars, but it has no part in Q.'s scheme of school work, nor in that of Dionysius Thrax (v. Art. 1914, p. 41); 'emendata lectio' here=Dionysius' ἐντριβὴς ἀνάγνωσις. The adjectives are added because, while the boy would learn to read before he went to the 'grammaticus,' he there learnt to read well and expressively.

iudicium. This faculty, Q. implies,

quidem ita severe sunt usi veteres grammatici, ut non versus
modo censoria quadam virgula notare et libros, qui falso
viderentur inscripti, tamquam subditos submovere familia
permiserint sibi, sed auctores alios in ordinem redegerint,
4 alios omnino exemerint numero. nec poetas legisse satis est:
excutiendum omne scriptorum genus non propter historias
modo, sed verba, quae frequenter ius ab auctoribus sumunt.
tum neque citra musicen grammatice potest esse perfecta, cum
ei de metris rhythmisque dicendum sit, nec si rationem siderum
ignoret, poetas intellegat, qui, ut alia omittam, totiens ortu
occasuque signorum in declarandis temporibus utuntur, nec
ignara philosophiae, cum propter plurimos in omnibus fere
carminibus locos ex intima naturalium quaestionum subtilitate
repetitos, tum vel propter Empedoclea in Graecis, Varronem

is not to be used in the limited sense of
κρίσις ποιημάτων, by which the Alexan-
drian grammarians formed their 'canons'
of accepted poets and excluded spurious
writings, but is required everywhere.
Thus 6, 3 it is needed for applying the
principle of analogy, 7, 30 in orthography
and so often in Book x. So in III. 3, 5
and VI. 5, 1 he deprecates the view that
'iudicium' can be regarded as a special
province in rhetoric. It is 'partibus
omnibus connexum et mixtum' (v. Art.
1914, p. 45).

censoria virgula, i.e. the obelus (—)
employed by Aristarchus and his predecessors. Cf. Isidore, Orig. 1, 20
(quoted in Forc.) 'obelus id est virgula
iacens apponitur in verbis, vel sententiis superflue iteratis, sive in iis locis,
ubi lectio aliqua falsitate notata est, ut
quasi sagitta iugulet supervacua atque
falsa confodiat.' This use of 'virgula'
is not illustrated from elsewhere by
Forc., but I have found it several times
in Jerome's letters, e.g. 61, 2 (Migne)
'tibi soli licet τῷ σοφωτάτῳ κρανίῳ de
cunctis et Graecis et Latinis tractatoribus
ferre sententiam et quasi censoria virgula
alios eicere de bibliothecis alios recipere,'
a passage probably reminiscent of this,
so 50, 4; 84, 7; 112, 19.

auctores...numero. Sp. who had been
tempted by the common use of the phrase
'in ordinem redigere' for 'reduce to the
ranks,' to regard it as having an unfavourable sense, rightly came to the
conclusion that this and 'eximere numero' were respectively equivalent to
ἐγκρίνειν and ἐκκρίνειν.

This passage, together with x. 1, 54
'Apollonius in ordinem a grammaticis
datum non venit, quia Aristarchus atque
Aristophanes neminem sui temporis in
numerum redegerunt,' is the chief authority for the existence of the 'Alex-
andrian Canon.' The reality of this
'Canon,' to which attention was originally
called by Ruhnken Hist. Crit. Or. Graec.,
has been much discussed. The best
treatment of which I know is that by
Usener, Dion. Hal. De Imit. (appendix).
It should be noted, I think, (1) that we
should speak rather of Canons, than a
Canon: the lists probably varied with
different schools at different times. (2)
There is no evidence that the term κανών
was actually used: the name generally in
use was perhaps τάξις = 'ordo' here (v.
my note, Class. Quart. Jan. 1919, p. 35).

4. nec poetas...sumunt. This sentence has been frequently misunderstood
(e.g. by Peterson on Tac. Dial. 30) to
mean that these authors were read in
the grammatical school at this time at
Rome. It is clear from ch. 8 that this
was not the case. The sentence gives
rather the necessary equipment for the
'grammaticus' to enable him to deal
properly with the poets.

citra, 'without.' 'Nemo frequentius
Quintiliano usurpat hanc dictionem:
saepe etiam Plinius.' Hand Turs. II.
p. 83.

utuntur. So Meister and Rad. with
A. Halm 'utantur' with B.

Empedoclea, i.e. the treatise περὶ
φύσεως τῶν ὄντων, v. Pauly-Wissowa.

Varronem. It is impossible to decide,

ac Lucretium in Latinis, qui praecepta sapientiae versibus tradiderunt. eloquentia quoque non mediocri est opus, ut de 5 unaquaque earum, quas demonstravimus, rerum dicat proprie et copiose. quo minus sunt ferendi, qui hanc artem ut tenuem atque ieiunam cavillantur. quae nisi oratoris futuri fundamenta fideliter iecit, quidquid superstruxeris, corruet: necessaria pueris, iucunda senibus, dulcis secretorum comes, et quae vel sola in omni studiorum genere plus habeat operis quam ostentationis.

Ne quis igitur tamquam parva fastidiat grammatices ele- 6 menta, non quia magnae sit operae, consonantes a vocalibus discernere ipsasque eas in semivocalium numerum mutarumque partiri, sed quia interiora velut sacri huius adeuntibus apparebit multa rerum subtilitas, quae non modo acuere ingenia puerilia, sed exercere altissimam quoque eruditionem ac scientiam

I think, whether this is Marcus or Publius (Atacinus); Cic. *Acad.* 1, 3, 9 'ipse (i.e. M. Varro) varium et elegans omni fere numero poema fecisti philosophiamque multis locis incohasti ad impellendum satis, ad edocendum parum' quoted by Sp. and others has no bearing on the matter (v. Reid's note). It means 'you have written poetry in almost every metre and touched on philosophy in several places' and merely shews that Varro then (18 years before his death) had written nothing solid on philosophy. Lactantius *Div. Inst.* 2, 12, 4 has 'Empedocles...de rerum natura versibus scripsit, ut apud Romanos Lucretius et Varro,' which I suspect to be one of Lact.'s reminiscences of Q. (v. intr. p. xliii). Though it has not been hitherto suggested, so far as I know, it seems to me not impossible that the work here referred to is the 'Chorographia' or 'Cosmographia' of Atacinus, the fragments of which would fit this passage very fairly.

5. iecit. Meister adopts 'iecerit,' with little MS. authority.

necessaria...comes. Cf. Cic. *Pro Arch.* 16 'haec studia adulescentiam agunt, senectutem oblectant, secundas res ornant, adversis perfugium ac solacium praebent: delectant domi, non impediunt foris, pernoctant nobiscum, peregrinantur, rusticantur.'

in omni. 'In' apparently in A only. Indeed Halm's note implies that it is absent there also. But the Director of

the Ambrosian Library assures me that A reads as in text.

6–29. These sections are an attempt to give, without dealing systematically with the subject, some idea of the 'quaestiones' or problems, with which the 'grammaticus' had to deal on the grammatical (as opposed to the literary) side of his art. They treat of (1) letters and sounds (6–17), (2) parts of speech (18–21), (3) nouns (22–26), (4) verbs (27–29). In each case the more obvious points are mentioned and contrasted with the more difficult problems, which shew that the science is neither 'tenuis' nor 'ieiuna' (v. Art. 1914, p. 37).

6. elementa. Perhaps here in the more restricted sense of the letters of the alphabet. After 'elementa' most MSS. (including A, B) insert 'de literis' which all edd. have no doubt rightly regarded as the intrusion of a marginal heading. Acc. to Fierville the only exceptions are Pratensis and Puteanus. But v. Intr. pp. xcii, xcvi.

semivocalium, i.e. according to all the Latin grammarians f, l, m, n, r, s, x.

adeuntibus. L.'s translation, 'as the *pupil* approaches,' misses, I think, the sense. The thought is throughout of the 'grammaticus' himself, who will find various problems, some of which are suited for the class-room (acuere ingenia puerilia), others for higher scholarship (altissimam eruditionem); v. note on 'at grammatici saltem omnes' below.

7 possit. an cuiuslibet auris est exigere litterarum sonos? non hercule magis quam nervorum: at grammatici saltem omnes in hanc descendent rerum tenuitatem, desintne aliquae nobis necessariae litterae, non cum Graeca scribimus (tum enim ab 8 isdem duas mutuamur), sed proprie in Latinis: ut in his 'seruus' et 'uulgus' Aeolicum digammon desideratur, et medius est quidam u et i litterae sonus (non enim sic 'optumum' dicimus aut 'optimum') et <in> 'here' neque e plane neque i

7. auris. So A, evidently rightly against B 'artis.'

exigere, to examine into and distinguish between, cf. 'aure exiguntur' 5, 19. The point of this will be appreciated by anyone who reads the discussions of the grammarians on the sounds of the various letters as quoted by Lindsay *L. L.* ch. 2.

at grammatici saltem omnes. Both A and B have 'aut.' Halm was right, I think, in adopting 'at' in spite of inferior support. While the phonetic questions just mentioned refer to 'altissima scientia,' all *grammarians* at any rate, though not necessarily their pupils, should go into the questions on which we now enter.

desint. In this and the next section Q. evidently alludes to the attempt of Claudius to introduce three new symbols (Suet. *Claud.* 41), (1) the inverted ⊣ for the consonantal *u*, (2) ⊢ to represent a sound intermediate between *u* and *i*, (3) Ɔ⊂ (antisigma) = ψ. The last of these took so little hold that no example of it remains in the inscriptions. Cf. 'quam psi non quaerimus,' § 9. For the literature of this subject v. Bücheler, *De Ti. Claud. Caes. Grammatico*, Lindsay *L. L.* (v. index 'Claudius'), cf. 7, 26.

duas, i.e. *y* and *z*.

8. in his = ἐν τοῖς. Q. regularly uses some such equivalent to the Greek article, when the noun has to be quoted in a case which does not fit into the construction. If possible he adapts the noun to the construction as in § 13. Here he would doubtless have preferred to write 'vulgo,' but 'servo' was impossible for the reason given below.

Aeolicum. This epithet is regularly applied to the digamma in Priscian, v. index in Keil. Though the letter is by no means confined to Aeolic, it was most familiar to Latin writers in the Aeolic poets.

desideratur. The need of the digamma seems to have been mainly felt

by the grammarians when the *w* sound was followed by *u* (cf. Aul. Gell. 14, 5), though Bücheler quotes plenty of inscriptions where it is followed by other letters: Sergius (K. IV. 476) 'praeterea et hoc proprium habet u ut digammon sonet, id est pingue quiddam, cum sibi ipsa praeponitur, ut servus, vulgus,' may perhaps suggest that some phonetic difference was felt in this connection, but § 11 below rather suggests that the objection to writing the ordinary *u* was largely a theoretical one to two identical letters in the same syllable.

non enim...'optimum.' This passage has been much discussed. Halm adopted the reading of B and older edd. 'sic dicimus optimum ut opimum,' which is surely quite impossible in view of the words just preceding. The reading here printed is that of A (except that the first hand has 'ut' for 'aut') and is adopted by Meister and, with 'vel' substituted for 'aut,' by Rad. Meister however bracketed 'sic,' for which Kid. proposed 'sincere.' I do not see much difficulty in 'sic' and take the words to mean 'we do not say either "optimum" or "optumum" as the written words (both of which were in use, cf. 7, 21) would indicate.' Ritschl's suggestion 'optimum d. ut aut optimum aut optumum' is worth considering. Keil 'non enim sic optimum dicimus ut scribimus optimum' is less probable.

et in 'here'...auditur. While the duplicate spelling is mentioned in 7, 22 and often in the grammarians, I can find no other instance where the sound is said to be intermediate between *e* and *i*, or that 'heri' and 'here' were not pronounced respectively as written, though Consentius (K. v. 394) says that such an intermediate sound is heard in 'hominem.' It seems to me not impossible that the words are an insertion, based on the juxtaposition of 'optimus,' 'optumus' and 'heri,' 'here' in 7, 21, 22.

⟨in⟩ 'here.' Assuming that the clause

auditur : an rursus aliae redundent, praeter illam adspirationis, 9
quae si necessaria est, etiam contrariam sibi poscit, ut k, quae
et ipsa quorundam nominum nota est, et q, cuius similis effectu
specieque, nisi quod paulum a nostris obliquatur, coppa apud
Graecos nunc tantum in numero manet, et nostrarum ultima,
qua tam carere potuimus, quam psi non quaerimus. atque 10

is genuine, it is probably best with edd.
to insert ' in,' against the MSS. However it is just possible that Q. may have
regarded ' here ' as an abl. Pompeius
couples it with ' vesperi,' as among the
adverbs ' quae a nomine veniunt,' K.
v. 244. In this case the absence of the
' in ' could be paralleled from ' libris
invenio,' 7, 22.
   9. illam (sc. **litteram**) **adspirationis.**
Halm, Meister and Rad. have all in-
serted ' notam,' I believe needlessly.
Whether ' h ' was a ' littera ' or ' nota '
was a disputed point amongst grammarians, influenced no doubt by Greek
usage, e.g. Diom. K. I. 423 ' h quoque
interdum consonans interdum adspirationis nota creditur,' cf. 5, 19. But it
was regularly reckoned amongst the
16 consonants, and I cannot think that
grammatical usage demands the insertion;
' illa (sc. littera) aspirationis,' i.e. ' that
letter which expresses aspiration,' is not
difficult. Meister and Rad. seem to have
been influenced by Sp.'s statement that
Gibson appeared to have found it in
his MSS. (Joann. and Bal.). But this is a
mistake. The Joannensis (v. Appendix)
has not got it, and the Baliolensis does
not begin till I. 5, 14; v. Add. Note.
   contrariam etc. Cf. Priscian K. II. 35
' H literam non esse ostendimus, sed notam aspirationis, quam Graecorum anti-
quissimi similiter ut Latini in versu
scribebant : nunc autem diviserunt et
dextram eius partem supra literam po-
nentes psiles notam habent...:sinistram
autem contrariae aspirationis.'
   ut k. ' Ut ' is a simple and almost
necessary correction for the ' et ' of
MSS., which Rad. has retained.
   et ipsa...est. Sp. explained ' et ipsa '
as a reference to the statement that ' h '
is also a ' nota '; and if this is right, it
might be regarded as a reason for in-
serting ' notam ' above. But the words
may simply mean ' even alone ' (cf.
Prooem. 27), the reference being of course
to K = Kaeso, Kalendae etc. The point
of the clause is not however quite clear,
since the main argument for the re-
dundancy of K is the availability of C

(cf. 7, 10). Possibly Q. may mean that
since it can only be used (v. again 7, 10)
in these few words, and in such cases K
alone is a sufficient symbol for the whole,
it is unnecessary as a ' consonans ' though
not as a ' nota.'
   obliquatur, i.e. Coppa has the shape ϙ.
   nostrarum ultima, i.e. *x*; it should
be unnecessary to state this, but that
Nettleship in his essay on ' Latin
Grammar in the first century ' actually
says it is *z*. Cp. Cic. *De Nat. De.* 2, 93,
where the alphabet is spoken of as con-
sisting of 21 letters. For the uselessness
of *x* cf. Serg. K. IV. 477, ' x quoque ideo
exclusione digna visa est, quod quasi una
consonans contra litterarum legem dua-
rum consonantium vim tenere desiderat.'
But though the grammarians regularly
note its composite nature, they do not
appear generally to share this view of
its superfluity.
   psi. This certain correction for the
' si ' of MSS. was made by P. Pithou
in the 15th century. It had however
apparently escaped the notice of edd.
till Sp. who, having printed ' qua tamen
c. p. si non quaesissemus,' noticed it in
the preface to his second volume.
   §§ **10, 11.** For a full discussion of these
difficult sections, especially the words
' at quae...fungantur,' I must refer to
Art. 1916, pp. 24-27. I am now inclined to think that the second of the
two solutions there offered is almost
certainly right, and have printed the text
as I think that explanation requires.
   The thesis is that *i* and *u* are sometimes really consonants. This is supported by the following arguments.
   (*a*) **at quae...fungantur.** If there is
more than one vowel in a syllable they
must either be really one, i.e. when we
write *aa* for *ā*, or two. There cannot be
three (this is assumed to be an absurdity).
But since we frequently write three, as
in ' seruae,' one of these must be a consonant.
   (*b*) **quaeret...' seruus.'** As it is elsewhere a universal law that a letter is
not repeated in a syllable, it is improbable that *u* or *i* should be repeated

etiam in ipsis vocalibus grammatici est videre, an aliquas pro
consonantibus usus acceperit, quia 'iam' sicut 'etiam' scribitur
et 'quos' ut 'tuos.' at quae ut vocales iunguntur, aut unam
longam faciunt, ut veteres scripserunt, qui geminatione earum
velut apice utebantur, aut duas, (nisi quis putat etiam ex tribus
vocalibus syllabam fieri), < quod nequit fieri >, si non aliquae
11 officio consonantium fungantur. quaeret hoc etiam, quo modo
duabus demum vocalibus in se ipsas coeundi natura sit, cum
consonantium nulla nisi alteram frangat. atqui littera i sibi
insidit ('conicit' enim est ab illo 'iacit') et u, quo modo nunc

thus, but the *symbol u* is actually repeated, e.g. 'seruus,' and *i* implicitly, for
'conicit' is really 'coniicit.'

(*c*) Cicero actually does repeat *i* in the
same syllable. We must therefore conclude that one of these *i*'s, as one of the
u's in the case above, is consonantal.

My belief that the sense of (*a*) is as
above rests on the fact that the same
argument appears not only in Priscian
(which I pointed out in Art. 1916) but
also in the far earlier authority Cornutus.
The quotations are given below.

If this is the sense of the whole passage, the question may be asked, how
does the problem so far as *u* is concerned differ from that suggested in § 7?
Perhaps in this way. The first subject
with which the grammarian deals is the
alphabet. Here the question will arise
whether other symbols such as the Clau-
dian digamma are required. The second
subject is the value of the letters, and
here the special 'quaestio' is whether
u and *i* are sometimes consonantal. This
would not be settled even for *u*, if the
digamma was admitted. For as we have
seen Q. would restrict the digamma to
cases where another *u* followed.

10. 'etiam.' MSS. 'tam.'

'tuos.' MSS. 'cos.' Halm also corrected 'quos' to 'vos,' and Meister has
followed him but not Rad. It seems to
me unnecessary.

unam longam; v. on 7, 14.

apice; v. on 7, 2.

quod nequit...fungantur. But this
result, i.e. that 'iunctae vocales faciunt
aut unam aut duas,' is only obtainable
on the assumption that some vowels are
really consonants; on any other assumption we should get the absurdity of three
in a syllable. For this argument cf.
Cornutus ap. Cassiodorum (K. VII. 148)
'tres vocales quibusdam esse videntur

sub una syllaba -vae. Errant si ita putant;
nam nusquam apud Graecos neque apud
Latinos ex tribus vocalibus syllaba constat; quare hic quoque digamma erit et
duae vocales.' Priscian K. II. 44 'nulla
syllaba tres vocales habet, unde u et i
non aliter iunguntur diphthongis nisi
loco positae consonantium.' The words
'quod nequit' are only found in 15th
century MSS. at any rate in the 1st hand
(v. Fierville). But I do not see how the
required sense (or any real sense) can
be obtained if they are omitted. Sp.
suggested that 'fieri' after 'nequit'
could be supplied from the former 'fieri.'
I have inserted it, as more likely to
account for the omission through the
two 'fieri's' from some MSS., and the
retention in the form 'quod nequit' in
others.

11. quaeret. This I understand not
to introduce a new 'quaestio,' but a
second reason for the view that *u* and *i*
are sometimes consonants.

frangat. Practically a synonym for
'coire,' but applicable to consonants as
that is to vowels. Cf. XII. 10, 29 'quae
(i.e. the letter 'f')...quotiens aliquam
consonantium frangit, ut in hoc ipso
"frangit" multo fit horridior.'

'conicit.' I have printed this instead
of 'coniicit,' as I understand Q.'s meaning to be that the common form 'conicit'
really involves two *i*'s. Otherwise like
Sp. I can see no force in the addition 'ab
illo "iacit."' But the correction I suggested in Art. 1916 '< ut conicit >, coniicit enim,' etc. seems to me very probable.
The sense will be the same, but better
expressed, i.e. 'conicit' is an example
of two *i*'s, for it is really 'coniicit' derived from 'iacit'; and this is supported
by Aul. Gell. 4, 17, where the derivation from 'iacit' is given as a reason for
writing 'subiicit' rather than 'subicit.'

scribitur 'uulgus' et 'seruus.' sciat etiam Ciceroni placuisse 'aiio Maiiamque' geminata i scribere: quod si est, etiam <i> iungetur ut consonans.

Quare discat puer, quid in litteris proprium, quid commune, 12 quae cum quibus cognatio: nec miretur, cur ex 'scamno' fiat 'scabillum' aut a 'pinno,' quod est acutum, securis utrimque habens aciem 'bipennis,' ne illorum sequatur errorem, qui, quia a pennis duabus hoc esse nomen existimant, pennas avium dici volunt. neque has modo noverit mutationes, quas adferunt 13 declinatio aut praepositio, ut 'secat secuit, cadit excidit, caedit excīdit, calcat exculcat' (et fit a 'lavando' 'lautus' et inde rursus 'inlotus' et mille talia), sed et quae rectis quoque casibus aetate transierunt. nam ut 'Valesii Fusii' in 'Valerios Furios-

---

sciat etiam, i.e. if anyone objects that 'conicit' is not actually written with two *i*'s, these examples from Cicero prove the point.

'aiio Maiiamque.' So Longus, K. VII. 54 'in plerisque Cicero videtur auditu emensus scriptionem, qui et Aiiacem et Maiiam per duo i scribenda existimavit.' Prisc., K. II. 494 'aio, quod in prima quidem persona i loco consonantis habet duplicis quae et geminabatur a vetustissimis aiio.' If I understand Q. rightly he does not really agree with the gramm., who apparently mean that the first of the two *i*'s belongs to the first syllable, *ay—yo*, v. Lindsay, p. 53.

quod...consonans. If this (i.e. what has been stated in the last two clauses) is true, *i* as well as *u* will come into the syllable as a consonant.

etiam <i> iungetur. I have ventured on this small correction which seems to me to improve the text at a minimum cost.

12. quare discat. I agree with Kiderlin that a new paragraph should begin here rather than at the end of the section. We now return to what the boy should learn as distinct from the higher problems which the grammarian should study, a digression which began at § 7.

'scabillum.' Cf. Scaurus (perhaps from Verrius) K. VII. 14. He gives as an instance of 'b cum m et p consentit,' 'alii scamillum, alii scabillum dicunt.' Presumably it was argued that 'scabillum' or 'scabellum' was a diminutive of 'scamnum' (and rightly too, though of course with no idea of the Latin phonetic law that a labial + *n* becomes *mn*, as e.g. 'omnis'). Hence a certain tendency

to assimilate the former to the latter. Thus Priscian, K. II. 111, accepts 'scamellum.' Champions of 'scabillum' had no doubt to meet the objection that the change was unusual and perhaps felt back on Varro who traced both to 'scand.' (*L. L.* 5, 168).

'pinno.' So A, other MSS. 'pinna.' 'Pinnus' (pinnum ?) is vouched for by Isidore, *Cr.* XIX. 19, 11, but not recognised by the dictionaries.

pennas. Sp. reads 'pinnas,' and explained the words as meaning that those who held that 'bipennis' must come from 'penna' and that therefore 'penna' meant 'acutum' argued conversely that 'pinna' must be the right form for a bird's wing. Surely this is absurd. Trans. 'would have it that the wings of birds are meant.' This sense of 'volunt' appears several times in Q.

13. excidit. Halm adopted the correction 'cecidit,' and so Meister, but not Rad. It is perhaps *prima facie* probable that the exx. of 'declinatio' and 'praepositio' should be two each. On the whole I think this is hardly sufficient reason for departing from the MSS. I presume that Q. would use the 'apex' with the second 'excidit.'

'lautus.' So later edd., for 'lotus' of MSS. The change was approved though not adopted by Halm and Sp. as better explaining 'inde rursus.'

mille talia. So Halm and Meister with A. Rad. 'alia' as other MSS.

sed et quae. So Meister and Rad. with B. Halm 'sed quae' with A.

rectis casibus = 'primis positionibus,' cf. 5, 6 and elsewhere.

Valesii etc. These well-known in-

que' venerunt, ita 'arbos, labos, vapos' etiam et 'clamos' ac
14 'lases' et 'asa' fuerunt: atque haec ipsa s littera ab his nominibus
exclusa in quibusdam ipsa alteri successit: nam mertare'
atque 'pultare' dicebant, quin 'fordeum faedosque' pro aspiratione f ut simili littera utentes: nam contra Graeci adspirare
f ut φ solent, ut pro Fundanio Cicero testem, qui primam eius
15 litteram dicere non possit, inridet. sed b quoque in locum
aliarum dedimus aliquando, unde 'Burrus' et 'Bruges' et
'Belena.' nec non eadem fecit ex 'duello bellum,' unde
'Duelios' quidam dicere 'Belios' ausi: quid 'stlocum stlitesque'?

stances of the law which changed intervocalic *s* to *r* within the historic period
were probably commonplaces of grammatical knowledge in Q.'s time. Note
that Varro mentioned 'Valerius,' 'Furius' and 'ara' together, Macrobius III.
2, 8. Cf. Scaurus (K. VII. 14) 'item Fu-
rios dicimus, quos antiqui Fusios, et aras
quas illi asas, et lares quos illi lases.'
ac 'lases' et 'asa' fuerunt. The MSS.
vary between 'aetatis fuerunt' (A), 'ac
lases as fuerunt' (B), 'ac lases et as
fuerunt' (Jo), 'ac lases fuerunt as' (N).
Under these circumstances I believe
the text I have adopted (suggested
by Sarpe) is right, v. quotation from
Scaurus above. The corruption 'aetatis,' which Sp. explained as = 'had their
day,' is surely impossible and was evidently induced by 'aetate' above. Halm,
Meister, Rad. all have 'ac lases fuerunt.'
14. 'mertare.' This like several other
exx. in this context is found in Paulus,
i.e. Verrius. The number is sufficiently
large to create a presumption of Q. having consulted Verrius, but hardly more.
pro aspiratione. Kiderlin, pointing
out (truly enough) that these examples
introduce a different point to that introduced by 'atque ipsa s,' would make
a stop after 'dicebant,' and insert 'pro-
nuntiabant' before 'pro.' The argument is, I think, insufficient: cp. a
similar continuance of construction with
a new point in 9, 2.
f ut simili. A certain correction due
originally to Christ for the 'vel' or 'velut
simili' of MSS.
adspirare f ut φ. Ritschl's correction
for 'adspirare φ' (A), 'adspirare ei' (B
and others). Kiderlin (who is followed by
Rad.) would omit 'ut φ' on the ground
that the Greeks could not be said to put
an aspirate into φ. But it is difficult to
account for the presence of φ in A, and

at any rate educated Latin considered
that φ was best represented by *ph*.
15. 'Burrus' et 'Bruges.' Cf. Cic. *Or.*
160 '"Burrum" semper Ennius, nusquam "Pyrrhum." "vi patefecerunt
Bruges," non "Phryges."'
'Belena.' I have retained, with all
other edd., this word against B 'balae-
na' (advocated by Lindsay, Nettleship,
and Usener), though with considerable
doubts. The facts are as follows. Paulus
(i.e. Verrius) 31 has on 'balena,' 'hanc
illi φάλαιναν dicebant antiqui consuetudine qua Πύρρον burrum, Πύξον buxum
dicebant.' This taken with other corre-
spondences in the section with Verrius is
certainly strong evidence. On the other
hand Priscian (K. II. 18) quotes this passage with 'Belena,' which he clearly regards as = Ϝελένη (a form of 'Ελένη which
he notes against II. 15, cf. Dion. Hal. *R.A.*
1, 20). One may indeed doubt whether
this digammated form of 'Helena' is
likely to have influenced literary usage,
so much as to produce 'Belena,' even if
the later confusion between *b* and *w*
can be traced back so early. On the
other hand the fact that Priscian (6th
cent.) had this reading is not negligible,
and Lindsay is not only too dogmatic
but hardly correct when he says that the
whole passage is taken from Verrius.
V. does not, to our knowledge, quote
'Bruges,' and L.'s statement ignores the
obvious connexion with *Or.* 160.
'duello'...'Duelios.' Clearly founded
on Cic. *Or.* 153, 'ausi sunt,' as Sp. says,
implying that it is a bolder step to apply the change to proper names.
quid 'stlocum stlitesque.' Sp. doubted
the acc. as compared with the nom.
'cognatio' and 'permutata.' But we
have the same alternation of cases in XII.
10, 23, where 'quid Aeschines?' 'quid
Demosthenes?' are followed by 'quid

quid t litterae cum d quaedam cognatio? quare minus mirum, 16 si <in> vetustis operibus urbis nostrae et celebribus templis legantur 'Alexanter' et 'Cassantra.' quid o atque u permutata invicem? ut 'Hecoba' et 'nutrix Culcidis' et 'Pulixena' scriberentur, ac ne in Graecis id tantum notetur, 'dederont' et 'probaveront.' sic 'Οδυσσεύς, quem 'Ολυσσέα fecerant Aeolis, ad 'Ulixem' deductus est. quid? non e quoque i loco fuit: 17 'Menerva' et 'leber' et 'magester' et 'Diove Victore,' non 'Diovi Victori'? sed mihi locum signare satis est: non enim doceo, sed admoneo docturos. inde in syllabas cura transibit, de quibus in orthographia pauca adnotabo.

Tum videbit, ad quem hoc pertinet, quot et quae partes orationis, quamquam de numero parum convenit. veteres 18

Periclea?' Or it is perhaps possible that Q. thinks of 'stlocum' as a neuter noun. The only other authority for the word in Paulus does not forbid this.

16. <in>. No MS. authority; v. note on 7, 22.

permutata. So Halm and recent edd. from A, B. Sp. 'permutatae.' Halm quotes § 8 '*u* et *i* litterae.'

'**nutrix Culcidis.**' A quotation presumably from Ennius or another tragedian. That Medea's nurse should be thus spoken of is probable enough. A, B have 'nutrix Culcides.' Edd. down to Rad. have mostly read 'notrix, Culcides,' for which there is some MS. authority. But the difficulty of reconciling the citation of a Latin word (even if that word is a possible one) with 'Graecis tantum nominibus,' seems to me insuperable. The solution here adopted was developed, if not originated, by Lane *Harvard Studies* (1890). There are perhaps the following objections: (1) there is a slight *prima facie* presumption in favour of two exx. of each kind, (2) why should 'Culcis' not be cited like the others by itself? Lane's comparison of 'Canopitarum exercitus' 5, 13, is not a complete answer to this. When we prove a usage by a quotation, the natural course is to indicate the source either by naming it as in 5, 13, or by giving enough of the context to make it easily recognizable. If an alternative is required I should suggest 'corotrophus.' Κουροτρόφος, while naturally Latinized as 'cur-,' might easily be found with an *o* as a side-form (cf. Varro's 'Dioscori' for the more usual 'Dioscuri'), and might have been glossed as 'nutrix' ('nymphae…ab alimonia infantum curotrophae nominantur,' Serv.

ad *Ecl.* 10, 62). But the above objections do not seem to me so serious as to make it necessary to look for any other explanation.

'Ολυσσέα. So A. Meister and Rad. have rightly rejected Halm's 'Υλυσσέα, which has no MS. authority, and spoils the sense. The Aeolic makes the change to *l*, but it is the Latin which changes *o* to *u*. Something might be said for Claussen's 'Ολιξέα.

17. fuit. Meister following Sp. 'fuit ut' but with little or no MS. authority. We have the same loose coupling of statement and example in § 20, 25 (?).

Menerva; v. Lindsay *L. L.* p. 190.

'**Diove Victore,' non 'Diovi Victori.'** There is little MS. authority for 'Victori.' I think there is much to be said for the reading given by Fierville as Pottier's, 'Deiove Victori non Deiovi.' We rather need something to shew that we are dealing with a dative.

in orthographia, i.e. in ch. 7 (§ 9 and elsewhere).

18, 19. Cp. Dion. Hal. *De Comp.* 2 ταῦτα δὲ Θεοδέκτης μὲν καὶ 'Αριστοτέλης καὶ οἱ κατ' ἐκείνους φιλοσοφήσαντες τοὺς χρόνους ἄχρι τριῶν προήγαγον, ὀνόματα καὶ ῥήματα καὶ συνδέσμους πρῶτα μέρη τῆς λέξεως ποιοῦντες. οἱ δὲ μετὰ τούτους γενόμενοι, καὶ μάλιστα οἱ τῆς Στωικῆς αἱρέσεως ἡγεμόνες ἕως τεττάρων προύβίβασαν, χωρίσαντες ἀπὸ τῶν συνδέσμων τὰ ἄρθρα. εἶθ' οἱ μεταγενέστεροι τὰ προσηγορικὰ διελόντες ἀπὸ τῶν ὀνοματικῶν πέντε ἀπεφήναντο τὰ πρῶτα μέρη. ἕτεροι δὲ καὶ τὰς ἀντονομασίας ἀποζεύξαντες ἀπὸ τῶν ὀνομάτων ἕκτον στοιχεῖον τοῦτ' ἐποίησαν. οἱ δὲ καὶ τὰ ἐπιρρήματα διεῖλον ἀπὸ τῶν ῥημάτων καὶ τὰς προθέσεις ἀπὸ τῶν συνδέσμων καὶ τὰς μετοχὰς ἀπὸ τῶν προσ-

enim, quorum fuerunt Aristoteles quoque atque Theodectes,
verba modo et nomina et convinctiones tradiderunt, videlicet quod in verbis vim sermonis, in nominibus materiam
(quia alterum est quod loquimur, alterum de quo loquimur),
in convinctionibus autem complexus eorum esse iudicaverunt:
quas coniunctiones a plerisque dici scio, sed haec videtur ex
19 συνδέσμῳ magis propria translatio. paulatim a philosophis ac
maxime Stoicis auctus est numerus, ac primum convinctionibus
articuli adiecti, post praepositiones: nominibus appellatio, deinde pronomen, deinde mixtum verbo participium, ipsis verbis adverbia. noster sermo articulos non

ηγορικῶν, οἱ δὲ καὶ ἄλλας τινὰς προσα-
γαγόντες τομὰς πολλὰ τὰ πρῶτα μόρια
τῆς λέξεως ἐποίησαν· ὑπὲρ ὧν οὐ μικρὸς ἂν
εἴη λόγος. Our passage is not as has
sometimes been said a translation of
this, but is evidently closely connected
with it. And though of course the view
that both are derived independently
from a common source is possible, it
would be, considering the knowledge of
D. H. shewn elsewhere by Q., an unnecessary multiplication of hypotheses.
Observe that the dependence only ex-
tends to the history of grammatical
development on which Q. probably had
no means of verifying D. H., and further
that he drops the question of chrono-
logical order and arranges the five later
parts according to their supposed connection with the original three. The
dependence of Q. on D. H. will be still
more marked if I am right in the interpretation of the words 'deinde mixtum
...adverbia.'
Aristoteles. This does not appear in
his texts as they stand. In *Rhet.* 3, 2, 5
we have only ὀνόματα and ῥήματα; in
Poet. 20, the genuineness of which is
doubted, σύνδεσμος, ὄνομα, ῥῆμα, ἄρθρον
(here ἄρθρον is often bracketed, apparently on account of the testimony of D. H.).
vim sermonis. This seems rather
different from the ordinary doctrine that
the verb signifies ἐνέργεια or πάθος, the
noun ὑπάρξεις τῶν πραγμάτων (Ammo-
nius quoted by Steinthal, *Sprach.* p. 591),
or Dion. Hal.'s that nouns give οὐσία,
and verbs τὸ συμβεβηκός (*De Comp.* 5).
It is nearer to the view of Theodosius
(quoted by Steinthal) ἔχει δὲ τὸ ῥῆμα
πλέον τι τοῦ ὀνόματος. τὸ μὲν γὰρ ὄνομα
σημαίνει πρᾶγμά τι μόνον, τὸ δὲ ῥῆμα καί
τι πλέον, οἷον τὸ λέγω σημαίνει καὶ αὐτὴν
τὴν ἐνέργειαν, ὅτι λέγω.

19. articuli. The plural because
Greek grammar recognised the post-
positive ὅς as well as the prepositive ὁ.
The implication that the ἄρθρα had
hitherto been regarded as σύνδεσμοι is
supported by the names; which were
probably originally synonyms. The distinction of the ἄρθρα was probably due to
the observation that they alone among
the σύνδεσμοι were inflected.
adiecti. This corresponds to D.
H.'s ἀποζεύξαντες and διεῖλον. To distinguish a new species is the same as
adding one.
pronomen. Observe that D. H. definitely assigns the separation of the
pronouns from the nouns to non-Stoic
influence. The Stoics in fact refused to
acknowledge the term, and whilst accepting the fact that pronouns were not
nouns preferred to class them with the
ἄρθρα, which they then rearranged as
ἄρθρα ὡρισμένα (pronouns) and ἄρθρα
ἀοριστώδη (articles).
ipsis verbis adverbia. Here again
Q. follows D. H. in a statement, which
can only mean that just as what were
now articles had been regarded as conjunctions etc., so adverbs had been
formerly regarded as verbs. The statement however can hardly be correct and
D. H. is probably misled by the word
ἐπιρρήματα and by later ideas on the
subject. When the function of the adverb became a matter of observation,
they were probably diagnosed as lying
between the verb and noun. Hence the
early name μεσότης, v. quotations in
Stephanus; and to some minds the connection with the verb may have seemed
so close as to justify the words of Pompeius K. v. 134 'multi adverbium tollunt
quia partem esse verbi volunt.' But in
the earlier period it is impossible to

desiderat ideoque in alias partes orationis sparguntur, sed
accedit superioribus interiectio. alii tamen ex idoneis dum- 20
taxat auctoribus octo partes secuti sunt, ut Aristarchus et
aetate nostra Palaemon, qui vocabulum sive appellationem
nomini subiecerunt tamquam speciem eius, at ii, qui aliud
nomen, aliud vocabulum faciunt, novem. nihilominus fuerunt,
qui ipsum adhuc vocabulum ab appellatione diducerent,
ut esset vocabulum corpus visu tactuque manifestum 'domus
lectus,' appellatio, cui vel alterum deesset vel utrumque 'ventus

suppose that κακῶς can have been thought
of as a verb. Rather it was an inflection
of the noun (so Ar. *Rhet.* 3, 9, 9 calls it
ὄνομα). The adverbs then were associated with nouns or verbs according to
their individual character and those that
could be associated with neither were
conjunctions. Cp. the early Greek name
πανδέκτης, which is explained (Charisius K. I. 190, 194) as referring to the
fact that they were drawn from all parts
of speech (v. note on 'tractio' § 20).

noster...desiderat. That there is no
'prepositive' article in Latin is obvious,
but why it was not held that 'qui' was
a post-positive or 'subjunctive' article
is not obvious. If I understand Priscian
(K. III. 125) aright, the idea seems to
be that 'qui' = ὅστις rather than ὅς,
because ὅς was capable of being used
'in dividendo' (ὅς μέν, ὅς δέ), and that
'qui' therefore contains something more
than the articular character of ὅς. Perhaps the truth is that the Latin doctrine
was founded on the Stoic view mentioned above, that the articles were to
be classed with the pronouns.

ideoque. Sp. boggles at this as illogical and would like to read 'ideo
quod.' The idea perhaps is that though
the Latin language has no special form
for the article, its functions have to be
performed somehow and therefore fall
on other agencies.

in alias partes sparguntur. Priscian
shews (K. III. 11) that the function of
the article may be performed by the
pronoun, (124) that the article + noun
is absorbed in the noun, (119) similarly
article + participle in the participle, (233)
article + inf. in inf. or gerund.

sed, i.e. still we reach the same
number by distinguishing the interjections from the adverbs. Expressions
like this and Diom. K. I. 301 'Latini
articulum, Graeci interiectionem non adsumunt,' suggest that this really was a

motive with the Latin grammarians for
making the distinction, though Charisius K. I. 191 repudiates such an idea.
The Greeks were of course alive to the
possibility of the distinction, and Apollonius argues against it.

20. dumtaxat, i.e. 'idonei' at any rate,
if nothing more, practically = 'certe.'
A rather rare shade of meaning; v.
Hand, who notes this passage, *Turs.* II.
p. 398.

Palaemon. As to his possible connection with Q. v. Intr. p. x. In Art.
1914 I have pointed out that the way
his opinion is here referred to, esp. in
§ 21, does not bear out Nettleship's
theory that this whole chapter is taken
from Palaemon's 'ars.'

vocabulum...speciem eius. This view
is found in Dionysius Thrax 5 ἡ γὰρ προσηγορία ὡς εἶδος τῷ ὀνόματι ὑποβέβληται.

speciem. A necessary correction for
'species' of MSS.

ut esset vocabulum...virtus. This
distinction or something like it is commonly made in Latin grammar, though
not to the extent of making the two
separate parts of speech, e.g. Diom. K.
I. 322 'haec (i.e. appellativa nomina)
in duas species dividuntur, quarum altera significat res corporales, quae videri
tangique possunt, ut homo, arbor, altera
incorporales, quae intellectu tantummodo percipiuntur, verum neque videri
neque tangi possunt, ut est deus, pietas,
iustitia, dignitas, sapientia, doctrina,
facundia.' In a similar passage in Exc.
Charisii K. I. 533, it is added that the
former are called by some 'vocabula.'
[Another classification by which 'appellationes' are 'animata' and 'vocabula'
'inanimata' is mentioned by Diom. K.
I. 320.] It is difficult however to
think that Q. can be right in classing
'cui *alterum* deesset' with the incor-
porals or in giving such exx. as 'ventus,'
'caelum.'

caelum deus virtus.' adiciebant et adseverationem, ut
'eheu,' et tractionem ut 'fasciatim': quae mihi non adpro-
21 bantur. vocabulum an appellatio dicenda sit προσηγορία
et subicienda nomini necne, quia parvi refert, liberum opinaturis
relinquo.

22   Nomina declinare et verba in primis pueri sciant: neque
enim aliter pervenire ad intellectum sequentium possunt. quod
etiam monere supervacuum erat, nisi ambitiosa festinatione
plerique a posterioribus inciperent, et dum ostentare discipulos
23 circa speciosiora malunt, conpendio morarentur. atqui si quis
et didicerit satis et (quod non minus deesse interim solet)
voluerit docere quae didicit, non erit contentus tradere in
nominibus tria genera et ea quae sunt duobus omnibusve com-
24 munia. nec statim diligentem putabo, qui promiscua, quae
ἐπίκοινα dicuntur, ostenderit, in quibus sexus uterque per
alterum apparet, aut quae feminina positione mares aut neutrali
feminas significant, qualia sunt 'Murena' et 'Glycerium.'

alterum = 'alterutrum,' as in 24, v.
exx. in Bonnell.
adseverationem; v. Art. 1916, p. 27,
where I have pointed out that 'eheu'
can hardly have been the example and
suggested as possible 'euhoe.' In Dion.
Thrax's system the 'asseverationes' are
adverbs ἀπωμοτικά, κατωμοτικά or βε-
βαιωτικά while the interjections are adverbs θαυμαστικά or σχετλιαστικά.
tractionem; v. Art. 1916, p. 18. I
have there tried to shew that the 'adverbium tractum' or παραγωγόν was an
adverb derived from a noun or verb as
opposed to the πρωτότυπον, such as
'nuper' or 'saepe.' When the conception of the adverb was grasped, there
was naturally an attempt to distinguish
between the adverbs 'quae a nominibus
aut verbis trahuntur' and those which
hitherto had been regarded as conjunctions; 'fasciatim' as a 'traction' from a
noun of the 1st declension might easily
head the list. The fact that it happens
to be a collective adverb led Sp. and
others into the fantastic notion that
'tractio,' or as it was read 'attrectatio,'
was 'a term applied to words which
denote a taking of many things together'
(v. L. and S. on 'attrectatio').
   22. Q.'s view that systematic 'declinatio' is necessary for the understanding
of the 'mother tongue' should be noted,
and also his statement that it was fre-

quently omitted. Whether the omission
was really due to the reasons he suggests, or whether there was a school,
who on reasoned grounds held it to be
unnecessary, is a point on which, so far
as I am aware, we have no knowledge.
   conpendio morarentur. Lewis and
Short quoting this passage, strangely
translate 'conpendio' 'only for a short
time.' It is hardly necessary to say that
the meaning is 'the short cut only
lengthens their journey' (L.).
   communia. Exx. commonly given
by the grammarians are 'homo,' 'sacerdos' for 'communia duobus generibus,'
'felix' for 'communia tribus.' The fact
that this in parts is 'duorum generum'
is curiously ignored.
   24. promiscua. For these (sometimes
called 'subcommunia') exx. given are
'passer' and 'aquila'; for while we say
of a priestess 'haec sacerdos,' we say
'haec aquila' of a male eagle.
   'Murena.' The fact that male names
(like Perpenna) appeared in -a had been
brought forward by the early anomalists.
The analogists had replied that though
used by men they remained feminine,
just as a woman's shoe may be worn by
a man, and yet remain a woman's shoe
(Varro *L. L.* 9, 40). Probably however Q. does not allude to these names
in general, which were too common for
notice (five such occur in the next sec-

scrutabitur ille praeceptor acer atque subtilis origines nomi- 25
num: quae ex habitu corporis 'Rufos' 'Longosque' fecerunt, ubi
erit aliud secretius 'Sullae Burri Galbae Plauti Pansae Scauri'
taliaque, et ex casu nascentium (hic Agrippa et Opiter et
Cordus et Postumus erunt), et ex iis, quae post natos eveniunt,
unde 'Vopiscus.' iam 'Cottae Scipiones Laenates Serani' sunt
ex variis causis. gentes quoque ac loca et alia multa reperias 26
inter nominum causas. in servis iam intercidit illud genus,
quod ducebatur a domino, unde 'Marcipores Publiporesque.'
quaerat etiam, sitne apud Graecos vis quaedam sexti casus et
apud nos quoque septimi. nam cum dico 'hasta percussi,' non

tion), but to names which as common
appellative nouns were feminine. Hence
the example 'Murena,' and the example
quoted by Donatus K. IV. 375, ' Fenestella,' is of the same character.
25. ille. Burman's conjecture confirmed by A. B and other MSS. 'mille.'
The suggestion of 'mi ille' is plausible,
but hardly necessary.
origines nominum. The following
passage from Plutarch *Coriolanus* 11
should be compared: ἐνίους δὲ συντυχίᾳ
γενέσεως μέχρι νῦν καλοῦσι, Πρόκλον μὲν
ἐὰν ἀποδημοῦντος πατρὸς γένηται, καὶ
Πόστουμον, ἐὰν τεθνηκότος· ᾧ δ' ἂν
διδύμῳ γενομένῳ συμβῇ περιβιῶναι, θατέ-
ρου τελευτήσαντος, Ούοπίσκον. τῶν δὲ
σωματικῶν οὐ μόνον Σύλλας, οὐδὲ Νίγρους
οὐδὲ 'Ρούφους, ἀλλὰ καὶ Καίκους καὶ Κλω-
δίους ἐπωνυμίας τίθενται.
In this section I have retained Halm's
reading but should prefer to insert 'et'
before 'ubi' and 'quae' after 'taliaque
et.' Meister as in 17 inserts 'ut' after
'secretius.'
'Rufos' etc. The meaning real or supposed of most of these names can be
found in Forcellini. I have given notes
only when I have something to add.
'Sullae.' On the possible origin of the
name v. Art. in Smith's dictionary.
Plutarch *Sulla* 2 has ἐξήνθει γὰρ τὸ ἐρύ-
θημα τραχὺ καὶ σποράδην καταμεμιγμένον
τῇ λευκότητι, πρὸς ὃ καὶ τοὔνομα λέγουσιν
αὐτῷ τῆς χρόας ἐπίθετον. If we take this
together with the passage quoted from
Plut. *Cor.*, which so closely corresponds
with Q., it seems likely that both regarded the word as indicating a tinge of
red, and this is rather confirmed than
otherwise by Charisius K. 1. 110 'qui
quod flavo et compto capillo fuit, similes Syllae sunt appellati.'
'Vopiscus.' Gronovius pointing out

that Valerius Maximus and Pliny explain
this as 'qui in utero matris geminus con-
ceptus, altero abortu eiecto, incolumis
editur,' wished to remove the name to the
list of 'nomina ex casu nascentium,' but
the περιβιῶναι in the quotation from
Plut. *Cor.* above confirms the text.
'Cottae.' De Vit's edition of Forcellini
quotes the 'vetus epigramma '
'irasci faciles Cottas, vultusque severos
fama refert, domui nomen et inde datum.'
If this is really an ancient epigram, it
suggests that the name was traced to
κότος. This derivation Sp. rejects as
impossible, but its impossibility is no
reason for supposing that Q. does not
allude to it. The reading of some MSS.,
'nam contra' for 'iam Cottae,' does not,
I think, deserve the consideration which
Sp. gives it.
26. intercidit. Cf. Pliny *N. H.* 33, 6
(quoted by Sp.) where the modern luxury
of many slaves is contrasted with the
ancient 'singuli Lucipores et Marcipores,'
and Varro *L. L.* 9, 22 'quotusquisque
iam servos habet priscis nominibus.'
casus...septimi. This doctrine of the
seventh case is mentioned by all or nearly
all the grammarians and as a rule without disapproval. Priscian K. 11. 190 is
an exception. The form it takes however
is that the true or false ablative is distinguished by the presence or absence
of 'ab,' and there is little attempt to lay
stress, as here, on difference of meaning.
We also have mentioned an eighth case,
' it clamor caelo' for 'in caelum,' v. K.
IV. 433. (Was this rather an attempt to
reduce to an absurdity the theory of the
seventh?) As to the remark on the Greek
sixth case, I have not found anything corresponding in the Greek grammarians.
Priscian indeed mentions a sixth Greek
case, but it is the θεν of οὐρανόθεν etc.

27 utor ablativi natura, nec si idem Graece dicam, dativi. sed in verbis quoque quis est adeo imperitus ut ignoret genera et qualitates et personas et numeros? litterarii paene ista sunt ludi et trivialis scientiae. iam quosdam illa turbabunt, quae declinationibus non tenentur. nam et quaedam participia [an verba] an appellationes sint dubitari potest, quia aliud alio

27. sed in verbis. From here to the end of the chapter, we have exx. of the more abstruse points that arise in connection with the verb (in which for this purpose the participle is included) prefaced, as in the case of the nouns, by a note on the commonplace lore of the subject. Thus 'sed...scientiae' correspond to § 24.

genera, 'voices,' the usual term, though 'significatio' is sometimes used. The regular Greek term is διάθεσις, and Q. himself uses 'modus' in 6, 26 and IX. 3, 7, v. next note. The 'genera' include deponent and neuter, which is distinguished from the transitive verb.

qualitates, 'moods.' Cf. 5, 41 'modos sive cui "status" eos dici seu "qualitates" placet.' All these three terms appear to be attempts to translate διάθεσις, and point to a derivation from some other Greek terminology in which διάθεσις (rather than the common ἔγκλισις) was used for 'mood,' and perhaps γένος for 'voice.' In fact there are still traces in the existing grammarians of the use of διάθεσις for 'mood' as well as 'voice.' (Steinthal p. 63). Sp. rightly notes that Charisius, while he uses the terms 'qualitas finita' and 'infinita' for the finite and infinitive verb, elsewhere admits 'qual.' as a synonym for 'modus.' But he is hardly correct when he says 'ceterum constantior usus grammaticorum est qualitates verborum appellantium, quatenus sunt inchoativa, frequentativa, cet.' Diomedes K. I. 342 uses 'qualitas' for this, more commonly called the 'forma' of the verb, but he also uses it (388) for the 'moods.' Donatus K. IV. 381 uses it to cover both 'forms' and 'moods,' and is followed by Cledonius, Pompeius and Consentius, while in Probus K. IV. 155 it covers 'genus' and 'forma.' Priscian, so far as I can see, does not use the term.

tenentur. I have retained this generally accepted reading though it has comparatively little support from the MSS. which mostly have 'teruntur.' This Rad. has retained, but what meaning he gives to it, I do not know. Claussen suggested 'feruntur' and took

the phrase to mean indeclinables like 'cedo,' and 'nam' to indicate transition. But (1) we should expect exx. of the indeclinables, (2) the instances of 'nam' transitional quoted are far less abrupt, (3) he gives no exx. of 'fero' but only of 'effero' in this sense. His point that 'declinatio' does not mean 'inflexion' is true, but it is not necessary here to take it as 'inflexion.' I understand it to refer to the *process* of 'declinatio' to which each verb as it occurred was submitted. In ordinary cases this process will locate or settle (tenere) the word. In other cases this fails and he proceeds to give a number of instances, which continue to the end of the chapter.

participia...appellationes. I have bracketed 'an verba' and translate 'whether some words are participles or nouns.' Halm etc. (with A) accept 'an verba,' i.e. 'whether some participles are verbs or nouns.' But would Q. suggest that a participle might sometimes be a verb and sometimes a noun? If it became either, it ceased to be, in the view of the grammarians, a participle, which is a distinct part of speech. B has 'part. an verbi (=verbales) appell.' The meaning will be as in my reading, but 'verbi app.' is an odd phrase.

'tectum.' I have (as Rad.) accepted this emendation of Lane (*Harvard Studies* 1890) for 'lectum' of MSS. Lane pointed out that 'lēctus,' a bed, was distinguished from 'lĕctus' the participle; and to this, which is perhaps not quite conclusive, it may be added that 'tectum' is actually one of the words cited by Priscian K. II. 125 which are sometimes participles and sometimes appellatives.

Lane's further objection that a nominative is needed might be met by supposing that Q. wishes to give a triple ambiguity between supine, participle and appellative. If 'lectum' is retained I should be inclined to read 'participia an participialia verba an appellationes' above.

loco valent, ut 'tectum' et 'sapiens.' quaedam verba appel- 28
lationibus similia, ut 'fraudator nutritor.' iam

'itur in antiquam silvam'

nonne propriae cuiusdam rationis est? nam quod initium eius
invenias? cui simile fletur. <tur> accipimus aliter, ut

'panditur interea domus omnipotentis Olympi,'

aliter, ut

'totis

usque adeo turbatur agris.'

est etiam quidam tertius modus, ut 'urbs habitatur,' unde et
'campus curritur' et 'mare navigatur.' 'pransus' quoque ac 29
'potus' diversum valet quam indicat. quid quod multa verba
non totum declinationis ordinem ferunt? quaedam etiam mutantur, ut 'fero' in praeterito, quaedam tertiae demum personae
figura dicuntur, ut 'licet piget,' quaedam simile quiddam
patiuntur vocabulis in adverbium transeuntibus? nam ut
'noctu' et 'diu,' ita 'dictu,' 'factu'; sunt enim haec quoque verba
participalia quidem, non tamen qualia 'dicto factoque.'

V

Iam cum oratio tris habeat virtutes, ut emendata, ut dilucida, 1
ut ornata sit (quia dicere apte, quod est praecipuum, plerique
ornatui subiciunt), totidem vitia, quae sunt supra dictis con-

28. '**sapiens**'...'**fraudator nutritor**.'
Cf. Diom. K. I. 322: 'sunt etiam alia
participium sonantia, ut demens, amens,
sapiens, ingens, alia verbis similia ut
contemplator, speculator, verbero, erro.'
And so other grammarians.

initium. I.e. 'prima positio'—there
is no 'eor.' Not as L. 'it has no *subject*.'

⟨**tur**⟩. I have ventured on this simple
correction, which I suggested in Art.
1916. This use of the syllable 'tur' to
indicate the 3rd pers. pass. is common
in the gramm. The accepted text (unless
the two 'ut's' are omitted as Sp. suggested) raises the question what is the
understood object of 'accipimus.' It
clearly refers to the 3rd pers. pass. in
general, but this has not been mentioned.

itur...panditur...turbatur. The reff.
are to *Aen.* 6, 179; 10, 1; *Ecl.* 1, 11.

tertius modus. This third form is
clearly that of verbs which are mainly
neuter, but are used in the passive by an
extension of the meaning; though 'urbs
habitatur' does not seem a very happy
instance. I do not think that exactly

the same point is made in the grammarians, for though Priscian (K. II. 375)
notes 'curritur spatium,' his point is
rather to distinguish between verbs
whose action can affect human beings,
and those which can not.

29. '**pransus**,' '**potus**.' So Diom.
K. I. 102: 'pransus, cenatus, potus, quae
participia esse aut significatio verborum
aut figura non patitur.'

patiuntur. Cf. on 2, 31.

'**noctu**' **et** '**diu**.' The grammarians
seem regularly to regard these as adverbs
simply (v. indices to Keil) and rather
oddly take no notice of the old use in
'qua noctu concubia' of Ennius mentioned by Macrobius. Q. may perhaps
have this usage in view.

V. The grammarian having treated and
classified the facts of language will pro-
ceed to apply his knowledge to establish
the laws of correct speech.

1. oratio. Meister ins. 'omnis,' which
does not improve the sense and is absent from B. The first reading of A is
uncertain.

tris virtutes. So in VIII. Pro. 31, what

traria: emendate loquendi regulam, quae grammatices prior
2 pars est, examinet. haec exigitur verbis aut singulis aut
pluribus. verba nunc generaliter accipi volo: nam duplex
eorum intellectus est, alter, qui omnia, per quae sermo nectitur,
significat, ut apud Horatium:
 'verbaque provisam rem non invita sequentur';
alter, in quo est una pars orationis 'lego scribo': quam vitantes
ambiguitatem quidam dicere maluerunt voces, locutiones, dic-
3 tiones. singula sunt aut nostra aut peregrina, aut simplicia aut
composita, aut propria aut translata, aut usitata aut ficta.
 Uni verbo vitium saepius quam virtus inest. licet enim
dicamus aliquod proprium, speciosum, sublime, nihil tamen
horum nisi in complexu loquendi serieque contingit: laudamus
4 enim verba rebus bene accommodata. sola est quae notari
possit velut vocalitas, quae εὐφωνία dicitur: cuius in eo
dilectus est, ut inter duo, quae idem significant ac tantundem
valent, quod melius sonet malis.
5   Prima barbarismi ac soloecismi foeditas absit. sed quia

is spoken must be 'Latina, significantia, ornata, apte collocata.' This is closely connected with the Stoic 'virtues' of speech Diog. Laert. VII. 59 viz. 'Ελλη-νισμός, συντομία, σαφήνεια, πρέπον, κατα-σκευή. Q. omits συντομία (so Cic. De Or. I, 144) and here includes πρέπον under κατασκευή.

2. **singulis aut pluribus.** This classification, which is retained in the eighth book, appears in Cic. Or. 80. It is really much the same as the common rhetorical division dating from Theophrastus (Volkmann p. 394 etc.) (1) ἐκλογὴ ὀνομάτων, (2) σχηματισμός, (3) σύνθεσις ὀνομάτων, the second and third of these mainly if not entirely belonging to 'plura verba.'

verbaque etc., A. P. 311.

3. **propria.** Observe this limited sense of the word, followed almost directly by the wider sense, for which v. note on Prooem. 31.

uni...inest. This somewhat doubtful doctrine (contrast Tennyson's 'all the charm of all the Muses often flowering in a lonely word') is reasserted in VIII. 3, 38, without any exception being made in favour of 'vocalitas.'

vitium. The other 'vitia in singulis' are discussed in VIII. 2, here only that which is opposed to 'emendata,' i.e. 'barbarismus.'

proprium, speciosum, sublime. The

words are carefully chosen and intended to contrast with each other. They perhaps correspond to the three styles, 'subtile,' 'medium' or 'floridum,' 'grande' (XII. 10, 58 and in rhet. lit. passim), intended respectively 'ad docendum, delectandum, movendum.' Thus we have VIII. 6, 48 'species ex arcessitis verbis venit, et intellectus ex propriis.' This contrast of charm with exactness frequently tends to give 'species' and 'speciosus' a suggestion of mere show.

4. **vocalitas.** So VIII. 3, 16 'vocalia.' I have not found elsewhere this version of εὐφωνία for which Q. apologises by 'velut.' Cic. Or. 80 has only 'quod optime sonat' and so Q. himself X. 1, 6 'melius sonantia.' The grammarians sometimes give 'suavitas' (cf. § 33), but also frequently adopt 'euphonia' itself.

cuius in eo dilectus est. A rather obscure phrase. The gen. may be either subjective, 'euphony exerts its powers of choice,' or objective, 'we choose euphony, but only under the specified conditions.'

5. **prima.** I am now inclined to take this not as in Art. 1914, v. note on 6, 1, but as meaning that the 'vitia' which affect the grammarian and the 'regula recte loquendi,' take precedence of those which affect the rhetorician and are treated in Book VIII.

interim excusantur haec vitia aut consuetudine aut auctoritate
aut vetustate aut denique vicinitate virtutum (nam saepe a
figuris ea separare difficile est): ne qua tam lubrica observatio
fallat, acriter se in illud tenue discrimen grammaticus intendat,
de quo nos latius ibi loquemur, ubi de figuris orationis trac-
tandum erit. interim vitium, quod fit in singulis verbis, sit 6
barbarismus. occurrat mihi forsan aliquis: quid hic promisso
tanti operis dignum? aut quis hoc nescit, alios barbarismos
scribendo fieri, alios loquendo (quia quod male scribitur, male
etiam dici necesse est, quae vitiose dixeris, non utique et
scripto peccant)? illud prius adiectione detractione inmutatione
transmutatione, hoc secundum divisione complexione adspiratione sono contineri? sed ut parva sint haec, pueri docentur 7
adhuc et grammaticos officii sui commonemus. ex quibus si
quis erit plane inpolitus et vestibulum modo artis huius ingressus, intra haec, quae profitentium commentariolis vulgata

ne qua. The older edd. had 'quem,'
but without MS. authority. Still the
phrase seems strange, unless indeed we
can take 'qua'=anywhere, for which I
can find no authority.
ibi, i.e. in IX. 3.
6. promisso, so A, B. Some MSS.
'promissor.' As Halm and his successors have retained 'promisso,' I have
followed them in deference to authority.
But my preference is for 'promissor.'
An allusion to Hor. *A. P.* 138 'quid
dignum tanto feret hic promissor hiatu?'
seems more than probable.
adspiratione, sono. Rad. has adopted
Claussen's suggestion to substitute 'spatio' for 'adspiratione' to harmonise with
§§ 18, 19. I have retained the accepted
text with hesitation, feeling that there
is much to be said for the insertion of
'spatio,' or some equivalent, but not so
much for the omission of 'adsp.'; though
this is supported by the 1st hand of A.
It is true as Cl. says that in 19 Q.
seems to speak of 'adsp.' as a species
of 'sonus,' rather than a genus by itself,
but he does so very hesitatingly. Cp.
Charisius K. I. 265 'fit inmutatio et per
sonos...sonus in pronuntiando invenitur,
similiter adspiratio ad sonum pertinet
tametsi nos h quasi litteram ponimus.
Sed hoc vitium in scripto invenitur,
cum aut choronam pro corona, aut umum
pro humo legimus.' Presumably if *h* is
a 'littera,' mal-aspiration is an 'adiectio'
or 'detractio litterae.' If it is only a

'nota' which can be omitted without
illiteracy, it is a 'vitium per sonum.'
But the doubt on this point would
naturally tend to give mal-aspiration
a place of its own in the list of 'barbarismi.' And so we find it in the
gramm., e.g. Donatus K. IV. 392 'barbarismus fit duobus modis pronuntia-
tione et scripto. His bipertitis quatuor
species supponuntur, adiectio, detractio,
inmutatio, transmutatio litterae, syllabae,
temporis, toni, adspirationis.' So too,
Servius, Pompeius, Consentius.
On the other hand the omission of
'spatio' (or perhaps 'productione, cor-
reptione') can only be regarded as an
oversight on the part of Q., if he did
omit it. It is regularly noticed by the
gramm. (e.g. 'temporis' in Donatus,
quoted above).
7. pueri docentur adhuc. We are
still dealing with juniors, and with the
grammatical school, and therefore elementary points must be mentioned. Cf.
I, 24.
intra. Cf. III. 1, 1 'intra quem modum plerique scriptores constiterunt,' v.
Hand *Turs.* III. 431. As in 2, 16 and
4, 23 Q. hints that the 'grammatici'
were often inadequately equipped for
their work.
barbarismum. Here and below in
9 B has 'barbarum...barbari,' which
Claussen would wish to adopt, with some
reason. In 10 Joann. has 'tertium est
illud barbari genus, vitium barbarismus.'

sunt, consistet, doctiores multa adicient; vel hoc primum, quod
8 barbarismum pluribus modis accipimus. unum gente, quale
sit, si quis Afrum vel Hispanum Latinae orationi nomen
inserat: ut ferrum, quo rotae vinciuntur, dici solet 'cantus,'
quamquam eo tamquam recepto utitur Persius, sicut Catullus
'ploxenum' circa Padum invenit, et in oratione Labieni (sive
illa Corneli Galli est) in Pollionem 'casamo' adsectator e
Gallia ductum est: nam 'mastrucam,' quod est Sardum, inridens
9 Cicero ex industria dixit. alterum genus barbarismi accipimus,
quod fit animi natura, ut is, a quo insolenter quid aut minaciter
10 aut crudeliter dictum sit, barbare locutus existimatur. tertium
est illud vitium barbarismi, cuius exempla vulgo sunt plurima,
sibi etiam quisque fingere potest, ut verbo, cui libebit, adiciat

8. **unum gente.** Distinguished by later grammarians from 'barbarismus' by the name of ' barbarolexis' (barbaros lexis). 'cantus,' Pers. 5, 71 ; 'ploxenum,' Cat. 97, 6. **Labieni.** Sp. can hardly be right in identifying this person with Q. Labienus the opponent of Antony, who was killed in B.C. 39. It is rather the orator and historian T. Labienus, an enemy of Augustus, who died about A.D. 12. For (1) we cannot separate the Lab. of this passage from that of IV. 1, 11 and IX. 3, 13 where the strictures of Pollio on him are mentioned, and (2) it appears from the first of these that Pollio and Labienus were opposed in the case of Urbinia's inheritance, which was tried acc. to Tac. to *Dial.* 38 'mediis Augusti temporibus,' (3) a hostile dictum of T. Lab. against Pollio is recorded, Sen. *Contr.* 4, Pr. 2. For Sp.'s view it may be said that, while Pollio's life covers the date of both Q. and T. Labienus, it is strange to find the authorship of a speech disputed between T. L. and Corn. Gallus who died c. 40 years before him. I suggest that the explanation is that both were distinguished as men who fell foul of Augustus and committed suicide in consequence, and the authorship of the speech here mentioned may have been inferred from the context. '**casamo' adsectator e Gallia ductum est.** So Meister and Rad. and Halm (except Meister 'adductum' for 'ductum'). This last follows B. The passage is wholly uncertain, but the following points may be noted. (1) The reading of the old editions 'casnar' has no MS.

authority and is an early and, though learned, improbable conjecture, founded on Varro and Festus, who mention 'casnar' as an Oscan (not Gallic) word, meaning 'senex' (not 'affectator' or 'assectator'). (2) A has 'casami affectator,' a by no means impossible reading. In this case the phrase is probably quoted (v. on 4, 16), while if we adopt the reading of B, 'adf(ads)ector' is the explanation of 'casamo.' (3) It seems to me highly probable that the true reading is 'casamo adfectato (or -e),' or possibly 'cas. adfectatum e Gallia dictum est.' Cp. 6, 40 of the 'adfectatio' of 'vetusta verba,' and Mart. Cap. 5, 512 'translatorum alienorumque verborum adfectatio.' The suggestion is by no means new, for Regius wrote 'quod vero "affectatum" fere ab omnibus legatur mihi non probatur, cum manifeste redundet et superfluum sit: omnia namque verba affectari dicuntur.' But this criticism misapprehends the meaning. Q. has adduced two foreign words used by the poets, he now gives two used by orators; one of these was an 'affectatio,' i.e. seriously intended to make a rhetorical impression, the other was merely quoted in derision. But though I can see little or no objection to this suggestion, I have thought it better to print the text as recent edd. **mastruca.** Cicero, i.e. in the *Pro Scauro* quoted by Isidore. 'Mastrucatus' also in *De Prov. Cons.* Both are given in Forc. As Sp. says 'apparet irrisio in utroque loco.'

9. **existimatur.** Meister 'existimetur,' needlessly, I think.

litteram syllabamve vel detrahat aut aliam pro alia aut eandem alio quam rectum est loco ponat. sed quidam fere in iacta- 11 tionem eruditionis sumere illa ex poetis solent et auctores, quos praelegunt, criminantur. scire autem debet puer, haec apud scriptores carminum aut venia digna aut etiam laude duci, potiusque illa docendi erunt minus vulgata. nam duos 12 in uno nomine faciebat barbarismos Tinga Placentinus, si reprehendenti Hortensio credimus, 'preculam' pro 'pergula' dicens, et inmutatione, cum c pro g uteretur, et transmutatione, cum r praeponeret antecedenti. at in eadem vitii geminatione 'Meteio Fufetteio' dicens Ennius poetico iure defenditur. sed 13 in prosa quoque est quaedam iam recepta inmutatio. nam Cicero 'Canopitarum exercitum' dicit, ipsi Canobon vocant, et 'Trasumennum' pro 'Tarsumenno' multi auctores, etiamsi est in eo transmutatio, vindicaverunt. similiter alia: nam sive est 'adsentior,' Sisenna dixit 'adsentio' multique et hunc et

12. Tinga. Mentioned by Cic. *Brut.* 172 as a celebrated wit, whose provincial pronunciation however put him at a disadvantage with the 'sapor vernaculus' of Granius. Hortensius' hit was clearly aimed at this.

in eadem vitii geminatione. Halm substituted 'eiusdem' for 'eadem' without authority. His successors have mostly refused to follow him. The case which follows must have 'duos barbarismos in uno nomine,' but these need not be of the same kind as those involved in 'precula.' Any combination of adiectio, detractio, inmutatio, transmutatio (§ 6) will satisfy the conditions.

Meteio Fufetteio. No certainty can be reached with regard to these words, and nearly every possible variation has been suggested or adopted by critics or edd. of Q. and Enn. I hope therefore I may be pardoned for printing a variant, which seems to me less unsatisfactory than the others. Of the MSS. A has 'mettioeo et furetioeo,' Bn 'etieo fufet (Bg e)ioeo.' Out of these edd. have developed, amongst others, the following:

(1) Halm: 'Mettoeo Fufettioeo.'
(2) Rad.: 'Mettioeo Fufetioeo.'
(3) Skutsch: 'Mettoeo(que) Fufe- tioeo.'
(4) L. Müller: 'Mettoi Fufetoi' (Vah- len 'Fubetoi').
(5) Meister and Bährens: 'Metteio Fufeteio.'
Of these I do not see how (1) and (2)

scan. (3) (possibly also (1) and (2)) is based on the idea that Ennius adopted the Greek genitive in 'οιο.' I am inclined to agree with L. Müller who speaks of this as 'portentosum inventum.' Nothing in any way parallel is adduced from Enn., and the gramm. could hardly have failed to notice it. L. Müller and Vahlen suppose -oi to be a dative, and compare 'populoi Romanoi.' But in this case what is the 'geminatio'? So with (5), for the form of which we may quote the variants 'Claudeius,' etc. Lindsay *L. L.* pp. 300, 320. Possibly those who adopt (4) or (5) suppose the 'geminatio' to consist in the repetition of the same 'vitium' in the two words. But this would require the change to 'eiusdem,' which Meister at any rate does not make. My own variant is based on the view that since Q. would find 'Met- tus' in Virgil and 'Mettius' in Livy, while Dion. H. has Μέτιος, he would see 'detractio' and 'adiectio' in 'Me- teio,' and a double 'adiectio' in 'Fufet- teio.' But it is no doubt against this, as also against (4) and (5), that the MSS. are fairly persistent in exhibiting '-oeo' in the second word.

13. Canobon. Cf. Herodian (Lentz, vol. I. 139) Κανῶβος, ὅπερ ἔδει γράφεσθαι διὰ τοῦ π. οὐδὲν γὰρ εἰς β λῆγον ὑπὲρ δύο συλλαβὰς τῷ ῶ παραλήγεται.

etiamsi, i.e. 'transmutatio' is a greater liberty than 'inmutatio.'

Sisenna. Q. is following Varro quoted

analogian secuti, sive illud verum est, haec quoque pars
14 consensu defenditur: at ille pexus pinguisque doctor aut illic
detractionem aut hic adiectionem putabit. quid quod quaedam,
quae singula procul dubio vitiosa sunt, iuncta sine reprehen-
15 sione dicuntur? nam et 'dua' et 'tre' [pondo] diversorum
generum sunt barbarismi, at 'dua pondo' et 'tre pondo' usque
ad nostram aetatem ab omnibus dictum est, et recte dici
16 Messala confirmat. absurdum forsitan videatur dicere barbarismum, quod est unius verbi vitium, fieri per numeros aut
genera sicut soloecismum: 'scala' tamen et 'scopa' contraque
'hordea' et 'mulsa,' licet litterarum mutationem detractionem
adiectionem habeant, non alio vitiosa sunt, quam quod pluralia

by Aul. Gell. 2, 25. The story is in accordance with the character ascribed to
S. by Cicero, *Brutus* 259, of 'emenda-
tor sermonis usitati.'
adsentio. Cf. IX. 3, 7 'pleraque utroque modo efferuntur: luxuriatur, luxuriat,
fluctuatur, fluctuat, adsentior, adsentio.'
14. pexus pinguisque. As Sp. says
the ordinary meaning of 'stupid' for
'pinguis' hardly harmonises with 'pexus,'
'trim,' or 'smart.' But I doubt whether
the idea is, as he thinks, 'nimia et af-
fectata accuratio,' so much as of ostenta-
tion and self-complacency. Cf. 'in iac-
tationem eruditionis' (§ 11). Perhaps the
same idea is present in Virgil's description of the grammarians (*Catalepton* 5)
'scholasticorum natio madens pingui.'
Possibly 'smug.'
15. et 'dua.' Halm was inclined to
omit 'et' and Meister has done so.
pondo. Recent edd. seem to be right
in regarding 'pondo' as an interpolation. It is difficult to think that Q. would
regard 'pondo' as a barbarism. The
grammarians treat it as a 'monoptoton.'
On the other hand the interpolation
would be natural and the difficulty of
taking 'iuncta' as = 'iuncta aliis' instead of 'inter se' is very small. Sp.
points out that we have really the same
usage in 'verba coniungimus' (27), and
I think we may add 'iungetur ut consonans' in 4, 11.
diversorum generum. L. gives 'of
different genders'; rather 'dua' is a case
of 'inmutatio,' 'tre' of 'detractio.'
'**dua pondo,' 'tre pondo.'** I think
these should be printed as separate words.
Regarded as single words they would
be 'composita ex corruptis et integris'
and would not illustrate Q.'s point.

Messala. Obviously M. regarded
'tre pondo' as an example of 'subtrahendae s litterae quotiens ultima esset
aliaque consonante susciperetur' IX. 4,
38; v. note on 7, 23.
16. 'scala'...'scopa.' The question
whether words like these are barbarisms or solecisms is discussed at length
by Consentius, K. v. 395. His conclusion is that they are not barbarisms,
'quoniam non dici potest melius Latine
in ipso numero,' i.e. 'scala' is not a
wrong substitute for some correct singular form. Q.'s view, as shewn by
'tamen,' apparently is that they are
barbarisms. The fact that they shew
'mutatio' etc. makes them necessarily
barbarisms, but obviously the mistake
lies in the fact 'quod pluralia' etc.,
and the conclusion is 'barbarismum
posse fieri per numeros.' Older edd.,
including Sp., inserted 'non' before
'habeant,' but with what sense I do
not understand. These particular words
are noted by Varro *L. L.* 8, 7; 9, 63
and elsewhere, and frequently in the
later grammarians.
'**hordea.'** Q. was doubtless aware that
this was used by Virgil. But throughout
this section it should be observed that
he has not fully developed the later distinction between metaplasms (I. 8, 14)
and barbarisms. To him the metaplasm
is still strictly speaking a 'vitium,' though
as being 'poetico iure defensum,' it is
not one for practical purposes.
detractionem, adiectionem. Kid.,
who is followed by Meister, would omit
these words on the ground that there is
nothing but 'mutatio' in these words, but
'scala' shews 'detractio' from 'scalae,'
and if the whole declension is thought

singulariter et singularia pluraliter efferuntur: et 'gladia' qui dixerunt, genere exciderunt. sed hoc quoque notare contentus 17 sum, ne arti culpa quorundam pervicacium perplexae videar et ipse quaestionem addidisse.

Plus exigunt suptilitatis quae accidunt in dicendo vitia, quia exempla eorum tradi scripto non possunt, nisi cum in versus inciderunt, ut divisio 'Europai Asiai,' et ei contrarium vitium, quod συναίρεσιν et συναλοιφήν Graeci vocant, nos complexionem dicimus, qualis est apud P. Varronem

'tum te flagranti deiectum fulmine Phaethon.'

nam si esset prosa oratio, easdem litteras enuntiare veris 18 syllabis licebat. praeterea quae fiunt spatio, sive cum syllaba correpta producitur, ut

'Italiam fato profugus'

seu longa corripitur, ut

'unius ob noxam et furias,'

extra carmen non deprendas, sed nec in carmine vitia ducenda sunt. illa vero non nisi aure exiguntur, quae fiunt per sonos: 19 quamquam per adspirationem, sive adicitur vitiose sive detrahitur, apud nos potest quaeri, an in scripto sit vitium, si h littera est, non nota. cuius quidem ratio mutata cum temporibus est saepius. parcissime ea veteres usi etiam in vocalibus, 20

---

of (v. 'efferuntur') e.g. 'hordeis' for 'hordeo' might be treated as 'mutatio'+'adiectio.'

'**gladia.**' Varro *L. L.* 9, 81 'dicitur a multis duobus modis,...hoc gladium et hic gladius.' Q. quotes the word in the plural because 'gladium' in his construction would not distinguish between masc. and neut. I have not found the word in the later grammarians. Consentius, l.c., to illustrate this point postulates a nom. 'fontis,' which he says would imply that the nom. was fem. and therefore the use of it would be an error in gender, i.e. a solecism rather than a barbarism.

17. quoque. As Sp. notes, referring to 4, 17.

'**Europai**' '**Asiai.**' I have followed recent edd. in reading this instead of the MSS. 'Europae Asiae.' Yet it might be possible to defend this last. The grammarians regularly give as an example of diaeresis this gen. in 'ai,' but add that it stands for 'ae' (e.g. Char. K. I. 27, 9). If it were retained, we should have to

take it to mean the division of 'ae' (the gen. doing double duty) into 'ai.' If it is objected that this would involve a 'mutatio litterae' as well as a 'divisio in dicendo' the answer is given in 7, 18, where Q. lays down that the gen. in 'ae' used to be spelt indifferently 'ae' or 'ai.'

συναλοιφήν. This 'vitium' (for which the example here quoted is often given) is generally called by the later grammarians ἐπισυναλοιφή, in consequence of which Meister and Rad. have adopted the word as a correction. But the form with ἐπι- does not appear in the Greek grammarians and Q.'s statement as it stands seems to be quite accurate, v. Art. 1916, pp. 23, 24.

18. Italiam...furias. Of these exx., viz. *Aen.* I, 2 and 41, the first is given by several grammarians and both by Don. and Consent.

ducenda. So Meister and Rad. Halm 'dicenda' with better MS. authority, but perhaps less intrinsic probability.

19. V. notes on 4, 9 and 5, 9.

20. Q. has clearly in mind Cic. *Orator*

cum 'aedos ircosque' dicebant. diu deinde reservatum, ne
consonantibus adspirarent, ut in 'Graccis' et 'triumpis.' erupit
brevi tempore nimius usus, ut 'choronae chenturiones prae-
chones' adhuc quibusdam inscriptionibus maneant, qua de re
21 Catulli nobile epigramma est. inde durat ad nos usque 'vehementer' et 'comprehendere' et 'mihi': nam 'mehe' quoque
pro 'me' apud antiquos tragoediarum praecipue scriptores in
veteribus libris invenimus.

22   Adhuc difficilior observatio est per tenores (quos quidem
ab antiquis dictos tonores comperi, videlicet declinato a
Graecis verbo, qui τόνους dicunt) vel accentus, quas Graeci
προσῳδίας vocant, cum acuta et gravis alia pro alia ponuntur,
23 ut in hoc 'Cámillus,' si acuitur prima, aut gravis pro flexa, ut
'Céthegus' (et hic prima acuta; nam sic media mutatur), aut
flexa pro gravi, †ut apice circumducta sequenti, quam ex
duabus syllabis in unam cogentes et deinde flectentes dupliciter
24 peccant. sed id saepius in Graecis nominibus accidit, ut

§ 160 'quin ego ipse cum scirem ita
maiores locutos, ut nusquam nisi in vocali aspiratione uterentur, loquebar sic
ut "pulcros Cetegos triumpos, Kartagi-
nem" dicerem; aliquando...usum loquendi populo concessi, scientiam mihi
reservavi; "Orcivios" tamen et..."coro-
nas lacrimas" dicimus, quia per aurium
iudicium licet.' Possibly also Varro
quoted by Charisius K. i. 82 'Graccus et
ortus sine adspiratione dici debere Varro
ait'; so too Scaurus K. VII. p. 20.
'triumpis'...inscriptionibus. Halm
has 'in' before both nouns, the first with
fair MS. authority, the latter with none.
Meister and Rad. omit both.
epigramma. I.e. 84.
21. 'vehementer' et 'comprehendere.'
Q. definitely admits 'deprehendere' IX.
4, 59.
'me.' Abl. or at any rate not merely
accusative, in which case Q. would have
written 'pro illo "me."' Though Cic.
can write 'in "optimus"' (*Or.* 161) Q.
never prefixes a prep. governing an abl.
to a quoted noun in another case;
v. Art. 1916, p. 20.
22-24. For a fuller discussion of these
sections I must refer to Art. 1916. I am
still inclined to think that the view there
expressed, that these 'vitia in accentibus'
are Graecisms and examples of the 'oris
vitia in peregrinum sonum corrupti'
mentioned in 1, 13, is right.

23. in hoc 'Cámillus.' This I think
supports the above theory. Q. does not
write 'in Camillo' (v. on 62). He thus
indicates that the transference of the
accent was not carried throughout the
noun, but only according to Greek usage
where the ultimate was short.
Céthegus. I.e. as Greek Κέθηγος.
ut...sequenti. I see no reason to
modify seriously the views stated in Art.
1916. The facts are as follows: A has
'aut apice circ. sequ.,' B etc. 'ut c. s.'
(omitting 'apice'). That 'apice' is an
attempt to represent something unintelligible in the archetype may be regarded
as certain. 'Appi' (Sp., Halm) is quite
possible (perhaps more so than I thought
in 1916). On Greek principles it would
be accented Appî, and the doctrine that
this contraction, however common in
practice, was an error was maintained
by Varro, Pliny, Scaurus etc. (v. reff.
in Goetz, Varro *L. L.* p. 231). Birt's
'Marcipor' adopted by Meister still
seems to me quite fantastic (for reasons
for and against, v. Art.). My own
suggestion there made is as follows. Q.
is thinking of adjectives in '-eus,' and is
noting that as χρύσεος becomes χρυσοῦς,
the 'peregrina corruptio' tended to
change 'aúreus' into 'aurêus.' On these
lines I propose 'ut appositis e circumducta sequentique, quam (quas?),' i.e.
'as when adjectives have the "e" and the

'Atreus,' quem nobis iuvenibus doctissimi senes acuta prima dicere solebant, ut necessario secunda gravis esset, item 'Nerei Tereique.' haec de accentibus tradita.

Ceterum scio iam quosdam eruditos, nonnullos etiam gram- **25** maticos sic docere ac loqui, ut propter vocum quaedam discrimina verbum interim acuto sono finiant, ut in illis

'quae circum litora, circum

piscosos scopulos,'

ne, si gravem posuerint secundam, 'circus' dici videatur, non **26** 'circuitus.' itemque cum 'quale' interrogantes gravi, con-

following syllable circumflexed.' A blot in the middle of the word would leave 'ap...ise' decipherable, the rest of the corruption following easily.

24. 'Atreus.' So MSS. Halm adopted 'Atrei' to harmonise with 'Nerei,' 'Terei.' I think with Meister and Rad. that it is unnecessary, even if we adopt 'Appî' above; 'id' need not mean more than this general principle of transferring the accent according to Greek usage from the first to the last syllable, and might well be illustrated from different cases. But 'item...Tereique' looks rather, as Sp. says, like an interpolation.

doctissimi senes. I.e. older scholars refused to adopt this accentuation even in Greek words (as in § 62). This is contrasted with the more recent tendency to throw the accent on to the ultimate in pure Latin, described in the next sections.

haec...tradita. If these words are to stand, they must mean that the rule *implied* in the last three sections, that the Latin accent cannot fall on the ultimate, is traditional, though it may not be fully accepted by the moderns. But as this rule has not been definitely stated the words are very awkward. They would come in better at the end of 31, but even there is a flaw as Claussen says they are awkward. I am inclined to think with him (*Quaest. Quint.* p. 324) that they are an insertion, something like the 'de literis' of 4, 6.

25. quae circum etc., *Aen.* 4, 254.

circum. Cf. Don. K. IV. 391 'separatae praepositiones acuuntur; coniunctae casibus aut loquellis vim suam saepe commutant et graves fiunt.' So Priscian K. III. 27, Diom. K. I. 433 and elsewhere in the grammarians.

26. 'quale.' Cf. Priscian K. II. 61 'interrogativum est, quod cum interrogatione profertur, ut "quis" "qualis" "quantus" "quot" "quotus" cum suos

servant accentus. Infinitum est interrogativorum contrarium, ut "quis" "qualis" "quantus" "quot" "quotus," cum in lectione gravi accentu pronuntiantur.' Ib. K. III. 9 'sciendum autem quod "qui," quando pro interrogativo vel infinito, id est pro "quis," ponitur, circumflectitur, quando autem pro relativo acuitur per se, in lectione vero gravatur.' There seems to be some confusion in these last two passages about the word 'infinitum' but apart from this the various doctrines may be summed up as follows. The earlier grammarians ('nonnulli grammatici') laid down that dissyllable prepositions and relatives were oxytone (monosyllables also, if naturally circumflex, became acute). The later grammarians modified this to the doctrine that before another word this oxytone accent became grave, i.e. the word as a whole was unaccented, though they still admitted that *by itself* (a condition which I suppose could only be satisfied when the word was quoted) it remained oxytone ('acuuntur per se, in lectione gravantur'). With this Q. on the main point agrees. When Charisius K. I. 111, states that in 'quando tot stragis acervos,' 'quando' is oxytone he does not really differ, as the word-group 'quando tot' would naturally be accented on the second syllable (on the whole subject v. Lindsay *L.L.* p. 167 etc.).

26. interrogantes. Besides the exx. quoted above, the following from Aul. Gell. 7, 2 well illustrates the point. In the lines of Ennius

'Hannibal audaci dum pectore de me hortatur
Ne bellum faciam, quem credidit esse meum cor
Suasorem summum et studiosum robore belli,'

Vindex put a stop at 'faciam' and thus

parantes acuto tenore concludunt, quod tamen in adverbiis
fere solis ac pronominibus vindicant, in ceteris veterem legem
27 secuntur. mihi videtur condicionem mutare, quod his locis
verba coniungimus. nam cum dico 'circum litora,' tamquam
unum enuntio dissimulata distinctione, itaque tamquam in
una voce una est acuta, quod idem accidit in illo

Troiae qui primus ab oris.

28 evenit, ut metri quoque condicio mutet accentum :

pecudes pictaeque volúcres.

nam 'volucres' media acuta legam, quia, etsi natura brevis,
tamen positione longa est, ne faciat iambum, quem non recipit
29 versus herous. separata vero haec a praecepto nostro non
recedent, aut si consuetudo vicerit, vetus lex sermonis abole-
bitur. cuius difficilior apud Graecos observatio est, quia plura
illis loquendi genera, quas διαλέκτους vocant, et quod alia
vitiosum, interim alia rectum est. apud nos vero brevissima

'quem acuto accentu legit quasi ad cor
referretur non ad Hannibalem,' i.e. he
made 'quem' an interrogative instead of
a relative. This at first sight seems the
opposite of what is stated here, but is
not really so. Acc. to both schools the
interrogative retained its natural accent,
which in the short monosyllable 'quem'
is acute. The relative according to the
older school remained acute, according
to the later lost its accent, when in
conjunction with other words.

adverbiis. The word is difficult.
Later grammarians carefully distinguished between the adverb and preposition in this matter and held that the
former retained the regular accent. Cf.
Priscian's statement that 'circum' in
'maria omnia circum' is made oxytone,
'ne si penultimam acuamus, nomen vel
adverbium putetur esse.' Other reff. in
Lindsay p. 168. It is possible no doubt
that these earlier gramm., to whom he
is referring, made the adv. 'circum' as
well as the preposition oxytone, and this
perhaps has some support from the
words 'ne circus dici videatur, non circuitus.' But even then it is difficult to
account for the omission of 'praepositionibus,' for Lat. grammar never
seems to have identified the two, though
admitting that many words might be both.
Possibly 'et praep.' has fallen out under
the influence of 'pronominibus.'

27. Troiae qui primus ab oris. Halm
and Meister accentuate 'Troiáe,' Rad.
'óris.' I think the point is that 'qui'

loses its accent in connection with 'primus,' and 'ab' with 'oris.' Cf. Priscian
K. III. 467, 468, where the whole line is
subjected to an elaborate analysis; the
latter of these two points is definitely
mentioned and the former implied, for
the fact that 'qui' loses its accent 'in
connexu' is noticed, though it is not
suggested that the accent of 'Troiae' is
changed.

28. pecudes etc., *Georg.* 3, 243; *Aen.*
4, 525.

volucres. Later grammarians do not
seem to have accepted this, v. Sergius
K. IV. 483 'in trisyllabis antepaenultima
accipit accentum, etiam si paenultima
sit longa positione ex muta et liquida
ut latebrae, colubri.' So Donatus ib. 371
and Servius on *Aen.* 1, 384, on which
v. Lindsay *L. L.* p. 130. The whole
sentence as Sp. says is really a paren-
thetic illustration of the effect position
may have on accent, and rather awk-
wardly interrupts the argument.

29. separata...abolebitur. Q. does
not definitely admit that words like
'circum' or 'quale' (rel.) became oxytone
in themselves, as we have seen the later
grammarians did, though the occasion
would seldom arise. But he contemplates
the possibility that usage (not 'the usage
in question' as L.) may overrule 'lex'
in this as so many other cases.

alia...alia. This has distinctly better
authority than 'alias...alias' and I follow
Halm against Meister and Rad. in accepting it. We might expect 'in,' but I

ratio. namque in omni voce acuta intra numerum trium syl- 30
labarum continetur, sive eae sunt in verbo solae sive ultimae,
et in iis aut proxima extremae aut ab ea tertia. trium porro,
de quibus loquor, media longa aut acuta aut flexa erit, eodem
loco brevis utique gravem habebit sonum, ideoque positam
ante se, id est ab ultima tertiam, acuet. est autem in omni 31
voce utique acuta, sed numquam plus una nec umquam ultima,
ideoque in disyllabis prior. praeterea numquam in eadem
flexa et acuta, quoniam est in flexa et acuta: itaque neutra
cludet vocem Latinam. ea vero, quae sunt syllabae unius,
erunt acuta aut flexa, ne sit aliqua vox sine acuta. et illa per 32
sonos accidunt, quae demonstrari scripto non possunt, vitia
oris et linguae: ἰωτακισμούς et λαβδακισμούς et ἰσχνότητας
et πλατειασμούς feliciores fingendis nominibus Graeci vocant,

take this as another example of Q.'s
tendency to omit it; v. on 7, 22.
interim. Bonnell says 'latet significatio tamen,' but this is unnecessary,
at any rate if we read 'alia.' I doubt
whether this sense can be given to the
word at all in Q. except in connection
with 'cum.'
31. quoniam...acuta. I have retained Halm's reading. A omits the clause
and so Meister and Rad. B has 'qui in
eadem flexa et acuta.' While some correction of this such as Halm's is required,
I think the clause in some form is almost
necessary, to explain the apparent contradiction in the words before.
cludet. This word like 'ultima'
does not apply to monosyllables.
32. ἰωτακισμούς. The grammarians
speak somewhat differently about this.
According to Diom. (K. 1. 453) it is
found 'cum i littera super iustum de-
corem in dictionibus extenditur' and so
perhaps Consentius (v. 394), who makes
it consist in sounding the i 'pinguius' as
the Gauls, or 'exilius' as the Greeks.
On the other hand Servius (IV. 445) and
Pompeius (V. 286) seem to say that when
i is followed by another vowel in the middle of a word as in 'Titius,' a 'sibilus'
is introduced and that the absence of
this constitutes 'iotacismus.' Mart. Cap.
explains it as a string of words beginning with i, which is surely absurd, and
Isidore of a doubled i as 'Troiia,' which
is hardly less impossible, for the fault
would then be reproducible in writing.
'Labdacismus' is also rather vague.
Diom. (ib.) 'si lucem prima syllaba vel

almam nimium plene pronunciemus.'
Servius 'si aut unum tenuius dicis ut
Lucius, aut geminum pinguius ut Metel-
lus.' Mart. Cap. and Is. treat it as
'iotacismus.' These doubtful and conflicting theories seem to me to make it
probable that the terms were traditional,
passed over from the Greek grammarians,
but had no real meaning to the later
Latin grammarians and possibly none to
the earlier. As the grammarians regularly
couple 'mytacismus' (often 'myotacis-
mus') with these two, and A and some
other MSS. have 'miot'—for 'iot'—
Claussen proposed the insertion of 'et
μυτακισμούς' here, and Meister and Rad.
have followed him. The insertion seems
to me unnecessary for (1) we need not expect a full list of the 'vitia,' (2) the reading of A is a natural corruption, (3) Q.
is here referring to Greek grammarians,
and as the term is applied by Latin
grammarians to a mispronunciation of
the final *m* elided before a vowel, a
phenomenon which has no place in
Greek, it seems more likely that the
term was invented by the Latin grammarians, (4) Servius points out that ' my-
tacism' concerned as it is with two words
is hardly a barbarism. (Cp. Gregory
the Great, quoted by Norden *A. K. P.*
531, 'non mytacismi collisionem fugio,
non barbarismi confusionem devito.')
ἰσχνότητας—not apparently found
elsewhere as applied to particular sounds.
πλατειασμούς. Cp. πλατειάσδοισαι of
Theocr. 15, 88, but it would be rash to
conclude that Q. means exactly the
same. Ernesti gives 'pinguitudo' as an

33 sicut κοιλοστομίαν, cum vox quasi in recessu oris auditur. sunt etiam proprii quidam et inenarrabiles soni, quibus nonnumquam nationes deprehendimus. remotis igitur omnibus, de quibus supra diximus, vitiis erit illa quae vocatur ὀρθοέπεια, id est emendata cum suavitate vocum explanatio: nam sic accipi potest recta.

34 Cetera vitia omnia ex pluribus vocibus sunt, quorum est soloecismus. quamquam circa hoc quoque disputatum est; nam etiam qui conplexu orationis accidere eum confitentur, quia tamen unius emendatione verbi corrigi possit, in verbo

35 esse vitium, non in sermone contendunt, cum, sive 'amarae corticis' seu 'medio cortice' per genus facit soloecismum (quorum neutrum quidem reprehendo, cum sit utriusque Vergilius auctor, sed fingamus utrumlibet non recte dictum), mutatio vocis alterius, in qua vitium erat, rectam loquendi rationem sit reddita, ut 'amari corticis' fiat vel 'media

equivalent, and 'exilitas' is the natural Latin equivalent for ἰσχνότης, but obs. that Q. does not think that there are any exact equivalents, v. below on 11, 4. **κοιλοστομίαν**—not apparently found elsewhere.

33. deprehendimus. MSS. 'reprehendimus.' I have accepted this correction of Burman with Meister (but not Halm or Rad.). We have 'deprehendo' with the same shade of meaning (but not the same construction) in 5, 56, and with virtually the same construction in 6, 5, v. other exx. in Bonnell. 'Quibus reprehendimus' is perhaps not altogether impossible, if we suppose Q. to have omitted 'in' after his manner, but it is awkward and gives an inferior sense.

ὀρθοέπεια. We may perhaps trace two meanings of this word—one when it denotes the correct use of individual words as opposed to 'verba coniuncta.' In this case it is opposed to ὀρθορρημοσύνη, cf. Themistius Or. 23, p. 289 D Πρωταγόρας ὀρθοέπειάν τε καὶ ὀρθορρημοσύνην μισθοῦ ἐκδιδάσκων, and is the negation of 'barbarismus' in general. In the other sense it is opposed to ὀρθογραφία (so frequently in Longus), and is the negation of the 'vitia in decendo' described in 17-33. The latter of these two meanings appears in this passage and the former in 6, 20.

explanatio. Sp. says this = 'accuratio.' But it is perhaps little more than 'utterance' (the stress being laid on 'emendata' and 'suavitas'), and is chosen

as carrying with it some idea of clearness and distinctness. Cf. XI. 3, 33 'dilucida vero erit pronuntiatio primum, si verba tota exierint, quorum pars devorari, pars destitui solet, plerisque extremas syllabas non perferentibus, dum priorum sono indulgent; ut est autem necessaria verborum explanatio, ita omnes imputare et velut adnumerare litteras molestum et odiosum.'

recta. The proposed addition 'locutio' based on 6, 20 seems to me quite unnecessary. Q. means that ὀρθο- (recta) may be legitimately regarded as embracing 'suavitas' as well as 'emendata.'

34–55. The treatment of solecisms in these sections runs much on the same lines as that in Diomedes, Donatus and other grammarians who frequently give examples identical with or very similar to those here. The parallel passages can be easily found from Keil's indices, s.v. 'soloecismus,' in the several volumes. I have only quoted them where there appears some difference, or something specially noteworthy.

34. nam etiam...contendunt. This objection does not seem to have been regarded by the grammarians as worthy of consideration, though they regularly deal with that propounded in 36, 37.

35. 'amarae corticis.' The grammarians vacillate between regarding this as a solecism and holding 'cortex' to be a noun of doubtful gender.

utriusque, i.e. Ecl. 6, 62; Georg. 2, 74.

cortice.' quod manifestae calumniae est: neutrum enim vitiosum est separatum, sed conpositione peccatur, quae iam sermonis est. illud eruditius quaeritur, an in singulis quoque verbis **36** possit fieri soloecismus, ut si unum quis ad se vocans dicat 'venite,' aut si pluris a se dimittens ita loquatur 'abi' aut 'discede.' nec non cum responsum ab interrogante dissentit, ut si dicenti 'quem video?' ita occurras 'ego.' in gestu etiam nonnulli putant idem vitium inesse, cum aliud voce, aliud nutu vel manu demonstratur; huic opinioni neque omnino accedo **37** neque plane dissentio. nam id fateor accidere voce una, non tamen aliter quam si sit aliquid, quod vim alterius vocis optineat, ad quod vox illa referatur: ut soloecismus ex complexu fiat eorum, quibus res significantur et voluntas ostenditur. atque **38** ut omnem effugiam cavillationem, sit aliquando in uno verbo, numquam in solo verbo. per quot autem et quas accidat species, non satis convenit. qui plenissime, quadripertitam volunt esse rationem nec aliam quam barbarismi, ut fiat adiectione 'nam enim, de susum, in Alexandriam,' detractione **39** 'ambulo viam, Aegypto venio, ne hoc fecit,' transmutatione, qua ordo turbatur, 'quoque ego, enim hoc voluit, autem non habuit': ex quo genere an sit 'igitur' initio sermonis positum dubitari potest, quia maximos auctores in diversa fuisse opinione video, cum apud alios sit etiam frequens, apud alios numquam reperiatur. haec tria genera quidam diducunt a **40** soloecismo, et adiectionis vitium πλεονασμόν, detractionis ἔλλει-

---

36. So Sext. Emp. (*adv. Gramm.* 261) argues that οὗτος speaking of a woman is neither a barbarism nor a solecism.

gestu...manu. Sp. aptly cites from Philostratus the story of an actor who stretched his hand to the ground when saying ὦ Ζεῦ and upwards when he said ὦ γᾶ, whereupon Polemon said σολοικίζει τῇ χειρί.

37. huic opinioni. This does not refer merely to the last sentence but to the whole suggestion that solecism can lie 'in singulis verbis.'

38. de susum. By a strange error the old edd. read here (in spite of the MSS.) 'de Susis.' Törnebladh seems first to have restored the true reading quoting Don. K. IV. 387 'praepositio non applicabitur adverbiis, quamvis legerimus...de sursum.'

in Alexandriam...Aegypto. As Pompeius K. V. 291 puts it 'si iungas praepositiones nominibus civitatum vel detrahas provinciis.'

ne hoc fecit. Though earlier edd. doubted it on the grounds that 'ne' = 'ne ...quidem' is supposed to be found in good authors and even made the impossible suggestion that the 'detractio' was 'an,' there can be no doubt that it is 'quidem,' v. Hand *Turs.* IV. p. 70.

'**igitur.**' Q. himself apparently uses 'igitur' at the beginning of a sentence 16 times to 139 in the 2nd or 3rd place (Lease *Class. Rev.* 1899). Merguet's Dict. gives 21 exx. in Cic. against many hundreds of the other.

40. diducunt. So Halm, Meister, Rad.—'deducunt' A, 'dicunt' B. Some MSS. 'dividunt,' which Fierville adopts.

ψιν, inversionis ἀναστροφήν vocant: quae si in speciem soloecismi cadat, ὑπερβατόν quoque eodem appellari modo posse.
41 inmutatio sine controversia est, cum aliud pro alio ponitur.
id per omnes orationis partis deprendimus, frequentissime in
verbo, quia plurima huic accidunt, ideoque in eo fiunt soloecismi per genera, tempora, personas, modos, sive cui 'status'
eos dici seu 'qualitates' placet, vel sex vel ut alii volunt octo
(nam totidem vitiorum erunt formae, in quot species eorum
42 quidque, de quibus supra dictum est, diviseris): praeterea
numeros, in quibus nos singularem ac pluralem habemus,
Graeci et δυϊκόν. quamquam fuerunt qui nobis quoque adice-
rent dualem 'scripsere legere': quod evitandae asperitatis
gratia mollitum est, ut apud veteres pro 'male mereris' 'male
merere,' ideoque quod vocant duale in illo solo genere consistit, cum apud Graecos et verbi tota fere ratione et in
nominibus deprendatur, et sic quoque rarissimus sit eius usus,

ἀναστροφήν...ὑπερβατόν. Cf. VIII. 6,
65 'verum id (i.e. hyperbaton) cum in
duobus verbis fit anastrophe dicitur,
reversio quaedam, qualia sunt vulgo
"mecum secum," apud oratores et his-
toricos "quibus de rebus." At cum
decoris gratia traicitur longius verbum,
proprie hyperbati tenet nomen: "ani-
madverti, iudices, omnem accusatoris
orationem in duas divisam esse partes."
Nam "in duas partes divisam esse"
rectum erat, sed durum et incomptum.'
cadat. So B and recent edd. 'Cadunt' A. 'Cadant' Sp. But both sing.
and subj. are necessary to the sense.
41. accidunt. So grammarians dealing with solecism regularly distinguish
between those concerned with 'partes
orationis' and those concerned with 'accidentia partibus orationis.' It may be
noted that the 'accidentia' are not the
different inflexions, but the categories
or forms of thought which were differ-
entiated by inflexion. The conjugations
or declensions are not 'accidentia,' at
least in the ordinary usage of the grammarians, though in 60 Q. uses 'accidebat' in this sense. Though we have
retained these categories in modern usage,
we have not so far as I know any general
name to cover them. The corresponding
term in Dion. Thrax is παρεπόμενα
(e.g. 12 Uhlig p. 24), but his scholiasts
give as a synonym συμβεβηκότα, which
is more likely to have given rise to
'accidentia.'

genera, 'voices,' as in 4, 27. L.
wrongly translates 'genders.'
'status'...'qualitates'; v. note on 4, 27.
sex...octo. The moods regularly acknowledged are 5, viz. ind., imp., subj.,
opt., inf. But many gramm. added
'impersonal,' e.g. Donatus, K. IV. 359,
381, and so Cledonius, and this is more
or less sanctioned by Priscian and Macrobius. The number 8 can be obtained
by adding 'promissive' (i.e. fut. ind.) and
'modus gerendi.' These are adopted
by Probus, Servius and Pompeius. (The
participle is of course excluded as a
separate part of speech.) Further suggested additions were 'hortandi' (as 'legat'), 'percontative' (as 'legisne'), 'concessive' (as 'legerim'). But these appear
very fitfully and are hardly likely to be
included in Q.'s eight.
42. quamquam...legere. This fantastic theory reappears to some extent
in later gramm., e.g. Don. K. IV. 384
'numeri verbis accidunt duo singularis et
pluralis, item secundum quosdam dualis
ut legere.' Other gramm. note it only to
condemn it. Macrobius besides 'con-
ticuere omnes' quotes 'una omnes fecere
pedem.' Many grammarians rightly note
'ambo' and 'duo' as genuine duals.
pro 'male mereris.' Note the omis-
sion of the article, cf. 'ex "cape si vis"' 66.
et sic...usus. Sp. was reasonably
puzzled as to the point of this, but his
suggestion of 'etsi sic' does not improve
matters. I take this to be an example

apud nostrorum vero neminem haec observatio reperiatur, quin **43**
e contrario
    'devenere locos'
    et 'conticuere omnes'
    et 'consedere duces'
aperte nos doceant nihil horum ad duos pertinere, 'dixere'
quoque, quamquam id Antonius Rufus ex diverso ponit
exemplum, de pluribus patronis praeco pronuntiet. quid? non **44**
Livius circa initia statim primi libri 'tenuere,' inquit, 'arcem
Sabini' et mox 'in adversum Romani subiere'? sed quem
potius ego quam M. Tullium sequar? qui in Oratore 'non
reprendo,' inquit, 'scripsere: scripserunt esse verius sentio.'
similiter in vocabulis et nominibus fit soloecismus genere, **45**
numero, proprie autem casibus, quidquid horum alteri suc-
cedet. huic parti subiungantur licet per comparationes et
superlationes, itemque in quibus patrium pro possessivo dicitur

of Q.'s tendency (v. on 9, 2) to continue a construction into what is really
a new context. Down to 'deprendatur' we have the argument that the
restriction of the so-called dual to one
tense in contrast to the Greek non-
restriction tends to shew that it is not
really a dual; 'et sic...pronuntiet' gives
a different statement, i.e. while in spite
of its wide distribution the Greek dual
is very rare, the Latin is really non-
existent as the quoted examples shew.
    43. devenere etc. *Aen.* 1, 365; 2, 1;
Ov. *Met.* 13, 1.
    quamquam id. So Halm and Rad.
with B. Meister 'quod' with A.
    Antonius Rufus. The only other
grammatical statement ascribed to this
person, viz. that he wished to spell 'locutio' with a *q*, because of its connexion with 'loqui,' suggests a penchant
for fantastic ideas. For other particulars about him v. Pauly-Wissowa.
    44. circa initia, i.e. ch. 12.
    qui in Oratore (§ 157). The point
of the quotation of course lies not
in Cic.'s modified approval of 'scripsere' (Q. himself uses these forms 5
times, 2 of them being 8, 12 and 10, 15,
v. Bonnell p. xxvii.), but in the fact
that Cic. here identifies 'scripsere' with
the undoubted plural 'scripserunt.'
    45. similiter. B and other MSS.
'similiter ne,' which Halm thinks may
have been a corruption of '-que.'
    genere. Here of course 'gender,'
but Q. seems to treat it as homogeneous

with 'genus' in verbs. It is *a priori*
possible that ancient grammarians did
see a close analogy between the male in
nouns and the active in verbs, and similarly between fem. and pass. But I have
not seen any positive evidence of it.
    vocabulis et nominibus. Cf. 4, 20, 21.
    proprie, i.e. which they do not share
with the verbs. L. wrongly 'more especially.'
    quidquid...succedet. The punctua-
tion of Sp., by which a full stop is placed
after 'casibus,' and these words made part
of the next sentence, is quite impossible.
    huic parti, i.e. 'soloecismis' in voc. et
nom.
    per comparationes et superlationes.
Thus in IX. 3, 19 amongst the schemata,
which are only licensed solecisms, we
have 'utimur vulgo et comparativis pro
absolutis, ut cum se quis infirmiorem
esse dicet.' Charisius K. 1. 267 suggests 'magis doctior' as an example of
sol. per comp., Don. K. IV. 394 and
others 'sancta dearum' as pos. for sup.
As 'per' throughout this section denotes the sphere within which the solecism takes place (e.g. 'per casus' implies the substitution of one case for
another), the phrase 'per compar. et sup.'
is not really suitable. I should suggest
that 'et sup.' is an interpolation. 'Comparationes' will then mean 'degrees of
comparison,' as in Donatus l. c., who
speaks of 'sancta dearum' as a 'soloecismus per comparationem.'
    patrium...contra. For 'patria' = 'pa-

46 vel contra. nam vitium quod fit per quantitatem, ut 'magnum peculiolum,' erunt qui soloecismum putent, quia pro nomine integro positum sit deminutum: ego dubito an id inproprium potius appellem; significatione enim deerrat: soloecismi porro
47 vitium non est in sensu, sed in conplexu. in participio per genus et casum ut in vocabulo, per tempora ut in verbo, per numerum ut in utroque peccatur. pronomen quoque genus, numerum, casus habet, quae omnia recipiunt huius modi
48 errorem. fiunt soloecismi et quidem plurimi per partis orationis: sed id tradere satis non est, ne ita demum vitium esse credat puer, si pro alia ponatur alia, ut verbum, ubi nomen esse
49 debuerit, vel adverbium, ubi pronomen ac similia. nam sunt quaedam cognata, ut dicunt, id est eiusdem generis, in quibus qui alia specie quam oportet utetur, non minus quam ipso
50 genere permutato deliquerit. nam et 'an' et 'aut' coniunctiones sunt, male tamen interroges 'hic aut ille sit.' et 'ne' ac 'non' adverbia: qui tamen dicat pro illo 'ne feceris' 'non feceris,' in idem incidat vitium, quia alterum negandi est, alterum vetandi. hoc amplius 'intro' et 'intus' loci adverbia, 'eo' tamen 'intus'
51 et 'intro sum' soloecismi sunt. eadem in diversitate pronominum, interiectionum, praepositionum accident. est enim soloecismus in oratione conprensionis unius sequentium ac
52 priorum inter se inconveniens positio. quaedam tamen et

tronymica' cf. Serg. K. IV. 539 'quae a Graecis patronymica a nobis patria dicuntur.' The grammarians (e.g. Diom. K. I. 324, Consentius V. 341) note that a possessive may be put for a patronymic as 'Agamemnonius Orestes,' but not the converse.

47. in participio...peccatur. What has become of the voice in participles? Andresen proposed to insert 'genus et' between 'per' and 'tempora.' But on the analogy of 45 we should rather expect 'per casum ut in voc....per genus et numerum ut in utroque.' It is perhaps better to retain the text and regard it as a slip.

48–50. Here having dealt with solecisms 'per accidentia part. or.' Q. passes on to 'per part. or.' These are subdivided into cases, (1) where one part is substituted for another, (2) where some 'species' of the part is wrongly substituted for another, though that 'species' is not to be classed with the regular 'accidentia.' This arrange-

ment is not very logical. The distinction between the 'species' and 'accidentia' is only one of convention; and solecisms 'per speciem part. or.' should really be classed with solecisms 'per acc. part. or.' rather than with solecisms 'per part. or.' But it is reproduced by Don. and later grammarians.

48. si pro alia...similia. Exx. suggested by the grammarians are adj. ('torvum') used as adv., conj. as adv. ('etiam' for 'etiam nunc'). In IX. 3, 9 Q. himself suggests 'vivere' for 'vita' as verb for noun, 'ferre' in 'magnum dat ferre talentum' as verb for part., 'volo datum' as part. for verb.

50. Donatus K. IV. 393 gives the same example of 'intro,' 'intus,' and also 'foris exeo' for 'foras,' 'apud amicum eo,' and 'in te tantum licuit' for 'de te.'

51. est enim...positio, 'for a solecism is a collocation involving disagreement between what precedes and what follows within the limits of a single clause.' So with A, reading 'enim' for

faciem soloecismi habent et dici vitiosa non possunt, ut 'tragoedia Thyestes,' ut 'ludi Floralia' ac 'Megalensia': quamquam haec sequenti tempore interciderunt numquam aliter a veteribus dicta. schemata igitur nominabuntur, frequentiora quidem apud poetas, sed oratoribus quoque permissa. verum schema 53 fere habebit aliquam rationem, ut docebimus eo, quem paulo ante promisimus, loco, sed id quoque quod 'schema' vocatur, si ab aliquo per inprudentiam factum erit, soloecismi vitio non carebit. in eadem specie .sunt, sed schemate carent, ut supra 54

the 'etiam' of other MSS. Sp. (who however only knew it as a conjecture of Regius) objected to 'enim' on the ground that a definition of a solecism at this point was out of place. It seems to me to follow quite suitably on the statement that solecisms may be found even in interjections and prepositions. Sp.'s other objection is that there is no parallel for this use of 'positio.' This may be so, but the usage is so natural that its rarity can hardly be set against the fact that it is impossible to give any satisfactory meaning to 'etiam.' Further the definition of sol. quoted in Aul. Gell. 5, 20 (from Capito) 'soloecismus est impar et inconveniens compositura partium orationis,' is sufficiently like this to suggest that we have here a definition, rather than a new species. Halm and Meister have accepted the reading of A, and I should have regarded the point as settled, but that Rad. has returned to 'etiam.' So too L. who gives as his note 'the meaning of this passage is uncertain, but the solecism in question is probably an anacoluthon.'

52. '**tragoedia Thyestes.**' So Don. K. IV. 375 notes 'Eunuchus comoedia,' 'Orestes tragoedia' and couples them with Fenestella, Glycerium etc. So too Sext. Emp. *adv. Gramm.* 261 gives Ὀρέστης καλὴ τραγῳδία, as an example of the apparent but not real solecism.

haec...interciderunt. Sp., who points out that Tac. and others use such forms as 'ludi megalenses,' asks pertinently what was the later form for 'trag. Thyestes.' It might be possible to regard 'haec' as only referring to the last two. This would become clearer if we read with the first hand of B 'haec sequentia.' But I have not found any instance of 'sequens' with so complete a suppression of the 'prior,' though some exx. in Bonnell perhaps approach it.

schemata...poetas; see 8, 14.

53. verum schema. I feel consider-

able doubt whether 'verum' is an adjective, or, as would probably be thought at first sight, a conjunction. 'Verus' in the sense of 'real' or 'genuine' is exceedingly common in Q., e.g. 'verus profectus,' 1, 28, and to take it so will add force to the antithesis with 'quod vocatur.'

rationem; v. IX. 3, 3 'verum auctoritate, vetustate, consuetudine (schema) defenditur, saepe etiam ratione quadam.' The 'ratio' seems to be then further defined in the words: 'virtus est si habet probabile aliquid quod sequatur: una tamen in re maxime utilis, ut et cotidiani ac semper eodem modo formati sermonis fastidium levet et nos a vulgari dicendi genere defendat.'

paulo ante, i.e. § 5.

sed id...carebit. So IX. 3, 3 'esset omne eiusmodi schema vitium si non peteretur, vel accideret.' Sp. quotes Sen. *Ep.* 95 'grammaticus non erubescet soloecismum si sciens facit, erubescet si nesciens.'

id. So A followed by Halm and Meister instead of the 'hoc' of old edd. MSS. mostly 'hic' which Rad. has printed, presumably as a contrast to 'eo loco,' i.e. 'I leave the other point to Book IX. but will note this here as well.' This seems to me impossible as the rest of the sentence stands, though if we could read 'carere,' and presumably also 'vocetur, 'factum sit,' it would make excellent sense.

54. schemate carent. Why are these names e.g. Glycerium and Murena (4, 24), 'schemate carentia'? Perhaps because they do not come under the definition of 'schema' given in IX. 1, 13 'quod sit a simplici atque in promptu posito dicendi modo poetice vel oratorie mutatum,' but are accepted elements in ordinary speech.

ut supra dixi. This has not been said in 4, 24. Possibly we should read 'quae' for 'ut.'

dixi, nomina feminina quibus mares utuntur, et neutralia
quibus feminae. hactenus de soloecismo: neque enim artem
grammaticam componere adgressi sumus, sed cum in ordinem
incurreret, inhonoratam transire noluimus.

55 Hoc amplius, ut institutum ordinem sequar, verba aut Latina
aut peregrina sunt. peregrina porro ex omnibus prope dixerim
56 gentibus ut homines, ut instituta etiam multa venerunt. taceo
de Tuscis et Sabinis et Praenestinis quoque (nam ut eorum
sermone utentem Vettium Lucilius insectatur, quemadmodum
Pollio reprendit in Livio Patavinitatem): licet omnia Italica
57 pro Romanis habeam. plurima Gallica evaluerunt ut 'raeda'
ac 'petorritum,' quorum altero tamen Cicero, altero Horatius
utitur. et mappam' circo quoque usitatum nomen Poeni sibi
vindicant, et 'gurdos,' quos pro stolidis accipit vulgus, ex
58 Hispania duxisse originem audivi. sed haec divisio mea ad
Graecum sermonem praecipue pertinet; nam et maxima ex
parte Romanus inde conversus est, et confessis quoque Graecis
utimur verbis, ubi nostra desunt, sicut illi a nobis nonnumquam
mutuantur. inde illa quaestio exoritur, an eadem ratione per
59 casus duci externa qua nostra convenIat. ac si reperias

inhonoratam. Meister has adopted
Kid.'s suggestion of 'inhonoratum.' Not
so Rad. The considerations are very
equally balanced. If we retain the fem.
the 'ordo' is the curriculum of studies,
the 'orbis doctrinae' (10, 1) necessary
for the student, and Q. here notices
in passing the principle on which the
book is constructed. If we read the
masc., the 'ordo' is the 'ordo institu-
tus' of the next section.
    55. institutum ordinem, i.e. in
§ 3.
    56. taceo...habeam. The form of
this sentence should be noticed. Rad.
who discussed it in *Rhein. Mus.* 1905,
p. 242, rightly places 'nam...Patavini-
tatem' in parenthesis. Thus 'ut' = 'tam
quam,' 'licet' = 'may be permitted' (not
'although') cf. 'subiungantur licet' (45).
The translation of L. and W., 'For although Lucilius...I may be allowed'
involves a use of 'ut' which I have not
paralleled in Q. Rad. however fails to
notice that the parenthesis apologises for
'Praenestinis quoque' only. Q. is noting
that not only national divisions but also
towns have, according to these authorities, their peculiarities of dialect.

Praenestinis. Plautus twice notes the
peculiar dialect of Praeneste, viz. *Trin.*
609 ('tam modo' = 'modo'), *Truc.* 691
('ciconia' cut down to 'conia').
    Vettium. In spite of the 'insectatur'
we can hardly doubt that this is the
Vettius (Vectius) Philocomus mentioned
by Suet. *De Gram.* 2, as one of the
friends of Lucilius and expounder of his
satires. A similar 'insectatio' of Scipio
Africanus for his peculiar pronunciation
is quoted by Festus, v. Marx' *Lucil.* 963.
    Patavinitatem. So again VIII. 1, 3.
    'raeda'...'petorritum'...'mappam'
...'gurdos.' For these words v. dict. For
illustrations of the use of 'mappa' at the
circus v. Mayor on Juv. 11, 193. Of
his quotations the most piquant is that
from Tert. *De Spec.* 16 'mappam missam
putant, sed est diaboli ab alto praecipi-
tati figura.' Μάππα = χειρόμακτρον is
given as a barbarism by the Greek
grammarians. For the supposed bearing
of 'gurdus' on Q.'s early life v. Intr.
p. xii n.
    58. nam et maxima...conversus est.
Cf. 1, 12 and 6, 31, also Charisius K. 1.
292 'cum ab omni sermone Graeco·
Latina lingua pendere videatur.'

grammaticum veterum amatorem, neget quidquam ex Latina ratione mutandum, quia, cum sit apud nos casus ablativus, quem illi non habent, parum conveniat uno casu nostro, quinque Graecis uti. quin etiam laudet virtutem eorum, qui potentiorem 60 facere linguam Latinam studebant nec alienis egere institutis fatebantur: inde 'Castorem' media syllaba producta pronuntiarunt, quia hoc omnibus nostris nominibus accidebat, quorum prima positio in easdem quas 'Castor' litteras exit, et ut 'Palaemo' ac 'Telamo' et 'Plato' (nam sic eum Cicero quoque appellat) dicerentur retinuerunt, quia Latinum, quod o et n litteris finiretur, non reperiebant. ne in a quidem atque s litteras exire 61 temere masculina Graeca nomina recto casu patiebantur, ideoque et apud Caelium legimus 'Pelia cincinnatus' et apud Messalam 'bene fecit Euthia,' et apud Ciceronem 'Hermagora,' ne miremur, quod ab antiquorum plerisque 'Aenea' ut 'Anchisa' sit dictus. nam si ut 'Maecenas Sufenas Asprenas' 62 dicerentur, genetivo casu non e littera, sed 'tis' syllaba terminarentur. inde 'Olympo' et 'tyranno' acutam syllabam mediam

---

59. grammaticum veterum amatorem. Rad. *Rhein. Mus.* 1905, p. 243 suggests that this is a definite reference to Valerius Probus (a contemporary of Q.), v. Suetonius *De Gram.* 24, on the ground that Probus is stated (Aul. Gell. 4, 7) to have pronounced 'Hannibalem' with the last *a* long (a point really different from 'Castōrem'). This is very speculative. The 'amator veterum' if he is an individual at all is not identified with the subject of 'pronuntiarunt,' and though he is said to have sympathised with the Latinisms of the next few sections, it is not really implied that he advocated the use of them in his own times. What he is stated to have advocated is that Greek case-endings should not be used.

60. 'Castorem.' Cf. Varro *L. L.* 10, 70. In answer to the anomalist, who argued that on analogical principles, 'Hectōrem' should follow 'quaestorem,' the analogist, after noting that foreign words do not necessarily follow the analogy of Latin words, goes on to say 'multi utuntur, non modo poetae, sed etiam plerique haec omnes, qui soluta oratione loquuntur, dicebant ut quaestorem praetorem sic Hectōrem, Nestōrem: itaque Ennius ait "Hectōris natum Troiano muro iactari." Accius haec in tragoediis largius a prisca consuetudine movere coepit, et ad

formas graecas verborum magis revocare, a quo Valerius ait "Accius Hectorem nollet facere, Hectora mallet."'

61. Caelium. This is probably the well-known orator of Cicero's time, though Sp. thought it might be Caelius Antipater, v. on 6, 42. As to the meaning of 'Pelia cincinnatus,' which Sp. found unintelligible, one may perhaps hazard a conjecture, that the words were applied to some elderly opponent, who appeared with 'cincinni' and had generally a rejuvenated aspect. The fact that the attempt to rejuvenate Pelias miscarried would not be fatal to such a use of the name.

Messala. Presumably this was in one of his numerous speeches. Sp.'s suggestion that it belongs to his translation of Hyperides (v. x. 5, 2) is fairly plausible. His preference of Latin to Greek words ('funambulus' to σχοινοβάτης) is noticed by Schol. Cruq. on Hor. *Sat.* 1, 10, 28.

Hermagora. This does not appear to be in agreement with our texts.

62. 'Olympo' et 'tyranno.' Commentators seem to me to have made too much difficulty out of these words. They have not sufficiently taken account of Q.'s habit, when he is speaking of a noun as a whole, of bringing it into construction with his sentence (v. Art. 1916, p. 20), e.g. in λῃστῇ 7, 17, 'si

dederunt, [quia duabus longis sequentibus primam brevem
3 acui noster sermo non patitur.] sic genetivus 'Ulixi' et
'Achilli' fecit, sic alia plurima. nunc recentiores instituerunt
Graecis nominibus Graecas declinationes potius dare, quod
tamen ipsum non semper fieri potest. mihi autem placet
rationem Latinam sequi, quousque patitur decor. neque enim
iam 'Calypsonem' dixerim ut 'Iunonem,' quamquam secutus
antiquos C. Caesar utitur hac ratione declinandi; sed auctori-
64 tatem consuetudo superavit. in ceteris quae poterunt utroque
modo non indecenter efferri, qui Graecam figuram sequi malet,
non Latine quidem, sed citra reprehensionem loquetur.

65   Simplices voces prima positione, id est natura sua constant,
compositae aut praepositionibus subiunguntur, ut 'innocens'
(dum ne pugnantibus inter se duabus, quale est 'inperterritus':

sulphuri et gutturi subicerent in genitivo
litteram O mediam' 6, 23. What he
means then is that the Latinisers kept the
words paroxytone throughout, not merely
in the genitive and dative, as the Greeks
did. He would certainly have made
himself clearer, if he had added 'per
omnes casus.'

The way in which Q. couples 'Olýmpus'with 'Castōrem'and other archaisms
seems to indicate that in his time Greek
loan-words were accented in Greek
fashion. The grammarians however
seem generally to have held that unless
the Greek declension was maintained,
Latin accentuation should be used, e.g.
Serv. K. IV. 427, who also on *Georg.* I,
59 declares for 'Epīrus,' but 'Épiros.'
On the other hand Serg. ib. 527, says
that 'Évandrum,' 'týrannum' are not
inadmissible.

quia...patitur. I am sure that this
nonsense should be omitted and not
emended, as so many have tried to do.
No explanation is required of the reason
why many preferred 'Olýmpus' to
'Ólympus,' but this ignorant glossator,
supposing that the word in question was
'Olympo,' added an explanation con-
cocted out of the facts before him. Let
anyone ask a schoolboy who knows that
accent has some relation to quantity, but
nothing more, why it is 'Ολύμπῳ not
῎Ολυμπῳ, and he will probably get the
same answer 'because the first syllable
is short and the other two long.'

63. sic genetivus...fecit. The phrase
seems strange, for (1) though Sp. quotes
Don. ad *Andr.* 1, 2, 25 'genetivus facit

Oedipi' to which add Char. K. I. 140
'genetivus pubis facit,' here no nominative
has been mentioned, (2) why are 'Achilli,'
'Ulixi' more Latin in formation than
'Achillis,' 'Ulixis,' or 'Achillei,' 'Ulixei'?
I should like to read 'sic genetivum
Ulixeus Ulixei, Achilleus Achillei fecit,'
the corruption of which to our present
text would not be difficult.

'Calypsonem'...Caesar. Attius, Pacuvius and Liv. Andr. are quoted by the
grammarians as preferring this form.
Pliny acc. to Charisius K. I. 127 declared
for 'Calypso.' For Caesar as a grammarian v. on 7, 34.

65. simplices...constant. The difficulties raised by Sp., who wished to
omit 'id est' and take 'prima positio'
as = the nominative, are imaginary. It
seems indeed to be true that 'prima pos.'
is not used of a simple as opposed to a
compound noun, nor is it identified with
'natura.' But it is found as indicating
analogous ideas, and is not restricted as
Sp. thought to the nom. of a noun, or
the 1st pers. pres. of a verb. Thus it is
applied to the original noun as opposed
to a derivative and in fact signifies any
word or form which constitutes the
starting-point for others. Again, while
to identify it with 'natura' is perhaps
loose in thought, the two ideas are
often closely connected. Thus of original
nouns we find Pomp. K. v. 143 'primae
positionis dicuntur nomina quae a natura
sic sunt facta.'

dum ne pugnantibus. So Bn, while
A, Bg, have 'dum rep.' That the
former is required for the sense rather

alioqui possunt aliquando continuari duae, ut 'incompositus reconditus' et quo Cicero utitur 'subabsurdum'), aut e duobus quasi corporibus coalescunt, ut 'maleficus.' nam ex tribus 66 nostrae utique linguae non concesserim, quamvis 'capsis' Cicero dicat compositum esse ex 'cape si vis,' et inveniantur, qui 'Lupercalia' aeque tris partes orationis esse contendant quasi 'luere per caprum': nam 'Solitaurilia' iam persuasum 67 est esse 'Suovetaurilia,' et sane ita se habet sacrum, quale apud Homerum quoque est. sed haec non tam ex tribus quam ex particulis trium coeunt. ceterum etiam ex praepositione et duobus vocabulis dure videtur struxisse Pacuvius:

Nérei repándirostrum incúrvicervicúm pecus.

iunguntur autem aut ex duobus Latinis integris ut 'superfui 68 subterfugi,' quamquam ex integris an conposita sint quaeritur, aut integro et corrupto, ut 'malevolus,' aut ex corrupto et integro, ut 'noctivagus,' aut duobus corruptis, ut 'pedisecus,'

than the 'interdum repugnantibus' of some MSS. and earlier edd., and that 'inperterritus' in spite of its Virgilian authority is definitely condemned seems clear. The later grammarians however (e.g. K. IV. 377) do not share this view and take 'inpert.' as the stock instance of a double compound. I have discussed this change of attitude in an article in *Class. Rev.* XXXIV. p. 29.

'**subabsurdum.**' *De Or.* 2, 274, ad *Att.* 16, 3, 4.

corporibus. Q. apparently holds that a preposition is not a 'corpus' though a conjunction ('si') is.

66. quamvis. I do not understand Q. to reject the three etymologies though it is not clear that he actually accepts them. As the compounds are formed 'ex particulis' an acceptance would not affect his general principle.

'**capsis.**' *Or.* 154.

'**Lupercalia.**' This derivation is noted by Serv. on *Aen.* 8, 343.

aeque. The word seems inappropriate here, for apparently Q. intends to em-phasize the point that while 'capsis' in-volves only two parts of speech, though three words, 'lupercalia' involves verb, preposition and noun. Possibly we should read 'adusque.' The exx. in the 'The-saurus' shew that this word is far com-moner in later prose-writers than is indicated by Forc. Or possibly 'uti-que.'

'**Solitaurilia**'...'**Suovetaurilia.**' We

may trace three different views on this question : (1) some held that 'suov-' was the right form and actually wrote and spoke it. The existing texts of Livy and Tac. point to this (v. Forc.), (2) others like Valgius (ap. Char. K. I. 108) held that 'solit-' was right and derived it from 'sollus' (or 'solidus'?) and 'taurus' in the sense of a male animal, (3) others again retained 'solit-' but still derived it from 'sus, ovis, taurus.' This view appears to be given by Festus (Verrius). Q. perhaps is mentioning this last, rather than the first ; 'ove' could hardly be called a 'particula.' Possibly we should read 'sue ove-taurilia.' B has 'suev-.'

68. integrum...corruptum. The cor-responding Greek terms are τέλειον, ἀπό-λειπον, e.g. Dion. Thrax p. 30 (Uhlig).

quamquam...quaeritur. Earlier edd. took this to mean 'it is questioned whether the two "integra" are really "in-tegra"' and supposed that the doubters pointed out that one of these words necessarily lost its accent. In Art. 1916, p. 20, I suggested (rightly, I think) that the meaning is 'are such words really "composita"? Are they not rather to be regarded as pairs of "apposita"?' So Apollonius *De Const.* IV. 316 thinks it necessary to shew that τὰ ἐκ τελείων φωνῶν συντεθειμένα have σύνθεσις and not merely παράθεσις.

duobus corruptis. Halm and Meister ins. 'ex.' I follow Rad., but regard the considerations as almost evenly balanced.

aut ex nostro et peregrino, ut 'biclinium,' aut contra, ut
'epitogium' et 'Anticato,' aliquando et ex duobus peregrinis,
ut 'epiraedium'; nam cum sit praepositio Graeca, 'raeda'
Gallicum (neque Graecus tamen neque Gallus utitur conposito),

69 Romani suum ex alieno utroque fecerunt. frequenter autem
praepositiones quoque copulatio ista corrumpit: inde 'abstulit
aufugit amisit,' cum praepositio sit 'ab' sola, et.'coit,' cum sit

70 praepositio 'con.' sic 'ignavi' et 'erepublica' et similia. sed
res tota magis Graecos decet, nobis minus succedit: nec id fieri
natura puto, sed alienis favemus, ideoque cum κυρταύχενα
mirati simus, 'incurvicervicum' vix a risu defendimus.

71 Propria sunt verba, cum id significant, in quod primo
denominata sunt, translata, cum alium natura intellectum,
alium loco praebent. usitatis tutius utimur, nova non sine
quodam periculo fingimus. nam si recepta sunt, modicam
laudem adferunt orationi, repudiata etiam in iocos exeunt.

72 audendum tamen: namque, ut Cicero ait, etiam quae primo
dura visa sunt, usu molliuntur. sed minime nobis concessa est
ὀνοματοποιία. quis enim ferat, si quid simile illis merito

aut ex nostro...'epiraedium.' While
the doctrine of the four combinations of
'integra' and 'corrupta' appears in most
grammarians, this last part is, as far as
I can see, only in Consentius K. v. 350.
He has 'sunt etiam plerique, qui ex
Graeco et Latino putant posse componi,
ut epiclinium, epiradium.' Here I think
we may fairly correct epic- to bic-. Perhaps too we should insert between epi-
and -radium ⟨-togium aut ex duobus
peregrinis ut epi-⟩. On the other hand
Cons. may perhaps have regarded 'rada'
or 'reda' as a genuine Latin word.
    aliquando. This correction for the
'aliquid' of MSS. is accepted by later
edd., but 'aliqua' or 'aliquot' would do
almost as well.
    sit praepositio. Meister and Rad. in-
sert 'epi.' As the balance of MS. evidence is for omission and it is not necessary to the sense, I have followed Halm.
    69. Most of the exx. in this section
are taken from Cic. Or. § 158.
    copulatio. I agree with Fierville and
Rad. against Halm and Meist. that the
authority of A which has 'compositio'
is not to be set against that of the other
MSS., supported by the fact that Cic. Or.
§ 154, which Q. clearly has in mind, uses
the phrase 'copulando verba iungebant'
of 'capsis' and similar combinations.

'coit'...'con.' Cf. 6, 17 'et "conire"
non "coire" his permittamus' (where v.
note). The grammarians seem never to
have regarded con- or com- as a corruption of 'cum' but as a preposition in
itself (though inseparable). V. reff. given
in Keil's indices under 'praepositio in
compositis,' e.g. Prisc. K. III. 29 'sunt
quae in compositione elisionem patiuntur, ut "con" sequente vocali, coeo, co-
arguo.'
    'erepublica.' The old reading 'erepti'
is hopelessly condemned both by the
authority of the MSS. and the fact that
'erepublica' is an example in Or. 158.
    70. sed res...decet. Cf. Liv. 27, 11,
4 (quoted by Lindsay L. L. p. 359)
'quos androgynos vulgus, ut pleraque,
faciliore ad duplicanda verba Graeco
sermone, appellat.' Κυρταύχην is not
known elsewhere.
    71. propria...translata. As this sub-
ject belongs for practical purposes to
rhetoric, it is here passed over, to be
treated in VIII. 3, 24 etc.
    usitatis. These remarks are repeated
and enlarged upon in VIII. 3, 30–37,
with the same quotation from De Nat.
De. 1, 34, 95, and the same recommen-
dation of 'audendum.'
    72. ὀνοματοποιία. Further treated
VIII. 6, 31 where it appears that Q.

laudatis λίγξε βιός et σίζεν ὀφθαλμός fingere audeamus? iam ne 'balare' quidem aut 'hinnire' fortiter diceremus, nisi iudicio vetustatis niterentur.

VI

Est etiam sua loquentibus observatio, sua scribentibus. 1 sermo constat ratione, vetustate, auctoritate, consuetudine. rationem praestat praecipue analogia, nonnumquam et ety-

does not deny the existence of many words such as 'sibilus,' 'murmur,' 'mugitus' of onomatopoeic origin, but merely forbids new creations. The subject is treated briefly by many grammarians, but without this caution.

λίγξε...σίζεν. The point is not merely that these words (*Il.* 4, 125; *Od.* 9, 394) are imitative, but that they are merely coined for their particular context and thus did not become real words. So Macrobius *Exc.* K. v. 628, notes of them 'in his verbis nec ulla persona nec modus declinationis quaeritur.'

iam. Sp. wished to correct to 'nam,' and Halm and Meister adopted it. Like Rad. I see no sufficient reason for the change.

VI. 1. est etiam...scribentibus. In Art. 1914 the theory was put forward that these words belong to the last chapter, and mean that onomatopoeic words might be more tolerated in speech than in writing. This was in connection with the further view there suggested that 'sermo' in this chapter = 'sermo coniunctus' or 'regula recte loquendi in pluribus verbis' and that Q. having (1) disposed of actual errors 'in singulis verbis' i.e. barbarisms, (2) of the same 'in pluribus verbis' i.e. solecisms, (3) having dealt with 'dubia in singulis verbis' § 55—end, now turns to 'dubia in pluribus verbis.' But the difficulty of identifying the disquisition on inflection which follows with a discussion on 'plura verba' now seems to me much greater than it did then. Further, another difficulty which then puzzled me, viz. the absence of any remarks on 'plura verba' to correspond with those on 'singula verba' in § 55—end, may be met by the supposition that everything in 'plura verba' beyond solecisms belongs to rhetoric and is therefore relegated to Book VIII. 3, 40 ff.

If we abandon this theory, can we find any coherent scheme in these chapters? Possibly in this way. Q. having

concluded his remarks on 'singula verba' and 'plura verba' so far as they affect the 'grammaticus' proceeds to deal with the general principles which examination will shew to govern spoken and written language. And he opens with the remark that these principles differ in the two cases. Spoken language depends on the four factors enumerated just below. The 'regula' or 'observatio recte scribendi' depends on other vaguer considerations treated in ch. 7. It is true that some grammarians did lay down similar canons for orthography as for orthoepy (v. below), and further that Q. shews some signs of following them, v. note on 7, 1. But he at any rate adds others, and so far as he follows the four does so in a very vague way.

ratione...consuetudine. I have discussed this formula at some length both in Art. 1914 and in another article in the *Classical Quarterly*, Jan. 1919 (henceforth referred to as Art. 1919), pp. 32, 33. The chief point is to determine its relation to that ascribed by Diomedes (K. I. 439) to Varro ' Latinitas...constat...ut asserit Varro his quatuor "natura, analogia, consuetudine, auctoritate."' I am now inclined to adopt the view put forward tentatively in Art. 1919. I suggest that the original formula was philosophical and described the processes by which words became what we find them. On this view the formula ran 'natura, vetustas, analogia, consuetudo, auctoritas,' and the meaning is that the true words (ἔτυμα) are given by nature, then modified by time ('vetustas') till we get the 'prima positio' of the noun or verb, which is then inflected by analogy, and this again is modified by usage and literary authority. (I must refer to that note for evidence for this use of 'vetustas' in this connexion.) The looser form of the formula sometimes dropped 'vetustas' and thus we get it as it appears in Diomedes. When

mologia. vetera maiestas quaedam et, ut sic dixerim, religio
2 commendat. auctoritas ab oratoribus vel historicis peti solet.
nam poetas metri necessitas excusat, nisi si quando nihil
impediente in utroque modulatione pedum alterum malunt,
qualia sunt

'imo de stirpe recisum'

et 'aëriae quo congessere palumbes'

et 'silice in nuda' et similia: cum summorum in eloquentia
virorum iudicium pro ratione, et vel error honestus est magnos
3 duces sequentibus. consuetudo vero certissima loquendi magistra, utendumque plane sermone ut nummo, cui publica forma
est. omnia tamen haec exigunt acre iudicium, analogia
praecipue, quam proxime ex Graeco transferentes in Latinum
4 proportionem vocaverunt. eius haec vis est, ut id, quod

the grammarians took it over, and used
it to describe the means by which they
might determine the correct word in
each case, it naturally underwent modification. For 'natura' is substituted
'etymologia,' the name of the science
which inquires into words in themselves,
and through the corruptions of 'vetustas' discerns their 'natura' or ἔτυμα.
This rendered the retention of 'vetustas'
unnecessary. But the memory of it lingered and by some schools it was retained
as a rather unnecessary variant to 'auctoritas.' If this is right, it does not
follow that Q. himself made the mistake.
He probably found the distinction between the two in his authorities and uses
it elsewhere as in 5, 5 and IX. 3, 3.
The formula should also be compared
with one of uncertain date put forward
as to ὀρθογραφία (*Anecd. Ox.* 4, 33
quoted by Rutherford *Chapter in Hist.
of Annotation* p. 79). According to this
the tests of ὀρθογραφία are διάλεκτος,
ἐτυμολογία, ἀναλογία, ἱστορία. This last
is defined as ἡ τῶν παλαιῶν παράδοσις,
and thus is equivalent to 'auctoritas.'
Διάλεκτος amongst later teachers seems
to have been applied to the Greek dia-
lects, but one cannot but suspect that
originally it meant 'the current speech'
and thus corresponds to συνήθεια
('consuetudo'). Scaurus K. VII. 12
has the three, 'historia, originatio, proportio,' as a means by which 'vitiosa
consuetudo' in orthography may be
corrected.

religio. We may compare X. 1, 88
'Ennium sicut sacros vetustate lucos
adoremus, in quibus grandia et antiqua

robora iam non tantam habent speciem,
quantam religionem.' For the application to language cf. Longus K. VII. 74
'mihi vero placet ut in latino sermone
antiquitatis religio servetur,' ib. 53, 60.

2. stirpe...palumbes...silice. The
gender of the first is discussed by some
of the grammarians (v. indices to Keil).
The general opinion seems to have been
that it was feminine of human stock,
masculine of trees. 'Silex' (fem.) is
sometimes coupled with 'cortex' as a
solecism or rather 'schema.' 'Palumbes'
is noticed once or twice but without
comment. Reff. to Virg. are *Aen.* 12,
208; *Ecl.* 3, 69; 1, 15.

honestus est. Halm says 'malim *sit*,'
which Rad. adopts. But the number of
semi-causal 'est's' after 'cum' in Q. is
considerable, v. Bonnell, esp. X. 3, 26
and Peterson's note. Here it is indeed
rather an illustrative reflection.

3. nummo. Of this idea Sp. gives
some apt illustrations including Ovid
A. A. 3, 480 'sermonis publica forma
placet,' Sext. Emp. *Adv. Gramm.* 255
where the idea is worked out at some
length, and Fortunatianus Halm *Lat.
Rhet.* p. 122. This last is really a quotation of this passage 'vir perfectissimus
(i.e. Q.) dixit: Verbis utendum est ut nummis publica moneta signatis.' To these
quotations we may add Hor. *A. P.* 59
'licuit semperque licebit Signatum praesente nota producere nomen' and Fronto
(N. 140) 'ne quod novum verbum ut aes
adulterinum percutiat.'

proportionem. This appears first in
the form 'pro portione' as a translation
of ἀνὰ λόγον, and this is the only form

dubium est, ad aliquid simile, de quo non quaeritur, referat et incerta certis probet. quod efficitur duplici via: comparatione similium in extremis maxime syllabis, propter quod ea, quae sunt e singulis, negantur debere rationem, et deminutione. comparatio in nominibus aut genus deprendit aut declina- 5 tionem: genus, ut, si quaeratur, 'funis' masculinum sit an femininum, simile illi sit 'panis': declinationem, ut, si veniat in dubium, 'hac domu' dicendum sit an 'hac domo,' et 'domuum' an 'domorum,' similia sint 'domus anus manus.' deminutio 6 genus modo detegit, et, ne ab eodem exemplo recedam, 'funem' masculinum esse 'funiculus' ostendit. eadem in verbis quoque 7 ratio conparationis, ut si quis antiquos secutus 'fervere' brevi media syllaba dicat, deprendatur vitiose loqui, quod omnia,

recognised by Varro. Cicero seems definitely to accept the noun 'proportio' in *Tim.* 13 and 24, but in the other places where he uses the phrase it is in the ablative and may very possibly be two words. Staberius Eros, who was somewhat older, is credited in Priscian K. II. 385 with a book 'de proportione' but MSS. there have 'perportione' or 'portione' and the latter may quite well be the true reading. The word, which is surely a monstrosity, gained such ground as it ever had, very slowly.

4. eius haec vis est. For further discussion of the theory of analogy I must refer to my article on the controversy (Art. 1919).

id quod dubium...probet. For the application of this principle to reasoning in general v. v. 10, 8 and 11.

in extremis maxime syllabis. For a full discussion of this passage v. Art. 1916, p. 21. I take 'extremis syllabis' to mean the whole of the last syllable not merely the inflection. By 'maxime' Q. indicates that all analogists did not lay stress on this point (v. on 13).

propter...rationem. Cf. Char. K. I. 138 'monosyllaba extra analogiam esse Plinius scribit.' Mart. Cap. III. 299 '"as" et "mas" cum sint monosyllaba analogia non tenentur.' If identity of the last syllable is accepted as essential to analogy, monosyllables must necessarily stand outside it.

debere. Rad. strangely adopts Capperonnier's emendation 'habere.' 'Debere' is admirably suited to the conception of ἀναλογία.

5. illi. Articular to 'panis.' Cf. 'illi simile "currit"' § 9.

'hac domu.' The articular 'hac' is used here to indicate that the gender is an essential part of the analogy between 'domus' and 'anus.'

'domus, anus, manus.' While it is true that Q. might have done as well or better to write 'domui,' I see no reason to bracket 'domus' with Halm and others. On the principle given in the note on § 13, the three nouns are 'similia.' Kiderlin (*N. J. P.* 1885) made an ingenious but perverse attempt to amend the passage. Arguing (1) that for analogy to hold, it was necessary to have identity of the last syllable, (2) that Q. would not support 'domu,' he wished to read 'similia sint domus ⟨pomus, ulmus non⟩ anus manus.' As to the first of these arguments v. note on 13. As to the second, Kid. I think mistakes Q.'s position. It is important throughout these sections to understand that he is quoting common analogistic arguments without definitely subscribing to them.

6. deminutio...ostendit. This obvious rule of Latin had been observed by Varro according to the grammarians, cf. Pomp. K. v. 164 'ait Plinius Secundus secutus Varronem "quando dubitamus principale genus, redeamus ad deminutionem, et ex deminutivo cognoscimus principale genus."' Varro had also observed exceptions as 'rana, ranunculus' acc. to Charisius K. I. 37.

et. Rad. adopts Usener's correction 'ut,' needlessly, I think.

'funem,' perhaps in special allusion to Lucretius' 'aurea funis' (2, 1154) which is commented on as unusual by Aul. Gell. 13, 20.

quae e et o litteris fatendi modo terminantur, eadem, si in infinitis e litteram media syllaba acceperunt, utique productam habent: 'prandeo pendeo spondeo prandēre pendēre spondēre.'
8 at quae o solam habent, dummodo per eandem litteram in infinito exeant, brevia fiunt: 'lego dico curro legere dicere currere,' etiamsi est apud Lucilium:

'fervit aqua et fervet: fervit nunc, fervet ad annum.'

9 sed pace dicere hominis eruditissimi liceat: si 'fervit' putat illi simile 'currit' et 'legit,' 'fervo' dicet ut 'lego' et 'curro,' quod nobis inauditum est. 'sed non est haec vera comparatio: nam "fervit" est illi simile "servit."' quam proportionem sequenti
10 dicere necesse est 'fervire' ut 'servire.' prima quoque aliquando

---

7. fatendi modo. This unusual form for the indicative has aroused a suspicion that it might be a corruption of 'faciendi.' But cf. Char. *Exc.* K. I. 562 'indicativus ut "amo," "facio" hic multifariam interpretatur. Nam et fatendi ex prima persona dicimus, ut amo, quia de se quisque profitetur, non de altero, et arguendi ex secunda persona...et nuntiandi ex persona tertia.' The fact that it actually is the first person with which we are here concerned, no doubt facilitates the use.

prandeo. Halm and Meister 'ut prandeo' with A. Rad. omits 'ut' with B.

prandēre etc. I think it may be assumed that Q. wrote these words with the 'apex' (cf. 7, 2), though no edition has previously printed them with a long mark. So too 'avēre' (21), where Rad. has adopted it.

8. exeant, here 'are formed' or 'declined' as in 14, not 'terminated' as in 5, 60, 61. Forc. rightly notes this meaning, which is ignored in Bonnell's Lex.

Lucilium, from Book IX. (Marx 357). It may seem strange that Q. ignores another line of Luc. 'fervere ne longum vero lectoribus tradam' (Nonius p. 503, Marx 356). But it would not really be to the point in this debate, which Q. represents, I believe, with some irony. The question is whether the old 'fervĕre,' which no doubt has 'vetustas' and 'auctoritas,'can be justified analogically. No, says the analogist, it is elsewhere a 2nd conj. word. 'But Lucilius does treat it as 3rd conj. in the 3rd person (fervit).' True, but no one supports 'fervo.' The supporter of Luc. is then (rather foolishly) supposed to justify 'fervit' by 'servit.' This of course will only make his case

worse, for then 'fervere' would have to become 'fervire.' The fact which has sometimes perplexed commentators, that Virgil's fairly frequent use of 'fervĕre' is here ignored, is not really surprising. Virgil's usage has no bearing on the analogical question. Lucilius' advocacy of 'fervit' is quoted partly because it does carry the argument for 'fervĕre' a step further and partly because Lucilius in Book IX. is speaking *ex cathedra* as a grammarian.

'**fervit ... annum.**' The older commentators seem to have thought that L. drew a distinction between 'fervit (fervo)' of water temporarily hot, and 'fervet (ferveo)' of water 'quae fervorem diu retinet.' I understand the line as follows. Luc. having declared for 'fervĕre' is asked whether he says 'fervit' or 'fervet.' He replies humorously 'I say both,' but 'fervit' is present, 'fervet' is future. 'Ad annum' not 'for a year' as L. but 'a year hence.' 'Cras,' or any other word which clearly marks some future date, would have done equally well, if it would have suited the metre. This interpretation is also, I think, supported by the fact that of the two grammarians who quote the line one, ps.-Prob. K. IV. 241, evidently takes both 'fervit' and 'fervet' as 3rd conj.

9. 'fervo'...inauditum. The grammarians are not so dogmatic, many of them regarding 'fervo' as a real form, though some argue from the inchoative 'fervesco' that 'ferveo' alone is correct.

sed non...'servit.' I believe that Rad. is right in putting these words in inverted commas. As stated above, I regard them as an alternative suggested by the disputant, which is refuted by the words 'quam...servire.'

positio ex obliquis invenitur, ut memoria repeto convictos a me, qui reprenderant, quod hoc verbo usus essem 'pepigi': nam id quidem dixisse summos auctores confitebantur, rationem tamen negabant permittere, quia prima positio 'paciscor,' cum haberet naturam patiendi, faceret tempore praeterito 'pactus sum.' nos praeter auctoritatem oratorum atque historicorum 11 analogia quoque dictum tuebamur. nam cum legeremus in XII tabulis ni ita pacunt, inveniebamus simile huic 'cadunt': inde prima positio, etiamsi vetustate exoleverat, apparebat 'paco' ut 'cado,' unde non erat dubium sic 'pepigi' nos dicere ut 'cecidi.' sed meminerimus non per omnia duci analogiae 12 posse rationem, cum et sibi ipsa plurimis in locis repugnet. quaedam sine dubio conantur eruditi defendere, ut, cum deprensum est, 'lepus' et 'lupus' similia positione quantum casibus numerisque dissentiant, ita respondent non esse paria, quia 'lepus' epicoenon sit, 'lupus' masculinum, quamquam Varro in eo libro, quo initia Romanae urbis enarrat, lupum feminam dicit Ennium Pictoremque Fabium secutus. illi autem idem, 13

11. 'pacunt'...'paco.' So Halm and Meister, but Rad. has returned to the 'pag-' of older edd. The point seems to me as unimportant as it is uncertain. Q. clearly intended it to be read as 'pag-' but was no doubt aware that the original orthography was 'pac-.'
12. sine dubio. Sp. well points out that here as frequently Q. uses these words (like our 'no doubt') to introduce something which is of less importance than something which follows. Other exx. are 38 below and II. 15, 6. In 10, 12 the use is different. Cic. (so far as we can judge from Merguet) does not use the combination at all.
similia. So Halm and recent edd. with A (preferably I think). Sp. 'simili' with B.
positione, 'prima' omitted as in 15 and 25. It is not really required, for the nominative is the true 'positio' or θέμα, the others being fallings away from it.
ita. Halm and Meister correct to 'ista,' but the prospective 'ita' followed by acc. and inf. appears in IX. 2, 92 and XII. 10, 1.
'lepus'...'lupus.' The anomalists pointed to the fact that analogy did not result, although the two words (1) had the same final syllable, (2) satisfied all the requirements mentioned in the note on

'aper' 'pater' below. Probably they also laid stress on general resemblance both of sound and meaning. The reason here given for the difference by the analogists, viz. that the two were not really of the same gender, is also given by Pomp. K. v. 198. On the other hand the analogist in Varro (*L. L.* 9, 91) who is also confronted with this pair, argues that the difference of vocative accounts for the difference of formation. The same pair is also mentioned Aul. Gell. 2, 25 (v. Art. 1919, p. 29).
eo libro. This may be very well one of the earlier of the 25 books of 'antiquitates rerum humanarum' of which some account is given by Augustine *C. D.* VI. 3, or again one of the three 'rerum urbanarum' mentioned in Jerome's catalogue of V.'s works. As J. also speaks of 'alia plura quae enumerare longum est,' it may also be one of these, or indeed of 10 'singulares' mentioned in the catalogue; v. Ritschl *Op.* III. p. 450, who considers, I think rightly, that in view of the popularity of the 'antiquitates' the first alternative is most probable.
Ennium. The line is given by Nonius 'Indo tuetur ibi lupus femina, conspicit omnis.'
Pictoremque Fabium. This is one of three passages which shew that besides

cum interrogantur, cur 'aper apri' et 'pater patris' faciat, illud nomen positum, hoc ad aliquid esse contendunt. praeterea quoniam utrumque a Graeco ductum sit, ad eam rationem
14 recurrunt, ut 'πατρός patris, κάπρου apri' faciat. illa tamen quomodo effugient, ut nomina quamvis feminina singulari nominativo 'us' litteris finita numquam genetivo casu 'ris'

the Greek history (vouched for by Cic.) of Fabius Pictor, there was a Latin work attributed to him. For the question whether the latter is a translation of the former or from the hand of a younger F. P., v. Pauly-Wissowa and Teuffel who take different views.

13. aper...pater. Here it is to be observed that the last syllables are not identical, a fact which shews that all analogists did not lay this down as a necessary condition for analogy. A passage in Char. K. I. 117 gives us a rule probably more regularly adopted. 'Huic (i.e. analogiae) Aristophanes quinque rationes dedit vel, ut alii putant, sex: primo ut eiusdem sint generis de quibus quaeritur, dein casus tum exitus, quarto numeri syllabarum, item soni (i.e. accent). Sextum Aristarchus discipulus eius illud addidit, ne unquam simplicia compositis aptemus' (the rule ascribed by Pompeius K. v. 197 to Caesar is slightly different), i.e. in the two nouns 'aper' and 'pater' we must be dealing with the same case, i.e. the genitive, and if we are to expect analogy must have in the nominative (1) the same termination -er, (2) gender, (3) number of syllables, (4) accent, and (5) both must be simple or both compound. It is obvious that all these conditions are here satisfied. Some grammarians laid down also that (1) the quantity of the penultimate vowel must be the same, (2) they must be the same εἶδος or part of speech. Thus we are told that analogy cannot be expected between ἱππότης (προσηγορία) and Σωκράτης (ὄνομα). Of these last two conditions, the first is obviously satisfied in the case of 'aper' and 'pater,' and to most people's minds the second also. But the hard-driven analogist took refuge in the plea that there was a real difference of εἶδος, as 'pater' is a relative and 'aper' an absolute noun. For further discussion v. Art. 1919, pp. 28, 29.

nomen positum. 'Positus' or 'positivus,' Greek θεματικός, is a synonym for 'absolutus' and the converse of 'ad aliquid' (πρός τι ἔχον). The insertion of an adverb as 'simpliciter' (Sp.) is quite

needless. For a definition of 'ad aliquid' nouns v. Consentius K. v. 339 'haec alium intellectum secum trahunt, patre enim dicto intelligas simul filium, et magistro dicto intelligas simul discipulum necesse est,' v. Art. 1916, p. 22.

praeterea...faciat. So Char. K. I. 83 'pater patris cum faciat et mater matris, cur dissimiliter aper apri et caper capri solet quaeri. Sed Graeca declinatio advertenda est ubi deprehendetur.' He goes on however to contrast πατρός 'patris,' μητρός 'matris' with κάπρου 'capri,' ἀγροῦ 'agri,' which last raises the suspicion that we should read 'ager agri' above.

κάπρου, 'apri.' Cf. Varro L. L. 5, 101 'apri ab eo quod in locis asperis, nisi a Graecis quod hi aproe,' where edd. have probably rightly corrected to '(c)aproe.'

14. nomina quamvis feminina. I have here returned to the old reading against Halm and later edd. The objection to it is the position of 'quamvis' as second word in its clause. Halm inserted 'cum' after 'ut.' But this is not really sense. It implies that all nouns in '-us' (including neuters) avoid '-eris.' Meist. and Rad. have 'non' for 'nomina' following A and apparently the 1st hand of Bn, though Fierville does not seem to recognise this. (Bg and N have 'nomina.') But the sense is not good. Presumably 'ut' is consecutive. What then exactly is 'illa'? Further it misrepresents the position of the analogist. He did not wish to alter the declension of 'Venus -eris,' but to justify it by adducing some reason why it should not 'owe analogy.' I cannot think that the position of 'quamvis' constitutes a fatal objection, and even if it does the reversal of the order of 'nomina quamvis' is as probable as the insertion of 'cum.'

numquam. Q. either forgets or ignores 'tellus.' The quantity of the ū would however have put it outside the controversy. But Q. does not treat the whole controversy with very full knowledge or understanding. The analogist would have replied both to this and the next point, that Venus (cf. Prisc. K. II. 269)

syllaba terminentur, faciat tamen 'Venus Veneris'? item, cum
'es' litteris finita per varios exeant genetivos, numquam tamen
eadem 'ris' syllaba terminatos, 'Ceres' cogat dici 'Cereris'?
quid vero? quae tota positionis eiusdem in diversos flexus eunt? 15
cum 'Alba' faciat 'Albanos' et 'Albensis,' 'volo' 'volui' et
'volavi.' nam praeterito quidem tempore varie formari verba
prima persona o littera terminata ipsa analogia confitetur, si
quidem facit 'cado cecidi, spondeo spopondi, pingo pinxi, lego
legi, pono posui, frango fregi, laudo laudavi.' non enim, cum 16

and Ceres being 'nomina' did not owe
analogy to appellatives.

terminentur. I have followed nearly
all edd. (but with hesitation) in reading
this for the almost universal 'terminantur' of the MSS. The fact that Q.
nearly always uses 'quamvis' with the
subj. (but ind. in VIII. 6, 73) coupled
with the dependence on another subj. is
perhaps sufficient justification for the
change.

'**Ceres'...'Cereris.**' A strange expression, hardly paralleled by the exx. quoted
by Sp. of the personification of words
such as 'analogia confitetur' below.

15. eunt. Meister and others 'exeunt,'
with N, v. Intr. p. xciii.

'**Alba.**' This was a stock case. Varro
L. L. 9, 35 puts into the mouth of
his anomalist 'ab isdem vocabulis dis-
similia apparet fingi, quod cum duae
sint Albae ab una dicuntur Albani, ab
altera Albenses.' So Char. K. I. 106:
'Albani dicuntur ab Alba, Albenses
autem ab Alba Fucente. Cuius rei causam
Varro ait esse, quod analogia in naturalibus nominibus tantum servatur, in
voluntariis vero neglegitur.' This last
sentence seems to be an inference of the
grammarians, for though this distinction
between 'voluntaria' (i.e. derivatives)
and 'naturalia' (inflexions) (v. Art. 1919,
p. 26) is put forward in the analogist
reply in Book IX., this special case is not
mentioned. According to Pomp. K. v.
144 Caesar in his *De Analogia* said
'duae sunt Albae; alia ista quam novi-
mus in Aricia, et alia hic in Italia.
Volentes Romani discretionem facere
istos Albanos dixerunt illos Albenses....
Plinius Secundus negat et ait sic "in-
differenter haec inveniuntur."' The context seems to suggest that Caesar gave
'discretio' as a sufficient reason for
violation of analogy, while Pliny rather
supported Varro's view that analogy
was not to be found in derivatives. But

the statement about Pliny seems opposed
to *Nat. Hist.* 3, 106 'Albensium Alba
ad lacum Fucinum.'

'**volo.**' The same example is quoted
by Varro *L. L.* 9, 103, but there is used
by the analogist to shew, if I understand
the passage rightly, that the difference
of conjugation proves that the two verbs
are intrinsically different. Cf. ib. 108,
109.

nam praeterito...laudavi. This appears to be an allusion to the analogist
theory (*L. L.* 9, 54, 55) that the present and perfect stems form separate
blocks for purposes of analogy. So long
as 'pingo,' 'pingam,' 'pingebam' follow
analogically on 'lego,' 'legam,' 'legebam'
and 'pinxi' etc. on 'legi' etc. no argument
against analogy can be drawn from the
dissimilarity of 'legi' and 'pinxi.' The
acceptance of this principle did to a very
large extent eliminate anomaly from the
Latin verb and thus narrow the controversy mainly to the noun, v. Art. 1919,
p. 27.

formari. Of inflexion. So 'forma' in
Varro *L. L.* 9, 37, 109.

o littera terminata. This is very in-
accurately expressed. While we have
little information about the analogists'
treatment of the verb, they cannot of
course have said that the variety of perfect stems was the only variety. Presumably they started with saying that
identity of conjugation was a condition
of analogy. To state the point fairly Q.
should have added after 'terminata,'
'quae per "is" exeunt,' and then eliminated 'spondeo' and 'laudo.' I do not
doubt however that the words are genuine
and take them as a sign that he has an imperfect understanding of the controversy.

16. enim. This does not give a reason
for the last sentence so much as for the
whole position taken up in 12-15.

non enim...caderet. Here Q. asserts
of analogy his favourite principle that

primum fingerentur homines, Analogia demissa caelo formam
loquendi dedit, sed inventa est, postquam loquebantur, et
notatum in sermone, quid quoque modo caderet. itaque non
ratione nititur, sed exemplo, nec lex est loquendi, sed observatio, ut ipsam analogiam nulla res alia fecerit quam consuetudo.
17 inhaerent tamen ei quidam molestissima diligentiae perversitate,
ut 'audaciter' potius dicant quam 'audacter,' licet omnes
oratores aliud sequantur, et 'emicavit,' non 'emicuit,' et 'conire,'
non 'coire.' his permittamus et 'audivisse' et 'scivisse' et 'tribunale' et 'faciliter' dicere: 'frugalis' quoque sit apud illos,

art is inductive 'non tam inventa a praeceptoribus quam cum fierent observata'
(VIII. pr. 12). In IX. 4, 115 we have it applied to metrical laws 'ante enim carmen
ortum est quam observatio carminis.'
More frequently it is applied to rhetoric,
III. 2, 3; V. 10, 120; VIII. Pr. 12. In
all these passages Q. is no doubt influenced by Cic. *De Or.* 1, 146 'verum
ego hanc vim intellego esse in praeceptis
omnibus, non ut ea secuti oratores eloquentiae laudem sint adepti, sed quae
sua sponte homines eloquentes facerent,
ea quosdam observasse atque collegisse'
(MSS. 'id egisse').

demissa caelo. For illustrations v.
Mayor on Juv. 11, 27 ('e caelo descendit
γνῶθι σεαυτόν').

quid quoque. Halm and Meister with
Sp. 'quo quidque,' a more natural
phrase, but with no MS. authority. I
follow Rad. doubtfully. A has 'quid quo'
which may very possibly be right.

caderet. In technical sense ('casus,'
πτῶσις).

non ratione nititur. There is, I think,
no real contradiction of the statement of
§ 1 that 'rationem praestat analogia.'
Men do not speak originally on 'ratio,'
in the sense of some reasoned principle,
but the observation of what they say may
be reduced to 'ratio' in the sense of a
system.

ut ipsam analogiam...consuetudo.
Here Q. follows Varro *L. L.* 9, 2 'consuetudo et analogia coniunctiores sunt
inter se quam ii' (i.e. analogists and
anomalists) 'credunt, quod est nata ex
quadam consuetudine analogia' (v. Art.
1919, p. 30). Cf. Sext. Emp. *adv.
Gramm.* 258 ὥστε καὶ ἡ σύστασις τῆς
ἀναλογίας ἐκ τῆς συνηθείας πρόεισι. The
dogma of Pindarion quoted ib. 259
ἀναλογία ὁμολογουμένως ἐκ τῆς συνηθείας
ὁρμᾶται· ἔστι γὰρ ὁμοίου τε καὶ ἀνομοίου
θεωρία is perhaps rather different, ἀνα-

λογία there standing for the science of
inflexion in general.

17. 'conire.' Usener (*Kleine Schriften*
I. 358) suggested 'comire,' quoting
'comes' 'comitium' 'comedere.' His
case might be strengthened by Varro
L. L. 5, 155 'comitium ab eo quod
coibant,' and still more by Plut. *Rom.*
19 ὅπου δὲ ταῦτα συνέθεντο μέχρι νῦν
Κομίτιον καλεῖται· κομῖρε γὰρ Ῥωμαῖοι
τὸ συνελθεῖν καλοῦσι. As however no
confirmatory evidence appears in the
grammarians, and 5, 69 (with Priscian
there quoted) seems to favour 'con,' I
have retained it with doubt.

'audivisse' et 'scivisse.' Cf. Cic. *Or.*
157 'quid quod sic loqui "nosse iudicasse"
vetant, "novisse" iubent et "iudica-
visse."' Q. appears to use the abbreviated
form in these cases always (Lease *C. R.*
June, 1899), though in IX. 4, 59 he
sanctions the longer form if 'compositio'
demands it. 'Etiam ubi aliud ratio, aliud
consuetudo poscet, utrum volet sumat
compositio, vitavisse vel vitasse, deprehendere vel deprendere.'

'tribunale.' So Char. K. I. 25 'multi
autem voluerunt nominativum per e
efferri ut hoc animale, tribunale, biden-
tale.' Later he condemns these (ib. 119)
on the authority of Pliny.

'faciliter.' The question is frequently
discussed by the grammarians who
generally hold that 'facile' is really a
noun. Charisius notes 'faciliter' as the
older form.

'frugalis.' The only place where
an apparently similar point is made is
in Varro *L. L.* 8, 77 quoted by Sp.
Here the anomalist argues 'si in his
dominaretur similitudo ... ut dicimus
doctus docta, doctissimi doctissima, sic
diceremus frugalissimus frugalissima,
frugus et fruga.' Sp. thought that here
we should read 'frugissimus'; but he
mistook the analogy intended, which is

non 'frugi': nam quo alio modo fiet 'frugalitas'? idem 'centum **18** milia nummum' et 'fidem deum' ostendant duplicis quoque soloecismos esse, quando et casum mutant et numerum: nesciebamus enim ac non consuetudini et decori serviebamus, sicut in plurimis, quae M. Tullius in Oratore divine ut omnia exequitur. sed Augustus quoque in epistulis ad C. Caesarem **19** scriptis emendat, quod is 'calidum' dicere quam 'caldum' malit, non quia id non sit Latinum, sed quia sit odiosum et, ut ipse Graeco verbo significavit, περίεργον. atqui hanc quidam **20** ὀρθοέπειαν solam putant, quam ego minime excludo. quid enim tam necessarium quam recta locutio? immo inhaerendum ei iudico, quoad licet, diu etiam mutantibus repugnandum: sed abolita atque abrogata retinere insolentiae cuiusdam est et frivolae in parvis iactantiae. multum enim litteratus, **21** qui sine aspiratione et producta secunda syllaba salutarit ('avere' est enim), et 'calefacere' dixerit potius quam quod

that if the superlatives run -us, -a, -um, the positives should too. The passage does not therefore really bear on ours (v. note on 29).

nummum...deum. 'Deum' with 'denarium' and 'assarium' is cited by Varro *L. L.* 8, 71 as a breach of analogy, but the passage which Q. has principally in mind is Cic. *Or.* 156 where both these exx. with many others are given.

nesciebamus etc. Clearly intended as an echo of Cic.'s words in the passage above quoted 'quasi vero nesciamus in hoc genere et plenum verbum recte dici et imminutum usitate,' which does not mean merely, as Sp. (quoting it elsewhere), that both the longer and shorter forms might be used, but that 'nummorum' follows anal. and 'nummum' 'consuet.' Q. rightly interprets Cic. to mean that following 'consuet.' with knowledge does not constitute a barbarism or solecism, as it would if 'per imprudentiam factum.' The stress is on 'nesciamus.'

19. C. Caesarem. Augustus' grandson. An interesting and rather charming extract is given by Aul. Gell. 15, 7. For Augustus' objection to anything pedantic or out of the way in language, v. Suet. *Aug.* 86.

emendat. The reading of A 'emendatius calidum...mavult' is interesting as an early correction, but obviously misses the sense.

'**calidum**'...'**caldum.**' The emenda-

tion 'calidam...caldam' is tempting, for the longer form seems to have been more general except in special cases, of which 'calda sc. aqua' is the most common. [Another perhaps is referred to in Sen. *Suas.* 3 'declamatores quos scholastici caldos vocant.'] But here again correction seems unnecessary in view of the possibility that A.'s view on these words may not have been the normal view. Q. does not adopt his judgment. He merely quotes a high authority who deliberately rejected an analogous in favour of an anomalous and presumably colloquial form.

odiosum. So MSS. Halm and Meister have both adopted 'otiosum' (given originally by Burman in the form 'quia i sit otiosum'). Rad. has returned to 'od-.' The milder word may suit περίεργον and perhaps the circumstances better, but hardly sufficiently so to justify the alteration. Cp. also Aug. to his granddaughter (Suet. 86), 'sed opus est dare te operam ne *moleste* scribas et loquaris.'

20. ὀρθοέπειαν: v. note on 5, 33.

solam. Not, I think, 'mere' as Watson or 'just a question of ὀρθ.' (L.), but 'the only really correct kind of speech.' 'Hanc' must refer to the whole type of purism discussed in 17, 18, 19.

21. avēre. If the reading is retained, we must suppose that Q. employed the apex. But the 'avete' of some older edd. is tempting. Sp. strangely fails to see the meaning of this, which would be

6

dicimus et 'conservavisse,' his adiciat 'face' et 'dice' et similia.
22 recta est haec via: quis negat? sed adiacet et mollior et magis
trita. ego tamen non alio magis angor, quam quod obliquis
casibus ducti etiam primas sibi positiones non invenire, sed
mutare permittunt, ut cum 'ebur' et 'robur,' ita dicta ac scripta
summis auctoribus, in o litteram secundae syllabae transferunt,
quia sit 'roboris' et 'eboris,' 'sulpur' autem et 'guttur' u litteram
in genetivo servent: ideoque 'iecur' etiam et 'femur' contro-
23 versiam fecerunt. quod non minus est licentiosum, quam si
'sulpuri' ut 'gutturi' subicerent in genetivo litteram o mediam,
quia esset 'eboris' et 'roboris': sicut Antonius Gnipho, qui
'robur' quidem et 'ebur' atque etiam 'marmur' fatetur esse,
24 verum fieri vult ex his 'ebura robura marmura.' quodsi anim-
adverterent litterarum adfinitatem, scirent sic ab eo, quod est
'robur,' 'roboris' fieri, quo modo ab eo, quod est 'miles limes,
militis limitis, iudex vindex, iudicis vindicis' et quae supra iam
25 attigi. quid vero quod, ut dicebam, similes positiones in longe
diversas figuras per obliquos casus exeunt? ut 'virgo Iuno,
fusus lusus, cuspis puppis' et mille alia: cum illud etiam accidat,
ut quaedam pluraliter non dicantur, quaedam contra singulari

of course that the plural greeting 'avete,'
not 'avite,' postulated 'avē.'
'**calefacere**.' This statement stands by
itself. There is no other evidence which
would lead us to suppose that 'calf-'
ever ousted 'calef-,' as far as I know.
'**face**' et '**dice**.' These have a certain
amount of authority. Cf. Char. K. 1.
256 'sed apud veteres salva est regula:
nam dixerunt face, dice, duce.'
22. non invenire sed mutare. Apparently the meaning is that while
forming imaginary nominatives to correspond to the oblique cases is harmless
(as Varro's analogist does *L. L.* 9, 76),
these analysts actually changed in
practice the existing nominatives. Or
is the thought 'they talk of discovering
the true nom., in reality they are merely
changing it'? In either case the expression
is strange. Baur has 'nicht nehmen wie
sie sind,' but we can hardly get this
meaning out of 'non invenire.'
summis auctoribus. Claussen would
insert 'a.' But for exx. of this dative
v. Bonnell, *Lex.* p. xlvi, and particularly
'claris auctoribus memoratas' 8, 18.
o litteram. 'Ebor' and 'robor' appear to be more or less accepted by Char.,
Prisc. and Phocas (v. indices to Keil).

23. Antonius Gnipho—presumably
from his *de sermone Latino,* v. Suet. *de
Gramm.* 7.
24. ab eo quod est. I have not
noticed this substitute for the article
elsewhere in Q. It is often used by
Longus, e.g. K. VII. 76 'in eo quod est
legere, scribere.'
iudex, vindex. The grammar of these
nominatives is not clear to me but it
might easily be corrected by transferring
them to after 'limes.'
quae supra iam attigi. The 'affini-
tas' of *o* with *u*, and *e* with *i* was dealt
with in 4, 16 and 17.
25. ut dicebam, i.e. in 12–24. The
recurrence to the point seems unnecessary.
virgo...puppis. The pairs seem to
be chosen to meet the two different
views of analogists. While the two last
pairs may be classed with 'lepus' and
'lupus,' as having identical final syllables, the first pair resemble 'aper'
and 'pater.' Some analogists would have
met this case by pointing out that 'virgo'
was an appellative, and 'Iuno' a 'nomen,' but Q. as we saw in 14 ignores
this test.
ut quaedam...'Iuppiter.' All these

numero, quaedam casibus careant, quaedam a primis statim positionibus tota mutentur, ut 'Iuppiter.' quod verbis etiam **26** accidit, ut illi 'fero,' cuius praeteritum perfectum et ulterius non invenitur. nec plurimum refert, nulla haec an praedura sint. nam quid 'progenies' genetivo singulari, quid plurali 'spes' faciet? quo modo autem 'quire' et 'urgere' vel in praeterita patiendi modo vel in participia transibunt? quid de aliis **27** dicam, cum senatus senatui 'senati' an 'senatus' faciat incertum sit? quare mihi non invenuste dici videtur, aliud esse Latine, aliud grammatice loqui. ac de analogia nimium.

four points are noted by Varro's anomalist, *L. L.* 8, 48, 49, and answered by the analogist, ib. 9, 63-71.

casibus careant, i.e. ἄπτωτα, words like 'nequam' usable in all cases, but unchanged. Some grammarians call these μονόπτωτα and keep the other name for Iuppiter, etc.

26. '**fero.**' The comparison between the position of 'Iuppiter' amongst the nouns and 'fero' amongst the verbs is made by Priscian, K. II. 454.

ulterius, i.e. the tenses 'quae praeteritum perfectum sequuntur.' B for 'fero' has 'tuli, fero,' which is impossible. Others 'fero tuli.' Sp., who read this, took 'cuius' to refer to 'tuli' only, in which case the words 'cuius... invenitur' must mean 'which has the perfect stem tenses and nothing more.' He himself however doubted if the words could mean this, and the use of 'praeteritum perfectum' in this wider sense is not, I think, in accordance with the practice of the grammarians. They usually reckon the fut. perf. as a fut. subj.

'**progenies**'...'**spes.**' The grammarians do not appear to have been struck with the non-usage of the gen. sing. of the 5th decl., though they frequently discuss the variety of forms, v. particularly Aul. Gell. 9, 14 (cf. Roby, vol. I. p. xci). On the other hand the rarity or the absence of the gen. (and dat.) plur. had been noticed by Cic. in *Top.* 30, where he advocates the translation of εἶδος by 'forma' rather than by 'species' because of this difficulty in the 'mutatio casuum.' Priscian, K. II. 367, quotes this passage of Cic. and notes the absence of the cases except in 'res' and 'dies.'

'**quire**' **et** '**urgere**'; 'urgere' is the reading of A and the 2nd hand of Bg. B etc. have 'ruere' which is retained by Halm

and Meister. The evidence of the grammarians, so far as it goes, is clearly for 'urgere,' which appears in Priscian's comprehensive list of verbs deficient in this way (K. II. 560); v. also Cledonius, K. V. 72. 'Ruo' on the other hand is not classed with these verbs, and considering the existence of 'ruiturus,' 'erutus' and the legal 'ruta caesa,' it is a poor, though perhaps not impossible, example for Q. to adduce. I confess to some suspicion of 'quire.' 'Quitus' was no doubt obsolete in Q.'s time, but so was 'quitur.' 'Luere' which is one of Priscian's verbs (l. c.) is a possible substitute.

patiendi modo; v. note on 4, 27.

27. cum senatus...incertum sit. The reading is doubtful. The text adopted has the best authority, B, N and A (2nd hand, the 1st having merely 'cum senatus faciat'). The old edd. with some MSS. read 'senatus senatus senatui an senatus senati senato.' Ritschl suggested 'senatus senatus senatui an senatus senati an senatus' was adopted by Halm, Meister and Rad. Fierville's adoption of B's text with the change of 'senatui' to 'senatuis' in view of Aul. Gell. 4, 16, who notes this form as used by Varro and Nigidius, is unacceptable, as Q. is clearly speaking of non-obsolete forms. I have retained the reading of B because I believe it on the whole to give the best sense. We are stating a final anomalistic point. Acc. to Halm's reading, the point is that analogy is unable to decide between two different declensions of the same noun. This is quite a sound point, and has not been made before, though that of 'Alba' and 'volo' is something similar. According to my reading we get the stronger point, that though 'senatui,' which has no rival 'senato,' fixes the declension as 4th, we still find 'senati' as well as 'senatus.'

28 Etymologia, quae verborum originem inquirit, a Cicerone
dicta est notatio, quia nomen eius apud Aristotelen invenitur
σύμβολον, quod est 'nota.' nam verbum ex verbo ductum, id
est veriloquium, ipse Cicero, qui finxit, reformidat. sunt qui
29 vim potius intuiti originationem vocent. haec habet aliquando usum necessarium, quotiens interpretatione res, de qua
quaeritur, eget, ut cum M. Caelius se esse hominem frugi vult
probare, non quia abstinens sit (nam id ne mentiri quidem
poterat), sed quia utilis multis, id est fructuosus, [unde sit ducta
frugalitas.] ideoque in definitionibus adsignatur etymologiae

28. etymologia. Q.'s treatment of
etymology in these sections should be
noticed. Etymology had to the ancient
student three different uses or interests:
(1) Rhetorical. An argument may be
founded on the 'true' meaning of a
word. This is the use noted in Cic.
Top. 35 and *Ac.* I. 32 (v. next note).
(2) As a test of and guide to correct
language. This is the conception involved in the formula 'sermo constat
analogia, etymologia etc.' (3) As a
branch of scientific study interesting in
itself. This is the point of view in
Varro, *L. L.*, where it is the science of
words in themselves as opposed to their
inflexions. This is also presumably the
point of view which makes Dionysius
Thrax include it in the branches of
grammatical study (v. note on 8, 13).
Q. should, strictly speaking, have confined himself to the second of these, but
as a matter of fact is carried away into
a general disquisition on it from all
three points of view. The first is treated
in 29, the 2nd very shortly in 30, and
the 3rd from 31–38 at some length, but
on the whole with a disparagement,
which prepares us for its exclusion
from the 'praelectio' in ch. 8.
notatio. Cic. *Top.* 35 'multa etiam
ex notatione sumuntur. ea est autem,
cum ex vi nominis argumentum elicitur;
quam Graeci ἐτυμολογίαν vocant, id est,
verbum ex verbo, veriloquium; nos autem novitatem verbi non satis apti fu-
gientes genus hoc notationem appella-
mus, quia sunt verba rerum notae. itaque
hoc idem Aristoteles σύμβολον appellat,
quod Latine est nota.' This attempt of
Cic. does not seem a happy one: σύμβολον, as used by Ar. (at any rate in
the books which survive, v. Bonitz,
index s.v.), merely expresses the relation
of the 'verbum' to the 'res,' and 'notatio' should mean the 'impositio nota-

rum,' not the science which enquires
into it. 'Veriloquium' is equally unhappy, for the termination -λογια is not
used as in φιλολογία, but as in ἀστρο-
λογία. Etymology is the science of
ἔτυμα. In *Ac.* I. 32 Cic. had suggested
'explicatio verborum' (an equivalent
possibly of the ἀνάπτυξις τῶν λέξεων,
which we find in later scholiasts), while
in *De Or.* 2, 165 the argument from
etymology is called 'ex vocabulo.' 'Notatio' does not seem to have taken root;
the only places where I have found it
or 'nota' are in Mart. Cap. 474 sq.
'nota, quam Graeci ἐτυμολογίαν vocant,'
ib. 483.
originatio. Forc. gives no other instance of this, but it is used by Scaurus,
K. VII. 12 'originatio, quam Graeci
ἐτυμολογίαν vocant.'
29. ut cum. So Meister and Rad.
with B. Halm omits 'cum' with A.
An evenly-balanced point.
mentiri. Halm 'ementiri' without
good authority and needlessly.
[**unde sit ducta frugalitas**]. I have
ventured to bracket these words, as the
sense seems to me very poor. It can
only be 'I claim "frugalitas," because
that is the quality of the "frugi," and
"frugi" means "fructuosus."' That might
stand if the ordinary sense of 'frugi'
was 'fructuosus,' but it is not. What we
expect is, 'I claim to be "frugi" because
by etymology that is "fructuosus."' Kid.,
who felt the difficulty, solved it by in-
serting 'quaeritur' before 'unde.' It
would then mean that when Caelius
pleads the etymology of 'frugi' he is
met by the objection that the undoubted
meaning of 'frugalitas' being 'abstinentia,' that of 'frugi' must correspond.
It is surely simpler to regard the words
as a muddle-headed insertion based on
§ 17 'quo modo fiet "frugalitas."'
definitionibus, i.e. 'argumenta ex

locus. nonnumquam etiam barbara ab emendatis conatur 30
discernere, ut cum 'Triquetram' dici Siciliam an 'Triquedram,'
'meridiem' an 'medidiem' oporteat, quaeritur, aliaque quae consuetudini serviunt. continet autem in se multam eruditionem, 31
sive ex Graecis orta tractemus, quae sunt plurima, praecipueque
Aeolica ratione, cui est sermo noster simillimus, declinata, sive
ex historiarum veterum notitia nomina hominum locorum
gentium urbium requiramus: unde Bruti, Publicolae, Pythici?
cur Latium, Italia, Beneventum? quae Capitolium et collem
Quirinalem et Argiletum appellandi ratio?

Iam illa minora, in quibus maxime studiosi eius rei fati- 32
gantur, qui verba paululum declinata varie et multipliciter ad

finitione.' Cf. v. 10, 54, 55, where etymology for this purpose is regarded as
a branch of definition. So too VII. 3, 25
where he quotes Cic. *Phil.* 8, 1, 3 'quid
enim est aliud tumultus nisi perturbatio
tanta, ut maior timor oriatur? unde
etiam nomen ductum est tumultus.'
There however such an argument is said
to be 'maxime rara'; v. also Reid's
note on Cic. *Ac.* I. 32.

30. barbara ab emendatis. Cf. Sext.
Emp. *adv. Gramm.* 266–268, where etymology as a test of Ἑλληνισμός follows
on analogy exactly as here. Sextus sets
himself to prove that both are equally
valueless.

'**Triquedram.**' Sp. questioned whether
the implied derivation was from 'quadra'
or ἕδρα. Probably the latter, based on
such geometrical terms as δωδεκάεδρος,
though these as belonging to solid geometry are not properly applicable.

'**medidiem.**' This point put strikingly
by Varro, *L. L.* 6, 4, where he supports
the *d* by his own observation of an old
dial at Praeneste, was a favourite one
with Latin philologists. Examples are
collected by Goetz on Varro l.c.

aliaque quae consuetudini serviunt.
So B; the reading of A 'aliquando
consuetudini servit' has been adopted by
Meister and Rad. I agree with Kid. that
the text of B is decidedly preferable.
Etymology is over-ruled by usage, but
can hardly be said to be controlled by
it as orthography is 7, 11. Moreover,
there is little point in the remark
here, where the object is to bring out
the uses of etymology. On the other
hand the statement that the grammarian may call in question the forms in
which usage has over-ruled etymology
(the etymologist thus taking the place

of the analogist) is quite to the point.
L.'s translation 'which depend on current usage' hardly gives the meaning,
rather 'which have been modified in
obedience to usage.'

31. sive ex Graecis: Meister 'sive illa
ex' from the 'si illa' of B.

Aeolica ratione. Meister inserts 'ab'
quite needlessly. 'Declinata' is here
used, not in the sense of terminal
inflexions, but as in 32 'formed and
modified.' Q. has already given us an
example of this in 4, 16. The doctrine
of the special affinity between Latin and
Aeolic is frequently mooted by Priscian,
e.g. K. III. 27 'Aeoles...quos in plerisque secuti in hoc (i.e. the accentuation
of the preposition) quoque sequimur.'
The doctrine was evidently largely
founded on the correspondence of the
digamma (cf. on 4, 8) with Latin consonantal *u* and was given a supposed
historical basis by the story that Evander
had introduced Aeolic into Latium, a
statement ascribed by Lydus to Varro,
v. Goetz, Varro *L. L.* p. 201.

Pythici. The older edd. had corrected
this to ' Pici' or ' Potitii,' but later edd.
have restored the MS. reading on the
evidence (first adduced by Meyer) of
Dion Cass. 63, 18, where Nero's freedmen put to death two Sulpicii, because
they continued to use the old family
surname of Pythicus and thus ἐς τοῦ
Νέρωνος νίκας τὰς Πυθικὰς ἐκ τῆς ὁμωνυ-
μίας ἠσέβουν. Of the other derivations it
is enough to say with Sp. 'consulenda
sunt lexica.'

32. paululum. So A. Most edd.
' paulum.' I have preferred the diminutive as bringing out better what I conceive to be the point of this sentence,
viz. that Q. looks with tolerance on this

veritatem reducunt aut correptis aut porrectis, aut adiectis aut detractis, aut permutatis litteris syllabisve. inde pravis ingeniis ad foedissima usque ludibria labuntur. sit enim 'consul' a consulendo vel a iudicando: nam et hoc 'consulere' veteres vocaverunt, unde adhuc remanet illud 'rogat boni consulas,'

33 id est 'bonum iudices': 'senatui' dederit nomen aetas, nam idem patres sunt: et 'rex rector' et alia plurima indubitata: nec abnuerim tegulae regulaeque et similium his rationem: iam sit et 'classis' a calando et 'lepus levipes' et 'vulpes volipes':

34 etiamne a contrariis aliqua sinemus trahi, ut 'lucus,' quia umbra

side of etymology, so long as it is confined to words, which deviate only slightly from the ἔτυμον, as e.g. rex, rector. He would have expressed himself more clearly if he had added 'and so long as the connexion of meaning is natural.' The exx. which he condemns mostly fail in this respect. For the principles of connexion which the etymologists postulated as justifying their derivations as 'per id quod efficiunt' (e.g. 'vincula' from 'vis'), 'per id quo continetur' (e.g. 'urbs' for 'orbis') and the like (amongst them of course the 'a contrariis' below) v. Augustine (?) *De Dialectica* (printed in Goetz' edition of Varro *L. L.*). V. also Art. 1919 p. 26.

veritatem, i.e. the ἔτυμον as in 7, 8.

aut correptis...syllabisve. Cf. Varro *L. L.* 5, 6 'litterarum enim fit (sc. commutatio verborum) demptione aut additione et propter earum traiectionem aut conmutationem, item syllabarum.' Varro explains that the etymologist must unravel these processes. In 5, 5 Q. has ascribed 'barbarismus' to the same causes. Most of them are illustrated in the exx. below, e.g. 'consul' (per syllabam ademptam), 'senatus' (per syll. adiectam), 'regula, tegula' (per litteram porrectam), 'classis' (per litteram permutatam).

porrectis. This synonym for 'productus' is used 7, 14. In x. 1, 29 we have 'extendere' which is also used by the grammarians.

'**consul.**' Sp. is misleading in saying 'aliam consulis originem tradit Varro.' Q. is actually reproducing Varro *L. L.* 5, 80 'consul nominatus qui consuleret populum et senatum, nisi illinc potius unde Accius ait in Bruto "qui recte consulat, consul ciat."' At the back of this view that 'consul'

= 'iudex' lay the tradition that the consuls had at one time been called 'iudices' Liv. 3, 55. A variant to these derivations appears in the 'argumentum ex vocabulo' noted in *De Or.* 2, 165 'si consul est qui consulit patriae.'

33. et 'rex.' Some edd. 'sit "rex."' Though it would ease the construction, it is hardly necessary.

rationem. I take this as meaning the analogy between these nouns with long *e* derived from verbs with short *e*. However it may mean merely the etymology commonly assigned.

'**classis' a calando.** Cp. Macrobius *Sat.* 1, 15, 10 where after noting that 'calata' = 'vocata' he continues 'verbum autem καλῶ Graecum est, id est "voco," hinc et ipsi curiae ad quam vocabantur Calabrae nomen datum est et classi, quod omnis in eam populus vocaretur.' The suggestion in Dion. H. *Ant.* 4, 18 that 'classis' = κλῆσις seems to be practically the same, for D. supports it by saying that the imp. κάλει is in Lat. 'cala.'

lepus...volipes. Of these two etymologies (both given by Aelius Stilo, v. Aul. Gell. 1, 18 and *L. L.* 5, 101) Varro had rejected the former in favour of a derivation from the Aeolic word λέπορις, and accepted the latter. Cic. probably accepts 'lepus = levipes,' when he writes 'levipes lepus' in his translation of Arat. *Phaen.* 121, as there is no corresponding epithet in the Greek.

34. a contrariis. This famous principle of etymology (κατ᾽ ἀντίφρασιν) was accepted by both Latin and Greek etymologists. In Latin we have, beside those mentioned here, 'bellum' 'parcae' 'foedus' and 'miles' (= mollis), 'lutum a lavando.' In Greek βάτος (ἄβατος), λίθος (λίαν θεῖν), ἐτώσιος (ἐτεός). The principle however fantastically applied, was not altogether irrational, as

opacus parum luceat, et 'ludus,' quia sit longissime a lusu, et 'Ditis,' quia minime dives? etiamne 'hominem' appellari, quia sit humo natus, quasi vero non omnibus animalibus eadem origo, aut illi primi mortales ante nomen inposuerint terrae quam sibi, et 'verba' ab aëre verberato? pergamus: sic perveniemus eo 35 usque, ut 'stella' luminis stilla credatur, cuius etymologiae auctorem clarum sane in litteris nominari in ea parte, quae a me reprenditur, inhumanum est. qui vero talia libris complexi sunt, 36 nomina sua ipsi inscripserunt, ingenioseque visus est Gavius 'caelibes' dicere veluti 'caelites,' quod onere gravissimo vacent,

the mere fact of euphemism shews. It is founded (as the rhetorical term ἀντί-φρασις suggests) on the truth that language is often made effective by saying the opposite of what is really meant, and antiphrasis in etymology is defined by Pompeius as 'ironla unius verbi.' When I was young 'Little Village' was an accepted colloquial term for London. It may be observed that Varro does not shew much sign of accepting the principle. The only two exx. I have noticed are 'vallum quod non varicatur' and 'caelum ab celando quod apertum est,' and neither of them does he accept definitely.

'**lucus**'...**luceat.** The stock example then as now, v. e.g. Char. K. 1. 276. Other references collected by Goetz, Varro *L. L.* p. 240.

'**ludus**'...**lusu.** So Festus 122 (88).

'**Ditis.**' For this nominative cf. Serv. on *Aen.* 6, 273 'dicimus autem et hic Dis et hic Ditis.' Here it is used possibly to shew the etymology more clearly.

'**Ditis**'...**dives.** Cic. *De Nat. De.* 2, 66 implies the same connexion of 'Dis' with 'dives,' following on Plato's derivation of Πλούτων (*Cratylus* 403), but the nature of the connexion here suggested is not, so far as I know, found elsewhere.

'**hominem**'...**natus.** This derivation appears to be found (apart from later and Christian sources) only in Hyginus (?) *Fables* 220, the date of which is very uncertain. Isidore 1. 29 perhaps takes it from Q.

'**verba**'...**verberato.** Also a common etymology, sometimes with the variant 'aurem' for 'aera,' v. exx. Goetz, Varro l.c. p. 238.

35. This etymology is not found elsewhere. I have adopted the reading of A 'quae' instead of the accepted 'qua' and understand the sentence as

follows. The author in question is not a grammarian, but a literary man of distinction (probably a contemporary), and the etymology in question is merely a casual utterance. As Q. has no occasion to acknowledge his merits elsewhere, he thinks it would be 'inhumanum' to name him in connexion with a subject, i.e. fantastic etymology, which he finds himself obliged to censure. 'Qua' would rather imply that the name should be suppressed, simply because this particular mention implies censure, and the inference would be that the individual in question had some personal claim on Q. Following this line, many edd. have supposed that Palaemon is intended, but this does not seem to me to agree well with the next sentence.

36. qui vero...**inscripserunt.** Clearly given as a proof that it is not 'inhumanum' to mention their names. This need not imply that the personage of the previous sentence wrote anonymously, but merely that these speak 'ex cathedra grammaticorum.'

Gavius. So B, as Burman had conjectured for the Gaius or Gabinius of other MSS. and Granius of the received texts. Gavius Bassus *de origine verborum et vocabulorum* is mentioned several times by Aul. Gell. (e.g. 2, 4 and 3, 19) who describes his method as 'inops et ieiuna.'

'**caelibes.**' The connexion with 'caelites' is accepted by Priscian K. 11. 18 and by others, including Isidore x. 34 and Jerome. In Christian hands it naturally gained new force from Matth. 22, 30. Reitzenstein (Varro and Joh. Maur. p. 35) is perhaps right in seeing in this etymology an example of the principle (found elsewhere in Latin etymologies, e.g. 'Dis') of tracing a word to an origin similar to that ascribed by Greek etymologists to the Greek equivalent.

idque Graeco argumento iuvit: ἠϊθέους enim eadem de causa dici adfirmat. nec ei cedit Modestus inventione: nam, quia Caelo Saturnus genitalia absciderit, hoc nomine appellatos, qui uxore
37 careant, ait; Aelius 'pituitam,' quia petat vitam. sed cui non post Varronem sit venia? qui 'agrum,' quia in eo agatur aliquid, et 'graculos,' quia gregatim volent, dictos Ciceroni persuadere voluit (ad eum enim scribit), cum alterum ex Graeco sit
38 manifestum duci, alterum ex vocibus avium. sed hoc tanti fuit vertere, ut 'merula,' quia sola volat, quasi mera volans nominaretur. quidam non dubitarunt etymologiae subicere omnem nominis causam, ut ex habitu, quem ad modum dixi, 'Longos' et 'Rufos,' ex sono 'stertere murmurare,' etiam derivata, ut a 'velocitate' dicitur 'velox,' et composita pleraque

Thus Varro suggests that 'memoria' = 'manimoria a manendo' to parallel the Greek derivations of μνεία and μνήμη from μένω. Such a principle would be a natural corollary to the Stoic view that the ἔτυμα are what they are φύσει.

ἠϊθέους, i.e. = ἀεὶ θεούς or as Reitzenstein ᾗ θεούς, though possibly the etymologists neglected the ἠι- as an 'additio.'

Modestus. A freedman of Hyginus (Suet. *Gram.* 20, cf. Martial 10, 21). His *Quaestiones confusae* is mentioned by Aul. Gell. 3, 9 (there too in connexion with Gavius Bassus). An etymology of his rather similar to this in type is mentioned by Diom. K. 1. 365. He supported 'inchoo' against 'incoho,' 'quia sit compositum a chao initio rerum.'

Aelius, i.e. L. Aelius Stilo; v. Suet. *Gram.* 2, and many other reff., for which v. dictionaries.

37. 'agrum' etc. A rather garbled statement, as what Varro says *L. L.* 5, 34 is 'ager dictus in quam terram quid agebant, et unde id agebant fructus causa. alii quod id Graeci dicunt ἀγρόν.'

'graculos,' *L. L.* 5, 76, where also 'merula.'

Ciceroni. Of the six books of the *L. L.* connected with etymology the first three are dedicated to Septumius, the others to Cicero. In adding the words 'ad eum scribit,' Q. evidently wishes to emphasise that he remembers this point.

38. sed hoc...vertere. L.'s translation 'V. had such a passion for derivation that etc.' misses the sense entirely, I believe. Rather 'it was worth while to V. to make this manipulation, in

order that' etc., i.e. the derivation of 'graculus' from 'gregatim volans' had the value of supporting the view that 'merula' etc. 'Vertere' = to turn about or manipulate by the processes of 'additio,' 'demptio' etc. I take the point to be that while it requires a serious amount of this treatment to produce 'graculus,' V. accepted it because it supported his contention about 'merula.'

etymologiae...causam. Not as L. 'to have recourse to etymology for the origin of every word,' but 'to regard every origin of name as coming under the head of etymology.' The view here spoken of corresponds to the first of Varro's four grades of etymology *L. L.* 5, 7 'nunc singulorum verborum origines expediam, quorum quattuor explanandi gradus: infimus quo populus etiam venit: quis enim non videt unde argentofodinae et viocurus.'

quem ad modum dixi, i.e. 4, 25.

stertere. So Rad. and Meister with A. B 'extrepere,' whence Halm 'strepere.'

a 'velocitate' dicitur 'velox.' I have fully discussed this passage in Art. 1916 pp. 30, 31. I now feel much more convinced of the view which I there put forward doubtfully, that the text is sound. It is true that elsewhere Q. treats 'beatitudo' as a 'declinatum' from 'beatus' (VIII. 3, 32), and 'frugalitas' from a supposed 'frugalis' (17 above), and that the later grammarians accept this view, which to us seems obvious. But Q. is here speaking of earlier etymologists and we have to reckon with Varro *L. L.* 8, 15 'declinata...ut a prudentia prudens, ab in-

his similia, quae sine dubio aliunde originem ducunt, sed arte non egent, cuius in hoc opere non est usus nisi in dubiis. Verba a vetustate repetita non solum magnos adsertores **39** habent, sed etiam adferunt orationi maiestatem aliquam non sine delectatione: nam et auctoritatem antiquitatis habent et, quia intermissa sunt, gratiam novitati similem parant. sed **40** opus est modo, ut neque crebra sint haec nec manifesta, quia nihil est odiosius adfectatione, nec utique ab ultimis et iam oblitteratis repetita temporibus, qualia sunt 'topper' et 'antegerio' et 'exanclare' et 'prosapia' et Saliorum carmina vix

genio ingeniosi...ut ab strenuitate et nobilitate, strenui et nobiles.' So Isidore I. 29 gives 'a prudentia prudens' as the example of 'facta ex nominum derivatione.' Nor is this view as unnatural as at first sight it may appear. On the accepted view in which 'demptio' played a part in the formation of words as well as 'additio,' there was nothing to decide whether 'velox' or 'velocitas' was the original. On the other hand in philosophical thought 'velocitas' is the cause of what appears in the 'velox.' It must be remembered that grammar was singularly slow in developing the distinction between adjective and substantive. If emendation is required, I should still consider that my suggestion of 'velo citato' for 'velocitate' is preferable to Meister's 'velo,' for which he quotes Priscian K. II. 140 'in "ox" verbalia vel denominativa "voco vox," "velum velox."' I should understand Q. to mean that the 'velox' possesses the qualities of a 'velum' when 'citatum.'

pleraque. In adopting this, the reading of A, instead of 'pluraque' I have differed from all edd. since Sp. I have done so, because I cannot see to what class of words the 'plura' could refer. I understand 'pleraque' to imply that not all 'composita,' but only those which in the simplicity of their origin resemble the 'derivata,' are excluded from etymology. Thus 'Publicolae' and 'Argiletum' § 31 are 'composita,' but the 'eruditio' needed to explain them brings them within the sphere of etymology.

39-41. The general thought of this passage is reproduced in VIII. 3, 24–30, where indeed it is much more appropriate. Here we are not really concerned with 'vetustas,' except in so far as it guarantees 'sermo' as 'emendatus' and thus has a place in the 'ars recte

loquendi.' There he deals with its rhetorical value in the 'ars bene dicendi.' Much of what he says here is really concerned with rhetorical values.

A large part of §§ 40, 41 together with the words 'abolita...iactantiae' in § 20 is quoted by Pope in his own note on *Essay on Criticism* 324 ff., v. Intr. p. lxxxvi, and the passage itself is clearly largely based on these sections.

'Some old words to fame have made pretence,
Ancients in phrase, mere moderns in their sense;
Such labour'd nothings, in so strange a style,
Amaze th' unlearn'd and make the learned smile.
....
In words, as fashions, the same rule will hold,
Alike fantastic, if too new or old:
Be not the first by whom the new are try'd,
Nor yet the last to lay the old aside.'

39. VIII. 3, 24 shews that he is specially thinking of Virgil.

sed etiam...delectatione. So VIII. 3, 25 '"Olli" enim et "quianam"'...adspergunt illam, quae etiam in picturis est gratissima, vetustatis inimitabilem arti auctoritatem,' a phrase which seems equivalent to the πίνος or εὐπίνεια of Dionysius.

40. sed opus...temporibus. So VIII. 3, 25 'sed utendum modo, nec ex ultimis tenebris repetenda.'

'**antegerio' et 'exanclare' et 'prosapia.'** We may be surprised to find 'exanclare' here, as Cic. uses it at least four times. He also uses 'prosapia' *Tim.* 39, but with the apology 'ut utamur vetere verbo.' 'Antegerio' and 'prosapia' are both mentioned again VIII. 3, 26. Other passages bearing on the use of archaic words are Cic. *De Or.* 3, 153, Aul.

41 sacerdotibus suis satis intellecta. sed illa mutari vetat religio
et consecratis utendum est: oratio vero, cuius summa virtus
est perspicuitas, quam sit vitiosa, si egeat interprete? ergo ut
novorum optima erunt maxime vetera, ita veterum maxime
nova.

42 Similis circa auctoritatem ratio. nam etiamsi potest videri
nihil peccare, qui utitur his verbis, quae summi auctores tradiderunt, multum tamen refert non solum, quid dixerint, sed
etiam quid persuaserint. neque enim 'tuburcinabundum' et
'lurcinabundum' iam in nobis quisquam ferat, licet Cato sit
auctor, nec 'hos lodices,' quamquam id Pollioni placet, nec
'gladiola,' atqui Messala dixit, nec 'parricidatum,' quod in
Caelio vix tolerabile videtur, nec 'collos' mihi Calvus persua-
serit: quae nec ipsi iam dicerent.

Gell. 11, 7, Suet. *Aug.* 86, and rather
casually Sen. *Ep.* 114 'multi ex alieno
saeculo petunt verba, duodecim tabulas
loquuntur.' These discussions should
be distinguished from those which deal
with the influence of old writers on style,
such as 11. 5, 21 etc.
  Saliorum carmina. Cf. Hor. *Ep.* 2,
1, 86–89.
  41. oratio...interprete. For this
emphasis on the *obscurity* of archaic
words cf. Sen. *Contr.* 9, 25, 26, where
he quotes a remark of Livy 'de oratoribus
qui verba antiqua et sordida consectan-
tur et orationis obscuritatem severitatem
putant.'
  **42. 'tuburcinabundum' et 'lurcina-
bundum.'** I have differed from former
edd. in spelling these words with 'cin-'
instead of 'chin-.' 'Lurcinor' does not
occur elsewhere, though 'collurcinatio'
does, and 'lurcho' for 'lurco,' though its
antiquity is attested by Probus K. iv.
10, can only be coupled with praecho
(4, 20): while in the few places where
'tuburcinor' occurs we do not find the
'h,' which is indeed against all ordinary
laws of Latin orthography. Sp. is hardly
right, I think, in regarding Q.'s disapproval as merely resting on the '-bundus,'
though it is true that in the other words
it is the formation and not the stem to
which exception is taken. But given
'lurcinor' what substitute could be found
for 'lurcinabundus'? It may however be
the case that the termination added to
the ugliness of an obsolescent word.
  'hos lodices,' i.e. making 'lodices'
masc. As some other grammatical views

are attributed to Pollio ('pugillares' masc.
and plur. only K. i. 97, 'nactum' not
'nanctum' ib. ii. 513, 'puer' fem. not
'puera' ib. i. 84), there seems to be
some presumption that he wrote a
grammatical work, and that this remark
on the gender of 'lodex' belongs to it is
perhaps suggested by 'placet.' On the
other hand the quotation of the word in
the plural with no apparent reason rather
looks as if Q. is quoting from some
speech, but v. on 7, 29.
  'gladiola.' Here as with 'collos' below the plural may be explained as used
to avoid the ambiguity of the acc. sing., v.
on 5, 16. Presumably Messala preferred
'gladium,' and his analogistic tendencies
led him to 'gladiolum.'
  'parricidatum.' A similar formation
to 'reatus,' viii. 3, 34.
  Caelio. Sp. infers from the words
'vix tolerabile videtur' that this is the
'omnino rudis' (Cic. *Or.* 230) Caelius
Antipater. But (1) the phrase need not
be more than a variation, (2) would
Antipater have 'auctoritas' for the
purposes of this section? (3) Caelius elsewhere in Q. clearly means the orator (5,
61 is a possible, but, I think, improbable
exception). For Caelius's eccentricities
of formation cf. viii. 6, 53. Possibly in
the same spirit as there, he gave 'parri-
cidium' a form which suggested an office,
as 'consulatus' or 'magistratus.'
  Calvus. Amongst the authors who
use 'collus' (v. Forc.) he is apparently
selected as the most recent. He is mentioned frequently by Q. (v. in particular
x. 1, 115).

Superest igitur consuetudo: nam fuerit paene ridiculum **43** malle sermonem, quo locuti sint homines, quam quo loquantur. et sane quid est aliud vetus sermo quam vetus loquendi consuetudo? sed huic ipsi necessarium est iudicium, constituendumque in primis, id ipsum quid sit, quod consuetudinem vocemus. quae si ex eo, quod plures faciunt, nomen accipiat, **44** periculosissimum dabit praeceptum non orationi modo, sed, quod maius est, vitae: unde enim tantum boni, ut pluribus quae recta sunt placeant? igitur ut velli et comam in gradus frangere et in balneis perpotare, quamlibet haec invaserint civitatem, non erit consuetudo, quia nihil horum caret reprensione (at lavamur et tondemur et convivimus ex consuetudine), sic in loquendo, non si quid vitiose multis insederit, pro regula sermonis accipiendum erit. nam ut transeam, quem **45** ad modum vulgo imperiti loquantur, tota saepe theatra et omnem circi turbam exclamasse barbare scimus. ergo consuetudinem sermonis vocabo consensum eruditorum, sicut vivendi consensum bonorum.

VII

Nunc, quoniam diximus, quae sit loquendi regula, dicendum, **1** quae scribentibus custodienda, quod Graeci ὀρθογραφίαν vocant,

43. igitur, referring to 'quae...dicerent.' The words 'superest igitur consuetudo' do not merely mean (as Sp.) that having dealt with the other four factors we have now only 'consuetudo' remaining. It is rather that 'vetustas' and 'auctoritas' cannot really claim against 'consuetudo,' being in fact merely the 'consuetudo' of the past. Q. here perhaps more definitely than elsewhere proclaims himself an anomalist, so long as 'consuetudo' is guided by 'iudicium.'
44. unde tantum boni. I understand 'unde' to suggest not so much origin as 'a qua parte.'
velli. So again II. 5, 12 and V. 9, 14. A number of parallels are given by Mayor on Juv. 8, 114.
comam in gradus frangere. So XII. 10, 47 (with much the same feeling) 'do tempori, ne hirta toga sit, non ut serica, ne intonsum caput, non ut in gradus atque anulos comptum.' Sp. well quotes Sen. *Contr.* I. Pr. 8 'capillum frangere' of the effeminate youth (called 'vulsi' ib. 10) and Suet. *Ner.* 51

'comam semper in gradus formatam.' He also notes Juv. 6, 502, but the edifice of the lady's hair there described is not attacked here. He also rightly notes that this use of 'frangere' for 'manipulate' is assisted by the suggestion of looseness and effeminacy so constantly associated with the word.
in balneis perpotare. Edd. quote Lampridius (11) of Commodus 'in balneis edebat.' Perhaps it is rather to be associated with Pers. 3, 98, and other passages where bathing after the 'cena' is described. A number of these are given by Mayor on Juv. 1, 143.
45. loquantur. So A for the 'loquuntur' of other MSS. and old edd.
tota saepe...omnem. The stress lies on these words. The audience no doubt included a large body of 'imperiti,' but also a more educated element, and even these are capable of frequent though not habitual barbarisms.
VII. In this chapter on orthography Q. does not use the canons of analogia, etymologia, auctoritas, consuetudo,

nos recte scribendi scientiam nominemus. cuius ars non
in hoc posita est, ut noverimus, quibus quaeque syllaba litteris
constet (nam id quidem infra grammatici officium est), sed
2 totam, ut mea fert opinio, suptilitatem in dubiis habet: ut
longis syllabis omnibus adponere apicem ineptissimum est,
quia plurimae natura ipsa verbi, quod scribitur, patent, sed
interim necessarium, cum eadem littera alium atque alium
3 intellectum, prout correpta vel producta est, facit: ut 'malus'
arborem significet an hominem non bonum apice distinguitur,
'palus' aliud priore syllaba longa, aliud sequenti significat, et
cum eadem littera nominativo casu brevis, ablativo longa est,
4 utrum sequamur, plerumque hac nota monendi sumus. similiter

though these were current amongst
writers on orthography, with the substitution of the term 'historia' for 'auctoritas' (v. note on 6, 1). Yet there are
some traces of them in his distinctly
rambling discourse. He opens with
what may have been another canon
διάκρισις τῶν ἀμφιλόγων (2-6). This
was a principle ascribed to Lucilius
(cf. 15), and the way in which Longus
K. VII. 56 argues against its general
applicability may imply that it was often
accepted by grammarians. In 7-10 we
have some vague allusion to etymology,
11-29 may be said to deal with the
conflicting claims of 'historia' and 'consuetudo,' while 30, 31 introduce a sixth
canon, viz. that spelling should be
phonetic. Sext. Emp. *adv. gramm.* 253
gives a division of the sphere in which
orthography operates into ποσότης, ποιότης, μερισμός. This fairly corresponds
with Q.'s arrangement in 2-9, viz.
ποσότης 2-4, ποιότης 5-8, μερισμός 9.
1. Halm following A, inserted 'hoc'
before 'nos.' Later edd. have not done
so, I think rightly.
2, 3. I have retained the accepted
punctuation and reading with all edd.
except Bonnell (who puts a full stop before 'ut' and has 'sic interim' for 'sed
interim'). It however implies some confusion of thought in Q. in making these
sentences an illustration of 'dubia.' In
the words 'sed...habet' he lays down
that in the department of orthography,
as in that of etymology (5, 38), the true
function of the grammarian is not to
state undoubted facts, but to discuss and
if possible settle questions where doubt
is reasonable. But the examples of
the 'apex' (and still more those which

follow) do not really illustrate this. In
these 'dubia' is really used in a different sense, for words which might
puzzle the reader, unless he had some
assistance. Still Bonnell's correction
would not avoid this confusion and
would merely make the sections un-
pleasantly abrupt.
2. **apicem**; v. Lindsay *L. L.* p. 4.
Cf. Scaur. K. VII. 33 'apices ibi poni
debent ubi isdem litteris alia atque alia
res designatur, ut vénit et venit, áret et
aret, légit et legit, ceteraque his similia.
super i tamen litteram apex non ponitur;
melius enim in longum producetur (i.e.
a tall I). ceterae vocales quae eodem
ordine positae diversa significant, apice
distinguuntur, ne legens dubitatione im-
pediatur, hoc est ne uno sono eaedem
pronuntientur.' This passage (like ours)
shews that the literary rule in the first
two centuries was that the 'apex' should
only be used, when needed for distinction of meaning. The inscriptions however do not lead to the conclusion that
this principle was generally observed
(v. Christiansen *De Apicibus* p. 12).
3. 'palus'...significat. L. strangely
translates '"palus" means a "stake,"
if the first syllable is long, a "marsh"
if it is short.' The real statement is:
pālus = stake, palūs = marsh. For another misapprehension v. Wilkins on
Hor. *A. P.* 65.
4, 5. Sp. goes too far, I think, in supposing that Q. definitely disapproves of
these spellings, and his argument that
'frigidiora' implies that these are 'fri-
gida' will hardly hold. His attitude is
rather one of detachment and he quotes
them as exx. of a principle held by
others.

putaverunt illa quoque servanda discrimina, ut 'ex' praepositionem si verbum sequeretur 'specto,' adiecta secundae syllabae s littera, si 'pecto,' remota scriberemus. illa quoque servata 5 est a multis differentia, ut 'ad,' cum esset praepositio, d litteram, cum autem coniunctio, t acciperet, itemque 'cum,' si tempus significaret, per quom, si comitem, per c ac duas sequentis scriberetur. frigidiora his alia, ut 'quidquid' c quartam haberet, 6 ne interrogare bis videremur, et 'quotidie' non 'cotidie,' ut sit quot diebus: verum haec iam etiam inter ipsas ineptias evanuerunt.

Quaeri solet in scribendo, praepositiones sonum, quem iunctae 7 efficiunt, an quem separatae, observare conveniat, ut cum dico 'optinuit' (secundam enim b litteram ratio poscit, aures magis

4. '**ex**'... '**specto**'... '**pecto**.' This view appears in Caesellius Vindex (2nd cent. A.D., preserved by Cassiodorus K. VII. 203). Longus, ib. 63 (though the passage is hardly intelligible as it stands), seems to declare for exp- and Scaurus, ib. 22, for exsp-. The fact that 'expecto,' 'comb out' is non-existent has made some critics suspicious, but the question of course centred round the verb 'ex-specto,' and the argument for the insertion of the *s* was that otherwise it would be taken to mean 'comb.'
5. '**ad**.' Q.'s apparent indifference on this is surprising and cannot, I think, be paralleled from the grammarians, though their remarks perhaps imply, what is confirmed by inscriptions, that the confusion was frequent; v. index to K. VII. 'at' and Nettleship's *Cont. to Lat. Lex.* s.v.
quom. The reading is very doubtful. Bn and other allied MSS. have as I have printed. Bg and A have erasures. All sorts of variations have been adopted by edd., q (Bonnell), qu et m (Halm); qu et um (Meister, Keil); qu (Rad., Becher). It seems to me that 'duas sequentes' suggests that the conjunction has been spelt out in four letters, and whether the third letter is *u* or *o* must depend on what (on other grounds) we believe to have been the usage of Q.'s time, a point on which I have not the knowledge to decide. Scaurus, the nearest of the grammarians to Q. in date, gives 'quom.' Longus, 2nd century, while maintaining the distinction between *c* and *q* d es not particularise further. I have preferred *o* to Meister's *u*, in deference partly to MS. authority,

partly to the views held on the spelling by scholars of the last generation, who seemed to regard 'quum' as a barbarism (v. Roby I. p. 35). If it should appear that 'quum' was an accepted spelling in Q.'s time, I should be inclined to suspect a transposition and read 'per q et duas u sequentis...per c' (A has *u* after 'duas').
6. '**quidquid**.' Caper (end of 2nd cent.?) and the later grammarians Marius Victorinus and Priscian support 'quicquid,' the last-named on the ground of the analogy of 'accidit' from 'adcidit' and not for the absurd reason here alleged.
'**quotidie**.' Cornutus (the philosopher of Nero's time), ap. Cass. K. VII. 149 supports 'quot-,' 'quotidie sunt qui per co cotidie scribunt, quibus peccare licet desinere, si scient quotidie tractum esse a quot diebus, hoc est omnibus diebus.' On the other hand Longus, ib. 79, declares against it, 'non est enim a quoto die sed a continenti die cotidie tractum.' So Mar. Vict. (v. indices to Keil).
verum...evanuerunt. L. 'such practices have disappeared into the limbo of absurdities.' Watson 'these notions have already passed away amidst other puerilities.' Neither of these translations takes any account of 'ipsas.' I understand the meaning to be 'they have passed away even out of that list of follies in which they might have hoped to maintain a place.' So substantially Sp., though he finds more difficulty in the phrase than I do.
7. I have adopted the punctuation suggested by Madvig, *Op. Ac.* 315, as better than, with other edd., placing the comma after 'solet' or 'praepositiones.'
'**optinuit**.' The question of the assimi-

8 audiunt p)et'immunis': illud enim, quod veritas exigit, sequentis
9 syllabae sono victum m gemina commutatur. est et in dividendis verbis observatio, mediam litteram consonantem priori
an sequenti syllabae adiungas. 'haruspex' enim, quia pars eius
posterior a spectando est, s litteram tertiae dabit, 'abstemius,'
quia ex abstinentia temeti composita vox est, primae relinquet.
10 nam k quidem in nullis verbis utendum puto nisi quae significat
etiam ut sola ponatur. hoc eo non omisi, quod quidam eam,
quotiens a sequatur, necessariam credunt, cum sit c littera,
quae ad omnis vocalis vim suam perferat.
11   Verum orthographia quoque consuetudini servit ideoque
saepe mutata est. nam illa vetustissima transeo tempora, quibus
et pauciores litterae nec similes his nostris earum formae fuerunt
et vis quoque diversa, sicut apud Graecos o litterae, quae
interim longa ac brevis, ut apud nos, interim pro syllaba, quam
12 nomine suo exprimit, posita est: ut a Latinis veteribus d

lation of prepositions is frequently treated
by the grammarians, Prisc. K. 11. 31;
Mar. Vict. VI. 18; Scaur. VII. 25; Long.
64; Corn. 151. While they note the
change of 'inm' to 'imm,' they do not
suggest that 'obt' passes into 'opt,' and
though the *p* is common in inscriptions,
I do not know of any literary parallel
to this, v. Lindsay *L. L.* p. 79.

8. illud enim. So all later edd. for
the 'illud n' of nearly all MSS. They
follow Sp. who objected to 'illud n' as
(1) abrupt, (2) illogical as compared
with 'm gemina,' (3) against Q.'s rule
of making the letters feminine. But the
true reading may well have been 'illud
enim nm,' which I am surprised that no
one has suggested.

veritas; v. on 6, 32.

9. For the rule of the grammarians,
not in ordinary cases to end a syllable
with a consonant, if that consonant can
be pronounced with the next syllable,
v. Lindsay *L. L.* pp. 125–6, where full
evidence is given. The rule was perhaps not so well established in Q.'s
time, for according to it 'a-ru-spex'
would be regular apart from etymo-
logical considerations. This passage,
as well as those in the grammarians,
shews that division of syllables was
regularly used in writing, v. Lindsay
l.c., who notes the use of dots for this
purpose in inscriptions as well as such
abbreviations as $\overline{MG}$ for 'magnus,'
$\overline{OMB}$ for 'omnibus.'

10. nam. The connexion is that
the question of *k* is only admitted in
deference to the views of 'quidam.'
Q. himself cannot place it amongst the
'dubia.' The grammarians vary considerably on this, from e.g. Diom. who
holds the view here ascribed to 'quidam,' to Priscian who declares *k* to
be 'supervacua,' while others merely
state that it cannot be used except before *a* (v. indices to Keil).

ut...ponatur, a concessive clause.
Meister has 'ubi...ponitur,' Rad. 'ita
ut...ponatur.' The former is unnecessary, the latter misses the sense. I
understand Q. to mean, that only those
words can be written in full with K
(as Kaeso, Kalendae) for which it is an
accepted symbol, even though alone.
The use of 'significat' is the same as
in 28 '"Gaius" C littera significatur'
('quae' being acc.).

vim suam perferat, i.e. can act as a
consonant.

11. quoque: either orthography is
controlled by 'consuetudo' as well as
by the above-mentioned considerations,
or orthography is controlled no less than
'orthoepeia,' see 6, 18.

sicut...posita est. Cf. Longus K.
VII. 49 'Graecorum vero qui de antiquis
litteris scripserunt commentaria, item
Latinorum qui illos secuti sunt, eadem
littera veteres solitos scribere ostendunt
μακρός, μακροῦ, μακρῷ, et confusas fuisse
o et ου et ω.' For the *name* of ου for

plurimis in verbis ultimam adiectam, quod manifestum est etiam ex columna rostrata, quae est Duilio in foro posita, interim g quoque, ut in pulvinari Solis, qui colitur iuxta aedem Quirini, 'vesperug,' quod 'vesperuginem' accipimus. de muta- 13 tione etiam litterarum, de qua supra dixi, nihil repetere hic necesse est: fortasse enim sicut scribebant, etiam loquebantur. semivocalis geminare diu non fuit usitatissimi moris, atque e 14 contrario usque ad Accium et ultra porrectas syllabas geminis,

the letter *o* v. evidence given in L. and S. on O, and Ausonius as quoted by Sp. and others. See also K. E. A. Schmidt *Beiträge zur Geschichte der Grammatik* p. 60. L. wrongly explains 'syllaba quam' etc. as meaning the interjection O!

12. ut a Latinis. Though this is accepted by all edd. it seems to me to have considerable difficulty. Are we to regard the clause as another illustration coordinate with 'sicut...posita est'? If so it is very abrupt (this may perhaps be met by reading 'ut et'), and it is difficult to suppose that Q. could speak of the ablatival *d* as an instance of an old letter with a 'diversa forma' or 'vis.' It seems possible to me that we should read 'at' (transition or rather resumption) and regard the clause as taking up the first sentence 'verum...mutata est' after the digression of 'nam illa vetustissima...posita est.'

columna rostrata. The inscription we now possess shews a number of ablatives in *d* and is no doubt what Q. refers to. The reasons which have led many scholars to consider that it 'is a restoration made in the time of Claudius may be found in Mommsen *C. I. L.* I. p. 37 and Pauly-Wissowa s.v. Duilius, v. also Wordsworth *Frag. and Spec. of Early Latin* pp. 170 and 412–414.

pulvinari. I can find no grounds for Sp.'s view that 'pulvinar' here stands for 'templum ubi pulvinaria sternuntur,' nor does there seem to be any difficulty in supposing an inscription on the 'pulvinar' itself. Sp.'s note on the temple of the Sun may be consulted by those interested in the topography of Rome. It hardly concerns the study of Q.

'vesperug.' No other notice of this so far as I know occurs anywhere, and I have no suggestion to make as to the real meaning of the word. As to Q.'s own view, Sp. thought that by 'accipimus' he meant to indicate that the

opinion though common was erroneous. This is possible, but it seems to me more probable that he accepts it and regards 'vesperug' as a neuter noun formed on the analogy of 'lac' etc. If he had thought of it as masc. he would presumably have written 'vesperugo' rather than 'vesperuginem,' as the termination which is the point in question would only belong to the nominative. I see no reason for Vollmer's correction of 'vesperum' for 'vesperuginem' mentioned by Rad.

13. supra, i.e. in 4, 13 etc.

14. semivocalis geminare. According to Festus (on 'solitaurilia' Lindsay, p. 374, cf. on 'porigam' ib. 244) the practice of doubling consonants was introduced by Ennius; v. also Mar. Vict. K. VI. 8. Q. has been accused of an error in limiting this statement to the 'semivocales,' i.e. the liquids, etc. But really his statement is very cautious, and amounts merely to saying that there was a time when these letters were more often found non-duplicated than otherwise. It may be noticed that all the duplications quoted by Festus and Mar. Vict. belong to this class, and indeed I doubt whether the question does often arise in other Latin words (if we leave compounded prepositions out of the question).

ad Accium et ultra. Here again it is generally assumed that Q. has blundered, and that the practice began with Accius. So Scaurus K. VII. 18 'Accius geminatis vocalibus scribi natura longas syllabas voluit,' Longus ib. 55 'nec Accium secuti sumus semper vocales geminantem.' To these perhaps may be added Mar. Vict. K. VI. 8, a passage which though as it stands in the MSS. it seems to ascribe the practice to Livius and Naevius, is probably to be emended in the same sense as Scaurus and Longus (v. Ritschl *Opusc.* 4, 142). The evidence of the inscriptions is said to be entirely for this view (Ritschl ib.). On the

15 ut dixi, vocalibus scripserunt. diutius duravit, ut e et i iungendis
eadem ratione qua Graeci ει uterentur: ea casibus numerisque
discreta est, ut Lucilius praecipit:

'iam "pueri venere" e postremum facito atque i,
    ut puerei plures fiant'
ac deinceps idem:
'mendaci furique addes e, cum dare furi
    iusseris.'

16 quod quidem cum supervacuum est, quia i tam longae quam

other hand Prisc. K. II. 298 by ascribing
the practice to 'vetustissimi' seems rather
to agree with Q. And whatever the
facts may be, I see nothing to shew that
Q. was not following a common tradition. The other authorities do not
actually say that Accius introduced the
practice, and the one thing on which all
are agreed is that he consistently advocated it.
porrectas...scripserunt. Mar. Vict.
K. VI. 8 notes that this does not apply
to long *i*, which Accius wrote *ei* (as a
matter of fact double *o* does not appear
to be found either). In the next sentence
Q. perhaps implies this. Observe that
he does not notice the use of the tall I,
which came into fashion in Sulla's time
(Lindsay *L. L.* p. 10).
15. ut...uterentur. The construction
requires that another 'uterentur' should
be understood after 'Graeci' governing
'ει,' but this is very awkward. I should
prefer to omit ει.
ratione. The 'ratio' common to both
languages is that the diphthong *ei* is used
in both to express the sound of long *i*, the
'discretio per casus et numeros' being
merely a Latin phenomenon.
iam 'pueri'...iusseris. I have discussed these two fragments of Lucilius
IX. (with other similar ones) in an article
in *Class. Quart.* Jan. 1921. Here the
following must suffice. The first is given
by Longus (K. VII. 56) with the addition

i si facis solum
pupilli, pueri, Lucili, hoc unius fiet.
Its meaning is of course that the gen.
sing. should be written with *i*, the plural
with *ei*. The second, which only occurs
here, appears to mean that the dat. sing.
of the 3rd declension is also to be written
with *ei*. Lachmann objected that 'iusse-
ris dare' for 'dabis' was meaningless
and proposed 'dato, Furi,' the meaning
in this case being that the voc. of

nouns in -ius should be written with
ei. So far as this objection goes it
might be met by substituting 'addet' or
'addent' for 'addes,' i.e. the correct
speller when you tell him to put 'fur'
in the dative will write 'furei.' But a
further difficulty seems to me to be raised
by the facts that (*a*) Lucilius from other
phrases used in this book seems to be
advocating a spelling in accordance with
what he believes to be correct pronunciation, though the grammarians
evidently held that these distinctions
were meant merely as διακρίσεις τῶν
ἀμφιλόγων, (*b*) in another fragment he
enjoins 'illei' (plur.), 'illi' (dat. sing.).
He seems therefore, if we accept the
ordinary reading, to be prescribing a
different pronunciation as well as spelling
for the datives of the 3rd decl. noun and
the pronoun. And if we are to suppose
that he represents the educated pronunciation of his own day, it would
follow that these two were pronounced
differently. Whether this is possible I
leave to the philologists. Prof. Lindsay
writes to me that he thinks it is.
iam 'pueri venere.' The punctuation
should be noticed (it is rightly given by
Rad.). 'Iam' introduces a new example,
i.e. 'again take the phrase "pueri venere."' There is considerable doubt as to the
choice between *i* and *ei* in the two lines,
and it is a point on which MS. authority
is of very little value. I have adopted
the spelling in the text, because it seems
to me to be Lucilius' practice to give
first the spelling which he condemns
and afterwards that which he prefers.
16. quod quidem...habet. Sp. found
himself unable to understand the logic
of this. I understand 'quod' to refer to
the general practice of writing *ei* for *i*,
not to Lucilius' special adaptation of it.
If taken so, it is logical enough. The
use of the diphthong could only be justified if there was a difference of quality

brevis naturam habet, tum incommodum aliquando; nam in iis, quae proximam ab ultima litteram e habebunt et i longa terminabuntur, illam rationem sequentes utemur e geminá, qualia sunt haec 'aurei argentei' et his similia: idque iis 17 praecipue, qui ad lectionem instituentur, etiam inpedimento erit, sicut in Graecis accidit adiectione i litterae, quam non solum dativis casibus in parte ultima adscribunt, sed quibusdam etiam interponunt ut in ΛΗΙΣΤΗΙ, quia etymologia ex divisione in tris syllabas facta desideret eam litteram. ae syllabam, 18 cuius secundam nunc e litteram ponimus, varie per a et i efferebant, quidam semper ut Graeci, quidam singulariter tantum, cum in dativum vel genetivum casum incidisset, unde 'pictai vestis' et 'aquai' Vergilius amantissimus vetustatis carminibus inseruit. in eisdem plurali numero e utebantur ⟨ut⟩ 19 his 'Syllae Galbae.' est in hac quoque parte Lucilii praeceptum,

in the sound thus represented from that of short *i*. Q. considers that there was no such difference. As to whether there actually was v. Lindsay *L. L.* pp. 27 sq. L. translates 'since *i* can be long no less than short.' But the phrase seems to me an odd one. I should be inclined to read '*i* tam longa quam brevis *i* (gen.) naturam habet,' words which would very easily be corrupted into what we have.

haec 'aurei argentei.' I know no other instance in Q. of this use of the neuter article with the nominative. Possibly it may be intended to mark that the forms quoted are individual cases and do not represent the noun as a whole. Rad. spells 'aureei argenteei.' This seems unnecessary. Q. is merely quoting exx. of words to which what he is saying applies.

17. ΛΗΙΣΤΗΙ. It is strange that Halm should have so little observed Q.'s usage as to write 'ipse malim ΛΗΙΣΤΗΣ.' This would be unprecedented, while 'in hoc ΛΗΙΣΤΗΣ' would confine the point illustrated to the nominative. For Q.'s use of the Greek dative after prepositions governing the ablative cf. ἐκ συνδέσμῳ 4, 18. At the same time the case serves to illustrate both the uses of the ι subscript, indicated in 'non solum...ascribunt.'

18. a et i. This spelling survives in inscriptions up to imperial times, v. Lindsay *L. L.* p. 43.

incidisset. I have adopted this correction of Kiderlin for 'incidissent.'

'Incidere in casum' is certainly more appropriately used of a termination than of a reader. Kid. quotes 5, 17.

'aquai.' Earlier edd. with little authority 'aulai.'

19. utebantur ⟨ut⟩ his 'Syllae Galbae.' All recent edd. 'utebantur hi Syllae Galbae.' So apparently A (according to Zumpt). The reading of B is not stated, but Joann. Nost. and Put. have 'his' (articular). In making the correction printed I have been guided by the following considerations: (1) while it is not clear how MS. authority stands between 'hi' and 'his,' the difference in this position is too slight to be taken into account; (2) I can find no parallel for such a use of 'hi.' There is no question of gender. If I am right in the note above on 'haec aurei,' the articular pronoun might be used on the same principle as there, but why not as there, neuter? (3) 'ut' (which indeed even with 'his' is not absolutely necessary) would easily fall out after 'utebantur.' For 'eisdem' Meister reads 'eadem' sc. 'syllaba.' This is unnecessary, at any rate if we insert 'ut.' I take 'eisdem' to mean nouns of the first declension.

Lucilii praeceptum. What was this? Some words of Mart. Cap. 266 'Lucilius in dativo casu a et e coniungit dicens huic Terentiae Orbiliae' seem to shew that Luc. did not agree with the 'quidam' above as to the dative. On the other hand Q. seems to imply that he agreed generally. Otherwise what is the point of 'si quis parum credet'? It can hardly

quod quia pluribus explicatur versibus, si quis parum credet,
20 apud ipsum in nono requirat. quid quod Ciceronis temporibus
paulumque infra, fere quotiens s littera media vocalium longarum
vel subiecta longis esset, geminabatur, ut 'caussae, cassus,
divissiones'? quomodo et ipsum et Vergilium quoque scripsisse
21 manus eorum docent. atqui paulum superiores etiam illud,
quod nos gemina dicimus 'iussi,' una dixerunt. iam 'optimus
maximus,' ut mediam i litteram, quae veteribus u fuerat,
acciperent, Gai primum Caesaris inscriptione traditur factum.

mean that the sceptic might doubt the
existence of such a passage. If he so
far agreed as to differentiate between
nom. plur. and gen. sing. and to set the
dative with the former, it would be in
line with the usual interpretation of 15.
20. media...longis. I have retained
the accepted text, though I feel much
drawn to Andresen's 'media vocalium
et subiecta longis' (or 'longae'). As he
says, in the MS. reading the first condition is unnecessary, as the quantity of
the posterior vowel is not relevant,
while the second is inadequate, for *s*
following a long vowel was not doubled
before a consonant (caespes, maestus).
Further, the alteration we find might
well be the work of the same bungler,
who I suggest corrected 5, 62 and 6, 29
in order to make the statement fit with
the exx. given. If we retain the text we
must suppose Q. to be saying in a very
awkward way that double *s* was found
between two long vowels and indeed
if only one of the two vowels was long.
As to the later disuse of the double *s*,
v. Lindsay *L. L.* pp. 110–111. The
grammarians in general were divided
as to whether it was impossible after a
long vowel, or only after a diphthong.
caussae etc. (plur.), v. on 29.
manus. Cf. Plin. *N. H.* 13, 26 (12)
'Iam vero Ciceronis et Divi Augusti
Vergiliique saepenumero videmus' (sc.
'manus').
There are several allusions to auto-
graph copies (real or supposed) of Virgil
in Aul. Gell., e.g. 9, 14, where, speaking
of the reading 'dies' genitive, which he
had found in old copies of Cic. *Pro
Sest.*, he continues 'quocirca factum
hercle est, ut facile iis credam qui scripserunt idiographum librum Vergilii sese
inspexisse in quo ita scriptum est "libra
dies somnique."' Other passages are
1, 21; 2, 3; 13, 20. All of these are
given in Lehrs' *Aristarchus* pp. 345,

346 (a very valuable disquisition on the
care taken by scholars of the time in
consulting old MSS.).
21. 'iussi.' If the quantity of the *u*
is otherwise doubtful (v. Lindsay *L. L.*
pp. 481, 498) this remark of Q. seems
to me to be an argument for its length.
If it is long, we have an instructive contrast to the point just mentioned. If it
is short, the double *s* is normal, and
the mention of it is a rather pointless
repetition of what has already been said
of the semivocales in 14.
Caesaris inscriptione. In deciding
the reading and interpretation of this we
have to deal with the two following
passages: (*a*) Longus K. VII. 67 'varie
etiam scriptitatum est mancupium aucu-
pium manubiae, siquidem C. Caesar
per i scripsit, ut apparet ex titulis ipsius,
at Augustus per u, ut testes sunt eius
inscriptiones,' (*b*) Cornutus ib. 150 'la-
crumae an lacrimae, maxumus an maximus, et siqua similia sunt, quo modo
scribi debeant, quaesitum est. Terentius
Varro tradidit Caesarem per i eiusmodi
verba solitum esse enuntiare et scribere:
inde propter auctoritatem tanti viri consuetudinem factam.' There can be little
doubt that Q.'s statement (and probably
Long.'s) depend on the passage in V.
(probably in the *de sermone Latino*)
which Cor. quotes. The proposed correction 'inscriptionibus' however is
unnecessary. The passage in V. may
well have quoted some particular inscription as having given the lead, at
the same time indicating that it did not
stand alone. (Halm's proposal of 'in
inscriptione' apart from what is said in
the next note on Q.'s use or non-use of
'in,' though easy enough, is unnecessary.)
The only points that raise a doubt are
(1) that Longus' statement would appear
at first sight to limit the inscriptional
evidence to these three particular words,
(2) A has 'instructione.' On these

'here' nunc e littera terminamus: at veterum comicorum adhuc 22
libris invenio 'heri ad me venit,' quod idem in epistulis Augusti,
quas sua manu scripsit aut emendavit, deprenditur. quid? non 23
Cato Censorius 'dicam' et 'faciam' 'dicae' et 'faciae' scripsit
eundemque in ceteris, quae similiter cadunt, modum tenuit?
quod et ex veteribus eius libris manifestum est et a Messala
in libro de s littera positum. 'sibe' et 'quase' scriptum in 24
multorum libris est, sed an hoc voluerint auctores nescio:
T. Livium ita his usum ex Pediano comperi, qui et ipse eum
sequebatur. haec nos i littera finimus. quid dicam 'vortices' 25
et 'vorsus' ceteraque ad eundem modum, quae primus Scipio
Africanus in e litteram secundam vertisse dicitur? nostri prae- 26

grounds Claussen proposed 'institutione.' But if we are to follow this line
at all, I should much prefer to read 'in
scriptione.' The use of 'scriptio' for
a particular form of spelling is frequent
in Longus, and though it does not
appear elsewhere in Q., we have to remember that this is the only chapter in
which he deals with spelling. Sp.'s explanation (repeated by L.) that by C.
Caesar is meant Caligula, who 'optimus
maximus vocabatur' (Suet. *Cal.* 22), is in
view of the evidence very improbable.

22. '**here**' **nunc e**. The later grammarians do not confirm this but appear
to allow both forms equally.

adhuc. If the words are taken strictly
the argument appears to be that if an
archaic spelling survives in *modern*
copies of an old writer, it is a *prima
facie* ground for supposing that he used
it. Q. however does not seem to accept
this as evidence in the case of 'quase'
and 'sibe' 24. I cannot help thinking
that he means that old copies still survive. Possibly 'veteribus' has fallen out
before 'veterum.'

libris. We should certainly expect
'in,' but Q. appears in many places to
have a tendency to dispense with the
preposition, e.g. x. 3, 3; xi. 2, 32 and
possibly viii. 6, 64.

'**heri ad me venit.**' A quotation from
Ter. *Phorm.* i. 1, 2 which does not fit
in very well with the preceding plural.
I should be inclined to read '⟨heri ut⟩
heri' etc.

epistulis Augusti. As Burman pointed
out, two of the surviving extracts (Suet.
Aug. 71, *Cal.* 8) contain this word.

sua manu. 'Autographa epistula'
Suet. *Aug.* 71. Cf. Plin. *N. H.* 13, 26
quoted on 20.

23. '**dicae**' **et** '**faciae**' ('dice et facie'
Rad. with N). This reading instead of
the 'dicem et faciem' of nearly all edd.
is proved by ix. 4, 39 'et illa Censori
Catonis dieae hac eque†ni littera in e
mollita. quae in veteribus libris reperta
mutare imperiti solent, et dum librari-
orum insectari volunt inscientiam, suam
confitentur.' Here the emendation to
'dicae(e) faciae(e)que' seems certain. Cf.
'dice pro dicam antiqui posuere' Fest. 63.

Messala in libro de s. For this book
cf. 5, 15 and ix. 4, 38 'quae fuit causa et
Servio, ut dixi, subtrahendae s litterae
quotiens ultima esset aliaque consonante
susciperetur, quod...Messala defendit.'
So too Mart. Cap. 244 's nonnulli litteram non putarunt, nam Messala quemdam sibilum dixit.' Clearly M. defended
his doctrine of the omission of *s* by the
analogous omission of *m* in 'dicam' etc.

24. nescio an. 'Q.'s use of "nescio
an" (like that of post-Augustan writers
generally) is vague: it is usually an expression of doubt, the "an" meaning
"whether" or "whether not" indifferently.' Peterson on x. 1, 65 (critical note).

Pediano. As Asconius lived till c. 88
A.D. Q. probably means that he learnt this
through personal intercourse and that
the statement applies to Livy's regular
practice in composition. This passage,
taken together with Asc. in Corn. 76,
where he speaks of 'Livius noster,' suggests that he was a native of Padua.

25. '**vortices**' **et** '**vorsus.**' Cf.
Corn. K. vii. 149 'vostra olim ita per o,
hodie per e ut advorsa adversa...vortex,
vertex.' Caper on the other hand ib. 99 has
'vortex fluminis est, vertex capitis,' while
Pliny (acc. to Char. K. i. 88) 'vertex
a vertendo, vortex a vorando.'

Scipio Africanus. Other innovations of

7—2

ceptores 'seruum ceruumque' u et o litteris scripserunt, quia
subiecta sibi vocalis in unum sonum coalescere et confundi
nequiret, nunc u gemina scribuntur ea ratione, quam reddidi:
neutro sane modo vox, quam sentimus, efficitur, nec inutiliter
27 Claudius Aeolicam illam ad hos usus litteram adiecerat. illud
nunc melius, quod 'cui' tribus quas posui litteris enotamus, in
quo pueris nobis ad pinguem sane sonum qu et oi utebantur,
tantum ut ab illo 'qui' distingueretur.
28   Quid? quae scribuntur aliter quam enuntiantur? nam et

spelling ascribed to him are 'rederguo'
for 'redarguo' and 'pertisum' for 'per-
taesum,' v. Festus 372. These two look
like attempts to introduce analogy into
both the spelling and pronunciation of
these words, his argument being that
compounds in 're' and 'per' should follow
the rule of compounds with other prepositions. If it is true (Lindsay *L. L.*
p. 467) that the 'vo-' was at this time
pronounced as 've-,' we have here another
conscious attempt on the part of Scipio
to promote 'ratio' in grammar (v. also
Lindsay, p. 228).

'**u**' et '**o**.' Cf. Prisc. K. II. 27 'Romanorum vetustissimi in multis dictionibus
loco eius (i.e. *u*) "o" posuisse inveniuntur...et maxime digammo ante-
cedente hoc faciebant, ut "servos" pro
"servus," "volgus" pro "vulgus,"
"Davos" pro "Davus."'

quia...nequiret. L. impossibly translates 'that the repetition of the vowel
might not lead to the coalescence and
confusion of the two sounds.' And so
Watson. I think it is clear that the
meaning is 'because as they held,
two identical vowels could not form a
diphthong,' cf. 4, 11. The reasoning is
(*a*) two vowels in a syllable must form
'unus sonus,' but (*b*) two identical vowels
cannot do this, therefore (*c*) one of these
must be altered. The later spelling accepted (*a*) and (*b*), but returned to *uu* on
the grounds that the first *u* was really a
consonant. This last is the 'ratio,' as I
understand it, to which Q. refers in the
next few words, and which he has stated
in 4, 10-11.

neutro...efficitur. Because (1) *o* is not
heard in 'seruom,' (2) the written *u*
does not properly represent the consonantal sound.

Claudius: v. on 4, 8.

litteram. Some MSS. prefix F,
others .f.

27. melius. I understand Q. to com-

pare the change from 'quoi' to 'cui'
with that from 'servom' to 'servum,'
and to regard the former as superior in
that it did serve to distinguish two forms
otherwise liable to confusion, whilst not
misrepresenting the sound. This seems
to me preferable to taking 'melius' (as
L. and W.) to mean that 'cui' is superior
to 'quoi.' That 'cui' was regarded as
having this usefulness is shewn by
Scaurus K. VII. 28, 'c autem in dativo
ponimus ut sit differentia "cui" et
"qui."' Very possibly he is right, and
the difference in spelling between the
two was really for purposes of distinction
and had no phonetic basis; v. Lindsay
L. L. 39, 44. This passage receives a
curious illustration in IX. 3, 8, where Q.,
quoting the last two lines of the Fourth
Eclogue 'cui non risere parentes, nec deus
hunc' etc., takes the first word as 'qui'
and treats the passage as illustrating
the change from plur. 'qui' to sing.
'hunc.' It has generally been supposed
that he found 'quoi' in his copy, but
is there any evidence for a nom. plur.
'quoi'?

posui. This has been accepted by
most edd. MSS. 'pposui,' but neither
'proposui' nor 'praeposui,' which Rad.
adopts, gives a very satisfactory sense.

pueris nobis. Cf. 'nobis iuvenibus,'
5, 24. If there is any distinction between
the two, it is that the first was a definite
rule laid down 'apud grammaticum,' the
other a general practice, which he had
observed. A good collection of these
reminiscences is given by Mayor on
x. 1, 24.

tantum... distingueretur. 'Nostri
praeceptores' no doubt gave this reason
and believed it. But the spelling really
represented the old pronunciation (Lindsay *L. L.* p. 445), which survived to
Longus' time, K. VII. 76, 'itaque audimus quosdam plena oi syllaba dicere
quoi et hoic pro cui et huic quod multo

'Gaius' C littera significatur, quae inversa mulierem declarat, quia tam Gaias esse vocitatas quam Gaios etiam ex nuptialibus sacris apparet: nec 'Gnaeus' eam litteram in praenominis nota 29 accipit, qua sonat, et 'columnam' et 'consules' exempta n littera legimus, et 'Subura,' cum tribus litteris notatur, C tertiam

vitiosius est.' Q.'s 'ad pinguem sonum' indeed recognises this.

28. quae...declarat. Cf. Longus K. VII. 53 'C conversum quo Gaia significatur; quod notae genus videmus in monumentis cum quis libertus mulieris ostenditur. Gaias enim generaliter a specie omnes mulieres accipere voluerunt.'

quia...apparet. Sp. was unable to see the connection of this with the preceding and believed it to be a gloss from the 'notae' of Petrus Diaconus (12th century), where the sentence appears bodily (Putsch, p. 1587). Apparently however it is an interpolation there (v. Keil's preface, IV. 331). I take the connexion to be this: the theory that inverted 'C' on the monuments indicated a woman in general and not one named Gaia was argued by the antiquarians of the time from the use of Gaia in the marriage ceremony. For this last we have abundant evidence.

Whether the further theory as to its use on the monuments has any foundation in fact, or was merely deduced from the special frequency of the name 'Gaia,' I leave to students of the inscriptions. In the particular instance quoted by Sp. it is clearly a proper name.

29. qua sonat. I have retained 'qua,' which is the reading of Halm and his successors, in deference to their judgment and the preponderance of MS. authority, but I am strongly inclined to the 'quae' of A (second hand?). I have not found any exx. of such a phraseology as 'verbum sonat litterā,' while on the other hand the 'littera' itself 'sonat,' VIII. 3, 16; cf. IX. 4, 40, and so several times in Longus.

et 'columnam'...legimus. The reading 'clarissimos et consules geminata eadem littera legimus,' which is found in the second hand of A and B and some other MSS. (in A on an erasure which however contained the crucial word 'geminata'), has rightly been rejected by all edd. except Bonnell. It is apparently founded on the idea that Q. is speaking of the use of 'C' in abbreviations. The statement that 'clarissimi' was expressed by 2 c's appears in Bede K. VII. 261 'v

geminata cum c duplici viri clarissimi,' cf. ib. IV. 290, but I know of no evidence that 'consules' was ever written in this way, and there cannot well be any allusion to the form 'coss.' The reading of the text is discussed by Hardie (*Cl. Rev.* Aug. 1913). He is undoubtedly right in rejecting the interpretation put on the words by Lindsay and others, that 'legimus' = 'we read aloud as,' so that Q. is made to say that 'consul' is written with an *n* and sounded without it. The meaning is exactly the opposite (cf. 6, 11 'cum in XII tabulis legeremus'), though probably the spelling does point to some pronunciation which was common (perhaps in earlier times) but is not recognised by Q. I think however that Hardie is wrong in assuming that the reference must be to abbreviations on inscriptions or elsewhere. For though it is true that most of the exx. are abbreviations, the point is that in each case a letter is used other than that which is pronounced. 'Cosul' for 'consul' is found on inscriptions, v. Thes. s.v., and it is this which presumably he has primarily in view, though he may also have the form 'Cos.' 'Columna n exempta' can hardly be an abbreviation. For the form 'columa' edd. quote Pompeius K. v. 283, where 'columa' and 'mamor' are given as exx. of barbarisms.

The plural 'consules,' on which Hardie attempts to found some argument, cannot, I think, be regarded as more than a variation. While some of the plurals used in these chapters have a purpose (e.g. 5, 16, and 6, 42) a large number have no special point (e.g. 'foedus,' 4. 14; 'stlites,' 4, 15; the names in 4, 25; 'aedos ircosque,' 5, 20; 'gurdos,' 5, 57; 'ignavi,' 5, 69; 'lodices,' 6, 42; 'divissiones,' 7. 20; 'vortices et vorsus,' 7, 25).

'Subura.' Cf. Festus 444 'Suburam Verrius alio libro a pago Succusano dictam ait...indicioque esse quod adhuc ea tribus per C litteram non B scribatur.' The text of Varro *L. L.* 5, 48 (after giving another view) has 'sed pago potius Succusano dictam puto Succusam nunc scribitur [space of three letters] tertia littera C non B.' This has been with

ostendit. multa sunt generis huius, sed haec quoque vereor ne
modum tam parvae quaestionis excesserint.

30   Iudicium autem suum grammaticus interponat his omnibus:
nam hoc valere plurimum debet. ego, nisi quod consuetudo
optinuerit, sic scribendum quidque iudico, quomodo sonat.

31 hic enim est usus litterarum, ut custodiant voces et velut de-
positum reddant legentibus. itaque id exprimere debent, quod
32 dicturi sumus. hae fere sunt emendate loquendi scribendique
partes: duas reliquas significanter ornateque dicendi non
equidem grammaticis aufero, sed, cum mihi officia rhetoris
supersint, maiori operi reservo.

33   Redit autem illa cogitatio, quosdam fore, qui haec, quae
diximus, parva nimium et inpedimenta quoque maius aliquid
agentibus putent: nec ipse ad extremam usque anxietatem

probability emended to 'sed ⟨ego a⟩
pago p. S. d. p. Succusam : ⟨nam etiam⟩
nunc scr. ⟨Suc.⟩ t. l. C n. B.'
tam parvae quaestionis. I.e. the subject of 28, 29, not orthography in general
which is too large to be called a 'quaestio.'
30–32. In these sections it might
be held that we still continue this subject of 'quae scribuntur aliter quam
enuntiantur.' On the whole it seems to
me that edd. are right in beginning a
fresh paragraph here. The type of spelling noticed in 28, 29, where 'scriptio'
and 'dictio' differed as much as they used
to in Sawbridgeworth and Cirencester,
is a special type. In 30 we pass on to
a general statement of the principles of
orthography. What these amount to is
that the rival claims of 'consuetudo' and
'scribendum quomodo sonat' are to be
settled by 'iudicium'; cf. note on 4, 3.
30. sic scribendum ... sonat. Cf.
Cornutus K. VII. 149 'nonnulli putant
auribus deserviendum atque ita scribendum, ut auditur. est enim fere certamen de recta scriptura in hoc utrum
quod audimus, an quod scribi oporteat,
scribendum sit. ego non omnia auribus
dederim.' Also Suet. *Aug.* 88 'ortho-
graphiam, id est, formulam rationemque
scribendi a grammaticis institutam non
adeo custodit, ac videtur eorum potius
sequi opinionem, qui perinde scribendum
ac loquamur existiment.' So also Longus
K. VII. 54 'ingredienti mihi rationem
scribendi occurrit statim ita quosdam
censuisse esse scribendum, ut loquimur
et audimus.' He replies that this principle would involve the omission of final

m in 'illum ego' and the doubling of *c*
in 'hoc erat.' The grammarians in fact
seem to have emphasised the point that
spelling should not always be phonetic.
Q. places his emphasis rather differently,
though his argument is substantially the
same.

32. significanter, i.e. clearly = 'per-
spicua' in the formula of 5, 1. So too
VIII. Pr. 31, 'Latina (=emendata), significantia, ornata.' So perhaps too X.
I, 49. Elsewhere e.g. IV. 2, 36, X. 1,
121, 'significans' and its cognate words
seem rather to suggest 'forcible, graphic,
full of meaning.'

non grammaticis aufero. These
qualities of speech had to be dealt with
by the grammaticus, both in his criticism
of authors, 8, 13–17, and in the 'progymnasmata' of ch. 9.

maiori operi reservo, i.e. in the eighth
book.

33. redit, referring to 4, 6. 'sedet'
adopted by Bonnell has less MS.
authority and inferior sense.

agentibus. So Halm and recent edd.
with A. Sp. with B 'agendi.'

nec ipse...credo. It is best to take
this 'I do not think we should, etc.,
such studies reduce the mind to fragments,' the negative being regarded as
extending only to 'descendendum'; but
it is perhaps possible that the present
inf. is loosely coordinated with the
gerundive. Burman who took this view
quoted Val. Max. 2, 6, 'patriae in-
columitatem fortiter tueri, et fidem
amicitiae constanter praestandam arbi-
trabantur.'

et ineptas cavillationes descendendum atque his ingenia concidi
et comminui credo. sed nihil ex grammatice nocuerit, nisi 34
quod supervacuum est. an ideo minor est M. Tullius orator,
quod idem artis huius diligentissimus fuit et in filio, ut epistulis
apparet, recte loquendi asper quoque exactor? aut vim C.
Caesaris fregerunt editi de analogia libri? aut ideo minus 35
Messala nitidus, quia quosdam totos libellos non verbis modo
singulis, sed etiam litteris dedit? non opstant hae disciplinae
per illas euntibus, sed circa illas haerentibus.

VIII

Superest lectio: in qua puer ut sciat, ubi suspendere spiritum 1
debeat, quo loco versum distinguere, ubi claudatur sensus, unde

concidi. Cf. Pr. 24.
comminui, cf. 12, 14. 'To descend
to these extreme anxieties and foolish
cavils of grammarians is able to break
a wit in pieces.' Ben Jonson, *Disc.* 118.
34. artis huius diligentissimus. Cf.
Tac. *Dial.* 30, 'in libris Ciceronis deprehendere licet non geometriae, non
musicae, non grammaticae, non denique
ullius ingenuae artis scientiam ei defuisse.' But C.'s knowledge of the
'methodical' side of 'grammatice' is
not very profound, and Q. is probably
thinking mainly of the *Orator*, which
he has already quoted.
in filio. Amongst the fragments of
these letters is an objection on the part
of C. to his son's phrase 'direxi duas
litteras' on the grounds that 'epistulas'
should be used for the plural (Serv. on
Aen. 7, 168).
ut epistulis. Meister, 'ut in ep.'
with A.
aut...libri. So Fronto (221 N.) who
may have had this passage in mind,
'fac memineris et cum animo tuo cogites
C. Caesarem atrocissimo bello Gallico
cum alia multa militaria, tum etiam
duos de analogia libros scrupulosissimos
scripsisse inter tela volantia de nominibus declinandis, de verborum aspira-
tionibus et rationibus inter classica et
tubas.' Caesar is however said by Suet.
Jul. 56 to have written it 'in transitu
Alpium, cum ex citeriore Gallia con-
ventibus peractis ad exercitum rediret.'
For these quotations and other information about the book v. Funaioli, *Gram.*
Rom. Frag. p. 145. I judge the book
to have been only mildly analogistic and

very possibly the title means nothing
more than 'inflection.'
vim. 'Vis' is again given in XII. 10,
11 as the predominant quality of Caesar's
oratory. Cf. also X. 1, 114, 'tanta in eo
vis est, id acumen, ea concitatio, ut
illum eodem animo dixisse quo bellavit
appareat; exornat tamen haec omnia
mira sermonis, cuius proprie studiosus
fuit, elegantia.'
35. nitidus. Messala is called 'nitidus et candidus' X. 1, 113. It is difficult
to get any clear idea of the meaning of
the adj. in Q. The clearest guides are
that in VIII. 3, 18, it is said to be the
opposite of 'humilis,' and in XII. 10, 79
'nitor' needs 'cultus virilis' as a cor-
rective. I do not think 'polish' (L.)
adequately expresses it here. 'Had M.
less charm and brightness' might possibly give the meaning.
verbis. Cf. Suet. *Gram.* 4 (discussing
the Lat. equivalents of γραμματικός),
'litteratores vocitatos Messala Corvinus
in quadam epistula ostendit.'
litteris. This of course includes the
treatise on 's.' No other is known and
not more than one such treatise is
necessarily implied.
circa illas haerentibus. Cf. VIII.
Pr. 27 'atqui plerosque videas haerentes
circa singula.'
VIII. 1. This section should be compared with the elaborate discussion of
'pronuntiatio' in rhetoric, Bk. XI. ch.
3, and still more with Dionysius
Thrax 2–4: ἀνάγνωσίς ἐστι ποιημάτων
ἢ συγγραμμάτων ἀδιάπτωτος προφορά.
ἀναγνωστέον δὲ καθ' ὑπόκρισιν, κατὰ
προσῳδίαν, κατὰ διαστολήν· ἐκ μὲν γὰρ

incipiat, quando attollenda vel submittenda sit vox, quo quidque
flexu, quid lentius celerius, concitatius lenius dicendum, de-

τῆς ὑποκρίσεως τὴν ἀρετήν, ἐκ δὲ τῆς
προσῳδίας τὴν τέχνην, ἐκ δὲ τῆς διαστολῆς
τὸν περιεχόμενον νοῦν ὁρῶμεν· ἵνα τὴν
μὲν τραγῳδίαν ἡρωικῶς ἀναγνῶμεν, τὴν
δὲ κωμῳδίαν βιωτικῶς, τὰ δὲ ἐλεγεῖα λιγυ-
ρῶς, τὸ δὲ ἔπος εὐτόνως, τὴν δὲ λυρικὴν
ποίησιν ἐμμελῶς, τοὺς δὲ οἴκτους ὑφειμένως
καὶ γοερῶς. τὰ γὰρ μὴ παρὰ τὴν τούτων
γινόμενα παρατήρησιν, καὶ τὰς τῶν ποιητῶν
ἀρετὰς καταρριπτεῖ καὶ τὰς ἕξεις τῶν ἀνα-
γινωσκόντων καταγελάστους παρίστησιν.
τόνος ἐστὶν ἀπήχησις φωνῆς ἐναρμονίου,
ἡ κατὰ ἀνάτασιν ἐν τῇ ὀξείᾳ, ἡ κατὰ
ὁμαλισμὸν ἐν τῇ βαρείᾳ, ἡ κατὰ περίκλασιν
ἐν τῇ περισπωμένῃ. Στιγμαί εἰσι τρεῖς·
τελεία, μέση, ὑποστιγμή (but v. Rutherford *Chapter* p. 168, on the text here)
καὶ ἡ μὲν τελεία στιγμή ἐστι διανοίας
ἀπηρτισμένης σημεῖον, μέση δὲ σημεῖον
πνεύματος ἕνεκεν παραλαμβανόμενον,
ὑποστιγμὴ δὲ διανοίας μηδέπω ἀπηρτισμένης ἀλλ᾽ ἔτι ἐνδεούσης σημεῖον.
In this extract ἀνάγνωσις καθ᾽ ὑπόκρισιν
appears to be explained by ἵνα τὴν μὲν
τραγῳδίαν...παρίστησιν, and κατὰ προσῳδίαν and κατὰ διαστολήν in the next
two sections. Q.'s 'ubi suspendere...
incipiat' clearly equals the last, and
(with the reading here adopted) καθ᾽
ὑπόκρισιν is represented by 'quando attollenda...dicendum,' and also by § 3,
while there is no equivalent for κατὰ
προσῳδίαν (on this point I went wrong
in Art. 1914). For an alternative view
v. note on 'flexu.'

**suspendere spiritum...versum dis-
tinguere...claudatur sensus.** These
three seem to correspond respectively
to the ὑποστιγμή 'subdistinctio,' στιγμὴ
μέση 'media,' τελεία 'finalis distinctio,'
of the Greek grammarians. Cf. the last
section of the quotation above from Dion.
Thrax, which even if garbled represents
a common grammatical view. So too
Diom K. I. 437, though from this it
might at first sight be thought that
'suspendere spiritum' here = στιγμὴ
μέση. But this is negatived by XI. 3,
35–38, where Q. applies his principles
to the first seven lines of the *Aeneid.*
There we are told that there is a 'sus-
pensio' after 'cano,' 'oris' (to mark the
end of the line), 'Italiam,' and 'profugus,' but no 'distinctio.' The first
'distinctio,' though a comparatively
light one (μέση) comes at the break in
the thought after 'litora' (line 3), but
there is no complete 'distinctio' till
'Romae' (line 7).

quo quidque flexu. So Halm and
later edd. following Sp.'s suggestion for
'quid quoque' of the MSS. Cf. 6, 16.
'Flexu' may either anticipate 'lentius'
etc., or more probably suggests the more
delicate modulations of the voice, as
again in § 3, and in 10, 23; v. also note
on 11, 12.

At the same time it may be worth
while to consider another interpretation,
which could be obtained by keeping the
MS. reading 'quid quŏque flexu,' or
possibly emending 'flexu' to 'flexa,' sc.
'voce.' According to this the words
would be taken closely with 'quando
att. vel subm. vox' ('quoque' almost =
'denique' as in VII. 10, 7 and XI. 3, 17
quoted below). The three verbs 'attollere, submittere, flectere vocem' would
then indicate the three accents. The
introduction of these would bring the
passage into closer harmony with Dion.
Thrax, and perhaps also with the words
in XI. 3 which most closely otherwise
resemble this passage, viz. § 17 'utendi
voce multiplex ratio, nam praeter illam
differentiam quae est tripertita acutae,
gravis, flexae, tum intentis, tum remissis,
tum elatis, tum inferioribus modis opus
est, spatiis quoque lentioribus aut cita-
tioribus.' Cp. also Ausonius, *Id.* 4,
47–50 :

'tu flexu et acumine vocis
innumeros numeros doctis accentibus
effer,
adfectusque impone legens : distinctio
sensum
auget et ignavis dant intervalla vigo-
rem,'

where clearly we have D.T.'s κατὰ προσῳδίαν, ὑπόκρισιν, διαστολήν.

My consideration for this view mainly
rests on the belief that it is *prima facie*
improbable that Q. would here omit the
question of accent, considering the persistent assumption by him and the
grammarians generally that Latin had
a system of accentuation similar to the
Greek, and also the fact that in this
chapter he has Greek schools in his
mind as well as Latin. Nor does the
awkwardness by which on this theory
'quid quoque flexu' is assimilated in
construction to what is less rather than
what is more connected with it seem to
me fatal. It may be paralleled by 9, 1
and perhaps 5, 42 and 43, where v.
notes. My chief objection is that we
need evidence of the use of 'attollere'

monstrari nisi in opere ipso non potest. unum est igitur, quod **2** in hac parte praecipiam: ut omnia ista facere possit, intellegat. sit autem in primis lectio virilis et cum suavitate quadam gravis, et non quidem prosae similis, quia et carmen est et se poetae canere testantur, non tamen in canticum dissoluta nec plasmate, ut nunc a plerisque fit, effeminata, de quo genere optime C. Caesarem praetextatum adhuc accepimus dixisse: 'si cantas, male cantas, si legis, cantas.' nec prosopopoeias, ut **3** quibusdam placet, ad comicum morem pronuntiari velim, esse tamen flexum quendam, quo distinguantur ab iis, in quibus poeta persona sua utetur. cetera admonitione magna egent, **4** in primis, ut tenerae mentes tracturaeque altius quidquid rudibus et omnium ignaris insederit, non modo quae diserta,

and 'summittere vocem' for the acute and grave accent.

2. unum...intellegat. To secure this, presumably the first reading by the teacher was accompanied by such comment as was necessary for the understanding of the poems, though such reading was primarily intended 'ut facile atque distincte pueri scripta oculis sequantur,' II. 5, 4.

canticum. Q. is probably thinking of Cic. *Or.* 57 (a passage which he develops at length in XI. 3, 58) where C. contrasts the 'cantus obscurus,' which is proper to rhetoric with the 'hic e Phrygia et Caria rhetorum epilogus, paene canticum.'

plasmate. What the exact meaning of this is, I will not pretend to say, but we may with fair certainty connect it with Pers. 1, 17, 'liquido cum plasmate guttur mobile collueris,' though the old interpreters took it there to mean a gargle. Sp. very appositely notes that Plin. *Hist. Nat.* 16, 66 while clearly adapting Theophrastus *De Plant.* 4, 12 renders μετὰ πλάσματος αὐλεῖν by 'ad flectendos sonos,' ἡνίκ' ηὔλουν ἀπλάστως by 'cum...simplici musica uterentur,' and ἐπεὶ δὲ εἰς τὴν πλάσιν μετέβησαν by 'postquam varietas accessit et cantus quoque luxuriae.' We may suppose then that the word suggested (a) variety, (b) artificiality, (c) softness and feebleness, all of them natural associations for a derivative of πλάσσω, and if so we may connect it with Cic. *De Or.* 3, 98 'quanto molliores sunt et delicatiores in cantu flexiones et falsae voculae quam certae et severae,' a passage which Sp. also quotes, v. note on 11, 6.

C. Caesarem praetextatum. One might conjecture that this remark is quoted from the 'dicta collectanea,' one of the works which Caesar is said to have written 'puer et adulescentulus' (Suet. *Jul.* 56), unless the statement which follows, 'quos vetuit Augustus publicari,' is to be taken to mean that they were effectively suppressed.

3. prosopopoeias. Here not in the common sense of the declamation exercise, in which the speaker assumed some personality, nor yet quite (as Bonnell) for the rhetorical figure, by which the orator puts words into the mouth of one of the personages mentioned or treated inanimate things as animate, but in a more general sense of the changes of speaker, which naturally occur in any narrative poem.

4. diserta. The well-known words of Antonius in *De Or.* 1, 94 'disertos cognosse me nonnullos, eloquentem adhuc neminem' (which Q. himself quotes VIII. Pr. 13) represents his usage well enough. The word indicates a certain position in the world of eloquence, and whether it is appreciatory or the reverse depends upon the context. In X. 1, 68 and ib. 3, 13 it is complimentary and in II. 12, 7 more positively so, while here as in VIII. Pr. 13 and 1, 10, 8 it is contrasted with the ideal orator. It may be noted that what the 'disertus' needs to bring him to the higher rank is sometimes moral as here (and XII. 1, 23 and 33), sometimes intellectual as in 10, 8. In this last passage L. translates 'fluent,' which does give the proper amount of appreciation. Here perhaps 'of literary worth' may give the meaning.

5 sed vel magis quae honesta sunt, discant. ideoque optime
institutum est, ut ab Homero atque Vergilio lectio inciperet,
quamquam ad intellegendas eorum virtutes firmiore iudicio
opus est: sed huic rei superest tempus, neque enim semel
legentur. interim et sublimitate heroici carminis animus
adsurgat et ex magnitudine rerum spiritum ducat et optimis
6 inbuatur. utiles tragoediae: alunt et lyrici, si tamen in his non

5–12. These sections giving Q.'s
views as to the authors most suitable
at this early stage must not be regarded
as an abridgement or anticipation of the
famous disquisition in X. 1 on the authors
suitable for reading. There we have
recommendations suitable (1) for the
rhetoric school, (2) for the improvement
of 'elocutio,' whereas here the primary
object is 'ingenium alere atque animum
augere,' (3) there the books are to be
read privately and not, as here, in
class.

Homero. For the practice of *beginning*
with Homer cf. Plin. *Ep.* 2, 14, 2 'sic
in foro pueros a centumviralibus causis
auspicari ut ab Homero in scholis.' We
may perhaps add the epigram ascribed
to Lucian, Teub. vol. III. p. 469, where
the physician sends his boy to school,
but when he reached the third line
πολλὰς δ' ἰφθίμους ψυχὰς "Αϊδι προΐαψεν
withdrew him, on the grounds that he
could teach him that as well himself.
Perhaps too Petron. 5 'det primos versibus annos Maeoniumque bibat felici
pectore fontem.' For other quotations
shewing the *predominance* of Homer,
v. Friedländer vol. IV. ch. 1 and Mayor
on Juv. 7, 227.

Vergilio. For V.'s predominance in
the schools v. the authorities mentioned
above, to which may be added Comparetti's *Vergil in the Middle Ages*,
Eng. Trans. ch. 3. I do not however
know of any passage but this which
suggests that Virgil was read at the
beginning of the school course, unless
'parvuli' in the quotation from Augustine below may be said to do so. It
would however naturally follow from
the obvious tendency of the schools to
balance the Latin against the Greek.
Whether Q. tacitly admits with H. and
V. other poetry of the 'heroic' type
seems to me doubtful. In Statius'
description of his father's school (*Silv.*
v. 3, 146 ff.) Hesiod and Theocritus are
coupled with Homer, and in *Theb.* XII.
815 he says of the *Thebaid* 'Itala iam
studio discit, memoratque iuventus,'

and cf. Suet. (Teub. p. 300) of Lucan
'poemata eius etiam praelegi memini.'
These leave little doubt as to the
practice, but Q. may himself have
thought that his judgment of 'multa
magis quam multorum lectio' applied
a fortiori to the lower school.

neque enim semel legentur. This
refers probably to the later private
'lectio' in the rhet. school.

interim. Here again Bonnell says
'latet significatio tamen,' but the natural
meaning 'until that more intelligent
reading is reached' is quite enough:
v. on 5, 29.

sublimitate...ducat. Cf. X. 1, 27 'ab
his (i.e. poetis) in rebus spiritus et
in verbis sublimitas...petitur.'

heroici. Halm and his successors
have adopted 'heroi' from A alone, as
elsewhere Q. uses 'herous' of the metre.
Though the considerations are closely
balanced, it seems to me best to follow
the weight of MS. authority. Here
though the metre is the predominant
consideration, there are other factors
which are not present in the other exx.
in Q.; and while the grammarians use
'herous' and 'heroicus' indifferently
with 'versus' and 'metrum,' I have not
found an instance of 'heroum carmen.'
Cf. Tac. *Dial.* 10 'heroici carminis
sonum.'

et optimis inbuatur, 'and thus be
baptised in the best.' 'Imbuere' is used
in its regular sense of *first* impressions,
a sense indeed general in Q., but not
always so emphatically as here. Cf.
Aug. *Conf.* 1, 13 'graecas litteras, quibus puerulus imbuebar,' and for the
general sense id. *De Civ. De.* 1, 3
(a passage which I am inclined to think
may be reminiscent of this) 'apud Vergilium, quem propterea parvuli legunt,
ut videlicet poeta magnus omniumque
praeclarissimus atque optimus teneris
ebibitus animis non facile oblivione
possit aboleri, secundum illud Horatii
"quo semel est" etc.'

6. tragoediae. This no doubt includes Ovid's *Medea* and Varius' *Thyestes*

auctores modo, sed etiam partes operis elegeris: nam et Graeci licenter multa et Horatium in quibusdam nolim interpretari. elegia vero, utique qua amat⟨ur⟩, et hendecasyllabi, qui sunt commata sotadeorum (nam de sotadeis ne praecipiendum quidem est) amoveantur, si fieri potest, si minus, certe ad firmius aetatis

(v. x. 1, 98) as well as the Greek tragedies. In Statius' list the only tragedian mentioned is Lycophron, and the phrase used 'latebras Lycophronis atri' rather suggests the *Cassandra* which is not a tragedy. Martial 8, 3, 13–16 'an iuvat ad tragicos soccum transferre cothurnos? | aspera vel paribus bella tonare modis, | praelegat ut tumidus rauca te voce magister, | oderit et grandis virgo bonusque puer?' points to the preference for epic and tragedy. As to whether Pacuvius etc. are here also meant v. note on § 8.

Horatium. Horace is classed with Virgil as a schoolbook in Juv. 7, 227 and Aus. *Id.* 4, 55, 56. If we can judge at all of his popularity from the quotations in the grammarians he stood third; Virgil occupying over 70 columns of the index, Terence 16, and Horace 8.

nolim interpretari. As the epodes are not included in the lyrical works either by Q. x. 1, 96 or Hor. himself, *Ep.* II. 2, 59, Q. was evidently at least as careful in this matter as modern schoolmasters.

elegia. The elder Statius' school admitted Callimachus at any rate. For the word, as Forc. only gives 'an elegy,' it may be noted that this general use recurs in x. 1, 58 and 93.

qua amat⟨ur⟩, i.e. in which there is love-making. Sp., Halm and Meister all read 'quae amat,' but apparently without MS. authority. Rad. has adopted the 'qua amat' of nearly all MSS., but this does not seem to me to diminish the oddity of the expression. Sp. paralleled it from 6, 22 'ebur et robur...transferunt,' and ib. 14 'Ceres cogat dici Cereris.' He might perhaps have added 'elementa... audebunt' 2, 26. But all these seem to me doubtful parallels. Andresen suggested 'utique amatoria.' The emendation I have printed has not been suggested before, but seems to me very probable. 'Amatur,' which actually occurs Plaut. *Pseud.* 273, is a natural formation recognised by Prisc. K. II. 414, 425. Confusions of -t and -tur are very common. To take two exx. from this book, in 7, 9 most MSS. have 'relinquetur' for 'relinquet' while in 6, 9 it is very

doubtful whether we should not read 'dicetur' for MS. 'dicet.' Edd. before Rad. have done so regularly.

hendecasyllabi...sotadeorum. Cf. Mar. Vict. K. VI. 153 'quinta autem hendecasyllabi species admixto anapaesto sotadium facit metrum. nam si ante dactylum, qui post spondeum sollemniter in hoc versu ponitur, anapaestum inseras, sotadium metrum propria modulatione formabis. erit exemplo versus hic

Carmen Pierides dabunt sorores.

huic si adieceris "lepidae" qui est anapaestus, inter spondeum et dactylum sequentibus tribus trochaeis fit versus sotadius ita

Carmen lepidae Pierides dabunt sorores.'

The same point is made by Terentianus Maurus ib. 409, who adds 'idcirco genus hoc Phalaeciorum, | vir doctissimus undecumque Varro | ad legem redigens Ionicorum | hinc natos ait esse sed minores,' so that perhaps Q. may owe this remark to Varro.

V. also Demetrius *De Eloc.* 189 σύνθεσις δὲ ἀναπαιστικὴ καὶ μάλιστα ἐοικυῖα τοῖς κεκλασμένοις καὶ ἀσέμνοις μέτροις οἷα μάλιστα τὰ Σωτάδεια. Here and in the illustrations which follow, Demetrius seems to associate the degeneracy of the Sotadean with its anapaestic character, but it is rather in its trochaic ending that the hendecasyllable resembles it, and so in IX. 4, 6 Q. says 'parvi pedes vim detrahunt rebus, ut Sotadeorum et Galliamborum.' It is clear that in these cases, as with the hexameter, Q. attributes real moral or immoral influence to the metre itself, but no doubt he also thinks of the subject-matter usually associated with them. For this view of the hendecasyllable v. Plin. *Ep.* 4, 14.

qui sunt commata. Sp. 'quibus sunt commata,' but the reading in the text, which is substantially that of A, is made certain by the quotations given above from the grammarians.

commata. 'Comma' for a portion of a verse is fairly common in the grammarians, e.g. Char. K. I. 290, Diom. ib. 494. In IX. 4, 22 Q. gives it the

7 robur reserventur. comoediae, quae plurimum conferre ad eloquentiam potest, cum per omnis et personas et adfectus eat, quem usum in pueris putem, paulo post suo loco dicam: nam cum mores in tuto fuerint, inter praecipua legenda erit. de **8** Menandro loquor, nec tamen excluserim alios. nam Latini quoque auctores adferent utilitatis aliquid.

Sed pueris, quae maxime ingenium alant atque animum augeant, praelegenda: ceteris, quae ad eruditionem modo pertinent, longa aetas spatium dabit. multum autem veteres

more regular meaning of a division determined by the sense (practically that which we mark off by a comma). For this meaning v. Sandys on Cic. *Orator* 211.

7. suo loco, i.e. 11, 12–14 of this book, not X. 1, 65 etc. where we have its use for 'iuvenes,' 'cum mores in tuto fuerint.'

praecipua. So Halm and later edd. Sp. 'praecipue' with little MS. authority.

Menandro. For the use of Menander in schools v. Ov. *Trist.* 2, 370 'fabula iucundi nulla est sine amore Menandri | et solet hic pueris virginibusque legi.' In Statius *Silv.* 11, 1, 114 and Aus. *Id.* 4, 46 he is coupled with Homer as being learnt by boys (though not in the list of *Silv.* v. 3).

8–12. The drift of these sections may be taken in two opposite ways, and the choice will largely depend on the meaning we give to the words at the end 'verum priora...pertinebunt.' Sp. interpreted them thus '"illa" sunt quae de legendis poetis praeceperat, "haec" quae de inserendis eorum versibus narraverat.' I do not think that this makes very good sense. The fact that the orator who quotes from the books he has read at school does not do so till after he has left school is too obvious and has no bearing on the subject. But if it is accepted, it will follow that the 'veteres Latini' are recommended for use 'apud grammaticum.'

I should however prefer to take the sections as follows. The main point is that 'quae ad eruditionem modo pertinent' are excluded at this stage, and this is summed up again in 'verum... pertinebunt.' 'Haec' then covers everything after the lyrical writers and includes 'veteres Latini.' But as Q. feels that these last have many qualities which fit them for early reading, he thinks himself bound to state this at

some length, though he still holds to his general view that they are better reserved. One consideration which inclines me to accept this view is that it does seem that the 'veteres' were not read in the grammatical schools at this period. Cp. Suet. *Gram.* 24 (of Probus) 'legerat in provincia quosdam veteres libellos apud grammatistam, durante adhuc ibi antiquorum memoria, necdum omnino abolita sicut Romae.' The fact that Horace read there Livius Andronicus (*Ep.* 11. 1, 70) is no evidence for our period, and the same is true of the frequency of their use in the second century (v. Friedländer vol. IV. ch. 1). Phaedrus, indeed, after quoting a line of Ennius (III. Epil. 33), says 'quem puer legi.' But Phaedrus' schooldays hardly fall within the period. On the other hand the persistency with which the later poets are spoken of in connection with the schools is remarkable. Cp. Suet. *Gram.* 16 of Caecilius Epirota 'dicitur...primus Vergilium et alios poetas novos praelegere coepisse.' Besides the actual instances of Virgil, Horace, Lucan, Statius we have the regular assumption that any poet who makes a reputation may expect to become a school text, e.g. Mart. 8, 3, 13 etc. (quoted above) and Persius 1, 29. Further this view receives, I think, some confirmation from the closely parallel passage in 11. 5, 21–23, where the student, who though still called 'puer,' has gone up to the rhetoric school and begun prose authors, is warned against both 'veteres' and the very recent till the age of 'firma iudicia iamque extra periculum posita.' I have marked my diffident acceptance of this view in the text by beginning a fresh paragraph at 'sed pueris.' In 'multum autem conferunt,' I should translate 'autem' ' no doubt.'

8. praelegenda. The reading in class is opposed to the later private 'lectio.'

etiam Latini conferunt, quamquam plerique plus ingenio quam
arte valuerunt, in primis copiam verborum, quorum in tragoediis
gravitas, in comoediis elegantia et quidam velut ἀττικισμός
inveniri potest. oeconomia quoque in iis diligentior quam in 9
plerisque novorum erit, qui omnium operum solam virtutem

ingenio)(arte. Sp. quotes Ov. *Trist.*
2, 424 and Cic.'s remarks on Lucr. in
ad Q. Fr. II. 11.
in primis copiam verborum. Kid.
wished to expunge these words and
Meister has followed him in bracketing
them. I regard them as very doubtful,
for (1) 'confero' in this sense is no-
where else followed by an acc. in Q.
(this might perhaps be corrected by
reading 'ad copiam,' as Claussen).
(2) The clause 'quorum...potest' raises
difficulty. If 'verborum' is the ante-
cedent of 'quorum' (as Bonnell and L.)
the whole clause is awkward; if 'veteres
Latini,' the separation of rel. and ante-
cedent is equally strange. (3) The
view expressed seems to me an unlikely
one for Q. to hold. It is true that
above (7) and in 11, 13 comedies presumably including the older Lat. comedies are said to contribute to eloquence.
But this evidently refers to their dramatic
force and variety. In the various remarks on the old Latin poets in x. 1
(and still more in those on the old
prose writers in II. 5, 21) there is nothing which bears out this view, except
possibly the 'pondus verborum' ascribed
to Pacuvius (x. 1, 97). On the other
hand a later student, conscious of the
fact that the old writers introduced him
to a vocabulary otherwise unknown,
might easily add this comment.
elegantia; v. Ernesti s.v. Auct. ad
Her. 4, 17 defines it thus 'elegantia
est quae facit, ut unum quidque pure
et aperte dici videatur. Haec tribuitur
in Latinitatem et explanationem. Latinitas est quae sermonem purum conservat
ab omni vitio remotum...explanatio est
quae reddit apertam et dilucidam orationem.' It seems thus to suggest
correctness, clearness, simplicity not
sinking to baldness, or rising to anything lofty, and is thus closely connected with the 'subtile genus dicendi'
as opposed to the 'grande' which is
found in the 'gravitas' of tragedy. So
Q. applies it in x. 1 to the old Greek
Comedy (65), Lysias (78), the Socratici
(83), Terence (99), Caesar (114).
ἀττικισμός. Cf. the remarks on 'urbanitas' VI. 3, 107 'nam meo quidem

iudicio illa est urbanitas, in qua nihil ab-
sonum, nihil agreste, nihil inconditum,
nihil peregrinum neque sensu neque
verbis neque ore gestuve possit depre-
hendi, ut non tam sit in singulis dictis
quam in toto colore dicendi, qualis apud
Graecos ἀττικισμός ille reddens Athena-
rum proprium saporem.' Edd. also
quote Cic. *ad Att.* 4, 19 'ille Latinus
ἀττικισμός,' but that is probably ironical
(v. Tyrrell). Judging from VI. 3, 107
we may suppose that the word here is
meant mainly for the 'sensus' of the
comedians, while 'elegantia' is restricted
to the 'verba.' 'Gravitas' in tragedy presumably applies to both, cf. the 'gravitas'
of Sophocles x. 1, 68. The high praise
of the ἀττικισμός of Latin Comedy here
is rather inconsistent with x. 1, 100
(in comedy) 'vix levem consequimur
umbram, adeo ut mihi sermo ipse
Romanus non recipere videatur illam
solis concessam Atticis venerem.'
9. oeconomia. For this important
term which covers the management,
arrangement and development of the
material and more or less superseded the
older τάξις, v. VII. 10, 11–13, where its
application to rhetoric is discussed. For
its application to poetry cf. (e.g.) Serv. on
Aen. 9, 745 where he says that according to some Turnus was killed at this
point, 'sed causa oeconomiae gloriam
a poeta Aeneae servatam esse'; Ps.-
Plut. *De Hom.* 162, where H.'s οἰκονομία is praised because οὐ πόρρωθεν
ἐμβαλὼν τὴν ἀρχὴν τῆς Ἰλιάδος ἐποιή-
σατο, ἀλλὰ καὶ καθ' ὃν χρόνον αἱ πράξεις
ἐνεργότεραι καὶ ἀκμαιότεραι κατέστησαν.
τὰ δὲ τούτων ἀργότερα, ὅσα ἐν τῷ παρελ-
θόντι χρόνῳ ἐγένοντο συντόμως ἐν ἄλλοις
τόποις παρεδιηγήσατο.
novorum. Clearly as in II. 5, 23
this does not include the Augustans.
And so too, I think, in x. 1, 43 (though
Peterson takes it otherwise) the 'veteres'
and the 'novi' stand at the two ends
with the true classics in between. Elsewhere undoubtedly 'veteres' or 'antiqui'
is used to cover all except the 'novi.'
Thus in IX. 3, 1 we have 'veteres
et praecipue Cicero,' and so x. 1, 122
and 126 and x. 2, 17. It should be
noted that while in II. 5, 21–23 the

sententias putaverunt. sanctitas certe et, ut sic dicam, virilitas
ab iis petenda est, quando nos in omnia deliciarum vitia dicendi
10 quoque ratione defluximus. denique credamus summis oratoribus, qui veterum poemata vel ad fidem causarum vel ad
11 ornamentum eloquentiae adsumunt. nam praecipue quidem
apud Ciceronem, frequenter tamen apud Asinium etiam et
ceteros, qui sunt proximi, videmus Enni, Acci, Pacuvi, Lucili,
Terenti, Caecili et aliorum inseri versus summa non eruditionis
modo gratia, sed etiam iucunditatis, cum poeticis voluptatibus
12 aures a forensi asperitate respirant. quibus accedit non
mediocris utilitas, cum sententiis eorum velut quibusdam

'novi' are definitely relegated with the
'antiqui' to a later stage, here there is
no such definiteness. Possibly Q. did
not wish to be dogmatic in a sphere
which was not his own and in which he
knew that living contemporaries like
Statius held an honoured place.

sententias. For this well-known and
special meaning of the word for striking
thoughts epigrammatically expressed or
'points' (to adopt a word which rather
inadequately expresses the meaning)
v. Bk VIII. 5, a chapter introduced by
the words 'sententiam veteres, quod
animo sensissent, vocaverunt...sed consuetudo iam tenuit, ut mente concepta
sensus vocaremus, lumina autem praecipueque in clausulis posita sententias,
quae minus crebrae apud antiquos nostris temporibus modo carent'; v. also
XII. 10, 48, and for an interesting dissertation on the 'pointed style' Summers'
Letters of Seneca Intr. pp. xv–xli.

sanctitas. Here applied to style, as
often also 'sanctus'; v. Nettleship
Contr. to Lat. Lexicography s.v. 'sanctus.' He quotes VIII. 3, 6 'ornatus
virilis et fortis et sanctus,' and ib. 24
ancient words 'sanctiorem et magis
admirabilem faciunt orationem,' ib. 44
'apud Sallustium dicta sancte et anti-
que,' so too of Calvus X. 1, 115; XII.
10, 11. His rendering of 'pure' however conveys other associations, nor do
I think that 'solemnity of style,' by
which Sellar renders the words here
(*Roman Poets of the Republic* p. 131),
is quite adequate. So close is the connexion of style with morality in Q.'s
mind (and that of his contemporaries,
v. particularly the opening of Sen.
Ep. 114) that the word carries with it
some ethical value. It is the opposite
of 'deliciarum vitia' and 'corruptum

genus dicendi,' and in view of this
perhaps the best rendering would be
'nobility.' On the other hand there is
no reference to the moral value of the
contents, of which Q. in the case of
comedy would evidently not have altogether approved.

defluximus. Cf. (of the imitators of
Seneca) 'tantum ab illo defluebant,
quantum ille ab antiquis descenderat'
X. 1, 126.

11. summa...iucunditatis. The presence of 'summa' makes it impossible
to take 'gratia' (as L.)='for the sake
of.' The sense must be 'such quotations
add great charm, a charm which lies not
only in the sense of learning (culture?)
given but also in their "iucunditas,"' for
the meaning of which v. next note.

iucunditatis)(**asperitate**. The same
antithesis appears in X. 2, 23. 'Asperitas'
seems to mean 'passion,' 'fierceness,'
'keenness' rather than mere harshness
or roughness, or (as L.) severity. That
'asperitas' is a quality markedly distinguishing oratory (especially forensic
oratory) from other forms of literature
is an idea which often appears; v. Cic.
De Or. 2, 64, where we are told that
in history 'verborum ratio et genus
orationis fusum atque tractum et cum
lenitate quadam aequabiliter profluens
sine hac iudiciali asperitate et sine
sententiarum forensibus aculeis perse-
quendum est' (v. Ernesti, s.v.). So
'iucunditas' gives the sense of something lighter and brighter, much as
we speak of a speaker as 'pleasant.'
Possibly 'pleasantness' might do as an
equivalent here.

respirant. So all MSS. Regius corrected to 'respirent,' which has been
accepted by Sp. (doubtfully), Halm
and Meister, but not by Rad. It seems

testimoniis quae proposuere confirment. verum priora illa ad pueros magis, haec sequentia ad robustiores pertinebunt, cum grammatices amor et usus lectionis non scholarum temporibus, sed vitae spatio terminentur.

In praelegendo grammaticus et illa quidem minora praestare 13 debebit, ut partes orationis reddi sibi soluto versu desideret et pedum proprietates, quae adeo debent esse notae in carminibus, ut etiam in oratoria compositione desiderentur. deprendat 14

to me unnecessary. Such quotations always have the 'gratia eruditionis.' *When* they relieve the 'forensis asperitas,' which is not always, they have also the 'gratia iucunditatis.' V. on 6, 2. **priora illa...haec sequentia**; v. note on §§ 8–12.

13—end. For a fuller discussion of these sections v. Art. 1914, pp. 43–46. I have there compared Q.'s method with the scheme of Dionysius § 1, who gives as the six parts of γραμματική 'πρῶτον ἀνάγνωσις ἐντριβὴς κατὰ προσῳδίαν, δεύτερον ἐξήγησις κατὰ τοὺς ἐνυπάρχοντας ποιητικοὺς τρόπους, τρίτον γλωσσῶν τε καὶ ἱστοριῶν πρόχειρος ἀπόδοσις, τέταρτον ἐτυμολογίας εὕρεσις, πέμπτον ἀναλογίας ἐκλογισμός, ἕκτον κρίσις ποιημάτων, ὃ δὴ κάλλιστόν ἐστι πάντων τῶν ἐν τῇ τέχνῃ.' It will be seen in the course of the notes how far Q. has developed this scheme. Here we may note that the fourth part ἐτυμολογίας εὕρεσις has no place in Q.'s method. In Art. 1914 I suggested that this omission was accidental, but I am now inclined to think in view of the general disparagement of the popular etymology in 6, 32 that it is deliberate, and that that part of it which he does approve (ib. 31) is reserved to a somewhat higher stage than that with which we are now dealing, as belonging to 'eruditio.'

illa quidem minora. These extending to the middle of § 15 include (*a*) parsing, (*b*) scansion, (*c*) treatment of irregularities, (*d*) homonyms. Of these properly speaking only (*a*) appears in Dionysius as the fourth part ἀναλογίας ἐκλογισμός, in which phrase ἀναλογία is used to cover the whole department of inflection. The others however are a natural development and shew how greatly the 'technical' or 'methodical' side of γραμματική had advanced during the interval.

reddi...versu. The best commentary on this is Priscian's 'partitiones XII versuum Aeneidos principalium' (i.e.

the first line of each book), where each word is carefully parsed and various grammatical remarks made on them, e.g. 'arma' leads to a discourse on its derivatives and the verb 'armo,' though probably Q. did not wish anything quite so elaborate. In 4, 22 we had 'nomina declinare et verba in primis pueri sciant,' but this was perhaps kept separate from the 'praelectio.' Priscian at any rate does not suggest that the whole declension or conjugation was rehearsed at this stage.

partes orationis. Presumably in the same sense as in 4, 17, though Prisc. l.c. uses 'pars orationis' also for an individual word. So on *Aen.* 1, 1 'quot partes orationis habet iste versus? Novem. Quot nomina? Sex...Arma quae pars orationis est? Nomen.'

soluto versu. I take this to mean that the words are grouped under their respective 'parts of speech' instead of the verse order. So Prisc., though in the actual parsing he returns to the verse order.

pedum proprietates, i.e. not merely 'scandere versum,' but to give a full discussion of the nature of the metre, as Prisc. l.c.

quae...desiderentur, i.e. the ear trained in verse metre will feel the need of it in prose. So substantially Sp. But this use of 'desidero' in two senses in the same sentence is awkward, and it may perhaps mean that the 'pedum proprietates' should be so well known in verse that the teacher can expect them to be given him in prose. If we take this meaning, I should be inclined to suggest 'ideo,' which might easily have been corrupted under the influence of 'adeo' below. 'Compositio' is such an important element in rhetoric that it might well be represented as the ultimate object of studying versification.

compositione. σύνθεσις in its technical sense. Cf. Auct. ad Her. 4, 18 'comp. est verborum constructio quae facit omnes

quae barbara, quae inpropria, quae contra legem loquendi sint
posita, non ut ex his utique inprobentur poetae (quibus, quia
plerumque servire metro coguntur, adeo ignoscitur, ut vitia
ipsa aliis in carmine appellationibus nominentur: μεταπλασμούς
enim et σχηματισμούς et σχήματα, ut dixi, vocamus et laudem
virtutis necessitati damus), sed ut commoneat artificialium et
15 memoriam agitet. id quoque inter prima rudimenta non inutile
demonstrare, quot quaeque verba modis intellegenda sint. circa
glossemata etiam, id est voces minus usitatas, non ultima
16 eius professionis diligentia est. enimvero iam maiore cura

partes orationis aequabiliter perpolitas.'
For the important part played in this
by 'numerus' or rhythm v. IX. 4, 45 ff.,
particularly 116 'ergo quem in poemate
locum habet versificatio, eum in oratione compositio'; v. also Cic. *Or.*
162 ff.
14. inpropria. Words used in the
wrong sense, ἄκυρα: cf. 5, 46. In VIII.
2, 3 Q. gives as an instance the Virgilian
'tantum sperare dolorem,' and adds
'non tamen quidquid non erit proprium,
protinus et improprii vitio laborabit.'
This is obviously the case where 'proprium' is the opposite of 'translatum,'
but it is also the case when it is used
in the higher senses indicated in the
note on Pr. 16. In *Aen.* 1, 410 'incuso'
may have more 'proprietas' (as Servius
says) than 'accuso,' but the latter would
be hardly an 'improprium.'
contra legem loquendi. Presumably
solecisms. Both these and barbarisms
in the poets have been several times
illustrated in ch. 5.
non...utique. In several places in Q.
'non utique' bears the natural sense
of 'not in every case' or 'not necessarily,' but sometimes, as here and
II. 5, 5 and X. 1, 57, this does not give
the required meaning. In these it seems
to equal 'utique non,' 'certainly not,' or
'not of course.' Peterson hardly treats
it adequately when he says on X. 1, 20
that it equals 'nullo modo.' It is decidedly stronger. So below 12, 14.
servire metro coguntur. Cf. X. 1,
29 'quod (poetica) adligata ad certam
pedum necessitatem non semper uti
propriis possit, sed depulsa recta via
necessario ad eloquendi quaedam de-
verticula confugiat.'
μεταπλασμούς etc. So regularly the
grammarians, e.g. Diom. K. I. 451 'hoc
vitium (i.e. barbarismus) in soluta oratione nomen suum retinet, ceterum apud

poetas metaplasmus vocatur, soloecismus
autem schema': cf. 5, 52.
et σχηματισμούς. Meist. and Rad.
have bracketed these words as suggested
by Sp. This, I think on the whole, is
unnecessary. It is true, as he says, that
'schematismus' or 'schematismi' do not
appear to be found in the Latin Gramm.,
but the plural is used in Greek, e.g. Dion.
H. *de comp.* 8, as a synonym for σχήματα,
and it is not remarkable that Q. should
give both forms, though we might
perhaps have expected two so closely
allied to be connected with 'vel' rather
than 'et.' If either is to be omitted, I
should choose 'schemata' as more likely
to have arisen from a gloss.
artificialium, not 'artifices of style'
as L., but technical terms or perhaps
rules. Thus Q. uses 'artificialis pro-
batio' as a translation for ἔντεχνος πίστις,
XII. 8, 14 and 'artificialiter' II. 17, 42.
The substantive however seems rare.
The Thes. quotes Aug. *adv. Cresc.* 3, 74
'grammaticorum artificialia.' I take the
gen. as governed by 'memoriam' as
well as 'commoneat.' This kind of
study does serve to impress rules and
terms on the memory, but hardly to
strengthen the memory as a whole.
15. quot ... intellegenda sint. So
Prisc. l.c. on *Aen.* 1, 1, dilates on
'arma' as 'homonymum, quod quidem
univocum dicunt,' and also on 'classi'
in VI. 1.
glossemata. The γλωσσῶν ἀπόδοσις
of Dion. Thrax. The form γλώσσημα
is not found, so far as I can see, in the
Greek grammarians, though it is implied
by γλωσσηματικός and its adv. One example is quoted from Marcus Aurelius.
It is found in Varro *L. L.* 7, 34 and
107, in the latter apparently in the sense
of an explanation of the γλῶσσα, a gloss
in our sense. For γλῶσσα v. note on
1, 35.

doceat tropos omnes, quibus praecipue non poema modo sed etiam oratio ornatur, schemata utraque, id est figuras, quaeque λέξεως quaeque διανοίας vocantur: quorum ego sicut troporum tractatum in eum locum differo, quo mihi de ornatu orationis dicendum erit. praecipue vero illa infigat animis, 17 quae in oeconomia virtus, quae in decore rerum, quid personae cuique convenerit, quid in sensibus laudandum, quid in verbis, ubi copia probabilis, ubi modus.

16. tropos omnes, i.e. Dionysius' second part ἐξήγησις κατὰ τοὺς ἐνυπάρχοντας ποιητικοὺς τρόπους, but v. note on 'schemata' below.

oratio. The point that these have a direct influence on rhetorical training, apart from the indirect influence which belongs to γραμματική as a whole, is emphasized.

schemata...vocantur. It would be out of place to write here at length on the very extensive subject of tropes and figures. But the following points may be noticed. (1) The distinction between the two—a trope uses words or phrases in a non-natural sense ('sermo a naturali et principali significatione translatus ad aliam,' IX. 1, 4), while a figure, though retaining the natural sense of the words, is a departure from the direct and obvious way of stating the thing ('conformatio orationis remota a communi et primum se offerente ratione etc.')—is a development of the original theory and probably Dionysius' included both under τρόποι. Indeed Rutherford (*Chapter on History of Annotation*, p. 188) may be right in saying that τρόπος ποιητικός properly meant nothing more than the poet's 'way' of saying a thing, and that the development was assisted by associating it with the idea of τρέπω = divert. (2) The distinction between 'figures of speech' and 'figures of thought' or 'meaning' is by no means so valueless as Rutherford represents it. The former applies to such devices as repetition of a name ('O Corydon, Corydon'), or 'hendiadys' or 'climax.' The latter is very widely used and covers not merely such devices as 'apostrophe,' or the putting of words into the mouth of an imaginary person, but sarcasm, assumed modesty and the like. For a full treatment of the three v. Book VIII. 6 for 'tropes,' IX. 2 for 'figures of thought,' IX. 3 for 'figures of words.' In all three the examples are frequently drawn from Virgil.

λέξεως, IX. 1, 17 'id est verborum vel dictionis vel elocutionis vel sermonis. διανοίας id est mentis vel sensus vel sententiarum.'

17. This section corresponds to the 'sixth part' of Dionysius, κρίσις ἃ δὴ κάλλιστόν ἐστι πάντων τῶν ἐν τῇ τέχνῃ. I still think (v. Art. 1914, p. 44) that this is not to be limited, as Rutherford thinks, to the determination of the genuineness of books or passages.

It is useful to observe how the six points here enumerated (*a*) structure, arrangement and development, (*b*) appropriateness and charm of incidents, (*c*) characterisation, (*d*) notable thoughts, (*e*) choice of words, (*f*) 'copia' and 'modus' reappear with various amplifications and additions in the remarks on Homer in X. 1, 46 ff., though there the direct connexion of poetry with oratory is the main consideration. (*a*), (*d*) and (*e*) 'in verbis, sententiis, figuris, dispositione totius operis nonne humani ingenii modum excedit?' (50). (*b*) 'hunc nemo in magnis rebus sublimitate, in parvis proprietate superaverit' (46). (*f*) 'tum copia, tum brevitate mirabilis' (46): 'narrare vero quis brevius, quam qui mortem nuntiat Patrocli, quis significantius potest, quam qui Curetum Aetolorumque proelium exponit?' (49). The least emphasised is (*c*), though it is to some extent recognised in the remarks on Homer's ἤθη and πάθη (48) and on Priam's prayers (50).

copia)(modus. Besides the quotations given above, cf. X. 1, 62 of Stesichorus 'si tenuisset modum, videtur aemulari proximus Homerum potuisse; sed redundat atque effunditur, quod ut est reprehendendum, ita copiae vitium est.' We may regard this point of 'copia' and 'modus' as constituting an elementary lesson in the χαρακτῆρες of style, which occupy so important a place in ancient rhetoric (e.g. Cic. *Or.* 20). 'Copia' is one of the marks of the ἀδρόν or 'grande genus,' and perhaps the one which could

18 His accedet enarratio historiarum, diligens quidem illa, non tamen usque ad supervacuum laborem occupata: nam receptas aut certe claris auctoribus memoratas exposuisse satis est. persequi quidem, quid quis umquam vel contemptissimorum hominum dixerit, aut nimiae miseriae aut inanis iactantiae est **19** et detinet atque obruit ingenia melius aliis vacatura. nam qui omnis etiam indignas lectione scidas excutit, anilibus quoque

most easily be grasped by boys. So Aul. Gell. 7, 14 translates ἁδρόs by 'uber.' 'Modus' is similarly a mark of the ἰσχνόs or 'gracilis.' Compare also Diom. K. I. 483, 'poematis characteres sunt quattuor μακρόs, βραχύs, μέσοs, ἀνθηρόs. μακρόs est character ut apud Virgilium in XI. ubi de Camilla facit narrationem ...aut ut se habeat II. et III. liber. βραχύs est ut in V. ubi de Ganymede strictim narrat' (i.e. V. 250–257). Here although Diom. by differentiating μέσοs from ἀνθηρόs (v. Q. XII. 10, 58) has made the χαρακτῆρεs four instead of three, he is clearly adapting the rhetorical doctrine.

18–end. The 'enarratio historiarum' corresponds to the ἀπόδοσιs ἱστοριῶν, which forms the second half of Dion. Thrax's third division. Q.'s reason for putting it at the end is (1) that by many grammarians it was given special importance, v. on 2, 14, (2) that he wishes to protest against the excessive labour spent on it.

historiarum; v. Art. 1914, p. 45 and Rutherford *Chapter on Annotation* pp. 381 etc. The word as used in the schools covers any information which is required or given about the personages, etc., in the poems, or any explanation of allusions. 'Historiae' are classified as τοπική, χρονική, περὶ τὰς πράξεις, περὶ τὰ πρόσωπα (Sext. Emp. *adv. gramm.* 270). The last of these was sometimes called γενεαλογική (ποίημα...συγκείμενον ἐκ τοπικοῦ καὶ πραγματικοῦ καὶ χρονικοῦ καὶ γενεαλογικοῦ εἰς ἃ διαιρεῖσθαι τὴν ἱστορίαν φασίν (οἱ παλαιοί)), Int. to Dionysius' περιήγησιs, Bernhardi p. 81 (quoted by Usener *K. S.* 11, p. 286). According to another classification they were divided into (1) μῦθοι, legendary matter, (2) πλάσματα, fictitious but possible matter as in comedies, (3) ἱστορία (in a limited sense) really historical matter, Sext. Emp. ib. 272. Cf. Aus. *Prof. Burd.* 21, 25 'ambo omnia carmina docti | callentes mython plasmata et historiam' (where 'mython' should not be taken as by Mayor and others, as

gen. plur.). These three are given by Q. II. 4, 2 as 'fabula, argumentum, historia.' Q. of course here uses the word in its wider sense. As the grammatical school dealt exclusively or almost exclusively (v. Intr. p. xxx) with poetry, the 'mythical' element naturally preponderated, though doubtless much that we should call 'myth' was to them 'historia' in the limited sense. The view expressed in these sections that the 'historiae' were frequently very frivolous and pedantic is common enough, v. Mayor on Juv. 7, 231 and 234. It may be noticed that while most of these sarcastic comments are directed against 'myths,' Sen. *De Brev.* 13 is quite as severe on the really historical 'historiae.'

receptas, i.e. αἱ διὰ στόματος καὶ δημώδεις ἱστορίαι (quoted by Steph. from Schol.). Their opposite is ξέναι ἱστορίαι, and a book with this title by Didymus himself (v. below) is quoted.

miseriae. This and similar words are frequently applied by Q. to excessive laboriousness, e.g. X. 1, 7 of the learning of synonyms by heart, 'cuiusdam infelicis operae,' VIII. pr. 27 excessive care for 'elocutio' is 'infelicitas,' 'miser enim...orator est, qui nullum verbum aequo animo perdere potest,' IX. 4, 112 of excessive care of rhythm, 'id cum miseri tum in minimis occupati est; neque enim qui se totum in hac cura consumpserit, potioribus vacabit.' Cf. 'miser' of Didymus in the quotation from Seneca below.

19. scidas : v. Cic. *ad Att.* 1, 20 'enitere...ne qua scida depereat.' On this Tyrrell says 'scida—a leaf, from scindo. The Greek σχέδη was probably a late corruption of the Latin word.' I accept this on his authority, though I do not know what the evidence is. Char. K. I. 105 notes that some wrote 'schida' ἀπὸ τοῦ σχίζειν. As to the meaning Sp. took it as 'pugillares' and identified it with the 'commentarii' below. But I see no clear example of this meaning. The usual sense is as in the passage from Cicero above.

fabulis accommodare operam potest: atqui pleni sunt eius modi impedimentis grammaticorum commentarii vix ipsis, qui composuerunt, satis noti. nam Didymo, quo nemo plura scripsit, 20 accidisse compertum est, ut, cum historiae cuidam tamquam vanae repugnaret, ipsius proferretur liber, qui eam continebat. quod evenit praecipue in fabulosis usque ad deridicula quaedam, 21 quaedam etiam pudenda, unde inprobissimo cuique pleraque fingendi licentia est, adeo ut de libris totis et auctoribus, ut succurrit, mentiantur tuto, quia inveniri qui numquam fuere non possunt: nam in notioribus frequentissime deprenduntur a curiosis. ex quo mihi inter virtutes grammatici habebitur aliqua nescire.

IX

[DE OFFICIO GRAMMATICI]

Et finitae quidem sunt partes duae, quas haec professio 1 pollicetur, id est ratio loquendi et enarratio auctorum, quarum illam methodicen, hanc historicen vocant. adiciamus tamen

impedimentis. In IX. 3, 1 the abl. with ‘plenus’ is noted as a modernism. Q. actually uses both.

commentarii. Gr. ὑπομνήματα. Sp. says ‘pugillares quibus illinunt quaecumque occurrunt observatu digna; non autem interpretationum libros.’ The first part of this is hardly adequate. The word means rather a body of notes, whether collected by pupil or teacher, not worked up into a literary or systematic form, and though it may not mean ‘liber interpretationum’ many ‘commentarii’ must have been of that nature.

20. Didymo. For this celebrated polymath v. Smith’s *Dict. Biog.* or better Pauly-Wissowa; cf. Sen. *Ep.* 88, 37 ‘quatuor millia librorum Didymus Grammaticus scripsit: miser si tam multa supervacua legisset. In his libris de patria Homeri quaeritur, in his de Aeneae matre vera: in his, libidinosior Anacreon an ebriosior vixerit; in his, an Sappho publica vixerit, et alia quae dediscenda erant, si scires.’ According to Athenaeus 139 c the epithet βιβλιολάθας was applied to him διὰ τὸ πλῆθος ὧν ἐκδέδωκε συγγραμμάτων. Sp. however cast doubt on the word, both as unsuitable to the reason given and also as not ‘analogice fictum’ and was inclined to suggest βιβλιοθήκην. I should certainly like to see more authority for such a

compound. Some self-contradictions of Did. are mentioned by Harpocration s.v. γαμηλία and ἔνθρυπτα (quoted by Rutherford *Chapter* p. 363).

21. curiosis. With an unfavourable sense, cf. VIII. 3, 55 ‘est etiam quae περιεργία vocatur, supervacua, ut sic dixerim, operositas, ut a diligenti curiosus et a religione superstitio distat.’ Cic. *Tusc.* I. 108 ‘permulta alia colligit Chrysippus, ut est in omni historia curiosus’ seems more neutral.

aliqua nescire. So Juv. 6, 451 of the Roman bluestocking ‘sed quaedam ex libris et non intellegat.’ Tac. *Hist.* 1, 83 ‘tam nescire quaedam milites quam scire oportet.’ Few quotations from Q. reappear more commonly in Renaissance and later writers than this.

IX 1. ratio…auctorum, v. on 4, 2.

methodicen…historicen. In Diom. K. I. 426 and elsewhere the names are given as ‘horistice’ and ‘exegetice.’ I do not think anything exactly corresponding to Q.’s statement is to be found elsewhere, and Usener (*Kl. Sch.* I. 358) proposes to read here ‘quarum illam methodicen alii, alii horisticen vocant.’ Q.’s terminology however is supported by the definition of γραμματική given by Chaeris (*Gram. Graec.* Part I. III. 118) ἕξις ἀπὸ τέχνης καὶ ἱστορίας διαγνωστικὴ τῶν παρ’ Ἕλλησι λεκτῶν, for though μέθο-

eorum curae quaedam dicendi primordia, quibus aetates nondum
2 rhetorem capientis instituant. igitur Aesopi fabellas, quae
fabulis nutricularum proxime succedunt, narrare sermone puro
et nihil se supra modum extollente, deinde eandem gracilitatem
stilo exigere condiscant: versus primo solvere, mox mutatis
verbis interpretari, tum paraphrasi audacius vertere, qua et
breviare quaedam et exornare salvo modo poetae sensu

δος is not the same as τέχνη, it is an inseparable accompaniment. Further, the
opposition between μέθοδος and ἱστορία
appears in the view of Tauriscus (Sext.
Emp. p. 268) where in the triple division
of γραμ. into λογικόν, τριβικόν and ἱστορικόν, the last is described as being
concerned περὶ τὴν προχειρότητα τῆς
ἀμεθόδου ὕλης. In fact both this and the
other triple division into τεχνικόν, ἱστορικόν and ἰδιαίτερον (v. on 2, 14) are
probably merely refinements on the
classification here mentioned. In this
classification I imagine that ἱστορία is
used in the wider sense of research and
indicates that each result stands by
itself and does not form part of a system.
The retention of the terminology however may well have been assisted by the
fact that 'histories' in the more limited
sense of the last chapter were to many
grammarians the most absorbing part
of 'exegetice.' Cf. the quotation from
Seneca given on 2, 14.

dicendi primordia. These are the
προγυμνάσματα or preliminary exercises
in composition, of which we have very
full accounts by Theon, Hermogenes,
and Aphthonius, as well as some later
writers. Of Hermogenes we have also
a Latin translation by Priscian. All
these follow much the same method,
and Q., who deals with them in this
chapter and in II. 4, does not differ
greatly; such differences as do exist
will be noticed in the sequel. Note
that all these are properly speaking
rhetorical ('dicendi primordia' not
'loquendi') though the more elementary
may be properly taken at this earlier
stage.

2. **Aesopi fabellas.** The μῦθος Αἰσώπειος (= our own 'fable') of the Greek progymnasmatists, Αἰσώπειος being added
to distinguish it from other μῦθοι—not
necessarily implying attribution of
authorship to Aesop, cp. Herm. *Prog.*
1. πάντες δὲ κοινῶς Αἰσώπειοι λέγονται
διότι τοῖς μύθοις Αἴσωπος ἐχρήσατο πρὸς
τὰς συνουσίας.

sermone...extollente. Compositions
begin with the fable because the childish
nature of the subject naturally tends to
produce a simple style appropriate to
this early stage. So Herm. *Prog.* ib. τὴν
δὲ ἀπαγγελίαν βούλονται περιόδων ἀλλο-
τρίαν εἶναι τῆς γλυκύτητος ἐγγύς. Theon.
Prog. 3 (175) ἐν τοῖς μύθοις ἁπλουστέ-
ραν (i.e. τῆς χρείας) τὴν ἑρμηνείαν εἶναι
δεῖ.

narrare)(**stilo exigere.** This in-
junction, that oral composition is to
precede written, is of great importance
and will, I think, commend itself to
most modern educationists.

exigere, v. on 4, 7.

versus...permittitur. The second
exercise conceded by Q. to the grammatical school is paraphrase of verse.
Paraphrase was a regular practice in
the schools, and according to Q. x. 5, 4
('ac de carminibus quidem neminem
credo dubitare') was universally admitted
in regard to poetry, though not by all
for prose. In Cic. *De Or.* 1, 154 however
Crassus puts forward the same objection
to paraphrasing Ennius as to paraphrasing Gracchus 'si iisdem verbis uterer,
nihil prodesse, si aliis, etiam obesse, cum
minus idoneis uti consuescerem.' Paraphrasing is not one of the 'progymnasmata' in Hermogenes etc., but Theon
in his introduction (152) speaks of it as
a regular means of training the orator,
and notes and answers the same objection as Crassus. Cp. also the mention
of paraphrase in the passage of Suet.
De Gram. 4, quoted in the note on
'aetiologiae' § 3.

versus...solvere, i.e. write the words
out in prose order.

interpretari. To give an exact version,
cf. x. 5, 5 'neque ego paraphrasin esse
interpretationem tantum volo, sed circa
eosdem sensus certamen atque aemula-
tionem.' This describes paraphrase in
the rhetorical school and indicates probably a wider liberty than is intended by
the words 'qua...permittitur.'

poetae. The majority, if not all, of

1-3] *INSTITUTIONIS ORATORIAE LIB. I* 117

permittitur. quod opus, etiam consummatis professoribus diffi- 3
cile, qui commode tractaverit, cuicumque discendo sufficiet.
sententiae quoque et chriae et aetiologiae subiectis

the commentators, misled, I think, by
the close connexion in construction of
the two halves of the section, have supposed that the material for paraphrasing
is restricted to a poetical version of
Aesop and have naturally gone on to
suppose that the poet here is Phaedrus.
If so we should have to couple with
him Babrius, as there is no reason to
suppose throughout this chapter, that
Latin exercises are thought of more
than Greek. But I can see no reason
for this assumption, against which I
have argued in *Class. Rev.* May—June
1919. In the treatment of the μῦθος
Αἰσώπειος in Herm. and Apth. there is
no suggestion of a poetic version being
used, or indeed any version. The child
is supposed to know the story and
write a little composition on it, and the
exercise described is as different from
paraphrase as possible. Again, it is
very unlikely that Q. should have wished
to restrict paraphrasing to the Phaedrus
stage. The 'poet' in question is any
poet who is being read in class, primarily no doubt Homer and Virgil.
It is interesting to note (though perhaps not evidence for Q.'s times) that
Augustine (*Conf.* 1, 17) takes as his stock
example of school work a rhetorical
paraphrase of this kind, and moreover
that the example is the earliest speech
in Virgil (*Aen.* 1, 38–50) 'proponebatur
enim mihi...ut dicerem verba Iunonis
irascentis et dolentis, quod non possit
Italia Teucrorum avertere regem, quae
nunquam Iunonem dixisse audieram.
Sed figmentorum poeticorum vestigia
errantes sequi cogebamur, et tale aliquid
dicere solutis verbis, quale poeta dixisset
versibus.'
.The introduction of paraphrasing at
this particular stage perhaps requires
some explanation. I understand Q. to
name these exercises in the order in
which he wishes them to be taken up.
The fable, based as it was on traditional
knowledge, could be employed at the
very earliest stage in the grammatical
school, while paraphrasing in its simplest form followed as soon as Homer
and Virgil were seriously begun.
   3. consummatis professoribus. Sp.'s
suggestion that this is abl., 'under accomplished professors,' is as he himself
felt too harsh. Sarpe's 'profectibus' is

very tempting. But the dat. does not
perhaps imply such an exaggeration as
at first appears. It was evidently a
common practice of the grammarians
to make such paraphrases. For the
practice of Aristarchus and others v.
Rutherford *Chapter* p. 336 ff. So perhaps (unless the reference is rather to
translation) in the account given by
Statius (*Silv.* 5, 3, 159) of his father's
school, 'sed quid parva loquor? tu par
adsuetus Homero | ferre iugum senosque
pedes aequare solutis | versibus et nun-
quam passu breviore relinqui.'
   difficile. Cf. x. 5, 8 (also of paraphrase) 'ipsa denique utilissima est
exercitationi difficultas.'
   sententiae quoque et chriae etc.—
end. I have discussed most of the
questions suggested by these sections
fairly fully in an article in *Class. Rev.*
Nov.–Dec. 1921. The notes which follow
agree with the opinions there expressed
except in a few points.
   sententiae, i.e. the γνώμη of the
progymnasmatists. For the difference
between this and the 'chria' v. note on
'personis continetur' below, p. 119.
   chriae. The meaning of the term as
used in the schools is sufficiently explained in the sequel, but it must be
remembered that it properly belongs
to the saying or action itself and not to
the exercise founded on it. Probably
indeed it was first introduced into the
schools as a valuable truth to be learnt
by heart and only afterwards utilised
for composition; cf. Sen. *Ep.* 33 § 7
'ideo pueris et sententias ediscendas
damus et has quas Graeci chrias vocant,
quia conplecti illas puerilis animus
potest, qui plus adhuc non capit.' As
to the original meaning of the term,
I agree with Rutherford *Chapter* p. 28,
that the explanation traditional amongst
the rhetoricians, that it is so named because of its special usefulness, is untenable and that it probably stands for τὸ
πρὸς τὴν χρείαν, i.e. something apposite
to a particular occasion. This seems to
follow from the quite early poem of
Machon χρείαι τῶν ἑταιρῶν when χρεία
= repartee. But the dominant use is of
the sayings of philosophers, and several
compilations of such χρείαι are mentioned by Diog. Laert.
   aetiologiae. So B, 'aethiol.' A, 'ethi-

mol.' or 'ethymol.' others; and so also below. I have returned to this reading against the 'ethologiae' of Regius adopted by all recent edd., not so much on account of MS. authority, as because I believe it gives a more satisfactory sense. The exercise in question clearly has these three marks; (*a*) it is closely connected with the γνώμη and χρεία, (*b*) it is, unlike the former, connected with some particular person (v. on 'personis continetur' below), (*c*) it is concerned with 'dicta.' 'Ethologia' is found in Sen. *Ep.* 95, 65 where we have it as a useful exercise in philosophy, 'descriptionem cuiusque virtutis: hanc Posidonius ethologiam vocat: quidam characterismon appellant, signa cuiusque virtutis ac vitii et notas reddentem, quibus inter se similia discriminentur.' It is also found in the accepted text of Suet. *De Gram.* 4, where he says that the old grammarians employed as preliminary exercises for rhetoric 'problemata, paraphrases, allocutiones, ethologias atque alia hoc genus'; and it is no doubt the apparent analogy of this passage with ours that has led edd. to accept Regius' emendation. If we followed the Senecan passage we might suppose here an elementary exercise in character-sketching —an embryo Theophrastus. But this fails to satisfy any of the conditions (*a*, *b*, *c*). A variant of this would be to suppose (with L.) the character-sketch of some famous individual. This will barely satisfy (*a*) and certainly not (*c*). Another view (apparently, to judge from his reference to VI. 2, 17, taken by Halm) is that it = the 'ethopoeia' of the progymnasmatists, i.e. an imaginary speech put into the mouth of some character real or fictitious, e.g. Andromache lamenting for Hector. Possibly 'ethologia' could = 'ethopoeia,' and Cic.'s use of 'ethologus' in *De Or.* 2, 242, 244 might be quoted to support this. But the meaning is quite untenable here. Not only does such an exercise fail to satisfy (*a*) and (*c*), but it is the very thing against which Q. is arguing. The 'ethopoeia' is hardly distinguishable from the 'prosopopoeia' (Q. indeed seems to use the latter word to include the former), and it is the fact that the Latin grammarians attempt such difficult exercises ('irrumpunt ad prosopopoeias' II. 1, 2) of which he is here complaining.

A fourth suggestion is that of Regius himself, 'ethologiam accipimus dictum mores alicuius exprimens, quale est illud Caesaris "si iusiurandum violandum est

propter regnum violandum."' Presumably the exercise would differ from the Chria in that it led up, not so much to an explanation and justification of the saying, as to remarks on the character of the speaker. This explanation would satisfy conditions *a*, *b*, *c*, but it seems to me to put a forced sense on 'ethologia' and moreover is it a sufficiently elementary exercise for the context? Still if we were in any way forced to accept 'ethologia,' I should regard this as the best explanation.

We may ask then whether the passage in Suet. does so force us. I think not. In the first place the reading there is uncertain, the MSS. having apparently 'ethio,' 'etymo,' 'ethimo,' 'aetho.' But even if we accept 'etho' there is no real parallelism between the two passages. S. is speaking of the exercises which the grammarians actually used; Q. is arguing that most of these were too advanced and pleading for the retention of a few only of the most elementary. The 'ethologia' of S. need not be of an elementary type, indeed probably is not, and obviously is not subject to our three conditions. It may in itself quite well have either of the two meanings just suggested above. There is a difficulty in equating it with 'ethopoeia,' for which the 'allocutio' preceding it in the list appears to be a regular equivalent (v. Priscian's trans. of Herm., Halm p. 557 and other reff. in Halm's index). But there is no difficulty in taking it as = 'descriptio virtutis' or 'vitii,' in which case it would be a form of 'communis locus'; or again as meaning the sketch of an individual, in which case it would correspond to the 'laudes,' 'vituperationes' or 'comparationes' of II. 4, 20.

To turn to 'aetiologia.' While it does not elsewhere appear amongst the progymnasmata, it is given as a 'figure of thought' and with language very similar to the language used here. Thus Cic. *De Or.* 3, 207 mentions amongst the figures 'ad propositum subiecta ratio,' and this Q., IX. 3, 93, identifies with αἰτιολογία. So Auct. Inc. (Halm *Rhet. Lat.* p. 73) 'αἰτιολογία est cum causam alicuius rei et rationem subicimus.' And when we observe that the αἰτία or reason of the saying is clearly the kernel of all these exercises (v. on 'subiectis dict. rat.' below, and 'ratio,' § 5) it is clear, I think, that αἰτιολογία is a very natural name for such an exercise. Observe that in II. 4, 26 Q., after mentioning such themes as 'cur armata apud Lace-

dictorum rationibus apud grammaticos scribantur, quia initium
ex lectione ducunt: quorum omnium similis est ratio, forma
diversa, quia sententia universalis est vox, aetiologia personis
continetur. chriarum plura genera traduntur: unum simile 4

daemonios Venus?' calls them a 'genus
chriae.' These particular themes are
of course too advanced for our context, but they suggest that the 'chria'
type might easily be headed with a 'cur.'
If it is asked why the exercise is never
elsewhere mentioned and how it differed
from the 'chria,' the same answer will
suffice for both questions. The difference
was so vague that the term died out. I
suggested in *Class. Rev.* l.c. that it may
have lain in the form in which the theme
was set.

One other point may be worth noting.
In *Ep.* 95, 65 where Seneca mentions
the philosophical 'ethologia' he also
notes the 'causarum inquisitio' or 'aetiologia,' and adds 'quam quare dicere
nos non audeamus, cum grammatici
custodes Latini sermonis suo iure ap-
pellent, non video.' This use of the term
by the grammarians may refer to the
'figure,' though that rather belongs to
rhetoric, but the words will certainly
acquire more force if the 'aetiologia'
was in Seneca's time one of the recognised exercises 'apud grammaticum.'

subiectis dictorum rationibus, i.e.
stating the reasons (αἰτία) for the sayings.
This suggests that in the earlier stages
the exercise consisted mainly if not entirely in writing out the saying which
had no doubt been committed to memory,
with the αἰτία. In the more elaborate
forms given in the progymnasmatists, we
begin (in the case of the 'chria') with
some remarks on the speaker. This is
followed by (1) a paraphrase of the saying, (2) αἰτία, including arguments ἐκ
τοῦ ἐναντίου, (3) παραβολή (illustration
from life), (4) παράδειγμα (illustration
from history), (5) μαρτυρία τῶν παλαιῶν,
i.e. quotations from the poets, (6) epi-
logue. For the further element of κλίσις
v. on § 5.

apud grammaticos scribantur, i.e.
'are suitable exercises for the school of
the grammarians.'

quia initium ex lectione ducunt. A
valuable remark shewing Q.'s desire to
correlate composition with reading. All
the instances of γνῶμαι in Herm. and
Apth. are drawn from poets, and Priscian
in his translation of the former draws
his exx. from Virgil and Terence. Most

of the examples of the 'chria' on the
other hand are sayings (or actions) of
philosophers such as those mentioned
below and would not be drawn directly
from the reading lessons in poetry.
Diom. indeed (K. I. 310) converts 'auri
sacra fames' and 'degeneres animos timor
arguit' from 'sententiae' into 'chriae'
by prefixing ' P. Verg. Maro dixit.' But
I imagine that Q. means that, even if
the text of the exercise did not come
directly from the poets read, it could
easily be connected with some passage,
which would then appear as μαρτυρία
τῶν παλαιῶν.

ratio, here used for 'general principle';
I do not think this is any objection to
the meaning I have given to it two lines
above. Q.'s use of 'ratio' is so wide,
that he was probably unconscious of the
difference.

**universalis vox...personis contine-
tur.** Cf. Aphth. *Prog.* 4 διενήνοχε δὲ ἡ
χρεία τῆς γνώμης τῷ τὴν μὲν χρείαν
δεῖσθαι τοῦ προσώπου, τὴν δὲ γνώμην
ἀπροσώπως ἐκφέρεσθαι, and so Herm.
and Theon, i.e. it is essential that the
'chria' should be attributed to some
particular person, about whom the
student is expected to make some remarks in his composition. Here however the distinction is made between the
γνώμη and the αἰτιο(ηθο)λογία, and not
the χρεία. Considering the persistence
with which the distinction between the
γνώμη and χρεία is repeated, I can hardly
think that the text is sound. I have suggested in *Class. Rev.* (l.c.) 'personis
continetur ⟨ut et⟩ chria. harum.' For the
phrase 'personis continetur' cf. III. 5, 11
'quidam putant etiam eas theses posse
aliquando nominari, quae personis cau-
sisque contineantur,' i.e. the name of
θέσις as opposed to ὑπόθεσις can sometimes be given even where there are
special limitations of persons and circumstances (the general distinction between θέσις and ὑπόθεσις is exactly
analogous to that indicated here).

4. plura genera. Distinctions more
or less corresponding to these are given
in progymnasmatists, though Herm.
passes them over lightly as used παρὰ
τοῖς παλαιοῖς. Theon comes closest to
Q. (§§ 203–206).

sententiae, quod est positum in voce simplici 'dixit ille' aut 'dicere solebat': alterum, quod est in respondendo 'interrogatus ille,' vel 'cum hoc ei dictum esset, respondit': tertium huic non 5 dissimile 'cum quis dixisset aliquid vel fecisset.' etiam in ipsorum factis esse chrian putant ut 'Crates, cum indoctum puerum vidisset, paedagogum eius percussit,' et aliud paene par ei, quod tamen eodem nomine appellare non audent, sed dicunt χρειῶδες, ut 'Milo, quem vitulum adsueverat ferre, taurum ferebat.' in his omnibus et declinatio per eosdem ducitur casus,

voce simplici. Theon and Herm. call this ἀποφαντική, which Prisc. translates 'indicativa.'
in respondendo. Theon ἀποκριτική.
tertium...fecisset. The reading of the old edd. (on little MS. authority) 'cum quis non dixisset, sed fecisset' was evidently the result of their wishing to draw a clear distinction between this and the preceding variety, and their failure to see that the distinction lay in the absence of 'ei.' The meaning is that the 'chria' in these cases is not called out by anything directly addressed to the speaker. Theon has a variant of the ἀποκριτική slightly different to this, where the 'chria' is uttered by Plato in answer to an invitation of Diogenes, though not to any direct question.
5. ipsorum. The conjecture of Regius 'ipsis' has rightly been rejected by all recent edd. The point is that the 'chria' may be some action of the philosopher himself, as well as his spoken comment on somebody else's action.
factis. The Greek progymnasmatists divide regularly into λογική, πρακτική and μικτή. The last named is exemplified by the Crates story (in Herm. attributed to Diogenes). This can be turned into a μικτή by the addition of the words τί γὰρ τοιαῦτα ἐπαίδευες; **indoctum puerum**; in Herm. and Aphth. μειράκιον ἀτακτοῦν (Prisc. 'indecenter agentem'). Theon παῖδα ὀψοφάγον, i.e. greedy. It is characteristic of Q.'s mentality and his belief that boys naturally wish to learn, that he has slipped into an expression, which implies that not only the misbehaving boy, but the dunce, is a disgrace to his teacher.
χρειῶδες. The point of distinction is that the person whose action or fortune supplies the moral does not supply it voluntarily or consciously. This is much the same as Theon's παθητική variety

of the χρεία πρακτική. After giving the story of the pedagogue above as ἐνεργητική he gives Δίδυμος ὁ αὐλητὴς ἁλοὺς ἐπὶ μοιχείᾳ ἐκ τοῦ ὀνόματος (διδύμων = ὄρχεων) ἐκρέματο as example of παθητική.
Milo...ferebat. In this instance Q. seems to have mixed two stories. Stob. *Flor.* 29, 69 gives it as γραῦν μόσχον μικρὸν ἀραμένην καὶ τοῦτο καθ᾽ ἡμέραν ποιοῦσαν λαθεῖν φέρουσαν τὸν ταῦρον, which is more to the point. So Petr. 25. In Cic. *De Sen.* 33 and Ath. x. 412 we have the story of M.'s carrying the bull, but no mention of the calf.
declinatio...casus. This evidently refers to the method described by Theon (210), γυμνάζονται κατὰ τὰς χρείας...τῇ κλίσει, and Diom. K. I. 310 by which the personage of the 'chria' was worked into different cases. We can begin not only with 'Cato dixit,' but with 'Catonis dictum est' or 'Catonem dixisse ferunt' or 'O Cato, dixisti.' This may possibly have had some value in teaching varieties of word-construction.—I take this to have been the purpose, rather than mere drilling in the inflections—but Theon and Diom. add the absurdity of putting the speaker into all numbers as well as all cases. Thus Theon gives us 'the two orators Isocrates said that their two clever disciples were sons of the gods.' Q., one is glad to see, does not add 'et numeros.' This treatment of the 'chria' etc. is also, I think, alluded to in Suet. *De Rhet.* I, where (describing the methods of the rhetoricians) the common text runs 'nam et dicta praeclare per omnes figuras, per casus et apologos aliter atque aliter exponere,' which I should be inclined to read 'dicta praeclara (i.e. chrias) per omnes figuras et casus, et apologos aliter atque aliter exponere' ('apologos' = the 'Aesopi fabellae' of Q.). All these exercises as noted above are theoretically rhetorical.

et tam factorum quam dictorum ratio est. narratiunculas a 6
poetis celebratas notitiae causa, non eloquentiae tractandas
puto. cetera maioris operis ac spiritus Latini rhetores relin-
quendo necessaria grammaticis fecerunt: Graeci magis operum
suorum et onera et modum norunt.

X

[AN ORATORI FUTURO NECESSARIA SIT PLURIUM ARTIUM COGNITIO]

Haec de grammatice, quam brevissime potui, non ut omnia 1
dicerem sectatus, quod infinitum erat, sed ut maxime necessaria.
nunc de ceteris artibus, quibus instituendos, priusquam rhetori
tradantur, pueros existimo, strictim subiungam, ut efficiatur
orbis ille doctrinae, quem Graeci ἐγκύκλιον παιδείαν vocant.

et...ratio est. The point of the sentence is that all these types of 'chria,' λογική, πρακτική and χρειώδης, are susceptible of both forms of treatment, i.e. training in word-structure by 'declinatio' and in thought-development by 'subiectio rationis.' It is misleading, I think, with Pottier (quoted by Fierville) to regard these two as representing 'grammatice' and rhetoric respectively. Rather they are both rhetorical and represent 'elocutio' and 'inventio' in their most elementary form.

6. narratiunculas. In the Greek progymnasmatists διήγημα takes the second earliest place between the μῦθος and χρεία. Q.'s attitude is distinctly different. 'Narratio' is only to be employed in the grammatical schools as a test of knowledge and to familiarise them with the stories and not as a regular progymnasma. Further when it reappears in II. 4, 2 as a rhetorical exercise, it is used in connection with history in the stricter sense. Narrative composition based on mythology or literary fiction seems therefore to have been considered unsuitable to either school by Q. It is not likely that scholastic practice followed him in this.

cetera...norunt. Cf. II. 1, 1 ff.
rhetores. So Halm etc. following A. Older edd. with B 'praeceptores,' which would naturally be followed as in II. 1, 1 by 'eloquentiae.' I follow Halm with hesitation. Q. is quite capable of thinking of his own profession as the 'praeceptores' *par excellence*, and A's reading

may easily have been an attempted improvement.
X. 1. orbis ille doctrinae. So 'disciplinarum circus,' Aug. *Cont. Ac.* III. 4: cf. Vitruv. I. 1, 12 'encyclios disciplina uti corpus unum ex his membris' (i.e. studies). It may be doubted, however, whether this idea of completeness really belongs to the Greek phrase, which perhaps rather means 'ordinary.' ἐγκύκλια or ἐγκ. παιδ. are frequently in philosophical writings set against philosophy (e.g. Diog. Laert., Theon *Prog.*, ps.-Plut. *De Lib. Ed.*, Philo) and in fact the question whether the ἐγκ. contributed to wisdom was one of the foremost philosophical questions (v. Intr. p. xxi). The word thus perhaps had a touch of disparagement, which Q. is glad to avoid.
As to the contents of the ἐγκ. παιδ., there is no doubt that it usually indicated the seven subjects (five if with Q. we class arithmetic and astronomy under geometry) which afterwards constituted the 'trivium' and 'quadrivium.' So Mart. Cap. speaks of the Seven as 'cyclicae.' The fact that the term is so often set over against philosophy need not raise doubts about the inclusion of dialectic; it merely implies that it did not embrace anything higher in philosophy. Not only is διαλεκτική not commensurate with λογική, but λογική itself was only the fence of the philosophical garden in which φυσική and ἠθική were respectively trees and fruits (Zeller *Stoics* p. 67). It has sometimes

2 nam isdem fere annis aliarum quoque disciplinarum studia
ingredienda sunt: quae quia et ipsae artes sunt et esse perfectae
sine orandi scientia possunt nec rursus ad efficiendum oratorem
3 satis valent solae, an sint huic operi necessariae, quaeritur. nam
quid, inquiunt, ad agendam causam dicendamve sententiam
pertinet, scire, quemadmodum in data linea constitui triangula
aequis lateribus possint? aut quo melius vel defendet reum vel
reget consilia, qui citharae sonos nominibus et spatiis dis-
4 tinxerit? enumerent etiam fortasse multos quamlibet utiles
foro, qui neque geometren audierint nec musicos nisi hac
communi voluptate aurium intellegant. quibus ego primum
hoc respondeo, quod M. Cicero scripto ad Brutum libro frequentius testatur: non eum a nobis institui oratorem, qui sit
aut fuerit, sed imaginem quandam concepisse nos animo perfecti
5 illius et nulla parte cessantis. nam et sapientem formantes

been thought, e.g. by Walden *Ancient
Universities* p. 198, that Q. here excludes both dialectic and rhetoric. This
is unnecessary: he has provided for
these subjects elsewhere, and here only
states that music and geometry are
necessary to complete the 'orbis.'
At the same time it is true that ἐγκ.
παιδ. is sometimes extended according
to individual ideas of complete education. In Strabo 14, 13 we have φιλοσο-
φίαν καὶ τὴν ἄλλην ἐγκ. παιδ. Max. Tyr.
Diss. 37 seems to include γυμναστικήν and
ποιητική. Stob. *Eth.* I. 20, Teub. I. p. 35
has φιλομουσίαν δὲ καὶ φιλογραμματείαν
καὶ φιλιππίαν καὶ φιλοκυνηγίαν καὶ καθ-
όλου τὰς ἐγκ. λεγομένας τέχνας. Vitruvius
l.c. appears to include medicine and
architecture, and these with the seven
may have made the 'novem disciplinae'
of Varro, though we have no evidence
that he used the term ἐγκ. or ἐγκ. παιδ.
2. **studia.** Sp. was inclined to read
'stadia' from 'ingrediuntur in stadium,'
in Cic. *De Or.* 1, 147. But the suggestion has rightly found no favour. The
whole passage in Cicero is based on
athletic metaphors.
perfectae...possunt. So B. A and
other MSS. have 'non possunt,' which
Sp. adopted or attempted to explain.
The statement might perhaps be justified
from *De Or.* 2, 36–38, but as far as I
can see, would have no possible bearing
on the argument. The emendation of
Regius 'perfecta sine his orandi scientia
non potest' is still more indefensible.
It is true that the received text is not

quite logical, for the irrelevance of
geometry and music does not follow
from their independence. Q. however
does not give the clauses 'quia...possunt'
as the reasons of the objector, but as a
fact, or apparent fact, which naturally,
though erroneously, predisposes him to
think these studies useless for the purpose.
3. **quemadmodum ... possint** = Euclid's ἐπὶ τῆς δοθείσης εὐθείας πεπερασ-
μένης τρίγωνον ἰσόπλευρον συστήσασθαι,
more correctly given by Mart. Cap. VI.
724 'quemadmodum possit super datam
directam terminatam lineam trigonum
aequilaterum constitui?' The omission
of 'finite' is natural enough, that of
'straight' less so. It is possible that
'directa' has dropped out. Several
MSS. have 'ducta' for 'data.'
triangula...possint. A has 'possit,'
which presumably induced Meister to
read 'triangulum...possit.'
4. **communi voluptate.** Cf. Arist.
Pol. v. 6, 4, where the proper and
educated appreciation of music is contrasted with merely χαίρειν τῷ κοινῷ τῆς
μουσικῆς, ὥσπερ καὶ τῶν ἄλλων ἔνια ζῴων
ἔτι δὲ καὶ πλῆθος ἀνδραπόδων καὶ παιδίων.
frequentius, i.e. *Orator*, esp. §§ 3–6,
and still more 7–10, 100, 101, cf. Prooem.
18–23.
et nulla parte cessantis. So later
edd. with A. Sp. 'ex nulla' with B and
others. Halm says 'ipse malim "et
ex."' But the 'ex' is better left out. The
usage is clearly that by which 'cesso' is
used of some part of the body refusing

eum, qui sit futurus consummatus undique et, ut dicunt, mortalis quidam deus, non modo cognitione caelestium vel mortalium putant instruendum, sed per quaedam parva sane, si ipsa demum aestimes, ducunt sicut exquisitas interim ambiguitates: non quia ceratinae aut crocodillinae possint facere sapientem, sed quia illum ne in minimis quidem oporteat falli. similiter **6** oratorem, qui debet esse sapiens, non geometres faciet aut musicus, quaeque his alia subiungam, sed hae quoque artes, ut sit consummatus, iuvabunt. nisi forte ἀντιδότους quidem atque alia, quae oculis aut vulneribus medentur, ex multis atque interim contrariis quoque inter se effectibus componi videmus,

to perform its function, cf. ps.-Quint. *Dec.* 6, 15 'de quinque rerum sensibus pars una (i.e. sight) cessabit?' **5. mortalis quidam deus**: v. exx. in Zeller *Stoics* Eng. Trans. p. 254. Q. has perhaps specially in mind Cic. *De Nat. De.* 2, 153 where, after speaking of man's knowledge of astronomy etc., he goes on 'quae contuens animus accedit ad cognitionem deorum, e qua oritur pietas, cui coniuncta iustitia est reliquaeque virtutes, e quibus vita beata existit par et similis deorum, nulla alia re nisi inmortalitate, quae nihil ad bene vivendum pertinet, cedens caelestibus.'

ceratinae aut crocodillinae. The explanation of these dialectical puzzles is given (1) Aul. Gell. 18, 2 and Sen. *Ep.* 49 'quod non perdidisti habes: cornua non perdidisti : habes igitur cornua.' (2) Lucian *De Vit. Auct.* 22, where Chrysippus puts to the purchaser as a specimen of his subtleties, τοῦτο (sc. τὸ παιδίον) ἤν πως κροκόδειλος ἁρπάσῃ, κᾷτά σοι ἀποδώσειν ὑπισχνῆται αὐτό, ἤν εἴπῃς τἀληθὲς ὅτι δέδοκται αὐτῷ περὶ τῆς ἀποδόσεως τοῦ βρέφους, τί φήσεις αὐτὸν ἐγνωκέναι; Both these quibbles seem to have become proverbial, cf. Luc. *Dial. Mort.* 1, 2 where Diogenes speaking of τοὺς ἀλαζόνας φιλοσόφους says κέρατα φύουσιν ἀλλήλοις καὶ κροκοδείλους ποιοῦσι, id. *Somn.* 11 (of the philosophical bore at a dinner) ἐνίοτε δὲ καὶ κέρατα ἔφασκεν εἶναί μοι. Cf. also Fronto *De El.* (Naber p. 146). Other reff. in Liddell and Scott, s.v. **6, 7. nisi forte…sentiuntur.** The general form of this sentence may be paralleled from II. 3, 6 and X. 5, 6 and 7. In all these the 'reductio ad absurdum' introduced as usual by 'nisi forte' consists in the incompatibility of the

two things combined, not in the impossibility of each singly. In II. 3, 6 also 'quidem' is used with the first limb, while in X. 5, 6 and 7 we have the same asyndetic combination as here. But apart from the unwieldy length of the sentence here, the combination is rather spoilt by the substitution of 'nos mirabimur etc.' for the simple 'oratio non eget.' The admission of A may make B impossible, but can hardly be said to make surprise at B impossible. These considerations give some, though I think on the whole inadequate, grounds for Andresen's conjecture of '<ne> antidotos quidem,' i.e. 'in that case we should have to disbelieve in compound medicines.' If this were adopted it would be necessary to put a full stop at 'sumit,' and insert 'cum' between 'et' and 'muta,' with a mark of interrogation after 'sentiuntur.' Such a mark is actually inserted by Rad. and L. in the accepted text, but is surely wrong.

6. oculis aut vulneribus. This collocation, which earlier edd. including Sp. avoided by reading 'morbis' for 'vulneribus,' is fully defended by Cic. *De Or.* 3, 132 'alios medicos qui morbis, alios qui vulneribus, alios qui oculis mederentur.'

effectibus. Either the antidote is composed of 'effectus' which is very loose, or we must read with Sp., who places 'atque …effectibus' between commas, suppose it to be an ablative of quality. Sp. also suggested that 'herbis' may have been lost after 'effectibus' and this he thought might account for the gender of 'earum.' Both these seem to me very harsh, and the same remark would apply to the possible alternative of taking 'effectibus' to be dependent on 'contrariis.'

quorum ex diversis fit una illa mixtura, quae nulli earum
similis est, ex quibus constat, sed proprias vires ex omnibus
7 sumit, et muta animalia mellis illum inimitabilem humanae
rationi saporem vario florum ac sucorum genere perficiunt: nos
mirabimur, si oratio, qua nihil praestantius homini dedit providentia, pluribus artibus egeat, quae, etiam cum se non
ostendunt in dicendo nec proferunt, vim tamen occultam
8 suggerunt et tacite quoque sentiuntur. 'fuit aliquis sine iis
disertus.' sed ego oratorem volo. 'non multum adiciunt.' sed
aeque non erit totum, cui vel parva deerunt; et optimum
quidem hoc esse conveniet, cuius etiamsi in arduo spes est, nos
tamen praecipiamus omnia, ut saltem plura fiant. sed cur
deficiat animus? natura enim perfectum oratorem esse non
prohibet, turpiterque desperatur quidquid fieri potest.

[DE MUSICE]

9   Atque ego vel iudicio veterum poteram esse contentus. nam
quis ignorat musicen, ut de hac primum loquar, tantum iam

diversis. This too is exceedingly
awkward. With what understood noun
does it agree? B has 'diversa' from
which Halm conjectured 'diversa vi.'
I should be inclined to suggest 'diver-
sitatibus.' The plural is not found, so
far as I know, but may be defended
from 'varietates,' and would account
for 'earum.'

earum. So all MSS. Halm thought
it was influenced by 'vires.' For other
explanations v. above, but it may be
noted that Sp.'s 'herbis' would also
require 'quarum.' Altogether the sentence if sound is very carelessly written.

proprias. Not 'its peculiar properties'
as L., but 'their own.'

7. inimitabilem. Sp. quotes II. 16,
16 'opera quaedam nobis inimitabilia,
qualia sunt cerarum ac mellis.'

tacite. I have returned to the reading of older edd. Sp. and later edd.
'tacitae.' Sp.'s note is as follows:
'Codd. quidem in talibus nulla auctoritas
(here no doubt he is right)....Quod
tacite sentitur id cum sentientis silentio
sentitur; cuius quidem sententiae equidem sensum hic nullum video: contra
quod *tacitum sentitur*, id sentitur etsi
vocem non mittens. Apte autem dicentur
tacere eae artes, quae *se non ostendunt
nec proferunt*.' But Sp. did not see that

in this usage 'tacit-' means 'unconscious' and is an attribute of the 'sen-
tiens' not of the 'sensum.' Cf. *De Or.*
3, 198 'tacite (al. taciti) tamen omnes
non esse illud, quod diximus, aptum
perfectumque cernunt.' So too ib. 195
'tacitus sensus' is ascribed to 'omnes,'
and to 'aures' in *Or.* 203. In Q. himself,
X. 1, 18, we have 'tacita verecundia'
for 'unconscious' shyness (v. Pet.'s note).
So too in VI. 3, 17 where 'urbanitas' is
described as 'sumptam ex conversatione
doctorum tacitam eruditionem,' the 'un-
consciousness' is an attribute rather
of the resultant quality than of the
factors which produce it; v. Nägelsbach
Stilistik p. 311, where all these exx.
are quoted.

8. disertus, v. note on 8, 4.

aeque. So Halm and recent edd.
with B etc. Earlier edd. 'utique.'

et optimum...conveniet. 'It will be
agreed that the whole is the ideal.'

cuius...fiant. Cf. Prooem. 20.

9–33. The sections on the educational
value of music may well be compared
with the second book of Aristides
Quintilianus. It is a pleasing possibility
that this writer may have been a freedman of Q.

These sections constitute by far the
most important evidence as to the posi-

illis antiquis temporibus non studii modo, verum etiam vene-
rationis habuisse, ut idem musici et vates et sapientes iudica-
rentur, mittam alios, Orpheus et Linus: quorum utrumque dis
genitum, alterum vero, quia rudes quoque atque agrestes
animos admiratione mulceret, non feras modo, sed saxa etiam
silvasque duxisse posteritatis memoriae traditum est. itaque **10**
et Timagenes auctor est omnium in litteris studiorum anti-
quissimam musicen extitisse, et testimonio sunt clarissimi
poetae, apud quos inter regalia convivia laudes heroum ac
deorum ad citharam canebantur. Iopas vero ille Vergilii nonne
canit

'errantem lunam solisque labores'

et cetera? quibus certe palam confirmat auctor eminentissimus
musicen cum divinarum etiam rerum cognitione esse con-
iunctam. quod si datur, erit etiam oratori necessaria, si quidem, **11**
ut diximus, haec quoque pars, quae ab oratoribus relicta a

tion held by music as a part of Roman
education. It is obvious that music was
not to the Roman what it was to the
Greek, at any rate in earlier times, but
I see no reason to doubt that it was a
normal part of the education of a boy of
the upper classes, and more so than it is
to-day, or at least was a generation ago,
in England. The mere fact that it is
regularly included in the 'liberal arts,'
as e.g. in Sen. *Ep.* 88, is a *prima facie*
proof of this: and it is confirmed for
Cicero's age by *De Or.* 3, 87, where
(in contrast to the professional who sings
every day) 'Numerius Furius, noster
familiaris, cum est commodum, cantat;
est enim paterfamilias, est eques Romanus; puer didicit quod discendum
fuit.' This passage indeed suggests, like
others, that musical performance had
not much place in the adult life of the
men, but this is after all what Aristotle
himself recommends for the Greeks.
The mention of choral performances
by boys as well as girls (e.g. Hor. *Odes*
I. 21, IV. 6, *Carm. Saec.*, Suet. *Cal.* 16)
tends to support the view that music
was commonly learnt by boys.

As to Q.'s own view, it is clear that
his belief in the value of music is largely
traditional. Except perhaps in § 31 he
shews little of the conviction that
appears in the *Republic*, the *Laws*, and
the *Politics*, that music really affects the
character permanently (ὅτι γινόμεθα

ποιοί τινες), though he is very conscious
of the powerful effect of music upon the
emotions, v. § 31, and IX. 4, 10, 11 (v.
on § 25).

9. Orpheus et Linus. The collocation
is probably suggested by *Ecl.* 4, 55, cf.
Tac. *Dial.* 12, where also the two are
spoken of as 'dis geniti.'

non feras...traditum est. This bit
of Euhemerism appears also in Hor.
A. P. 391–393:
'Silvestres homines sacer interpresque
    deorum
Caedibus et victu foedo deterruit Or-
    pheus,
Dictus ob hoc lenire tigres rabidosque
    leones.'
Cf. Dion Chrys. 53, 8 (of Orpheus)
τὸ γὰρ λίθους τε καὶ φυτὰ καὶ θηρία
κηλεῖν καὶ ἄγειν τί ἐστιν ἕτερον ἢ τὸ
βαρβάρους ἀνθρώπους ἀσυνέτους τῆς Ἑλληνικῆς φωνῆς οὕτως ἄγαν χειρώσασθαι
...πρὸς κιθάραν κηλουμένους;

10. Timagenes, v. *Class. Dict.*, Q. X. 1,
75, Hor. *Ep.* 1, 19, 15. Presumably, this
is from one of his historical works.

poetae, i.e. Homer of Demodocus,
Virgil of Iopas, though, strictly speaking,
the statement is only true of the first.

canebantur. Sp. is right, I think, in
saying that the imperfect for present is
unusual. But it is not an unnatural
use.

Iopas. *Aen.* 1, 742.

11. ut diximus. Prooem. 10 ff.

philosophis est occupata, nostri operis fuit ac sine omnium
12 talium scientia non potest esse perfecta eloquentia. atqui claros
nomine sapientiae viros nemo dubitaverit studiosos musices
fuisse, cum Pythagoras atque eum secuti acceptam sine dubio
antiquitus opinionem vulgaverint mundum ipsum ratione esse
conpositum, quam postea sit lyra imitata, nec illa modo
contenti dissimilium concordia, quam vocant ἁρμονίαν, sonum
13 quoque his motibus dederint. nam Plato cum in aliis quibusdam
tum praecipue in Timaeo ne intellegi quidem nisi ab iis, qui
hanc quoque partem disciplinae diligenter perceperint, potest.
de philosophis loquor, quorum fons ipse Socrates iam senex
14 institui lyra non erubescebat? duces maximos et fidibus et
tibiis cecinisse traditum, exercitus Lacedaemoniorum musicis
accensos modis. quid autem aliud in nostris legionibus cornua
ac tubae faciunt? quorum concentus quanto est vehementior
15 tantum Romana in bellis gloria ceteris praestat. non igitur
frustra Plato civili viro, quem πολιτικόν vocat, necessariam

12. **dubitaverit...fuisse.** For this use
of 'dubito' with the inf. v. Peterson on
x. 1, 73, who says that it is on the whole
a silver usage.
mundum...imitata. Cf. Cic. *Somn.
Scip.*, Macr. *Comm.* II. 1, 3, which Q.
may have specially in mind, where after
speaking of the music of the spheres he
says 'quod docti homines nervis imitati
atque cantibus aperuerunt sibi reditum
in hunc locum.'
sonum. For other reff. v. Heath's
Aristarchus (Index s.v. 'Harmony of
Spheres').
13. **aliis quibusdam,** e.g. *Rep.* III.
398 etc., *Phileb.* 7.
Timaeo, i.e. the theory of the use of
the διαστήματα by the Creator in forming
the 'anima mundi' 36, 37. So Sp. who
aptly quotes also Plut. *De Mus.* 22.
ne intellegi quidem...potest. Cf. Cic.
De Fin. 2, 15 'rerum obscuritas non
verborum facit, ut non intellegatur oratio,
qualis est in Timaeo Platonis.'
fons. Sp. quotes Cic. *De Or.* 1, 42
'fonte et capite Socrate,' i.e. of the
'philosophorum greges.'
de philosophis. Earlier edd. 'quid
de,' to which Meister has returned. It
has little MS. authority. Rad. omits the
mark of interrogation after 'erubescebat.' The sense of this I do not understand. L. translates 'why speak of
philosophers only?' Perhaps rather,

'why speak of them at all?' the evidence
of their 'fons' is enough.
Socrates...erubescebat. The story is
originally derived from Plato *Euthyd.*
272 c (cf. id. *Menex.* 235 E), where S.
tells how the boys in the school laughed
at him and derided his teacher Connus
as γεροντοδιδάσκαλος. Cicero alludes to
it *De Sen.* 26. It would seem, however,
to have had wider currency as a 'chria,'
in which S. supplied the moral that it
was better to be ὀψιμαθής than ἀμαθής.
So Val. Max. VIII. 7, 8, Sext. Emp. 359.
14. **duces maximos.** Q. has especially
in mind (as in 19) Cic. *Tusc. Disp.* 1, 4.
Who is meant besides Epaminondas
there mentioned is not clear. Sp. notes
Alcibiades who, according to Plat. *Alc. I*,
107, Plut. *Alc.* 192 D, learnt the lyre,
but refused to learn the flute. The list
of well-known musical men in Ath. IV.
184 has no great generals except possibly
Callias and Alc.
15. **non igitur...credidit.** I cannot
see that P. actually makes this statement.
Q. is perhaps thinking of *Rep.* III., and
identifies the guardians with the πολιτι-
κός; also perhaps *De Legg.* II. and VII.
and *Prot.* 326 B where boys are taught
music ἵνα χρήσιμοι ὦσιν εἰς τὸ λέγειν τε
καὶ πράττειν.
vocat. So Halm and later edd. with
A. Other MSS. 'vocant.' I should feel
more certain of the reading, if we could

musicen credidit. et eius sectae, quae aliis severissima, aliis asperrima videtur, principes in hac fuere sententia, ut existimarent sapientium aliquos nonnullam operam his studiis accommodaturos, et Lycurgus, durissimarum Lacedaemoniis legum auctor, musices disciplinam probavit. atque eam natura 16 ipsa videtur ad tolerandos facilius labores velut muneri nobis dedisse, si quidem et remigem cantus hortatur; nec solum in iis operibus, in quibus plurium conatus praeeunte aliqua iucunda voce conspirat, sed etiam singulorum fatigatio quamlibet se rudi modulatione solatur. laudem adhuc dicere artis 17 pulcherrimae videor, nondum eam tamen oratori coniungere. transeamus igitur id quoque, quod grammatice quondam ac musice iunctae fuerunt: si quidem Archytas atque Euenus etiam subiectam grammaticen musicae putaverunt, et eosdem

find that P. used the word in connexion with a musical education. The nearest approach to this I have found is *Rep.* IV. 425 A, where those who through music receive εὐνομία are contrasted with the restless people who οἴονται τῇ ἀληθείᾳ πολιτικοὶ εἶναι 426 D. As it is, there is not much, I think, to choose between the two readings.

eius sectae. No doubt the Stoics; the Cynics certainly held no such view. But no definite remark of this kind from any Stoic seems to have been preserved. I am inclined to think that Q. by the cautious way in which he speaks (aliquos nonnullam) refers to the rather dubious and half-hearted way in which the Stoics regarded the ἐγκύκλια in general (and therefore music by inclusion) as useful.

quae..videtur. L. goes strangely wrong here, translating 'in other respects the strictest and most severe of all schools of philosophy.' The meaning no doubt is 'most extreme in what some call seriousness, others harshness.' For the antithesis cf. XI. 3, 159 'vultus severus, non maestus,' XII. 10, 80 'severa, non tristia,' XI. 1, 90 'verborum etiam moderatione detrahi solet si qua est rei invidia, si asperum dicas nimium severum.'

Lycurgus. Sp. quotes Plut. *Lac. Inst.* p. 238 B ὁ γὰρ Λυκοῦργος παρέξευξε τῇ κατὰ πόλεμον ἀσκήσει τὴν φιλομουσίαν, ὅπως τὸ ἄγαν πολεμικὸν τῷ ἐμμελεῖ κερασθὲν συμφωνίαν καὶ ἁρμονίαν ἔχῃ.

16. Cf. Arist. Quint. II. 4 (Meib. p. 65) οὔκουν ἔνεστι πρᾶξις ἐν ἀνθρώποις, ἥτις ἄνευ μουσικῆς τελεῖται. θεῖοι μὲν ὕμνοι καὶ τιμαὶ μουσικῇ κοσμοῦνται, ἑορταὶ

δὲ ἴδιαι καὶ πανηγύρεις πόλεων ἀγάλλονται· πόλεμοι δὲ καὶ ὁδῶν πορεῖαι διὰ μουσικῆς ἐγείρονται καὶ καθίστανται· ναυτιλίας τε καὶ εἰρεσίας καὶ τὰ χαλεπώτατα τῶν χειρωνακτικῶν ἔργων ἀνεπαχθῆ ποιεῖ, τῶν πόνων γινομένη παραμύθιον. A similar passage in the fragments of Philodemus *De Mus.* IV. 8 (Teub. p. 71).

singulorum... solatur. Q. may be thinking of *Ecl.* 9, 64. Watson quotes from Boswell (ann. 1782):
Verse sweetens toil, *however rude the sound*:
All at her work the village maiden sings,
Nor, while she turns the giddy wheel around,
Revolves the sad vicissitude of things.
Johnson also quotes the stanza in the Dictionary, s.v. wheel. It is from a poem called 'Contemplation' by the Rev. R. Gifford (v. *D. N. B.*), and apart from its attraction for Johnson, has the interest that it may probably have been inspired by this passage.

17. iunctae fuerunt. For the close connexion v. Plat. *Prot.* 325 E ff. Q. is perhaps rather confused by the use of μουσική sometimes for ἡ ἐπὶ ψυχῇ παιδεία, e.g. *Rep.* II. 376 E (and quotation from the *Knights* below), sometimes for music in the narrower sense.

Archytas ... putaverunt. Probably these writers pointed out that in the wider usage music included γραμματική, and used this fact to glorify music in its narrower sense.

Archytas. This may well come from the τὸ ἁρμονικόν, which whether genuine

utriusquereipraeceptoresfuissecum Sophron ostendit,mimorum
quidem scriptor, sed quem Plato adeo probavit, ut suppositos
18 capiti libros eius,cum moreretur,habuisse credatur,tum Eupolis,
apud quem Prodamus et musicen et litteras docet et Maricas,
qui est Hyperbolus, nihil se ex musice scire nisi litteras confitetur. Aristophanes quoque non uno libro sic institui pueros
antiquitus solitos esse demonstrat, et apud Menandrum in
Hypobolimaeo senex, qui reposcenti filium patri velut rationem
impendiorum, quae in educationem contulerit, exponens psaltis
19 se et geometris multa dicit dedisse. unde etiam ille mos, ut in
conviviis post cenam circumferretur lyra, cuius cum se im-
peritum Themistocles confessus esset, ut verbis Ciceronis utar,

or not is quoted as such by Nicomachus,
Q.'s contemporary. The fragment there
given, Arith. I. 3, 4, speaks of music,
arithmetic and geometry as μαθήματα.
Euenus. Pre-Halmian edd. read
'Aristoxenus,' but with no early MS.
authority. B and others have 'Euenus,'
while A originally had 'nus' following
on a space of three, or, as I should say
from a personal inspection, of four letters.
At the same time some doubt may be
felt whether the real name has not been
lost. There is nothing in the record of
Euenus (poet, sophist and possibly the
author of a rhetorical τέχνη, Plat.
Phaedr. 267 A) which suggests a reason
why he should be mentioned in this
connexion. The name of Eudemus would
suit well enough, for the remark might
easily have come in his history of geometry, possibly as a repudiation of the
view which ranked music as a branch
of geometry. But the corruption in
MSS. would not be easy to account
for.
subiectam. 'Branch of.' Cf. 'appellatio...subicienda nomini' 4, 21.
Plato...credatur. The story is given
by Diog. Laert. 3, 18, Val. Max. 8, 7, 3.
18. Prodamus. A character probably
in the *Goats* of Eupolis, v. the statement of Theodosius (Bekk. *Anec.* III.
p. 1168): ὅτι δὲ ποιητικοῦ τινος ἀνδρὸς
καὶ μουσικοῦ ἢ τῶν στοιχείων εὕρεσις ἦν
σημεῖον τὸ πάλαι τοὺς αὐτοὺς εἶναι διδασ-
κάλους μουσικῆς καὶ γραμματικῆς, ὡς ὁ
Εὔπολις εἰσάγει ἐν Αἰξί. In view of this
the suggestion to emend the name to
Prodicus or Pronomus, who taught
music to Alcibiades (v. Halm's note),
seems quite unnecessary.
nihil...litteras. A literal equivalent

of οὐδὲ μουσικὴν ἐπίσταμαι πλὴν γραμ-
μάτων Ar. *Eq.* 188. I cannot rule out
the possibility that in ascribing this to
Eupolis Q. has made a slip. While it
is true that in *Nub.* 553 Ar. says that
the *Maricas* was a mere travesty of the
Knights (a point rather complicated by
Eupolis' own claim to have collaborated
in the latter), it seems rather improbable
that he should have transcribed the
phrase ; and if it did occur in both plays
Q. would be more likely to quote it
from what was at any rate the earlier,
if not the better known of the two. On
the other hand the similarity of the two
plays would easily excuse such a slip of
memory. Confusions between Eup. and
Ar. occur elsewhere. Cicero himself in
the original edition of the *Orator* made
one (cp. *Or.* 29 with *ad Att.* 12, 6).
non uno libro. Neither Sp.'s suggestion of 'loco' nor the fantastic idea that
Ar. of Byzantium is referred to can be
sustained in view of Pers. 1, 76 'venosus
liber Atti' and perhaps Prop. 4, 21,
28 'librorumque tuos, docte Menandre,
sales.'
The references here are to *Ran.* 729,
Nub. 966, also perhaps Δαιταλεῖς, v.
Meineke *Fr. Com.* II. p. 1038.
Hypobolimaeo. Otherwise called Ἀγ-
ροικος. The situation alluded to seems
very uncertain, and hardly concerns us.
Sp.'s explanation cannot be reconciled
with Cic. *Pro Rosc. Am.* 46.
qui reposcenti. Sp. and earlier edd.
omit 'qui' but with little authority.
exponens. So A. Sp. and earlier
edd. 'opponens' with B.
psaltis ... dedisse. ψάλταις δέδωκα
πολλὰ καὶ γεωμέτραις (?).
19. Ciceronis. *Tusc. Disp.* I. 4.

'est habitus indoctior.' sed veterum quoque Romanorum epulis 20
fides ac tibias adhibere moris fuit: versus quoque Saliorum
habent carmen. quae cum omnia sint a Numa rege instituta,
faciunt manifestum ne illis quidem, qui rudes ac bellicosi
videntur, curam musices, quantam illa recipiebat aetas, defuisse.
denique in proverbium usque Graecorum celebratum est, 'in- 21
doctos a Musis atque a Gratiis abesse.' verum quid ex ea 22
proprie petat futurus orator, disseramus.

Numeros musice duplices habet, in vocibus et in corpore:
utriusque enim rei aptus quidam modus desideratur. vocis
rationem Aristoxenus musicus dividit in ῥυθμόν et μέλος,
quorum alterum modulatione, alterum canore ac sonis constat.
num igitur non haec omnia oratori necessaria? quorum unum
ad gestum, alterum ad conlocationem verborum,· tertium ad
flexus vocis, qui sunt in agendo quoque plurimi, pertinet: nisi 23

20. habent carmen. Presumably 'have
a tune of their own' as perhaps in 32.
To take the words to mean 'are in
metrical form' would make 'versus'
rather otiose, though Sp. thought it
possible, and the fact that Q. is reproducing Cicero quoted below might
excuse the weakness of the remark to
some extent.

quae...omnia. Referring to 'sed...
fuit' as well as to 'Saliorum versus.'
Q. is merely reproducing *De Or.* 3, 197
'quorum illa summa vis carminibus est
aptior et cantibus, non neglecta, ut mihi
videtur, a Numa rege doctissimo maiori-
busque nostris, ut epularum sollemnium
fides ac tibiae Saliorumque versus indicant'; though Cicero may no doubt have
meant to ascribe 'fides ac tibiae' to
'maiores,' and only 'Sal. vers.' to
Numa.

21. indoctos...abesse. The nearest
approach to this which I can find is
Aelian *De Nat. An.* 12, 6 where οἱ
ἀπὸ τῶν Μουσῶν καὶ Χαρίτων (noted as a
proverbial phrase) are contrasted with
ἐπαΐοντες τῆς Μούσης. Cp. also Theoc.
Id. 16, 109 ἀεὶ Χαρίτεσσιν ἅμ' εἴην.

22. proprie. Not as L. 'reasonably,'
but 'for his own special sphere.'

ῥυθμόν et μέλος. B has 'ῥυθμόν
et μέλος μέτρον' which seems to have
given rise to the μέλος ἔμμετρον read by
earlier edd. including Sp. While nothing,
so far as I can see, is to be said for this
last, 'μέλος et μέτρον' would in itself be
in accordance with Arist. Quint. I. 4
(Meibom. p. 6), where μέλος in its fuller

sense (μέλος τέλειον) is divided into
μελωδία, ῥυθμός, λέξις, this last being
later called μέτρον. So too ib. I. 5 τοῦ
δὲ μέρη τρία, ἁρμονικόν, ῥυθμικόν, μετρι-
κόν. This doctrine, which goes back to
Rep. III. p. 398 D τὸ μέλος ἐκ τριῶν ἐστι
συγκείμενον, λόγου τε καὶ ἁρμονίας καὶ
ῥυθμοῦ, ran no doubt parallel to the other,
according as the whole song, or only the
musical part of it was thought of; cf.
Aul. Gell. 16, 18 where μετρική is
introduced rather as an outlying subject.
Thus even in Ar. Quint. we find the
double classification, e.g. II. 7 (Meibom.
p. 75). Here the μέτρον cannot be
reconciled with the rest of the passage,
and I should regard it as an addition
by someone who was familiar with the
triple classification. Mediaeval students
might naturally take this view from
Augustine *De Musica,* who includes
'metrica,' and still more from what was
for some centuries the most familiar
source of knowledge, Isidore, v. *Or.* III.
18, where the triple classification is definitely adopted.

modulatione. Here the word is evidently restricted to the 'measures' or
the rhythm of the song, as opposed to
the variations of the notes of the melody.
A similar restriction of meaning appears
in IX. 4, 139. It can no doubt, however,
be used of both elements in music, and
presumably was so above § 16, as below
§ 25, where v. note.

omnia. I.e. 'modus (or 'ῥυθμός')
corporis' as well as the 'ῥυθμός and
μέλος vocis.'

9

forte in carminibus tantum et in canticis exigitur structura
quaedam et inoffensa copulatio vocum, in agendo supervacua
est, aut non conpositio et sonus in oratione quoque varie pro
24 rerum modo adhibetur sicut in musice. namque et voce et
modulatione grandia elate, iucunda dulciter, moderata leniter
canit totaque arte consentit cum eorum, quae dicuntur, adfecti-
25 bus. atqui in orando quoque intentio vocis, remissio, flexus
pertinet ad movendos audientium adfectus, aliaque et conlo-
cationis et vocis, ut eodem utar verbo, modulatione concitationem
iudicis, alia misericordiam petimus, cum etiam organis, quibus
sermo exprimi non potest, adfici animos in diversum habitum
26 sentiamus. corporis quoque aptus et decens motus, qui dicitur
εὐρυθμία, et est necessarius nec aliunde peti potest: in quo
pars actionis non minima consistit, qua de re sepositus nobis
27 est locus. age, non habebit in primis curam vocis orator? quid

23. carminibus et canticis. Hardly
as L. 'poetry, lyric or otherwise,' rather
'songs whether of the higher or lower
type.' Cf. Ter. Maur. 296, K. VI. 334:
'Verba si non appetita nec remota plurimis,
Sed fere communis usus, et tamen non
obvia,
Carminis servant honorem, non iacentis
cantici.'
This is supported by the frequent use of
'canticum' in connexion with revelry
and the like, cf. 'obscenis canticis,'
above 2, 8.
    conpositio et sonus. Here 'sonus
in oratione' clearly refers to the management of the voice in 'pronuntiatio,' a
subject developed in XI. 3, 14–65. Cp.
§42 of that chapter 'mediis ergo utendum
sonis, hique tum augenda intentione
excitandi, tum submittenda sunt tem-
perandi.' 'Sonus' therefore = 'flexus...
vocis' above, and corresponds to μέλος
in music. So 'conpositio' corresponds
to ῥυθμός. Sp. however not unreasonably
questioned 'conpositio' as being a mere
repetition of 'structura...vocum' above.
There may not be much, if any, distinction between them. But the two halves
of the sentences are really different in
meaning. The first notes that the ear
requires rhythm both in music and
oratory; the second that *variety* of
rhythm, and also *variety* of that element
which is melody in music and 'sonus'
in oratory, serve to express variety of
subject.

24, 25. For the general sense of these
sections cf. IX. 4, 10–13.
    24. canit. Sc. 'musice,' certainly
not 'eloquence' as L. If proof is required of this, the use of 'atqui,' as Sp.
says, is sufficient. Possibly 'ea' may
have fallen out either before or after
'namque.' For the former cf. 'is namque' VIII. 6, 71.
    25. ut eodem utar verbo. The point
clearly is that 'modulatio' having been
previously used exclusively of rhythm,
Q. is conscious of a weakness in using
it here of the 'flexus vocis,' but apparently can find no better word.
    cum etiam...sentiamus. Cf. IX. 4,
10 'neque enim aliter eveniret, ut illi
quoque organorum soni, quamquam
verba non exprimunt, in alios tamen
atque alios motus ducerent auditorem.'
    26. εὐρυθμία. Cf. IX. 4, 50 'metrum
in verbis modo, rhythmus etiam in corporis motu est.'
    actionis. Not to be translated 'elo-
quence' as L., and even 'delivery' is
rather too wide, cf. XI. 3, 1 'pronuntiatio
a plerisque actio dicitur, sed prius nomen
a voce, sequens a gestu videtur accipere.'
The 'locus sepositus' is XI. 3, 65–149,
where after dealing with 'pronuntiatio'
in the stricter sense of the management
of the voice, he turns to the discussion
of gesture, face, dress, etc.
    27. age, non. So A. B has 'locus
agendus' on which Halm says 'fortasse,
locus agendi.' The 'age, si' of Sp.
and earlier edd. has little authority.

tam musices proprium? sed ne haec quidem praesumenda pars
est: uno interim contenti simus exemplo C. Gracchi, praecipui
suorum temporum oratoris, cui contionanti consistens post eum
musicus fistula, quam τονάριον vocant, modos, quibus deberet
intendi, ministrabat; haec ei cura inter turbidissimas actiones 28
vel terrenti optimates vel iam timenti fuit. libet propter quosdam imperitiores etiam 'crassiore,' ut vocant, 'Musa' dubita-
tionem huius utilitatis eximere. nam poetas certe legendos 29
oratori futuro concesserint: num igitur hi sine musice? ac si
quis tam caecus animi est, ut de aliis dubitet, illos certe, qui
carmina ad lyram composuerunt. haec diutius forent dicenda,
si hoc studium velut novum praeciperem. cum vero antiquitus 30
usque a Chirone atque Achille ad nostra tempora apud omnis,
qui modo legitimam disciplinam non sint perosi, duraverit, non
est committendum, ut illa dubia faciam defensionis sollicitudine.
quamvis autem satis iam ex ipsis, quibus sum modo usus, 31

Cf. XII. 1, 8 'age, non ad perferendos
studiorum labores necessaria frugalitas?
Quid igitur ex libidine ac luxuria spei?'
where also the phrase serves to introduce
a new but allied thought.
sed ne...pars est. Referring to XI. 3,
1–65.
uno interim ... ministrabat. The
story is given by several (reff. in Sp.).
Q. probably follows Cic. *De Or.* 3,
225 'Gracchus...cum eburneola solitus
est habere fistula qui staret occulte post
ipsum, cum contionaretur, peritum
hominem, qui inflaret celeriter eum
sonum, quo illum aut remissum excitaret
aut a contentione revocaret.' Aulus
Gellius 1, 11 commenting on these
words adopts a version (also found in
Plutarch *Tib. Gracch.* 2, 4), that the
pipe was only used 'ad reprimendum
sedandumque impetum vocis eius.'
Possibly Q. connects the 'remissum' of
C.'s version with the period of 'timenti
optimates,' and the 'contentione' with
'terrenti.'
τονάριον. 'Pitch-pipe,' not found elsewhere. Plutarch calls it φωνασκικὸν
ὄργανον and συρίγγιον.
modos. L. gives 'tones.' Perhaps
rather 'key.'
ministrabat. So Meist. and Rad.
with B. A has 'monstrabat' which
Halm printed, but doubtfully, pointing
to Aul. Gell. l.c. 'praeisse ac praeminis-
trasse modulos ferunt.'
28. fuit. So Sp. Halm, and later edd.

with B. A has 'profuit,' with, I think,
almost equal probability.
29. num igitur hi sine musice?
It has been suggested that 'legendi'
should be understood, and that the words
refer to the recitative in which poetry
was read (cf. 8, 2). I do not think that
anything more is meant than that poetry
is inseparably bound up with music.
illos. The construction is loose, but
hardly presents the difficulty which Sp.
found in it. Understand 'concesserint
non sine musice esse.'
30. Chirone atque Achille. For the
specific inclusion of musical teaching in
the legend of the education of Achilles
v. Juv. 7, 210, Plut. *De Mus.* 40. In
Il. 11, 831 it is confined to medicine,
nor is music mentioned in Pind. *Nem.*
3, 75 ff. The legend was probably
developed (as in Plut. l.c.) from the
representation of Achilles as playing
the lyre in *Il.* 9, 186 ff. I think Q. has
this last passage in mind (τῇ ὅ γε θυμὸν
ἔτερπεν, ἄειδε δ' ἄρα κλέα ἀνδρῶν) in the
words of the next section 'qua laudes'
etc.
31. These rather vague limitations as
to the nature of the music and instruments to be employed may be partly
reminiscent of Plat. *Rep.* III. 398, 399,
and Ar. *Pol.* v. 6. Cp. also Plut. *De
Mus.* 15 οἱ δὲ νῦν τὰ σεμνὰ αὐτῆς
παραιτησάμενοι, ἀντὶ τῆς ἀνδρώδους ἐκεί-
νης καὶ θεσπεσίας καὶ θεοῖς φίλης κατεα-
γυῖαν καὶ κωτίλην εἰς τὰ θέατρα εἰσάγουσι.

exemplis credam esse manifestum, quae mihi et quatenus
musice placeat, apertius tamen profitendum puto, non hanc
a me praecipi, quae nunc in scaenis effeminata et inpudicis
modis fracta non ex parte minima, si quid in nobis virilis
roboris manebat, excidit, sed qua laudes fortium canebantur
quaque ipsi fortes canebant: nec psalteria et spadicas etiam
virginibus probis recusanda, sed cognitionem rationis, quae ad
32 movendos leniendosque adfectus plurimum valet. nam et
Pythagoran accepimus concitatos ad vim pudicae domui ad-
ferendam iuvenes iussa mutare in spondium modos tibicina
conposuisse, et Chrysippus etiam nutricum illi quae adhibetur
33 infantibus adlectationi suum quoddam carmen adsignat. est
etiam non inerudite ad declamandum ficta materia, in qua

inpudicis modis fracta. For this
use of 'frangere'=to enervate or emas-
culate, cf. infra 11, 1 and Sen. *Ep.* 90,
19 'molles cantus et infractos,' ib. 114,
1 'oratio infracta et in morem cantici
ducta.' So Cicero was called by Brutus
'fractus et elumbis,' Tac. *Dial.* 18. Cp.
Persius 1, 18 'patranti fractus ocello.'
The use of θρύπτω in Greek is very
similar, compare also κατεαγότες, e.g.
Dion. Hal. *De Comp.* 18 ὑπὸ γυναικῶν ἢ
κατεαγότων ἀνθρώπων, and Plut. quoted
above. The usage is not very adequately
treated in Forc.

psalteria ... recusanda. Are these
instruments regarded as in themselves
lascivious and demoralizing? Possibly
so, cf. the association of the psaltery
with Clodius, Cic. *De Har. Resp.* 44.
Nothing further seems to be known of
the 'spadix.' On the other hand the
idea may be that as they are complicated and outlandish an acquaintance with them implies more attention
to music than is consistent with
respectability. If so, the thought is
very similar to Sall. *Cat.* 25 'psallere
...elegantius, quam necesse est probae.'
By 'etiam' is implied that a girl may
rightly carry her musical training further
than a boy, though she too, if of the
virtuous classes, has her limit. For girls
learning music v. exx. quoted by Grasberger III. p. 525, particularly Stat.
Silv. III. 3, 63, where also it is hinted
that 'ars' of this kind may throw suspicion on 'probitas.' Cp. also Plat.
Rep. III. 398 E ἄχρηστοι (sc. θρηνώδεις
ἁρμονίαι) γὰρ καὶ γυναιξὶν ἃς δεῖ ἐπιεικεῖς
εἶναι, μὴ ὅτι ἀνδράσιν.
sed cognitionem. Q. must not be

understood as barring direct instruction
either in singing (v. on 'moduletur,' 12,
13) or in the proper instruments. He
does not indeed specify these, but no
more does Aristotle in the parallel passage. He no doubt holds with him (if
he is not directly following him), that
a real knowledge of the theory, or power
of exercising proper judgment, is hardly
obtainable without practice at some
point in life.
32. nam et Pythagoran. The story
is frequently told with slight variations
(reff. in Sp.). In Galen *De Plac. Hipp.
et Plat.* v. 6 and in Mart. Cap. IX. 926
it is told of Damon. Q. clearly takes it
from Cic. *De Consiliis Suis*, a fragment of
which is given in substance by Boeth. *De
Mus.* 1, 1 'cum vinolenti adulescentes
tibiarum etiam cantu, ut fit, instincti mulieris pudicae fores frangerent, admo-
nuisse tibicinam, ut spondeum caneret,
Pythagoras dicitur. Quod cum illa
fecisset, tarditate modorum et gravitate
canentis illorum furentem petulantiam
consedisse.' For another story about
Pythagoreans and music v. IX. 4, 12.
accepimus. So N, all other MSS.
'accipimus.'
concitatos. Not as L. 'led astray by
their passions,' but = 'cantu instincti'
of C., as indeed Q. implies by 'mutare.'
spondium. Cf. Dion. Hal. *De adm.
vi dic. Dem.* 22 σπουδαῖος γίγνομαι καὶ
πολὺ τὸ εὐσταθὲς ἔχω τῆς γνώμης, ὥσπερ
οἱ τῶν σπονδείων αὐλημάτων...ἀκροώ-
μενοι.
Chrysippus : cf. 1, 4 and 16.
nutricum...adlectationi. I have little
doubt that Chrysippus used the word
καταβαυκάλησις (Athenaeus XIV. 618 E)

ponitur tibicen, qui sacrificanti Phrygium cecinerat, acto illo in insaniam et per praecipitia delato accusari, quod causa mortis extiterit: quae si dici debet ab oratore nec dici citra scientiam musices potest, quomodo non hanc quoque artem necessariam esse operi nostro vel iniqui consentient?

[DE GEOMETRIA]

In geometria partem fatentur esse utilem teneris aetatibus: 34 agitari namque animos et acui ingenia et celeritatem percipiendi venire inde concedunt, sed prodesse eam non ut ceteras artis, cum perceptae sint, sed cum discatur, existimant. ea vulgaris

or some word from βαυκαλάω (Hesychius βαυκαλᾶν, κατακοιμίζειν, τιθηνεῖν, παιδία μετ' ᾠδῆς κοιμίζειν). As these terms in themselves denoted the relation of nurse and infant, Q. is driven to this rather awkward periphrasis to explain it. Sp. thought that the 'adlectatio' (if genuine, which he doubted) was 'ad sugendum.' Much more probably 'ad dormiendum,' but Hesychius' definition would not exclude the former.

Phrygium. Cf. Ar. *Pol.* v. 7, 8 where he censures Plat. *Rep.* III. p. 399 for admitting the 'Phrygian' which he says is ὀργιαστικὸς καὶ παθητικός, and amongst harmonies what the flute is among instruments. In some of the other versions of the Pythagoras story above, the minstrel excites the youths with the 'Phrygian.' In the declamation, no doubt a special point was made of 'sacrificanti,' i.e. that this mode was inappropriate to the solemn occasion.

ponitur ... tibicen ... accusari. Sp. thought this construction intolerable, and that to correct to either 'tibicinem' or 'accusatus' was necessary. Later edd. have wisely rejected this view. The construction may be paralleled even from Cicero, v. Madv. *L. G.* 400 C. 'Ponitur' is of course the natural word for the subject of a 'thema.'

34-49. It is a commonplace amongst historians of mathematics, that the Romans had little or nothing of mathematics. Cicero's words (*Tusc.* I. 5) 'in summo apud illos (i.e. Graecos) honore geometria fuit; itaque nihil mathematicis illustrius. At nos metiendi ratiocinandique utilitate huius artis terminavimus modum,' are true of the centuries that followed him, in the sense that nothing was produced beyond the work of the 'agrimensores,' which, except perhaps for a few very small points in Balbus,

has nothing which we should call mathematics. But this is quite a different thing from saying that educated Romans knew nothing of, and took no interest in, mathematics. While it may be said that the length at which Q. insists on so elementary a truth as that discussed in §§ 39-45, looks as if neither he nor his readers were much versed in mathematics, the questions mentioned in 49 point to a rather more extended knowledge than the Romans are usually credited with. The chapter certainly shews that Roman boys were taught geometry. Further the wording of § 37, particularly 'illa propositarum...syllogismis' clearly implies deductive geometry and something more than the formulae and definitions of the 'agrimensores.' And as (1) we have every reason to believe that Euclid was the universally accepted text-book of Geometry in the Greek world, and (2) the first proposition of Euclid is represented (§ 3) as the typical example of school geometry, quoted by opponents, I see no reason to doubt that Euclid himself was taught at Rome. At any rate the statement of Gow (*Gr. Math.* p. 203) that 'Euclid does not seem to have been known at all in Italy' is far too sweeping. And indeed Euclid is quoted by name Aul. Gell. I, 20. The fact that no Latin translation of Euclid is known prior to that of Boethius is no objection to this. It is probable enough that he was read and expounded in Greek, or if in Latin (and possibly the use of 'constituere' = συστήσασθαι both in Q. and Mart. Cap. may point to the existence of regular Latin equivalents for Euclidean terms) only to so limited an extent that no authorised translation of the book was needed.

agitari ... opinio est. Cp. Isocrates

35 opinio est. nec sine causa summi viri etiam inpensam huic
scientiae operam dederunt. nam cum sit geometria divisa in
numeros atque formas, numerorum quidem notitia non oratori
modo, sed cuicumque saltem primis litteris erudito necessaria
est. in causis vero vel frequentissime versari solet: in quibus
actor, non dico, si circa summas trepidat, sed si digitorum
saltem incerto aut indecoro gestu a computatione dissensit,

περὶ ἀντιδ. 264 (Bekker 283), a passage
which Q. may have definitely had in
mind. After saying that he agrees with
the common view that astronomy and
geometry are not directly useful πρὸς τὰς
πράξεις, he goes on to say that he still
believes in their value. Τὰ μὲν γὰρ ἄλλα
τότ' ὠφελεῖν ἡμᾶς πέφυκεν, ὅταν λάβωμεν
αὐτῶν τὴν ἐπιστήμην, ταῦτα δὲ τοὺς μὲν
ἀπηκριβωμένους οὐδὲν ἂν εὐεργετήσειε
πλὴν τοὺς ἐντεῦθεν ζῆν προῃρημένους,
τοὺς δὲ μανθάνοντας ὀνίνησι· περὶ γὰρ
τὴν περιττολογίαν καὶ τὴν ἀκριβείαν τῆς
ἀστρολογίας καὶ γεωμετρίας διατρίβοντες,
καὶ δυσκαταμαθήτοις πράγμασιν ἀναγκαζό-
μενοι προσέχειν τὸν νοῦν, ἔτι δὲ συνεθιζό-
μενοι λέγειν καὶ πονεῖν ἐπὶ τοῖς λεγομένοις
καὶ δεικνυμένοις, καὶ μὴ πεπλανημένην
ἔχειν τὴν διάνοιαν, ἐν τούτοις γυμνασθέντες
καὶ παροξυνθέντες ῥᾷον καὶ θᾶττον τὰ
σπουδαιότερα καὶ πλέονος ἄξια τῶν πραγμάτων ἀποδέχεσθαι καὶ μανθάνειν δύνανται.
Cf. also Cic. De Rep. 1, 30 'istae quidem
artes (i.e. geometry and astronomy) si
modo aliquid valent, id valent ut paulum
acuant et tamquam irritent ingenia puerorum, quo facilius possint maiora discere.' Philo's view is rather more philosophical (De Cong. 4) γεωμετρία δ' ἰσότητος
καὶ ἀναλογίας ἐμβαλλομένη τὰ σπέρματα
εἰς ψυχὴν φιλομαθῆ γλαφυρότητι συνεχοῦς
θεωρίας δικαιοσύνης ζῆλον ἐμποιήσει,
where the words γλαφ. συν. θεω. mean
presumably 'the symmetrical beauty of
its logical continuity.' Ib. De Somn. 1,
35 παρὰ δὲ ἀριθμητικῆς καὶ γεωμετρικῆς τὸ
ἀνεξαπάτητον ἐν οἷς ἀναλογίας καὶ λογισ-
μῶν ἐστι χρεία sc. λήψεται.

ea...opinio est. For 'ea' MSS. have
'id.' Rad. rejects the clause as a gloss,
for which I can see no reason.

35. in numeros atque formas. Here
we have arithmetic definitely treated as
a subdivision of geometry. So Sen. Ep.
88, 10 'metiri me geometres docet lati-
fundia...numerare docet me et avaritiae
commodat digitos.' Philo in the passage
quoted from De Cong. (evidently a complete list of the Encyclia) no doubt intends to include arithmetic in geometry,
though in the passage from De Somn. they

are named separately. Cic. De Or. 1, 187
has 'in geometria formae, lineamenta,
intervalla, magnitudines,' v. Wilkins'
note. Here arithmetic seems to be ignored, but in the passage quoted above
from Tusc. 1. 5 it is recognised probably
by 'ratiocinandi,' though included in
geometry. [It is generally thought, but
seems to me doubtful, that arithmetic is
one of the 'novem disciplinae' of Varro.]
On the other hand Plin. N. H. 35, 76,
recognises it as a separate science, and
after his date the two are distinguished
by Sext. Emp., Max. Tyr., Aug., and
Mart. Cap. and of course in the later
quadrivium. The fact perhaps is, that
during the two centuries preceding Q.
arithmetic was largely neglected (v. Gow
Greek Math. p. 88). It was taught of
course (v. Hor. A. P. 325-330), but
perhaps to such an elementary extent,
that it hardly ranked as part of the
encyclic training. With the rise of Nicomachus (about Q.'s date) it again came
into prominence, but may have taken
some time to assert itself as a separate
science. So far as I know we never
hear of a separate teacher for it.

cuicumque saltem. Rad. brackets
'saltem,' apparently on the ground of
its reappearance two lines down. But
the sense is quite good. The totally
uneducated may dispense with it, but
no one else.

si digitorum ... dissensit. Here as
also XI. 3, 117, Q. alludes to the well-
known system of finger symbolism, by
which the units were indicated by nine
different movements (gestus), the tens
by nine other movements, of the fingers
of the left hand, and the thousands and
hundreds by identical movements with
the right. For an account of this system
(the original authorities for which, Nico-
las Smyrnaeus (13th cent.?) and Bede
De Ratione Temporum c. 1, though late,
seem to agree with earlier allusions)
v. Gow Greek Math. pp. 25 ff., and
for a collection of allusions and illustrative passages v. Mayor on Juv. 10,
249 (to which add Jerome Ep. 48, 2 and

iudicatur indoctus. illa vero linearis ratio et ipsa quidem cadit 36
frequenter in causas (nam de terminis mensurisque sunt lites),
sed habet maiorem quandam aliam cum arte oratoria cogna-
tionem. iam primum ordo est geometriae necessarius: nonne 37
et eloquentiae? ex prioribus geometria probat insequentia et
certis incerta: nonne id in dicendo facimus? quid? illa propositarum quaestionum conclusio non fere tota constat syllogismis? propter quod plures invenias, qui dialecticae similem
quam qui rhetoricae fateantur hanc artem. verum et orator,
etiamsi raro, non tamen numquam probabit dialectice. nam 38
et syllogismis, si res poscet, utetur et certe enthymemate, qui
rhetoricus est syllogismus. denique probationum quae sunt
potentissimae γραμμικαὶ ἀποδείξεις vulgo dicuntur: quid autem

123, 9, and Firmicus Maternus 1, 4, 13
'vides ut primos computos discentes
digitos tarda agitatione deflectant').
Our passage suggests (as also does Apuleius, *Apol.* 89) that public speakers
were accustomed to employ this symbolism simultaneously with the spoken
numbers. It is not very easy to understand how this assisted the audience.
As the units (and thousands) were mainly
indicated by the three last fingers, and
the tens (and hundreds) by the thumb
and forefinger, it may have been possible
for a speaker to exhibit a number of
three or four figures at the same moment.
He could not however thus exhibit more
than one number, and to follow an addition sum the audience would require
to use their memory, as much as we do.
Possibly the practice of thus accompanying on the fingers any numerical statement had become instinctive.
  The natural translation of our passage
is as L. 'I will not say if he hesitates
in making a calculation, but even if he
contradicts the calculation which he
states in words by making an uncertain
or inappropriate gesture with his fingers.' But it is possible, I think, that
'computatio' was the technical term for
this finger-symbolism. This is borne
out by Apuleius l.c. He is apparently
referring to the similarity of the 'gestus'
for ten and thirty, and says 'si triginta
pro decem dixisses, posses videri com-
putationis gestu errasse.' Cf. Sen. *De Ira*
3, 33 of the gouty usurer, 'manibus non
ad computandum relictis.' This term later
appears in the shortened form of 'com-
putus.' So Firmicus Maternus l.c., and
several times in Bede, where also the

chapter is headed 'de computo vel lo-
quela digitorum.' If this is right we
should rather translate 'if through uncertain or awkward movements he fails
to shew the proper finger symbolism.'
  37. ordo. Cp. Proclus (ed. Friedlein
p. 69) who notes as one of the chief merits
of Euclid the τάξις...τῶν...θεωρημάτων
καὶ προβλημάτων, and again the οἰκονομία
καὶ τάξις τῶν προηγουμένων καὶ ἑπομένων,
i.e. in each separate proposition, the
parts of which he gives elsewhere as
πρότασις, ἔκθεσις, διορισμός, ἀπόδειξις,
συμπέρασμα. I should suppose that Q.
is especially thinking of the resemblance
between these and the regular divisions
of a speech (cf. Cic. *De Or.* 2, 307)
though no doubt the phrase has also a
more general meaning. 'Ordo' (τάξις) is
chosen rather than 'dispositio' (οἰκονομία) as suggesting 'recta collocatio'
(VII. 1, 1), while 'disp.' suggests rather
the thought of 'utilitas,' which is not so
germane to geometry.
  et certis. Halm 'ex,' but without
any clear MS. authority.
  illa...conclusio. Geometrical terms,
= τῶν προτεινομένων ζητησέων συμπέρασμα—'illa' seems to me to point to a
certain amount of familiarity with and
appreciation of Euclid. 'Constat' here
as often in Q. 'is based on.'
  38. rhetoricus ... syllogismus. A
definite quotation from Arist. *Rhet.* 1,
2, 8 καλῶ δ' ἐνθύμημα μὲν ῥητορικὸν
συλλογισμόν. Enthymemes are treated
by Q. in v. 14. For the literature of the
subject v. Ernesti, Volkmann *Rhet.* and
Cope's *Intr. to Ar.'s Rhet.*
  γραμμικαὶ ἀποδείξεις. Also in v. 10,
7, where the MSS. seem to have got

39 magis oratio quam probationem petit? falsa quoque veris
similia geometria ratione deprendit. fit hoc et in numeris per
quasdam, quas ψευδογραφίας vocant, quibus pueri ludere
solebamus. sed alia maiora sunt. nam quis non ita proponenti
credat: 'quorum locorum extremae lineae eandem mensuram

the word right—here they have 'grammaticae.' The phrase is translated by
'linearibus probationibus' in 49. The
words here seem to imply that γρ. ἀπ.
was applied to a cogent proof *outside
the sphere of geometry.* I have found
no clear example of this, though the
following from Galen περὶ ἰδ. βιβ. II
approaches it. His philosophical studies
would have led him to scepticism, but
for his training in mathematics. ἔγνων
δεῖν ἀποστῆναι μὲν ὧν ἐκεῖνοι λέγουσιν,
ἀκολουθῆσαι δὲ τῷ χαρακτῆρι τῶν γραμ-
μικῶν ἀποδείξεων.

39. falsa quoque veris similia. It
is, I think, fairly probable that Q. has
in mind the treatise of Euclid called
ψευδάρια, which Proclus (Fried. p. 70)
couples with the Elements. Proclus
speaks of Euclid as thereby γυμνάσας
ἡμῶν τὴν διάνοιαν παντοίοις θεωρήμασι,
καὶ τῷ ψεύδει τὸ ἀληθὲς παραθεὶς καὶ
τῇ πείρᾳ τὸν ἔλεγχον τῆς ἀπάτης συναρ-
μόσας.

geometria. So MSS. and Meister.
Halm adopted the correction 'geometrica,' 'oratio' being understood as
subject to 'deprehendit.' I have not
followed him, believing that the correction spoils the sense. If adopted, it
would limit the meaning to the use of
geometry by the orator in dealing with
technical questions. But this was disposed of in § 36, and we were then
bidden to take a wider view of the
mental effects of geometrical training.
Reading 'geometria,' the statement is
that geometry employs scientific methods
('ratione,' for this absolute use v. § 12,
and Prooem. 27) to distinguish the true
from the false ; and the inference to be
drawn is, that the geometrically trained
will carry on into wider spheres this
faculty 'falsa ratione deprehendendi,'
just as they carry on 'ordo' and 'pro-
batio' The prolixity of the examples
makes him forget to state this inference
—a fault in style no doubt, which the
correction would emend, but at the
expense of sacrificing the homogeneity
of the whole passage.

ψευδογραφίας. This and the cognate
forms — γράφημα, γραφῶ, γράφος—

though sometimes applied to fallacies
in general, seem to have been specially
used of fallacies in geometry caused by
inaccurate drawing (v. exx. in Steph.
from Aristotle and elsewhere). One
example (not in Steph., but originally adduced by Capperonnier on this passage)
is noteworthy. Origen (pref. to *Cont.
Cels.*) says οὐ τὸ τυχὸν τῶν ψευδομένων
ἐν γεωμετρικοῖς θεωρήμασι ψευδογραφού-
μενόν τις ἂν λέγοι, ἢ καὶ ἀναγράφοι,
γυμνασίου ἕνεκεν τοῦ ἀπὸ τούτων. This
suggests that the terms ψευδογραφία etc.
were especially applied to such exercises
for educational purposes as the ψευδάρια
of Euclid mentioned above.

I see no difficulty (as Sp.) in the
transference of the word to arithmetical
catches. Indeed Stob. *Phys.* 724 (Teub.
1. p. 197) quotes from Archytas ψευδο-
γραφίαι ἐν γαμετρίᾳ κατὰ σχήματα καὶ
ἀριθμοὺς ἐμφαίνονται. As suggested by
Camerarius such traps might easily be
made out of 'inverse rule of three' or
'double rule of three,' like the old
schoolboy catch of 'if a man and a half
eat a herring and a half in a day and a
half,' etc., or from the dunce's tendency
to reason that as 3 and 4 make 7, ∴ ⅓
and ¼ will make ⅓. An allusion to
questions of this kind, which probably
might be multiplied to any extent, suits
the context better than the suggestion
of a reference to the method afterwards
called 'falsa positio,' or 'regula duorum
falsorum,' though this method (v. Gow
p. 100) may well have been employed
by ancient arithmeticians. This method
runs as follows: e.g. you think of a
number, treble it, subtract 2, quadruple
the result, subtract the original number
and give the result as 102. The solver
tries 8 and gets 80, then 11 and gets
113, whence he infers that the answer
is 8 + 2. This suggestion would have
the slight advantage that ψευδ- would
then really be the agency by which the
correct result is reached. On the other
hand, apart from the fact that the name
'falsorum regula' is said to be translated
from the Arabic, it is not really analogous
to the geometrical example which here
follows.

colligunt, eorum spatium quoque, quod iis lineis continetur,
par sit necesse est?' at id falsum est: nam plurimum refert, **40**
cuius sit formae ille circuitus, reprehensique a geometris sunt
historici, qui magnitudinem insularum satis significari naviga-
tionis ambitu crediderunt. nam ut quaeque forma perfectissima,
ita capacissima est. ideoque illa circumcurrens linea, si efficiet **41**
orbem, quae forma est in planis maxime perfecta, amplius
spatium complectetur, quam si quadratum paribus oris efficiat,
rursus quadrata triangulis, triangula ipsa plus aequis lateribus
quam inaequalibus. sed alia forsitan obscuriora: nos facillimum **42**
etiam imperitis sequamur experimentum. iugeri mensuram
ducentos et quadraginta longitudinis pedes esse dimidioque
in latitudinem patere, non fere quisquam est qui ignoret, et qui
sit circuitus et quantum campi claudat, colligere expeditum.
at centeni et octogeni in quamque partem pedes idem spatium **43**

---

40. reprehensique...historici. The
allusion no doubt is partly to Thuc. 6,
1, where after giving the perimeter of
Sicily in terms of the time of circum-
navigation he goes on καὶ τοσαύτη οὖσα.
Other passages illustrating the frequency
of misapprehension on the point are
(1) Polybius 9, 21, where, after speaking
of the surprise felt that while the perimeter of Megalopolis is forty-eight stades
against the fifty stades of Lacedæmon,
the latter is double (of the former, he
adds ἂν δὲ καὶ συναυξῆσαί τις βουλό-
μενος τὴν ἀπορίαν εἴπῃ ὅτι δυνατόν ἐστι
τετταράκοντα σταδίων πόλιν ἢ στρατοπε-
δείαν ἔχουσαν τὴν περιγραφήν, διπλασίαν
γίνεσθαι τῆς ἑκατὸν σταδίων ἐχούσης τὴν
περίμετρον τελέως ἐκπληκτικὸν αὐτοῖς
φαίνεται τὸ λεγόμενον. τούτου δ' ἐστιν
αἴτιον, ὅτι τῶν ἐν τοῖς παιδικοῖς μαθήμασι
παραδιδομένων ἡμῖν διὰ τῆς γεωμετρίας
οὐ μνημονεύομεν. (2) Proclus (Fried.
p. 237) speaking of the conditions of
equality in triangles, καὶ ἤδη τινὲς κοινω-
νοὺς ἑαυτῶν ἐν διανομαῖς χωρίων παρε-
κρούσαντο διὰ τῆς κατὰ τὴν περίμετρον
ἰσότητος μεῖζον λαβόντες χωρίον.
Pliny *N. H.* 6, 208 goes very near
falling into this error, as he estimates
the magnitude of Europe and Africa by
adding length to breadth.
41. The mathematical truths in this section were proved, with a good deal more,
in a treatise περὶ ἰσομέτρων σχημάτων by
Zenodorus, preserved both by Pappus
and Theon of Alexandria (fourth century

A.D.). Cantor (*Gesch. Math.* vol. 1. p.
308) and Hultsch (Pappus p. 190) have
used this section to determine the limits
of Zenodorus' possible date. (All that
we know otherwise is that he was later
than Archimedes.) Gow, reproducing
Cantor's view, erroneously says that Q.
mentions Zenodorus. I cannot think
that this reasoning is conclusive. The
facts here mentioned are surely ascer-
tainable by experiment, and may well
have been known before the time of Z.
It would appear from Polybius quoted
above that the paradox of perimeter
and area was a commonplace of ordinary
education in his time.
quae...perfecta. Cf. Cic. *De Nat.
Deorum* 2, 47 'cumque duae formae
praestantes sint, ex solidis globus...ex
planis autem circulus,' where v. Mayor's
note. The idea is ascribed to Pythagoras
in almost identical words, Diog. Laert.
8, 19, 35. Cp. also Proclus (Fried. p. 82)
φύσει κρείττων ὁ κύκλος (sc. τῶν εὐθυ-
γράμμων).
42. sed...obscuriora. L.'s translation
'But there are other points which perhaps present greater difficulty' is misleading. Rather 'but since other cases
perhaps present some difficulty, let us
take etc.' 'Alia' serves to contrast the
more difficult relations just mentioned
between circles, quadrilaterals and rect-
angles, with the simple case of the
rectangle which follows. Halm suggested, but did not adopt 'set talia.'

extremitatis, sed multo amplius clusae quattuor lineis areae
faciunt. id si computare quem piget, brevioribus numeris idem
discat. nam deni in quadram pedes quadraginta per oram,
intra centum erunt. at si quini deni per latera, quini in fronte
sint, ex illo quod amplectuntur quartam deducent eodem cir-
44 cumductu. si vero porrecti utrimque undeviceni singulis
distent, non plures intus quadratos habebunt, quam per quot
longitudo ducetur: quae circumibit autem linea, eiusdem spatii
erit, cuius ea, quae centum continet. ita quidquid formae
45 quadrati detraxeris, amplitudini quoque peribit. ergo etiam
id fieri potest, ut maiore circuitu minor loci amplitudo cludatur.
haec in planis; nam in collibus vallibusque etiam imperito
46 patet plus soli esse quam caeli. quid quod se eadem geometria
tollit ad rationem usque mundi? in qua, cum siderum certos
constitutosque cursus numeris docet, discimus nihil esse in-
ordinatum atque fortuitum: quod ipsum nonnumquam pertinere
47 ad oratorem potest. an vero, cum Pericles Athenienses solis
obscuratione territos redditis eius rei causis metu liberavit, aut
cum Sulpicius ille Gallus in exercitu L. Pauli de lunae defectione
disseruit, ne velut prodigio divinitus facto militum animi
48 terrerentur, non videtur esse usus oratoris officio? quod si
Nicias in Sicilia scisset, non eodem confusus metu pulcherrimum
Atheniensium exercitum perdidisset: sicut Dion, cum ad
destruendam Dionysii tyrannidem venit, non est tali casu
deterritus. sint extra licet usus bellici, transeamusque, quod

43. areae. Does Q. use the word in
its technical geometrical sense = Greek
ἐμβαδόν, or more generally = open space
as 'campi'? Probably the former, as it
is so used several times in Vitruvius
9, 1. It is found once or twice in the
'agrimensores' and in Boethius, whence
no doubt it passed into modern use.
In Aul. Gell. 1, 20 'triquetra et quadrata, quae in area fiunt sine altitudine,'
the use is somewhat different for 'super-
ficies.' This geometrical use is inadequately treated in the Dicts.
46. tollit...mundi. For this extension of geometry v. Sen. *Ep.* 88, 13
(addressing the geometrician) 'intervalla siderum dicis, nihil est quod in
mensuram tuam non cadat.' The sequel
shews that this does not extend to
astrology, which is regarded by S. as a
separate science. V. also Maximus Tyrius
Diss. 37, who in a long passage shews

that Geometry's main province is not
what the name implies. That is merely
the harbour in which the ship geometry
rests. Leaving the harbour, it will take
us to τὸ ὑπὲρ κεφαλῆς θέαμα τὸ καλόν,
τὸ ποικίλον, ἐληλαμένον περὶ γῆν ἐν κύκλῳ
καὶ περὶ αὐτὴν ἐλιττόμενον, μεστὸν
ἄστρων, ἥλιον φέρον, σελήνην ἔχον.
47, 48. Sp. gives reff. for these four
stories: Pericles, Plut. *Per.* p. 171:
Gallus, Liv. 44, 37, Val. Max. 8, 11,
1: Nicias, Thuc. 7, 50, 51, Plut. *Nic.*
p. 538: Dion, Plut. l.c. and id. *Dion*
p. 968; Plut. like Q. points the contrast
between Nic. and D., a contrast which
no doubt was a favourite means of pole-
mic against superstition.
48. usus bellici. L.'s translation
'however we are not concerned with the
uses of geometry in war' seems to take
these words as referring to the cases just
mentioned. This is surely impossible,

Archimedes unus obsidionem Syracusarum in longius traxit: illud utique iam proprium ad efficiendum quod intendimus, **49** plurimas quaestiones, quibus difficilior alia ratione explicatio est, ut de ratione videndi, de sectione in infinitum, de celeritate

for these cases have been cited as 'pertinentia ad oratorem.' I take the words as referring to military mechanics, such as those contained in the collection called 'veteres mathematici' (v. Gow p. 277). Cp. Proclus (Fried. p. 41) where he gives as a subdivision of geometry ἡ ὀργανοποιϊκὴ τῶν κατὰ πόλεμον ἐπιτηδείων ὀργάνων, οἷα δὴ καὶ 'Αρχιμήδης λέγεται κατασκευάσαι τῶν πολεμούντων τὴν Συράκουσαν ἀμυντικὰ ὄργανα. **sint extra…utique.** 'Even if we grant that "usus bellici" are beside the point and pass over etc. at any rate the next point is germane.' Q. does not definitely accept the view that they 'non ad oratorem pertinent' (the orator might conceivably talk of them), but is willing to concede it. 'Extra' must I think = 'extra rem,' but though several exx. are to be found in Q. of 'extra' adv. (v. Bonnell), Sp. is right in saying there is no exact parallel.

49. de ratione videndi, i.e. ὀπτική. The fact that I have had the audacity to return to the MS. reading in place of the correction 'dividendi,' originally made by Regius, and since then adopted by all edd. (I think) without exception, requires a full and lengthy explanation. (1) The MS. authority is almost entirely on this side. Halm and other edd. note as giving 'videndi,' Bern., Bamb., Mon., Arg., Nost., Tur., Flor., Jo. The only MS. stated to have 'dividendi' is the fifteenth century Vallensis (Par. 7723), a codex which, though exhibiting many useful readings, is open to the doubt whether such readings are not the result of post-Poggian scholarship rather than of the use of some superior archetype, v. Intr. p. xciv. A has 'vivendi,' which of course entirely supports 'videndi' as against 'dividendi.' (2) No editor has given the smallest reason for the correction, or done more than repeat Regius' words, 'ita legendum, non "videndi" ut quidam ad opticen, quae perspectiva dicitur, referentes.' As a matter of fact the meaning of 'rat. div.' is by no means clear. Sir T. Heath writes to me 'it may mean almost anything.' If it was otherwise certain, I should understand it in one of the following ways: (a) that a division sum of any

magnitude requires some mathematical knowledge. The subject of division seems to be little noticed in the arithmeticians, but that there was such difficulty is likely enough, and it may be noted that Cantor seems inclined to regard the method of 'complementary division,' described by Boethius, as Roman in origin (Cantor I. 495, 496). Or again it might be referred to the elaborate calculations which, according to Marquardt (*Privatleben* pp. 96-101), were needed to turn the Roman duodecimal system of fractions of the 'as' into decimal fractions (with which he seems inclined to connect Hor. *A. P.* 325 ff.). (b) Geometrically, and if we credit Q., as I should not be unwilling to do, with a general knowledge of Euclid's work, we might connect it with the partially extant treatise of διαιρέσεις (v. Gow p. 214). But these, though plausible explanations if the reading was forced upon us, are far too indefinite to support an emendation. Moreover they (or at any rate the latter) do not really suit the 'quaestiones,' which seem rather to imply problems in themselves of a general character, but capable of assistance from mathematics. (3) On the other hand 'videndi ratio' can be definitely connected with such 'quaestiones.' Optics provided problems which might be and were discussed philosophically, but at the same time had a connexion with geometry which is constantly emphasised (e.g. Arist. *An. Post.* I, 12). Thus Proclus (Fried. p. 63) says of geometry πολλὰς ἀφ' ἑαυτῆς ἐπιστήμας ἐκδίδωσιν, οἷον τὴν γεωδεσίαν, τὴν μηχανικήν, τὴν ὀπτικήν, δι' ὧν καὶ τὸν θνητὸν βίον εὐεργετεῖ. Again (p. 40) πάλιν ὀπτικὴ καὶ κανονικὴ γεωμετρίας εἰσὶ καὶ ἀριθμητικῆς ἔκγονοι, ἡ μὲν ταῖς ὄψεσι γραμμαῖς χρωμένη καὶ ταῖς ἐκ τούτων συνισταμέναις γωνίαις. In Aul. Gell. 16, 18 we have a passage very similar to this last beginning 'pars quaedam geometriae ὀπτική appellatur, quae ad oculos pertinet; pars altera, quae ad aures, κανονική.' Both writers go on to divide ὀπτική into (1) the science which accounts for illusions in sight (ὀπτικὴ ἰδίως καλουμένη), and (2) κατοπτρικά or the phenomena of the mirror.

These last, or some of them, are discussed by Seneca *N. Q.* 1, 4 ff. with the remark 'rationes quae non persuadent, sed cogunt, a geometris afferuntur.' So id. *Ep.* 88, 27 'quae causa in speculo imagines exprimat, sciet sapiens; illud tibi geometer potest dicere, quantum abesse debeat corpus ab imagine et qualis forma speculi quales imagines reddat.' Cp. also Lucr. 4, 269–323, and particularly the last words 'ad aequos reddita flexus' (on which Munro says 'He refers no doubt to the angle of reflexion being equal to the angle of incidence, a fact well known to the Greek and Roman geometers of his day'), and with this the discussion on ἡ ἐν ἴσαις γωνίαις ἀνάκλασις in Plut. *De Fac. in Orb. Lun.* 17, a discussion which is described earlier (ib. 3) as ὥσπερ ἀφ' ἑστίας τῆς γεωμετρίας ὁρμώμενον.

(4) These points seem to me so clear that the only reason I can assign for edd. preference for 'dividendi' is that they doubted whether 'ratio videndi' is a natural rendering for ὀπτική. It is more or less true that in the cases where Q. uses 'ratio' with the gerund to express theory, science, doctrine, principles etc. (e.g. rat. dicendi, declamandi, inveniendi) the subject of the gerund (is qui dicit etc.) *consciously* employs the 'ratio,' while here 'is qui videt' merely supplies the phenomena which the 'ratio' explains. I say 'more or less,' for in Q.'s inductive view of these arts, some speakers etc. have unconsciously supplied the phenomena which are reduced to the 'ratio' which other speakers etc. afterwards use. Still this case goes further and the phrase 'ratio videndi' though in form analogous to the cases just mentioned is in thought nearer to the cases where the genitive expresses the subject-matter with which the 'ratio' deals, e.g. 'ratio siderum' 4, 4, and in this chapter 'ratio mundi' (46), 'vocis' (22), 'linearis' (36). The phrase does thus perhaps stand alone, but is not this also the case with ὀπτική? I can recall no other science-noun in -κη which is formed from an *active* verbal noun, and yet does not express the activities of the subject of the verb, as e.g. πλαστική does. At any rate there is none which Q. has occasion to translate.

(5) What else in fact could Q. have said? If he had wished to limit himself to the 'catoptric' branch of the science he might (as Sen. l.c.) have employed 'specularis ratio.' But to indicate ὀπτικὴ

in general, I know of nothing but this or the interchangeable 'ratio visus.' 'Visionis' was hardly available in view of the fact that Q. (VI. 2, 29) like Cic. uses it = φαντασία with its quite different associations; while 'r. ocularis' or 'ocularia' would suggest the medical art of the oculist. (Regius' 'perspectiva' is not given at all in Forc.)

sectione in infinitum. I.e. τομὴ εἰς ἄπειρον, the doctrine of the infinite divisibility of matter. On this v. Reid on Cic. *Ac. Post.* 27, who gives a summary of the chief philosophical opinions on the subject. For its connexion with mathematics cf. Sext. Emp. *adv. geom.* p. 329 τὴν ἀρεσκομένην αὐτοῖς (i.e. γεωμέτραις) εἰς ἄπειρον τῶν ὄντων τομήν: Galen *De plac. Hipp. et Plat.* VIII. 2 (referred to by Reid) περὶ δὲ τῆς κατὰ μέγεθος τομῆς τῶν σωμάτων ἐπιδέδεικται τοῖς γεωμετρικοῖς ἀνδρασιν, ὡς οὐδέποτε στῆναι δυναμένης, ἀλλ' αἰεὶ τοῦ τεμνομένου μικρότερον ἑαυτοῦ τὸ μέγεθος ἔχοντος. He goes on to contrast it with ἡ κατ' εἶδος τομή, in which indivisibility does exist. Proclus (Fried. p. 278) proves or thinks he proves it from the existence of incommensurable magnitudes, 'so that we shall not arrive at the indivisible which is the least common measure of magnitudes'; v. also Nicom. *Ar.* 1, 2. The πρόβλημα of τομὴ τῶν ἀορίστων mentioned in Plut. *De Aud.* 10 is not, I think, the same as this, v. Wyttenbach's note.

de celeritate augendi. The MS. authority is fairly equally divided between the 'augenda' of B and 'augendi' of A. Halm, Meister and Rad. have adopted the former, which would make the 'quaestio' to be that of acceleration. This would be suitable enough, if there was any evidence that ancient mathematics took account of this problem. In the absence of this I have adopted (with Sir T. Heath's approval) 'augendi.' This may I think be taken in two ways, though I believe the first to be more probable. (1) Rate of increase in geometrical progression, especially as contrasted with that in arithmetical progression. So Gesner, Watson, Fierville and also Sir T. Heath, who has supplied me with an excellent illustration in Aristotle (*Anal. Post.* 1, 12, 77 b. Here Kaineus had argued that fire followed πολλαπλάσιος ἀναλογία i.e. geometrical progression, because this is generated *rapidly* and also is fire. οὕτω δ' οὐκ ἔστι συλλογισμός· ἀλλ' εἰ τῇ ταχίστῃ ἀναλογίᾳ ἕπεται ἡ πολλαπλάσιος, καὶ

augendi, linearibus illis probationibus solvi solere, ut, si est oratori, quod proximus demonstrabit liber, de omnibus rebus dicendum, nullo modo sine geometria esse possit orator.

XI

[DE PRIMA PRONUNTIATIONIS ET GESTUS INSTITUTIONE]

Dandum aliquid comoedo quoque, dum eatenus, qua pro- 1 nuntiandi scientiam futurus orator desiderat. non enim puerum, quem in hoc instituimus, aut femineae vocis exilitate frangi volo aut seniliter tremere. nec vitia ebrietatis effingat nec 2

τῷ πυρὶ ἡ ταχίστη ἐν τῇ κινήσει ἀναλογία).
The subject of progressions (ἀναλογίαι συνεχεῖς) was a favourite branch of Greek Mathematics, e.g. Euclid, Books VIII. and IX., Nicomachus *Ar.* II. 21 ff. Geometrical progression, which alone was ἀναλογία κυρίως καλουμένη, is of course, if it starts from unity, a series of successive powers of a given number. Its suitability for a general 'quaestio' lay no doubt largely in its ταχυτής, especially as contrasted with arithmetical progression. The rapidity with which high numbers are reached in geometrical progression has probably always been a trap for the unwary. Simple and compound interest are a striking example, and the fact that a sum put out at τόκος ἐπίτριτος would in twenty years be seven times, but at ἀνατοκισμὸς ἐπίτριτος some three hundred times the original, would be startling then as now. One may also remember the demonstration in *Rep.* 587 that the kingly man is seven hundred and twenty-nine times as happy as the tyrant, and the surprise with which Glaucon receives this ἀμήχανος λογισμός.

(2) The other possible way of taking the words would be as = the question of how to multiply with rapidity. For specimens of ancient multiplication, bringing out the obvious difficulties attendant on Greek and Roman symbolism, v. Gow, p. 50. Friedlein *Zahlzeichen* pp. 76, 77. It seems probable that some abridged method of multiplication was set forth by Apollonius of Perga, and in a treatise called ὠκυτόκιον (Cantor I. 297), and if so we have a close parallelism of phrase. Of course

'augendi' would in this case include 'raising to a higher power.'
The use of the verb is too natural under either supposition to require defence. It will be remembered, however, that Plato several times uses αὔξη, αὐξάνω in the *Republic*, sometimes as in 528 B of the multiplication of any factors, sometimes as in 587 D of raising to a power or creating a new term in geometrical progression. Thus too Nicomachus II. 15, '9 being thrice 3 by another 3 ἐπ' ἄλλο διάστημα αὐξεται and becomes 27,' while Boethius II. 43 has 'si tres septies augeantur, in XXI. numerum cadant.'

XI. 1-14. The elements of 'pronuntiatio' are here dealt with. The fuller treatment is reserved to Book XI. 3.
1. comoedo. The word, I presume, is to be taken literally, and implies that actors eked out their living by giving lessons in elocution and deportment at this early stage. Later apparently the pupil in the rhetorical school is handed over to more specialised instruction; v. infr. 14 and note.
pronuntiandi. Otherwise called 'actio,' ὑπόκρισις. Cf. XI. 3, 1 'pronuntiatio a plerisque actio dicitur, sed prius nomen a voce, sequens a gestu videtur accipere.'
femineae...exilitate. Cf. XI. 3, 19 'ne ad spadonum et mulierum et aegrorum exilitatem vox nostra tenuetur.'
frangi. Not as Watson 'to be broken *to* the shrillness,' but as in 10, 31. The boy himself becomes 'fractus,' i.e. loses manhood by assuming 'exilitas.'
tremere, probably of voice. Cf. XI. 3, 91, where the comedians playing a young man's part are blamed, if 'cum

servili vernilitate imbuatur nec amoris, avaritiae, metus discat
adfectum: quae neque oratori sunt necessaria et mentem
praecipue in aetate prima teneram adhuc et rudem inficiunt:
3 nam frequens imitatio transit in mores. ne gestus quidem
omnis ac motus a comoedis petendus est. quamquam enim
utrumque eorum ad quendam modum praestare debet orator,
plurimum tamen aberit a scaenico, nec vultu nec manu nec
excursionibus nimius. nam si qua in his ars est dicentium, ea
prima est, ne ars esse videatur.

4   Quod est igitur huius doctoris officium? in primis vitia si
qua sunt oris emendet, ut expressa sint verba, ut suis quaeque
litterae sonis enuntientur. quarundam enim vel exilitate vel
pinguitudine nimia laboramus, quasdam velut acriores parum

in expositione aut senis sermo...aut
mulieris...incidit, tremula vel effeminata
voce pronuntiant.' It might however
be possible to take it of more general
imitation of old age.

2. imbuatur; v. on 8, 5.

quae neque oratori sunt necessaria.
As the orator in the Forum spoke always as an advocate, it would of course
be absurd for him to imitate the
characters he defended. In the declamations on the other hand the speaker
regularly impersonated the person at-
tacking or defending. This contrast
between the schools and the forum is
noted two or three times by Q. Thus
in III. 8, 51 'enimvero praecipue de-
clamatoribus considerandum est quid
cuique personae conveniat, qui paucis-
simas controversias ita dicunt ut advo-
cati, plerumque filii, parentes, divites,
senes, asperi, lenes, avari, denique
superstitiosi, timidi, derisores fiunt.'
So VI. 2, 17 'non parum significanter
etiam illa in scholis ἤθη dixerimus,
quibus plerumque rusticos, supersti-
tiosos, avaros, timidos secundum condicionem propositorum effingimus.' So
too X. I, 71. He does not however in
these passages condemn these imperso-
nations, nor does he mention the point
in his criticism of the declamation
methods in II. 10. Presumably his
view is that at this later stage they may
be educational, but as they are not part
of the orator's final equipment there is
no need to incur the moral risk in this
early stage.

**3. frequens imitatio transit in
mores.** Cp. the Ovidian ' abeunt studia
in mores ' (*Her.* 15, 83).

excursionibus. Cf. XI. 3, 126 'procursio opportuna brevis, moderata, rara.
conveniet etiam ambulatio quaedam...
quamquam Cicero (*Orator* 59) rarum
incessum neque ita longum probat.
discursare vero...ineptissimum; urbane-
que Flavus Verginius interrogavit de
quodam suo antisophiste, quot milia
passuum declamasset?' Here perhaps
' excursio' might cover both 'procursio'
and 'ambulatio,' but as in Cic. (l.c.)
'excursio'='procursio,' it is better to
limit it thus. L.'s 'extravagance of
gait' is too vague.

ne ars esse videatur. This famous
canon of ' ars est celare artem' is again
given by Q. in II. 5, 8 'ea sola in hoc
ars est quae intellegi nisi ab artifice non
possit,' and IX. 3, 102 'cum...ubicumque
ars ostentatur, veritas abesse videatur.'
The only earlier examples of it which
I have been able to find are Ov. *Met.*
10, 252 'ars adeo latet arte sua,' and
ad Herenn. 4, 10, where we are told
that examples from orators of rhetorical
points are not so well adapted to shew
the theory ('accommodata ad artem '),
because in actual oratory ' leviter unusquisque locus plerumque tangitur, ne
ars appareat.'

4–7. These sections are referred to
in XI. 3, 31 'sunt enim multa vitia, de
quibus dixi, cum in quadam primi libri
parte puerorum ora formarem, oppor-
tunius ratus in ea aetate facere illorum
mentionem, in qua emendari possunt.'

4. exilitate...pinguitudine. Possibly
equivalent to the ἰσχνότητες and πλα-
τειασμοί of 5, 32, though (1) as pointed
out there Q. does not seem to find any
adequate equivalents in Latin for these,

efficimus et aliis non dissimilibus, sed quasi hebetioribus per-
mutamus. quippe et rho litterae, qua Demosthenes quoque 5
laboravit, labda succedit, quarum vis est apud nos quoque, et
cum c ac similiter g non evaluerunt, in t ac d molliuntur. ne 6
illas quidem circa s litteram delicias hic magister feret, nec
verba in faucibus patietur audiri nec oris inanitate resonare
nec, quod minime sermoni puro conveniat, simplicem vocis
naturam pleniore quodam sono circumliniri, quod Graeci κατα-

(2) there they are 'vitia' while here
they are characteristics of the letters
themselves. As 'acriores')('hebetiores'
below appears to refer to consonants,
it is probable that ' exilitas ')(' pinguitudo ' applies to vowels. This will agree
with Q.'s use of 'pinguis' in 7, 27, and
with the general use of these two contrasted adjectives in Longus; v. Lindsay
L. L. pp. 25 ff.

hebetioribus. Cf. Plut. *Quaest. Rom.*
54, where after noting that γ perhaps
becomes κ in ' macellum,' he goes on τὸ
λ πάλιν ἀπολισθάνουσι τοῦ ρ διὰ ἀμβλύ-
τητα τῆς γλώττης ὑποκεῖται τραυλιζό-
μενον.

5. quippe rho...succedit. Q. follows
Cic. *De Or.* 1, 260 'cumque ita balbus
esset (Demosthenes), ut eius ipsius artis
cui studeret primam litteram non posset
dicere, perfecit meditando, ut nemo
planius esse locutus putaretur.' To the
same effect id. *De Div.* 2, 96 (perhaps also Diog. Laert. II. 108). In the
next words he evidently alludes to the
well-known τραυλότης of Alcibiades
(Ar. *Vesp.* 44, 45), but does not commit
himself to the statement that Dem.
changed ρ into λ.

quarum...quoque. I understand Q.
to mean that the historical and literary
examples are confined to Greek, but
that as the Latin corresponding letters
have the same value, the same phenomena may be expected.

c...g...in t ac d. Halm quotes the
correction of Baiter (though it is really
much older) 'c...t...in g ac d.' He adds
'recte ut videtur.' I am inclined to
agree with him. It may be true that
small children make the mispronuncia-
tions of the received text (I have noticed
the *c* to *t* myself), but we are not here
dealing with infantine phonetics, but
with faults which if not early corrected
last through life. The suggested correction will imply that the 'tenues'
were 'acriores,' the 'mediae' 'hebetiores,' and this is fairly in accordance

with the evidence that the former required more energy of articulation
(v. Lindsay *L. L.* p. 71 ff.). Cp. also
Terentianus Maurus (quoted ib. p. 86),
where *g* is said to produce its sound
'obtusius' than *c*. On the other hand
it may be said that in other places
where confusions between 'tenues' and
'mediae' are noted (by Q. himself 4, 16
and 5, 12, Plut. *Quaest. Rom.* 54, Luc.
Jud. Voc. 10) it is the 'mediae' which
become 'tenues.' If the MS. text is
retained, we may perhaps refer the
change of *c* to *t* to the confusion between the two letters in words where *i*
follows, e.g. 'solacium, solatium.' So
apparently Lindsay *L. L.* p. 88.

6. ne illas...delicias. The meaning of this must be left as uncertain.
Lindsay's suggestion that it refers to
the tendency, which appeared in later
centuries, to put a vowel sound before
initial *sp* etc., is open to the objection
that there is no early evidence for it.
Sp. quotes a story in Eustathius of
Pericles' efforts to avoid the sibilancy
of *s* which, if supported, might be worth
considering (v. his note). It seems to
me possible that Q. is following *Orator*
161, and referring to the case of final *s*.
Cic. there says that the practice of
dropping the *s* 'iam subrusticum videtur,
olim autem politius.' As the practice
was defended at a rather later date than
Cicero's by Messala (v. IX. 4, 38 and
note on 7, 23) there may quite possibly
have been a tendency towards it in Q.'s
time, which the orthodox elocutionist
had to correct. If this is possible, we
might explain the word 'delicias' as
implying that Q. regards the practice
as a piece of literary and archaistic
affectation, perhaps also with reference
to C.'s implication that it had a 'suavitas.'

nec...resonare. Perhaps = the κοιλο-
στομία of 5, 32.

circumliniri. So Halm and later
edd. for the MSS. 'circumlinire' from

7 πεπλασμένον dicunt: sic appellatur cantus tibiarum, quae praeclusis, quibus clarescunt, foraminibus, recto modo exitu 8 graviorem spiritum reddunt. curabit etiam, ne extremae syllabae intercidant, ut par sibi sermo sit, ut, quotiens exclamandum erit, lateris conatus sit ille, non capitis, ut gestus ad 9 vocem, vultus ad gestum adcommodetur. observandum erit etiam, ut recta sit facies dicentis, ne labra distorqueantur, ne inmodicus hiatus rictum distendat, ne supinus vultus, ne deiecti 10 in terram oculi, ne inclinata utrolibet cervix. nam frons pluribus generibus peccat. vidi multos, quorum supercilia ad singulos vocis conatus adlevarentur, aliorum constricta, aliorum etiam dissidentia, cum alterum in verticem tenderent, altero paene 11 oculus ipse premeretur. infinitum autem, ut mox dicemus, in his quoque rebus momentum est, et nihil potest placere quod non decet.

the MS. of Julius Victor, who quotes it in the passive. V. Intr. p. xcii.

8. ne...intercidant. Cf. xi. 3, 33 '(verborum) pars destitui solet, plerisque extremas syllabas non perferentibus, dum priorum sono indulgent.'

ut par...sit. Cf. ib. 43 'prima est observatio recte pronuntiandi aequalitas, ne sermo subsultet imparibus spatiis ac sonis.'

gestus ... adcommodetur. L. carelessly translates 'that gesture and voice are mutually appropriate.' The three elements 'vox, gestus, vultus' appear in the same order in xi. 3 with the remark (72) 'dominatur autem maxime vultus.'

9. recta...dicentis. Not as L. 'that the speaker face the audience,' but merely that the face is natural and uncontorted. The words sum up in fact the details which follow. Cf. ix. 3, 101 'orator habet rectam quandam velut faciem, quae ut stupere immobili rigore non debebit, ita saepius in ea, quam natura dedit, specie continenda est.' So of the almost equivalent 'caput' xi. 3, 69 'decoris illa sunt, ut sit (sc. caput) primo rectum et secundum naturam; nam et deiecto humilitas et supino arrogantia et in latus inclinato languor et praeduro ac rigente barbaria quaedam mentis ostenditur.'

ne labra...distendat. Cf. xi. 3, 81 'labra et porriguntur male et scinduntur et adstringuntur et diducuntur, et dentes nudant et in latus ac paene ad aurem trahuntur.' The 'rictus' is the open mouth, and immoderate distension of it

corresponds to 'labra diducuntur et dentes nudant.' The 'discindat' of A adopted by Bonnell is out of place, and cannot be defended by 'scinduntur labra' of xi. 3, which rather corresponds to 'distorqueantur' here. The 'jaws parted to a grin' of L. misses the sense.

distorqueantur. Rad. reads 'detorqueantur' with B and Julius Victor. Halm and Meister 'dist-' with A. The latter seems the more appropriate word.

10. nam frons...peccat. L.'s translation 'for there are a variety of faults in facial expression' cannot, I think, be right. I know no authority in Q. for the use of 'frons' for the face in general, and the sequel shews that only the upper part of the face is being dealt with. The corresponding sections in xi. 3, 78 etc. are introduced by 'multum et superciliis agitur.' 'Nam' is used in the transitional way so common in Q.

dissidentia. Cf. xi. 3, 79. Gesn. and Sp. quote Cic. *in Pis.* 14 'altero ad frontem sublato, altero ad mentum depresso supercilio.'

alterum in verticem. So A. Rad. has 'altero' with B. Surely 'tendere supercilio' is a strange expression.

11. mox, i.e. in xi. 3. As L. translates 'shortly,' it is as well to note that here and elsewhere Q. uses it for 'later.' The interval between Books i. and xi. can hardly be called short. The 'his' is perhaps best limited to §§ 9-12, in which case the statement anticipates the 'dominatur maxime vultus' of xi. 3, 72.

Debet etiam docere comoedus, quomodo narrandum, qua 12
sit auctoritate suadendum, qua concitatione consurgat ira, qui
flexus deceat miserationem. quod ita optime faciet, si certos
ex comoediis elegerit locos et ad hoc maxime idoneos, id est
actionibus similes. idem autem non ad pronuntiandum modo 13
utilissimi, verum ad augendam quoque eloquentiam maxime
accommodati erunt. et haec, dum infirma aetas maiora non 14
capiet: ceterum cum legere orationes oportebit, cum virtutes
earum iam sentiet, tum mihi diligens aliquis ac peritus adsistat
neque solum lectionem formet, verum ediscere etiam electa ex
iis cogat et ea dicere stantem clare et quem ad modum agere
oportebit, ut protinus pronuntiationem, vocem, memoriam
exerceat.

Ne illos quidem reprehendendos puto, qui paulum etiam 15
palaestricis vacaverunt. non de iis loquor, quibus pars vitae in
oleo, pars in vino consumitur, qui corporum cura mentem

12. quomodo...miserationem. This is dealt with more fully in XI. 3, 63–65, where corresponding to 'narrandum' we have 'in expositione...recta et inter acutum sonum et gravem media' (sc. vox); to 'suadendum,' 'suadentium... gravis' (vox); to 'concitatione...ira,' 'atrox in ira et aspera ac densa et respiratione crebra'; to 'qui flexus deceat miserationem,' 'miseratione flexa et flebilis et consulto quasi obscurior.' For the last cp. ib. 170 'si misericordia commovendos, flexum vocis et flebilem suavitatem,' and 172 'tamen infinito magis illa flexa et circumducta sunt "me miserum, me infelicem."' Also Cic. *Orator* 56 'voce inflexa miserabilis.' All these passages shew clearly that 'flexus' is not merely 'tone' (Watson) or 'change of tone' (L.). It is rather a special quality of voice, 'a plaintive modulation' (as Sandys on *Or.* l.c.), peculiar to 'miseratio.'
14. cum...oportebit, i.e. in the rhetorical school, v. II. 5; learning by heart passages from the orators is again recommended in II. 7.
mihi; v. on 2, 1.
diligens aliquis ac peritus. The function of the 'comoedus' ceases when the boy is promoted to the upper school. Q. does not expect the 'grammaticus' to understand 'pronuntiatio,' but he does expect it of the 'rhetor.'
15–19. It will be seen that Q. shews no interest in the older aspect of Greek

gymnastic as developing health and strength and endurance, e.g. in Plat. *Prot.* 326. This can hardly be accounted for by saying that he is here merely thinking of the orator's special training, for he is fully conscious that these qualities are necessary to the orator. Cf. Prooem. 27. It must be rather that he does not believe in gymnastic serving these purposes, and he perhaps carries further than most the common depreciation of the athlete. Cf. XI. 3, 26 and X. 1, 33, where Mayor has accumulated a large stock of reff., to which add Lucan 7, 271 and Galen *Utrum med. an gymn.* ch. 46 and elsewhere. In this view of the 'palaestra' Q. is in marked contrast to ps.-Plut. ch. 11, where the boy is sent to the παιδοτρίβης, ἅμα μὲν τῆς τῶν σωμάτων εὐρυθμίας ἕνεκεν, ἅμα δὲ καὶ πρὸς ῥώμην, a theme which he develops at some length.
15. palaestricis. Sp. notes the remark in Stephanus that the word in itself does not mean a teacher of the 'palaestra,'v. II. 8, 7. But like 'musicus,' 'geometres,' and in Greek at least ῥήτωρ, while covering the proficient, it is naturally applied to the teacher.
pars...obruerunt. Cf. Sen. *Ep.* 15, 3 of the athletes 'homines inter oleum et vinum occupati,' and ib. a few lines before 'maiore corporis sarcina animus eliditur.' The whole passage is very similar and may have been in Q.'s mind.

obruerunt (hos enim abesse ab eo, quem instituimus, quam
16 longissime velim): sed nomen est idem iis, a quibus gestus
motusque formantur, ut recta sint brachia, ne indoctae, rusticae
manus, ne status indecorus, ne qua in proferendis pedibus
inscitia, ne caput oculique ab alia corporis inclinatione dis-
17 sideant. nam neque haec esse in parte pronuntiationis negaverit
quisquam neque ipsam pronuntiationem ab oratore secernet:
et certe, quod facere oporteat, non indignandum est discere,
cum praesertim haec chironomia, quae est ut nomine ipso
declaratur lex gestus, et ab illis temporibus heroicis orta sit et
a summis Graeciae viris atque ipso etiam Socrate probata, a
Platone quoque in parte civilium posita virtutum, et a Chrysippo
in praeceptis de liberorum educatione compositis non omissa.
18 nam Lacedaemonios quidem etiam saltationem quandam tam-

16. The higher lore of the subject
is given in XI. 3, 65 ff. For ' brachia'
v. particularly 84, 'manus' 85–116,
'status' and 'pedes' 124 ff. For 'ne...
dissideant' v. 69 'tum (sc. caput) accipiat aptos ex ipsa actione motus, ut cum
gestu concordet et manibus ac lateribus
obsequatur.'
ne indoctae, rusticae manus. So
Halm and later edd. for 'rusticaeve'
of earlier edd., which does not seem
to have any MS. authority. Fierville
further justifies the omission of 've' on
the grounds of its rarity in Q. But
though undoubtedly rare it appears at
least seven times in Halm's text (v. exx.
in Bonnell's *Lexicon*). I confess to a
feeling that the asyndeton is harsh.
'Rusticae' gives a lower depth than
'indoctae,' v. VI. 3, 13, where 'non
indocti modo, sed etiam rustici' are
said to speak occasionally with wit.
So XII. 10, 53 and XI. 3, 117. But if
any insertion is adopted, ' ne rusticae'
would be as likely as ' rusticaeve.'
17. chironomia. For the connexion
of the term with the ' palaestra' cf.
Dion Chrys. *Or.* 32, 20 οἱ ἀγεννεῖς τῶν
ἀθλητῶν, οἳ τὰς παλαίστρας ἐνοχλοῦσι
καὶ τὰ γυμνάσια, χειρονομοῦντες καὶ
παλαίοντες, εἰς δὲ τὸ στάδιον οὐκ ἐθέ-
λουσιν ἰέναι. Plut. *Quaest. Conv.* 15,
p. 747 ὠρχήσατο γὰρ πιθανῶς τὴν πυρ-
ρίχην καὶ χειρονομῶν ἐν ταῖς παλαίστραις
ἐδόκει διαφέρειν τῶν παίδων.
ut nomine. So Halm with A. Rad.
'in' with B. Meister ' uti.'
ab illis...virtutum. Q. appears here
to identify χειρονομία with ὄρχησις, or

at least to regard the latter as a branch
of the former (though they are distinguished in Xen. *Symp.* 2, 19). Sp. is
probably right in referring ' illis temporibus heroicis' to the Homeric instances
of dancing, *Il.* 16, 617; 18, 590 ff.; *Od.*
8, 262 ; 'Socrate' to Xen. *Symp.* 2, 16,
and 'Platone' to the *Laws*. (These
are also mentioned by Lucian in the
De Salt.) As to the particular place
in the *Laws* Sp. noted VII. 795 D to
796 E, where Pl. concludes οὗτοι γὰρ
(sc. dancers) χρήσιμοι εἴς τε πολιτείαν
καὶ ἰδίους οἴκους. Radermacher not so
well, 813 B ff. Perhaps also II. 653, 654
where παιδεία, of which ὄρχησις is given
as a part, is spoken of as ἀρετή. What
is meant by ' summis Graeciae viris'?
Possibly Solon is included, whose laws
regulating the gymnasia are given by
Aesch. *Contra Tim.*
a Chrysippo. Rad. with B omits ' a.'
I cannot find that we have any other
evidence as to the Stoic view on this
question (unless indeed we reckon ps.-
Plut. 11 quoted above). Seneca in *Ep.*
15 merely recommends a certain amount
of *mild* exercise. Cp. ib. 83, 1 'minimum
exercitationi corporis datur.' The σωμα-
τικὴ ἄσκησις of Musonius is rather bodily
self-denial and hardiness.
18. etiam saltationem quandam,
i.e. the πυρρίχη, v. *Dict. Ant.* s.v. The
word 'etiam' may be thought otiose if,
as seems certain from the last section,
Q. draws no distinction between ' chironomia' and 'saltatio.' Perhaps the
point is that the L.'s might have been
expected to take a more severe view,

quam ad bella quoque utilem habuisse inter exercitationes accepimus. neque id veteribus Romanis dedecori fuit: argumentum est sacerdotum nomine ac religione durans ad hoc tempus saltatio et illa in tertio Ciceronis de Oratore libro verba Crassi, quibus praecipit, ut orator utatur 'laterum inclinatione forti ac virili non a scaena et histrionibus, sed ab armis aut etiam a palaestra.' cuius disciplinae usus in nostram usque aetatem sine reprehensione descendit. a me tamen nec ultra pueriles annos **19** retinebitur nec in his ipsis diu. neque enim gestum oratoris componi ad similitudinem saltationis volo, sed subesse aliquid ex hac exercitatione puerili, unde nos non id agentis furtim decor ille discentibus traditus prosequatur.

XII

[AN PLURA EODEM TEMPORE DOCERI PRIMA AETAS POSSIT]

Quaeri solet, an, etiamsi discenda sint haec, eodem tempore **1** tamen tradi omnia et percipi possint. negant enim quidam, quia confundatur animus ac fatigetur tot disciplinis in diversum tendentibus, ad quas nec mens nec corpus nec dies ipse sufficiat, et, si maxime patiatur hoc aetas robustior, pueriles annos

or it may be that 'etiam' goes closely with 'quandam,' the selection of a particular form being regarded as a specially valuable testimony. Sp. notes that Ath. XIV. 631 c says καλεῖται δὲ ἡ πυρρίχη καὶ χειρονομία.

sacerdotum nomine ac religione durans. A rather vague expression, which Nettleship (*Contributions*, s.v. 'religio') translates 'in the name and with the sanction of the priests.' But 'nomine' clearly refers to the name 'Salii.' I understand Q. to mean that the survival of the institution is due to the name of 'the dancers' given to the priests as well as to their sanctity. For this use of 'religio' v. above 6, 1.

Crassi, 3, 220. The supposed date of the speech being 91 B.C., Cr. may fairly be called 'vetus Romanus.'

inclinatione. Cic. 'inflexione.'

19. For the limitation of palaestric discipline (apart from the fear of athleticism) to the little which will give some instinctive grace, cf. IX. 4, 56, where the statement that metre in prose is as undesirable as absence of rhythm, is

followed by 'sicut etiam quos palaestritas esse nolumus, tamen esse nolumus eos qui dicuntur ἀπάλαιστοι' (where surely we should read ἀπάλαιστροι as in Cic. *Or.* 229, which Q. is following). In *De Off.* 1, 130 Cic. says 'palaestrici motus saepe sunt odiosiores.'

neque...volo. Cf. 12, 14 below and XI. 3, 89 'abesse enim plurimum a saltatore debet orator.'

non id agentis, 'instinctively.' Cf. 'tacite sentiuntur' above 10, 7.

furtim etc. Edd. quote Tibullus IV. 2, 7–8 'illam, quicquid agit, quoquo vestigia movit,
cómponit furtim subsequiturque decor.'

Cf. *De Or.* 1, 73 'qui pila ludunt, non utuntur in ipsa lusione artificio quodam proprio palaestrae, sed indicat ipse motus didicerintne palaestram an nesciant.'

XII. 1. si maxime, εἰ τὰ μάλιστα. So 'ut maxime' IX. 3, 94. Madvig on *De Fin.* 1, 2 remarks on the fact that Hand ignores this usage though 'pervagatissimum,' and mistakes the mean-

2 onerari non oporteat. sed non satis perspiciunt, quantum
natura humani ingenii valeat, quae ita est agilis ac velox, sic
in omnem partem, ut ita dixerim, spectat, ut ne possit quidem
aliquid agere tantum unum, in plura vero non eodem die modo,
3 sed eodem temporis momento vim suam intendat. an vero
citharoedi non simul et memoriae et sono vocis et plurimis
flexibus serviunt, cum interim alios nervos dextra percurrunt,
alios laeva trahunt, continent, praebent, ne pes quidem otiosus
4 certam legem temporum servat, et haec pariter omnia? quid?
nos agendi subita necessitate deprensi nonne alia dicimus, alia
providemus, cum pariter inventio rerum, electio verborum,
compositio, gestus, pronuntiatio, vultus, motus desideretur?
quae si velut sub uno conatu tam diversa parent simul, cur non
pluribus curis horas partiamur? cum praesertim reficiat animos
ac reparet varietas ipsa, contraque sit aliquanto difficilius in

ing of exx. of it. It is also ignored by
Forc.
3. Cf. v. 10, 125 where the instinctive-
ness of the musician's action is compared
with that of the orator.
cum interim. The phrase is common
in Q., meaning 'and yet all the same,'
without implying actual simultaneousness; v. Peterson on x. 1, 18. Here
probably the usage is the same, for the
simultaneousness is given by 'et haec
pariter omnia.'
percurrunt. Sp. and other earlier edd.
'percutiunt,' with little MS. authority.
cum interim ... omnia. For the
general picture cf. Philostratus Jun.
Imagines (Orpheus) 871, where after
the description of his appearance, dress,
etc. we have καὶ τοῖν ποδοῖν ὁ μὲν λαιὸς
ἀπερείδων ἐς τὴν γῆν ἀνέχει τὴν κιθάραν
ὑπὲρ μηροῦ κειμένην, ὁ δεξιὸς δὲ ἀναβάλ-
λεται τὸν ῥυθμὸν ἐπικροτῶν τοὔδαφος τῷ
πεδίλῳ, αἱ χεῖρες δὲ ἡ μὲν δεξιὰ ξυν-
έχουσα ἀπρὶξ τὸ πλῆκτρον ἐπιτέταται
τοῖς φθόγγοις ἐκκειμένῳ τῷ ἀγκῶνι καὶ
καρπῷ ἔσω νεύοντι, ἡ λαιὰ δὲ ὀρθοῖς
πλήττει τοῖς δακτύλοις τοὺς μίτους. A
shorter but similar description in Philostratus himself, *Imagines* (Amphion)778.
praebent. The word clearly describes
some action by which the left hand
offers or prepares strings for the right
to strike. If by 'continent' it is meant
that the left-hand finger holds the
string at a certain place, so as to alter
the length and therefore the pitch of
the part which is presented to the right

hand to strike, 'praebent' may imply
that, by removing the finger, the string
in its natural condition is offered to the
right hand. In this case the translation
'release' (L.) is practically right. The
use however seems to me strange, for
the held string is also 'offered' or
presented. Canon Galpin, a well-known
authority on ancient instruments, suggests to me that 'continent' may describe the process called 'damping,'
i.e. when the string has been struck, the
application of the *soft* finger 'restrains'
or 'checks' the vibration. On the
other hand 'praebent' will give the
process by which *before* the string is
struck the *hard* nail is applied to it,
thus shortening or 'stopping' and thereby 'preparing' or 'presenting' what is
practically a new string of higher pitch
for the hand or 'plectrum' to strike.
Canon Galpin mentions a curious survival of the 'cithara,' in which the finger-
nail was thus used.
4. The requirements of the extempore
speaker are worked out at length in x. 7,
v. esp. § 9. Here the catalogue is not
exhaustive: 'dispositio' is omitted, or
perhaps included in 'inventio,' as in
Prooem. 22. Of the three parts of 'elocutio' we have here two, 'electio verborum' (ἐκλογὴ ὀνομάτων) and 'compositio'
(σύνθεσις), i.e. euphonious arrangement.
The other (σχηματισμός or use of figures
and tropes) is omitted. The other four
items are sufficiently explained by the
last chapter.

labore uno perseverare. ideo et stilus lectione requiescit, et
ipsius lectionis taedium vicibus levatur. quamlibet multa 5
egerimus, quodam tamen modo recentes sumus ad id, quod
incipimus. quis non optundi possit, si per totum diem cuiuscumque artis unum magistrum ferat? mutatione recreabitur
sicut in cibis, quorum diversitate reficitur stomachus et pluribus
minore fastidio alitur. aut dicant isti mihi, quae sit alia ratio 6
discendi. grammatico soli deserviamus, deinde geometrae
tantum, omittamus interim quod didicimus? mox transeamus
ad musicum, excidant priora? et cum Latinis studebimus
litteris, non respiciamus ad Graecas? ut semel finiam, nihil
faciamus nisi novissimum? cur non idem suademus agricolis, 7
ne arva simul et vineta et oleas et arbustum colant? ne pratis
et pecoribus et hortis et alvearibus avibusque accommodent
curam? cur ipsi aliquid forensibus negotiis, aliquid desideriis
amicorum, aliquid rationibus domesticis, aliquid curae corporis,
nonnihil voluptatibus cotidie damus? quarum nos una res
quaelibet nihil intermittentis fatigaret: adeo facilius est multa
facere quam diu.

ideo et stilus etc. L.'s translation
'*consequently* we *should* give the pen
a rest' etc. gives quite a wrong idea.
Rather 'this is the reason why we give'
etc. Q. illustrates his point (which
properly concerns the lower school)
from the practice in the higher rhetorical
school. The relation of written composition to reading and the variety of
authors to be studied are both discussed
in Book x.

5. pluribus minore fastidio alitur,
'increase of variety brings diminution
of satiety.' Cf. 'non enim vox illa praeceptoris ut cena minus pluribus sufficit,'
2, 14.

6. geometrae. A, B and others
have 'geometri.' Halm's query whether
this is 'ex γεωμέτρῃ' has led Rad. to
print the Greek form. But it seems to
me unlikely that Q. should have a
Greek for such a thoroughly naturalised
word.

respiciamus, i.e. *Keep up* our Greek
'grammatice,' which was begun before
the Latin: cf. 1, 12 and 4, 1.

7. idem, acc. to Halm = 'iidem.'
Sp. corrected to 'item.' With all respect
to their authority I see no difficulty in
taking it as neut. sing.

arbustum. L. translates 'orchard

trees.' There is no reason to depart
from the usual meaning of a plantation
of trees intended for vines. In this
sense it is frequently compared with
and distinguished from 'vinea,' e.g.
Columella *De Arb.* 15 'quoniam de
vineis abunde diximus, de arbustis
praecipiamus,' where the precepts which
follow are entirely confined to planta-
tions for this purpose. So Cic. *De Sen.*
54 'nec vero segetibus solum et pratis
et vineis et arbustis res rusticae laetae
sunt, sed hortis etiam et pomariis.'

avibusque. Omitted by B etc., also
by Sp. The word is much wider than
our poultry and includes 'columbae,'
'turdi' and 'pavones,' v. Col. *R. R.* VIII.

rationibus domesticis. Possibly as
L. 'domestic affairs' in general. But
wide as Q.'s use of 'ratio' is, I know
of no exact parallel. 'Accounts' as in
10, 18 will give an adequate sense.

multa facere quam diu. Many in-
sertions between 'quam' and 'diu'
have been proposed, 'multum,' 'idem,'
'unum,' 'quidquam' (to which I should
add 'unum quidquam'; cf. in a similar
context XI. 3, 44 'nihil eorum pati unum
diu possumus'). But I am inclined to
think that the text, which thus emended
would do little more than repeat 'cum

8   Illud quidem minime verendum est, ne laborem studiorum
pueri difficilius tolerent; neque enim ulla aetas minus fatigatur.
mirum sit forsitan, sed experimentis deprendas; nam et
9 dociliora sunt ingenia, priusquam obduruerunt. id vel hoc
argumento patet, quod intra biennium, quam verba recte
formare potuerunt, quamvis nullo instante omnia fere locuntur:
at noviciis nostris per quot annos sermo Latinus repugnat!
magis scias, si quem iam robustum instituere litteris coeperis,
non sine causa dici παιδομαθεῖς eos, qui in sua quidque arte
10 optime faciant. et patientior est laboris natura pueris quam
iuvenibus. videlicet ut corpora infantium nec casus, quo in
terram totiens deferuntur, tam graviter adfligit nec illa per
manus et genua reptatio nec post breve tempus continui lusus
et totius diei discursus, quia pondus illis abest nec se ipsi
gravant: sic animi quoque, credo, quia minore conatu moventur
nec suo nisu studiis insistunt, sed formandos se tantummodo
11 praestant, non similiter fatigantur. praeterea secundum aliam
aetatis illius facilitatem velut simplicius docentis secuntur nec
quae iam egerint metiuntur: abest illis adhuc etiam laboris

praesertim...perseverare' in 4, is stronger
as it stands. I should not suppose as
some that 'unam rem' is understood,
but that the idea is rather something
like this. Labour may be measured
either by the number of things effected,
or by the length of time covered, but
in estimating the difficulty the latter is
the more important factor. In fact
'adeo...diu' is a 'sententia' such as
Seneca would have employed. 'Non
multum praestant sed cito' in 3, 4 is
not altogether unlike it.

9. noviciis...repugnat. Varro on the
other hand seems to have been struck
by the rapidity with which the grammar
of the language was acquired, v. *L. L.*
8, 6 'etiam novicii servi empti in
magna familia cito omnium conservorum
nomina recto casu accepto in reliquos
obliquos declinant.'

παιδομαθεῖς. Cp. Hippocrates νόμος
(Kühn, 1, p. 4) where φύσις, διδασκαλία,
τρόπος εὐφυής, παιδομαθία, φιλοπονία,
χρόνος are given as the necessary factors
for acquiring medicine. In the agri-
cultural parable that follows παιδομαθία
is τὸ καθ' ὥρην αὐτὰ (i.e. τὰ σπέρματα)
πεσεῖν ἐς τὴν ἀρούραν. Sp. is, I think,
right in saying that while the opposite
ὀψιμαθής does sometimes simply equal

'ignorant,' we have no clear evidence that
παιδομαθής simply equals 'proficient.'
Q.'s statement on this is closely parallel
to his statement about γραμμικαὶ ἀποδείξεις in 10, 38.

**11. nec quae iam egerint...cogi-
tatio.** I understand the meaning of
this passage as follows. The child on
completing the task does not estimate
its difficulty ('nec...metiuntur'). He does
not even do so while the work is in progress ('abest...iudicium'). Consequently he comes under the general rule that
the consciousness that exertion is needed
tells on us more than the exertion itself.
So Huet (quoted by Kid.) 'minus affi-
ciuntur cum fatigantur, quam cum cogi-
tant se fatigari.' Kid. himself would
read 'fatigationis,' which he takes as
genitive both after 'sensus' (nom.) and
'cogitatio,' 'adficit' being used absolutely. He quotes IV. Pro. 7 'ipsa cogi-
tatione suscepti muneris fatigor.' This
will give the same sense, perhaps à little
more easily, but I doubt whether the
gain is worth the change.

Sp.'s note is 'cogitatio est eius, qui
ipse aliquid excogitat, fatigatio eius qui
nonnisi mandata peragit sive corpore
sive mente.' This seems to me (as to
Kid.) not so good. I see no real con-

iudicium. porro ut frequenter experti sumus, minus adficit sensus fatigatio quam cogitatio.

Sed ne temporis quidem umquam plus erit, quia his aetatibus 12 omnis in audiendo profectus est. cum ad stilum secedet, cum generabit ipse aliquid atque componet, tum incohare haec studia vel non vacabit vel non libebit. ergo cum grammaticus 13 totum occupare diem non possit nec debeat, ne discentis animum taedio avertat, quibus potius studiis haec temporum velut sub-siciva donabimus? nam nec ego consumi studentem in his 14 artibus volo: nec moduletur aut musicis notis cantica excipiat, nec utique ad minutissima usque geometriae opera descendat. non comoedum in pronuntiando nec saltatorem in gestu facio: quae si omnia exigerem, suppeditabat tamen tempus; longa est enim quae discit, aetas, et ego non de tardis ingeniis loquor. denique cur in his omnibus, quae discenda oratori futuro puto, 15

nexion between such a meaning and the words that precede. I note that Montaigne clearly took it as I have. He writes Lib. III. 12: 'il est certain qu'à la plus part la preparation à la mort a donné plus de tourment, que n'a faict la souffrance. Il fut jadis veritablement dict et par un iudicieus autheur "minus afficit sensus fatigatio quam cogitatio."' I think Jonson means the same, though he is not so clear (*Discoveries*, 117): 'The sense of the paine, the judgement of the labour is absent, they doe not measure what they have done. And it is the thought and consideration, that affects us more, than the wearinesse itselfe.'

porro = 'in fact.' It is rather Bonnell's 'porro explorantis aut concluden-tis' than the 'porro continuantis' under which he classes it (v. Lex.). V. also Madvig's criticism of Bonnell's classifi-cation in his note on *De Fin.* 2, 25, though he does not mention this passage. L.'s 'finally' is wrong, I think.

13. velut subsiciva. As Sp. suggests 'velut' implies that the word is felt to be a metaphor from its use in land-surveying. So too *De Or.* 2, 364, 'sub-sicivis operis, ut aiunt,' where Wilkins' 'Odds and Ends' gives the feeling of the word well. Compare the 'lucrativa opera' of X. 7, 27.

14. consumi...artibus. The 'com-minui...partibus' of A are possible read-ings, and were adopted by Bonnell.

moduletur. This has been generally understood (by Sp., L. and Watson) as

simply = 'sing.' This view seems to me to be contrary both to Aristotle and common sense, v. on 10, 31. What is it supposed that the musical student did learn? Cf. particularly the passage from *De Or.* 3, 87 quoted on 10, 9, which clearly shews the practice for Cicero's time. I am inclined to take 'modulor' as 'compose music,' or more properly 'set words to music,' a sense which the word seems to bear in *Ecl.* 5, 14 'carmina descripsi et modulans alterna notavi.'

aut...excipiat. Sp. 'neque aliorum cantum fidibus prosequatur,' and so Watson. L. has 'learn to read music.' Sp. originally read 'modis,' but the later note Praef. p. lxxx. (in which he accepted 'notis') does not shew any change of view as to the meaning. I hold the obvious view to be that suggested by Burman 'i.e. to take down or express a tune in notes.' This is exactly analo-gous to the use of 'excipio' in connexion with the 'notarii' in VII. 2, 24; cf. Prooem. 7.

nec utique, v. on 8, 14.

15. The sense of this section can hardly be as L., 'why did Plato bear away the palm etc.?' I answer 'because he was not merely content etc.' (so too Watson). The moral of this, viz. that if you take pains, you will be successful in geometry etc., is not to the point, nor will the Latin bear the sense. It is rather 'why unless these things are valuable, should Plato have taken such trouble?' Cf. XII. 11, 22 'quae tandem

eminuit Plato? qui non contentus disciplinis, quas praestare
poterant Athenae, non Pythagoreorum, ad quos in Italiam
navigaverat, Aegypti quoque sacerdotes adiit atque eorum
arcana perdidicit.

16 Difficultatis patrocinia praeteximus segnitiae; neque enim
nobis operis amor est, nec, quia sit honesta ac rerum pulcherrima
eloquentia, petitur ipsa, sed ad vilem usum et sordidum lucrum
17 accingimur. dicant sine his in foro multi et adquirant, dum sit
locupletior aliquis sordidae mercis negotiator et plus voci suae
debeat praeco. ne velim quidem lectorem dari mihi, quid studia
18 referant, computaturum. qui vero imaginem ipsam eloquentiae

ars digna litteris Platoni defuit?' Q.
regards Plato not merely as a philosopher, but as a model for the orator, v.
his judgment of him X. 1, 81, and the
statement that he was 'praeceptor
Demosthenis' XII. 10, 24.
qui non contentus...perdidicit. Cf.
Cic. *De Rep.* 1, 16 'audisse te credo
Platonem Socrate mortuo primum in
Aegyptum discendi causa, post in Italiam
et in Siciliam contendisse, ut Pythagorae
inventa perdisceret.' Q.'s placing the
Egyptian visit last is probably not a
mere slip, as the same order is given in
Diog. Laert. III. 6.
Q. is also perhaps thinking of *De
Fin.* 5, 50 'quid de Pythagora, quid
de Platone aut de Democrito loquar?
a quibus propter discendi cupiditatem
videmus ultimas terras esse peragratas.'
This and the surrounding sections in
Cicero seem to have several echoes in
this chapter. Thus compare 55 'videmus
igitur ut conquiescere ne infantes quidem
possint' with § 10 of this chapter, also
48 of Cic. with 18, 19 of this.
16—end. The 'communis locus' which
follows is in many ways admirable, but
is surely out of place here. It is not the
boy's fault that he is not sent to these
various masters, and though the parent
is at fault, it can hardly be said to be
'segnitia,' at any rate the sort of 'segnitia' which is described in § 18, that
prevents him. It is true that Q. contemplates the 'iuvenis' continuing these
studies, and such continuance was often
prevented by the attractions mentioned
in § 18; but that has nothing to do with
the argument of this chapter which is
merely concerned with the advantage
or disadvantage of variety of studies for
boys.
16. Q. discusses the ethics of the

advocate's fee in XII. 7, 8–12, with the
conclusion 'nihil acquirere volet orator
ultra quam satis erit; ac ne pauper
quidem tamquam mercedem accipiet.'
rerum pulcherrima eloquentia. Cf.
XII. 1, 32 'hoc...procul eximatur animo,
rerum pulcherrimam eloquentiam cum
vitiis mentis posse misceri.'
vilem. So Meister and Rad. with B.
Halm 'venalem' with A.
accingimur. Sp.'s note 'inest venusta
aviditatis, servo aut caupone digna,
significatio' is fanciful.—The associations of the verb are rather of an opposite
kind, and the feeling perhaps is 'we
arm ourselves for a battle unworthy
of us.'
17. dum sit locupletior etc. I do
not think L. can possibly be right in
translating 'but it is my prayer that
every dealer etc.' The sense required
is clearly 'Many make an income at
the bar without these: yes, and if income
is the only question, the huckster makes
still more.' As Sp. puts it 'fateor ego,
sed tu vicissim fatere.' I do not, however, know of any exact parallel. II. 12,
7 and Ov. *Met.* 10, 309, which he
quotes, are rather of the nature 'I do
not object to A so long as B is involved.'
praeco. To translate 'town-crier' as
L. is misleading, rather 'auctioneer.'
For illustrations of their wealth and
small reputation v. Mayor on Juv. 7, 6.
lectorem. Sp.'s idea that this refers
to the employed ἀναγνώστης is rightly
rejected by later edd. and translators.
No doubt 'reader of this book.'
18. A less exalted view is taken in
X. 7, 17 'adeo pretium omnia spectant,
ut eloquentia quoque, quamquam plurimum habeat in se voluptatis, maxime
tamen praesenti fructu laudis opinionis-
que ducatur.'

divina quadam mente conceperit quique illam, ut ait non
ignobilis tragicus, 'reginam rerum orationem' ponet ante oculos
fructumque non ex stipe advocationum, sed ex animo suo et
contemplatione ac scientia petet perpetuum illum nec fortunae
subiectum, facile persuadebit sibi, ut tempora, quae spectaculis,
campo, tesseris, otiosis denique sermonibus, ne dicam somno
et conviviorum mora conteruntur, geometrae potius ac musico
inpendat, quanto plus delectationis habiturus quam ex illis
ineruditis voluptatibus. dedit enim hoc providentia hominibus
munus, ut honesta magis iuvarent. sed nos haec ipsa dulcedo 19
longius duxit. hactenus ergo de studiis, quibus, antequam
maiora capiat, puer instituendus est: proximus liber velut
novum sumet exordium et ad rhetoris officia transibit.

divina quadam mente. Cf. xii. 2,
21 'si divina nostris animis origo.' The
apologetic 'quidam' is often used by
Cicero with 'divinus,' e.g. *Mil.* 21
'divina quadam mente praeditus.'
reginam rerum orationem. 'O
flexanima atque omnium regina rerum
oratio,' assigned by Nonius (s.v. flexanima) to the Hermione of Pacuvius.
Edd. quote Eur. *Hec.* 816 πειθὼ δὲ τὴν
τύραννον ἀνθρώποις μόνην. Q. is clearly

drawn to the line by the fact that it is
quoted in *De Or.* 2, 187, as said 'a bono
poeta.'
tempora, quae spectaculis etc. Cp.
the very similar account of the distrac-
tions of the adult in xii. 11, 18.
19. ipsa dulcedo. 'Ipsa' is missed
by L. and wrongly given by Watson as
'the very pleasure of these reflexions.'
Rather 'this self-same pleasure in what
is noble' (honesta).

ANALYSIS AND SUMMARY

Letter to Trypho the bookseller:
'I had not intended to publish my treatise till after some considerable time had elapsed from its completion, but I yield to your representation
of the urgency of the demand. I trust to you to issue it as correctly as
possible.'

PROOEMIUM

The scope and character of the whole work

(**I**—**2**) When to those who asked me to write on this subject I pleaded
that so many distinguished authors had treated it already, I was told that
the fact that so great a variety of views had been expressed made an
authoritative treatise the more necessary. (**3**—**5**) When I began my work I felt drawn to take a different line from
my predecessors. They confined themselves to the highest stages of rhe-
toric. Knowing that to make the orator the foundations must be well laid,
I describe his education from the first. (**6**—**8**) I dedicate the book to you,
Marcellus, the father of a promising boy, and trust that it may be of use to
him. I do so the more gladly because the previous publications of my
lectures, made without my consent, were so imperfect.

(**9**—**13***a*) The true orator must needs have every virtue, and the study
of virtue must not be abandoned to the philosophical schools (though we
cannot afford to neglect what philosophers have written). The orator has
often to speak on ethical subjects. In fact, as Cicero shews, philosophy
and eloquence in old days were not divided. (**13***b*—**14**) Then there came
a schism. Eloquence sold itself for wealth. Ethics fell into weaker hands,
who began to arrogate to themselves the title of 'the wise,' a name which
should have a wider significance. (**15**) Still I do not deny that those older
philosophers were often men of worth. It is in our own day that the profession has become hypocritical and degraded. (**16**—**17**) Its claim to
monopolize philosophy is untenable, for all three sides of philosophy, logic,
physics and ethics, are really matters of common knowledge, and we have
a right to regard the results obtained by the old philosophers as our own
heritage. (**18**—**20**) My ideal orator then is the truly 'sapiens' of high
moral worth and enriched with every form of knowledge, and if I am told
that this ideal has never been realised, still let us aim at it. He who aims
high achieves more than he who does not aim at all.

(**21**—**22**) In accordance with this view my work will embrace all that
an orator can need. The first book will treat of early education before the
rhetorical school; the second will give a general introduction to that
school and also discuss the nature of rhetoric. The next five will treat of
'invention' or provision of the material, including its arrangement. Four

more deal with style, memory and delivery, while the last discusses various points connected with the orator considered as a man, rather than with his work. (**23—25**) I hope in treating all these subjects, to avoid the dry and lifeless method which characterises most text-books, and this implies avoidance of prolix discussion of details. (**26—27**) But the reader must remember that no rules or precepts can be effective where intelligence is absent, and that the trinity,—nature, practice, teaching—can never be dispensed with.

CHAPTER I

Early training—Infancy and primary instruction

(**I—3**) A father should hope the best for his child from birth onwards and act upon that hope. He may reasonably do so, for total want of ability is almost unknown. Mental activity is as natural to man, as flying to birds, and we see this in the brightness of children so often extinguished by bad handling. (**4—II**) The following points are to be observed in treating infancy. The nurse should speak correctly. The child is sure to adopt her language, in accordance with the usual law that what is first learnt is longest retained. As for the parents, the more educated they are the better. I include the mother—there are well-known cases of highly educated women. What was said of the nurse applies to the 'vernae' also. As for the 'paedagogus,' a little learning is a dangerous thing. A false conceit of learning often breeds in him a tyrannical spirit. The pedagogue's example too may be morally mischievous, as was Leonides' with Alexander. That all these evils may be avoided may be much to ask, but not too much, considering how important is the task before us. If these counsels of perfection are rejected, the responsibility rests with the individual, not with the principle. At any rate we may neutralise any evil influence by associating with the child some supervisor who can correct what is amiss.

(**I2—I4**) The first medium of instruction should be Greek, but Latin should follow close behind. Long confinement to Greek often taints the Latin. (**I5—I9**) Some have limited the age for beginning education to over 7 years. Chrysippus thought better, who said that education of a kind began from the first, and if character can be affected in these early years, attainments can too. The gain will be small, but it will be something, and that something will be felt throughout life. And in those early years there is one faculty more susceptible than it ever will be again—the memory. (**20**) Of course I do not mean that small children should be set tasks. It should all be a matter of emulation, of the joy of activity, possibly too of the inducement of rewards.

(**2I—24**a) Elementary all this, but it is none the less necessary for future success, and if it is the parent's duty to carry out this early training aright, I cannot be blamed for bringing it to the notice of the reading public. Indeed care and skill are more important in the elementary stage, when the mind is most flexible, than in the later, and so Philip thought when he gave the infant Alexander into the hands of Aristotle. I will suppose an Alexander and give a few notes as to the conduct of his primary education.

(**24** *b*—**26**) (*a*) The names and order of the letters must not be learnt apart from their shapes. (*b*) The representations of the letters which are put before the children should be of an attractive kind. (**27**—**29**) (*c*) In writing, to use grooved tablets is better than to guide the hand of the beginner. Incidentally I emphasize the importance of good and quick writing in later years and therefore the need of learning it young. The upper-class habit of relying on an amanuensis is a fatal one. (**30**—**34** *a*) (*d*) Syllables must be learnt by heart just as they come, not selected for their easiness. Even when regular reading begins, drill in them is required. More haste, worse speed, is eminently true of learning to read. The instinctive action of looking on to what comes next only becomes an instinct by long practice. (**34** *b*—**37**) (*e*) In the earliest writing exercises the words should be chosen for the knowledge they give, and in connexion with this we may note that at a slightly later stage the maxims given for copies should be of moral value. This again suggests the wisdom of making children learn by heart such thoughts expressed in prose or poetry, and this will also strengthen the memory. Finally (*f*) the tongue should be trained to say difficult combinations of syllables without stumbling.

CHAPTER II

The second stage—question between school and private tuition

(**1**) We must now pass on to the stage where the nursery is left and serious instruction begins; and here the old question between school and private education becomes important. (**2**) While the former is supported by the most eminent authorities, the latter is often defended on two grounds (*a*) fear of moral corruption in schools, (*b*) the belief that the individual pupil gets better attention. (**3**) The first consideration is of course the more important; for according to my definition a vicious boy can never become an orator at all.

(**4**—**8**) To the argument that morals are corrupted at school, I answer that they are equally corrupted at home amidst loose surroundings, while on the other hand careful guardianship can protect them at school. Unfortunately we ourselves insist on corrupting our own children by the luxury with which we surround them. Indeed we encourage them in precocious wickedness and accustom them to the sight of our bad example. They do not learn vice from the school: they bring vice to the school. (**9**—**10**) To the objection that individual teaching is superior we may answer—in the first place you may supplement the school teaching with some private help, and if this is impossible, the best teachers are to be found in schools, attracted by their atmosphere of stimulating activity, while only inferior men are attracted by private work. (**11**—**13** *a*) But suppose that somehow you get a good private teacher, how will you employ his time? His pupil does not always require him. Intervention is often but a hindrance. The boy must read by himself and a few minutes will suffice for direction. (**13** *b*—**14**) Besides most instruction is of a nature to reach a whole class at the same time, as the sunlight reaches the world. This is true not only of the declamations of the ' rhetor,' but of the lectures of the 'grammaticus.' (**15—16**) True, numbers are a slight drawback in catechizing individuals, but consider the positive gains. First however let me say that a good teacher will not take too many pupils. Sympathetic treatment by the parent and his own pride in his work will safeguard the individual against neglect, and to grant the danger of large schools is not to condemn schools in general.

(**17—20**) Now for the positive advantages. The would-be orator should be accustomed from the first to his future publicity. Isolation produces either apathy or conceit and undue nervousness when the world has to be faced. The school too is the seed-ground of friendships: it is a social education. (**21—25**) The boy moreover learns from the corrections, warnings, and praises given to his companions. Above all school means competition and emulation. I remember how this stimulus worked when I was at a school where the system of determining by competition the order of declaiming at the speech-day was in force. (**26—29** *a*) Again, with the younger pupils, it is well that they should have someone to imitate. The teacher is too far above them (and indeed he must always remember how limited are their receptive powers and that it must be drop by drop with them). (**29** *b*—**31**) Further the teacher himself finds inspiration from a large audience. Indeed eloquence with its physical accompaniments would be ridiculous when addressed to a single auditor.

CHAPTER III

Boy-nature ; some hints to the teacher

(**1—2**) The teacher's first business is to take stock of his pupil. In the early stages the chief signs of ability are (*a*) memory (*b*) power of imitation, though the latter should not degenerate into malicious mimicry. (**3—5**) The best type of pupil is receptive and ready with questions, though not with that readiness which leads rather than follows. For precocity and superficial quickness, though pleasing for the time, are deceptive and wither away without bearing fruit. (**6—7**) After the diagnosis comes the treatment. Slackness, resentment of control, and timidity are found in different boys. Give me the sensitive and ambitious. (**8—13**) All however need relaxation. So indeed do things inanimate, but the learner even more so, because in learning zest is all-important. And for this reason delight in play is good and apathy at games bodes ill for success at books, though no doubt such relaxations must be carefully limited. Games it should be noted may also be applied to intellectual uses, and in them the simplicity of childhood often reveals itself to the observing schoolmaster, who must however remember that it is just this simple age which most needs moulding and in which impressions have most permanence.

(**13—18**) Corporal punishment for failure in class I entirely reject. It is degrading, ineffective, unneeded if proper supervision is given, leaves nothing in reserve for the more difficult tasks of a later age, and is liable to gross abuse in unworthy hands.

CHAPTER IV

*The scope of 'grammatice': character of the philological
questions with which it deals*

(**1—5**) We now turn to the branches of study. After the primary elements or 'grammatistice,' we enter the province of the 'grammaticus.' The range of study needed by the 'grammaticus,' whether Greek or Latin, is a wide one. Its two main divisions are (*a*) the laws of correct speech, (*b*) the interpretation of poetry, but the former of these includes orthography and the latter the art of good reading. Critical judgment too is needed, a word not to be limited, as often, to the arbitrary admission or exclusion of writers to or from the accepted classics. Wide prose reading also he must have, some knowledge of music and rhythm, astronomy and philosophy, ability also to lecture with eloquence. In fact 'grammatice' is the foundation of higher education as well as the lifelong solace of the cultured man.

(**6—11**) Even what seem the elements of the art are not contemptible. They lead on to problems of higher scholarship which the 'grammaticus' himself if not his pupils should deal with. Amongst these is the need of further letters for unrepresented sounds [such as those which Claudius tried to introduce], or the question whether some, as h, k and q, are superfluous. In the case of the vowels we may ask whether u and i are not sometimes consonantal, since otherwise we should sometimes have two identical vowels in the same syllable, as ' seruus,' and also three vowels in a syllable [as ' seruae'] (both breaches of the ordinary rules of language).

(**12—17** *a*) The boys themselves should learn the various changes produced by the affinity of letters in compounds or inflections and also those in uncompounded or uninflected words, e.g. the change of intervocalic s to r, of t to s, h to f, ph and p to b, d to t, alternations between o and u and between e and i. The lore of single letters should be followed by that of syllables, though this belongs rather to orthography. (**17** *b*—**21**) Then come the parts of speech which have been gradually evolved from the three of Aristotle to the eight of our own time, or nine if we distinguish between nouns proper and vocables, to say nothing of other fanciful distinctions which have been sometimes made.

(**22—26**) The declension of nouns and verbs is a necessary part of a boy's drill, and this in nouns will lead up to various miscellaneous problems such as the origin of various names and whether there are really six or seven cases. (**27—29**) In verbs, besides the ordinary classification of moods, tenses, etc. we have the ambiguous words which belong according to their meaning to both noun and verb, or again there are the varieties of the verb-forms in -tur, the defectives, the anomalous verbs, and those hybrids of verb, noun and adverb, the supines.

CHAPTER V

The philological side of 'grammatice' continued: the principles of correctness in language

[These are examples of the phenomena of language with which the 'grammaticus' has to deal, and they will shew how varied and interesting the study may be made. But he has also to shew how to distinguish correct from incorrect speech.] (**I**—**3** *a*) Eloquence indeed has other characteristics besides correctness, but these belong rather to rhetoric. We may test correctness either in single or in combined words. (I am here using 'verba' in its wider sense, not as in the last chapter.) Single words again may be (*a*) native or foreign, (*b*) simple or compound, (*c*) literal or metaphorical, (*d*) established by usage or newly coined. (**3** *b*—**6**) The single word cannot well have any merit, but euphony. Of its faults 'barbarism' stands foremost (the others belong to rhetoric), and solecism holds the same place in combined words. Both these it should be remembered may under certain circumstances cease to be faults. Of course every one knows what barbarism is, that it is caused by addition, subtraction, substitution and transposition of letters whether in speech or writing. (**7**—**10** *a*) But the scholarly 'grammaticus' will go far beyond this. He will master for instance the various senses in which the word 'barbarous' can be used ; one of these is the employment of a non-naturalised foreign word, and the last is the grammatical use now in question. (**10** *b*—**14** *a*) Examples can be found at pleasure, and it is better not to take them from the authors read in class, for their poetical character justifies these. So too to some extent in prose, as with Cicero's 'Canopitae' or Sisenna's 'adsentio.' (**14** *a*—**17** *b*) The scholar too will notice various irregularities to which the name is really inapplicable. All these, if vices at all, are vices of writing. (**17** *b*—**21**) The vices of pronunciation cannot be indicated in writing, except in verse. Such are unusual quantities or contractions of vowels. Some not even in verse (and here we may note in passing that mal-aspiration lies on the borderline between vices of writing and those of speech, according as we regard h as a letter or not, also that the fashion of aspiration has varied greatly at different times). (**22**—**28**) To this genus of non-indicables belongs accentuation, a difficult subject. Errors arise from the application of Greek principles to Latin words. The traditional Latin principle is that the accent is never on the final syllable of disyllables or polysyllables. Some scholars, I know, accent the final of disyllabic prepositions (and adverbs?) and relative pronouns. My own view is that in such cases the word is neither oxytone nor paroxytone, but forms part of the preceding word. (**29**—**31**) Apart from these special cases the Latin rule is simple, i.e. the accent is never further back than the ante-penultimate and belongs to that or the penultimate according to whether this last is short or long (by position). In this last case the accent may be acute or circumflex (according to whether the syllable is long or short by nature). As the accent cannot be on the final syllable, it follows that in disyllables it must be on the first, and as the circumflex includes the acute, every word, including monosyllables, must have an acute. (**32—33**) There are other nondescript faults of sound, which we cannot reproduce. Avoid all these faults in sound, and we have 'orthoepy' or right pronunciation.

(**34—38***a*) To turn to words in combination. The fault under this head which concerns the grammarian is 'solecism,' though as a solecism can be emended by the substitution of another single word, some contend that it does not come under the head of faults in combination of words. But this is a quibble. If I say 'amarae corticis' instead of 'amari corticis' the fault does not lie in the word itself, but in its combination with the noun. Another question raised is whether such a word as 'venite' addressed to a single person is a solecism—a doubtful point. The fact is that while solecism does lie in a single word, it does not lie in a single word without a context. (**38***b*—**40**) Some would give the same fourfold classification of solecisms as of barbarisms. Others give different names to these misuses which come through addition or omission of necessary words or inversion of order, and confine the name of solecism to the substitution of right for wrong forms. (**41—44**) This last is found in all parts of speech, particularly in verbs, because of the great number of 'accidents,' i.e. mood, tense, person, number etc. (The mention of 'numbers' leads incidentally to a condemnation of the theory that the forms in -ere for -erunt are duals.) (**45—51**) Solecisms are also possible in nouns, in degrees of comparison, in varieties of adjectives, in participles and pronouns. Again, one part of speech or one type of pronoun, adverb, conjunction, preposition or interjection may be wrongly substituted for another. In fact solecism may be defined as "a collocation involving disagreement between what precedes and what follows within the limits of a single clause." (**52—54**) Licensed solecisms like 'tragoedia Thyestes' may be regarded as 'figures of speech,' and something of the same kind may be said of male names in female form and the like. Here we may leave the subject.

(**55—58***a*) Following the arrangement laid down at the beginning of the chapter we discuss the use of foreign as opposed to Latin words. [By foreign here we mean words of foreign origin but naturalized, as distinguished from the non-naturalized 'barbara' of § 8.]

Italian dialectical words may be regarded as Latin in a sense; and though we get many from Gaul or elsewhere, our main source of foreign words is the Greek. (**58***b*—**64**) This leads to the question of the declension of Greek names. The older school held to the Latin inflexions in the quantity of the -or in -ωρ nouns, the dropping of the n in the nominative of -ων and of the s in that of -ας -αν, i.e. Castōris, Plato, Aenea. So too with accent, Olýmpus, not Ólympus. Lately the Greek forms have become more common, and though I prefer the Latin, I admit the others.

(**65—70**) Simple and compound words. We may have compounds formed with preposition and verb or noun (even two prepositions if they are not contradictory), also by joining two words other than prepositions, hardly however more than two, though some doubtful instances are quoted. We can also have two nouns etc. and preposition. The elements thus joined may exhibit various combinations of 'integral' and 'corrupted' forms and of native and foreign words. The preposition itself is often corrupted by the process. Altogether composition is much more congenial to Greek than to Latin, though this may be due merely to our predilection for Greek. (**71—72**) The question of literal and metaphorical words [belongs rather to rhetoric]. As for our final division into accepted and newly coined, the latter should be occasionally ventured, but only occasionally. The 'onomatopoeia' of the Greeks is impossible in Latin.

CHAPTER VI

The same continued : the factors or forces which create language, and their respective value

[We have still to consider the fundamental forces or tendencies which create language and on which correct speaking depends.] (**1—3**) They differ somewhat from those of correct spelling, and may be given as (1) analogy, (2) etymology, ((3) antiquity, (4) literary authority, (5) usage) [that is to say one word or form may be adopted in preference to another, on the ground that it conforms with one or other of these]. It should be noted that in the case of the fourth, literary authority, we mean prose writers rather than poets, whose licences are not to be extended to ordinary language, and that the fifth is really our safest guide. To take these in order. (**4—6**) Analogy is traced mainly in terminations and diminutives. We may decide the gender of some noun on the grounds that it has the same termination as a noun whose gender is certain, or that the gender of its diminutive is known. (**7—11**) Another example is the question of fervĕre or fervēre. Can the former, the literary authority of which is acknowledged, be justified analogically? Lucilius adduced 'fervit,' but he ought also to produce 'fervo' to make good. Sometimes we may recover analogically the original noun or verb from its apparently irregular inflexions. Thus 'pepigi' seems anomalous, but the archaic 'paco' ('pago') is analogical. (**12—16**) But analogy is on the whole an uncertain guide, and the arguments by which the analogist party endeavour to shew that there is no anomaly in 'lepus, leporis' compared with 'lupus, lupi,' or 'aper, apri' compared with 'pater, patris,' are very far-fetched. And for the declension of 'Venus' and 'Ceres' there is no possible analogy with other nouns of similar nominative and gender. As for the vagaries of the perfect, analogists themselves surrender the whole province. In fact analogy is merely observed usage. (**17—21**) So we must avoid the perversity of trying to speak analogically (e.g. 'conire') in defiance of usage. Cicero indeed derides, as did Augustus, this pedantry, which to some minds seems the true 'orthoepy,' an excellent thing no doubt, and worth fighting for, where possible, but though your archaisms may be the orthodox road, the path of usage gives better travelling. (**22—27**) Still more painful is the practice employed by some of adapting nominatives to the other cases, or the converse, e.g. to form 'robor' from 'roboris' or 'roburis' from 'robur.' As a matter of fact in the nouns there are numberless exceptions to analogy, e.g. virgo, Juno etc., and indeed the sequence in many nouns and verbs breaks down altogether. Strict grammar and good Latin, it has been well said, are different things.

(**28—31**) Etymology, which is variously rendered in Latin, may serve to define the meaning of a word or to determine the correct form. It is a scholarly study, when we trace the Greek origin of words, or of the names of persons or places. (**32—38***a*) The etymology of words obtained by various manipulations of letters is of less value and is often carried to ludicrous lengths, and while the accepted derivations of many words such as 'rex,' 'senatus' may be right, the 'lucus a non lucendo' type, or 'verbum' from 'aer verberatus,' or 'stella' from 'stilla' are absurd. Gavius, Modestus, and above all Varro, were offenders in this way. (**38***b*) The term 'etymology' is sometimes used to cover all derivations however obvious, but the science is really only needed where there is some doubt.

(**39—41**) Antiquity lends a certain charm to words, but great moderation must be used. Obsolete words have a sacredness which fits them for religious observances, but oratory eschews the disused. As a modern word is better for not being too modern, so an old word is better for not being too old.

(**42**) Authority is closely connected with antiquity. We must look not only to what our best authors have said, but to what they have been able to establish. There are words or forms which have the sanction of Cato, Pollio, and others, which even they would not use if they were living now.

(**43—45**) We are left then with usage as the final arbiter, but we must define 'usage.' It is not what most people use: that is a most dangerous principle. In life it is only what is felt to be right that bears the name, and so in speech, usage means the usage of the educated.

CHAPTER VII

The same continued: laws of correct spelling

(**1—6**) Orthography or the laws of correct spelling [cannot be judged solely or mainly by the canons discussed in the last chapter.] It becomes worthy of study by the 'grammaticus' only when points of real doubt arise (just as the use of the 'apex' is only justifiable when otherwise there would be doubt about the meaning, and so with other differences of spelling, which vary with the meaning, according to some). (**7—10**) Among the doubtful or difficult points are the questions of the modification of letters in composition, as immunis and inmunis, and of the divisions of syllables, aru-spex as compared with abs-temius. Amongst such some would reckon the question of k or c, though I have no doubt on the point. (**11—13**) Orthography is controlled by usage, and thus (to pass over the fact that the letters themselves have often changed their form and value) we have lost the old ablative in -d, and nouns in -g. (**14—25**) Amongst these changes are the doubling of the semivowels [e.g. porrigam for porigam], and the abandonment of the practice of doubling vowels in long syllables [e.g. paacem for pācem] and of writing ei in some cases for ī (puerei, nom. plur., pueri gen. sing.), ai for ae in 'aquai' etc., double s in a long syllable (caussa), u in 'optimus' and other archaisms. (**26—27**) A noticeable change is -uus for the old -uos (though neither really expresses the sound heard), and 'cui' for 'quoi.' (**28**—**29**) There are some spellings quite different from the actual sound, as e.g. C for Gaius, and Suc. for Subura. (**30** -**32**) On the whole, questions in spelling must be settled by private judgment, always remembering that, where usage does not forbid, the spelling should represent the sound. Here we may leave the subject of the correct use of language, whether written or spoken. The other qualities of right speech, lucidity and adornment, are not indeed outside the province of the grammarian, but are better treated as part of rhetoric. (**33**—**35**) No doubt the points we have discussed will seem to some unworthy of our purpose, but they are only so if treated with exaggerated care. The examples of Cicero, Messala and Caesar shew that interest in them is compatible with genius. Traverse them, do not be imprisoned in them.

CHAPTER VIII

The literary side of 'grammatice': how to teach literature in the school

[We may now turn to the second main division of 'grammatice,' viz. the 'enarratio poetarum' or interpretation of poetical literature.] (**I**—**3**) Reading [in the higher sense] involves proper punctuation and expression [and accentuation?]. These can only be demonstrated by practice, and therefore the only rule I lay down is that we cannot read well without understanding what we read. But I may add that poetry must be read in a way which is pleasant without losing strength, which marks the difference from prose and yet does not become a sing-song, and that characters must be distinguished without aiming at histrionic effect. (**4**—**8** *a*) The most important point is that the literature laid before the young should be the best. Thus we do well in beginning with Homer and Virgil in spite of their difficulty. Metre and subject are alike inspiring. Tragedy and lyrics (carefully chosen) are useful, amatory elegiac poetry and hendecasyllables not so; comedy, more especially Menander, is most valuable at a later stage, in the earlier only under limitations laid down hereafter (Ch. 11). (**8** *b*—**12**) In fact in the grammatical school the books should be of the character-forming and inspiring type. Scholarly study will come later. [Some might include in this earlier reading the old Latin tragedians and comedians.] They are no doubt of great value, particularly by their careful structure and by a certain nobility of style, and we know with what effect they are quoted by Cicero and later writers. Still I adhere to the view that the early reading should be limited as suggested above and that these others should be left to a more advanced age. 'Grammatice' is not for schools only but is a life-long study.

(**13**—**17**) The subjects treated in a literary lesson under the 'grammaticus' will include parsing, prosody (the knowledge of which is valuable to teach rhythm in prose), irregularities (though in poetry these are not faults), the use of words in different senses, or homonyms, and the meaning of the rarer words (glosses). Tropes and figures are more important. But above all comes criticism, i.e. indicating the beauties of structure, diction, incidents, striking thoughts, characterization, and style from the point of view of brevity or fullness. (**18—21**) The explanation of 'histories,' i.e. of allusions to personages, places or events which occur in the poems, must not be neglected, but undue attention to this element shews pedantry and conceit and is a waste of time and energy. Researches of this kind load the notebooks of the 'grammatici,' and Didymus was once confuted in his denial of some statement out of his own earlier work. Indeed such statements are often invented wholesale. Thus the 'grammaticus' will do well not to try to be omniscient.

CHAPTER IX

'Progymnasmata' or exercises in composition suited to the school of the grammaticus

(**1—3 a**) We have now traversed the two branches of 'grammatice' (sometimes called respectively 'methodice' and 'historice'). But something must be said about the composition exercises or 'progymnasmata' appropriate to the grammatical school. We begin with fables, of which the pupil is asked to give a version (oral or written) in very simple language. Then he may give a version of a passage in the poetry he is reading, rising from the mere transposition of the words from their verse order to a paraphrase in the proper sense. (**3 b**) Next come little essays on moral sayings or maxims—the 'sentence,' where the author of the saying is not stated, the aetiology and chria, where he is, [and where therefore the student is expected to say something about the author]. (**4—5**) Chrias may be classified as simple sayings, answers to some other remark, or sayings (not given as answers) but founded on some other saying or action. Also a chria may describe an action intended to convey a moral, and even an action which only does so unintentionally may be considered to be akin to the chria. In all these [the main point is that] the pupil has to give an explanation or justification of the saying or action, and they may all be used as exercises in 'declension' [i.e. in word-structure by varying the form of the introductory sentence]. (**6**) Short narratives from the poets may be written out to impress the story on the memory, but not as exercises in composition. Higher 'progymnasmata' should properly be left to the rhetorical school, though as the Latin rhetors (unlike the Greek) have neglected them, they have fallen into the hands of the 'grammatici.'

CHAPTER X

Additional subjects needed to complete the course— Music and mathematics

(**1**) Besides 'grammatice' there are other subjects to be taken at the same stage, without which the student will fail to complete the regular curriculum or 'encyclopaedia.' (**2—5**) Some argue that these subjects (music and mathematics) are unnecessary to the orator, and no doubt many have been in a sense successful speakers without them. But *our*

orator is the ideal orator corresponding to the Wise Man of the philosophers. As *he* is trained in logical subtleties, trivial in themselves, to
set him above the possibility of deception, (**6—8**) so music and mathematics will contribute to the completeness of the orator. Medical drugs
and honey are the result of the combination of many ingredients. Can
we wonder that eloquence needs many elements, the effect of which is felt
but cannot be specified? That effect may be small but it is something.
Once more, I say, aim at the complete ideal, and we shall accomplish
more than by lower aims. And indeed even of the ideal we need not
despair.

(**9—11**) As to the value of music, the testimony of the ancients embodied in the stories of Orpheus and Linus ought to be enough. Timagenes' view that it is the oldest of studies is supported by Homer and
Virgil. The latter connects music in his account of Iopas with astronomy,
and as astronomy is a branch of philosophy which we hold to be necessary
to the orator, we have a connecting link between music and oratory.
(**12—17** *a*) The great estimation in which philosophers held music appears
in the Pythagorean theory of the music of the spheres, in Plato's *Timaeus*,
and in the life of Socrates himself. Its military value is shewn in the
Spartan as well as in our own armies. Thus Plato, the Stoics and Lycurgus
have all, in their way, shewn their approval of it, while nature has given it
as the great soother of toil. But this hardly proves its connexion with
oratory. [It will carry us a step nearer if] (**17** *b*—**22** *a*) we note its close
connexion with 'grammatice.' The two arts had of old the same professors. There are well-known passages in the comic poets where this
connexion is emphasized. Another piece of evidence is that in Greece
and indeed in old Rome ignorance of music was considered a sign of
defective education. But we still have to ask what the orator directly gains
from it, [apart from that indirect influence which I have already mentioned].

(**22** *b*—**26**) Music is concerned both with the motions of the body and
with the voice, and as the music of the latter is subdivided into rhythm
and melody we have in music three things that are necessary to the orator.
The first affects his deportment, the second his arrangement of words, the
third the inflexions of his voice. The orator, like the singer, must have
rhythmical flow and mastery of the voice to express the various emotions
to which he appeals, and he too needs the music of the body, as will be
shewn in a later book (XI). (**26—30**) [To return to the voice.] A single
example, that of Gracchus and the flute-player whom he employed to give
him the proper note for his speeches, should be enough. Once more
remember the close connexion of music with poetry, at any rate lyric
poetry, and poetry is admitted to be necessary to the orator. But I must
not prolong the argument. To do so would be to give the impression that
this certainty, accepted from the days of Achilles, was not a certainty. (**31**)
I should at the same time point out that I am not supporting the present
decadent music of the stage, but the martial and manly style, not the use
of effeminate instruments, but the knowledge of an art of soul-moving
power. (**32—33**) [How true this description is, is shewn by the story how]
Pythagoras controlled the passions of youth by a change in melody and
how Chrysippus acknowledged its value even with infants. And lastly, the

very fact that we have a declamation turning on the question whether a musician is responsible for the suicide of another, committed under the influence of his music, shews that a speaker may easily need to know something about it.

(34—38) Everyone admits the use of mathematics for training the mind and sharpening the intelligence, but they usually confine its value to the process of learning. [But it is also of real practical value.] On the arithmetical side the proper use of the fingers in calculations is indispensable to the orator and others, and geometrical questions often enter into lawsuits, though really its chief bearing on oratory is of a broader kind,—its use of order and deductive proof and its power of detecting fallacies. (39—45) Simple specimens of such fallacies often serve to amuse children, but there are others of a higher kind. Such is the common idea that the size of a given area varies as its periphery, which has deceived even historians. Geometry shews this to be false. A circle of given periphery is greater than a square of that periphery, a square than an equilateral triangle, an equilateral triangle than a scalene. To take a simpler example, a rectangle of 240 × 120 ft. is much less than a square of 180 ft., though the periphery is the same, or, a still simpler example, a rectangle of 15 × 5 is only ¾ of a square of 10. (46—48 *a*) Again geometry leads to astronomy, and thus tends to shew the immutability of the natural order, and orators have sometimes calmed armies by their knowledge of this. The stories of Pericles, Sulpicius and Dion illustrate this, while Nicias is an example of the contrary. (48 *b*—49) Its use in military mechanics, e.g. by Archimedes, is perhaps hardly to our purpose. But it comes into many questions of general discussion with which the orator may well have to deal, such as optical illusions, the philosophical problem of infinite divisibility, and the rate of increase in geometrical progression.

CHAPTER XI

Physical and vocal training needed at this stage of education

(I—3) Lessons should also be taken from a professor of acting, though only within the limits which the orator needs. We do not want our pupil to be able to mimic weaknesses or the effect of vice, or to copy the actor in movement and gesture. He must indeed avoid the histrionic. (4—II) Yet an actor can do much to correct and clarify his enunciation of such sounds as r and s, in which so many are uncertain, and to prevent the thick deadened sounds sometimes heard, and the dropping of final syllables. He can promote harmony between the parts of the body employed and cure the pupils of tricks with their mouths, eyes, eyebrows and foreheads. (I2—I4) He can also teach him how to use his voice to express various emotions, and to effect this he will do well to make him learn selected passages from comedies. At a later stage [i.e. in the rhetorical school] the student will need to be instructed in the delivery of speeches by some trained specialist.

(I5—I8 *a*) Even the gymnastic master is not useless, though we must avoid athleticism. He can do much for the deportment, and the management of arms, hands, feet and head. What is called 'chironomia' [which is practically the same as dancing] had the support of the great men of Greece from the earliest times and even the Spartans recognised its importance. (18 *b*—19) So too the old Romans had their Salii, while Cicero recommends the use of the 'palaestra.' So do I in moderation and for the earlier years only. The orator does not need to be a dancer, but to have imbibed some of the unconscious grace which such training gives.

CHAPTER XII

The value and practicability of the wider training sketched in the foregoing chapters

(1—5) But some ask, 'is it well to learn all these things at once?' The mind of the child, they say, will become weary and confused. This view ignores the power of the human mind to perform many functions simultaneously—a power which we see in the musician and also in the orator himself; who in some crisis often supplies all the different elements of oratory instinctively and simultaneously. Much more then is it possible to spread a variety of occupations over a period of time. Indeed such a variation is much more congenial than concentration on one. (6—7) Do our opponents propose that we should study 'grammatice' alone for a prolonged period and then geometry only and the like? In agriculture and domestic life we adopt the opposite plan. (8—11) And as a matter of fact boyhood is just the time when this multiplication of interests is easily borne. The boy's mind is very malleable. Observe how instinctively he learns the mother tongue, compared with the imported slave. Again boys are very unsusceptible to fatigue, largely because they do not consciously measure their effort. It is this consciousness which really wearies us elders more than the effort itself. (12—14) Further there is no time so good for this generalization of work as the years in the grammatical school. In the rhetorical school, when the era of original composition begins, he will be too absorbed for such multiplicity. Remember that I do not wish him to go deeply into these extra subjects, but only to employ on them the odd hours which his work under the 'grammaticus' must necessarily leave, though indeed life is long enough to enable him to get a full knowledge of them. [And how valuable such knowledge may be to the orator is shewn by that master of oratory Plato.] (15) If Plato had not thought them necessary he would not have travelled so widely to acquire them.

(16—19) No, this variety of knowledge is not difficult; it is we who are lazy. We do not seek the ideal; we think too much of gain, which no doubt is possible without these additional acquirements. He who loves true eloquence for its own sake will readily acknowledge that geometry and music are more worthy occupations than games, gossip, and the like. It is one of the greatest gifts of God to man that he enjoys best what is worthiest. [My own theme is of that nature], but I must not allow my joy in it to lead me too far, and we will here leave the boy on the threshold of the rhetorical school, which will be discussed in the following book.

ADDITIONAL NOTES

Intr. p. xviii.: Perhaps to the statement that we know nothing of Q.'s subsequent life, I should add that, if we may take for granted that Juvenal never discusses or criticizes living persons, Q. must have died before the sixth satire was published, that is before 116 A.D.: v. Duff's *Juv.* Intr. p. xv.

Intr. p. xxx. (note): Ausonius *Id.* 4 in modern editors is given as 'Ep. 22.' This remark applies to other cases where reference is given to the same poem, viz. on pp. 34, 36, 104, 107, 108 of the commentary.

Intr. p. lxxxvi.: The admitted use of Q. in the *Essay on Criticism* justifies us in setting down as reminiscences resemblances which otherwise we might regard as accidental. Sp. himself quoted on I. 11, 19 'as those move easiest who have learn'd to dance' (l. 363). Wakefield noted the resemblance in l. 262 'for not to know some trifles is a praise' to the concluding words of I. 8. But I suspect that there is a more striking example. It was only when I found myself instinctively giving in the analysis 'a little learning is a dangerous thing,' as a summary of I. 1, 8, that it occurred to me that the original inspiration of this now proverbial line probably came from that passage. Cp. Petrarch's use of it, Intr. p. lvii.

Intr. p. xcv.: Mr Previté-Orton points out that it has recently been shewn (R. L. Poole, *Eng. Hist. Rev.*, July, 1923) that John of Salisbury was for some years in Rome not long before he wrote the *Metalogicus*. When we remember (1) that John's quotations shew some striking resemblances to the text of Prat. and Put., (2) that these MSS. come from a Roman source, the fact may have some significance.

Ep. ad Tryph. 3: **emendatissimi.** The danger here suggested is described in an interesting passage in Strabo (13, p. 609). The Aristotelian library brought by Sulla from Athens to Rome was corrupted by βιβλιοπῶλαί τινες γραφεῦσι φαύλοις χρώμενοι καὶ οὐκ ἀντιβάλλοντες, ὅπερ καὶ ἐπὶ τῶν ἄλλων συμβαίνει τῶν εἰς πρᾶσιν γραφομένων βιβλίων καὶ ἐνθάδε (i.e. Rome) καὶ ἐν Ἀλεξανδρείᾳ.

Prooem. 4: **[in] eloquentia.** Peterson in his Intr. p. lxxv. notes that the D'Orville MS. in the Bodleian (15th cent.) actually shews the reading suggested by Regius and Sp. 'inde eloquentiae.' The same MS. has 'Getae' in Pr. 6, a remarkable fact, as A is otherwise the only MS. known to exhibit this undoubtedly correct reading. In the same section it has in the margin the variant 'festinabimus,' which also is otherwise confined to A.

Pr. 6: **manifestum iam ingenii lumen.** If Peterson is right in his view of the relation of H. to the later MSS. (v. my Introduction p. xcvii.), we may find in it the origin of the 'iter ad ingenii lumen' read by Sp. etc. H. has 'it ingenii,' which is evidently intended for 'iter ingenii,' but might be easily a misreading of iā. The Turicensis reproduced this as 'iter ingenii,' the Florentinus omitted the 'iter.' The later 'iter ad' was an obvious correction for the reading of H. and T.

Pr. 21 : **substantia.** As Q. appears to be the first writer in whom we find this important word with any frequency, it may be worth while to examine his usage. Here it = 'nature' (rather than 'essence' as L.) and so in II. 15, 34 'huic eius (i.e. rhetorices) substantiae maxime conveniet finitio, rhetoricen esse bene dicendi scientiam,' and II. 14, 3 'nos ipsam nunc volumus significare substantiam.' In these cases we may say that of the three main 'status' or issues laid down by the rhetoricians 'an sit,' 'quid sit,' 'quale sit,' it is the second to which the 'substantia' is the answer. Elsewhere however it is the (affirmative) answer to the first and = 'reality.' Thus when we have the person or thing in question before our eyes ('substantia ante oculos venit' VII. 2, 5), 'non potest quaeri an sit?' So we get to 'something real or substantial': figures are no use without the 'substantia' of thoughts and facts IX. 3, 100: the 'substantia rerum' is contrasted with mere words II. 21, 1, and the 'substantia altae mentis' with 'igniculi ingenii' VI. Pr. 7. In the status-lore itself 'de substantia' seems to have been an accepted alternative name for the 'an sit' (commonly called 'coniecturalis' or στοχαστική) status IX. 1, 8, and presumably there it was a translation of περὶ οὐσίας used by Theodorus in the same connexion (Halm *Lat. Rhet.* p. 142). Other rhetoricians, however, seem to have used it for a combination of the 'an sit' and 'quid sit' (III. 6, 39). It is the 'an sit' sense which we find in the only quotation given from Seneca in the Dict., and also, I think, in Tac. *Dial.* 8; but it is the 'quid sit' sense which led up to the grammatical idea of a 'substantive,' and, I imagine, to its use in theological controversy and medieval philosophy.

Three questions may be added to which I am unable to give an answer:

(1) Did the term arise in the status-lore, which is certainly the earliest place where we find it technically used? The 'status' were a very fundamental and a much discussed part of rhetoric.

(2) Was it by Q.'s time the accepted equivalent for οὐσία, as it certainly was later? and if so, how is it that in III. 6, 23 he says that the only Latin rendering of οὐσία is 'essentia'?

(3) Was it a definite translation of ὑπόστασις? I observe with interest that ὑπόστασις appears in two famous verses of the Epistle to the Hebrews (i. 3 and xi. 1), and that the meaning differs in these two exactly as does the meaning of 'substantia' in the contemporary *I. O.*

Ch. 1. **Quemadmodum...sunt.** It is difficult to know how to treat this and subsequent headings. They belong to the earliest manuscript tradition, being found both in A and B; but no one can suppose that they come from the author. Nor are they always well chosen. The composer has been unable to find anything more definite than 'de grammatica' (B), or 'de grammatice' (A), for the whole of chs. 4—8 comprising nearly half the book, and 'de officio grammatici' is a very misleading title for ch. 9. Halm relegated them to his critical apparatus; Meister printed them without any indication as to their genuineness; Rad. treated them as I have done. In this first heading 'sunt' is as the MSS. have it, but the analogy of the others requires 'sint.' Similarly in the heading of ch. 3, 'quae tractanda sint' seems to be a mistake for 'qua (sc. 'ratione') tr. s.'

1, 8: **primas litteras.** Not to be limited (as L.) to 'a knowledge of the alphabet,' but as an equivalent to γραμματιστική.

interim. Here as very frequently in Q. (and so also in Seneca and Pliny) 'interim'=interdum. In 5, 5 we have this sense followed in a few lines by the ordinary meaning of 'meanwhile' or 'for the present.'

1, 9: si quidem Leonides etc. I am inclined to think that Jerome's curious addition of 'et in incessu' in his adaptation of this story (v. other note) may be explained as follows: J. has combined the story with Q.'s warning against allowing boys to imitate 'ingressum et si quid in peius notabile est' (3, 1). Of course the two kinds of imitation are really quite different, that of 3, 1 being derisive mimicry. But the two passages are sufficiently alike to have made it easy for J. to confuse them, if he wrote from memory. Or possibly he may have combined them deliberately. Knowing the *I. O.* so well, he may also have remembered 11, 3 where 'frequens imitatio (here 'mimicry') transit in mores,' and formed a theory that A. mimicked L. in the way denounced in 3, 1. Perhaps the theory would not be altogether absurd. We hear of boys sometimes being unable to get rid of tricks which they originally acquired in mimicking their seniors.

1, 14: Latina...debent. Rad. in his addenda seems to be inclined to Vollmer's suggestion 'debet.' But (1) 'lingua,' which alone could justify the feminine, has not preceded, and (2) the neuter plural used substantivally is found in X. 5, 4 'illa ex Latinis conversio' following 'vertere Graeca in Latinum' ib. 2. Perhaps too in I. 4, 7. In this book we have the neuter sing. in 6, 3. Peterson on X. 5, 2 quotes Cic. *Tusc.* 3, 29 'in Latinum illa convertere.'

1, 19: per singulos. Edd. up to Sp. (also Fierville) added 'annos.' Halm and his successors have followed A Bg in omitting it. It can easily be understood out of 'anno' above.

1, 21: ideo nec. For this use of 'nec' v. Madvig, *De Fin.* Exc. III.

1, 24 ff. The following passage from the *De admirabili vi dicendi in Demosthene* of Dion. Hal. (ch. 52) is worth noting in connexion with these sections. It may be observed that he does not distinguish between 'grammatistice' and 'grammatice' (unless indeed we should emend γραμματικήν below to γραμματιστικήν), and that the course he suggests differs in some respect from Q.'s. The names of the letters are not learnt concurrently with the shapes, and the parts of speech etc. are taught before the child begins to read. He is speaking of the necessity of constant drill in rhetoric, and goes on οἷόν τι γίνεται καὶ περὶ τὰς ἄλλας τέχνας, καὶ οὐχ ἥκιστα περὶ τὴν καλουμένην γραμματικήν. ἱκανὴ γὰρ αὕτη καὶ τὰς ἄλλας τεκμηριῶσαι, φανερωτάτη πασῶν οὖσα καὶ θαυμασιωτάτη. ταύτην γὰρ ὅταν ἐκμαθῶμεν, πρῶτον μὲν τὰ ὀνόματα τῶν στοιχείων τῆς φωνῆς ἀναλαμβάνομεν, ἃ καλεῖται γράμματα· ἔπειτα τύπους τ' αὐτῶν καὶ δυνάμεις. ὅταν δὲ ταῦτα μάθωμεν, τότε τὰς συλλαβὰς αὐτῶν, καὶ τὰ περὶ ταῦτα πάθη· κρατήσαντες δὲ τούτων, τὰ τοῦ λόγου μόρια· ὀνόματα λέγω καὶ ῥήματα καὶ συνδέσμους· καὶ τὰ συμβεβηκότα τούτοις, συστολάς, ἐκτάσεις, ὀξύτητας, βαρύτητας, γένη, πτώσεις, ἀρίθμους, ἐγκλίσεις, τὰ ἄλλα παραπλήσια τούτοις μυρία ὀνόματα. ὅταν δὲ τὴν τούτων ἁπάντων ἐπιστήμην περιλάβωμεν, τότ' ἀρχόμεθα γράφειν τε καὶ ἀναγινώσκειν, κατὰ συλλαβὴν μὲν καὶ βραδέως τὸ πρῶτον, ἅτε νεαρᾶς οὔσης ἔτι τῆς ἕξεως· προβαίνοντος δὲ τοῦ χρόνου, καὶ τόνον ἰσχυρὸν τῇ ψυχῇ περιτιθέντος ἐκ τῆς συνεχοῦς μελέτης, τότ' ἀπταίστως τε καὶ κατὰ πολλὴν εὐπέτειαν· καὶ πᾶν ὅ τι ἂν ἐπιδῷ τις βιβλίον,...ἅμα νοήσει διερχόμεθα.

1, 26: non excludo autem, id quod est notum etc. Mr Duff suggests (rightly I think) that the comma should be omitted after 'autem.' The inf. 'offerre' must be regarded as explanatory of 'id quod est notum,' not as direct object of 'excludo.' The same applies to the emended versions of Halm and Rad.

1, 35: quas...vocant. From the fact that B etc. (though not A) insert 'id est' before 'quas,' Becher inferred that the whole clause is a gloss, and Rad. in his addenda agrees. I think the clause is really wanted, as the phrase 'secretior lingua' would be hardly understood by Q.'s readers without the accepted Greek equivalent, cf. 8, 15.

2, 1: publicis. I should perhaps note that Fierville accepted the reading of Bg 'publicatis,' and explained it as 'en vogue, bien connus du public': and perhaps the 'se publicare' quoted by Forc. from Suet. *Nero* 21 (in the sense of 'to appear in public') might give this some support. I hardly think however that it can be right.

2, 13: ideoque...tradenda sunt. We might translate 'even where individual instruction is necessary, it can be given to a considerable number in succession.'

2, 17: quid ipsi sequamur. This is, I think, a little more than 'my own views' (L.). For this shade of meaning I cannot find any exact parallel in Q., and the refutation which precedes the words is really just as much his own view as what follows. Rather 'aim at' as in 'nihil sequatur praeter voluptatem,' III. 8, 28. The word thus serves to introduce the positive advantages which Q. and those who think with him hope to gain.

2, 19: omnia nova offendit. Mr Duff is inclined to doubt whether I am right in preferring the rendering 'stumble over (or 'knock against') everything new' to 'find everything new.' The latter use of 'offendo' is not noted by Bonn. elsewhere in Q., though no doubt it is fairly frequent in Cic. On the other hand the following passage in Q. (XI. 3, 21) seems to me to support my rendering: 'finditur etiam spiritus obiectu aliquo, sicut lapillo tenues aquae, quarum cursus etiamsi ultra paulum coit, aliquid tamen cavi relinquit post id ipsum, quod offenderat.' Here 'quod' seems to be acc., for I cannot find any instance of 'offendo' with the stationary obstacle as subject, which would justify us in taking it as nom. At any rate Cic. *Rosc. Am.* 79 'ubi scopulum offendis eiusmodi' is beyond dispute. But my main reason for preferring this interpretation is that it carries on so well the idea of 'caligat in sole.'

2, 26: sed sicut...imitatio est. I am now inclined to withdraw most of my original note. The difficulty I felt about the irrelevance of 'quam praeceptoris' may perhaps be explained as follows. The argument is that the presence of 'condiscipuli' is valuable at both stages. In the later stage it produces 'aemulatio.' In the earlier stage it is assumed that the child is sure to imitate somebody. If there are no fellow-pupils he will necessarily imitate the teacher: if there are fellow-pupils he will naturally imitate them with a better result. This is much the same as Sp.'s view, and necessitates the insertion of a comma after 'facilior.' (Meister and Rad. as well as Halm omit it.)

4, 4: sed verba...sumunt. This point is further developed in 6, 42.

4, 5. In the quotation from Cic. *Pro Arch.* 16, with which Q. was no doubt familiar, even if he was not here consciously reproducing it, edd. have corrected the difficult 'agunt' of the MSS. to either 'alunt' or 'acuunt.' The educational use of either word can be paralleled from Cic.; the former in the *Ep. ad Titinnium* (quoted Intr. p. xxxii.), the latter in *De Rep.* 30 (quoted in note on 10, 34, p. 134), and both are used in the same way by Q., e.g. 'acuere' just below, 'alant' in 8, 8.

4, 9: illam adspirationis. Gibson's note actually runs as follows. After quoting the words without 'notam,' he adds 'MS. Bodl. Ald. Sich. Codices alii vocabulum *notam* agnoscunt.' It is an example of his general carelessness that he did not write 'MSS. Bodl. Joann.,' but he obviously could not have meant by 'Codices alii' to indicate Joann. and Bal. To do him justice he does not cite Bal. till it actually begins in 5, 14. Presumably he refers to some second-hand knowledge, real or supposed, about other MSS. beyond his regular three, v. p. 184.

effectu specieque. Meister prints 'effectus speciesque' with A. I think this is a mere misprint. M. does not include it in the list of his variations from Halm, and though other editions, including Burman, have it, I do not see myself how it can be translated.

coppa. A certain correction for the 'kappa' of MSS., due (according to Halm) to Boherius and Gallaeus. So too in Longus K. VII. 16, a very similar statement, MSS. have 'kappa.'

4, 10: ⟨quod nequit fieri⟩. The MSS. which here have 'quod nequit' are, according to Fierville, Carcassonensis (second hand), Gothanus, Parisini 7725, 7727 (all fifteenth century), and the margin of Turicensis. I have seen no reason to suppose that these are of any particular value. When I wrote the main note I was inclined to think that they did add some, though slight, support to my view of the passage, but experience makes me doubt this more and more, and though, as I have said (Intr. p. xciv.), I have no right to deny the existence of a purer tradition outside that of A and B, I think this particular insertion may well have been a scholar's emendation. I can hardly indeed believe that the emender took my view of the passage, the central point of which is that 'nisi... syllabam fieri' is a parenthetical statement of an acknowledged absurdity, and that 'quod' refers back to 'aut unam longam faciunt...aut duas.' Certainly the edd. who accepted the insertion did not mean this. But the fact is that if 'nisi quis putat' etc. is taken as a serious supposition, the insertion becomes almost as natural as on my view. This is excellently shewn by L., who, though he does not read 'quod nequit,' actually makes the insertion in his translation. He gives 'though some hold that even three vowels can form a single syllable; *this however is only possible* (my italics of course) if one or more assume the rôle of consonants.'

A corollary to this is that if we take this view of the insertion in some MSS., viz. that it is an emendation made on a wrong interpretation of the passage, but accidentally capable of admitting the right interpretation, that interpretation does not demand this particular insertion, though it does demand a similar one. The lost words may as well have been 'sed fatendum erit ex tribus nonnumquam fieri,' or other variants. The reader will doubtless echo the words of Q. on analogy 'ac de hoc loco nimium.'

4, 14: **haec ipsa s littera...ipsa alteri successit.** Meister brackets the second 'ipsa' on account of its awkwardness. No doubt it is awkward, but the sense of the word is slightly different in the two cases. No one who translates 'this very letter S has itself superseded another' would feel any tautology. Even if it were tautologous we could hardly expunge it on that ground alone: v. Peterson on Q.'s 'inadvertent repetitions,' Intr. to Book X., p. lv.

4, 24: **diligentem putabo.** Halm and Meister adopted Meyer's easy emendation 'diligentem eum putabo'; very possibly they are right.

4, 25: **Serani.** It should be noted that this is a correction for the MSS. 'Sera.' While it is probable enough (cf. *Aen.* 6, 844 and other reff. in *Dict. Biog.*), it is not perhaps to be regarded as an absolute certainty. 'Sura,' which has been suggested to me, must perhaps be ruled out on the ground that it would presumably be explained as a 'nomen ex habitu corporis,' a class which has been disposed of. 'Pera' is another possibility. And finally I would ask, though I am quite prepared to find the question answered in the affirmative, whether our knowledge of Roman cognomina is exhaustive enough to put 'Sera' itself out of the question. (There is no particular presumption in favour of a plural, for 'Cotta' B is almost as well supported as 'Cottae' AN.)

The name 'Serranus' (I have not elsewhere seen it spelt with one *r*) occurs again in X. 1, 89. Curiously enough, there too it is a conjectural emendation.

4, 27: **tectum.** This correction is to my mind put beyond doubt by a passage in Scaurus (K. VII. 25) which I have recently noticed. Sc. selects two words to exemplify ambiguities of this kind. One is 'caveas,' which may be a noun or verb, the other is 'tectis' (the abl. probably only because it fits his construction), which may be noun or participle.

5, 5: **ne qua.** Mr Duff points out that an example of 'ne quā' occurs Lucr. 1, 267.

observatio. A favourite word with Q. (Bonn. gives between 30 and 40 exx.), rather vaguely used. The senses in which it occurs in the *I.O.* may perhaps be reduced to four: (1) the observation or classification of examples with a view to obtaining a general rule (so Greek τήρησις, on which v. Stephanus): (2) a question which calls for such an observation: (3) the rule or body of rules thus obtained: (4) the practice or observance of such a rule. In our book I should class under (1) this passage, and 'difficilior obs.' 5, 22 and 29 (though v. add. note on this last): under (2) 'est et in dividendis verbis obs., mediam litteram consonantem priori an sequenti syllabae adiungas' (7, 9), under (3) 'est sua loquentibus obs., sua scribentibus' 6, 1, and 'nec (analogia) lex est loquendi sed obs.' 6, 16: under (4) 'apud nostrorum neminem haec obs. reperiatur' 5, 43. Good examples elsewhere of (3), which is perhaps the dominant sense, are VI. 3, 11, where it is said that 'risus' (i.e. the ridiculous) may be reduced to some extent to an art 'quia nonnullam obs. habet,' and IX. 4, 115 'ante carmen ortum est quam obs. carminis.'

5, 6: **quid hic promisso.** If 'promissor' is read, 'tanti operis' must depend upon it. It is not to be supposed that Q. would use a gen. after 'dignum.'

5, 8: quale sit. Halm reads 'est' against A, B. Like Meister and Rad., I see no reason for the change.

5, 10. I think L. and others have missed the sense here to some extent. He translates: 'A third and very common kind, of which anyone may fashion examples for himself, consists in the addition or omission etc.' It is rather this: the third kind is the well-known fault which we call 'barbarism,' of which there are plenty of examples to be found (i.e. both in writers and current speech), and also the teacher can invent them for himself, by adding or omitting, etc. That is to say, the teacher can choose between using existing examples, several of which are suggested below, and purely fictitious ones. This last kind is well illustrated by Charisius, K. I. 51, and others, who give 'scrimbo' as an example of a word distorted from its proper form. I do not imagine that anyone actually said 'scrimbo.' I take 'ut adiciat' as a quasi-consecutive clause, and differing therefore from the 'ut existimatur' above, which is purely comparative. Meister probably thought otherwise: hence his correction to 'existimetur.' I may add that the way in which I have taken the first words of the sentence goes far to make me believe that the 'barbarum' (7) and 'barbari' (9) of B should be adopted.

5, 18: sed nec. V. note and add. note on 1, 21.

5, 20: reservatum. So Rad. with B. Halm and Meister 'servatum' with A. The point seems to me very doubtful. I have a very slight preference for 'res.' as giving a rather fuller sense. The objectors to non-aspiration, when defeated in one quarter, still maintained their position in another.

5, 29: a praecepto nostro. Here again Rad. has followed B, while the other two editors omit 'nostro' with A. This also is a very doubtful point. But Fierville, who rejects 'nostro' on the ground that there is here no question of any rule of Quintilian, mistakes the meaning. 'Nostro'= 'Latino,' and is to some extent supported by the reference to Greek in the next sentence, followed by 'apud nos' etc.

cuius...Graecos. L. has 'this law is more difficult for the Greeks to observe.' Rather, I think, 'the rules of accent amongst the Greeks are more difficult to reduce to a system.' V. add. note on 'observatio' above.

5, 31: nec umquam ultima. Cf. XII. 10, 33, where this rule is said to make the Latin accents 'cum rigore quodam, tum similitudine ipsa minus suaves' than the Greek.

5, 36. The question here discussed is dealt with by Apollonius *De Const.* 198 (Uhlig, Vol. II. p. 273). Some people, he says, have questioned the law that μιᾶς λέξεως κακία ἐστὶν ὁ βαρβαρισμός, ἐπιπλοκῆς δὲ λέξεων ἀκαταλλήλων ὁ σολοικισμός, on the ground that οὗτος, when speaking of a woman or a number of people, is a σολοικισμὸς ἐν μιᾷ λέξει. He replies that, since it would not be a solecism if the speaker was in the dark, it cannot be a solecism at all. But he does not deal, I think, with a case like 'ego' in response to 'quem video,' and would probably regard it like Q. as a virtual solecism, since the pronoun and the verb understood are ἀκατάλληλα.

5, 37: quibus res significantur et voluntas ostenditur. I take these two to mean nouns and verbs (or their equivalents): v. on 4, 18. For the conception of the verb involved in 'voluntas' cf. the definition of Apollonius (*Gramm. Graec.* Part I. Vol. 3, p. 76), in which the verb ψυχικὰς διαθέσεις δηλοῖ. This is, properly speaking, limited to the finite verb, but Heliodorus (ib.) says more generally that noun and verb are ὥσπερ σῶμα καὶ ψυχή.

5, 67 ff. Munro has some interesting remarks on these sections (*Lucr.* p. 313).

5, 72: iam ne 'balare' quidem. I am inclined to go further than in the original note and to say that the substitution of 'nam' actually weakens the sense. 'Iam' in these cases = 'indeed,' and introduces an example more striking than the preceding. V. Hand III., p. 148.

6, 4—27. Analogy, and the controversy between the analogists and anomalists.

Mr Duff suggests to me that to refer readers to my long article in the *Classical Quarterly* on this little-known subject is not a very practical method. I therefore subjoin the following attempt at a summary.

Though to our minds the controversy, or at any rate many of the arguments, may seem very unreal, it has some interest in the history of ancient thought. I venture to reproduce some of the opening sentences of my article.

"The interest of the controversy lies in the spirit in which it was conducted. Anyone who reads for instance Varro *De Ling. Lat.* VIII. 31-32, where the anomalist argues that as in life variety of furniture and the like is necessary for aesthetic enjoyment, so in language anomaly is desirable; or IX. 24, etc., where the analogist argues from the unchanging order that prevails in the heavenly bodies, in the tides, in the continuity of species, will feel that he is moving in a world of thought very different in one way from our own, though in another rather like it. By the analogist language is conceived as a world in itself, much as we conceive of the visible world. Its phenomena are being laid bare and constantly reveal fresh signs of law and order. The investigator sometimes finds facts which *prima facie* suggest anomaly, but he is as confident that behind them must lie some unifying principle as the scientific man of to-day is with regard to the phenomena of the visible world, as impatient of the suggestion of disorder as he is of any miraculous interference with the order of nature. Even the anomalist, sceptic as he is, approaches the question not in a spirit of mere denial, but of aesthetic consideration. We get a glimpse of a lost point of view. The world of words had a glamour and a wonder for them which it cannot have for us."

A very complete view of the main questions discussed is given in Varro's *De Lingua Latina*, Book 8 contra analogiam, 9 pro analogia, 10 de analogia (in which V.'s own views are given). The arguments brought forward by one party and answered by the other are sufficiently illustrated in the notes on 6, 4–27, particularly those on 'lepus'...'lupus' (12), 'aper' ...'pater' (13), 'Alba' and 'nam praeterito...laudavi' (15).

As to the results of the controversy (apart from the fact that it gave a great impulse to the systematic study of grammar) we may note the following points:

(1) Some analogists may have attempted to correct language so as to

bring it into complete agreement with analogy, and examples of this tendency are given by Q. in 6, 17 ff. But this tendency may not have been very widespread, for (2) the orthodox analogist did not really need to make much change. Rather he argued, largely by means of such shifts as are mentioned in the note on 6, 13, that language as it stood was analogical, and that real exceptions were as abnormal as the 'luscus homo' or 'claudicans equus' (*L.L.* 9, 33).

(3) Even if he did not take this line the analogist could argue that analogy might well be universally right, yet impossible to attain at the present time. The people do not speak analogically, and the orator has to make himself understood. Analogy thus, though under protest, tolerates anomaly *L.L.* 9, 5. As Charisius says in effect 'consuetudini indulget non accedit.'

On the other hand (4) the anomalist, even if he did not go so far as to hold that anomaly for aesthetic reasons was actually desirable, often argued that analogy itself rested on 'consuetudo' and therefore could not claim to supersede it. This need not necessarily have prevented him from admitting that analogical forms were preferable 'in dubiis.'

Q.'s position is on the whole as this last, though perhaps with some admixture of (3), e.g. 6, 22.

An account of the controversy bringing out some points not mentioned here will be found in Sandys *Hist. Class. Schol.* I. pp. 179–181.

6, 12: **Romanae urbis.** Rad. has followed Claussen *Quaestiones Quintilianeae* p. 328 in bracketing 'Romanae.' Claussen's argument was that (1) the fact that the common text in the old editions was 'urbis Romae,' while A and B give the words 'Romanae' and 'urbis' in a different order, suggested that the first was an interpolation, (2) Q. three times calls attention to the point that 'urbs' by itself would be understood to mean Rome without further addition, and indeed himself in v. 13, 40 uses it in this way. This last however is in a context where the addition of the adj. is obviously unnecessary and would be almost absurd, and the semi-colloquial use alluded to in the other references stands on rather a different footing from the formal title of a treatise. The value of the first argument seems to me doubtful. Anyhow I think it safer to retain 'Romanae' with Halm and Meister.

6, 14: **nomina quamvis feminina.** In writing the original note I had overlooked the following in Halm's *Addenda*, p. 367 '*Keilius recte monet coniecturam Gallaei* ut, cum nomina quamuis feminina...terminentur *parum probabilem uideri, ipse scribit* ut, quamuis nomina feminina *etc. an deleto uoc.* nomina, *cuius loco Ambrosianus et prima manu Bernensis* non *habent,* ut, quamuis feminina *etc. scribendum est?*' This agrees with the views expressed in my note as to the readings 'ut cum nomina' and 'ut non.'

6, 16: **quid quoque.** There is similar doubt with regard to 'quo quaeque' X. I, 2, v. Peterson's crit. note.

6, 32: **qui verba paululum** etc. 'Qui' is a correction (originally due to Regius) for 'quae paululum' (A) or 'quae verba paulum' (B and other MSS.). Rad. has retained this last, but it is difficult to translate. The reading of A would be a little less awkward, but I feel no hesitation in adopting the correction.

6, 37 : **graculos.** So B. A and the text of Varro have grag- which Rad. has adopted. I have not, however, seen any other authority for the *g*, which may have been due to a wish to assimilate the word to 'gregatim.' V. would not, I think, have been deterred by the *c*, which will give more force to Q.'s criticism of the etymology.

6, 38. (Quotation from *L.L.* 5, 7 in note on 'etymologiae...causam') 'Argentofodinae' is the reading in Goetz' edition. Elsewhere he has 'argentifodinae,' and I do not know what authority there is for the -to. The MSS. have 'aretofodine,' for which I should suggest creti(o) fodinae. But the point does not affect the reason for which the passage is cited.

7, 19: ⟨ut⟩ his 'Syllae Galbae.' In the original note I said that the insertion of 'ut' was not absolutely necessary. I am now inclined to think that it is unnecessary, in view of Q.'s constant habit of appending his examples without the conjunction (cf. on 4, 17).

I remain, however, quite convinced of the superiority of 'his' to 'hi.' In fact it seems to me very difficult to construe the latter. Sp., Bonn., and L. put a comma after 'utebantur.' With this the 'Syllae Galbae' becomes a mere 'nominativus pendens.' Halm, Meister and Rad. have no comma, in which case we are told that the forms 'Syllae Galbae' used to use -ae. Surely this is a strange expression.

'**Syllae.**' Should this be corrected to 'Sullae'? The name appears in five other places in the *I.O.* In the first of these, I. 4, 25, the MS. authority, to judge from Halm's silence, is for 'Sullae' (so certainly Joann.). In the others the best MSS. available (A, B or G) have Syll-, which the edd. have corrected to Sull-, in accordance with the accepted orthography of the name, while here they have unanimously retained 'Syllae.' Presumably this is because they supposed that Q., though he wrote 'Sulla' himself, *believed* that earlier writers used 'Sylla.' I do not see much ground for this idea. It is true that there was a tradition (recorded by Char. (K. 1, 110) and Macrobius) that the name was originally an abbreviation of 'Sibylla,' and it is also the case that both these late authorities give the secondary form as 'Sylla.' The story itself is old, for Char. gives as his authority Epicadus, (presumably the freedman of Sulla mentioned by Suet. *De Gram.* 12), who, in a treatise 'de cognominibus,' apparently tried to harmonize this tradition with the other view that 'Sulla' denoted some tinge of colour, by suggesting that the original bearer of the name had 'flavus capillus,' and that thus the term, while derived from 'Sibylla,' came to indicate persons of a particular colour. But (1) the way in which Q. groups the name in 4, 25 gives us no reason for thinking that he accepts this derivation, (2) it does not follow that those who maintained it held that the name in its abbreviated form should be spelt with a '*y*.' Roman etymologists regularly derived Latin words from Greek, without assimilating the spelling, e.g. Varro *L.L.* 6, 96 'putere a πύθεσθαι,' (3) even if Q. thought of the name as a genuine Greek loan-word he was quite aware that the fashion of writing such words with a *y* and not a *u* was a later, not an earlier use. Cf. his mention of 'Burrus' and 'Bruges' in 4, 15. And perhaps we may add that the introduction of the point here would be out of place, as he is only concerned with the second syllable of the word.

Another passage which may have influenced editors is Mar. Vict. (K.

VI. 20) "'gylam,' 'myserum,' 'Syllam' (MSS. syllabam), 'proxymum' dicebant antiqui." But this merely refers to pronunciation, and moreover it is called 'consuetudo paucorum hominum.'

On the whole I should prefer to read 'Sullae' here, but I have kept the accepted text largely in deference to the opinion of Prof. Lindsay.

7, 27 : illud nunc melius. I am now inclined to think that it is better to explain these words as indicating the superiority of 'cui' to 'quoi,' in view of the fact that the very similar passage from Longus quoted in my note on 'tantum—distingueretur' also speaks of this superiority. Q. and Longus may have found the comparison made in their common authority (Verrius?).

8, 6: nolim interpretari. B. has 'notis,' which is probably a mistake for 'nolis.' This last, in view of Q.'s use of the 2nd pers. sing. for the indefinite 'one,' is by no means impossible.

8, 9: oeconomia. The following passage from Headlam, *Cambridge Praelections*, p. 111 (quoted by J. T. Sheppard, *The Pattern of the Iliad*), illustrates excellently the ancient idea of 'oeconomia,' at any rate as it was understood by the best critics. "The more we study them (i.e. the plays of Aeschylus), the more, I think, we shall discover in them what is to my mind the highest of artistic qualities, the power of construction, of designing a composition from the beginning to the end, and controlling the relations and proportions of one part to another: the power that corresponds to strategy as opposed to tactics; or the statesman's power as opposed to the mere politician's, the power that in art is exhibited in the highest degree by Beethoven."

8, 11 : cum...respirant. Perhaps a reminiscence of Cic. *Pro Arch.* 12 'Quaeres a nobis cur tanto opere hoc homine (i.e. Archias) delectemur. Quia suppeditat nobis ubi et animus ex hoc forensi strepitu reficiatur, et aures convicio defessae conquiescant.'

8, 14: laudem virtutis necessitati damus. Do we owe our proverbial equivalent to this passage? It seems possible. The next appearance of it in point of time, according to Bartlett's *Dict. of Quotations*, is 'to maken vertue of necessite' in the *Knight's Tale.*

8, 20. (Quotation from Sen. *Ep.* 88 in note on 'Didymo.') For 'miser si tam' the Teubner text has 'misererer si tam.' If this is right, the last sentence of the note on 'miseriae' on the preceding page will have to be cancelled.

8, 21: aliqua nescire. Cf. Grotius 'nescire quaedam, magna pars sapientiae est' (quoted by Sandys *Hist. Class. Schol.* II. p. 277).

10, 3: in data linea. So Halm and Meister with B (A's original hand is illegible). Rad. omits 'in.' Halm himself felt doubts and pointed out that the proper geometrical terminology, as seen in Boethius, was 'super lineam.' (Cf. also quotation from Mart. Cap. in my first note.) Others however may have felt that 'super' was not exactly the same as the Greek ἐπί, and indeed 'in' on the analogy of 'in equo' 'in capite' is at least as good an equivalent.

10, 25: iudicis. So A. B has 'iud' without any sign of abbreviation, and Joann. reproduces this. So too N. according to Chatelain, but Fierville gives 'iudicum: N. Prat.' Prat.'s reading here is of little importance in itself. If Stephen of Rouen, who has evidently sometimes deliberately altered his text, found 'iud' he would be sure to alter it to either 'iudicis' or 'iudicum.' Fierville does not tell us what Put. has, which would be more to the point. Halm while reading 'iudicis' adds '*ipse malim* iudicum.' But as far as meaning is concerned, I see no difference whatever between the two.

10, 34: **ea vulgaris opinio est.** I think it is possible that something has fallen out between these words and 'nec sine causa' etc. The sections which follow do not justify the view that mathematics serve only to sharpen the wits. They are intended to shew that mathematics give valuable practical knowledge, as well as the ideas of 'ordo' etc., and though these last might be regarded as agreeing fairly well with 'agitari —concedunt,' they hardly agree with 'sed prodesse—discatur.' Possibly we might conjecture something which would enable us to retain the 'id' of the MSS., e.g. 'id vulgaris opinio ⟨accipit, sed et adultis nonnihil prodesse verior opinio⟩ est.' Some such insertion would also suit better the words 'summi viri,' which suggest that not only 'tenerae aetates' but grown men with abilities already powerful have found value in the study.

11, 1: **quem in hoc instituimus.** I.e. as Sp. 'ut fiat orator.' Cf. Pr. 7 '(libri) neque in hoc comparati.' Hand, III. p. 320, calls attention to the frequency of this use of 'in hoc' in Q.

11, 3: **ne ars esse videatur.** As Dr Reid reminds me, I should have noted as another earlier example, *Ars Amoris* 2, 313, 'Si latet ars, prodest.' Another example in Q. himself is IV. 2, 126 'cum desinat ars esse, si apparet.'

12, 4: **desideretur.** So MSS. Rad. has corrected to 'desiderentur,' and so many of the older edd.

12, 7: **adeo...diu.** Cf. X. 2, 10 'adde quod plerumque facilius est plus facere quam idem.'

12, 14: **moduletur.** For my view of the meaning of this passage cf. Plin. *Ep.* 4, 19 (in praise of his wife), 'versus quidem meos cantat etiam formatque cithara, non artifice aliquo docente sed amore, qui magister est optimus.'

For the word itself cf. Suet. *Cal.* 16 'nobilibusque pueris ac puellis carmine modulato laudes virtutum eius canentibus.' Here 'in an ode set to music' will give a good sense.

12, 18: **facile persuadebit...voluptatibus.** Evidently inspired by *Pro Arch.* 13 'Quis me reprehendat...si, quantum ceteris ad suas res obeundas, quantum ad festos dies ludorum celebrandos, quantum ad alias voluptates et ad ipsam requiem animi et corporis conceditur temporum, quantum alii tribuunt tempestivis conviviis, quantum denique alveolo, quantum pilae, tantum mihi egomet ad haec studia recolenda sumpsero?'

ineruditis. Rad. has corrected this to 'ineruditi'(nom. plur.). The correction is certainly attractive. It adds force to the comparison, and 'ineruditae voluptates' is not an expression to which I can find any parallel.

hoc providentia. A has 'hoc quoque prov.' And so Halm and Meister. It is perhaps supported by the fact that we have already had one 'gift of providence' mentioned, 10, 7. It may be noted that this semi-personified use of 'providentia,' though quite common in Stoic literature, is more frequently found in Q. than we should expect in a writer not strictly philosophical; v. exx. in Bonnell.

CONSPECTUS OF PLACES WHERE THE TEXT OF THIS EDITION AND OF THOSE OF HALM, MEISTER AND RADERMACHER DIFFER FROM ONE ANOTHER

	HALM	MEISTER	RADERMACHER	THIS EDITION
PROOEM.				
4	[in] eloquentia	as H	in eloquentia	as H
6	Victori	Vitori	as M	as M
	quamquam sunt	as H	quamquam sint	as H
17	ad eos aliquando	as H	ad eos [aliquando]	as H
22	informandus est ubi	inf. est et	as H	as H
CHAP. I				
2	hi pauci admodum fuerunt. argumentum	as H	as H	hi pauci admodum. fuerit argu mentum
3	quam maxime curam	as H	quam maxime datur curam	as H
5	imbuas	as H	imbuas vasa	as R
	quo deteriora	quae deteriora	as M	as M
	num quando	quando	as M	as M
8	plene	plane	as M	as M
11	defuerint	defuerit	as H	as H
13	hoc enim	hinc enim	as H	as H
15	is primus	as H	is primum	as H
17	dissenserunt	as H	as H	id senserunt
20	fecisse	as H	scisse	as H
26	inventum	notum	motum	as M
	vel si quid	et si quid	as M	as H
36	usque ad mores	usque ad mortem in mores	as H	as H
CHAP. II				
3	si potest	si posset	as H	as H
4	tam hercule quam	tam hercule laesae quam	as H	as H
5	timebantur	timebuntur	as H	as H
11	num tamen	as H	non tamen	as H
29	velis	velit	as M	as M
30	loquitur	loquimur	as H	as H
CHAP. III				
12	maxime formanda	maxime mens est formanda	as H	as H
14	quamlibet receptum	quamlibet et receptum	as M	as M
	iniuria est	iniuria	as M	as M
CHAP. IV				
1	grammatici	as H	grammaticis	as H
3	cum loquendo	cum loquendi	as H	as M
	enarrationem	as H	narrationem	as H
5	iecit	iecerit	as H	as H
	in omni studiorum genere	as H	omni studiorum in genere	as H
8	sic optimum dicimus ut opimum	[sic] optumum d. aut optimum	sic optumum d. vel optimum	sic optumum d. aut optimum
9	illam notam adspirationis	as H	as H	illam adspirationis

	HALM	MEISTER	RADERMACHER	THIS EDITION
CHAP. IV				
9	ut k	as H	et k	as H
	effectu specieque	effectus speciesque (but v. Add. note)	as H	as H
10	uos ut tuos	as H	quos ut tuos	as R
	aut duas	as H	aut diphthongum. iungimus autem non plures quam duas	as H
	fieri si non	as H	as H	fieri quod nequit fieri si non
11	coniicit	as H	as H	conicit
	etiam iungetur	as H	as H	etiam i iungetur
13	cadit cecidit	as H	cadit excidit	as R
	a lavando lotus	a l. lautus	as M	as M
	mille talia	as H	mille alia	as H
	sed quae	sed et quae	as M	as M
	lases fuerunt	as H	as H (but 'lasis')	lases et asa fuerunt
14	ipsa alteri	as H	[ipsa] alteri	as H
	f ut φ solent	as H	f solent	as H
16	notrix, Culcides	as H	nutrix Culcidis	as R
	Ῑλυσσέα	'Ολυσσέα	as M	as M
17	fuit Menerva	fuit ut Menerva	as H	as H
24	diligentem eum putabo	as H	diligentem putabo	as R
25	secretius Sullae	secretius ut Sullae	as H	as H
	taliaque et ex	as H	talia quae et ex	as H
27	tenentur	as H	teruntur	as H
	participia an verba	as H	as H	participia [an verba]
	lectum	as H	tectum	as R
28	et quaedam verba	quaedam verba	as M	as M
	fletur accipimus	as H	as H	fletur. tur acc.
29	dictu factu	as H	dictu factuque	as II
CHAP. V				
1	cum oratio	cum omnis oratio	as H	as H
6	adspiratione	as H	spatio	as H
8	quale est	quale sit	as M	as M
	adductum est	ductum est	as M	as M
9	existimatur	existimetur	as H	as H
12	in eiusdem vitii geminatione	in eadem v. g.	as M	as M
	Mettoeo Fufettioeo	Metteio Fufeteio	Mettioeo Fufetioeo	Meteio Fufetteio
15	nam et dua	nam dua	as H	as H
16	inmutationem detractionem adiectionem	mutationem [detractionem adiectionem]	mutationem detractionem adiectionem	as R
17	συναλοιφήν	ἐπισυναλοιφήν	as M	as H
18	dicenda	ducenda	as M	as M
20	servatum	as H	reservatum	as R
	in triumpis	triumpis	as M	as M
	in inscriptionibus	inscriptionibus	as M	as M
23	ut Appi circumducta	ut Marcipor circumducta	ut †apice circumducta	as R
	Atrei	Atreus	as M	as M
29	praecepto	as H	praecepto nostro	as R
	alia...alia	alias...alias	as M	as H
31	quoniam est in flexa et acuta	[quia in eadem flexa et acuta]	om.	as H

	HALM	MEISTER	RADERMACHER	THIS EDITION
CHAP. V				
32	ἰωτακισμούς et λαβδακισμούς	ἰωτακισμούς et μυτακισμούς et λαβδακισμούς	as M	as H
33	reprendimus	deprehendimus	as H	as M
43	quamquam id Antonius	quod Antonius	as H	as H
51	accident	accidunt	as H	as H
	est enim	as H	est etiam	as H
53	sed id	as H	sed hic	as H
54	inhonoratam	inhonoratum	as H	as H
62	quia duabus longis sequentibus primam brevem acui noster sermo non patitur	quia longa sequenti ('primam patitur' as Halm)	as Halm but 'duabus — sequentibus' bracketed	the whole bracketed
64	sed tamen citra	as H	sed citra	as R
68	sit praepositio	sit 'epi' praepositio	as M	as H
	ex duobus corruptis	as H	duobus corruptis	as R
69	compositio	as H	copulatio	as R
72	nam ne balare	as H	iam ne balare	as R
CHAP. VI				
2	honestus est (but 'sit' suggested)	h. est	h. sit	as M
4	debere	as H	habere	as H
5	[domus]	as H	domus	as R
6	et ne	as H	ut ne	as H
9	'fervo' dicetur	as H	f. dicet	as R
11	pacunt...paco	as H	pago...pagunt	as H
12	ista	as H	ita	as R
	romanae urbis	as H	urbis [romanae]	as H
14	ut cum nomina	ut non	as H	ut nomina
	flexus eunt	f. exeunt	as H	as H
16	quo quidque	as H	quid quoque	as R
19	otiosum	as H	odiosum	as R
26	ruere	as H	urgere	as R
27	senatus senati an senatus	as H	as H	senatus senatui senati an senatus
29	ut M. Caelius	ut cum M. Caelius	as M	as M
	ementiri	mentiri	as M	as M
	unde sit ducta frugalitas	as H	as H	[unde...frugalitas]
30	aliaque quae consuetudini serviunt	aliquando consuetudini servit	as M	as H
31	sive ex Graecis	sive illa ex Graecis	as H	as H
	praecipueque aeolica	praecipueque ab aeolica	as H	as H
32	qui verba	as H	quae verba	as H
	paulum	as H	as H	paululum
35	parte qua	as H	as H	parte quae
37	graculos	as H	gragulos	as H
38	strepere	stertere	as M	as M
	velocitate	velo	as H	as H
	pluraque	as H	as H	pleraque
42	tuburchinabundum et lurchinabundum (but tuburci- lurci- suggested)	turburchi- lurchi-	as M	tuburci- lurci-

	HALM	MEISTER	RADERMACHER	THIS EDITION
CHAP. VII				
1	hoc nos	nos	as M	as M
5	per qu et m	per qu et um	per qu	per q u o m
10	etiam ut sola ponatur	etiam ubi sola ponitur	ita ut sola ponatur	as H
16	aurei argentei	as H	aureei argenteei	as H
18	incidissent	as H	as H	incidisset
19	in eisdem	in eadem	as H	as H
	hi Syllae Galbae	as H	as H	ut his Syllae Galbae (but v. Add. Note)
23	dicem et faciem	as H	dice et facie	dicae et faciae
27	posui	as H	praeposui	as H
34	ut epistulis	ut in epistulis	as H	as H
CHAP. VIII				
5	heroi	as H	as H	heroici
6	quae amat	as H	qua amat	qua amatur
8	in primis copiam verborum	[in primis copiam verborum]	as H	as H (but v. note)
11	respirent	as H	respirant	as R
14	et σχηματισμούς	[et σχηματισμούς]	as M	as H
CHAP. IX				
3	ethologiae ... ethologia	as H	as H	aetiologiae ... aetiologia
CHAP. X				
3	in data linea	as H	data linea	as H
	triangula...possint	triangulum...possit	as H	as H
7	tacitae	as H	as H	tacite
13	de philosophis loquor...?	quid de philosophis loquor...?	de philosophis loquor.	as H
27	monstrabat	ministrabat	as M	as M
34	ea vulgaris opinio est	as H	[id vulgaris opinio est]	as H
35	cuicumque saltem	as H	cuicunque [saltem]	as H
37	ex certis	et certis	as M	as M
39	geometrica ratione	geometria ratione	as M	as H
49	dividendi	as H	as H	videndi
	augenda	as H	as H	augendi
CHAP. XI				
9	distorqueantur	as H	detorqueantur	as H
10	alterum...tend e ret	as H	altero...tenderet	as H
17	ut nomine	uti nomine	in nomine	as H
	a Chrysippo	as H	Chrysippo	as H
CHAP. XII				
4	desideretur	as H	desiderentur	as H
6	geometrae	as H	γεωμέτρη	as H
16	venalem	vilem	as M	as M
18	ineruditis	as H	ineruditi	as H
	hoc quoque providentia	as H	hoc providentia	as R
ADDENDA				
IV, 4	utantur	utuntur	as M	as M
VI, 7	ut prandeo	as H	prandeo	as R

THE CODEX JOANNENSIS

This MS., which belongs to the library of St John's College, Cambridge, was written in the twelfth century[1] and shews the same lacunas[2] as A, B, N etc. (v. Intr. p. lxi). Its age entitles it to considerable respect: whether a careful study will maintain this respect is a point on which I have considerable doubt. I was originally interested in it as the property of my own college; but as, owing to circumstances stated below, it has been imperfectly known by editors of Q., yet at the same time has received a certain consideration, I have added the subjoined collation[3] of the first book in order that future students of the text who have before them the apparatus of Halm and Fierville may be able to judge what value, if any, is to be attached to its variants.

The MS. was first used by Edmond Gibson, afterwards Bishop of London, who edited Q. in 1693. He tells us in his preface that he had before him three MSS., all of Oxford or Cambridge, the Bodleianus, the Baliolensis and the Joannensis. As the two first are of much later date[4], the Joannensis was his best authority. And indeed, as on the whole it follows B very closely, Gibson was really in a better position for constructing a revised text of Q. than most pre-Halmian editors. I doubt whether he actually followed it to any great extent, but his apparatus was studied by Burman, Spalding and Zumpt and till the present day has been the only source of knowledge as to the readings of the Joannensis, in the first three books, at any rate.

The last words are of importance, for Spalding, who had depended on Gibson throughout his first volume, obtained better information while he was at work on the second, which was published five years after the first. "Joannensis Codicis," he writes in the preface of Volume II., "interiorem notitiam conciliavit mihi vir iuvenis, eleganter doctus, Georgius Butlerus, Universitatis Cantabrigiensis alumnus et sodalis. Impetravit mihi is manu doctissimi Porsoni perscriptam codicis huius collationem in iis quidem locis, quae a Gibsono negligenter essent tractata." Butler also supplied some account of the MS. and its lacunas. I presume that Spalding made due use of this "interior notitia" in his 2nd and 3rd volumes[5], though I have not examined the point. But I do not think that Butler's (or Porson's) collation can have dealt with the first three books; as there is no allusion to any corrections to be made in consequence of the new knowledge, though

---

[1] Peterson assigns it to the thirteenth century; but I am assured on the best authority that the earlier date is right.

[2] It began originally with the second chapter, but as the upper part of the first page has been cut off, we have it only from 'constaret' 2, 3, and this also involves the loss of from 'modo paedagogorum' 2, 10 to 'non tamen' 2, 16.

[3] In this I owe everything to the help and kindness of Mr Previté-Orton.

[4] Apparently they belong to the fifteenth century.

[5] He had comparatively little opportunity of doing so, since the lacunas extend to more than half these volumes. The fourth volume was left by Sp. in an incomplete state.

the error into which he had been led by Gibson on 'notam' in 4, 9[1] was sufficiently serious to call for correction.

If Spalding was unfortunate in his opportunities of knowing the Joannensis, Fierville was still more so. He describes in his introduction how a friend wrote on his behalf to the Librarian of the University of Cambridge to ask for some account of the MS., but received no answer. Presumably the letter miscarried somehow in passing from one librarian to the other. Fierville, who clearly did not grasp the distinction between the College and the University, made no further attempt. He received another rebuff from an English library, of which he gives a rather amusing account, and came to the conclusion that English savants were not as ready to promote scholarship as those of other countries. In consequence his account of the Joannensis is almost a blank. In his apparatus criticus, however, he notes the variants as supplied by Gibson.

Peterson, who examined the MS. for his edition of the Xth book, was the first to give any full account of it. I may refer to his Introduction (p. lx.) for details as to some of its characteristics. He states that it generally agrees with the Bernensis, though there are striking resemblances to the Pratensis, and also notes some readings in which it agrees with the Vossiani I. and III.[2] The results of his collation for the Xth book are given in his critical appendix.

My examination of the codex in the Ist book more than confirms the first part of this judgment. The general agreement with the Bernensis and Bambergensis (B), on which I have therefore based my collation, is very close. All B's worst errors, with the exception of 'de litteris' in 4, 6, are reproduced. To give a few examples among many, Joann. like B has 'ait ξεβιος' for λίγξε βιός (5, 72), 'notis interpretari' for 'nolis' or 'nolim interpretari' (8, 6), 'magistra' for 'magis trita' (5, 21), 'oratione' for 'oratore' (6, 18), 'vitandum' for 'videor nondum' (10, 17), 'iud' (without any sign of abbreviation) for 'iudicis' or 'iudicum' (10, 25). On the other hand the merest glance at my collation will shew that the identities with Voss. I. and Voss. III. are far more striking than Peterson's words would lead us to expect[3], while the resemblances to Prat. (and Put.), though by no means absent, are less obvious[4]. As however I am anything but an expert in tracing the pedigrees of MSS., I do not put forward any theory as to the exact relation of these codices to each other. I state the facts, which it must be remembered only apply to the first book, for future critics to interpret.

I would speak rather more positively, though still with diffidence, as to the *value* of the Joannensis, so far as I can judge it from the first book, compared with the value set on it by former editors. Spalding clearly paid some respect to what he believed, rightly or wrongly, to be the readings

---

[1] V. note and additional note on this passage.

[2] Two MSS. in the library of the University of Leyden (v. Intr. p. lxi.). Their variations from Burman's text are given in the Addenda to his edition.

[3] On the other hand Joann. does not contain the fragment X. 1, 46–107 (v. Intr. p. lxi.), and so far belongs to the group of Bn, Bg and N rather than to that of Prat., Put. and Voss. I. and III.

[4] As I have only cited the variants from B, the collation does not contain the numerous cases where J agrees with B and disagrees with Prat. and Put.

of the 'Codices Britannici,' particularly the Joannensis. I need not enter again into the question of 'notam' (4, 9). But he was also inclined to adopt 'nam contra' for 'iam Cottae' (4, 25), primarily on the authority of Joann. Another and perhaps more serious source of error was the idea that where Gibson did not quote his MSS. as giving a variant they were in agreement with his text. Thus on 'ne indoctae rusticae[ve] manus' (11, 16), Spalding, after noting that 've' is omitted in most MSS., adds 'videntur tamen habere Codd. Britannici,' evidently meaning that as Gibson inserts the 've' without citing any opposing authorities, he probably found it in his MSS. Meister and Radermacher seem to have shared this idea. They both allege Gibson as the authority for the reading 'cadit cecidit' for 'cadit excidit' in 4, 13, and I presume thought like Spalding that Gibson's silence implied MS. authority, an idea which, in this case at least, was quite erroneous.

My own impression is that though Joann. would be a most valuable substitute for B and the other 'mutilati,' whose readings are given by Fierville, it adds practically nothing to our present-day knowledge. The variations recorded below are largely pure blunders, and give no suggestion that the scribe had access to a purer tradition than the others possessed. When his peculiar readings are possible, they are hardly ever likely to be accepted. This is a very negative conclusion, but I hope that the negation may possibly be of use to some future critics, who may feel that so early a manuscript ought to be taken into account.

I should add that in citing the text of B I have understood Halm's *silence* to imply that B reads as he prints. I presume that Halm's reputation justifies me in this assumption better than Spalding was justified in making the same assumption with regard to Gibson.

B = consensus of Bn and Bg (where they differ these are given separately).

P = consensus of Prat. (where available) and Put. Where Prat. is wanting P = Put. only.

V_1 and V_3 = Vossianus I. and III. respectively as given by Burman.

† means that the text of Joannensis agrees with that of Burman. As Burman records in his Addenda the variants of V. I. and III. from the text which he adopts, it may be presumed that in passages marked † the Joannensis agrees with both V_1 and V_3[1].

---

[1] One odd fact as to Burman's 'Addenda' seems never to have been noticed. He cites readings from "Voss. tert." seventeen times in the Prooemium, though not in Chap. I. But the Vossianus III. has always been known to begin with Chap. II. Enquiry at Leyden confirms this, and the custodian of the MSS. there tells me that he can give no explanation as to what Burman can have meant.

	JOANNENSIS	B
II, 3	de hac igitur	de hac re igitur
4	tam lese hercule (as P)†	tam hercule
	cuiusque tantum totum (as V₁ V₃)	cuiusque totum
5	timebunt (as P V₃)	timebuntur
6	cocum	coccum
7	licentius dixere	licentius dixerint
	concubinos viderunt (as V₁)	concubinos vident
8	cantibus	canticis
17	refutabimus (as V₃)	refutavimus
18	media republica vivendum (as P V₁)	media rei publicae luce viven-dum Bn (but 'luce' expunged); rei vivendum Bg
	qui huiusmodi	quae in huiusmodi
19	caligant (as V₁ V₃)	caligat
20	religiose	religiosa
23	ordinem discendi (as Prat. V₁)	ordinem dicendi
26	vix enim prima (as V₃)	vix enim se prima
27	ipsi etiam magistri (as V₃)	ipsius etiam magistri
28	excipere possunt (as A)	excipere possint
	aptos (as V₁)	apertos
31	unium	unum
	dimittere (as A P V₃)	demittere
III, 1	retinere (as V₁ V₃)	continere
4	praecoquum (as Prat. V₃)	praecox
	quidquid illud possint	quidquid illud possunt
	quod in proximo est verbo (as V₃)	quod in proximo est ! verba
8	quod studium discendi quod volun-tate	quod studium discendi voluntate
14	quamquam illud (as V₁ V₃)	quamlibet id
	iniuria†	iniuriae
	exstiterit	adstiterit
17	minus esse quod (as V₃)	nimium est quod
IV, 5	oratori futuro†	oratoris futura
	minus ostentationis (as V₁ V₃)	quam ostentationis
6	elementa non (as P V₁ V₃)	elementa de litteris non
7	an grammatici (as V₁)	aut grammatici
	descendunt (as V₁ V₃)	descendent
9	habundent (as V₁ V₃)	redundent
	paulatim (as V₃)	paulum
	q......k (as V₁ V₃)	k......q
10	unam enim longam	unam longam
13	ab aetate (as P V₁ V₃)	aetate
	lases et as fuerunt (as V₁ V₃)	lases as fuerunt
15	unde proprium Burrus (as V₁)	unde Burrus
19	vel maxime (as V₁ V₃)	ac maxime
20	deduxerunt (as P V₁ V₃)	diducerent
23	docere quod didicit (as V₃)	docere quae didicit
	et quae sint†	et quae sunt
24	mares aut neutrali (as A, P)	mares neutrali ?
	significat (as V₁)	significant
25	scrutabitur (as A, P†)	scrutabit
	ex habitu corporis scilicet ut Allo-bros Cicero Rufos (as V₁ *fere*)¹‡	ex hab. corp. Rufos
	nam contra (as V₁, iam contra V₃)	iam Cotta

¹ This curious gloss, as Mr Previté-Orton at once pointed out to me, is clearly based on Juv. 7, 214,
Rufum, quem totiens Ciceronem Allobroga dixit.

	JOANNENSIS	B
IV, 26	quaerant etiam (as V_3)	quaerat etiam
28	est quidam	est etiam quidam
V, 1	loquendi regula (as P †)	loquendi regulam
	igitur ex verbis (as P V_3)	exigitur verbis
4	delectus	dilectus
7	multis modis	pluribus modis
9	quod fiet animi (as N P V_1 V_3)	q. fiat a.
10	illud barbari genus vitium barbarismus (as V_3)	illud vitium barbarismus (Bg barbarismi)
	sibi et	sibi etiam
12	et ti eo fufetii	Bn etieo fufetioeo
		Bg etieo fufecio eo
13	pro Tarsumennum	pro Tarsumenno
14	ducuntur (as V_1 V_3)	dicuntur
15	duo et tre (as V_3)	et dua et tre
	at duo pondo	at dua pondo
17	Europae et ei (as P V_1 V_3)	Europae Asiae et ei
	apud Varronem (as V_1)	apud P. Varronem
20	haedos hircosque (as V_1)	aedos ircosque
	manent (as V_1)	maneant
22	derivato a Graecis verbo declinato	declinato a Graecis verbo
23	*om.* et hic prima acuta (as V_1 V_3)	*ins.*
26	ne circuitus (as V_3)	non circuitus
	om. itemque	*ins.*
28	heroicus (as P †)	herous
29	alias...alias (as P? †)	alia...alia
31	quin eadem flexa et acuta	qui in eadem f. et a.
34	contextu vel complexu	complexu
35	amarae cortices (as V_1 V_3)	amarae corticis
	reprehensio	reprehendo
	sic reddit ut †	Bn sic redditur aut
		Bg sic reddit...ut
36	dicit venite	dicat venite
38	fit aliquando †	sit aliquando
39	in vitio sermonis (as V_1)	initio sermonis
40	quidam dividunt (as N P V_1)	quidam dicunt
42	adiecerent	adicerent
47	ideo num quoque genus (as Bn acc. to Zumpt)	idoneum q. g. (acc. to Halm)
48	pronomen esse debuerit ac similia (as V_1 V_3)	pronomen ac similia
50	intro et intus unius loci (as P V_1V_3)	intro et loci
57	mappalia (as P V_1 V_3)	mappam
58	nam maxime (nam maxima N P) (as V_1 V_3)	nam et maxima
59	latina oratione	latina ratione
62	sed s terminarentur (as P)	Bn sed s. syllaba term.
		Bg (?) sed syllaba term.
65	interdum repugnantibus † (P interdum pugnantibus)	Bn dum ne pugnantibus
		Bg dum repugnantibus
	quod Cicero utitur	quo Cicero utitur
67	trium constant vel coeunt (as V_1 V_3)	trium coeunt
68	*om.* ut biclinium aut (as V_1 V_3)	ut biclinio aut
VI, 5	ha domu dicendum sit an hac domu ('domu' as V_3)	hac domu d. s. an hac domo
12	urbis romae †	romanae urbis
20	retinere cuiusdam (as V_1 V_3)	retinere insolentiae cuiusdam
22	permittant (as N P V_1)	permittunt

	JOANNENSIS	B
VI, 28	sunt qui inde (as V_1)	sunt qui vim
	vocant (as $V_1 V_3$)	vocent
32	veteres appellaverunt †	veteres vocaverunt
34	ab usu (as $V_1 V_3$)	a lusu
37	*om.* ad eum enim scribit †	*ins.*
VII, 1	constat	constet
	multum officium grammatici est	infra grammatici officium est
	infra	
8	victum etiam gemina m	victum in gemina
18	vel in genetivum (as P)	vel genetivum
	his Syllae (as N P)	hi Syllae
20	quotiens media littera (as V_3)	quotiens s media littera
21	iussi via una	iussi una
33	atque in his (as V_1)	atque iis
34	vim Caesaris (as N P)	vim C. Caesaris
VIII, 1	quando attollenda quando vel submittenda (as $V_1 V_3$)	quando attollenda vel submittenda
	quod quoque flexu	quid quoque flexu
2	Caesarem	C. Caesarem
	accipimus (as V_3)	accepimus
11	summam…gratiam	summa…gratia
14	deprehendatque barbara	deprendat quae barbara
16	mihi hic de ornatu	mihi de ornatu
17	insensionis laudandandum (insensionis as V_3)	in sensibus laudandum
18	hominum est dixerit (as V_1)	hominum dixerit
	melius salus	melius aliis
19	aut qui pleni (as V_1)	atqui pleni
20	profertur (as V_3)	proferretur
21	quaedam nescire (as $V_1 V_3$)	aliqua nescire
IX, 4	cum quis dixisset aliquis (as $V_1 V_3$)	c. q. d. aliquid
5	audient (as V_3)	audent
X, 1	quem encyclon paedian (as V_1)	quam e. p.
2	quae et ipsae	quae quia et ipsae
3	aequis lateribus possit (as A)	ae. l. possint
5	sapientes	sapientem
	sed quaedam (as V_1)	sed per quaedam
9	quis ignoret (as N $V_1 V_3$)	quis ignorat
17	iuncta fuerunt (as $V_1 V_3$)	iunctae fuerunt
22	PIEMON et ΜΕΝΕΛΟC ΜΕΛΟC ΜΕΤΡΟΝ	ῥυθμόν et μέλος μέτρον
27	suorum temporis oratoris (as V_3)	suorum temporum oratoris
28	vel etiam iam timenti (as V_3)	vel iam timenti
31	esse mihi manifestum (as $V_1 V_3$)	esse manifestum
	nam psalteria (as V_3)	nec psalteria
	repudianda et recusanda (as $V_1 V_3$)	recusanda
32	suum quondam modum adsignat carmen (quoddam modum carmen $V_1 V_3$)	suum quoddam carmen adsignat
33	dici debeat (as A $V_1 V_3$)	dici debet
35	incerto indecoro (as V_1)	incerto aut indecoro
37	geometrice necessarius (as N)	geometriae necessarius
39	per quosdam quas	per quasdam quas
48	destruendum	destruendam
49	proprium efficiendum	proprium ad efficiendum
XI, 1	in hoc loco instituimus (as $V_1 V_3$)	in hoc instituimus
7	catapeplasmēn	catapeplasmen
9	rictus (as V_3)	rictum

	JOANNENSIS	B
XI, 10	*om.* cum alterum—premeretur (as $V_1 V_3$)	*ins.*
XII, 1	eodem tempore tradi non omnia (as $V_1 V_3$)	eodem tempore tamen tradi omnia
	fatigatur (as V_3)	fatigetur
4	alia discimus (as $V_1 V_3$)	alia dicimus
	pluribus horis diversa partiamur	pluribus curis horas partiamur
5	egerimus tamen modo	egerimus quodam tamen modo
7	fatiget	fatigaret
9	cepis	coeperis
13	subsidia †	subseciva
14	musicis modis †	musicis notis
	minutissima geometriae † (munitissima V_3)	munitissima usque geometriae

BIBLIOGRAPHICAL NOTES

I have not attempted to furnish any full bibliography of modern works dealing with the various subjects with which the First Book of Quintilian is concerned. The nearest approach I can give to this is the Index of modern writers quoted or referred to in this volume (Index No. III.). But there are some matters which, as I have hitherto had no occasion to deal with them, may be properly mentioned here, especially as they are not discussed to any extent by Halm, Peterson or Fierville.

A. EDITIONS.

A complete list of these up to the year 1810 is given in the seventh volume of Lemaire's edition of Quintilian, *Bibliotheca Classica*, pp. 277–279. The list contains nearly 130 items. From them I select as the most important the following[1]:

Date	Name[2] by which the edition is known, generally that of the editor, in one or two cases of the printer	Place
1470	Campanus (Campani). The *Editio Princeps*	Rome
1470	Andrea de Bussi	Rome
1471	N. Jenson	Venice
1493	Locatelli(us) (with the notes of Regius[3] and embodying his corrections)	Venice
1512	Aldus (Navagero)	Venice
1516	J. Badius Ascensius[4] (containing his notes as well as those of Regius and Georgius Merula. A later edition (1528) added those of Petrus Mosellanus)	Paris

[1] I have not verified for the most part the statements as to the editions made by Lemaire. Where I have been able to do so I have found them accurate.

[2] Except where a special note is added, some information about nearly all the persons named will be found in Sandys *Hist. Class. Schol.*

[3] Raphael Regius is not mentioned by Sandys, nor in the *Enc. Brit.*, nor even in the Italian *Biographia Universale*. The only place where I have found any mention of him is in Zedler's *Universal-Lexicon*. According to this he lived at Padua, learnt Greek when 70 years old, and translated the *Odyssey*. He also edited the *Metamorphoses*, and there are copies of this in the Cambridge Library (1513 and 1527).

In an 'Epistula ad lectorem' at the end of this, after speaking of the delinquencies of the 'librarius,' he adds the warning 'ne in emendatis quoque nostris in Quintilianum annotationibus decipiaris, quae eiusdem imperiti ineptiis foedatae citra ullam praefationem nostram venales circumvehuntur.'

Regius was certainly the father of Quintilianean criticism and must have held a higher place among the scholars of his time than the scantiness of the record would suggest. In some verses on the title-page of the *Ovid* he is called
Lumen Romani Regius eloquii.

[4] Badius, printer and scholar, and father-in-law of Robert Estienne (Stephanus), is also left without mention by Sandys. There is a short article on him in *Enc. Brit.* His date is given as 1462–1535.

Date	Name by which the edition is known, generally that of the editor, in one or two cases of the printer	Place
1531	Epitome of Jonas Philologus[1]	Paris
1534	J. Sichard[2] with his notes and those of Longolius and Camerarius. An earlier edition (Basle 1529) had contained those of Sichard only	Cologne
1538	P. Galland[3]	Paris
1554	Epitome of Patrizi, published by Jean du Tillet (v. Intr., p. lxix.)	Paris
1556	T. Richard (this edition claimed to include notes by Turnebus, but these, though often quoted by later editors, have been generally held to be spurious)[4]	Paris
1693	Gibson[5,6] (Text and App. Crit.)	Oxford
1698	Obrecht (Text and App. Crit.)	Strasburg
1715	Epitome of Rollin	Paris
1720	P. Burman, often spelt 'Burmann,' perhaps because the name was from the first Latinized as 'Burmannus.' Even the article in the last edition of the *Enc. Brit.* has the double *n*. There seems, however, to be no doubt that 'Burman' is the true Dutch form. This is the first real commentary, but like Capperonnier's which followed it, it consists largely of 'notae variorum' quoted without any remarks of the editor himself	Leyden
1725	C. Capperonnier. This edition, like Burman's, contains a reprint of Dodwell's *Annales Quintilianei* (1698)	Paris
1738	J. M. Gesner. A somewhat meagre commentary	Göttingen
1810	F. G. Pottier. This is apparently a commentary, but I have never seen a copy of it, and only know it from the occasional quotation of the notes by Fierville	Paris

I now come to the great edition of G. L. Spalding (Berlin). The first volume was published in 1798, and two more appeared before his death in 1811. He had then nearly completed the fourth and last volume of the

---

[1] His real name was Gonthier of Andernach, and he was physician to Francis I. So at least Fierville, Intr. p. xxxiv. There is a copy of the book in the Cambridge Library dated 1531. It only deals with parts of Books II.–IX.

[2] Sichard again is only known to me from Zedler. His birth and death are given as 1499 and 1552. Primarily a jurist, though some of his works are theological, he held in the latter part of his life the 'Professionem Codicis' at the University of Tübingen.

[3] v. Intr. p. lxxv.

[4] If this is right, in notes on 2, 1, and 3, 1 I should have written 'ps.-Turnebus' for 'Turnebus.'

[5] This long interval is bridged over by some twenty editions in Lemaire's list. But they do not appear to include any important additions. Even in number they fall far short of the output of the ninety preceding years, and bear testimony to the decline in interest noticed in the Intr. pp. lxxv. ff.

[6] v. p. 184.

commentary. This was revised and seen through the press by Buttmann in 1816. Zumpt added a fifth volume of supplementary critical notes in 1829, and the whole work was crowned in 1834 by the invaluable *Lexicon Quintilianeum* of Bonnell[1]. In connexion with Spalding I may note Sarpe's tractate called *Analectorum ad G. L. Spaldingii M. Fabium Quintilianum specimen*, Halle 1815, which contains several interesting and some perverse suggestions.

After Spalding we have the following:

Gernhard, L., Leipsic, 1830 (with some notes mainly critical).

Zumpt, 1831, Leipsic. Text only with a few footnotes of variants. (Zumpt, however, no doubt intended it to be read in connexion with his volume of critical notes in Spalding's edition.)

Meyer, Leipsic, 1833, Books I–III only, a commentary with some good critical suggestions.

Bonnell (Teubner text), with short critical notes; first published in 1854.

After these we have the editions of Halm, Meister, Fierville and Radermacher, all of which have been discussed at length in Intr. ch. v. There are many editions of Book X, which do not properly concern us; but Peterson's Introduction and many of his notes are exceedingly useful to the student of Book I.

B. TRANSLATIONS.

English. Guthrie. London, 1756.

Patsall. London, 1774. (This omits the parts omitted by Rollin in his epitome, *e.g.* nearly all of I. 4–7.)

Watson. London, 1856. (In Bohn's series, but a by no means contemptible piece of work.)

Butler. London, 1921. (Loeb series.)

French. Michel de Pure. Paris, 1663.

Gédoyn. Paris, 1718.

In the series edited by Nisard. Paris, 1853.

German. Baur. Stuttgart, 1863.

Italian. Toscanella[2]. Venice, 1566.

Besides these the following are only known to me as mentioned by Lemaire, Vol. VII. p. 300, Fierville, Intr. p. xxvii., and Peterson, Intr. p. lxxvi.[3]:

French. Ouisille. Paris, 1829.

Baudet (Collection Nisard)[4]. Paris, 1842.

---

[1] Spalding's work is not included in Lemaire's list simply because the edition to which this list is appended is, for the first four volumes, merely a reproduction of Sp.'s text and commentary with some additional notes by Dussault. The fifth and sixth volumes contain the *Declamations*. In the seventh, besides the list of editions, are prefaces by various editors, other matter of the same kind and a good-sized index. [2] v. Intr. p. lxxx.

[3] As Lemaire and Fierville give Patsall's name as 'Pastel,' I do not vouch for their accuracy in other cases.

[4] Perhaps the same as the Nisard translation mentioned above. My copy does not give the name of the translator.

German. Henke. Helmstädt, 1775.
Herzog. Leipsic, 1829.
Alberti. Leipsic, 1858.
Lindner. Vienna, 1881.
Italian. Gariglio. Vercelli, 1780.

C. Recent work on Quintilian outside the regular editions
(mostly but not entirely dealing with textual questions).

Claussen, *Quaestiones Quintilianeae.* Leipsic, 1883.

Usener, two articles originally published in 1889 and 1892, reproduced in *Kleine Schriften*, Leipsic and Berlin, 1912, I. 369 ff. and II. 265 ff. For special reference to Q., v. index.

Meister, *Philologus* 1876, Vol. XXXV., esp. pp. 543–549[1] and 688–691.

Kiderlin. This critic published many papers on textual points in the *Institutio*. The most important are to be found in *Blätter für das bayerische Gymnasialschulwesen* 1886, *Neue Jahrbücher für Philologie und Pädagogik* 1893, and *Neue Philologische Rundschau* 1887. For the others, references will be found in Bursian (v. below), 1887, 1901.

Andresen, *Rheinisches Museum*, 1887, vol. 43, p. 506 ff.

Nettleship's Essay on *The Study of Latin Grammar among the Romans in the first century* A.D. Originally published in the *Journal of Philology*, 1886, and reprinted in *Lectures and Essays*, Oxford, 1895. I must digress here for a moment to explain why I have made no use of this essay in my notes. So far as it concerns Quintilian, it is mainly directed to discovering the authorities which Quintilian used in I. 4-7. The conclusions arrived at are that ch. 7 is from Verrius Flaccus, 4, 1–5, 54 from Palaemon (but Palaemon is supposed to have borrowed part of this from Verrius), and 5, 54 to the end of 6 from Pliny. Not only do the specific arguments for the last two conclusions at any rate seem to me very weak (I have argued against some of them in my article in *Class. Quart.* 1914), but the whole enquiry appears to me misdirected. I cannot think that this kind of Higher Criticism, though applicable enough to historical books like the Pentateuch, is applicable to a tractate like I. 4-7, which deals with what at the time is a growing and living science, in which each successive student and teacher takes or leaves what he wishes of his predecessors' work. Moreover, Nettleship failed, I think, to appreciate how deeply rooted and widely understood grammar was at the time, and when he finds two writers agreeing in a terminology, which was probably familiar to thousands, infers some connexion far too easily[2].

---

[1] These pages are of importance, as in them Meister discusses briefly the points in Book I. in which he disagreed with Halm's text. It was written before the publication of his edition, and in the latter he did not always follow his earlier opinion. Still the paper makes a valuable supplement to the edition.

[2] To give one instance out of many, Nettleship thinks that Pliny made several original attempts at terminology, and as Charisius, who frequently quotes Pliny, says (K. I, 225) that P. gave the name of 'relativae ad aliquid' to conjunctions (not comparative adverbs as N. says) such as 'magis,' 'potius,' 'immo,' he assumes

For notes or papers of minor importance, the best course will be to refer the reader to the periodical surveys in Bursian's *Jahresbericht*. These surveys are at least as accessible as the work which they record, and in many cases give sufficient discussion to save the student from the need of consulting the originals. These surveys are as follows:

1876: Vol. 6, pp. 262–293, Iwan Müller.
1879: Vol. 18, pp. 157–170, Iwan Müller.
1887: Vol. 51, pp. 1–61, F. Becher.
1901: Vol. 109, pp. 86–144, G. Ammon.
1910: Vol. 148, pp. 166–253, G. Ammon.
1922: Vol. 192, pp. 214–308, G. Ammon.

Besides those which deal with the text, there are among those noticed several which, as they treat of style or subject-matter generally, have partial reference to Book I.

[I should add that the 1922 Bursian has only come into my hands at the very last moment. While there are many items which suggest points of interest to the student of the First Book, I do not think there are any of very great importance.]

Additional note on Regius and the quotation from Virgil in 3, 13.

[The reading 'a teneris' in the quotation from Georg. 2 in 3, 13 evidently appeared in Locatelli's edition, though I have been unable to verify it from an actual copy: for Badius (1516) while adopting 'in' remarks 'a teneris': omnes codices praeterquam Raphaelis habent 'in teneris.' Regius seems to have had a special MS. which Zumpt (Sp., vol. 4, p. 10) believed to be the 'Florentinus.' But there is no suggestion in Zumpt's *App. Crit.* that F has 'a.' I suspect that it was merely one of the mistakes against which Regius inveighs in the letter above noted, p. 191 n. 3. There is no mention of the reading in Regius' own notes which are incorporated in Badius' edition; and as said in the note on 3, 13 no edition known to me has it. I cannot but wonder why successive editors of Virgil should repeat this misstatement, instead of taking down a Quintilian from their book-shelf and looking out the passage.]

without any reason that Pliny was the first to use the term. Then elsewhere, as Q. speaks of 'ad aliquid' nouns in I. 6, 13, he suggests that Q. got the term from P. How is it supposed that the πρός τι ἔχοντα of Dion. Thrax had been rendered in the Roman Schools in the century or century and a half which had elapsed between him and P.?

I here take this opportunity of explaining, with a slight correction, the statement made in the note on 'nostrarum ultima,' 4, 9, that Nettleship *says* this is z. N. *implies* this by quoting as a parallel Longus 50 'Z lingua Latina non agnoscit' (Essay, p. 152).

NOTE ON SOME VARIATIONS IN SPELLING
IN THE TEXT

The reader is entitled to know why the spelling of certain classes of words varies so much. He will find both *is* and *es* in the accusative plural, and also *np* and *mp*, *nb* and *mb*, *pt* and *bt*, *adc* and *acc*, *ads* and *as*; and this variation is not restricted to classes, but appears in individual words. Thus 'art*is*' is found side by side with 'art*es*,' 'co*n*paro' with 'co*m*paro,' 'i*n*buo' with 'i*m*buo,' 'su*p*tilitas' with 'su*b*tilitas,' '*ad*commodo' with '*ac*commodo' and '*ad*spiratio' with '*as*piratio.' The explanation is that I have followed Halm's spelling[1], while Halm, as occasional indications shew, followed or wished to follow his MSS., presumably in this book A, Bn and Bg. While I have not thought the point of sufficient importance to justify a difficult and distant enquiry in Milan, Berne or Bamberg, I have roughly tested the extent of Halm's agreement in this book with the manuscript tradition, by comparing his text with Chatelain's collation of N (v. Intr. p. xciii.), and with the two MSS. accessible to me, viz. H and Jo, and also with the specimen pages of A and Bn given in Chatelain's *Paléographie*. From this it would appear (1) that N is in general, but only general, agreement with Halm's text, (2) that much the same may be said about H, except in the matter of *is* for *es*, where the discrepancy is very marked, (3) that Jo agrees with Halm better than H as to *is*, but not so well in other respects. As to the specimen pages, there is of course little opportunity for judging, but I observe that with regard to another variable, *nm* or *mm*, A has 'i*m*mutatio,' where Halm has 'i*n*mutatio' without any indication that his MSS. differ, and also that Bn uses abbreviations for *comp* or *conp*, which, one would think, make it difficult to decide which form should be printed in each particular case. It seems to me then that the MS. tradition on these points is rather uncertain, and even if these tenth or eleventh century MSS. are in agreement, are they any evidence for the first; and even if they are, are we to suppose that Quintilian himself, as opposed to the scribes, capriciously varied his spelling of these words from page to page and almost from line to line? My natural inclination would be to follow Meister who in each case adopts the same spelling throughout. But as the main purpose of textual enquiry, to my mind, is to ascertain what the writer wrote with the further object of ascertaining what he meant, and on this these variations in spelling have no possible bearing, I have preferred to submit to Halm's authority. I should add that while in the headings of the notes words of these classes have been (with the aid of the readers of the Press) assimilated to the text, I have felt myself at liberty, within the body of the notes, to use of the alternative forms that which is most familiar to me.

[1] The text was actually printed from that of Radermacher, who follows Halm in the vast majority of cases. I have noticed some four or five variants in words of these kinds. In two of them Rad. is supported by N, and he may have had some reason for the others. I have not thought it worth while to alter them.

One detail in Halm's spelling may be criticised on other grounds. His adoption of 'Appi' in the 'locus vexatus' 5, 23 implies that Q. regarded the contraction of genitives in -ii as an error. If so, it would surely be necessary to correct 'Horati' in Ep. ad Tryph. 2 to 'Horatii.' Spalding is here more consistent than Halm.

There is another point which is not likely to escape criticism, viz. my use of v for the consonantal u. Here I have gone with Meister and Radermacher against Halm. This seemed to me a question of modern usage rather than ancient spelling, and in following the two most recent German editors I followed also my own prejudices. But I must admit that the book itself does supply a strong argument against using a different form for the consonant and the vowel; for in chapters 4 and 7, where the argument turns on their identity, it is necessary to print u for v. Further a high authority tells me that I have sinned against the 'Cambridge Tradition,' and though another equally high reassures me, it will perhaps be better to ask for pardon rather than to attempt justification.

FURTHER ADDITIONS TO COMMENTARY

10, 49. de celeritate augendi. As the reading adopted and the first interpretation proposed will receive confirmation, if it appears that the *rapidity* of increase in geometrical progression is a suitable subject for a 'quaestio' which would appeal to the ordinary intelligence, a modern illustration may not be out of place.

"'He (i.e. Mr Stiggins) borrows eighteenpence on Monday, and comes on Tuesday for a shillin' to make it up half-a-crown; calls again on Vensday for another half-crown to make it five shillin's; and goes on, doubling, till he gets it up to a five pund note in no time, like them sums in the 'rithmetic book 'bout the nails in the horse's shoes, Sammy.'

Sam intimated by a nod that he recollected the problem alluded to by his parent." *Pickwick Papers*, ch. XXVII.

(I understand that in the question the customer agrees to pay 1*d.* for the first nail, 2*d.* for the second, 4*d.* for the third, and so on.)

11, 3. frequens imitatio transit in mores. Cf. Plat. *Rep.* III. 395 D ἢ οὐκ ᾔσθησαι ὅτι αἱ μιμήσεις, ἐὰν ἐκ νέων πόρρω διατελέσωσιν, εἰς ἔθη τε καὶ φύσιν καθίστανται καὶ κατὰ σῶμα καὶ φωνὰς καὶ κατὰ τὴν διάνοιαν; There are other resemblances in the context to these sections of Q., and when we remember also that in Ch. 10 we have had signs of the influence of *Rep.* III. (v. particularly the resemblance of 398 E to 10, 34, mentioned in the note on that passage) I think it is probable that here too Q. has P. definitely in mind.

12, 1. si maxime (correction to note). I have perhaps somewhat misrepresented Madvig's note. He blames Goerenz for describing the usage as rare while it is really 'pervagatissimum,' and Hand for mistaking the exx.

INDEX I

NAMES OF PERSONS REFERRED TO AND AUTHORS QUOTED IN THE TEXT

(N.B. Names quoted as words are not included.)

INDEX II

AUTHORS QUOTED OR REFERRED TO IN THE INTRO-DUCTION AND NOTES, MAINLY ANCIENT AND MEDIEVAL

Such modern writers are included as are quoted not as authorities, but as illustrating Quintilian or the use made of Quintilian.

The names of books are usually given when more than one by the same author is quoted, or when references have been given in an abbreviated form, which might possibly cause difficulty.

The Roman numbers refer to pages of the Introduction; the Arabic numbers to the chapter and section of the text, and the notes upon them.

The addition "and A" means that the point is dealt with both in the original and the additional note (v. pp. 168–179). The addition 'A' means that the point is dealt with in the additional note only.

INDEX III

MODERN AUTHORITIES (APART FROM EDITIONS AND TRANSLATIONS) REFERRED TO IN THE INTRODUCTION AND NOTES

(For explanations v. headings to Index II.)

The following articles or papers by the editor are also referred to:

The Grammatical Chapters in Quintilian in Classical Quarterly, Jan. 1914
chs. 4–8 *passim*
Problems in the Grammatical Chapters in Quintilian in Class. Quart., Jan. 1916
chs. 4–6 *passim*
The Analogist and Anomalist Controversy in Class. Quart., Jan. 1919 6. 4 A and
elsewhere

For other papers by the editor v. xxiii.: xxxiii.: Pr. 27: 5. 65: 7. 15: 9. 2;
9 3 f.

INDEX IV

OTHER WORDS AND MATTERS IN INTRODUCTION AND NOTES

(For explanations v. headings to Index II.)

For EU product safety concerns, contact us at Calle de José Abascal, 56–1°,
28003 Madrid, Spain or eugpsr@cambridge.org.

www.ingramcontent.com/pod-product-compliance
Ingram Content Group UK Ltd.
Pitfield, Milton Keynes, MK11 3LW, UK
UKHW040619240426
470322UK00010B/208